NORTHUMBERLAND FAMILIES

VOLUME TWO

W. PERCY HEDLEY

THE SOCIETY OF ANTIQUARIES OF NEWCASTLE UPON TYNE 1970

©W. Percy Hedley, M.A., F.S.A., 1970
Published by the Society of Antiquaries of Newcastle upon Tyne
The Black Gate, Newcastle upon Tyne
SBN 901082 03 1

ACKNOWLEDGMENT

The publication of this volume has been made possible by generous grants towards
its cost from the Sir James Knott Trustees and from the University of Newcastle,
and by interest-free loans from the Northumberland County Council and from
the University of Durham. All these the Society thanks for their interest and support.

Printed in Great Britain by Northumberland Press Limited, Gateshead.

PUBLICATIONS OF THE SOCIETY OF ANTIQUARIES
THE BLACK GATE, NEWCASTLE UPON TYNE

Editor: John Philipson, M.A., F.S.A.

NORTHUMBERLAND FAMILIES

INTRODUCTION

VOLUME I of *Northumberland Families* began with the Pre-Conquest and immediate Post-Conquest families of native origin, some Anglo-Saxon, some Danish and some Scottish which held power or lands in Northumberland before 1166; and was completed with an account of the families mainly Norman and French that held lands *in capite* of the Crown at that date.

This second volume also contains two almost distinct sections. It begins with certain baronial families of Norman-French extraction which acquired baronies in Northumberland after 1166, and then deals with the under-tenants of 1166 who held by knight service.

There are many families of whom we only get passing glimpses as we turn over the pages of history. Surnames were derived from almost every vill and hamlet in the county, but the majority of these lasted only a few generations, sometimes only three or four, and then failed in the male line. This process is still continuing and every century sees the loss of many surnames. No account will be given of these ephemeral families of the 12th and 13th centuries.

Before the time of our Tudor monarchs, all but two of the 22 baronies which had existed in Northumberland in 1166 had passed from the families of their descendants or had been broken up. The surviving baronies were those of Seaton Delaval which remained in the Delaval family until 1814, and Bradford retained by the Bradfords until 1624. The Bertrams of Bothal became extinct in the male line in 1364 although Bothal still remains in the possession of their lineal descendants in the female line. Of the later baronial families there were Percys at Alnwick in Tudor times and there is a Percy there today. In the male line the present duke of Northumberland is a Smithson. His ancestor, sir Hugh Smithson, married the daughter and heiress of Algernon Seymour, duke of Somerset, who had married the only daughter and heiress of Josceline Percy, earl of Northumberland.

The greater part of this volume is concerned with the four families of Heron, Widdrington, Ogle and Lisle. There are now no Widdringtons at Widdrington and no Ogles at Ogle, but the surnames are still with us. The scattered estates of the Lisles at East Woodburn, Chipchase, Newton Hall, Felton and Gosforth, have long since passed from the family. Estates belonging to various branches of the Heron family were scattered all over the county and although there are persons bearing the name in Northumberland today it seems unlikely that any of them has a proven descent from the Middle Ages. In Tudor times these families were amongst the greatest and most powerful in Northumberland. We shall see their reactions to some of the principal episodes of English history—the Rising of the North, the Pilgrimage of Grace, the Civil Wars that heralded the Commonwealth and the Jacobite Risings of 1715 and 1745.

All these episodes were concerned in one way or another with Religion—the greatest war maker of all time. In Northumberland many of the old families clung to the old faith and suffered more than once in life and estates for their belief. In this most northerly county of England there seems to have been little or no enmity between Papist and Protestant. In the case of the Widdringtons of Cheeseburn Grange a Roman Catholic succeeded to the family estates by the will of his Protestant brother. In 1673 sir John Swinburne of Capheaton, a staunch Roman Catholic, applied to lord Ogle for an office or employment for Thomas Ogle a son of his neighbour at Bradford. Part of sir John's recommendation is that Ogle 'is a gentleman both by father and mother, always great loyalists and professors of the church of England'.

In Northumberland the relationship of these great manorial families with the town merchants on the one hand and the rural yeomen on the other hand was very close. In the south of England the yeoman was a retainer or attendant in a lord's household but here in the north he was a man who owned his own farm and farmed it. In most generations of the manorial families there were younger sons to be provided for; many of them were apprenticed to town merchants but others were given a farm or farms which they worked themselves. In later generations the younger sons of the merchants became craftsmen and tradesmen in the towns and the descendants of the yeomen when there was no land available for them became rural craftsmen and landless labourers. The landless men steadily provided for overseas colonization, for trade and for war.

The principal towns in Northumberland, Newcastle in particular, but also the lesser market towns of Hexham, Morpeth, Alnwick and Berwick-on-Tweed had their merchant and craft guilds in the Middle Ages. By an Act of Parliament of 1405, repeated in 1562 (7 Henry IV, *c.*17 and 5 Elizabeth *c.*4) it was stipulated that merchants' apprentices were to be sons of men possessed of landed property, and that no one was to set up trade or even work for wages as a journeyman artisan until he had served seven years of apprenticeship. It is obvious from this that a high standard of blood and breeding was maintained by the town guilds. The law about apprenticeship was not repealed until 1814, and the rights and privileges of the Merchants' Company, largely disused before the close of the 18th century were finally abrogated by sect.14 of the Municipal Corporations Reform Act, 1835.

It is again a pleasure to record my thanks to all those who have so willingly assisted in the publication of Volume I of this series and the preparation of Volume II. The committee appointed by the Society of Antiquaries of Newcastle upon Tyne to guide Volume I through publication has performed its task in an admirable way. My thanks are due to each and every member of the committee—John Philipson, M.A., F.S.A.; Professor G. W. S. Barrow, M.A., B.Litt.; W. Tynemouth, F.L.A.; C. R. Hudleston, M.A., F.S.A.; John

F. Brown, T.D. Additional thanks are due and most willingly given to my friend C. R. Hudleston for his great labour in examining on my behalf so many Durham wills, administrations and inventories now kept in the Durham Records Office. Mr R. M. Gard, M.A., the Northumberland County Archivist, and his staff at the Northumberland Record Office have also been unfailingly helpful. Dr A. M. C. Forster of Burradon has again allowed me to draw from her immense knowledge of Roman Catholic families; without this my work could never have been completed.

Without the painstaking help of my wife it is true to say that this work could never have been finished. Her assistance in the preparation of Volume I had already been recorded before the index was made. The index which took many weeks to complete was largely her work. She has typed Volume II many times over and has made helpful suggestions for its improvement. The index again owes much to her labours.

CONTENTS

ABBREVIATIONS

The following abbreviations have been used in this work: —

AA.   *Archaeologia Aeliana*—publications of the Society of Antiquaries of Newcastle upon Tyne.

adm.   administration of personal effects.

bap.   baptised (date of baptism).

BNFC   Berwickshire Naturalists Field Club transactions.

b. of m.   bond of marriage.

bur.   buried (date of burial).

c.   *circa* = about (that date).

CBP.   Calendar of Border Papers—2 vols.

CDS.   Calendar of Documents relating to Scotland.

chap.   chapelry.

co.   county.

coh.   coheir, coheiress.

d.   died.

dr.   daughter.

ex.   executed.

HN.   rev. John Hodgson's *History of Northumberland.*

inv.   inventory of goods (and valuation of effects).

i.p.m.   *inquest post mortem* (normally called for in the case of tenants *in capite*).

m.   marks (used besides the normal abbreviations £, s., and d.).

m.   married.

m.lic.   marriage licence.

m.sett.   marriage settlement.

Nc.   Newcastle upon Tyne.

Nd.   Northumberland.

NCH.   *Northumberland County History.*

NDD.   *Northumberland and Durham Deeds* being vol. VII of the *NRS.*

NRS.   *Newcastle upon Tyne Record Series* published by the Records Committee.

par.   (ecclesiastical) parish.

PRO.   Public Record Office.

PSAN.   Proceedings of the Society of Antiquaries of Newcastle upon Tyne.

s.   son.

s.p.   *sine proelii*—without issue.

SS.   Publications of the Surtees Society.

unm.   unmarried.

Vis.Ped.   Visitation Pedigree entered at a Herald's Visitation.

w.d.   will dated (preceding the date of the will).

w.pr.   will proved = date of probate of the will.

C.R.H.   These are the initials of Mr C. Roy Hudleston, M.A., F.S.A., and their appearance over and over again in this work, shows only part of the great help and encouragement the author has received from him.

OTHER BARONIAL FAMILIES

An account has already been given of the families of those Northumberland barons who held *in capite* in 1166. An anomalous case also included was that of the barony of Wark. Walter Espec, baron of Wark, died in 1153 leaving three sisters as his coheiresses. One of these sisters, Adeline, married Piers de Ros and their descendants eventually obtained the whole barony. Philip de Humez answered for the barony in 1166 and although his position is uncertain he may have been acting as guardian of Everard de Roos, and for this reason the family of Roos was included in the first part of this work.

In the 12th and 13th centuries certain of the Northumbrian baronies passed by purchase or by marriage with an heiress, to persons who were descendants of Norman-French baronial families. These are now dealt with. Some short time after 1173 Radulf de Wirecestre was succeeded in his barony of Hadston by his son-in-law Jordan Hairun. (*See* HAIRUN OF HADSTON).

On the death of Adam de Gaugy in 1279 the barony of Ellingham passed to his cousin Robert de Clifford, who to judge by his name was a descendant of the family taking its name from Clifford in Herefordshire. (*See* CLIFFORD OF ELLINGHAM). Walter son of Gilbert (d.1206), baron of Bolam, left two daughters Alesia and Alina who married two brothers James de Cauz (d.1248) and John de Cauz (d.1234), between whom the barony of Bolam was divided. Sometime between 1293 and 1295 Hugh de Raymes of Wherstead in Suffolk purchased one half of the barony. The Raymes family had held the barony of Rayne in Essex from the time of the Domesday Survey. (*See* RAYMES OF SHORTFLATT).

About the same time as Hugh de Raymes acquired half the barony of Bolam, Henry de Percy bought the barony of Alnwick. William de Vesci III, the last male heir of the earlier barons died without legitimate children 19 July 1297; he had made a settlement of the barony in 1295 on the legitimate heirs of his body with remainder to Anthony Bek, bishop of Durham. The bishop succeeded to the barony and sold it to Henry de Percy. (*See* PERCY OF ALNWICK).

Another family to be included here is that of Taylbois. On the death of vice admiral sir Robert Umfravill, K.G., on 27 January 1436, the heir to his lordship of Redesdale was sir Walter Taylbois, son and heir of sir Walter Taylbois (d.1418), son and heir of Henry Taylbois (d.1368) by his wife Alianora de Burrowden, daughter and heiress of Gilbert de Burrowden by his wife Elizabeth, sister and heiress of Gilbert de Umframville (d.1381). The Taylbois family also held the thegnage of Hepple (changed to a barony in 1212) by the marriage of Ivo Taylbois to Elizabeth daughter and coheiress of William son of William son of Waltheof (*See* TAYLBOIS OF REDESDALE).

Other families to be included in this section are Mauduit, Valoignes and Bulmer. The Mauduits acquired two southern baronies by marriage, those of Hanslope in Buckinghamshire, and Castle Holgate in Shropshire. From the beginning of the 13th century they held the manors of Eshot and Bockenfield in the barony of Mitford (*See* MAUDUIT OF ESHOT). At the time of the Domesday Survey, Peter de Valoignes held the barony of Benington in Hertfordshire. Before the end of the 12th century a cadet of the family was holding the manor of Newham in the barony of Alnwick (*See* VALOIGNES OF NEWHAM).

The Bulmers are in a different category from the other families in this section. Like the Cliffords they took their name from their property in England; Bulmer is in the North Riding of Yorkshire. In neither case is it known from what part of Normandy or France they originated. Stephen de Bulmer (d.1171-72) married as his second wife the heiress of the barony of Wooler and their descendants assumed the surname of Muschamp. A son of Stephen de Bulmer by his first wife married Johanna daughter and coheiress of Hugh de Ellington, whose second wife was coheiress of the barony of Ellingham. In the 13th century sir John de Bulmer (d.1299) married one of the coheiresses of the barony of Chevington. As the territorial possessions of the Bulmers were mainly in Yorkshire, the account of the family to be given here will be restricted to the family connections with the three Northumbrian baronies referred to (*See* BULMER OF BULMER, YORKS.).

CLIFFORD

THREE brothers Drogo, Richard and Simon, sons of Ponz, evidently of Norman-French extraction, appear in England in the reign of William I. Drogo and Simon were tenants *in capite* in 1086. From Simon descended the baronial family of Poyntz, extinct in 1376; a cadet line of Poyntz of Iron Acton in Gloucestershire 'maintained its importance down to the seventeenth century and substantial and clearly proved younger branches have continued to the present day' (Wagner, *English Genealogy*, p.68). Richard son of Ponz took part in the Norman invasion of Wales and his son Walter (d.1190) acquired the surname of Clifford from his castle of Clifford in Herefordshire. Walter's granddaughter was the Fair Rosamund, mistress of Henry II. Walter had two sons, Richard, who seems to have died *s.p.* in 1199, and Walter II (d.1221). Walter de Clifford III (d.1263), son of Walter II married Margaret, daughter of Llewelyn, prince of Wales. Their daughter and heiress Maud was wife firstly of William Longespee (d.1257) and secondly of John Giffard (d.1299) of Elston, Wilts.

Roger de Clifford (d.1282), a cadet of the Cliffords of Clifford, married Isabel daughter and coheiress of Robert de Vipont, baron of Appleby in Westmorland. Their grandson Robert de Clifford II (d.1344) acquired the other half of the barony from John de Cromwell and his wife Idoine, the other Vipont coheiress. Henry, lord Clifford, was created earl of Cumberland in 1525 but his male line expired in 1644.

CLIFFORD, BARONS OF ELLINGHAM

AT the beginning of the 13th century a Robert de Clifford appears in Northumberland and it can hardly be doubted that he was a cadet of the Cliffords of Clifford. He married Mabilla daughter of Radulf de Gaugy, baron of Ellingham, and their grandson Robert de Clifford III succeeded to the barony in 1278. Between 1207 and 1217 Henry de Orde transferred to Philip de Ulecotes the services due from Robert de Clifford for the vill of Murton in Norhamshire. Robert was appointed sheriff of Norham *c.*1214 by the king when the see of Durham was vacant; he was still sheriff in 1226 (*AA4.* XXI, p.73).

A second Robert de Clifford was instructed 23 April 1251 by bishop Walter de Kirkham to do homage to the prior and convent of Durham for a moiety of Murton. Sir Robert de Clifford III succeeded to the barony of Ellingham on the death of Adam de Gaugy the leper in 1279. Mandate was given to the king's escheator Thomas de Normanvill to accept security from Robert de Clifford, cousin (*consanguineus*) and heir of Adam de Gaugy for his reasonable relief for all the lands which the said Radulf (*sic*) held of the king *in capite* (*Originalia* in *HN.* iii, II, p.284). In 1292 Eva widow of Adam de Gaugy claimed dower from him. In 1304 when

Ralph de Meryng laid claim to the barony, Robert de Clifford III set out that he was son of Robert de Clifford, and grandson of another Robert de Clifford; he claimed also that his grandmother was Mabilla, aunt and heiress of Radulf de Gaugy who died *s.p.* in 1278. This Radulf was elder brother and predecessor of Adam the leper who only held the barony for one year. In 1306 Robert de Clifford III settled on his son Robert de Clifford IV and his wife, a house and lands at Ellingham. Robert IV married Elizabeth daughter of John de Vaux and died in his father's lifetime; his widow died on 28 March 1357.

On 18 May 1330 Robert de Clifford enfeoffed Michael de Presfen of the manor of Ellingham in trust for Robert for life with successive remainders in tail to his grandsons Robert son of Robert son of Robert de Clifford, John and Thomas, his brothers, Andrew son of Robert de Clifford, Roger and John his brothers, and finally to his own right heirs (*Feet of Fines*).

Sir Robert de Clifford III was sheriff of Norham in 1314 and died in 1339; writ for his *i.p.m.* dated 6 July 1339. Sir Robert had a younger brother Walter de Clifford who in 1256 had been given the manor of Heaton by Newcastle by his father Robert de Clifford II; Walter was then under age and he and his land were to remain in the custody of William Hayrun (*SS.* 88, p.17 and *Feet of Fines*). Walter was still alive in 1279 when Andrew Russell and Alicia his wife called him to warrant them against Robert son of Robert de Clifford for a messuage, 24 acres of land and 2 acres of meadow in Heaton (*SS.* 88, p.232).

Sir Robert de Clifford III had been predeceased by his son Robert IV and his grandson Robert V, and was succeeded by his grandson John de Clifford, aged 18 in 1334. Margaret, widow of Robert V survived her husband and had one third of Morton in dower.

In 1343 (*Feet of Fines* 23 May) Gilbert de Trewyke settled the manor of Middleton by Belford on Michael de Presfen and his male issue, with remainders to William de Presfen and Mary his wife and their male issue; to Alexander de Baumburghe and Margery his wife and their male issue; on Isabel, Alexander's daughter, and to John de Clifford and Elizabeth his wife and their male issue (*NRS.* XI, p.99). In 1344 John de Clifford, lord of Newstead conveyed to John Heron the reversion of the third part of the manor which Margaret widow of Robert de Clifford, then held in dower of his inheritance (*NDD.* p. 103).

John de Clifford was sheriff of Northumberland 1348. He was concerned in the death of John de Coupland 20 December 1362 and his lands were confiscated by the Crown 10 February 1366. In 1399 Christiana de Clesseby and Henry de Heton, *chivaler*, unsuccessfully claimed the manor of Ellingham as heirs of Robert son of Robert son of Robert de Clifford by virtue of the entail made by Robert the grandfather in 1330.

Henry de Heton (d.1399) was son of Thomas de Heton (d.1362) by his wife Joan daughter and coheiress of Robert de Clifford V, Christiana de Clesseby being the other daughter and coheiress (*de Banco Roll* 1399. R. 552, m. 98, and 1405. R. 577). Thomas de Heton was an illegitimate son of sir Thomas de Heton (d.1353) of Lowick.

CLIFFORD OF ELLINGHAM

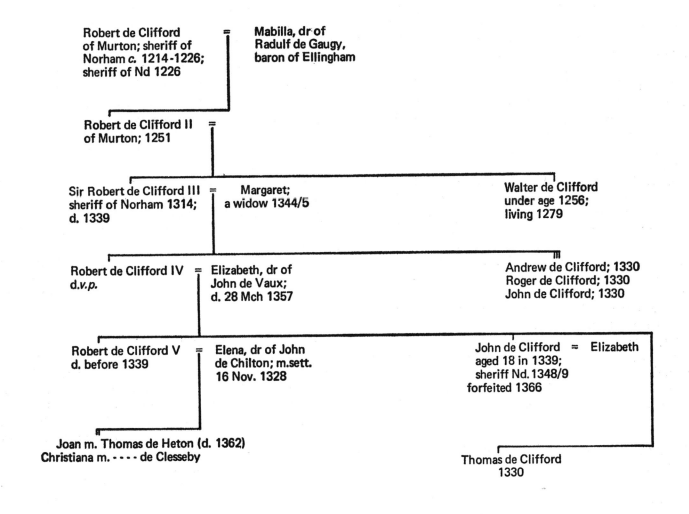

3

TAILBOIS

Ivo TAILLEBOIS has been used by several authors of historical novels as the prototype of the ruthless baron in the years following the Norman Conquest. Taillebois is perhaps a nickname and is said to signify 'the woodcutter'. The original bearer of the name was a substantial tenant *in capite* at the time of the Domesday Survey. He may have acquired most of his estates with his wife Lucia, who was heiress to Bolingbroke, Lincs., and other lands. Lucia may have been daughter to Aelgar, earl of Mercia, and thus a sister of Morcar, earl of Northumbria. She seems to have been closely related to Thorold, the English sheriff of Lincolnshire, and it has been suggested that she was his daughter, niece or greatniece. She was niece of Robert Malet, lord of Eye, and of Alan of Lincoln, lord of Thoresway (Sanders, *English Baronies*, p.18). All that seems to be certain is that she was a wealthy heiress and of Anglo-Saxon parentage.

Ivo Taillebois was *dapifer* to William Rufus and received from his master the barony of Kendal, Westmorland, as well as lands in the upper Eden Valley in Cumberland (*CW*. ns. LXII, p.95). When Ivo died in 1094 he was survived by his wife, who married secondly Roger son of Gerold de Roumare, and thirdly, *circa* 1098, Ranulf le Meschin (d.*circa* 1129), earl of Chester. According to Peter de Blois, Ivo 'had an only daughter nobly espoused' (Duchess of Cleveland's *Battle Abbey Roll*, III, 345). Many guesses have been made as to this daughter's identity, but none of them is quite satisfactory. The barony of Kendal was later held by William de Lancaster (d.1170) and by his son William de Lancaster II (d.1184). The latter's only daughter and heiress Helewise married Gilbert son of Renfrid, and they confirmed some of Ivo de Taillebois' grants to the abbey of St Mary at York.

TAILLEBOIS, BARONS OF HEPPLE, LORDS OF REDESDALE

It can be taken as certain that Ivo had no legitimate son. A little over a hundred years after his death his namesake appears in Northumberland. In 1207 this second Yvo Taillebois married Elizabeth one of the three daughters and coheiress of William son of William son of Waldef, thegn of Hepple. She had previously been married to William Bardulf but seems to have had no issue by him; William Bardulf may have died abroad for in 1205 it was reported that he was going overseas with the king (*Cur. Reg. Roll*). Yvo must have died in 1213 for Elizabeth was again a widow in 1214. Her third husband was Nicholas de Farendon who answered for the barony in 1230 and 1231; in 1242 he was fined 5m. for not going with the king to Gascony (*Pipe Roll*).

Yvo Taillebois was succeeded by his son and heir, Robert Taillebois, who died in 1257. After her husband's death Margery 'who was the wife of Robert Tayleboys' claimed against Robert le FrAunceys the third part of lands at Cliburn, Askham and Bampton, Wmd, as her dower; Robert le FrAunceys called Robert Tayleboys to warrant and the sheriff was instructed to summon him in the county of Northumberland (*Nd Pleas*). Robert Tayleboys' heir was his son, a second Robert, of full age in 1257. On 24 June 1279 sir Robert (de) Taylboys gave certain common or common rights in Hepple to the abbot of Newminster (*NDD*. p.185, No. 104).

Sir Robert Tayleboys died in 1281 and was succeeded by his son Luke. On 11 May 1287 Luke Taylebois had a conveyance from Richard son of Philip de Chartenaye of land in Hepple called the little Cruche (*Ib.*, No. 105). He granted to the abbey and convent of Newminster free way and passage through all his lands in the barony of Hepple (*SS. 66*, p.163). Sir Luke died in 1316 when his son and heir William was aged 30. He had a younger son Robert; Theofenia, widow of John de Bulmer granted to sir Luke Tailboys and Alice his wife and Robert his son and the heirs of Luke, all her lands in Hudspeth, Elsdon and Monkridge and her forest in Redesdale (*NDD*. p.186, No. 108). Sir Luke also had a daughter Alice; Thomas son of Hugh Bykertoun, lord of Bickerton, granted to Hugh his son in frank marriage with Alice daughter of sir Luke Tailleboys, lord of Hepple, his land and meadow of Farinley in Bickerton to hold in tail of the chief lord (*Ib.*, p.186, No. 107).

On 5 November 1337 sir William Tailboys had licence from the king to grant lands in Hepple and Great Tosson to his son Henry and Alianor de Boroudon in tail (*Ib.*, p.187, No. 111). Alianor was the only daughter and heiress of Gilbert de Borouden of Burradon in Coquetdale, by his wife Elizabeth, only sister of Gilbert de Umframville, baron Umframvill, earl of Angus. After the death of sir Robert Umframvill, KG., on 27 January 1436, the lordship passed by family settlement to the descendants of Gilbert de Boroudon.

In 1351 sir William Taylboys granted to sir William Heron a rentcharge of 100m. out of his lands in Northumberland (*NDD*. p.220, No. 1). On 24 June 1354 he leased the manor of Hepple to sir Robert Umframville, and on the following day he gave him quitclaim of the same (*Ib.*, p.188, Nos. 113, 114). Sir William died 28 July 1364 and was succeeded by his son Henry then aged 30; Henry was apparently only three years old when he was married unless his specified age of 30 means 30 plus. Henry's younger brother, Robert Taylboys, on 9 February 1357 quitclaimed to Henry the lands and advowson of Horthewort (Hurworth, co. Dur.) which he had of sir Henry son of Hugh and Henry his son, except two bovates which Robert had of sir William his father (*Ib.*, p.220, No. 2).

Sir Henry Taylboys died in 1364; his son Walter was then under age but came of age in 1371. On 20 May 1352 Walter had received lands in Warton from his father and mother (*Ib.*, p.188, No. 112). Elianor, 'late wife of Henry Tailboys' conveyed to her son Walter the manor of Fawdon North, the manor of Flotterton, and other lands (*Ib.*, p.221, No. 5). In February 1387 Walter exchanged with sir Robert Ogle, four husbandlands in Hepple for Ogle's moiety of the manor of Hurworth except the advowson of the church of Hurworth (*Ib.*, p.221, No. 6). Hurworth was part of the barony of Hepple, and like the manor of Hepple, had been divided into moieties after the death of William the thegn in 1200. As a result of the exchange of 1387 the two moieties of Hurworth became the property of the Taylboys family, whilst the whole of Hepple passed to the Ogles. Sir Walter Taylboys was at one time a prisoner in Scotland and a royal mandate was issued 1380/1 to the effect that Patrick de Cromby, a Scotsman, was to be delivered to him to assist in the purchase of his freedom.

Sir Walter Taylboys died on St Matthew's day 1416 when his son and heir Walter was aged 46. The second sir Walter succeeded in 1436 to the lordship of Redesdale together with the lordship of Kyme in Lincolnshire.

Walter Taylboys was living at Goxhill in Holderness 8 August 1432 when he confirmed William Clennel in his office of constable of Harbottle castle. He was then an esquire but before his death on 21 April 1444 had been knighted. His son, sir William Taylboys, was aged 26 in 1447.

When we consider little episodes in sir William's life, it is not too difficult to identify him with Willam Taylboys of Enfield, Middlesex, esquire, whose name appears on a list presented to parliament in 1459 as 'universally throughout all this realm famed and noised, known and reputed severally for open robbers, ravishers, extortioners and oppressors' (*Rolls of Parl.* V, 367). The identification is not at all certain, but at a later date sir William was fined £3000 for a riot and assault on lord Cromwell. He was captain of Alnwick castle in 1461 and fought at the battle of Towton on the Lancastrian side. After the battle of Hexham he was taken prisoner and executed at Newcastle shortly afterwards. Confiscation of his lands followed.

Sir William's son Robert was restored in 1472 (*Ib.*, VI, 18). In his w.d. 16 October 1494 he styles himself lord of Kyme and Redesdale. His body is to be buried in the priory of Kyme on the north side of the quire; his tomb is to have a 'picture' of himself and another of his wife. He bequeaths to his son George six silver bowls with a covering, a bason and ewer of silver, two pots of silver and other items. His sons William, Robert and John are each to have a silver cup. He leaves the manor of Faldingworth and the advowson of the church of Metringham, Lincs., for life to his son William. Robert is to have the manors of Newton, Kyme, Oxton and Horington, for life. His four sons John, William, Robert and Richard and his daughter each have legacies of 100m., and in addition Robert is to have £100. Sir Robert mentions in his will a marriage between his eldest son George and Elizabeth daughter of sir William Gascoigne. This was George's second wife, his first being a daughter of sir Thomas Borough of Gainsborough, Lincs.

Sir Robert died 30 June 1495 when his eldest son George was 28 years old. Sir George died 21 March 1538. His eldest son Gilbert had been summoned to parliament as baron Tailboys of Kyme in 1529. He doubtless owed his elevation to the peerage to the fact that he was the husband of the king's mistress, his wife being Elizabeth daughter of sir John Blount of Kinlet, Salop, the mother of Henry VIII's illegitimate son Henry Fitzroy, earl of Nottingham, duke of Richmond (d.1536 aged 17). Within a few months of becoming a baron, lord Tailboys died; the inscription on his monument states that he died 15 April 1530 (*Genealogist* OS. vol. II, quoted by J. Horace Round, *Peerage and Family History*, p.350n.). His widow married secondly Edward, lord Clinton.

Lord Tailbois' eldest son George, 2nd baron, was still a minor in 1538, but in April or May 1539 he married Margaret daughter of sir William Skipwith. He died *s.p.* before 15 February 1541 when the name of 'Robert lord Talboys', a minor, occurs in a royal grant. Robert, 3rd baron Tailboys of Kyme, died *s.p.* 12 March 1541. In 1542 Harbottle castle is described as the inheritance 'of the lord Taylboys' heirs' (*HN.* iii, II, p.212).

Elizabeth only sister and heiress of Robert, lord Tailboys, married for her first husband Thomas Wymbyshe of Necton, Lincs. Wymbyshe claimed to be entitled to be lord Tailboys in the right of his wife, but Henry VIII on the advice of the two chief justices, the bishop of Winchester and Garter king of arms ruled 'that neither Mr Wymbish, nor none other from thenceforth should use the style of his wife's dignity, but such as by courtesy of England, hath also the right to her possessions for term of his life'. This decision has been quoted in many subsequent peerage claims. Elizabeth's second husband was Ambrose Dudley, earl of Warwick. In the lifetime of her first husband she had exchanged the lordship of Redesdale with the Crown for the manor of Brailes in Warwickshire and other lands in Worcestershire.

Henry VIII was alleged to have designated on his deathbed, 'Sir—Wymbishe' as one of those who were to be created barons (*Acts of the Privy Council*, 1547-1550, p.16, quoted by Dr J. Horace Round, *Peerage and Pedigree*, I, p.23n.).

TAILLEBOIS—BIBLIOGRAPHY

Tailbois of Hurworth, co. Dur.; Surtees, *Durham*, III, p.254 with pedigree.
Tailbois, lords of Redesdale. *HN.* ii I, pp.60-67; pedigree pp. 6-7.
Tailbois, lords of Hepple, *NCH.* XV, pp.382-384.
Complete Peerage, XII, pp. 602-605.

TAILBOIS OF HEPPLE

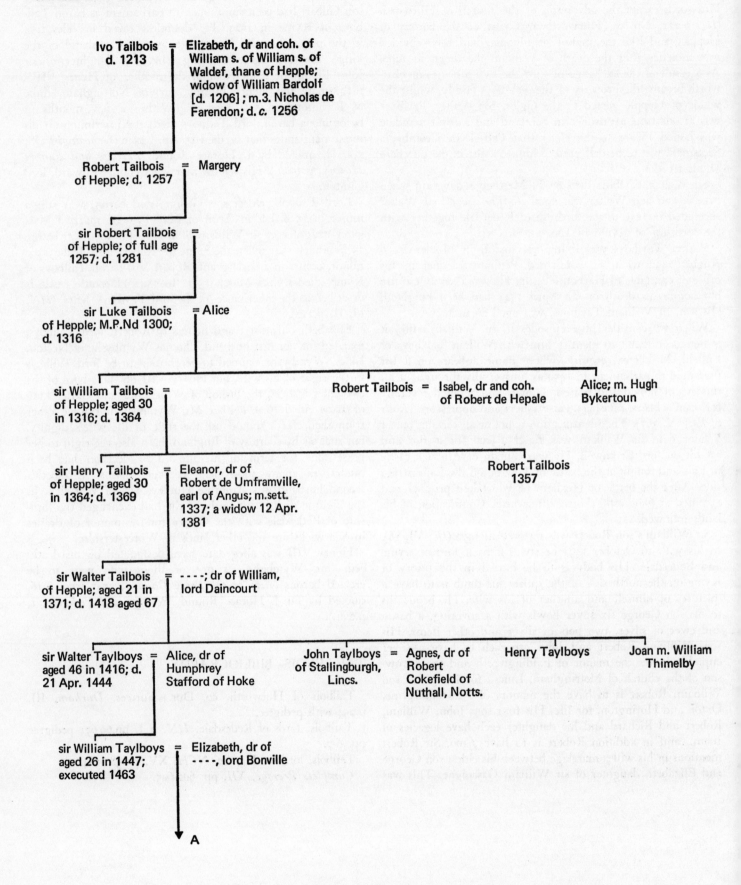

Ivo Tailbois
d. 1213
= Elizabeth, dr and coh. of
William s. of William s. of
Waldef, thane of Hepple;
widow of William Bardolf
[d. 1206] ; m.3. Nicholas de
Farendon; d. *c.* 1256

Robert Tailbois
of Hepple; d. 1257
= Margery

sir Robert Tailbois
of Hepple; of full age
1257; d. 1281
=

sir Luke Tailbois
of Hepple; M.P.Nd 1300;
d. 1316
= Alice

sir William Tailbois
of Hepple; aged 30
in 1316; d. 1364
=

Robert Tailbois = Isabel, dr and coh.
of Robert de Hepale

Alice; m. Hugh
Bykertoun

sir Henry Tailbois
of Hepple; aged 30
in 1364; d. 1369
= Eleanor, dr of
Robert de Umframville,
earl of Angus; m.sett.
1337; a widow 12 Apr.
1381

Robert Tailbois
1357

sir Walter Tailbois
of Hepple; aged 21 in
1371; d. 1418 aged 67
= ----; dr of William,
lord Daincourt

sir Walter Taylboys = Alice, dr of
aged 46 in 1416; d.
21 Apr. 1444
Humphrey
Stafford of Hoke

John Taylboys = Agnes, dr of
of Stallingburgh,
Lincs.
Robert
Cokefield of
Nuthall, Notts.

Henry Taylboys

Joan m. William
Thimelby

sir William Taylboys = Elizabeth, dr of
aged 26 in 1447;
executed 1463
----, lord Bonville

A

6

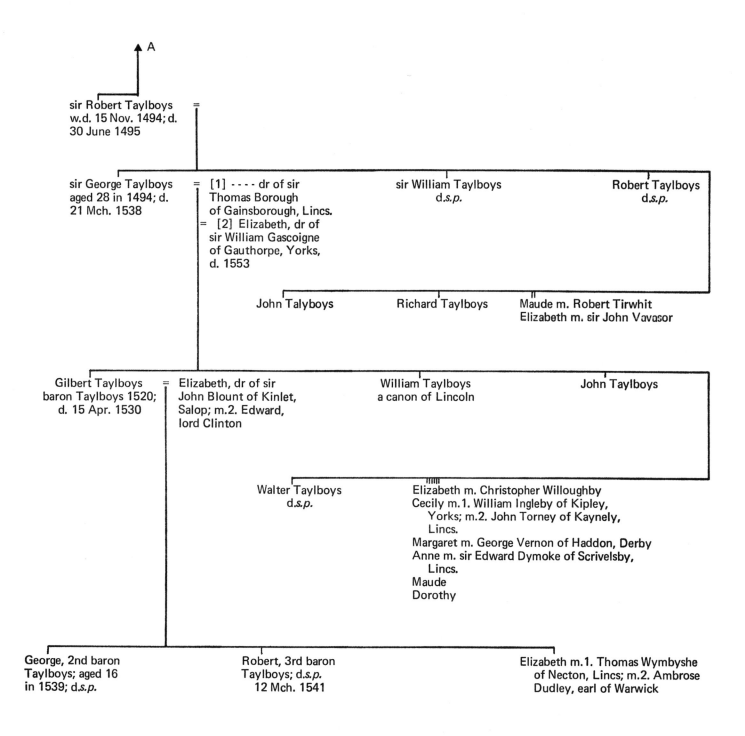

▲ A

sir Robert Taylboys
w.d. 15 Nov. 1494; d.
30 June 1495 =

sir George Taylboys   = [1] - - - - dr of sir   sir William Taylboys   Robert Taylboys
aged 28 in 1494; d.   Thomas Borough   d.*s.p.*   d.*s.p.*
21 Mch. 1538   of Gainsborough, Lincs.
                      = [2] Elizabeth, dr of
                         sir William Gascoigne
                         of Gauthorpe, Yorks,
                         d. 1553

                         John Talyboys   Richard Taylboys   Maude m. Robert Tirwhit
                                                                              Elizabeth m. sir John Vavasor

Gilbert Taylboys   = Elizabeth, dr of sir   William Taylboys   John Taylboys
baron Taylboys 1520;   John Blount of Kinlet,   a canon of Lincoln
d. 15 Apr. 1530   Salop; m.2. Edward,
                         lord Clinton

                         Walter Taylboys   Elizabeth m. Christopher Willoughby
                         d.*s.p.*   Cecily m.1. William Ingleby of Kipley,
                                                        Yorks; m.2. John Torney of Kaynely,
                                                        Lincs.
                                                    Margaret m. George Vernon of Haddon, Derby
                                                    Anne m. sir Edward Dymoke of Scrivelsby,
                                                        Lincs.
                                                    Maude
                                                    Dorothy

George, 2nd baron   Robert, 3rd baron   Elizabeth m.1. Thomas Wymbyshe
Taylboys; aged 16   Taylboys; d.*s.p.*   of Necton, Lincs; m.2. Ambrose
in 1539; d.*s.p.*   12 Mch. 1541   Dudley, earl of Warwick

7

PERCY

IT is not necessary in a work of this character to give any great detail to the history of the family of Percy. From the time of Dugdale every peerage work has contained such an account, but most of them have drawn largely from a 16th century chronicle which is mainly fantasy. It was not until early in the 14th century that the Percys obtained their first foothold in Northumberland. They held the barony of Topcliffe in Yorkshire at the time of the Domesday survey, and somewhat later obtained the honour of Petworth in Sussex. Once the family became resident in Northumberland they acquired many other baronies, lordships and manors.

Besides the barony of Alnwick (bought 1310) they added to the family possessions the barony of Warkworth and the manors of Corbridge, Newburn and Rothbury (1328), the *serjeanty* of Beanley (1333), the baronies of Prudhoe and Langley (1381), the lordship of Redesdale (1750) and the manor of Wark in Tyndale (1835).

Separate Percy family histories have been written by Edward Barrington de Fonblanque (1887) and by Gerald Brenan (1902). Another detailed account appears in Tate's *History of Alnwick* (1866). It is unfortunate that all these works have been tainted more or less by a fantastic poetical work written by William Peeris, clerk, chaplain to the fifth earl of Northumberland. *The Metrical Chronicle of the Percye Family* is packed from beginning to end with a romantic account of the early Percys produced and made up from his own imagination.

Dugdale (1675) states that 'This antient and right Noble family, do derive their descent from Mainfred de Perci. Which Mainfred came out of Denmark into Normandy, before the adventure of the famous Rollo thither'. He then gives four generations 'all born in Normandy; and from the last Geffrey, two sons, William and Serlo, who came into England with William the Conqueror' (*Baronage*, I, p.269). All this is pure romance, except for the statement that William de Perci came into England at the Conquest. At the time of the Domesday Survey he held Hambledon in Hampshire, 32 manors in Lincolnshire and 86 manors in Yorkshire; his chief properties in Yorkshire were Topcliffe in the North Riding and Spofforth in the West Riding.

The family of Perci took its name from Perci-en-Auge, dept. Calvados, arr. Lisieux and canton Mezidon.

William de Perci, the Domesday lord of Topcliffe, died on the first crusade in 1096. In addition to the lands which he held *in capite*, he held of Hugh d'Avranches, earl of Chester, the lordship of Whitby in Yorkshire, on which he founded an abbey for Benedictine monks. William came to England in 1067 with the earl of Chester; very much later, long after his death, he was given the nickname *al grenon*, a term meaning he had moustaches, unlike other Normans who were usually cleanshaven. William de Perci's wife was Emma de Port, probably a daughter of Hugh de Port (d.1096), baron of Basing in Hampshire; she was not the Saxon heiress of Semar in Yorkshire.

In the Royal Collection of MSS in the British Museum (7A, III) is a manuscript written in the 12th century, perhaps at Bardney abbey, by an anonymous monk. The monk is particularly anxious to impress on his readers the necessity of propitiating St Julian the Harbinger before and during a long journey. As an example he quotes the case of a man of Norman race, called William de Perci, who before accompanying his sovereign in one of his wars against Scotland, gave explicit directions to his chaplains to make the necessary invocations to St Julian. On account of this, both he and his fellow soldiers had unbroken successes in Scotland. On his return, however, when he was only a day's journey from his house at Topcliffe he decided that he would have no further use for the saint and gave instructions accordingly to his chaplains. The result of this, as we can imagine, was disastrous, for within a mile of Topcliffe it was discovered that his house was on fire. Being built in country fashion of wood and thatched with straw it was soon burnt out. Moving to Tadcaster it was found that all Perci's granaries and barns there had also been burnt out, and the same destruction had overcome his mansion house in York and his other house at Nafferton where his wife had been staying. It was then decided to move on to his manor of Immingham in Lincolnshire. Unknown to their lord, his followers now put in a special prayer to St Julian for mercy. This was entirely successful, for on arrival at Immingham they were greeted by the reeve who had gathered together provisions for three or four hundred men for forty days. He had received instructions to do this five weeks before although neither the notary nor the chamberlain had in fact written. It was evident that St Julian had been busy. Perhaps the most interesting part of the tale is the description of Perci's house at Topcliffe, evidently a typical Saxon timber-built and thatched hall.

William de Perci had a brother Serlo who was prior of Whitby, and their nephew William became the first abbot. A niece Alice de Perci married, firstly Reginald Buscel and secondly Hugh de Boythorpe.

William de Perci was succeeded by his eldest son Alan; he also had three younger sons, Walter, William and Richard. From Richard descended the Percys of Dunslay. Alan was one of the witnesses to the charter of Henry I whereby he confirmed the foundation of Bardney abbey in Lincolnshire by Walter de Gant. The latter was Alan's brother-in-law for Alan married Emma daughter of Gilbert de Gant, baron of Folkingham in Yorkshire.

Alan de Perci and his sons were considerable benefactors of the abbey of Whitby which the first William de Perci had founded. Alan had three legitimate sons, William his heir, Walter and Henry. Walter married as her third husband

Avice daughter of William Meschin; she inherited from her father Rougemont in Harewood, and on account of this Walter was sometimes termed 'de Rugemond'. He had a son Robert. Henry de Percy lived in Scotland and confirmed to Whitby lands in Oxnam and Heton, co. Roxburgh, given by his brothers Alan and Geoffrey, his charter being witnessed by Geoffrey and Robert de Perci, his brothers, John son of Robert de Perci, Geoffrey the clerk his brother, Robert son of Walter de Perci and Gilbert son of Hugh de Perci (*Whitby Chartulary*, i, No. 60).

Besides these legitimate sons, Alan de Perci had three illegitimate sons, Alan, Gaufrid and Gosfrid. Alan is described as *magni Alani filius nothus*. He fought for the Scots at the battle of the Standard in 1138. In 1152-53 for the health of his lord king David and earl Henry and the soul of Alan de Perci his father he gave to Whitby abbey a carucate in Oxnam and one in Heton, his charter being witnessed by William and Henry de Percy his brothers. Geoffrey de Perci witnessed his brother Alan's gift to Whitby, and added another carucate in Oxnam which had been given to him by king David. His charter is witnessed by Gosfrid the clerk, his brother. He gave a carucate in Heton to Kelso abbey with the consent of Henry his brother and heir.

Alan de Perci of Topcliffe died 1130 x 1135 and was succeeded by his eldest son William de Perci II. In 1138 William fought on the English side at the battle of the Standard. In 1166 he reported to the king that his barony had 28 knights' fees of the old feoffment, 8 of the new and a small fraction from his mesne lands. In later years his barony was charged scutage on 30 fees (Sanders, *English Baronies*, p.148n.). William de Perci II was twice married; his first wife Adelidis de Tunbridge was apparently the daughter of Richard son of Gilbert de Clare. His second wife was Sybil de Valoines, widow of Robert de Ros (d.1162/3), baron of Wark. She married thirdly, Ralph d'Aubigny.

William de Perci II is said to have had three sons Alan, Walter and Henry, but Alan died in his father's lifetime and Walter and Henry were illegitimate and when William died 1174/5 his heirs were his two daughters, Maud wife of William de Newburgh, earl of Warwick, and Agnes wife of Jocelin de Louvain. The earl of Warwick died *s.p.* 1184; the countess of Warwick in her widowhood made a grant to the monks of Salley for the health of the souls of William de Perci her father, Adelidis de Tunebrigge her mother, William, earl of Warwick, her late husband, Alan her brother and Agnes her sister. When the countess of Warwick died in 1204, the heir to her half of the barony of Topcliffe was her great nephew William de Percy, grandson to her sister Agnes.

When king Henry I's only legitimate son and heir, William the Atheling perished in the wreck of *Le Blanche Nef* on 24 November 1120 the position with regard to the crown of England became a problem. The heir now was Henry's only daughter, the empress Matilda, but the time had hardly come when a queen would be accepted in her own right by the magnates of England. The king had many bastard sons but the time was past for the acceptance of an illegitimate son as ruler such as had occurred when William I succeeded to the duchy of Normandy. After nine weeks' mourning the king married again 'with special view to male issue and to chastity', and by the advice of the archbishop of Canterbury and of the barons and 'that he might not lead a dis-

solute life'. Envoys were sent to Godfrey, duke of Lower Lorraine, previously count of Louvain, demanding in marriage his daughter Athelis. In the train of the new queen came her brother Jocelin.

A suitable wife was found for Jocelin in the person of Agnes the daughter of William de Perci II, baron of Topcliffe. The persistent tale that he 'wedded this dame Agnes Percye upon condition that he should be called Jocelyn Percy, or else that he should bear the arms of the lord Percy' is completely false (J. H. Round, *Studies in Peerage and Family History*, pp.41-42). It is known that he did not take the name of Percy and it is very doubtful whether his wife was an heiress in his lifetime or, at any rate, when he married her. The blue lion first borne by the Percys on their coat of arms in the reign of Edward I which has been blazoned as 'the ancient arms of the duke of Brabant and Lovaine', was never the arms of that family. Fifty years later when their coat of arms is first recorded they bore a gold lion. Agnes de Perci's husband in his own charters is regularly termed *Jocelinus frater Adelide regine* (*Percy Chartulary*, p.385, No. CM); Henry I in a charter of confirmation calls him *Jocelinus frater regine* (*Ib.*, No. CMV).

The honour of Arundel in Sussex, forfeited by Robert de Belesme in 1102, was granted to Adeliza, widow of Henry I as her dower. Part of this great fief, the honour of Petworth, was given to the queen's brother and remained part of the Percy estates until the 18th century when it passed by will to the Wyndhams, earls of Egremont, and from them to their illegitimate descendants, the lords Leconfield.

As a tailpiece to this account of Jocelin the queen's brother and his wife Agnes de Perci it is perhaps interesting to record here that sir Hugh Smithson, the founder of the present line of dukes of Northumberland, demanded a dukedom of Brabant in right of his wife's descent. As a compromise he was made duke of Northumberland (1766).

Jocelin the queen's brother died 1179/80 and his widow Agnes 1201 x 1204. Their eldest son Henry, who took his mother's name of Percy, had livery of his mother's land and in 1211 paid scutage on fifteen knights' fees.

After the death of the countess of Warwick, her half share of the Percy lands was acquired by Jocelin de Louvain's younger son sir Richard who also took his mother's surname of Percy. He died in 1244. He was twice married but left no legitimate issue. His illegitimate son was sir Henry de Percy of Settle, Yorks. The editor of *Percy Chartulary* referring to a deed (No. XXVII) by which Henry son of Richard de Percy gave lands in Erghum to his son Alexander, suggests that Alexander was a brother to sir Henry and not a son. There are, however, several other deeds where Alexander is called son of sir Henry (Nos. CXLIII, CCCLXXXII, CCCLXXXVIII, CCCCI, and CCCCVI). By a family arrangement, the lands taken, perhaps illegally, by sir Richard were later transferred to the senior branch of the family. In 1244 Bernard de Baillol had a grant of the marriage of Agnes the widow of Richard de Percy to the end he might take her to wife if he could obtain her consent (*Patent Roll*). By 8 November 1251 Agnes had married John de Eyncurt and was claiming dower from Henry son of William de Percy (*Percy Chartulary*, III). John de Eyncurt (Aincourt) was lord of Blankney in Lincolnshire, and died in 1257 (Sanders, *op. cit.* p.16).

Henry de Percy married Isabella daughter of Adam de Brus, baron of Skelton, and with her acquired the manor of Leconfield in Yorkshire which for many years was one of the principal residences of the family. In 1222 William son and heir of Henry de Percy was pardoned for scutage on 15 knights' fees in Yorkshire and 28 in Sussex. In 1244 he had livery of the lands which had been held by his uncle Richard. William de Percy died in 1245 and was succeeded by his eldest son Henry who paid £900 for livery of his lands and that he might marry as he pleased. Henry died in 1272 and it is with his eldest surviving son and successor, another Henry, that the family's connection with Northumberland commences.

PERCY, BARONS OF ALNWICK

IN 1310 Henry de Percy II acquired the barony of Alnwick by purchase, and in the following year was knighted by Edward I at Berwick. He fought in Scotland in most of king Edward's campaigns and was rewarded by a grant of the lands in Scotland and England forfeited by Ingelram de Baliol. Under Edward II Henry de Percy was governor of the castles of Bamburgh and Scarborough but joined the barons who revolted and put to death the king's favourite, Piers de Gaveston. For this, the king's escheator was ordered to seize all his lands, tenements, goods and chattels. When peace was concluded between the king and his barons Percy was restored. He was only 42 or 43 years old when he died in 1315.

Henry de Percy III was sixteen when his father died and his estates in Northumberland were committed to John de Felton. Whilst still a minor he acquired in 1316 the serjeanty of Beanley forfeited by Patrick, earl of Dunbar and March. In 1333 he was present at the battle of Halidon Hill, and was made governor of Berwick and one of the guardians of the eastern side of Scotland. From Edward Baliol, king of Scotland, he had a grant of the pele of Lochmaben and the valleys of Annandale and Moffatdale. These Scottish lands were later exchanged for the castle and town of Jedburgh, the towns of Bon-Jedburgh and Hassyden and the forest of Jed. By 1342 the English had been driven out of the whole of Scotland. Henry de Percy was present at the battle of Neville's Cross in 1346 where with Gilbert de Umfraville and other northern barons he commanded the right wing. He made his will on 13 September 1349 (*Testamenta Eboracensia*, p.57) and died on 26 February 1352.

He leaves numerous bequests to religious establishments. Because formerly he had intended to go on pilgrimage to the Holy Land, but had been unable to do so, 1000 marks which he had set aside for his own journey are to be given to his son Henry if the latter should make the journey on his father's behalf. His sons Henry, Thomas and Roger and his daughters Margaret and Isabella all have legacies. He leaves £200 to any one in those parts of England through which he had passed either in time of peace or war, who might have complaint of anything taken from him by the testator or his people against his will. By a series of deeds dated from 1 May 1334 to 20 April 1335 Henry de Percy had settled the manor of Starbotton in Craven, Yorks., for the benefit of his third son Roger (*Percy Chartulary*, DXCIV to DCII); Roger died childless.

Henry de Percy IV had fought at the battle of Crecy in his father's lifetime. He was governor of Berwick in 1359. His first wife was a royal Plantagenet, being Mary daughter of Henry, earl of Lancaster. He died on Ascension Day 1368 and was buried in Alnwick abbey. His son and heir Henry de Percy V was then 26 years of age.

Henry de Percy V served for many years in the French campaigns of Edward III. In 1376 he was appointed marshal of England, and the following year he was made general of all the English forces in France. At the coronation of Richard II in 1377 he was raised to the dignity of earl of Northumberland. At the battle of Otterburn in 1387 his sons sir Henry and sir Ralph were taken prisoner by the Scots and held to ransom. In 1399 the Percys incurred the displeasure of Richard II owing, it is said, to words spoken which were derogatory to the king. The earl, summoned to appear before the king, refused to do so and was proclaimed a traitor and sentenced to banishment. With the assistance of Ralph Nevill, earl of Westmorland, and other barons, Percy openly rebelled and succeeded in deposing the king and placing the duke of Lancaster on the throne as Henry IV. Rich rewards followed this, the earl being made constable of England, and to him and his heirs was given the Isle of Man to hold by carrying the sword of Lancaster on the day of the king's coronation. He and his son Hotspur also received very substantial grants of land mainly in Scotland and Wales.

In spite of these great rewards, the rapacity of the earl and the haughty character of his son Hotspur demanded more, which the king was unwilling or unable to give. In June 1403 the Percys were in revolt and active rebellion. On 21 July 1403 Hotspur's forces, about 14,000 men, faced the royal army of almost equal numbers at Shrewsbury; the earl with additional forces had not yet arrived. Hotspur would not wait for his father and made a determined attack on the king's army. His rashness was his undoing for he was badly supported and an arrow from an unknown hand pierced his brain. His body was afterwards drawn and quartered and the remains exhibited at Shrewsbury, London, Newcastle, York and Chester. His father surrendered to the king at York and was pardoned on asserting that Hotspur had acted contrary to his express wishes and orders.

Notwithstanding the king's leniency, the earl of Northumberland was again in rebellion in 1405. He escaped to Scotland but his lands were confiscated. For four years he remained a fugitive in Scotland and Flanders. Returning to England in 1409 he advanced into Yorkshire with a small band of followers, but was defeated and killed at Bramham Moor.

The earl's grandson Henry, son of Hotspur, remained in Scotland but was restored to the earldom in 1414 and liberated by the Scots in 1415. From now on the Percys were staunch supporters of the Lancastrian kings. When Henry VI was defeated and captured at the battle of St Albans by the duke of York on 22 May 1455 the earl of Northumberland was killed.

Henry Percy, 3rd earl of Northumberland, was knighted by the duke of Bedford at the same time as Henry VI. He was then only two years old. His wife was Eleanor, only daughter and heiress of Richard Poynings, son and heir of Robert, baron Poynings. In right of his wife, Henry Percy succeeded to the estates belonging to the baronies of Poynings, Bryan and Fitzpayne, and on 14 December 1446 was summoned to

PERCY. First line

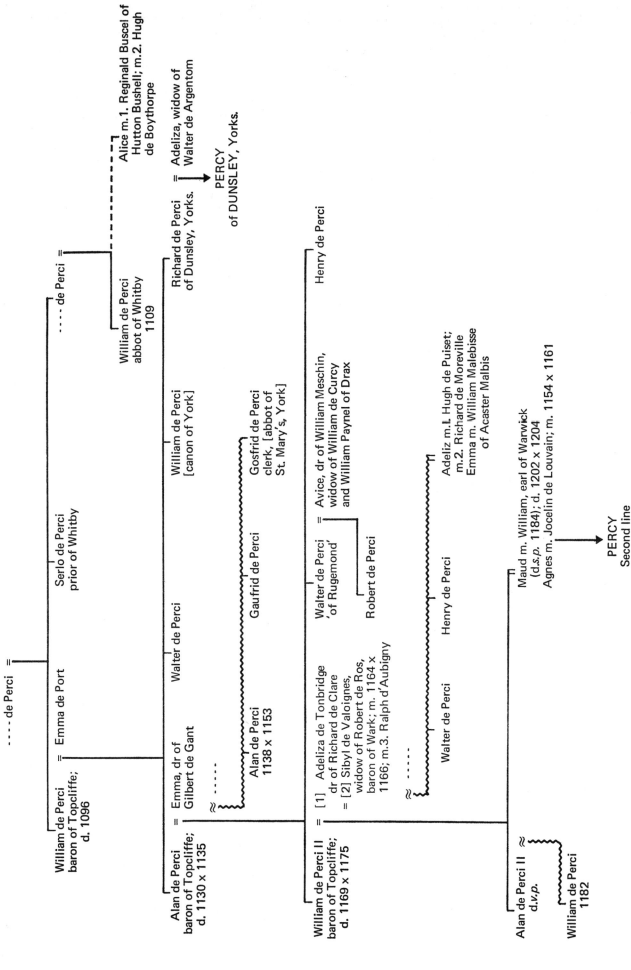

II

parliament as Henry Percy de Poynings, *chevalier*. Still faithful to the Lancastrians, the earl fought for them at the battle of Northampton in 1460 and at Towton in 1461. In the latter conflict, when it is said that 38,000 Englishmen were killed, the earl was amongst the fallen. He was attainted by the parliament which met on 4 November 1461 and all his estates were confiscated.

The earldom and estates were bestowed on John Nevill, lord Montagu. Henry Percy, son and heir of the third earl, was imprisoned in the Tower of London but was given his liberty on 27 October 1469. He was restored to his earldom and estates, lord Montagu being created a marquis in compensation. By Richard III, the earl of Northumberland was made lord high chamberlain of England, but when the king stood against Henry Tudor, earl of Richmond, at Bosworth field 22 August 1485, he remained neutral with his men during the course of the battle. He may have already had some secret arrangement with Henry Tudor for he was much in the latter's favour when he became Henry VII.

On 28 April 1489 he was killed in his own house at Coxlodge, near Thirsk in Yorkshire, by a mob who was dissatisfied by a special levy imposed by parliament and the haughty manner by which the earl was enforcing its collection. His funeral at Beverley was particularly impressive; 13,340 poor folk who attended received 2d., each, and the total cost was more than £1500, a considerable sum for those days. He had made provision in his w.d. 27 July 1485 (shortly before Bosworth Field) for his sons Henry, William, Aleyne and Gessilyne, his daughters Alianor and Anne, his nephews sir Ralph and George Percy, and for the children of sir Henry, another nephew. His son Gessilyne (Jocelin) was ancestor of the Percys of Beverley, Cambridge and Rochester, of whom an account will be given later.

The fifth earl of Northumberland besides being called Henry was given the additional name of Algernon, coined from the description *al grenon* the imagined nickname of his ancestor William de Perci (d.1096). At the age of 10 he was created a Knight of the Bath at the same time as Arthur, prince of Wales; before 1498 he was a Knight of the Garter. It has been said of him that 'he was more at home in gaudy shows than in battle-fields'. For the marriage of Margaret, eldest daughter of Henry VII to James IV of Scotland, he escorted the princess on her way to Scotland. They were received at Lamberton by the Scottish king and his nobles who were richly apparelled for the occasion, but the earl of Northumberland outshone them all 'in the richness of his coat being goldsmith's work, garnished with pearl and stones; and for the costly apparel of his henchmen, and gallant trappings of his horses, besides 400 tall men well horsed and appareled in his colours, he was esteemed both of the Scots and Englishmen more like a prince than a subject'. He was not engaged in the battle of Flodden, 9 September 1513, but his brother sir William Percy was there, and a distant kinsman, sir Lionel Percy. He died 19 May 1527; by his wife Catherine daughter and coheiress of sir Robert Spencer of Spencer Combe, Devonshire, he had three sons, Henry his successor, sir Thomas and sir Ingelram, and two daughters.

Henry, the 6th earl, was brought up in the household of cardinal Wolsey, and whilst in attendance on the cardinal met at the royal court and fell in love with Anne Boleyn. About the same time she had caught the fancy of Henry VIII who instructed Wolsey to dissuade Percy from pressing his suit. The 6th earl changed to the reformed religion but his brothers clung to the old faith. Both sir Thomas and sir Ingelram joined in the Pilgrimage of Grace.

Sir Thomas was taken, condemned as a traitor, and executed at Tyburn in 1537; Sir Ingelram died in 1538. The earl died 30 June 1537 without issue. The children of his brother sir Thomas could not succeed to the title for he had been attainted. Until queen Mary came to the throne the Percy family remained in obscurity, but she being attached to the church of Rome looked with favour on Thomas Percy son of the attainted sir Thomas. By letters patent on 30 April 1557 he was created baron Percy and on the following day advanced to the earldom of Northumberland, the succession being restricted to the male heirs of his own body, and failing them, to the heirs male of his brother Henry.

On the succession of Elizabeth in 1559, earl Thomas was for some time in favour, but his religion was against him. In 1568 he was intriguing to place Mary, queen of Scots, on to the throne of England. He was commanded to appear before queen Elizabeth by orders dated 14 November 1569; fearing to obey he broke into open revolt but less than a hundred men joined him. Escaping over the Border into Liddesdale he was betrayed by Hector Armstrong of Harelaw, and turned over for a sum of money to James Stewart, earl of Murray. He was imprisoned in Lochleven castle until July 1572 when for a large bribe he was given up to lord Hunsdon, governor of Berwick. In almost indecent haste he was hurried to York and there beheaded on 22 August. By his wife Anne daughter of Henry Somerset, earl of Worcester, he had an only son who died in infancy, and five daughters.

The Percy titles and estates passed to his brother Henry who had conformed to the Protestant religion in 1560. Henry may, however, have had a secret attachment to the old faith, for he became an object of suspicion to the government and was not allowed to leave London. This was not sufficient for his enemies and he was trapped by counterfeit letters. He was never brought to trial but remained a prisoner in the Tower of London until his death. Under very mysterious circumstances he was found on the morning of 21 June 1585 dead in his bed with three bullets in the chest. A jury brought in the extraordinary verdict of suicide. The eighth earl had eight sons, all of whom died without issue except the eldest son Henry.

Henry, 9th earl of Northumberland, was strongly attached to James VI of Scotland and assisted him to become James I of England. He soon lost his popularity with that monarch owing to the treasonable conduct of his kinsman, Thomas Percy, who was involved in the Gunpowder Plot and killed on 8 November 1605. Thomas was grandson of Joscelin Percy, fourth son of the fourth earl. The earl was convicted of treason, 27 June 1606, on the most slender of evidence, but his enemies were numerous and powerful. He was sentenced to life imprisonment and a fine of £30,000. The fine was paid in 1614 and he was released on 18 July 1621. Until his death on 5 November 1632 he lived in obscurity at Petworth. He was survived by his two sons Algernon and Henry.

Algernon, 10th earl of Northumberland, had been created baron Percy on the accession of Charles I in 1625 and remained a strong supporter of the king. During the Commonwealth he lived in retirement at Petworth where he died 13

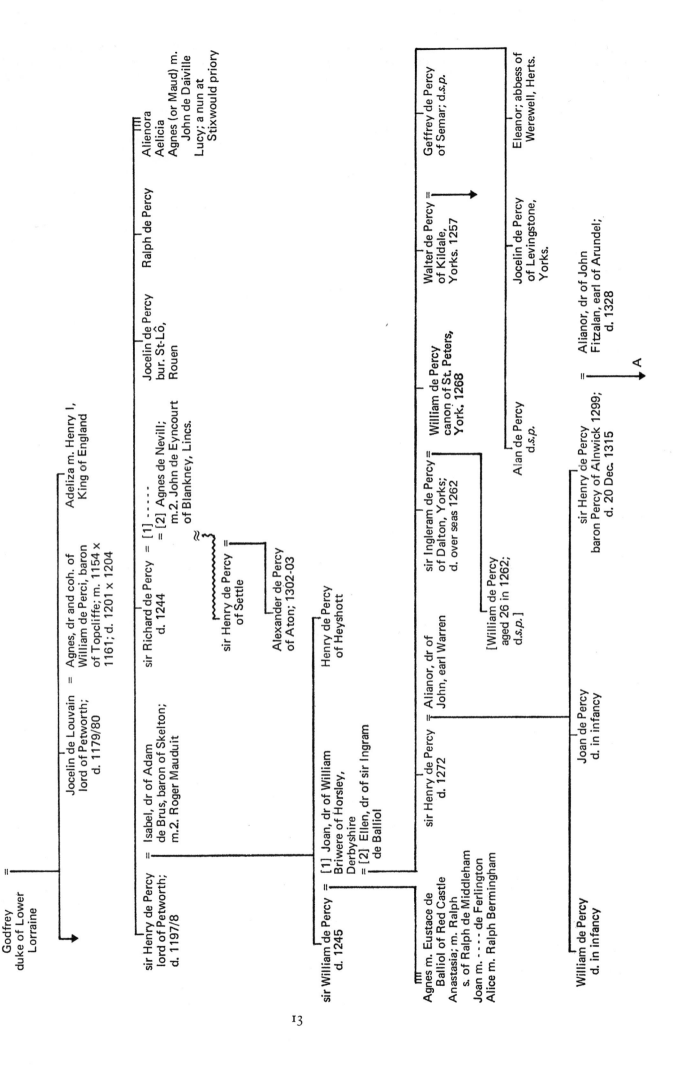

13

October 1668. By his first wife Anne daughter of William Cecil, earl of Shrewsbury, he had five daughters, and by his second wife Elizabeth daughter of Theophilus Howard, earl of Suffolk, an only son Josceline.

Josceline, 11th earl of Northumberland, died 21 May 1670 and left an only daughter Elizabeth, then four years of age.

It is now necessary to consider in some detail the cadet lines of the Percys throughout the 15th and 16th centuries, for after the death in 1670 of Josceline, earl of Northumberland, it was believed that the male line of the family was extinct. On the death without children of the 6th earl in 1537 and the attainder of his brother sir Thomas at the same time, the earldom created in 1377 became extinct. A large portion of the Percy estates was taken over by the Crown. As Roman Catholics the family remained in obscurity until the reign of queen Mary, herself an ardent believer in the Romish faith.

On 30 April 1557 queen Mary by letters patent created Thomas Percy, nephew of the 6th earl and eldest son of the attainted sir Thomas, baron Percy of Cockermouth 'in consideration of his noble descent, constancy, virtue, and valour in deeds of arms, and other shining qualifications'. The following day Thomas was advanced to the earldom of Northumberland and the Percy estates remaining in the possession of the Crown were restored to him. The succession to both the title and the estates was to be restricted to the heirs male of his own body, and failing them, to the heirs male of his brother Henry. In 1670 it was certain that there were no male heirs living of the bodies of earl Thomas (d.1572) and earl Henry (d.1585). In 1674 Charles II created George Fitzroy, his illegitimate son by Barbara, duchess of Cleveland, earl of Northumberland; in 1683 he was made duke of Northumberland. The Percy estates were given to James, duke of Monmouth.

Henry Percy, 2nd earl of the creation of 1557 had, besides his eldest son and heir, seven younger sons, Thomas (d. unm. April 1587), sir William (d.s.p. 1648), sir Charles (d.s.p. 1648), sir Richard (d.s.p. 1628), sir Alan (d.s.p. 1613), sir Josceline (d.s.p. 1631) and George (d. unm. 1532). It could, however, be argued that the creation of 1557 was but a restoration of the earldom created in 1377 lost by the attainder of 1407 but restored in 1414.

Henry, first earl of Northumberland (d.1408), had two younger sons, sir Thomas and sir Ralph who married two sisters, Elizabeth and Philippa, daughters and coheiresses of David de Strathbogie, earl of Athol. Sir Ralph was killed in the Holy Land in 1399 and had no children. Sir Thomas, called of Athol, died in Spain in or before 1388. He had two sons sir Henry Percy of Athol and Thomas Percy. The latter died in infancy at Carlisle. The former died 25 October 1433 when the estates which had belonged to his mother passed to his two daughters.

Henry, second earl of Northumberland (d.1455), had five younger sons. Of these sir Thomas, created baron Egremont in 1449 was killed at the battle of Northampton in 1460; he left a son sir John Percy, born 1459, living 1480, and believed to have died unmarried. George Percy, 6th son of the 2nd earl, was prebendary of Beverley, rector of Rothbury and Colbeck, and died unmarried in 1474. The 8th son sir Richard was killed at Towton Field 1461 s.p. The 9th son William was bishop of Carlisle and died 1462.

Sir Ralph Percy, 7th son of the 2nd earl, was killed at the battle of Hedgeley in 1464. By his wife Eleanor daughter and heir of Lawrence Acton of Acton, par. Felton, he had three sons, sir Henry, sir Ralph and George, and a daughter Margaret wife of sir Ralph Harbottle. Little is known about the younger sir Ralph except that he was living in 1489; George married Alianore daughter of sir William Hilton, widow of Owen, 2nd lord Ogle, and died about 1500. So far as is known neither of these brothers left children. The elder brother sir Henry Percy died in 1486. Besides his son and heir John he had a daughter Catherine who married sir Simon le Grand. Both sir Ralph Percy and his son sir Henry had been constables of Dunstanburgh castle; the latter became bailiff of Embleton in 1485 (NCH. II, p.36); John Percy who was bailiff in 1520 was presumably his son. It has been stated that about this time John Percy settled at Worcester and that he left descendants, amongst them Dr Thomas Percy, author of *The Hermit of Warkworth*. No proof of this has been seen.

Henry, 4th earl of Northumberland (d.1489), had three younger sons, sir William, Alan and Josceline. Sir William was present at the battle of Flodden in 1513 and took part in the Pilgrimage of Grace in 1536; he is said to have married Agnes, daughter of sir Robert Ughtred, and to have had children, but he seems to have had no male descendants living in 1670. In 1532 sir William had a wife called Margaret, for his brother Josselyn Percy of Newlands by his w.d. 7 September 1532 leaves 'to my dearly beloved sister Dame Margaret Percy, wife of my brother, sir Wm Percy, to pray for me, 6s.8d.'. Alan Percy was Warden of Trinity College, Arundel, 1545 and never married. The youngest son Josceline had lands in Sussex from his father and died in 1532. He married Margaret daughter and coheir of Walter Frost of Beverley and through her inherited lands at Beverley which remained with their descendants for several generations. One of these descendants was Thomas Percy, at one time constable of Alnwick castle, who became infamous for his part in the Gunpowder Plot. (*See* PERCY OF BEVERLEY).

Henry, 5th earl of Northumberland, besides his two elder sons Henry, 6th earl (d.1537) and Thomas (executed 1537), had a younger son, sir Ingelram. Sir Ingelram took part in the Pilgrimage of Grace in 1536 and died in 1538; he never married, but he had an illegitimate daughter Isabella who married Henry Tempest of Broughton, Yorks.

Immediately after the death in 1670 of Josceline, 11th earl of Northumberland, one James Percy put forward a claim to the earldom and the estates attached to it. He had at one time been a trunkmaker in Dublin but was now a prosperous merchant in that town. His knowledge of his ancestors was very slight for he could not name his great grandfather. He was the eldest surviving son of Henry Percy of Horton, Northants, by his wife Lydia daughter of Robert Cope of Horton. Henry Percy was the third son of another Henry Percy of Pavenham Bury, co. Bedford, by his wife Jane daughter of James Tibbot of Pavenham Bury. Further than that James could not go, but there was a tradition in his family that his grandfather was one of four brothers and sisters brought secretly in hampers from the north of England shortly after 1559. There were few persons prepared to give any credence to this tradition. Anne, countess of Pembroke, however, openly stated at Court and elsewhere that 'if the Trunkmaker really came from Pavenham, he must be one of those four Percy children that in the time of the

PERCY [LOVAINE] —cont.

↑ A

sir William Percy
K.B; d.s.p. 1355

Henry de Percy
2nd baron; w.d.
13 Sept. 1349; d. 26
Feb. 1353
= Idonea (Imania)
dr of Robert, lord
Clifford; d. 1365

Henry Percy
aged 30 in 1349;
d. 1368
= [1] Mary, dr of Henry
Plantagenet, earl of
Lancaster; d. 1 Sept.
1362
= [2] Joan, dr and heiress
of John de Orby; d.s.p.

Richard Percy
of Semar, Yorks;
1335; d.s.p.

Thomas Percy
bishop of Norwich;
w.d. 25 May 1368;
d. 1369

Roger Percy
1335-1354;
d.s.p.

sir William Percy
of Kirk Levington;
d.s.p. 1355

Robert Percy
1335; d.s.p.

Margaret; m.1. Robert Umframville;
m.2. William, lord Ferrers of
Groby. (d. 1372); d. 1375
Maud; m. Ralph, lord Nevill of Raby
Eleanor; m. John, lord Fitzwalter
Isabel; [m. William de Aton]; d.s.p.

Mary; aged 2 in 1368;
(m. John, lord Roos of Hamlake]

Henry Percy
3rd baron; aged 26
in 1368; marshal of
England 1376; constable
1399; earl of Northumberland 16 July 1377; k.
19 Feb. 1407/8
= [1] Margaret, dr of Ralph,
lord Nevill of Raby; m.12
July 1358; d. 1372
= [2] Maud, dr of Thomas,
lord Lucy, widow of Gilbert
Umframville, earl of Angus;
d. 18 Dec. 1398

sir Thomas Percy
K.G.; earl of Worcester
1398; ex. 21 July 1403
s.p.

Isabel m. Gilbert de Aton

sir Henry Percy, K.G.,
'Hotspur'; b. 20 May
1364; k. 2 July 1403
= Elizabeth, dr of Edward
Mortimer, earl of March;
m.2. Thomas, lord Camoys;
d. 20 Apr. 1417

sir Thomas Percy
of Athol; d. 1386
= Elizabeth, dr and coh.
of David Strabolgy,
earl of Athol

sir Ralph Percy
k. in Palestine
1399
= Philippa, dr and coh.
of David Strabolgy,
earl of Athol

Alan Percy

Margaret

sir Henry Percy,
of Athol; d. 1432
= Elizabeth, dr of William,
lord Bardolph. [widow of
lord Scales]

Thomas Percy
d. in infancy

Elizabeth; m.1. sir Thomas Burgh;
m.2. sir William Lucy
Margaret; m.1. lord Grey of Codnor;
m.2. sir Richard de Vere

Henry Percy, 2nd earl
b. 3 Feb. 1392/3; constable
of England; k. 22 May
1455
= Eleanor, dr of Ralph
Nevill, e. of Westmorland,
widow of Richard, lord
le Despencer; d. 1463

Elizabeth; m.1. John, lord
Clifford; m.2. Ralph
Nevill, e. of Westmorland

→ B

15

PERCY [LOVAINE] —cont. 2

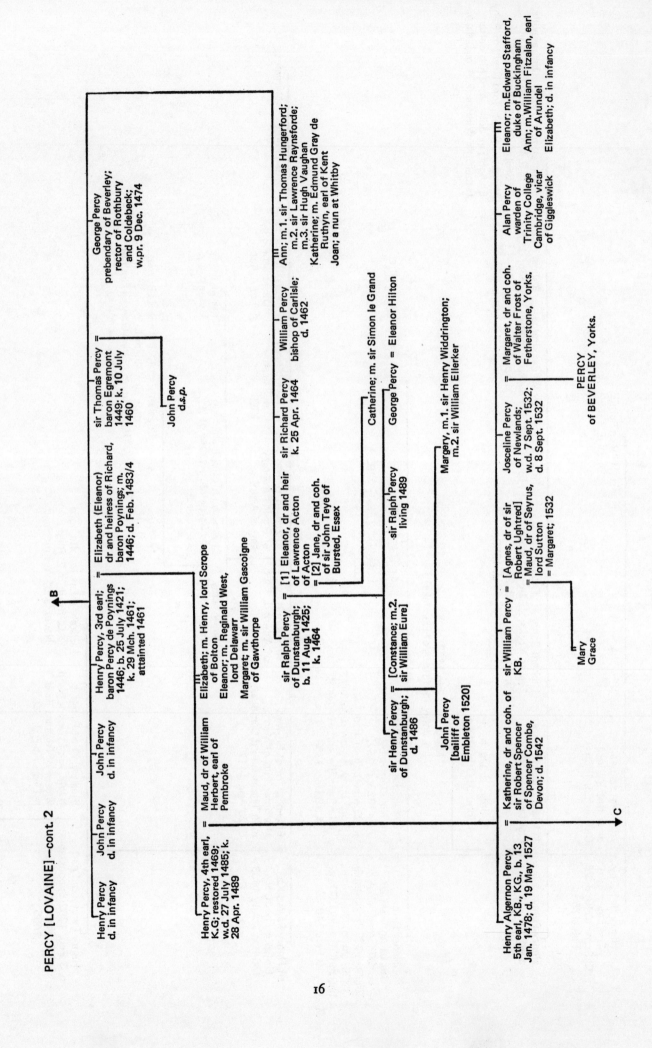

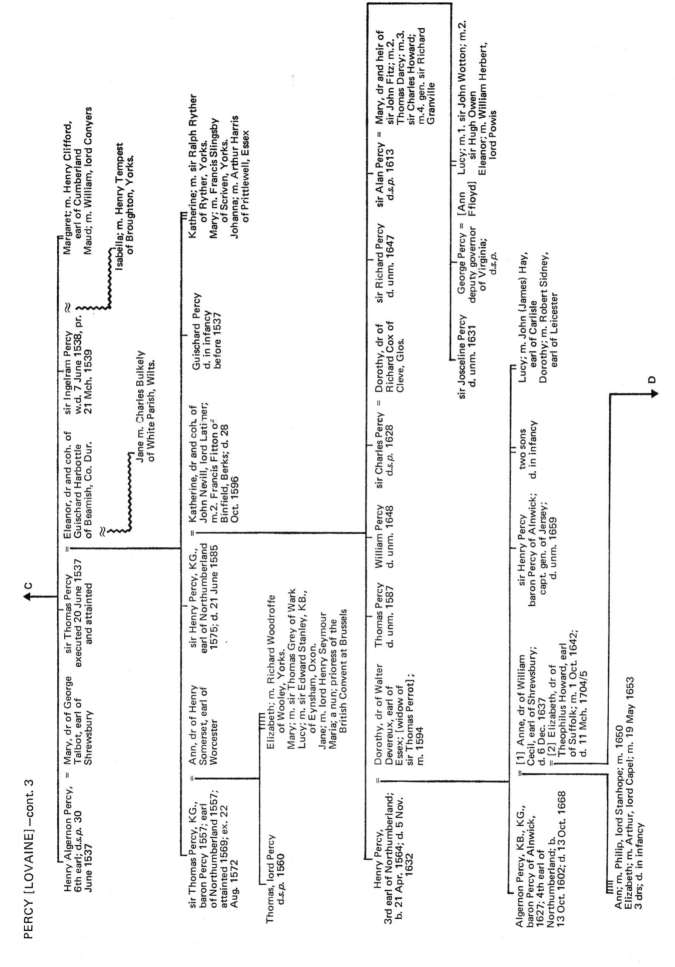

troubles in 1559 were sent out of the North in Hampiers to old Dame Vaux at Harrowden in Northamptonshire'. Dame Vaux was probably the widow of Thomas (d.1556), 2nd lord Vaux of Harrowden. In the hope of establishing the ancestry of his grandfather, James Percy applied to the Heralds' College. Sir Edward Walker, then Garter King of Arms, produced a book dealing with the family history of the earls of Northumberland. Unfortunately for the claimant a page of the book was missing, the very page the claimant thought that might have proved his ancestry. After the hiatus caused by the missing page the account continued '——ard Percy who married and had issue'. Garter suggested that the person whose name was half missing was sir Richard Percy, whom we now know to have died unmarried in 1648.

To have been the great grandfather of James Percy, sir Richard must have become a grandfather at the age of sixteen! The claim was considered in the House of Lords in 1673 and easily refuted. About this time a second claimant, William Percy, a London glover, put forward a pedigree in which he set out that he was an elder brother of the trunkmaker. The latter easily proved that William was his half brother, an illegitimate son of his father Henry Percy of Horton by one Mary Varnum.

James Percy returned to the attack with a revised claim, in which he set forth that his grandfather was a son of sir Ingelram Percy, third son of Henry Percy, 5th earl of Northumberland. He claimed that sir Ingelram 'married and had issue 2 sons, (viz) Henry and Robert'. 'Henry had issue 3 sons, James, William and Henry' of whom Henry was father of James the claimant. According to the claim, Robert, 2nd son of sir Ingelram 'had issue 3 sons, Robert, Thomas and one more'. He went on to state that 'Now for Alexander Percy, gent. of Ireland, that rides in the Life-guard, and Mr Roger Percy shoe-maker at Charing-cross; and Mr Francis Percy stone-cutter in Cambridge, and his brother a taylor: I acknowledg them to be Cousins, and Descended from the Sons of Robert Percy, my Great Unkle. And by reason I know not which is the Eldest and nearest of Kin of that Collateral Line' (*This book makes appear the Claim, Pedigree and Proceedings of James Percy Now claimant to the Earldom of Northumberland, Humbly presented to both Houses of Parliament.* Printed in the Year 1680).

James Percy's second attempt at his 'pedigree' was no more satisfactory than his first, for we know for certain that sir Ingelram Percy had no legitimate children, and there is no evidence that he was ever married. In his w.d. 7 June 1538, pr. 21 March 1539 sir Ingelram makes no mention of any children except a daughter Isabel to whom he leaves £20; her mother is to have 20 marks; from the wording of the will it is evident that Isabel was illegitimate. Isabel married Henry Tempest of Broughton, Yorks., and in the 1563/4 visitation pedigree of Tempest of Broughton she is called 'base' daughter of sir Ingram.

In 1681 Francis Percy, the Cambridge stone-cutter, cousin of James Percy the claimant, came to London to consult the Heralds' College. Sir William Dugdale the well-known genealogist was now Garter King of Arms. Francis Percy knew the tradition of the four children brought from the north of England in 1559 and believed that his grandfather Robert Percy was one of them. It is probable that Francis had missed out a generation in his pedigree. His grandfather Robert

Percy who married in 1615 can hardly have been James Percy's great uncle for James' parents were married in 1614. It seems more likely that Robert Percy (m.1615), grandfather of Francis the stone-cutter, was a son, the 'one more' son of James' great uncle Robert. He had inherited another tradition that Robert was a very near relative of Thomas Percy, the conspirator in the Gunpowder Plot. Dugdale, misled as his predecessor Garter Walker had been, by the hiatus in the book recording the family pedigree, suggested that the common ancestor of Francis and his cousin James could be (Guisch)ard Percy, the youngest son of sir Thomas Percy, executed and attainted in 1537. He made this Guischard father of Thomas the conspirator.

Dugdale was hopelessly at sea in this. It is quite certain that Guischard died in early childhood; he was certainly dead in 1537 when his father was executed. Thomas the conspirator belonged to the family of PERCY of BEVERLEY. Josceline Percy (d.1653) of Beverley admitted that he was playing at primero with other pages of the earl at Essex House on the night preceding the 5th of November 1603 when his 'uncle' Thomas the conspirator called upon him (Singer, *Treatise on Cards*, quoting an original state paper in the *Public Record Office*).

On 3 April 1688 James Percy wrote to his cousin Francis Percy of Cambridge pointing out that Francis was of a junior line to his own. 'My father was Henry Percy of Horton in Northamptonshire, who was second son of Henry Percy of Pavenham in Bedfordshire who was the first son of sir Ingelram Percy, third son of Henry Percy, fifth earl of Northumberland: and your father was Francis Percy, the son of Thomas Percy, who was the son of Robert Percy, second son of sir Ingelram Percy'. Later in the letter he states 'but there is one Roger Percy who was the son of Henry Percy, who was the son of Richard Percy, who was the son of Robert Percy, second son of sir Ingelram Percy, who sent those two sons and two daughters in hampires: Anne married Eson a miller in Cookhoo (Cogenhoe) in Northamptonshire; and Eleanor married and had a daughter Mary, grand-daughter of sir Ingelram, who is yet living aged 85: but whether Thomas your grandfather, or Richard his grandfather was the eldest, I cannot tell'. Perhaps Francis was influenced by this letter for he ceased prosecuting his own claim to the title in 1689. By now James Percy's money was at an end, and all he had to live on were the small sums sent from Ireland by his sons.

James' eldest son, sir Anthony Percy, became the lord mayor of Dublin. From him, and from another son John Percy of Norwich there are many descendants living today, mainly in Ireland. Sir Anthony Percy's son, Henry Percy of Seskin, co. Wicklow, Ireland, unsuccessfully claimed the Percy estates from the duke of Somerset in 1725.

In 1679 the young heiress Elizabeth, only surviving child of Josceline Percy, 11th earl of Northumberland, was married to Henry Cavendish, lord Ogle, 'a sickly boy of appalling ugliness, certainly weak-minded if not indeed, an absolute idiot'. Lord Ogle assumed the surname of Percy, but fortunately for his bride he died on 17 November 1679 about six months after the marriage, before the couple had actually lived together. The next husband chosen for Elizabeth was a wealthy commoner Thomas Thynne of Longleat, Wiltshire. Thynne was assassinated by captain Christopher Vratz in February

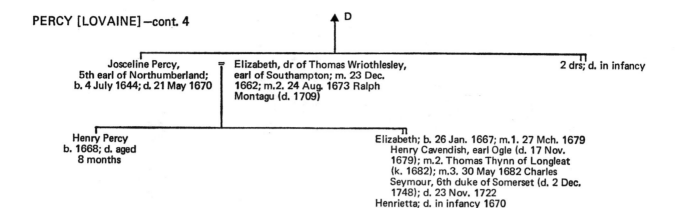

D

| Josceline Percy, 5th earl of Northumberland; b. 4 July 1644; d. 21 May 1670 | = Elizabeth, dr of Thomas Wriothlesley, earl of Southampton; m. 23 Dec. 1662; m.2. 24 Aug. 1673 Ralph Montagu (d. 1709) | 2 drs; d. in infancy |

Henry Percy
b. 1668; d. aged
8 months

Elizabeth; b. 26 Jan. 1667; m.1. 27 Mch. 1679
Henry Cavendish, earl Ogle (d. 17 Nov.
1679); m.2. Thomas Thynn of Longleat
(k. 1682); m.3. 30 May 1682 Charles
Seymour, 6th duke of Somerset (d. 2 Dec.
1748); d. 23 Nov. 1722
Henrietta; d. in infancy 1670

1682; it was said at the time that Vratz had been persuaded to do the deed by Charles John von Koningsmarck, a Swedish nobleman, who had developed a consuming passion for lady Elizabeth. With rather unseemly haste the heiress was married to her third husband, Charles Seymour, 6th duke of Somerset. The duke of Somerset died 2 December 1748. His only surviving son and heir, Algernon Seymour, 3rd baron Percy (under the writ of 1625) and 7th duke of Somerset, was created earl of Northumberland and baron Warkworth in 1749 with special remainder to his daughter Elizabeth and her husband, sir Hugh Smithson, 5th bart, of Stanwick, Yorks.

In 1750 sir Hugh Smithson succeeded his father-in-law as 2nd earl of Northumberland and baron Warkworth, and took the name and arms of Percy by Act of Parliament. In 1776 he was created 1st duke of Northumberland and earl Percy. The present duke of Northumberland is his lineal descendant.

PERCY OF BEVERLEY, YORKS.

Gosslyne Percy, youngest son of the 4th earl, was provided for by his father with lands of 300 marks annual value in Sussex, of which the manor of Poynings was to form part, 'to the intent that the said Gosslyne shall be of loving and lowly disposition toward the said Henry his brother and give him next his allegiance, and that I charge him to do and to be, upon my blessing as he will answer before God'. Josselyn was living at Newland, near Wakefield, Yorks., when he made his w.d. 7 September 1532. It is remarkable that no mention is made in the will of the testator's son and heir Edward. Josselyn died the day after making his will, and on 19 September his brother sir William Percy, writing to Cromwell, asked for the wardship of his nephew Edward Percy, then nine years old and already 'married to one Waterton, a sorry bargain, his blood considered'. Edward's wife was Elizabeth daughter of sir Thomas Waterton of Walton, Yorks.

Three of Josselyn's servants were accused of killing their master by poison and it was said also that they had taken the dead man's money and moveable goods and had been harboured at Walton in the house of sir Thomas Waterton. Eventually custody of the heir was given to sir William Percy and he was allowed £20 a year out of his brother's estate to bring up the boy. Edward Percy was perhaps the person of that name who was admitted to Gray's Inn in 1544. He died on 22 September 1590 when his eldest son and heir Alan Percy of Beverley was aged 30 years and unmarried. The younger son Thomas later became infamous as one of the leading conspirators in the Gunpowder Plot in 1603.

Alan Percy was member of parliament for Beverley from 1599 to 1603 and died 24 June 1632. His two surviving sons Josceline and Edward both entered the service of their cousin, the earl of Northumberland. Edward died at Petworth 20 August 1630 aged 32, and there is no evidence that he was ever married. Josceline was a page in the service of the earl in 1603. In later life the notoriety caused by his uncle's treason caused him to live in retirement. He made his will on 30 September 1652 when he was living in the parish of St Paul's, Covent Garden. His two surviving sons Alan (d.1687) and Charles were probably the last male representatives of Gosslyne Percy (d.1532).

After the death of earl Josceline in 1670, Alan Percy of Beverley was almost certainly his heir male. He could not, however, claim the earldom created in 1557 for he was not descended from the recipient of that title. He was, however, a descendant of Henry Percy, 4th earl (of the creation of 1377), and would appear to have been entitled to the earldom of 1377. No claim was ever made.

Thomas Percy the conspirator was brought up a protestant but later in life became a Roman Catholic when he married a Catholic lady, Martha daughter of Robert Wright of Plowland in Holderness, Yorks. He had been intended for the law but never qualified. As a young man he was constantly in trouble and more than once was in danger of imprisonment. His cousin, the earl of Northumberland, was taken in by his plausible manners and appointed him constable of Alnwick. In this post his behaviour was greatly objected to by the earl's tenants and he was even charged with dishonesty. After this, although he retained the office of constable he had to exercise it through deputies whilst he lived in London. In London he joined in many of the intrigues of the Catholics which culminated in the attempt to blow up the Houses of Parliament on 5 November 1603. Betrayed by his confederates he was shot down on 8 November and died the following day. He was buried in the garden of the house at Holbeach, Staffs., where the conspirators had met.

THE PEDIGREE of JAMES PERCY of DUBLIN

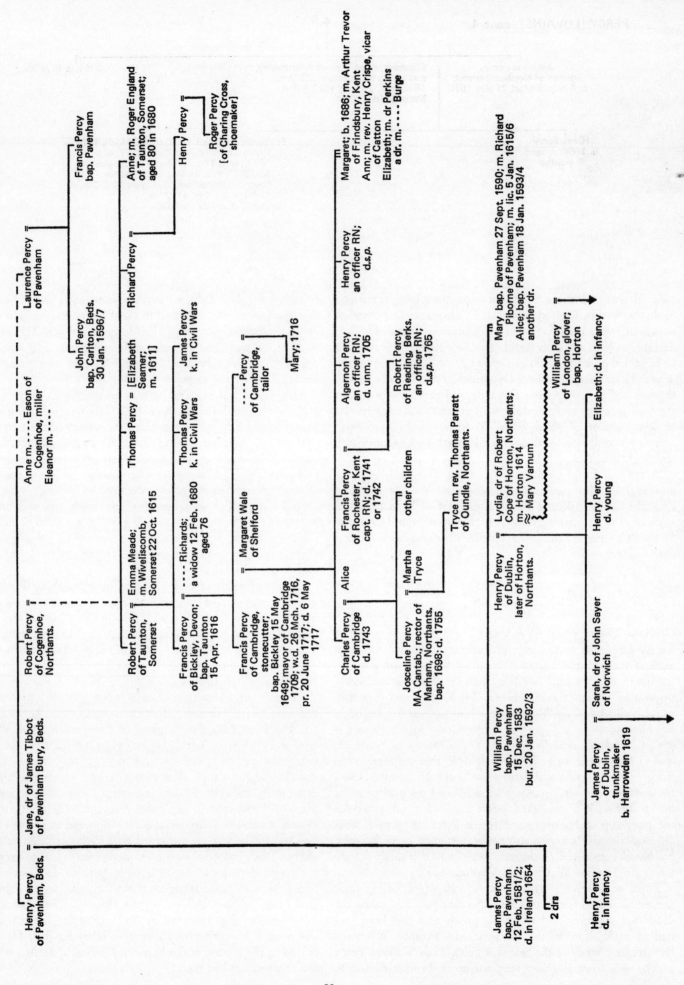

Henry Percy = Jane, dr of James Tibbot
of Pavenham,   of Pavenham Bury, Beds.
Beds.

Robert Percy =
of Cogenhoe,
Northants.

Anne m. - - - - Eason of
Cogenhoe, miller
Eleanor m. - - - -

Laurence Percy
of Pavenham

Francis Percy
bap. Pavenham

Robert Percy =
of Taunton,
Somerset

Emma Meade;
m. Wiveliscomb,
Somerset 22 Oct. 1615

John Percy
bap. Carlton, Beds.
30 Jan. 1596/7

Thomas Percy =
[Elizabeth
Seamer;
m. 1611]

Anne; m. Roger England
of Taunton, Somerset;
aged 80 in 1680

Richard Percy =

Henry Percy =

Roger Percy
[of Charing Cross,
shoemaker]

Francis Percy
of Bickley, Devon;
bap. Taunton
15 Apr. 1616

- - - - Richards;
a widow 12 Feb. 1680
aged 76

Thomas Percy
k. in Civil Wars

James Percy
k. in Civil Wars

Francis Percy
of Cambridge,
stonecutter;
bap. Bickley 15 May
1649; mayor of Cambridge
1709; w.d. 26 Mch. 1716,
pr. 20 June 1717; d. 6 May
1717

Margaret Wale
of Shelford

- - - - Percy
of Cambridge,
tailor

Mary; 1716

Charles Percy
of Cambridge
d. 1743

Alice

Francis Percy
of Rochester, Kent
capt. RN; d. 1741
or 1742

Algernon Percy
an officer RN;
d. unm. 1705

Henry Percy
an officer RN;
d.s.p.

Margaret; b. 1686; m. Arthur Trevor
of Frindsbury, Kent
Ann; m. rev. Henry Crispe, vicar
of Catton
Elizabeth; m. dr Perkins
a dr. m. - - - - Burge

Robert Percy
of Reading, Berks.
an officer RN;
d.s.p. 1765

other children

Joseline Percy
MA Cantab.; rector of
Marham, Northants,
bap. 1698; d. 1755

Martha
Tryce

Tryce m. rev. Thomas Parratt
of Oundle, Northants.

Henry Percy
of Dublin,
later of Horton,
Northants.

Lydia, dr of Robert
Cope of Horton, Northants;
m. Horton 1614
≋ Mary Varnum

Mary bap. Pavenham 27 Sept. 1590; m. Richard
Piborne of Pavenham; m. lic. 5 Jan. 1615/6
Alice; bap. Pavenham 18 Jan. 1593/4
another dr.

William Percy
of London, glover;
bap. Horton

Henry Percy
d. young

Elizabeth; d. in infancy

William Percy
bap. Pavenham
15 Dec. 1583
bur. 20 Jan. 1592/3

James Percy
bap. Pavenham
12 Feb. 1581/2;
d. in Ireland 1654

2 drs

James Percy
of Dublin,
trunkmaker
b. Harrowden 1619

Sarah, dr of John Sayer
of Norwich

Henry Percy
d. in infancy

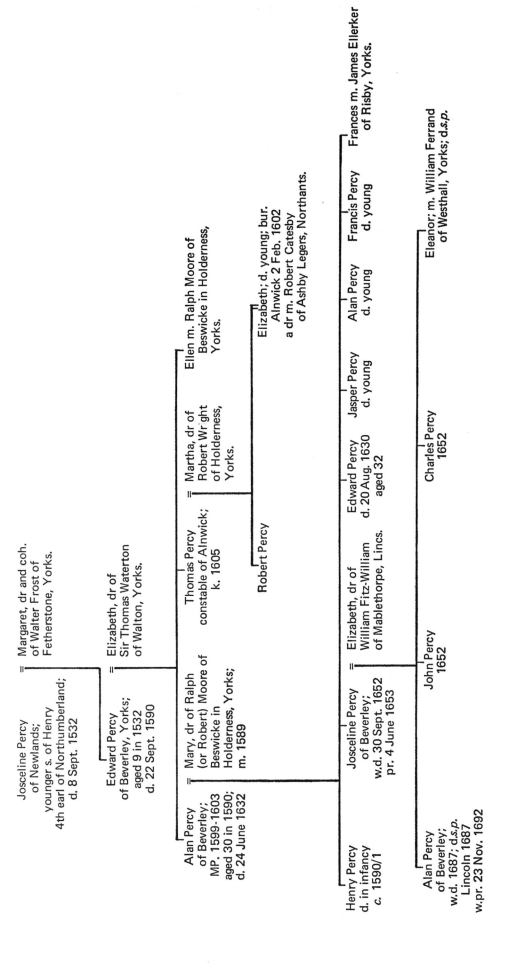

Josceline Percy
of Newlands;
younger s. of Henry
4th earl of Northumberland;
d. 8 Sept. 1532
= Margaret, dr and coh.
of Walter Frost of
Fetherstone, Yorks.

Edward Percy
of Beverley, Yorks;
aged 9 in 1532
d. 22 Sept. 1590
= Elizabeth, dr of
Sir Thomas Waterton
of Walton, Yorks.

Alan Percy
of Beverley;
MP. 1599-1603
aged 30 in 1590;
d. 24 June 1632
= Mary, dr of Ralph
(or Robert) Moore of
Beswicke in
Holderness, Yorks;
m. 1589

Thomas Percy
constable of Alnwick;
k. 1605
= Martha, dr of
Robert Wright
of Holderness,
Yorks.

Ellen m. Ralph Moore of
Beswicke in Holderness,
Yorks.

Robert Percy

Elizabeth; d. young; bur.
Alnwick 2 Feb. 1602
a dr m. Robert Catesby
of Ashby Legers, Northants.

Henry Percy
d. in infancy
c. 1590/1

Josceline Percy
of Beverley;
w.d. 30 Sept. 1652
pr. 4 June 1653
= Elizabeth, dr of
William Fitz-William
of Mablethorpe, Lincs.

Edward Percy
d. 20 Aug. 1630
aged 32

Jasper Percy
d. young

Alan Percy
d. young

Francis Percy
d. young

Frances m. James Ellerker
of Risby, Yorks.

Alan Percy
of Beverley;
w.d. 1687; d.s.p.
Lincoln 1687
w.pr. 23 Nov. 1692

John Percy
1652

Charles Percy
1652

Eleanor; m. William Ferrand
of Westhall, Yorks; d.s.p.

21

There is some evidence that Thomas Percy left descendants. Sir William Dugdale, Garter King of Arms, when he was investigating in 1680 the pedigree of Francis Percy of Cambridge to substantiate the latter's claim to the earldom of Northumberland took depositions from many old persons who had known Francis' grandfather.

John Swinton, clerk of the parish church of Alnwick in Northumberland, above 80 years of age, affirmed that he had heard his father say that he had known Thomas Percy and his wife when they lived in the castle of Alnwick; they had children and after the Powder Plot when Thomas lost his life, his wife went to London and lived there privately. Matthew Scott of Gateshead, co. Durham, aged 99 certified that he had known Thomas Percy, and that he had a son called Robert and two daughters and that Robert had been a schoolboy at Alnwick. Dugdale produced an extract from the Alnwick Parish Registers of the burial on 2 February 1602 of Elizabeth daughter of Thomas Percy of Alnwick Castle. Other deponents gave evidence that Robert Percy, grandfather of the claimant, had told them he was a son of Thomas Percy the conspirator. There is no doubt that Dugdale was misled in accepting this hearsay evidence.

Thomas' widow kept a dame's school in High Holborn for many years after her husband's death. It is known that a daughter married Robert Catesby, son of one of the conspirators.

OTHER PERCYS

YOUNGER sons of sir William de Percy (d.1245) and of Henry, 2nd baron Percy of Alnwick (d.1353) founded cadet lines of the family. The principal branch was that of Scotton, Yorks. It is not necessary here to give a detailed account of this branch for it does not appear to have had any contact with Northumberland.

Sir Robert Percy of Scotton was comptroller of the household and captain of the guard to Richard III and fell with his master at Bosworth Field 22 August 1485. Although the family was now attainted it was restored in 1495 by Henry VII in the person of another Robert Percy. If one were to judge by the selection of Christian names in a family, it could be thought that the Percys of Pavenham were closely connected to those of Scotton. The names Robert, Francis and Thomas are common to both (*Familiae Minorum Gentium*, Harl. Soc. p. 873).

The Percys of Dunsley, par. Whitby, Yorks., were descended from Richard a younger son of William de Perci I (d.1096). His direct male descendant Peter son of Simon de Percy living in the 14th century was succeeded by Margaret de Percy wife of Robert Man of Sneaton.

An Ernald de Perci witnesses the charter of William de Percy I to the monks of Whitby, *c*.1090-1096. He was probably a near kinsman of William but his connection with the main line is not known. His Yorkshire estates were held of the Brus barony and included Kilnwick Percy. The family continued in the male line until early in the 16th century.

Picot de Percy, a tenant at the time of the Domesday survey of William de Perci I was ancestor of the Percys of Bolton Percy who died out in the male line in 1321.

PERCY—BIBLIOGRAPHY

Edward Barrington de Fonblanque, *Annals of The House of Percy*. 2 vols. London 1887.

Gerald Brenan, *A History of the House of Percy*, 2 vols. London 1902.

George Tate, *The History of the Borough, Castle and Barony of Alnwick*. 2 vols. Alnwick 1866. His account of the early Percys is derived mainly from Dugdale.

This Book makes appear the Claim, Pedigree and Proceedings of James Percy now Claimant to the Earldom of Northumberland, humbly presented to both Houses of Parliament. Printed in the year 1680.

Dugdale, *Baronage*, vol. I, pp.269-286. That part of the genealogy of the early Percys derived by Dugdale from '*MS. penes Wil. Pierpont*' appears to be very inaccurate.

A. R. Wagner, *English Genealogy*, Oxford 1960. (Sir Anthony Wagner points out that if there remain any direct male descendants of Joceline de Louvain, they have the distinction of direct male descent from Griselbert, count of the Maasgau (840 x 870). Joceline's half brother Godfrey, was ancestor of the dukes of Brabant and Hesse, from whom a male line descent can be proved for earl Mountbatten of Burma).

J. M. W. Bean, *The Percies and their estates in Scotland*, in *AA*4. xxxv, pp.91-99.

G. R. Batho, *The Percies and Alnwick Castle*, in *AA*4. xxxv, pp.48-63.

J. M. W. Bean, *The Percies' acquisition of Alnwick*, in *AA*4. xxxii, pp.309-319.

The Percy Chartulary. SS. 117.

Whitby Chartulary I. SS. 69.

W. H. D. Longstaffe, *The Old Heraldry of the Percys* in *AA*2. IV, pp.157-228.

G. E. C. *Complete Peerage*, new edition, vol.X, *s.v.* Percy.

Julius P. Gilson. St Julian the harbinger and the first of the English Percys in *AA*3. IV, pp.304-312.

Early Yorkshire Charters. vol.XI. *The Percy Fee*. Edited by sir Charles Travis Clay, C.B., F.B.A. This is the most recent (1963) and most accurate account of the first line of Perci.

PERCY—NOTES

1. The family histories compiled by Fonblanque and Brenan are extremely inaccurate and are both well padded with romantic nonsense. Both have drawn very largely upon Peeris' *Metrical Chronicle*, which they have accepted as historical, whereas it is mainly fantasy. Tate who was an extremely able historian has given a careful account of the Percy family and evidently saw through most, but not all, of Peeris' fables. The origins of many of the cadet lines of the family who held manors in Yorkshire are obscure and it is unwise to accept Fonblanque or Brenan's guesswork.

2. Besides the 'standard' histories of the Percys many other works, including Collins' *Baronage*, insist on giving the title of 'lord Percy' to all the holders of the barony of Topcliffe and later that of Alnwick commencing with the 11th century William de Perci. The first baron Percy was sir Henry de Percy summoned to parliament by writ in 1299.

RAYMES

At the time of the Domesday Survey, Roger de Raimes held *in capite* Rayne in Essex, and other lands in Essex, Norfolk, Suffolk and Middlesex later assessed as ten knights' fees. His name was derived from Rames, Seine Inf., arr. Le Havre, cant. Saint-Romain de Colbosc, comm. Gommeville (*Harl. Soc.* 103, p.84).

After the death of William de Raimes, Roger's son and successor, his lands were divided between his two sons Robert and Roger. Robert died *s.p.* and his lands passed to his younger brother Roger whose wife was a daughter of Aubrey de Vere, lord of Hedingham in Essex, 1st earl of Oxford. After Roger's death, possibly before 1159, his lands were divided between his sons Richard and William. In 1166 the *carta* for Richard's lands, which still appears under the name of Robert, stated that he owed the service of ten knights.

When Richard de Reimes died in 1204 his lands were divided amongst his four daughters, one unnamed, wife of Roger son of Ivo de Mestinges; Joan wife firstly of Brian Aquarius and secondly of William Herlawe; Amicia wife firstly of William de Marini and secondly of Roger le Messager; and Alice wife firstly of William de Wudeham and secondly of Roger de Marini (Sanders, pp.139-140).

William's share of the Raymes' lands descended after his death in the Holy Land in 1195 to his son William II (d.1203) and his grandson William III (living 1235). The later descent of the family is unknown.

About 1200 Henry son of William de Raimes had a grant of land at Wherstead, near Ipswich. Robert and Hamon de Raimes are witnesses to the deed, and another deed of about the same date is witnessed by Henry de Raimes and Hamon and William his brothers. Throughout the 13th century there are many references to the family in connection with Wherstead and Ipswich, many of the family becoming burgesses of the latter place (*AA*3. IV, pp.2-3).

RAYMES OF SHORTFLATT, PAR. BOLAM

In 1286, Robert son of Hugh de Reymes was concerned in land transactions near Wherstead and in the same year Robert de Reymes acted as attorney for Hugh de Gosebek in a plea of assize of *mort d'ancestor*. At this time Gosebek held half the barony of Bolam in Northumberland. Before 1295 he alienated this half barony to Hugh de Reymes and to Robert his son, without licence from the king. Hugh died in 1295. The king restored it to Robert in 1296 'by a fine made with him in the exchequer'. After the death of Hugh de Gosebek 'Robert son of Hugh de Reymes of Wherstead, appeared by his attorney on the 4th day of April 1309 against Richard de Gosebek, on a plea that he should warrant to him a moiety of the manor of Bolam with its appurtenances which he holds and claims to hold of him and for which he has a charter of

Hugh de Gosebek, father of the said Richard, whose heir he is' (*de Banco Roll*). The manor of Wherstead passed to Alice, daughter and heiress of Robert de Ramis who married sir Robert de Reydon. In 1296 Albreda and Nicola, daughters of the late Gilbert de Reymes, released to sir Robert de Reydon all right which had accrued to them after the death of sir Robert de Reymes their brother, formerly rector of the church of Eston Gosebekes, in lands in Wherstead and elsewhere. Hugh and sir Robert were brothers and evidently sons of Gilbert de Reymes of Wherstead. We can therefore identify Hugh as the Hugh son of Gilbert de Reymes who became a sworn burgess of Ipswich in 1277. Gilbert had become a burgess in 1240, and was perhaps the Gilbert son of Robert de Reymes to whom Gilbert, prior of the monastery of St Peter and St Paul in Ipswich, had granted 1225 x 1251 land in Wherstead.

In 1304 Robert de Reymes and Maud his wife are returned as holding half the manor of Bolam, half the vill of Aydon, the hamlet of Little Whittington, half the hamlet of Greenleighton and the vill of East Brunton. His wife Maud was a daughter of sir Nicholas de Worteley; she was living 6 January 1311/2 but died in her husband's lifetime. Robert had licence to crenellate his house at Aydon and to have free warren in his lands 5 April 1305. He had letters of protection dated 21 October 1309 to go in the king's train to Scotland. About 1315 Robert de Reymes petitioned the king for a lease of the park of Plumpton in Inglewood; he stated that he had been in all the king's wars in Scotland and had there lost horses, armour and other possessions to the value of 100 marks; the Scots had burned, spoiled and destroyed his dwellings and lands in Northumberland to the loss of £1,000; moreover he had been taken prisoner by the Scots and put to ransom at 500 marks for which his son was still living in Scotland as hostage. King Edward instructed his chancellor and treasurer 25 March 1316 to consider the petition and eventually Raymes was granted a ten year's lease of Plumpton park (*PSAN* 3. IV, pp.91-92). He was knight of the shire for Northumberland in 1322, and died in 1324. The inquest taken after his death found that he had died seised of half the barony of Bolam, with the manor of Aydon, 100 acres of pasture in 'lightinton' (now Greenleighton), the manor of Shortflatt, 14s. rent in South Middleton and half the mill. His son and heir Robert was then aged 23. The effigy in Bolam church of a knight in armour, his shield bearing a cross engrailed, is perhaps the memorial to the first Robert de Reymes (d.1324). Besides his son and heir Robert II, the first Robert de Reymes had a daughter Lucy, and in 1311/2 Thomas de Tyndale granted to William his son and to Lucy his wife, daughter of Robert de Reymes, his lands in Corbridge with the reversion of all the lands which Margery who was the wife of William de Tyndale held there (*NDD*. p.191, No. 7, where the date should be 5 E.II and not 5 E.I). Henry de Reymys, clerk, vicar of Bolam, who

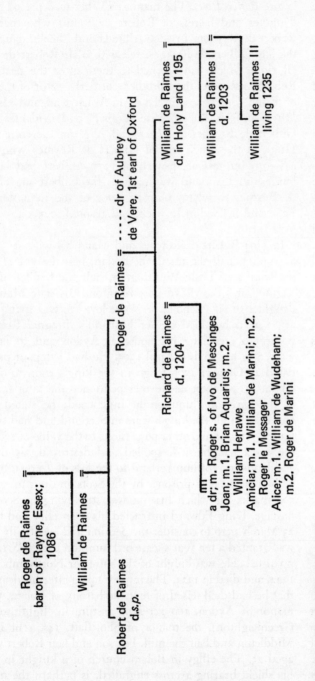

RAIMES, barons of Rayne, Essex

Roger de Raimes baron of Rayne, Essex; 1086

William de Raimes

Robert de Raimes d.s.p.

Roger de Raimes = - - - - - dr of Aubrey de Vere, 1st earl of Oxford

William de Raimes d. in Holy Land 1195

William de Raimes II d. 1203

William de Raimes III living 1235

Richard de Raimes d. 1204 =

a dr; m. Roger s. of Ivo de Mescinges
Joan; m.1. Brian Aquarius; m.2. William Herlawe
Amicia; m.1. William de Marini; m.2. Roger le Messager
Alice; m.1. William de Wudeham; m.2. Roger de Marini

RAIMES of WHERSTEAD, Suffolk

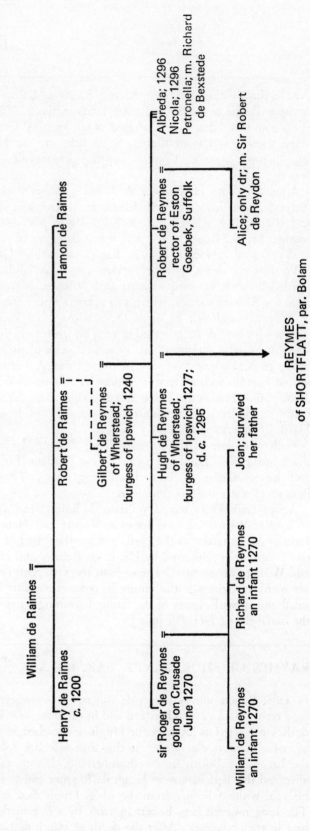

William de Raimes

Hamon de Raimes

Henry de Raimes c. 1200

Robert de Raimes =

Gilbert de Reymes of Wherstead; burgess of Ipswich 1240

Robert de Reymes rector of Eston Gosebek, Suffolk

Hugh de Reymes of Wherstead; burgess of Ipswich 1277; d. c. 1295

Albreda; 1296
Nicola; 1296
Petronella; m. Richard de Bexstede

Alice; only dr; m. Sir Robert de Reydon

sir Roger de Reymes going on Crusade June 1270

Joan; survived her father

Richard de Reymes an infant 1270

William de Reymes an infant 1270

REYMES of SHORTFLATT, par. Bolam

died in 1339, may have been a younger son of Robert I.

Robert de Raymes II in 1343 was a commissioner for keeping the truce with Scotland and a justice for punishing violators of it. He was knight of the shire for Northumberland in 1346 and sheriff in 1347. He died 10 October 1349 seised of the same lands which his father had held. At the inquest taken on 30 November 1349 the jurors stated that Robert had died 'in the pestilence' (*i.e.* the Black Death) and that Nicholas de Raymes, then 30 years of age was his son and next heir. His widow Agnes had Shortflatt in dower, married secondly in 1361 Robert de Lowther of Halton, and died 8 October 1363. She was probably a Delaval as sir Henry Delaval in 1372 settled certain lands on Nicholas de Raymes and John de Selby; the latter was son of sir Walter de Selby and his wife Katherine Delaval; Agnes Raymes and Katherine Selby were perhaps sisters, and great aunts of sir Henry Delaval.

The eldest son and heir of Robert de Raymes II was Robert de Raymes III, aged 22 at his father's death. In 1354 he settled on (his brother) Hugh de Raymes 400 acres of pasture in Leighton, half the manors of Bolam and Aydon, and lands in Shortflat and South Middleton, with remainder to himself. Hugh fined 8 marks to the Crown for licence to acquire these lands. Robert III died in 1360 and was succeeded by his brother Hugh. Before 1362 the latter was also dead and Nicholas his brother had succeeded. They had a sister Joan wife of William de Swynburne of Capheaton, whose names occur in a settlement of Capheaton dated 7 June 1349 (*NDD.* p.207, No. 59), and whose marriage settlement is dated 27 October 1348 (*Swinburne Charters* I/66).

Nicholas de Reymes of Shortflat was knight of the shire for Northumberland in 1378 and 1385; on the latter date he is termed *miles* signifying that he had received knighthood. He served in the campaigns in France in 1355 and 1359, was keeper of Roxburgh castle, and chancellor and chamberlain of Berwick in 1383. In 1383 he was commissioner of array in Northumberland, and in 1390 ambassador to treat with the Scots. Sir Nicholas died 11 October 1394 when his son and heir Robert de Raymes IV was aged 14; his widow Maud married secondly John de Whitfield and was living at Flotterton in 1415.

Robert Raymes IV was married, perhaps whilst still a boy, to Margaret daughter of sir Robert Ogle of Bothal. His father-in-law in 1374/5 settled lands in Longwitton on them, and by his w.d. 7 February 1410/11 leaves Robert *duas equas cum suis sequelis* (*SS.*2. p.48). Robert Raymes was living at Flotterton, a property belonging to the Ogles, in 1415. In 1415 the *fortalicium* of Shortflat had been in the ownership of Robert 'Ramese', whilst the castle of Aydon was in the hands of Robert 'Ramsey' and sir Ralph Grey (*AA2.* XIV, pp.15-16). Robert Raymes IV was a commissioner of oaths in Northumberland in 1434 and died 5 October 1450. His wife Margaret Ogle having died, he had married (before 1424) a second wife Alice and she survived him and had assignment of dower on 24 December 1450.

Robert Raymes IV was succeeded at Shortflat by his son Robert Raymes V who was then aged over 30. There may have been younger sons. There was a Nicholas Raymes mentioned in 1415, perhaps the person of that name living at Middleton in 1442. In 1440 William Crauster sued Thomas Ramys, son of John Ramys, late of Shortflat, esquire, executor of the will of the said John Ramys, and John Manners the elder, gent.,

son of sir John Maners of Etal, knight, and Margaret his wife, coexecutrix of the said will, for 40s. (*de Banco Roll*, 717 mem. 346d.).

Robert V died 1 September 1479 when his brother and heir was John Raymes aged over 60.

John Raymes was living in 1481. He gave his younger son John 40s., rent for life out of Aydon; John the son was still living 30 June 1511. John's eldest son and heir was Robert Raymes VI who died 4 April 1490. Robert's wife was Joan daughter and coheiress of David Witton of Longwitton; she survived him and was living 18 April 1512 when she settled two tenements in Longwitton on her daughter Joan for life.

When Robert Raymes VI died in 1490 his son and heir Robert Raymes VII was seven years old. The latter married Anne daughter of John Clavering of Callaly, but died at the early age of 26 on 24 May 1509; his widow married secondly John Swinburne of Chopwell and was living on 15 January 1544/5. Robert Raymes VIII, son and heir, was four years old when his father died, and his wardship was granted to Nicholas Turpyn in 1511. Robert Raymes VII also had a daughter, Anne wife of Christopher Swinburne of Wylam. In 1538 Raymes was in fee with the warden of the marches. On 7 April 1541 he exchanged Aydon Hall with sir Reynold Carnaby for the manor of Hawkwell.

Robert Raymes VIII made his will on 10 October 1544. By it he directs that his lands are to be divided into three parts, 'one part to my wife, another to my heir, and the third part to the upbringing of my children, and the child that my wife is with to be partner in all in general'. The third part is to be divided equally amongst the male children when they reached the age of 18 years 'by the sight of my father John Swynborne, my brother John his son, and my brother Thomas Myddelton, esquire, for the term of their natural lives and then to return to my heir'. The tithe of Bradford 'after the decease of my mother Elizabeth Fenwicke of Little Harle, and my cousin Isabell Aynesley, late wife to Robert Aynesleye', is to remain to the testator's heir. 'My aunt of Little Benton Elizabeth Killingeworthe and Jane' are to have the tithe of Trewick, ferm free for their natural lives 'and the keeping of my two daughters, that is to say Ursula and Margaret'. The ferm of the tithes of Bolam and Harnham is 'to run to' the marriage of the testator's daughters, the eldest to have 40 marks and the other £20 'and my wife to receive the said ferm to the behoof of my children during her widowhood'. His wife and his son Robert are to be together 'whilst some of my children be preferred, they being both content'.

Robert Raymes died ten days after he had made his will. The will is extremely vague about the testator's relatives but we can deduce from it the following:

1. His first wife was a sister of Alexander Heron of Meldon who was a witness to the will. Heron's mother Elizabeth had married for her second husband Thomas Fenwick of Little Harle.

2. His mother had married secondly John Swinburne of Chopwell, called 'my father' in the will, by whom she had a son John Swinburne whom Raymes calls 'my brother'.

3. 'my cousin Isabell Aynesley late wife to Robert Aynesley' was widow of Robert Aynsley of West Shafto, and was a daughter of John Fenwick of Little Harle. Raymes' mother-in-law's second husband Thomas Fenwick must have been John's brother.

4. 'my aunt of Little Benton, Elizabeth Killingworthe and Jane' were both probably his father's sisters.

5. 'my brother, Thomas Myddelton, esquire' must have been a brother of Robert Raymes' second wife, who was therefore a daughter of John Middleton of Belsay.

6. Raymes' wife was with child when he made his will. The expected child seems to have been a daughter Isabel who became the wife of Roland Shafto of Anvil, co. Durham. When the latter entered his pedigree at the 1575 visitation he stated that his wife was 'Isabel, dau. of Robert Rames of Shortflatt in Northumberland'.

7. Raymes' two daughters Ursula and Margaret are otherwise unknown.

8. Raymes only mentions one son by name, his eldest son and heir Robert, but there were evidently younger sons for he directs that a third part of his lands is to be divided 'amongst my children male when they come to the age of 18 years', and later in the will mentions that his wife and his son Robert should remain together 'whilst some of my children be preferred'. There appear to have been three younger sons who were all educated at Cambridge, viz:

John Raymes; matriculated at Christ's College, Cambridge, November 1550; BA. 1553/4; fellow of St John's College, Cambridge 1554; MA, 1557; master of Westgate Hospital, Newcastle, 25 April 1558; resident at Louvain University in 1567; took part in the rebellion of 1569 for which he was imprisoned in Durham gaol; deprived of his mastership for contumacy 29 May 1579.

Thomas Raymes; matriculated at Christ's College, Cambridge, November 1552; BA, 1555/6.

Roger Raymes; matriculated at Christ's College, Cambridge, May 1561; BA, 1563/4.

Robert Raymes IX was aged 22 when his father died. On 10 January 1568 he sold the manor of Hawkwell to John Swinburne of Wylam. He was sheriff of Northumberland in 1569. He died 20 March 1599/1600 and administration was granted 24 April 1601 to his widow Anne. She was a daughter of sir John Delaval of Seaton Delaval and died 1 January 1612/3. When Sir Ralph Delaval entered his pedigree at the herald's visitation in 1666 he recorded that Anne daughter of sir John Delaval was 'wife of Robert Raymes of Shortflatt, and had 5 sons, John, Roger, James, Robert and Edward'.

It is convenient to deal with the younger sons first. Roger Raymes was aged about 50 in 1607; he resided at South Shields and held copyhold lands at Whitburn. In 1591 he was vice-admiral of the palatinate of Durham. He seems to have had the manor of Longwitton from his father and he sold it to William Fenwick of Stanton in 1605. His wife Margaret was party to the sale and died in 1621 (bur. 12 January 1620/1). A William Raymes of Whitburn had been buried at Whitburn 14 October 1596 and the like entry appears in the parish registers under the date 22 January 1596/7. Was this the same William Reymes of Shortflatt who on 8 August 1586 had taken out a licence to marry at Ware, Elizabeth Hill of Ware, spinster, daughter of Gilbert Hill, late of the same, gent., deceased?

James Raymes of South Middleton was aged about 51 or 52 in 1607; in his w.d. 22 January 1608/9 he mentions his wife Isabel, who was a daughter of Roger Heron of Riplington. He devises his lands in South Middleton and Longwitton to his daughter Dorothy, who with her husband Thomas Fenwick sold them in 1617 to William Fenwick of Stanton.

Robert, 4th son of Robert Raymes (d.1600), was a freeholder in Longwitton in 1628, and sold five farms there and Raymes' Close in Greenleighton to William Fenwick of Stanton. A Thomas Raymes was rated for lands in Longwitton in 1663.

Of Edward Raymes, the 5th son, nothing further is known. Robert Raymes IX (d.1600) had a daughter Anne wife of Joshua Delaval of Rivergreen. On 6 June 1596 her father had assigned to her on her marriage a lease of the tithes of Bolam.

John Raymes who succeeded in 1600 to his father's lands in Shortflat, Bolam and Aydon only held them for a very short time. He made a settlement of his lands in 1604 and administration of his goods was granted on 4 September 1605 to his widow for their sons Robert, George, William, Philip and Joseph, and their daughters Margaret, Grace and Ursula. She was Dorothy daughter of John Heron of Chipchase. They had been married before 26 April 1576 for her great uncle Gawyne Swinburne of Cheeseburn Grange in his will of that date leaves 'to Dorethye Raymes two quyes' (SS. 2, p.409). Johne Raymes is a witness to the will. In the w.d. 5 December 1590 of John Heron no mention is made of Dorothy Raymes or her husband John, but their two elder sons Henrye and Robert Rames are to have 'to each three whyes of two years old' (SS. 38, p.201).

The eldest son Henry must have been born about 1580 or earlier for it was stated in 1621 that he was then over 41 years of age. He seems to have been particularly unfortunate or very extravagant for within a few years he had sold all the family estates. He parted with his moiety of Aydon in 1604, and the manors of Bolam and Shortflat and his lands in South Middleton and Longwitton in 1611. An annuity which had been retained out of Aydon Castle was sold in 1608 to Robert Fenwick of Netherton and the following year his mother released her dower thirds in Aydon Castle to Robert Fenwick of Little Harle. All that was left of a considerable estate was some burgage property in Corbridge which had been acquired by Robert Raymes VI with his wife Joan Witton in the 15th century. Henry Raymes was living at Hartley 15 July 1630 when he conveyed his Corbridge property to his brother Philip. He had married at Witton-le-Wear 9 February 1602 Elizabeth Hutton and a son William had been baptised there on 26 May 1605. It is not known when or where Henry Raymes died or if he had any surviving children. His wife Elizabeth had not long survived the birth of her son for she was buried at Witton-le-Wear 27 November 1605.

In 1634 there was a chancery suit about the Raymes' property. Four of the younger brothers were plaintiffs. They were Robert Raymes, George Raymes of Chirton, Philip Raymes of Cramlington, and William Raymes. They claimed against Roger Fenwick and others that their father had charged Bolam, Shortflat, Aydon and Longwitton with an annuity of £20 to be paid to themselves and their brother Joseph, who had since died, and to be continued to the last survivor (Chan. Bills and Answers, 1634). The other brother Joseph had died about 1608. George Raymes of Chirton was buried in Tynemouth chancel 4 February 1638/9.

Philip Raymes of Hartley had a son and a daughter baptised at Earsdon, John 3 February 1624/5 and Dorothy 20 June 1622.

Hodgson, *History of Northumberland*, pt ii, vol.I, pp.366-369 with pedigree.

Northumberland County History, vol.X, pp.343-350 with pedigree.

Shortflatt Tower its Owners, by A. L. Raimes in *AA*4. XXXII, pp.126-159 with pedigree.

Robert de Reymes of Bolam, Shortflatt and Aydon Castle, and his connection with Suffolk, by Frederick Raimes in *AA*3. IV, pp.313-318.

The family of Raimes of Wheldrake, Acaster Malbis and Stockton-on-Tees, traces its descent from a George Raymes who, on 3 March 1537/8, took a lease from the prioress of Thicket of a house and lands in Wheldrake, Yorks (*Augmentation Office Transcripts of Leases*, 23 Eliz. No. 133). His will was proved at York 9 February 1545. 'That George Raymes was a cadet of the family of Raymes of Shortflat is made probable by the fact that the contemporary rector of Wheldrake, Simon Weldon (1514-1535), almost certainly had Northumbrian ancestry, and that sir William Percy son of the fourth earl of Northumberland was in 1535, seneschal of the neighbouring priory of Thicket' (*NCH*. X, p.350).

RAYMES of SHORTFLATT, par. BOLAM

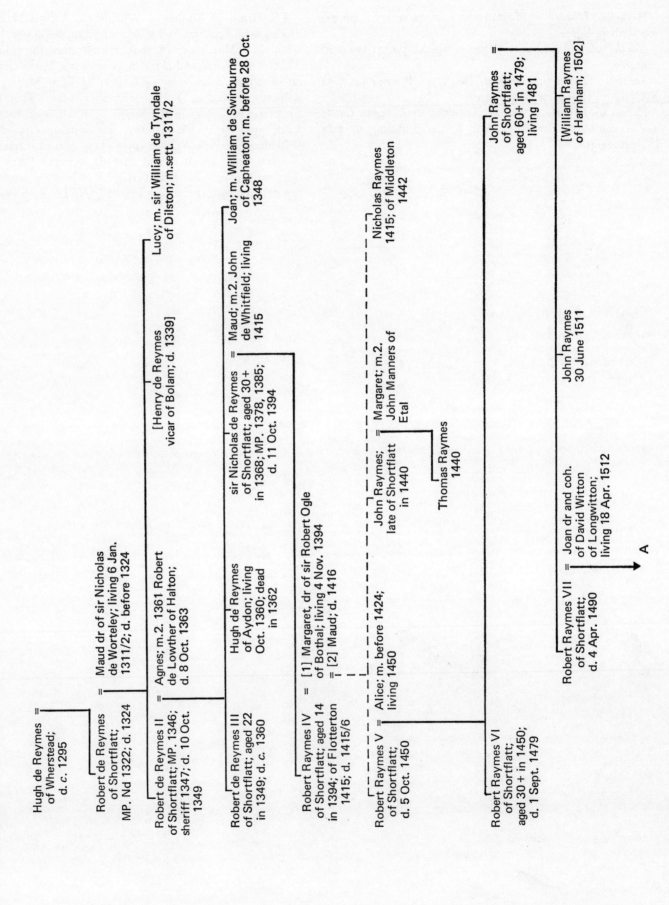

Hugh de Reymes =
of Wherstead;
d. c. 1295

Robert de Reymes = Maud dr of sir Nicholas
of Shortflatt;   de Worteley; living 6 Jan.
MP. Nd 1322; d. 1324 1311/2; d. before 1324

Robert de Reymes II = Agnes; m.2. 1361 Robert   [Henry de Reymes   Lucy; m. sir William de Tyndale
of Shortflatt; MP. 1346;   de Lowther of Halton;   vicar of Bolam; d. 1339]   of Dilston; m.sett. 1311/2
sheriff 1347; d. 10 Oct.   d. 8 Oct. 1363
1349

Robert de Reymes III   Hugh de Reymes   sir Nicholas de Reymes = Maud; m.2. John   Joan; m. William de Swinburne
of Shortflatt; aged 22   of Aydon; living   of Shortflatt; aged 30+   de Whitfield; living   of Capheaton; m. before 28 Oct.
in 1349; d. c. 1360   Oct. 1360; dead   in 1368; MP. 1378, 1385; 1415   1348
                         in 1362   d. 11 Oct. 1394

Robert Raymes IV = [1] Margaret, dr of sir Robert Ogle
of Shortflatt; aged 14   of Bothal; living 4 Nov. 1394
in 1394; of Flotterton   = [2] Maud; d. 1416
1415; d. 1415/6

Robert Raymes V = Alice; m. before 1424;   John Raymes; = Margaret; m.2.   Nicholas Raymes
of Shortflatt;   living 1450   late of Shortflatt John Manners of   1415; of Middleton
d. 5 Oct. 1450   in 1440   Etal   1442

                                                        Thomas Raymes
                                                        1440

Robert Raymes VI   John Raymes = Joan dr and coh.   John Raymes = [William Raymes
of Shortflatt;   of Shortflatt;   of David Witton   of Shortflatt;   of Harnham; 1502]
aged 30+ in 1450;   aged 60+ in 1479; of Longwitton;   30 June 1511
d. 1 Sept. 1479   living 1481   living 18 Apr. 1512

Robert Raymes VII =
of Shortflatt;
d. 4 Apr. 1490

→ A

28

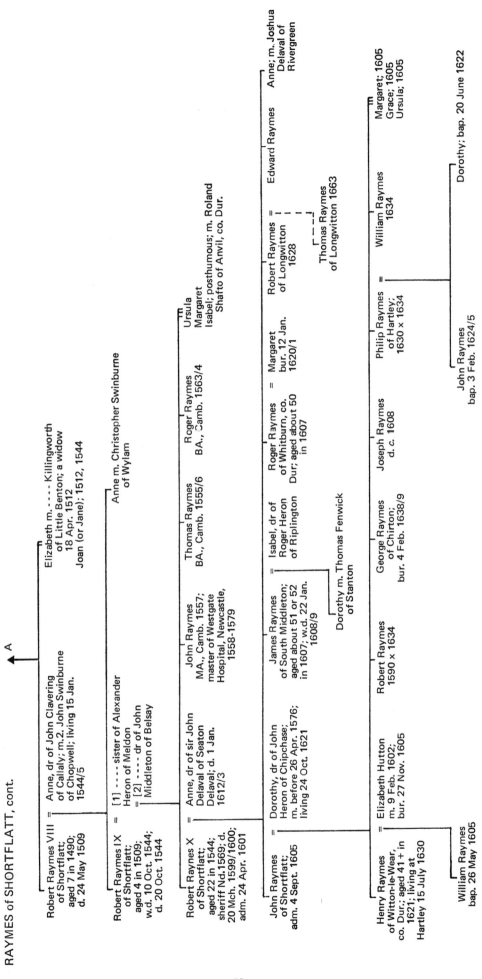

Robert Raymes VIII of Shortflatt; aged 7 in 1490; d. 24 May 1509 = Anne, dr of John Clavering of Callaly; m.2. John Swinburne of Chopwell; a widow 18 Apr. 1512; living 15 Jan. 1544/5

Elizabeth m. - - - - Killingworth of Little Benton; a widow 18 Apr. 1512; Joan (or Jane); 1512, 1544

Robert Raymes IX of Shortflatt; aged 4 in 1509; w.d. 10 Oct. 1544; d. 20 Oct. 1544 = [1] - - - - sister of Alexander Heron of Meldon = [2] - - - - dr of John Middleton of Belsay

Anne m. Christopher Swinburne of Wylam

Robert Raymes X of Shortflatt; aged 22 in 1544; sheriff Nd.1569; d. 20 Mch. 1599/1600; adm. 24 Apr. 1601 = Anne, dr of sir John Delaval of Seaton Delaval; d. 1 Jan. 1612/3

John Raymes MA., Camb. 1557; master of Westgate Hospital, Newcastle, 1558-1579

Thomas Raymes BA., Camb. 1555/6

Roger Raymes BA., Camb. 1563/4

Ursula
Margaret
Isabel; posthumous; m. Roland Shafto of Anvil, co. Dur.

John Raymes of Shortflatt; adm. 4 Sept. 1605 = Dorothy, dr of John Heron of Chipchase; m. before 26 Apr. 1576; living 24 Oct. 1621

James Raymes of South Middleton; aged about 51 or 52 in 1607; w.d. 22 Jan. 1608/9 = Isabel, dr of Roger Heron of Riplington

Dorothy m. Thomas Fenwick of Stanton

Roger Raymes of Whitburn, co. Dur; aged about 50 in 1607 = Margaret bur. 12 Jan. 1620/1

Robert Raymes of Longwitton 1628 =

Thomas Raymes of Longwitton 1663

Edward Raymes

Anne; m. Joshua Delaval of Rivergreen

Henry Raymes of Witton-le-Wear, co. Dur.; aged 41+ in 1621; living at Hartley 15 July 1630 = Elizabeth Hutton m. 9 Feb. 1602; bur. 27 Nov. 1605

Robert Raymes 1590 x 1634

George Raymes of Chirton; bur. 4 Feb. 1638/9

Joseph Raymes d. c. 1608

Philip Raymes of Hartley; 1630 x 1634 =

William Raymes 1634

Margaret; 1605
Grace; 1605
Ursula; 1605

William Raymes bap. 26 May 1605

John Raymes bap. 3 Feb. 1624/5

Dorothy: bap. 20 June 1622

A

MAUDUIT

BEFORE the end of the 12th century a family called Mauduit was holding the vills of Eshot and Bockenfield, par. Felton. These places were members of the barony of Mitford but had been sub-enfeoffed to the barons of Whalton.

There is a place called Mauduit or Malduit in Saint Martin du Bosc, Eure, arr. Les Audelys, cant. and comm. Etrepagny in Normandy. A family called Mauduit owned land here in the early 13th century. It is remarkable that the Northumbrian Mauduits refrained from using the territorial 'de' with their surname.

A William de Mauduit who held Hartley Maudit and Porchester in Hampshire, was chamberlain of the exchequer and by his marriage with Maud, heiress of Michael de Hanslope acquired the barony of Hanslope, Bucks. He died before February 1158 and was succeeded by his son William de Mauduit II. The latter married Isabel daughter of Simon (d.1153), earl of Huntingdon, a grandson of Waltheof (d.1076), earl of Northumberland. William de Mauduit II died in 1195, and was succeeded by his son Robert de Mauduit (d.1222) and he by his son William de Mauduit III. William III (d.1257) married Alice sister and heiress of Henry de Beaumont (de Newburgh), earl of Warwick. Their son, William de Mauduit IV became earl of Warwick but dying *s.p.* in 1268 was succeeded in his earldom and the barony of Hanslope by his brother-in-law William de Beauchamp (d.1269) who had married his sister Isabel.

A Robert Mauduit of Warminster, Wilts., who may have been a younger son of the chamberlain of the exchequer also acquired a barony by marriage. His wife was Agnes daughter and heiress of Robert de la Mare and heiress of Herbert de Castello, baron of Castle Holgate, Shropshire. Robert Mauduit died *circa* 1193 and his widow married secondly Ralph de Ardene. Robert's son and heir Thomas came of age in 1204 and died 1244. His son William Mauduit alienated the barony of Castle Holgate 1256 x 1258 to Richard de Cornwall.

MAUDUIT OF ESHOT, PAR. FELTON

WHEN William Bertram, baron of Mitford, died in 1199 or earlier, his son Roger who was under age was placed under the guardianship of William Briewere, lord of Horsley in Derbyshire. Either now or a little later Godefrid Mauduit became Briewere's bailiff; it is possible that he had been sent north for this purpose. On 24 April 1200 king John confirmed to him the vills of Eshot and Bockenfield which he held of the barony of Whalton (*Charter Roll*). At Martinmas 1201 William de Coigners stood surety for him in a plea *versus* William Briwer. In 1205 Sibilla widow of Ralph de St Peter, sued her father-in-law William de St Peter for her dower, which he had withheld from her on the grounds that he had not consented to her marriage (*Nd Pleas*). Before Easter 1206 Mauduit

had married the widow and was acting as her attorney. Sibilla's parentage is unknown; after the death of her second husband she married Richard de Hedley.

By a grant witnessed by Philip, bishop of Durham (1197-1208), and others, sir Godfrid Mauduit with the consent and assent of his heirs and for the souls of Constance daughter of Walter son of William, and of his and her ancestors, gave to Brinkburn priory a carucate of land in Eshot, Bockenfield and Upper Felton (*Brinkburn Chartulary*, p.57). In 1208 he gave to Brinkburn a toft in Bockenfield for the health of his own soul and those of his wife, his heirs, ancestors and successors (*Ib.*, p.59).

At Easter term 1210 Constance de Crammaville who had been heiress of the barony of Whalton, claimed in the *curia regis* that after William Briewere had received custody of the lands and heir of Roger Bertram, Godefrid Mauduyt, bailiff of the said William, had disseised her of lands in her barony. Godefrid produced his charter of enfeoffment, the confirmation by Constance's children, and a royal confirmation by king Henry (*NCH.* VII, p.328n). A boundary dispute between sir Godfrid Mauduith and the monks of Brinkburn was settled by an award dated 6 Kalends June (27 May) 1224.

When the northern magnates rose against king John in Easter week 1215 and later in the year did homage at Felton to Alexander II, king of Scots, one of the rebels is named as William Mauduit, probably a relation of the lord of Eshot.

Sir Godfrid Mauduit had been succeeded by his son Roger before 1242. Between 1242 and 1268 Roger witnesses several grants of land made to the prior and monks of Brinkburn. In December 1244 he confirmed the grants made to Brinkburn by his father. He is described as a knight when he witnesses with sir William Heron, sheriff 1246-1257, a grant to Brinkburn. He witnesses another grant when sir Gwychard de Charron was sheriff 1268-1272. His death must have occurred in 1268. In 1258 Fulk de Tibenham and Dionisia his wife, and Roger Mauduit and Isabella his wife were summoned before the justices of assize by John de Lexington for two carucates and 24s., rent in Newsham; Dionisia and Isabella refused to ratify the gift to Lexington made by their husbands, alleging that the lands were of their private inheritance (*SS.* 88, p.49). Dionisia and Isabella were sisters and coheiresses and besides lands in Newsham had succeeded to property in Earsdon and Tritlington. At the assizes in 1269 Radulph son of Robert le Breton of Morpeth claimed from Roger son of Roger Mauduit a messuage and a carucate of land in Earsdon. Roger came and stated that a certain Isabella, mother of the said Roger, held the messuage by hereditary right and after her death it had descended to him (*Ib.*, p.170). For the health of his soul, that of his wife Isabella and those of all his ancestors and heirs, Roger Mauduit gave 20s., a year out of his mill at Eshot to Newminster abbey for which the monks were to give a general absolution on the feast of the translation of St Thomas the Martyr (7 July) being the anniversary of his wife's death (*SS.* 66, p.17). On the petition of his wife Isabella he had given to Newminster a quarter of wheat, or four shillings annually for making the hosts, the rent to be paid out of the lands in Tritlington held by Robert Blund.

Sir Roger Mauduit II was knight of the shire in 1297. To a deed of 7 May 1317 is attached his seal on which his name is given as MAVDEVTS (*NDD.* p.81, No. 25). His eldest son and heir Roger Mauduit III married between 1325 and 1327 Eleanor, widow of sir Richard Marmaduke and of Robert de Umfreville (d.1325) earl of Angus.

It appears that Roger Mauduit III had an only daughter Margaret and in order that part of his estates should pass to her he made a settlement on two trustees Edmund de Esshate and William de Wakefield. On 14 April 1331 the trustees conveyed a messuage, 14 tofts, the mill, 14 bovates and two acres of land, 16s., rent and the third part of Bockenfield and Tritlington to Roger and the heirs male of his body by Eleanor his wife. Other lands which were held for life by other members of the family were also brought into settlement; these were a messuage, two bovates and two acres in Eshot held by Weland Mauduyt; two bovates and ten acres in Eshot held by William Mauduyt and Juliana his wife; ten tofts and twelve bovates in Tritlington held by the same William; eight tofts, four bovates and 3 acres of land and 6s., rent in Earsdon held by Adam Mauduyt; five tofts, four bovates and 3 acres of land in Earsdon held by Master John Mauduyt; and eight tofts, four bovates and 3 acres of land in Earsdon which master Robert Mauduyt held. If Roger should die without an heir male by his wife Eleanor, all the settled lands were to go to his daughter Margaret and her heirs male, and then them failing to Roger's right heirs. Weland, William, master John and master Robert Mauduyt were consenting parties to the settlement (*Feet of Fines*).

It would seem that the other Mauduyts mentioned in this settlement were younger brothers of Roger Mauduyt III. Two of them, William and Adam, were probably the persons of these names who with others had the king's licence 25 September 1318 to go to the papal court at Rome there to obtain absolution for offences committed on the Scottish marches (*Patent Roll*).

On 29 August 1332 Roger Mauduit and Alienor his wife recovered a third part of the manor of Fawdon which was Alienor's dower. Both Roger and Alienor's seals are attached to the deed his inscribed s' ROGERI MAVDVYT TCII (tertius) and her's s'ALIENORE COMITISSE.

Sir Roger Mauduyt was empowered by an inquisition held on 25 June 1332 to found a chantry in St Michael's church, Felton, and to endow it with 100s. rent in Eshot and Bockenfield to maintain a chaplain to say masses daily for his soul and for the souls of his heirs and ancestors. On 14 September 1553 Roger Mauduyt, '4th lord of Eshot' gave to Edmund de Esshet certain rights of common of pasture in Eshot (*NDD.* p.95, No. 13). Shortly after this he forfeited his lands. In 1358 the king restored to Roger Mauduyt the castle, vill and manor of Eshot and all other lands and tenements with appurtenances in Northumberland which were Roger Mauduyt's his father, deceased. It seems that he had been concerned in Gilbert de Middleton's rebellion.

On 7 July 1358 immediately after his restoration, sir Roger Mauduit made a settlement of the manor of Eshot. Robert Tatmane and Robert de Thorpe, chaplains, who held the manor by the enfeoffment of John Mauduyt and John Mauduyt and Johanna his wife, granted it to sir Roger Mauduyt with successive remainders to John Mauduyt and Joan his wife; to John brother of Roger Mauduyt father of their feoffor; to Robert son of Roger father of John Mauduyt; to Welard son of Roger Mauduyt father of John their feoffor; to John son of Roger Mauduyt their feoffor, and his right heirs (*NDD.* p.96, No. 15). The remainder men in this settlement were Roger Mauduit's younger brothers John, Robert and Welard (Wyland) and his uncle John.

Roger Mauduit IV seems to have died *s.p.*, his heir being his brother John. In 1347 John son of Roger Mauduit as 'cousin' and heir of John Bekard succeeded to the manor of Burton Leonard, Yorks. On 11 November 1374 John Mauduyth of Burton Leonard, 'lord of Eshot', released to Robert Mauduyth son of sir Roger Mauduyth certain lands in Eshot. These lands descended to Robert's son Wyland Mauduyth who, after the death of Isabell his wife, settled them 16 January 1419 in the hands of trustees. Subsequently on 20 May 1422 Wyland sold his lands in Eshot to Edward Bertram, to whom the trustees released their rights on 20 June 1422. Wyland's heir was his brother John who had an only daughter Agnes wife of Richard Park of Bedlington. The latter on 10 June 1473 released all Agnes' rights 'which was nothing in effect' to Edward Conyers and Jane his wife, which Jane was granddaughter of Edward Bertram, the purchaser of 1422.

MAUDUIT—BIBLIOGRAPHY

NCH. VII, pp.327-341 with pedigree.
Sanders, *English Baronies*, pp.28-29, 50-51.

MAUDUIT of ESHOT, par. FELTON

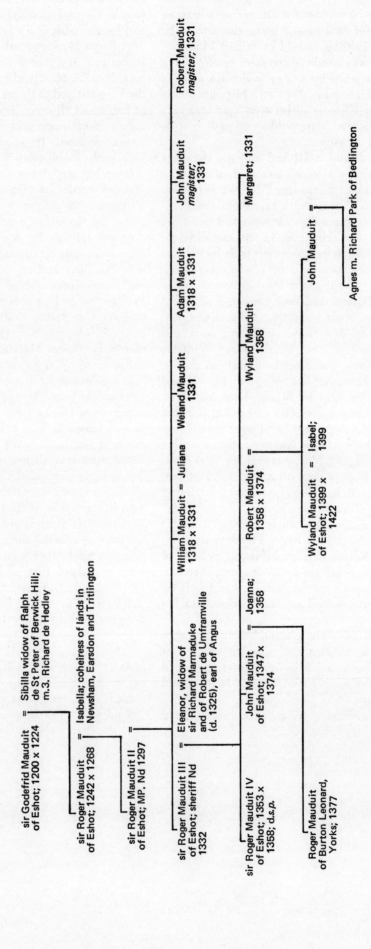

VALOIGNES

PETER DE VALOIGNES was lord of Benington in Hertfordshire at the time of the Domesday survey. He witnesses documents the last of which dates definitely from 1109. (Sanders, *English Baronies*, p.12n.). Valognes is an arrondisement and canton in Manche (*Harl Soc.* vol.103, p.108). Peter was succeeded in his barony of Benington by his son Roger who died 1141/2. It seems likely that Roger's wife was Agnes, sister of Pagan son of John. About 1185 it was stated that 'Agnes de Valuines, sister of Pagan son of John, is in the gift of the king, and aged over 60 years; her daughter and heir is given to Durando de Ostili' (*Rotulus de Dominabus*, p.46). Actually Durando's wife was a granddaughter of Roger de Valoignes. Pagan son of John was brother of Eustace son of John, baron of Alnwick.

'A case in 1234-35 relating to the descent of land in Dersingham, Norfolk, which formed part of the barony of Valognes, where it is stated that Peter the eldest of the three Valognes brothers had held the land and died without an heir of his body, and he had a certain wife Gundreda de Warauna who had held the land for her life in the name of dower; and the judgment shows that the land had descended to the issue of Robert, Peter's next brother, and that the ultimate heirs were the granddaughters of Philip the third brother' (Bracton's *Note Book*, No.1128; *Early Yorkshire Charters* VIII, pp.28 *et seq*). In fact Roger had at least five sons.

The eldest son, Peter de Valognes II, married Gundreda daughter of Reginald de Warenne. Peter died *s.p.* in 1158 and Gundreda married secondly William de Curcy and thirdly Geoffrey Hose; she died in 1224 having had issue by her second husband. Peter's heir was his brother Robert who rendered account of 200m. for his land at Michaelmas 1160 (*Pipe Roll*). In 1165 he paid scutage on 30 knights' fees, and in 1166 he answered for 30⅓ fees of old feoffment and 4½ of new. Robert's wife was called Hawise but her parentage is unknown. Robert died in 1184 leaving an only daughter and heiress Gunnora.

Gunnora married before 1185 Durand de Ostilli. As chamberlain he was with Henry II at Le Mans 1182 x 1186 (*Cal. documents preserved in France*, p.361) and in 1190 he paid £15. 3s. 4d. for scutage on 30⅓ knights' fees. He was dead in 1194 when Gunnora de Valoignes herself paid the scutage. Gunnora's second husband was Robert son of Walter, leader of the barons in their struggle for Magna Carta. In 1207 Gunnora had livery of lands in Burton, Yorks., until then held in dower by Emma de Humet after the death of Geoffrey de Valoignes her husband (Dugdale). Geoffrey de Valoignes married before 1163, Emma daughter of Bertrande Bulmer (d.1166) and heiress to her brother William de Bulmer; after Geoffrey's death in 1169 she seems to have married Guy de Humet. Her third husband was Geoffrey de Nevill of Ashby in Lincolnshire; Nevill died in 1193. His widow died in 1208 when her son Henry de Nevill was charged £100 and one

palfrey for the lands which he had inherited from his mother Emma in Raskelf and Sutton in the Forest, Yorks. (*Pipe Roll*). At Easter 1209 Philip de Valoignes had a plea against Robert son of Walter and Gunnora his wife concerning both the land which he demands against them and the land which they demand against him. These lands in dispute were in Northumberland, Herefordshire, Lincolnshire and Yorkshire (*Nd Pleas* in *NRS*. II, p.37). Philip and Geoffrey de Valoines were younger brothers of Robert de Valoines and therefore uncles of Gunnora.

VALOIGNES OF NEWHAM, PAR. BAMBURGH

GEOFFREY DE VALOIGNES had held the manor of Newham in Northumberland and presumably his lands passed after his death to his niece Gunnora. When William de Vescy made a return of his barony of Alnwick in 1166 he reported that Galfrid de Vall' held half a knight's fee of him; the enfeoffment had been made since he had succeeded to the barony in 1157. An undated grant of lands in Preston, par. Ellingham, by Robert son of Brian to Alnwick abbey is witnessed by William de Vesci, Hugh de Valoniis *dapifer*, and others (*NCH*. II, p.319n.). In 1187 the sheriff of Northumberland rendered account of 62s.8d. of the donum of the land which was Henry de Valoignis in the county; 31s.4d. was then paid and a further 10s., in 1188 or 1189; the balance of 21s.4d. was carried forward in the *pipe rolls* for 1190 and 1191, but for the next three years the *pipe rolls* are not extant. It is not known if or how Henry was related to Geoffrey but there is no record of lands in Northumberland other than Newham belonging to anyone of the name of Valoignes.

Gunnora de Valoignes by her husband Robert son of Walter had two daughters who became coheiresses not only to the barony of Benington but to the manor of Newham. The daughters were Maud wife of Geoffrey de Mandeville, earl of Essex, and Christiana wife of William de Mandeville, earl of Essex. Both the earls of Essex died *s.p.*, Geoffrey in 1216 and William in 1227. On the death of the countess Christiana in 1232 her heirs were the three granddaughters of Philip de Valoignes.

Before 1166 Philip de Valoignes had moved to Scotland probably with his younger brother Roger. Roger was lord of Easter Kilbride as early as 1175 x 1189 (*Notes and Queries*, 6th ser. V, pp.142, 143). Philip was a surety for the Scottish king in the treaty of Falaise in 1174. About this time he was in attendance on the king at a tourney in France (*L'histoire de Guillaume le Marechal*, 1901, iii, 21). In or before 1166 he had been made hereditary chamberlain of Scotland and had been granted the lands of Panmure and Bervie in Fifeshire by William the Lion. In 1191 he gave £100 for livery of the lands of Geoffrey his brother.

The *Chronicle of Melrose, s.a.* 1215 records that 'On the nones of November (5 November) died Philip de Valoniis, the chamberlain of our lord William, king of Scots, who was conveyed to Melrose, and honourably interred in the chapter-house of the monks'. Philip's son and heir William died four years later. 'William de Valoniis died at Kelso, and his body was carried to Melrose (contrary to the wishes of the monks of that house) and there honourably buried in the chapter house of the monks, near the burial place of his father' (*Chronicle of Melrose, s.a.* 1219). By his wife Lora daughter of Saher de Quincy, earl of Winchester, William de Valoignes had three daughters who were not only his coheiresses, but heirs to Christiana, countess of Essex, their second cousin.

The three daughters were Lora (Lauretta) wife of Henry de Balliol of Cavers, co. Roxburgh; Christiana wife of Peter de Maune, and Isabel wife of David Comyn of Kilbride, Lanarkshire. The hereditary office of chamberlain of Scotland passed to the Balliols. The Comyns acquired the lands of Easter Kilbride in Scotland and the manor of Newham in Northumberland.

In 1238 (*circa* 15 April) the king granted to David Comin and Isabella his wife that they might pay in instalments the debt to the exchequer of £100 for which Henry de Bayllol and Lora his wife, Peter de Maun and Christina his wife, and themselves, made a fine with the king for their relief of the manors which were Gunnora de Waloynes (*CDS*. I, No. 1416). On 3 May 1253 inquisitions were taken in Suffolk, Hert-fordshire, Essex and Norfolk of the extent of the lands of Isabella de Valoynes, deceased; her son and heir William was aged 16 (*Ib.*, Nos. 1920, 1921, 1922, 1923). In 1257 and again in 1258 writs were sent to the sheriff of Northumberland to present the executors of the testament of Isabella de Valoynes to answer to the king with William Comyn her son and heir, for £4. 17s., that she owed the king for the scutage of Gascony (*Ib.*, Nos. 2096, 2135). On 29 October 1258 the sheriffs of Norfolk, Suffolk, Essex and Herts were advised that the king had taken William Comyn's homage (*Ib.*, No. 2134).

It would seem that the male heir of William de Valoynes (d.1219) had some claim to the manor of Newham for at the assizes in 1269 William Comyn had an assize of *mort d'ancestor versus* William de Waloynes of the manor of Newham (*SS.* 88, p.170) Was this the William de Valoynes who with his wife Laderana, had a plea of trespass in Middlesex 1266 against Johanna, widow of Gilbert de Basseville?

VALOIGNES—BIBLIOGRAPHY

J. Horace Round, *Comyn and Valoignes* in the Ancestor, No.11, pp.129-135.
Dugdale, *Baronage*, I, p.44.
Ritchie, *The Normans in Scotland*, p.358n.
Sanders, *English Baronies*, pp.12-13.

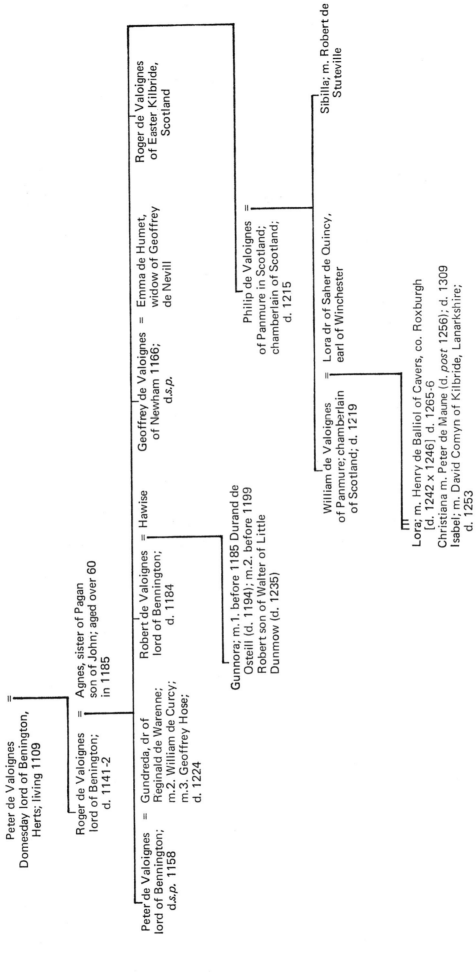

VALOIGNES of NEWHAM, par. BAMBURGH

Peter de Valoignes
Domesday lord of Benington,
Herts; living 1109
=

Roger de Valoignes
lord of Benington;
d. 1141-2
=
Agnes, sister of Pagan
son of John; aged over 60
in 1185

Peter de Valoignes
lord of Benington;
d.s.p. 1158
=
Gundreda, dr of
Reginald de Warenne;
m.2. William de Curcy;
m.3. Geoffrey Hose;
d. 1224

Robert de Valoignes
lord of Benington;
d. 1184
=
Hawise

Geoffrey de Valoignes
of Newham 1166;
d.s.p.
=
Emma de Humet,
widow of Geoffrey
de Nevill

Roger de Valoignes
of Easter Kilbride,
Scotland

Gunnora; m.1. before 1185 Durand de
Osteill (d. 1194); m.2. before 1199
Robert son of Walter of Little
Dunmow (d. 1235)

Philip de Valoignes
of Panmure in Scotland;
chamberlain of Scotland;
d. 1215
=
Lora dr of Saher de Quincy,
earl of Winchester

Sibilla; m. Robert de
Stuteville

William de Valoignes
of Panmure; chamberlain
of Scotland; d. 1219

Lora; m. Henry de Balliol of Cavers, co. Roxburgh
[d. 1242 x 1246] d. 1265-6
Christiana m. Peter de Maune (d. post 1256); d. 1309
Isabel; m. David Comyn of Kilbride, Lanarkshire;
d. 1253

BULMER

The surname is from the small village of Bulmer, North Riding of Yorkshire, a few miles north-east of York.

The earliest known member of the family is Aschetil de Bulemer who witnesses a charter of Nigel Fossard, a Yorkshire baron *c*.1100-*c*.1115. The Christian name is the Old Norse *Asketil*, compound of *ass* and *Ketal*. The corresponding Old English form is *Oscytel*. The Norman forms of the name are Ansketil, Anketil and Anketin. It seems possible that the Bulmers acquired their Yorkshire lands by marriage. Round suggested that Ansketil may have married the heiress of Peter de Humez of Brancepeth (*Early Yorkshire Charters*, II, p.128).

On the death of Ansketil de Bulmer *circa* 1129 he was succeeded by his eldest son and heir Bertram who was sheriff of York 1130-1163. Bertram's wife Emma was probably a daughter of Robert Fossard, a Yorkshire tenant-in-chief, for Bertram held four knights' fees of the Fossards. Bertram was dead in 1166 when a return of the fees that he had held was made by David the lardener (*Ib.*, p.113). A grant made by Bertram de Bulemer 1147 x 1163 is witnessed by Aschetil his son, but the son died in his father's lifetime and Bertram's heir was a young son William who came of age between 1163 and 1168 and died *s.p.* 1176 x 1178.

William's heir was his sister Emma wife of Geoffrey de Nevill (d.1193) of Burreth, Lincs. She had previously been married to Geoffrey de Valoignes (d.1169). When Emma died in 1208 her only son and heir Henry de Nevill succeeded to the Bulmer estates. Henry died *s.p.* in 1227. His sister and heiress Isabel married Robert son of Meldred (d.1253), lord of Raby, and they became ancestors of the second line of Nevill.

Stephen de Bulmer who married Cecily sister and heiress of Thomas and Ranulf de Muschamp, barons of Wooler, was probably a younger brother of Bertram de Bulmer (d.1166). From this marriage sprang the second line of Muschamp, barons of Wooler. By an earlier marriage Stephen was father of Robert de Bulmer (living 1181, d. before 1202). It was this Robert who married Joanna daughter and coheiress of Hugh de Ellington. Ellington held half the barony of Ellingham in Northumberland in right of his wife Alice sister and coheiress of William de Grenvile; Joanna however was not Alice's daughter. The descendants of Robert and Joanna seem to have assumed the surname of Ferlington.

The male line of Bulmer was carried on by John de Bulmer, living in 1205. Round thought that he was probably a younger son of Stephen de Bulmer (d.1171-72). From John de Bulmer descended three generations of Bulmers all called John. It was the third John (d.1299) who married Theophania one of the daughters and coheiresses of Hugh de Morwick, baron of Chevington.

The main line of the family was of Wilton, Yorks. Sir William Bulmer a younger son of this family married Eliza-

beth daughter and heiress of William Elmeden and their descendants were of Tursdale, co. Durham.

BULMER OF NEWCASTLE UPON TYNE

Although the Bulmers were primarily a Yorkshire family, younger sons (or more likely younger sons of younger sons) were forced to the big towns by the pressure of over population in the countryside and attracted to where great fortunes could be made. Many young men from Yorkshire came to Newcastle, amongst them Bulmers who could have been descended from any of the different branches of the family. The earliest of these seems to have been Edward Bulmer, master and mariner, who became a freeman of Newcastle in 1607.

Shortly before 17 April 1634 Edward Bulmer addressed a petition to Charles I concerning great abuses on the river Tyne. As one of the Society of the Trinity House of Newcastle, and as steersman of the royal barge when the king had made a trip down the river on 4 June 1633, he complained that the mayor and aldermen 'have taken for great and inveterate malice against your petitioner'. He was evidently concerned about the overbearing attitude of the Newcastle merchants who wished to have control of all the river trade. They had brought a suit at York against Bulmer for instigating certain boys in pulling down a house and limekiln. In his absence, Bulmer was fined 500 marks, and he now petitions the king to remit the fine or to refer it to the Lords Commissioners for the Admiralty (*AA*2. XXI, p.85). The result of the appeal was that the fine was reduced to £40, which Bulmer paid just before Christmas.

Two sons of the royal steersman became freemen of Newcastle, both as master mariners, Charles in 1642 and Edward in 1652. The father made his will 8 July 1635. To his 'now' wife and her heirs for ever he leaves a burgage in Hornsbye's Chair near the Quay side in Newcastle. Two cellars with lofts over the Plumber Chair he leaves to his son Charles Bulmer for his life and then to the heirs of his body lawfully begotten and in default to his son Edward Bulmer for his life and then to his heirs and in default to the testator's right heirs for ever. His son Charles is to have a large silver beaker 'which hath the Emdons arms upon the same'; his son Edward is to have another large silver beaker 'which hath the merchaunts marke upon the same'. He leaves to his daughter Margaret Bulmer 'a silver cann' and to his sister Alice Fell a hood and a 20s., piece of gold for a token. The will was proved by his widow Anne, the executrix, 14 January 1638/9.

In 1639 Anne Bulmer, the widow, submitted an account of her executorship. Her late husband's goods were valued at £250. 4s. 9d. The total amount of debts paid and to be paid was £440. 13s. Included in these payments were £56. 1s. to the

BULMER OF BULMER, Yorks.

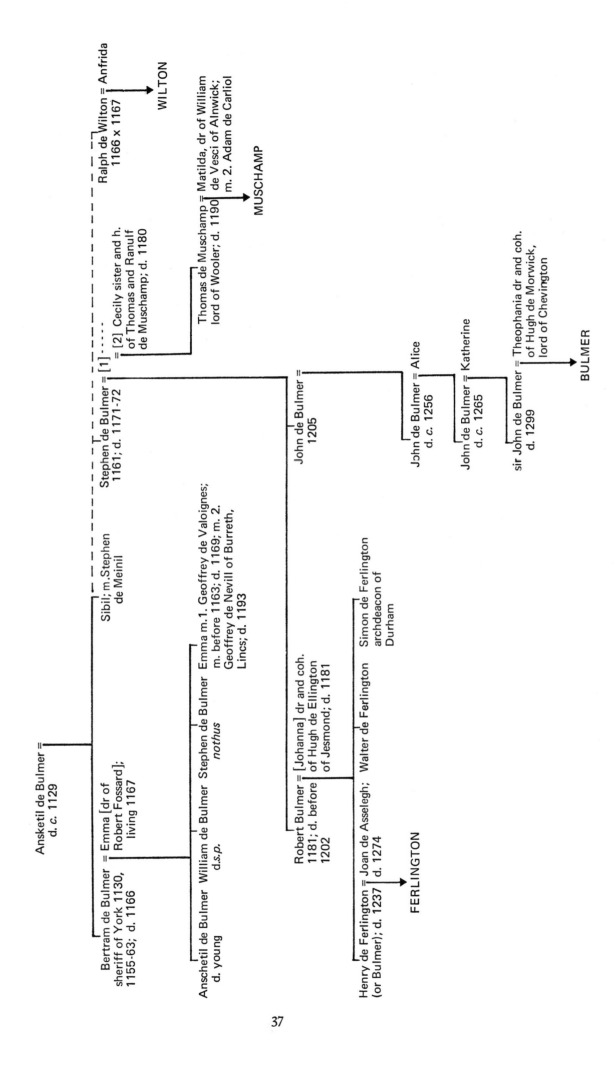

37

Master of the Trinity House at Newcastle upon Edward's bond; £60 to Margaret Bulmer for a legacy given her by the will of Margaret Peacocke which was received by the testator and was in his hands at his death; to the mate to her husband in the ship where he was master, for his funeral expenses and debts in the Eastland £50 (*Dur. Prob. Off.* by C.R.H.).

It is evident that the two sons were half brothers. The name of Charles' mother is unknown. Edward's mother was Anne Peacock, widow of William Clavering. She had married William Clavering at All Saints, Newcastle on 27 November 1620; Clavering died in 1624. After Edward Bulmer's death she married Robert Babington.

If the silver beaker with the arms of Emdon on it was a family heirloom it might suggest that Edward Bulmer was descended from sir William Bulmer (d.1531) of Wilton in Cleveland, Yorks. Sir William's younger son William married Elizabeth daughter and heiress of William Elmeden, and left descendants.

On a complaint made by a brother of the Merchants company of Newcastle upon Tyne that divers apprentices were not conforming to the Company's rules concerning their hair, apparel and behaviour, it was directed that some of the apprentices concerned should be summoned to a court to be held on 21 March 1655. Seven, including George Bulmer, failed to put in an appearance (*SS.* 93, p.185). A few years later, on 9 February 1658/9 a report was made of 'the uncivil and lascivious carriage' of George Bulmer, apprentice to Mr Peter Burwell, with a woman at Shields. The woman had been committed to prison at Morpeth gaol for her lewdness and it was ordered that the Justice of the Peace responsible for this committal should be asked to certify the truth so that Bulmer might be 'proceeded against according to his demerit' (*Ib.*, p.194). On 30 September 1659 Bulmer appeared before a merchants' court when it was decided that his misdeeds should be taken notice of in the margin of his enrolment so that when he desired his freedom of the fellowship further enquiry might be made about his behaviour (*Ib.*, p.198).

In the 17th century Edward Bulmer, weaver (1670), and John Bulmer, master and mariner (1698) became freemen of Newcastle. Other freemen with the surnames of Bowmer and Boomer may have had no connection with the Bulmers. Edward Bulmer of Newcastle, weaver, died before 28 February 1699/1700; two of his sons, Christopher and John were butchers in Newcastle, and Christopher's sons Christopher and Thomas followed their father's occupation.

Another family of Bulmers in Newcastle in the 18th century were house carpenters. Of this family were three brothers who later migrated to London; they were sir Fenwick Bulmer, Blackett Bulmer and William Bulmer. A daughter of sir Fenwick married Pierre de Sales La Teniere and their grandson Fenwick Bulmer de Sales La Teniere was a member of the King's Bodyguard. Both sir Fenwick and Blackett Bulmer voted at the election in 1774 as freemen of Newcastle. The youngest of the three brothers was a well-known London typographer and has achieved a place in the *Dictionary of National Biography*.

Perhaps the last Bulmer immigrant from Yorkshire was Joseph Bulmer (d.1807), a Newcastle builder, who came from Skelton in Cleveland, Yorks. He has left his name to Bulmer Street, off Gallowgate, Newcastle. His great-great-grandson William Bulmer was President of the Society of Antiquaries of Newcastle upon Tyne in 1965.

BULMER of NEWCASTLE UPON TYNE. Line I

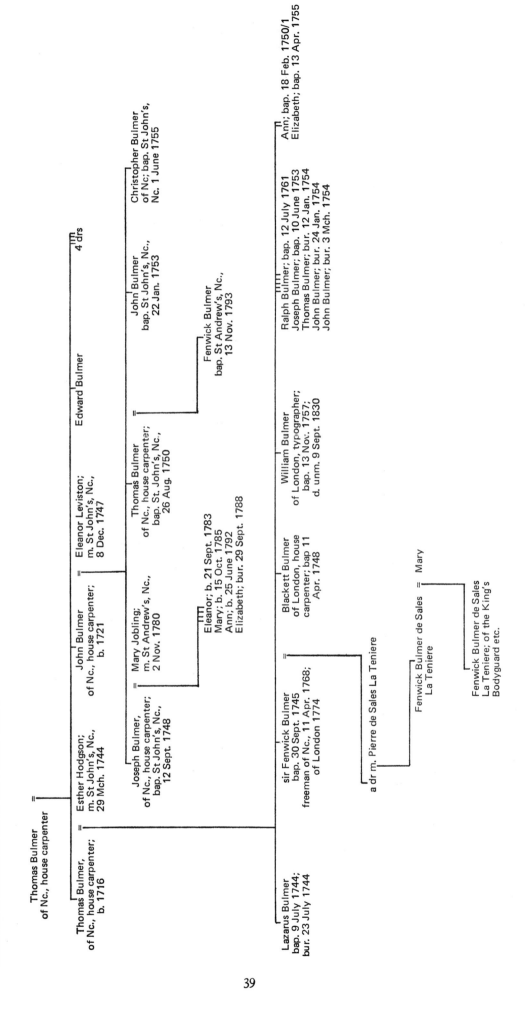

BULMER of NEWCASTLE UPON TYNE. Line II

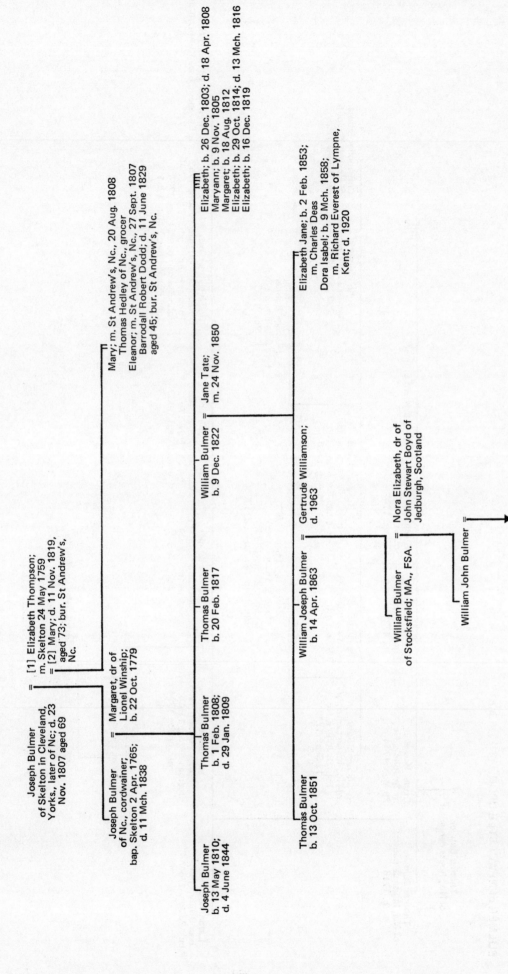

Joseph Bulmer
of Skelton in Cleveland,
Yorks., later of Nc; d. 23
Nov. 1807 aged 69

= [1] Elizabeth Thompson;
   m. Skelton 24 May 1759
= [2] Mary; d. 11 Nov. 1819,
   aged 73; bur. St Andrew's,
   Nc.

Joseph Bulmer
of Nc., cordwainer;
bap. Skelton 2 Apr. 1765;
d. 11 Mch. 1838

= Margaret, dr of
   Lionel Winship;
   b. 22 Oct. 1779

Mary; m. St Andrew's, Nc., 20 Aug. 1808
Thomas Hedley of Nc., grocer
Eleanor; m. St Andrew's, Nc., 27 Sept. 1807
Barrodall Robert Dodd; d. 11 June 1829
aged 45; bur. St Andrew's, Nc.

Joseph Bulmer
b. 13 May 1810;
d. 4 June 1844

Thomas Bulmer
b. 1 Feb. 1808;
d. 29 Jan. 1809

Thomas Bulmer
b. 20 Feb. 1817

William Bulmer
b. 9 Dec. 1822

= Jane Tate;
   m. 24 Nov. 1850

Elizabeth; b. 26 Dec. 1803; d. 18 Apr. 1808
Maryann; b. 9 Nov. 1805
Margaret; b. 18 Aug. 1812
Elizabeth; b. 29 Oct. 1814; d. 13 Mch. 1816
Elizabeth; b. 16 Dec. 1819

Thomas Bulmer
b. 13 Oct. 1851

William Joseph Bulmer
b. 14 Apr. 1863

= Gertrude Williamson;
   d. 1963

Elizabeth Jane; b. 2 Feb. 1853;
   m. Charles Deas
Dora Isabel; b. 9 Mch. 1858;
   m. Richard Everest of Lympne,
   Kent; d. 1920

William Bulmer
of Stocksfield; MA., FSA.

= Nora Elizabeth, dr of
   John Stewart Boyd of
   Jedburgh, Scotland

William John Bulmer   = →

40

HERON

The use of the Christian name Jordan, probably derived from the old German personal name Jordanes, suggests that the Heron family may have been of Flemish extraction. Many Flemings received grants of land in Clydesdale from Malcolm IV of Scotland (1153-1165). A charter of Robert, bishop of St Andrew's, *circa* 1150 is witnessed by 'Baldewinus flam' (*i.e.* the Fleming), 'Hugo fil. Fresechin', 'Jordane Heyrum' and others (Ritchie, p.375). In the middle of the 12th century, many families were holding lands on both sides of the Border. Gilbert de Umframville, a member of the family that held the barony of Prudhoe and the lordship of Redesdale, was constable to William and Henry, the Scottish earls of Northumberland, and had a near relative called Jordan de Umframville. About the same time Henry I of England founded a Flemish colony in Pembroke, and one of the settlers gave his name to Jordanston in Rhos.

Jordan Hairun in 1144 witnesses a charter of king David granting Lesmahagow to the abbey of Kelso (Lawric, CLXXII). About 1153-1157 he witnesses a confirmation by Malcolm IV of Scotland, of the gift of Ranulf de Sules, the king's butler, of a carucate of land in the vale of Liddell to the hospital of St Peter at York. Shortly after this he seems to have been resident in Yorkshire, where perhaps he already held lands in Allertonshire of the bishop of Durham. *Circa* 1150-1157 he witnesses a confirmation by William de Vesci of the gifts made by his father, Eustace son of John, to the nuns of Walton of the church and vill of Walton (Farrer II, No. 1110). Besides witnessing two Yorkshire charters of Hugh, bishop of Durham, between 1153 and 1157, about the same time he witnesses Robert de Lasceles' grant of a carucate in Morton Grange to the monks of Rievaulx (*Ib.*, No. 727). Whilst German was prior of Durham (1163-1186) Jordan Hairun witnesses a grant of a carucate of land at Silksworth, co. Durham, by Gaufrid son of Richard to Philip son of Hamund (*SS*. 58, p.125n.). About the same time he is named as a witness to a confirmation by William de Vesci of a grant by Radulf de Caugi to the monks of St Cuthbert at Durham of the church of St Maurice at Ellingham, Northumberland (*Ib.*, p.101n.).

HERON, BARONS OF HADSTON

In the returns made by the tenants in chief in 1166 we find Jordan Hairun holding a ninth part of a knights' fee of Gilbert Hansard in Yorkshire; he held Great and Little Chilton, co. Durham, of the bishop of Durham, and Gilbert Hansard was his under tenant of these lands. In Northumberland he held of Radulf de Wirecestre a quarter of a knight's fee in the barony of Hadston. Before 1184 he had succeeded to the barony of Hadston in right of his wife who was daughter and heiress of Radulf de Wirecestre. As holder of a barony he found himself in rather a peculiar position with regard to

Gilbert Hansard. Hansard was Hairun's overlord in Yorkshire though in Northumberland he held West Chirton, and in Durham the vills of Great and Little Chilton as under tenant of Hairun. In a later generation complications were to arise from this relationship.

Jordan Hairun, Radulf his son, Jordan brother of the same, and Robert Hairun are witnesses to a grant from Roger de Aepplingdene to Thomas son of Hamund of 6 bovates in Silksworth, co. Durham (*SS*. 58, p.124n.). Jordan the father was dead in 1191 when his son and heir Radulf is charged 40s., in the *Pipe Roll*, apparently for relief of his lands, and 10s., for a recognition. The debt of 40s., was carried forward to 1195. By the following year Radulf also was dead and Jordan Hairun his brother and heir rendered account to the sheriff of 40m., for having his lands which were in the hands of the king.

From now on the younger Jordan appears with unfailing regularity in the *Pipe Rolls* until 1233. He had quittance for the sixth scutage in 1205, and for the scutage for Scotland in 1213, so perhaps served in person. He is a regular witness to the charters of the prior and convent of Durham, in the later ones being described as *dominus*, signifying that he had received knighthood. In 1201 began a series of disputes between Hairun and Gilbert Hansard, the latter claiming that Hairun would not take his homage for the vill of Chilton. Hairun's answer was 'that he ought not to take homage for that land, because it was the heritage of his mother, and not of his father, and if his father gave it to Gilbert's father, he gave it wrongfully, because he neither ought nor could, as he was only the guardian of his mother's heritage'; the justices decided 'that Jurdan should take Gilbert's homage, saving his right and quarrel, and he took his homage before the justices' (*Nd pleas* in NRS. II, p.14). In 1220 they again went to law when Hairun claimed against Hansard three carucates in Chirton. This was settled at Easter Term 1221 when Hansard gave one mark for licence to make an agreement with Hairun (*Ib.*, p.65).

Jordan Hairun was succeeded by his son William Hairun. In 1245 for the aid given to the king for the marriage of his eldest daughter, Jord. (amended to Will.) de Hayrun was charged 20s. In 1256 William Hairun gave West Chirton in free alms to the prior and convent of Tynemouth. At Easter 1242 Robert son of Adam gave a mark for leave to agree with Michael de Ryhull and his parceners, in a plea of land, by pledge of William Hayrun (*NRS*. II). At Michaelmas 1250 William made a covenant with Simon de Dyveleston to render to Simon every year for Simon's whole life 24m. for the manor of Dilston until the lawful age of Thomas, the son and heir of Simon and Lucy his wife (*Ib.*). Thomas de Dyveleston married Lucy daughter of William Hairun. On 29 December 1251 Hairun had a grant of free warren in his demesne lands of Hadston. He was keeper of Bam-

HERON, barons of Hadston

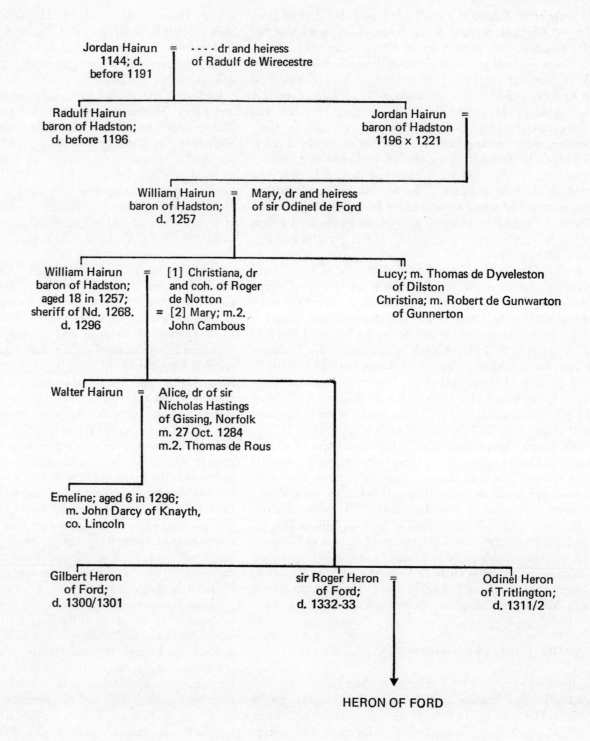

Jordan Hairun
1144; d.
before 1191
= - - - - dr and heiress
of Radulf de Wirecestre

Radulf Hairun
baron of Hadston;
d. before 1196

Jordan Hairun =
baron of Hadston
1196 x 1221

William Hairun =
baron of Hadston;
d. 1257
Mary, dr and heiress
of sir Odinel de Ford

William Hairun =
baron of Hadston;
aged 18 in 1257;
sheriff of Nd. 1268.
d. 1296
[1] Christiana, dr
and coh. of Roger
de Notton
= [2] Mary; m.2.
John Cambous

Lucy; m. Thomas de Dyveleston
of Dilston
Christina; m. Robert de Gunwarton
of Gunnerton

Walter Hairun =
Alice, dr of sir
Nicholas Hastings
of Gissing, Norfolk
m. 27 Oct. 1284
m.2. Thomas de Rous

Emeline; aged 6 in 1296;
m. John Darcy of Knayth,
co. Lincoln

Gilbert Heron
of Ford;
d. 1300/1301

sir Roger Heron =
of Ford;
d. 1332-33

Odinel Heron
of Tritlington;
d. 1311/2

HERON OF FORD

42

burgh castle in 1248 and of Scarborough castle in 1255. In 1245 he had protection going to Wales with John Maunsel. He was sheriff of Northumberland between 1246 and 1257 and during this time made himself so unpopular that when he died in 1257 the historian Matthew Paris wrote of him 'he ground down the poor and oppressed the monks. His thirst for riches was immense, and now he has gone to thirst in Hell'. The writ for the inquisition after his death is dated 20 January 1257/8. By his wife Mary daughter and eventually heiress of sir Odinel de Ford, he had a son William Heron, aged 18 at his father's death on 11 November 1257, and at least two daughters Lucy wife of Thomas de Dyveleston and Christina wife of Robert de Gunwarton (NCH. IV, p.325).

William Hairun II was sheriff of Northumberland in 1268 and constable of Bamburgh castle before 11 February 1278. He was a conservator of the peace and a commissioner for the Statutes of Winchester in Northumberland 20 January 1287. On 3 June 1291 he was summoned to serve against the Scots, and had been MP for Northumberland in 1290. Before 1292 he succeeded to his mother's estates comprising the manor of Ford, the vills of Crookham and Kimmerston, with lands and rents in Howburn and Holy Island. By this date William's eldest son and heir was dead leaving a baby daughter, and in order to provide for his younger sons, in 1292 he settled his mother's estates on his son Gilbert with remainders to his other surviving sons Roger and Odinel.

William Hairun II heads the Subsidy Roll for Hadston in 1296 and died at Newcastle on the Sunday before 21 December 1296. He was twice married, his first wife being Christiana, daughter and coheiress of Roger de Notton, Yorks., who was probably the mother of his children. The family name of his second wife Mary is unknown but her seal bears the arms checky and a chief (AA3. XX, p.160); she had one third of Hadston in dower and on 25 March 1299 made an agreement about her dower with her step-son Gilbert Heron. After the death of William Hairun she married John Cambous who was killed in 1303. William Hairun's heir was his grand daughter Emeline aged 6 and then under the guardianship of her mother. Walter Hairun had married at Alverstayn, Yorks., on 27 October 1284 Alice daughter of sir Nicholas Hastings of Gissing, co. Norfolk. In 1294 Alice Hairun claimed dower in Ford, Crookham and Kimmerston from her brother-in-law Gilbert Heron. She married secondly Thomas de Rous. The heiress married John Darcy of Knayth, co. Lincoln, and the barony of Hadston passed to their descendants.

HERON OF FORD, PAR. FORD

WILLIAM HAIRUN was succeeded in the manor of Ford by his second but eldest surviving son Gilbert.

Gilbert Heron was sued by Robert Heron, parson of Ford, in 1294 (AA3. VIII, p.233n.). He was living at Ford before his father's death and was assessed for the Subsidy of 1296 on his goods there. He died between Easter 1300 and Trinity 1301, his heir being his brother Roger.

Sir Roger Heron was constable of Bamburgh castle 1300-1316. He had a grant of free warren in Ford and Crookham in 1304. In 1309 he had an action with Roger Mauduit of Eshot about trespass (NCH. VII, p.334). He acquired lands in Crawley from Michael de Middleton 26 September 1312, and granted Hedgeley 21 September 1330 to Robert de Manners. He was living in 1332 when he was appointed a justice of oyer and terminer, but was dead in 1333. His widow Margery is mentioned in 1337. She was his second wife and after his death married Gilbert de Burradon. Roger's first wife was Elizabeth, daughter and coheiress of Adam de Swinburne. By this marriage the Herons of Ford acquired the manors of Simonburn and Sewingshields and lands in Espleywood. Sir Roger Heron's younger brother Odinel Heron paid for the Subsidy at Tritlington in 1296, was a commissioner of array in 1311, and was dead in 1312.

Sir Roger Heron had three sons, William, his son and heir, Roger and John. Roger was a witness to a lease dated 19 June 1362 of the manor of Tarset by David, earl of Athol, to sir William Heron his brother. Sir John Heron was given the manor of Crawley by his father and founded the family of HERON OF ESHOT, PAR. FELTON.

In 1333 sir William Heron claimed money from the Crown in connection with his father's office of constable of Bamburgh castle. He made settlements of his lands in 1337 and 1340. By the first he settled the manor of Ford and the advowson of the church there, except two messuages, four carucates of land and thirty shillings of rent in the said manor. The excepted lands and rent were held in dower by Margery formerly wife of Roger Heyron. The settlement was on William Heyroun (by the name of William son of Roger Heyroun) and Isabel his wife and their male issue with successive remainders to Roger son of William and his male issue; William brother of Roger and his male issue; John brother of William and his male issue; Thomas brother of John and the right heirs of William son of Roger. The dower lands of Margery Heyron which after her death should revert to William son of Roger, were to go with the settled lands (Feet of Fines 25 November 1337 in NRS. XI, p.94). In the settlement of 1340 the remainders are to William brother of Roger, John his brother, and Walter his brother and the heirs male of their bodies respectively; the dower lands which Gilbert de Boreudone and Margery his wife held as her dower were to go with the settled lands after Margery's death (Feet of Fines 13 Oct. 1340 and 27 Jan. 1341 in NRS. XI, p.94). William Heron on 21 April 1340 had a grant of free warren in his demesne lands at Bockenfield, Ford, etc., and licence to crenellate his house at Ford. In 1345 William Heroun made a settlement of the manor of Pigdon; the manor was held for life by Katherine formerly wife of John de Denum; after her death it was to go to William Heroun for life, then to Walter his son and his male issue in perpetuity; them failing to Thomas his brother, John his brother and then to the right heirs of William Heroun (Feet of Fines 11 Apr. and 6 Oct. 1345—NRS. XI, p.103). On 6 January 1348 he had a grant of the manor of Thornton in Norhamshire from the bishop of Durham. Thornton became the property of William's third son John Heron. On 9 September 1348 sir Robert de Lisle of Chipchase made an agreement with sir William Heron of Ford, whereby it was arranged that Cecily de Lisle, sir Robert's granddaughter and heiress should marry William, John or Walter Heron younger sons of sir William. In accordance with this agreement the manor of Chipchase was conveyed to sir William Heron 11 October 1348 and was settled on Walter Heron who married the heiress. Walter was also provided for by his father with the manor of Pigdon conveyed to him on 5 October 1360. In June 1377 sir William Heron settled on his son Andrew Heron the vill of West Whelpington with remainders to Roger son of Walter Heron of Chipchase, Thomas Heron, Robert Heron, Walter Heron, John Heron and sir Roger Heron. Sir William was keeper of Berwick castle in 1350, a commissioner for array in Northumberland in 1367 and a knight of the shire of Northumberland in 1371. In 1376 he and others were excused payment of £1500 which they owed to the king (*AA4*. XI, p.54). He died before 1382 when his executors John Heron of Thornton, Walter Heron and Edward Heron sued sir John Heron, senior, for a debt of £60 (*AA3*. VI, p.63). John Heron and Walter Heron were two of sir William's sons. Edward Heron is otherwise unknown, and the name is perhaps an error for Andrew Heron, sir William's youngest son. The sir John Heron, senior, who was sued by the executors was sir John Heron of Crawley, sir William's younger brother.

Sir William Heron's wife Isabel who is mentioned in the settlements of 1337 and 1340 was living in 1351 (*Ib.*, p.53) but her parentage is unknown. Sir William was succeeded by his eldest son sir Roger in the manor of Ford. Of the younger sons William Heron founded the family of HERON OF CORNHILL and Walter Heron the family of HERON OF CHIPCHASE. Thomas Heron appears to have been ancestor of the HERONS OF MELDON. It is not known if Robert and Andrew Heron left any descendants. A daughter of sir William Heron was Elizabeth, wife of William Lilburn of Beanley (*AA3*, XIX, p.63).

Sir Roger Heron is stated to have held the manor of Ford in 1350 but to have given it to his younger brothers Thomas and Robert Heron. This must have been some sort of family arrangement as Roger was still under age in 1351. With his father he attorned for three knights' fees in Ford in 1373. As sir Roger Heron, knight, son of William Heron he had a lease 1 June 1368 of tenements in Gauxton.

On 27 December 1374 William Heron son of sir Roger Heron is described as lord of Ford when he granted the vill of Hetherslaw to his younger son Walter Heron and to William de Flixburgh, rector of Ford, and Nicholas de Raymes, apparently in trust. Under the same description on 1 February 1377 he granted lands in Hetherslaw to Jordan son of Agnes de Kirkton (not Kirkheaton). Jordan de Kirkton was probably William Heron's illegitimate son, and in a lawsuit of 1424 mention is made of the manor of Bockenfield which William Heron, knight, son of Roger Heron, knight, gave to Jordan son of Agnes de Kirkton and his heirs, with remainder to Odinel son of Agnes de Kirkton and brother of said Jordan and his heirs, and further remainder to Liell son of Agnes de Kirkton (*AA3*. VI, p.173). Sir William was MP for Northumberland in 1385 (*AA4*. XI, p.74). He was dead by 1404 in which year William Heron, a minor, son and heir of William Heron is mentioned as holding his lands in the barony of Wooler by knight service. By 1415 the young heir was not only of age but had received knighthood and was then the owner of Ford castle. He was sheriff of Northumberland in 1424 and came to a violent end on 20 January 1427/8. A quarrel with his neighbour John Manners of Etal, culminated in an attack by Heron on Etal castle where there was 'great assault in shooting of

arrows (and) striking with swords'. Heron and his servant Robin Atkinson were both killed, and Isabel Heron the widow claimed against John Manners the payment of her husband's debts of £666 and the cost of the legal proceedings consequent on his death of £137. 5s. 3d. She also demanded that Manners should have the king's hand removed from the land of the heir who was a minor, alleging that the wardship had been claimed by the Crown 'by the procuring, stirring and assent of the said John Manners and his friends'. Although arbitrators were appointed by both sides, no settlement was reached until the priors of Durham and Tynemouth were asked to adjudicate. They issued their award on 31 September 1431 which was to the effect that Manners and his associates should on an appointed day at Newcastle 'lawfully submit them with words and deeds of humbleness and submission'; Manners was to have 500 masses sung within the year for the repose of the soul of William Heron and pay the widow 250 marks, one hundred of which were to be devoted to masses for the soul of Atkinson. It would appear that even this decision did not finally settle the matter as some time later Manners complained that he had had to pay for 800 masses. It is obvious that only the church financially benefited from its own decision.

The young heir, John Heron, was only ten years old at his father's death, and his lands were taken into the king's hands and on 8 July 1428 were granted with his marriage to the earl of Northumberland, William Carnaby and Henry Trollop. In this grant the name of the heir was mistakenly given as William and a fresh grant correcting the name was issued on 14 September 1429. Sir Robert Umfreville and nine others then claimed that on 2 January 1427 William Heron had conveyed all his lands to them in trust. The Crown accepted this claim and cancelled the grant to the earl of Northumberland and William Carnaby, Henry Trollop having died in the interval. On 11 July 1438 John Heron had a papal dispensation to marry Elizabeth daughter of sir William Heron knight. The bride's father was possessed of lands at Cornhill, Tweedmouth and Benwell, and was probably descended from William Heron a younger son of sir William Heron of Ford (d. *circa* 1382). If this is so the couple were third cousins. On 24 March 1443 John Heron, esquire, lord of Ford, and his wife Elizabeth had letters of attorney about two tenements in Newcastle. He was sheriff of Northumberland in 1440, 1451 and 1456. In 1445 he was on a commission to enquire into the smuggling of wool into Scotland. The following year the Crown seized some of his lands in Ford by way of distress and he was again prosecuted for debt in 1447 when he was described as 'late' of Ford. In 1449 he and his wife received pardon for all entries and intrusions made by them into their inheritances or any lands or possessions suing livery thereof out of the king's hands, and of all felonies, misprisions and contempts, debts, prests, arrears of account, impeachments and respites, and all actions and demands which the king could have against them. John Heron was appointed constable of Bamburgh castle in 1452 and retained the office irrespective of whether the Yorkists or Lancastrians were in power. In 1456 he was knighted and three years later, when the Lancastrians controlled the government, the office of constable of Bamburgh was given to him and to his son Roger for the term of their lives. In 1460 the Yorkists appointed him as royal ambassador to Scotland. Sir John ultimately sided with the Lancastrians for whom he fought at the battle of Towton. He was attainted and his estates forfeited, but it seems that he had been killed in the battle as the order for the sequestration of his property describes him as dead, and includes an order for the arrest of his son and heir, Roger.

In 1472 Roger Heron was pardoned and had a regrant of his father's lands together with all rights and privileges enjoyed by his ancestors. He was appointed constable of Norham castle 20 April 1475, and was sheriff of Norhamshire 1475-81. On 6 July 1477 he quitclaimed the lands of Mollawe by Chipchase to John Heron of Chipchase. He received knighthood on 22 August 1482 and died before 1485 when his heir was his eldest son John Heron, a child under the age of sixteen.

As a very young man John Heron was appointed lieutenant of Redesdale and constable of Harbottle castle by sir Robert Tailbois 26 December 1493, and in the following year was made lieutenant of the East and Middle Marches. His brother William Heron appointed him attorney to deliver seisin 13 May 1500 of lands which he had granted to his brother Henry Heron. John Heron was only 26 when he died on 20 June 1498 (*AA*2. XVI, p.39). His heir was his brother William Heron who also succeeded him as lieutenant of the Middle Marches which office he was holding in 1500. On 17 February 1498 (probably 1498/9) he is described as William Heron of Ford, esquire, when he consented to a grant by dame Elizabeth Heron, whose heir he was, of a tenement in Bayly Highgate in Newcastle. In 1504 he was granted a pardon for all offences previous to 1st January in that year, but two years later he was involved in a border feud on account of his illegitimate brother John Heron of Crawley. This John Heron 'the bastard' had killed sir Robert Carr, warden of the Middle Marches of Scotland, and had fled to unknown parts. William Heron was handed over to the Scots as a hostage for his brother. He was apparently still in Scotland in 1509 when he is described as owner of Ford castle but not 'inhabitant'. On 22 August 1513 James IV entered England in the memorable invasion which culminated in his defeat and death on the field of Flodden on 9th September. One of the fullest accounts of the battle, that by Robert Lindsay of Pitscottie, has an involved description of improper relations between the king of Scotland and lady Heron of Ford, and this has been taken by sir Walter Scott for an episode in the verses of *Marmion*. Lindsay states that 'On the morrow the king went to Wark and Norham and cast them down, and thereafter went to Ford and cast it down. Great slaughter was made of the king's men that stood about the house in the flyings of the timber. Some say the lady of Ford was a beautiful woman, and that the king melled with her, and also his son, Alexander Stuart, bishop of St Andrews, with her daughter, which was against God's commandment and against the order of all good captains of war'. He goes on to state that the king continued at Wark for twenty days without battle till at last all the victuals in the castle were spent. The story is undoubtedly malicious gossip. The whole campaign only lasted eighteen days of which six were spent in the siege of Norham castle. William Heron was only 35 years old in 1513 and is unlikely to have had a daughter old enough to have had an affair with Alexander Stuart.

After the battle William Heron was released from his imprisonment in Scotland in exchange for George Hume. In 1524 royal commissioners were sent to Northumberland to gather forces for an invasion of France found Heron very intractable. The commissioners reported:—

'As many of the gentlemen of Northumberland as appeared before us at Newcastle were well minded to serve your grace . . . sir William Heron only excepted, who, being in the town, would not appear before us on two of the clock at afternoon, and at his coming (in froward manner, rather like as a quarrel than otherwise) said openly "the lieutenants undoes the country", with divers other froward words, and if his power had been better than ours further trouble had been like to have grown among us'. (Welford, II, p.81). He eventually agreed to raise sixteen men though the commissioners thought this very small considering his power and authority; Sir William was sheriff of Northumberland in 1523 and 1531. He died on 18 June 1535 leaving a widow Agnes, evidently his second wife. During his lifetime he made provision for his two younger brothers. To Henry he gave 13 May 1500 lands in Temple Thornton, North Gosforth, Little Benton, Clifton, Coldwell, Duddo, Little Ryle and Thropton. On 3 May he granted lands in Tundehouse in Norhamshire to his younger brother Odinel.

Sir William Heron's only son and heir William Heron died in his father's lifetime. He had married in 1524 Margaret daughter of sir Thomas Forster of Adderstone and their only child Elizabeth, aged 3 years, was her grandfather's heir. The widow Margaret married as her second husband sir George Heron of Chipchase. It has been stated over and over again that between these two marriages she also married John Heron of Thornton. A letter of her brother sir John Forster to Walsingham on 6 March 1586/7 is quite clear about this. He writes 'having first sir George Heron that married my sister, and John Heron another sister, slain' (*CDS*., I, p.248).

On 10 March 1537 the custody and the marriage of the young heiress was granted to sir Thomas Audley. She married Thomas Carr, a younger son of John Carr, captain of Wark. In 1551 both sir George Heron of Chipchase, and Alexander Heron of Meldon laid claim to the Ford estate each as heir male to sir William Heron, and from this developed the Carr-Heron feud, in which many of the Northumbrian gentry took sides. Details of this feud are best reserved to be dealt with in the account of the Herons of Chipchase. Both the claimants were descended from younger sons of that sir William Heron of Ford who died about 1382, which suggests that there were no surviving male descendants from any of the later generations of the Herons of Ford. The Carrs in fact made good their claim to Ford.

HERON OF CRAWLEY, PAR. EGLINGHAM

Sir Roger Heron of Ford had an illegitimate son John Heron, usually termed 'the bastard', to whom he gave the estate of Crawley, then a part of the manor of Hedgeley. About 1509 sir Robert Ker of Caverton, the Scottish warden of the Middle Marches, had been set upon and slain by three Englishmen, one of whom was the bastard Heron. Lilburn, another of the killers was arrested by the Scots, but Heron and the third man, Starhead, escaped and were outlawed. Sometime later Starhead was kidnapped, carried across the

HERON of FORD, par. FORD

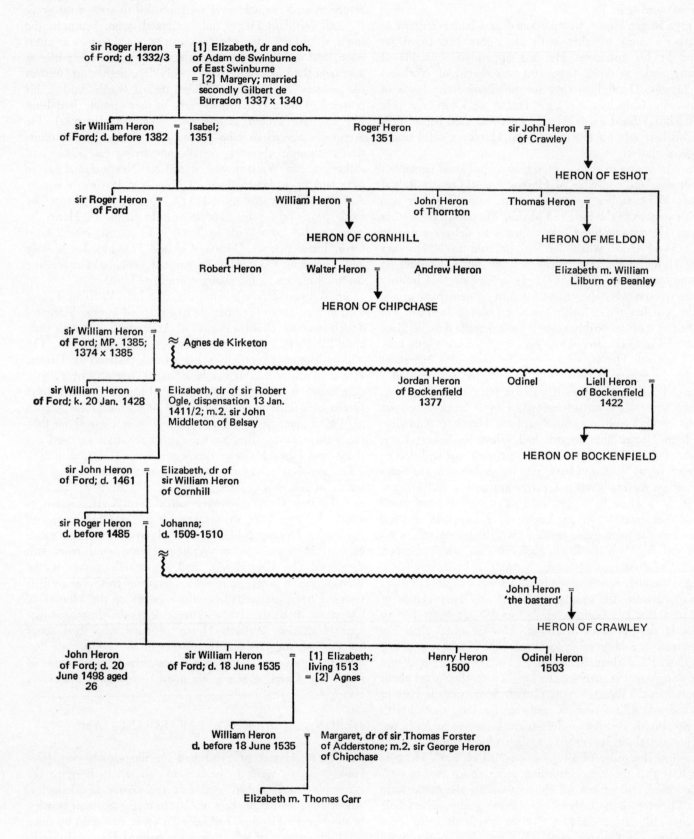

sir Roger Heron of Ford; d. 1332/3 = [1] Elizabeth, dr and coh. of Adam de Swinburne of East Swinburne = [2] Margery; married secondly Gilbert de Burradon 1337 x 1340

sir William Heron of Ford; d. before 1382 = Isabel; 1351

Roger Heron 1351

sir John Heron of Crawley =

HERON OF ESHOT

sir Roger Heron of Ford =

William Heron =

John Heron of Thornton

Thomas Heron =

HERON OF CORNHILL

HERON OF MELDON

Robert Heron

Walter Heron =

Andrew Heron

Elizabeth m. William Lilburn of Beanley

HERON OF CHIPCHASE

sir William Heron of Ford; MP. 1385; 1374 x 1385 = ≈ Agnes de Kirketon

Jordan Heron of Bockenfield 1377

Odinel

Liell Heron of Bockenfield 1422 =

sir William Heron of Ford; k. 20 Jan. 1428 = Elizabeth, dr of sir Robert Ogle, dispensation 13 Jan. 1411/2; m.2. sir John Middleton of Belsay

HERON OF BOCKENFIELD

sir John Heron of Ford; d. 1461 = Elizabeth, dr of sir William Heron of Cornhill

sir Roger Heron d. before 1485 = Johanna; d. 1509-1510

John Heron 'the bastard' =

HERON OF CRAWLEY

John Heron of Ford; d. 20 June 1498 aged 26

sir William Heron of Ford; d. 18 June 1535 = [1] Elizabeth; living 1513 = [2] Agnes

Henry Heron 1500

Odinel Heron 1503

William Heron d. before 18 June 1535 = Margaret, dr of sir Thomas Forster of Adderstone; m.2. sir George Heron of Chipchase

Elizabeth m. Thomas Carr

border and put to death by sir Robert Ker's son. Heron remained in hiding, and his brother sir William Heron of Ford was handed over to the Scots as a hostage. In 1511 it was reported that Heron the bastard had died of the pestilence somewhere between Newark and Northampton. His death by pestilence was a fiction put out by his servants. He had in fact been hiding in his own house, the secret known to none save his wife and three servants.

When hostilities with Scotland broke out in 1513, Heron came out of hiding and on 13 August he defeated a Scots raid, on account of which he was pardoned on 18 August for the earlier killing. He distinguished himself at the battle of Flodden on 9 September 1513. Sir Edmund Howard who was with the Cheshire and Lancashire contingent on the English right wing had been cut off from the main body of his men and left almost surrounded with only his standard bearer and two of his servants. Heron, already sorely wounded, came up to him and according to an Elizabethan 'Ballad of Flodden Field' (*BM. Harl. MSS* 3526) said to him:—

'There was never a nobleman's son so like to be lost as you this day;
But for all my hurts I shall here live and die with you.'

They were saved by lord Dacre who arrived in the nick of time with his troop of horsemen previously held in reserve. Before the battle Heron, according to the same ballad had made the statement:—

'And so for murthering Englishmen I never hurt man, maid, or wife,
Howbeit, Scots some nine or ten at least I have bereaved of life.'

For this gallantry in the battle he had £20 reward from the king. He continued his services on the Border till 21 May 1524 when he was killed in a skirmish with the Scots on the banks of the Tweed. His son William Heron also served with distinction and in the year of his father's death received a pension of £10 a year.

In 1565/6 William Heron with his eldest son John conveyed Crawley to the second son Thomas Heron. The reason for this seems to have been the fact that John had no sons. William Heron died late in 1570 or early in 1571. The inventory of his goods dated 26 January 1570/1 states 'The debts of late William Heron as doth appear by his testament and last will amounts to £43. 19s. 3d.' (*SS.* 2, p.335). It is unfortunate that his will has not survived, as the pedigree of the family about this time is rather obscure. Besides his second son, Thomas Heron who was a Newcastle merchant, William Heron had a daughter Isabel who married another Thomas Heron. Previous pedigrees of the Herons of Crawley have confused these two Thomas Herons. Thomas Heron the merchant had been apprenticed 10 October 1553 to Henry Anderson the elder, of Newcastle, boothman, and admitted to the Merchant Adventurer's Company of Newcastle 15 October 1563. He has a legacy of 5 marks by the w.d. January 1558 of his master Henry Anderson (*Ib.*, p.165).

William Heron of Clerkenwell, gent., in his w.d. 12 July 1580, proved 22 August 1580, mentions Thomas Heron of Newcastle, and leaves a legacy of £6. 13s. 4d. to Roger Heron 'of Rochester in Northumberland' (*SS.* 121, p.219). There was evidently some property in London involved in the will for on 28 February 1580/1 John Heron of Crawley released to his brother Thomas Heron of Newcastle the messuage in the city of London lately belonging to his kinsman William Heron of the parish of Clerkenwell, co. Middlesex, gent. (*PSAN*2. VI, p.202). Was he the William Heron of London to whom Ralph Claxton of the parish of Hart, co. Durham, was bound 'in one bond obligatory in a certain sum of £20', as he mentions in his w.d. 4 February 1567/8? (*SS.* 2, p.276).

Thomas Heron the merchant made his will on 6 August 1582, proved 9 November 1582. He leaves to his mother the third part of his demesnes of Crawley. He had two daughters Margaret and Barbary and his wife was expecting another child. His cousin Henry Mitford is appointed Margaret's guardian and he mentions 'that land in Mickle Benton which my daughter Margaret must have'. His cousin Henry Chapman is to be Barbary's guardian, and another cousin Henry Anderson is to be guardian of the expected child. The three Newcastle merchants, Henry Anderson, Henry Chapman and Henry Mitford, whom Thomas Heron calls 'cousins', were all related to each other, Chapman being a son of Anderson's aunt Marion and Mitford a son of another aunt Jane, but it is not known how Heron was related to them. Perhaps his mother was an Anderson?

In the inventory of Thomas Heron's goods dated 30 October 1582 mention is made of his wife Marion and of Thomas Heron of Crawley and Mrs Heron mother of Thomas Heron. His wife Marion was a daughter of Roger Thornton of Newcastle, merchant, who in 1570 had settled half of Longbenton on them in marriage (*NCH.* XIII, p.411).

Thomas Heron's mother, Katherine Heron of Crawley, widow, made her will on 1 October 1584 in which she leaves a legacy to Elizabeth Heron daughter of her son John, and mentions 'Thomas Herrone and my daughter Isabell his wife and her children'. This cannot have been her son Thomas Heron the merchant who had died two years earlier.

Marion's expected child was evidently a son as in a survey of the lordship of Beanley taken in 1586, 'John Hearon son and heir of Thomas Hearon' is returned as freeholder of Crawley. (*AA*3. XIX, p.67). In 1628 Thomas Hearon of Crawlaw, gent., voted as a freeholder, and was probably the same Thomas Heron the administration of whose goods was granted 6 May 1635 to his widow Dorothy for their children Anne, John, Hanna, Henry, Robert, Margaret and Susanna. Thomas Heron's widow Dorothy died about 1643, and on 27 May of that year the administration of her goods was granted to John Collingwood, one of her creditors (Raine, *MS. Prob. and Adm.* II, p.33). John Collingwood was in fact her brother as in the declaration of account which he produced in 1649 he is described as Dorothy Heron's brother and administrator.

John Heron, the heir, was rated for Crawley in 1663, and in 1665 he was defendant in a chancery suit regarding the property. At that time he had two brothers who had become lunatics. In 1683 John Heron sold Crawley to John Proctor of Shawdon. It is not known if he had any descendants.

John Hearon, esq. who was a sponsor at the baptism 23 October 1670 at Eglingham of Sara daughter of Henry Jackson, gent., of Crawley, was no doubt the last John Heron

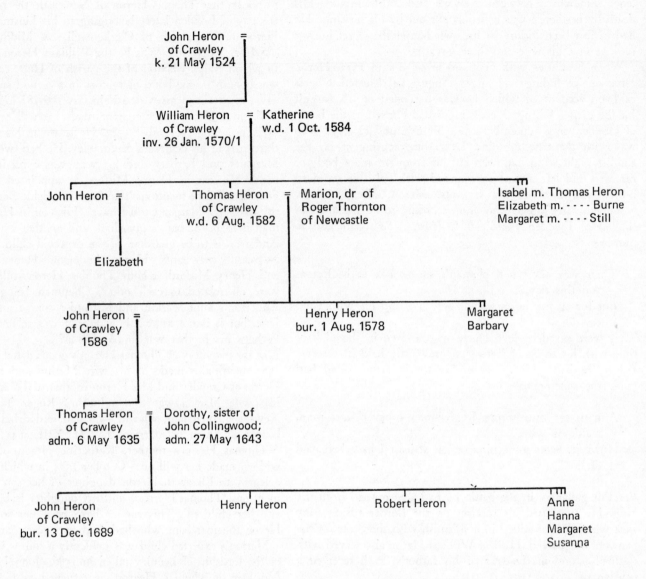

John Heron
of Crawley
k. 21 May 1524
=

William Heron
of Crawley
inv. 26 Jan. 1570/1
= Katherine
w.d. 1 Oct. 1584

John Heron =

Thomas Heron
of Crawley
w.d. 6 Aug. 1582
= Marion, dr of
Roger Thornton
of Newcastle

Isabel m. Thomas Heron
Elizabeth m. - - - - Burne
Margaret m. - - - - Still

Elizabeth

John Heron
of Crawley
1586
=

Henry Heron
bur. 1 Aug. 1578

Margaret
Barbary

Thomas Heron
of Crawley
adm. 6 May 1635
= Dorothy, sister of
John Collingwood;
adm. 27 May 1643

John Heron
of Crawley
bur. 13 Dec. 1689

Henry Heron

Robert Heron

Anne
Hanna
Margaret
Susanna

of Crawley (*Eglingham Registers*). As Mr John Heron he was buried at Eglingham 13 December 1689. Not for 100 years does the surname of Heron again appear in the *Eglingham Registers*.

HERON OF CHIPCHASE, PAR. CHOLLERTON

On 9 September 1348 sir Robert de Lisle of Chipchase granted to sir William Heron of Ford the custody of his granddaughter and heiress Cecily de Lisle to the intent that she should marry William, John or Walter, sons of sir William Heron 'if God permitted them to live until Cicely and one of them should be of age to consort with her'. Walter, the youngest son, became husband of the heiress. On 11 October 1348 sir Robert de Lisle conveyed to sir William Heron the manor of Chipchase with 'Rowechestreshele', and these lands were presumably settled on Walter Heron and his wife. From his father, Walter Heron had a grant 5 October 1360 of the manor of Pigdon in tail male paying £100 a year to his

father during his lifetime. He had a grant 1 October 1375 from Agnes Hunter of lands in Bellingham and Conheath. As Walter Heron, knight, he was a witness 19 June 1388 to a settlement of the Vaux lands in Bewclay and Portgate.

In June 1377 Roger Heron son of Walter Heron of Chipchase was a remainderman in a settlement of the vill of West Whelpington by his grandfather sir William Heron. On 28 October 1368 Roger Heron was in remainder to the castle and manor of Haughton, the vill of Humshaugh and Stonecroft in Tyndale in a settlement made by John de Widdrington, being then described as son of sir Walter Heron. His relationship to the Widdringtons is unknown. He had succeeded his father before 3 May 1395 when he demised the vill of Pigdon for two years to sir Ralph de Eure, knight. The next owner of Chipchase was Alexander Heron, who was probably Roger's son.

Alexander Heron is a witness to a settlement 20 September 1403 of the Horsley lands in Thirnham, Togston, Aydonshields and Linshields. He was party to deeds of 28 July and 5 August 1404 with Ralph Wallas of Knarsdale (*HN*. ii, III, p.84n.). Described as lord of Chipchase 16 May 1408 he conveyed all his lands in Pigdon to William de Themilby, clerk, and William Scryvane, apparently in trust. He has a small legacy by the w.d. 7 February 1410/1 of sir Robert Ogle. Alexander Heron was owner of a tower at Chipchase in 1415 (*AA2*. XIV, p.18). On 6 July 1426 he appointed sir John Bertram and sir John Widdrington as trustees for the manor, tower, vill and mill of Chipchase, and they, on 26 June 1430, gave a power of attorney to John Horsley and John Carlele to deliver seisin of Chipchase and Whittle which they had by the grant of Alexander Heron esq. It is very unfortunate that we have no details of this settlement, which might have given a clue to the younger members of the family living at this time. John Heron who succeeded Alexander Heron was no doubt his eldest son and heir. Gerard Heron, Alexander Heron and Norman Heron mentioned about this time as trustees of the Chipchase estate were perhaps younger sons or nephews.

On 20 May 1443 William Harbottle gave letters of attorney to Gerard Heron of Chipchase, gent., to deliver seisin to John Heron of Chipchase, esq., of lands in the vills of 'Halyland', Harbottle, Dissington, Corbridge, and elsewhere in Northumberland. As sheriff of Northumberland on 29 September 1444 John Heron gave a receipt to William Swinburne of Capheaton for 28 shillingsworth of green wax. He was keeper of Tyndale in 1455 (*HN*. i, p.320). Sir John Heron married Isabel daughter of Robert, 1st lord Ogle, by his wife Isabel daughter and heiress of sir Alexander Kirkby of Kirkby Irelyth in Lancashire, and was dead by 2 January 1477/8 when his mother-in-law Isabel, lady Ogle, made her will. By this will she leaves lands in Lancashire to John Heron of Chipchase esq., eldest son of her daughter Isabel, formerly wife of John Heron, knight, and to Robert Widdrington esq., son to the same Isabel.

John Heron, the heir, was apparently a minor at his father's death, and Chipchase was occupied by his step-father John Widdrington. In 1482 Richard Musgrave of Hartley, Wmd, esquire, had a plea of £100 debt against John Wyderyngton of Chipchase, esq. This was no doubt in connection with the marriage settlement of the heir, as John Heron married Richard Musgrave's daughter Margaret. On 24 October 1488 John Heron and three others were bound in the sum of 2000 marks each for the good behaviour of Roger Hastings of Pickering Lythe, Yorks. (*CDS*. IV, p.315). On 12 February 1489/90 as bailiff of sir Robert Talyboys in the liberty of Redesdale, he bound himself before the king in Chancery under a penalty of £500 to execute the duties of his office in capturing felons and evil-doers and bringing them to justice, and to allow no conventicles or privy meetings between English and Scots on the Marches or elsewhere in the liberty (*Ib.*). He was one of the commissioners for England, 26 March 1494, who entered into an indenture at Coldstream with the commissioners for Scotland to consider a complaint by the tenants of Canoby against North Tyndale men for cattle thieving (*Ib.*, p.418). John Heron was sheriff of Northumberland in 1494 and on 13 December 1495 he took a 40 years lease of the vill of Hallington from the archbishop of York. On 4 February 1497 he was a trustee of Giles Horsley in a settlement of Thirnham, Bradley hall and Crawcrook. Giles Horsley was perhaps a godfather of John Heron's grandson Giles Heron born about this time. On

6 July 1515 John Heron was party to a demise of the manor of Horton, with the consent of Margaret, lady Ogle, to Thomas Lisle.

On 20 March 1516, Giles Musgrave and Roger Heron at the special request of John Heron of Chipchase conveyed to him the manor of Chipchase and lands in Chipchase, Whelpington, Ray, Pigdon and Whittle, which they with John Heron of Chollerton and Norman Heron, both since deceased, had recovered in Hilary Term 1506 before the Justices *de Banco* against the said John Heron of Chipchase; this was a settlement in tail male on John Heron, with remainders to the heirs male of Gerard Heron, late of Errington, and then to William Heron of Ford. John Heron of Chollerton was one of the sons of Gerard Heron of Errington and on 12 March 1484 he had a grant from John Swinburne of Capheaton of lands in Chollerton in marriage with Constance sister of the grantor, and for her lifetime. On 15 June 1490 John Swinburne of Capheaton gave a rent-charge to Roger son of Alexander Heron, deceased, and on 13 February 1506 Roger Heron gave this to John Heron of Chollerton.

As sir John Heron of Chipchase, knight, he granted 22 November 1524 to sir Ralph Fenwick of Wallington the receivership of the rents of the Brough lands in Tyndale. The last mention of sir John Heron is on 6 August 1529 when he let to Roger Heron of Corbridge, gent., a burgage and lands in Corbridge.

Sir John Heron's first marriage to Margaret Musgrave is confirmed by Glover's Visitation of Yorkshire 1584/5, *sub* Musgrave and by St George's Visitation of Cumberland and Westmorland 1615, *sub* Musgrave. On 22 April 1507 Edward Musgrave esq., son and heir of Richard Musgrave had licence of entry without suing livery on all his father's lands and a pardon for receiving and assisting John Heron of Chipchase, William Heron of Ford, and John Heron the bastard (*Cal. Pat. Rolls*, H.VIII, 1494-1509, p.521). It is not known what misdemeanour the Herons had committed. Sir John Heron's second wife was Cecily daughter of Roger Thornton of Netherwitton, widow of George Middleton of Belsay. Between 11 August 1502 and 11 May 1503 John Heron and Cecily his wife, 'late the wife of George Middleton', complained in the Court of Chancery that they held the manor of Belsay and other Middleton lands as in the right of the said Cecily but were unable to obtain the title deeds (Sir Arthur Middleton, bart., *MS Account of the Family of Middleton of Belsay*, vol.V, pp. 47-49). Mention is made of the marriage settlement of George and Cecily Middleton, the trustees being Cecily's brothers sir Roger Thornton, knight, and Giles Thornton (*Ib.*).

The payment of rent for the farm of the demesne lands of Birtley was made in 1503/4 by Cecily, wife of John Heron of Chipchase (*Duke of Nd's MS—Accounts of the manor of Birtley*).

Sir John Heron died between 1529 and 1533 and was succeeded by his son John, the third of that name to own Chipchase. A daughter Margaret married Hugh Ridley of Willimontswick; Glover's Yorkshire Visitation pedigree of 1584/5 calls him (blank) Ridley, heir to Nicholas Ridley; Hodgson wrongly calls her Isabella in his pedigree of Ridley of Willimontswick and Blagdon (*HN*. ii, II, p.323). There was perhaps another daughter Sybil wife of John Ogle of Kirkley

John Heron III, described as John Heron of Chipchase junior, with John Heron his son took the manor of Birtley to farm 9 May 1517. As John Heron of Chipchase, *armiger*, he witnesses a Dilston deed of 20 February 1521/2 (*NCH*. X, p.264n.). He was appointed a trustee by sir Nicholas Ridley of Willimontswick 17 May 1532 (*Cal. inq. p.m.* vol. 57, No. 57). On 8 March 1532/3 as John Heron of Chipchase esq., son and heir of sir John Heron, knight, he had a lease for life at the yearly rent of 6s of Carryhouse and other lands in the manor of Birtley. In 1536 he held the corn tithes of Chipchase, 'Stewden', and Birtley by lease at the rent of £4. 6d. 8d. On the collapse of the Pilgrimage of Grace in Yorkshire in 1536 and the coming of sir Thomas Percy, one of the leaders, out of Yorkshire to his house at Prudhoe, 'the most notable offenders both of Tyndale and Hexhamshire' resorted to him, and especially John Heron of Chipchase and his friends Edward Charlton, Cuthbert Charlton, Geoffrey Robson, Anthony Errington and others. Cuthbert Charlton was a nephew of Edward Charlton (of Hesleyside) and was Heron's son-in-law having married his daughter. At one time sir Thomas Percy tried to act as lieutenant of the Middle Marches and with John Heron went to Harbottle castle intending to meet with the officers of Scotland, but they refused to meet him. John Heron of Chipchase, called 'Little John Heron', tried to have the men of Tyndale and Hexhamshire 'to break' in order to prevent the royal commissioners from dissolving Hexham Priory. Heron was at enmity with the Carnabys of Halton and attempted to take Halton castle by guile, but in this was unsuccessful. The Council of the North wished to arrest Heron but others recommended that he should remain at liberty but be bound with sufficient sureties in the sum of 2000 marks to appear before the king 13 February 1536/7. In April 1537 Jerrye Charlton accused him of the murder of Roger Fenwick, keeper of Tyndale (*SS*. 44, p. cxx *et seq.; State Papers* H.VIII, p.142). On 8 July 1537 Norfolk wrote to Cromwell, 'also where I wrote to you concerning John Heron and his son George and the other John Heron, yesterday was with me Lionel Grey and brought with him one of the men that hath detected the matter, who confessed the same to me' (*State Papers* H.VIII, V, p.92). There were many who did not believe that Heron was guilty of Fenwick's death. In another letter to Cromwell of 27 August 1537, Norfolk writes 'I shall do my best to put order for Tyndale, with using all the policies I can to apprehend Edward and Cuthbert of Charlton and John Heron's son, which John I require your good lordship may be secretly conveyed hither and so delivered to the officers of my house to be by them conveyed to me to Newcastle, to be ordered according to justice. I would he should be here the 20th day of September, and conveyed with a hood on his head and so secretly kept by the way that no man should know him, unto his deliverance, which would be also in the night because I have many pledges of Tyndale and Redesdale here. For, and if it were known he were here, I should neither take his son nor the others that I would have. And if it be not known in the flete (*i.e.* prison) whither he shall go, but conveyed in the night, the better' (*Ib.*, p.102). Wharton writing to Cromwell on 7 November 1538 reported that at a march meeting the previous day at Baittinge Bushe, John Heron, one of the murderers of Roger Fenwick was 'in the utter part of the Scotes men', and on the same day writing to James V of Scotland, Wharton asks that commandment should be given to lord Maxwell to deliver up John Heron being a rebel and a traitor (*Ib.*, pp. 140, 141). On 8 December 1538 the Council of the North reported to Henry VIII that amongst the prisoners lately taken by sir Reynold Carnaby and imprisoned at Warkworth was Jerrye Charleton *alias* Jerrye Topping the only accuser of John Heron of Chipchase and others for the murder of Roger Fenwick (*Ib.*, p.142). An undated report of about this time from the Privy Council to Henry VIII states that they have considered the contents of a letter from sir Thomas Wharton concerning John Heron; with it they had considered the malice between the Carnabys and John Heron and the favour between Wharton and the Carnabys; they think it may be that Charlton the accuser of Heron knowing of this displeasure between the Carnabys, Wharton and John Heron 'hath thrown out this bone, as it were, to please the Warden'; they are therefore persuaded that 'John Heron is not to be yet impeached' of Roger Fenwick's death (*Ib.*, p.203). A royal pardon to John Heron senior esq., John Heron junior and George Heron, gents, all of Chipchase, Roger Heron of Hallington, gent., and others may date from this time (*NDD*. p.117 dates it 4 December 1418 which must be incorrect; the copy of the pardon in the *Hodgson MSS* in the *County History Committee Papers* gives the date as '4 *die December, Anno regni,* (illegible) *sexto*'—surely 36 H.VIII, *i.e.* 1544/5).

In 1539 John Heron held the rectories of Alwinton, Corsenside and Holystone and the site and lands of the late dissolved priory of Holystone (*AA3*. IV, pp.11-12). A rather obscure reference to him is contained in a letter from Wharton to Cromwell on 27 January 1540 in which he says that he had written to John Heron 'but he will not make me privy to any of his doing there' (*State Papers* H.VIII, vol. V, pt. IV, p.171). By the Council Register of 17 August 1540 it was intended to appoint Heron as keeper of Tyndale, but he refused unless he had Redesdale also, and on the 30th it was resolved to appoint him to both (*Ib.*, p.203n.).

'John Heron, squier', one of the commissioners of the marches 26 September 1541 is probably John Heron of Chipchase (*Ib.*, p.192). He was one of the commissioners for the Survey of the East Marches made by sir Robert Bowes and sir Ralph Ellerker on 15 October 1541 (*Hamilton Papers*, vol.I, p.106). In the Survey his castles at Chipchase and Sewingshields are thus described: 'At Chypchase is a fair tower and a manor of stonework joined thereunto of the inheritance of John Heron of the same, esquire, kept in good reparations', and 'at Sewyngshealles is an old tower of the inheritance of John Heron of Chipchase in great decay in the roofs and floors, and lieth waste and unplenished' (*AA2*. XIV, p.47). At the same time he held one quarter of Filton Moor where he intended 'to build a stone house upon his said part at a place called Towland' (now Tone). John Heron joined sir Robert Bowes on a raid into Scotland with the Tyndale and Redesdale men on 24 August 1542; he was in the van leading one foray when he was taken prisoner by the laird of Edmonston's servant; on 27 August he was taken to Edinburgh (*Hamilton Papers*, vol.I, p.347). Later in the year there were 'advertisements' out of Scotland from John Heron, prisoner, sent by a servant of sir Robert Bowes, also a prisoner (*Cal. State Papers*—Scotland, 1509-1603, vol.I).

On 20 June 1543 the bishop of Durham wrote to Parr about the ransoming of prisoners with the Scots, *viz.* sir Cuthbert Radcliffe, sir Robert Bowes, Parson Ogle, John Heron and others (*Cal. State Papers*, H.VIII, vol.V, pt. IV, p.307). On his release from captivity in Scotland, Heron again found himself in disfavour with the authorities. Suffolk wrote to the Privy Council on 21 August 1543, 'And as concerning John Heron of Chipchase and George his son, the king's pleasure shall be followed in proceeding against them. . . . We fear lest the country will find little against John Heron and his son. . . . And as touching March treason which is for treating with the Scots or bringing in of them contrary to the law of the Borders, we think there is no matter against John Heron or his son, nor other thing than the misordering of them in their office' (*Hamilton Papers*, vol.I, p.427).

There is no further record of John Heron being employed on the Borders. In 1546 he was in arrears with the rent of the rectory of Alwinton (*NCH*. XV, p.469). The farm of the water mill at Hallington is described in 1547 as late in the tenure of John Heron esq. He must have recently died, and on 6 May 1548 sir Thomas Hilton, sir John Forster, and John Lumley, Nicholas Ridley, John Ogle and John Beadnell, esquires, were appointed to make inquisition of the lands and heir of John Heron, esquire, deceased (*Cal. Pat. Rolls*, E.VI, 1547-8, p.416).

On 1 September 1491 there was a dispensation for John Heron and Johan Ridley to marry in the third and fourth degree. This is John Heron of Chipchase and his wife Joan daughter of sir Nicholas Ridley of Willimontswick. The close relationship was through their mothers who were both Musgraves.

References to another John Heron about this time are very confusing. A general pardon was granted 15 April 1504 to John Heron of Chipchase, '*alias* gentilman' of offences previous to 1 January last (*Cal. Pat. Rolls* H.VII, p.349). He can hardly have been a son of John Heron of Chipchase by his wife Joan Ridley who were not married until 1491, and from his description we can presume that he was illegitimate. In May 1517 John Heron of Chipchase junior is mentioned with John Heron his son. John Heron junior is no doubt the John Heron of Chipchase who died in 1547, his father sir John Heron being still alive in 1517. There can be no reason to doubt the legitimacy of 'John Heron his son'. We have seen that Norfolk in 1537 wished to apprehend John Heron, which John was to be secretly conveyed to him, for if it were known he would be unable to take his son. This must mean that John Heron the father was to be conveyed to him, and that he hoped to apprehend a son of John Heron. A month earlier Norfolk had written concerning John Heron and his son George, and "the other John Heron". It seems therefore that it was probably the son George whom Norfolk wanted to take into custody, and perhaps the other John Heron was George's illegitimate half-brother.

The whole relationship is further complicated by the uncertain date of the pardon granted to John Heron senior esquire, John Heron junior and George Heron, gents, all of Chipchase. If we are correct in dating this to 4 December 1544 (*i.e.* 36 H.VIII) it would seem that John Heron senior had two legitimate sons, John and George living at that time. The eldest son John must have predeceased his father, as when the latter died in 1547 George was his heir. If the date

of the pardon was 4 December 1534 (*i.e.* 26 H.VIII) the position would be easier to understand, except that we do not know of any misdeeds committed at this time by the Herons which would warrant such a pardon. In any case it seems quite certain that John Heron III had an eldest son John who died in his father's lifetime, and he probably also had an illegitimate son of the same Christian name.

It would seem that George Heron acted as deputy keeper of Tyndale whilst his father was a prisoner in Scotland. Rutland and his council writing to Henry VIII on 28 August 1542 state 'George Heron hath shewed unto me at this present hour, that there is come to Jedworth (Jedburgh) and Kelso 2000 men, whereof he saith his father being prisoner in Scotland did send him word he saw 1000 horsemen' (*Hamilton Papers*, vol.I, 1532-1543, p.164). He is again mentioned in a letter to Henry VIII, from the earl of Hertford, 19 November 1542, who says 'After these my letters were enclosed, George Heron came unto me and declared that he with the Tyndale and Redesdale men, entered Scotland, as before I had appointed, and burnt there a town called Abbotes Rowle, three miles from Jedburgh and another town called Harwood with all the corn within the same, and took there 3 prisoners, 140 head of nolt, 204 score of sheep and 30 nags and mares' (*Ib.*, p.305). On 5 December 1542 'George Heron, with three of his brethren with him and 100 men in his company, made a rode into Scotland and there burnt a town called Dolfynstunne, 7 miles within Scotland and took and brought away 11 prisoners and 4 score head of cattle, besides mares and nags, and such gear' (*Ib.*, p.319). He is referred to about this time as 'young George Heron' (*Ib.*, p.321). Lisle writing to Henry VIII on 19 December 1542 reports 'I had taken order to send letters to all your Grace's pensioners of Northumberland, and to George Heron, your Grace's keeper of Redesdale and Tyndale, that they should have been to the number of 1200 horsemen, and to have met me at a place indifferent between the East and Middle Marches called Stone on Crokemore (Coquetmoor), at which time they so assembled should there know further what should be done'; and later on in the same letter, 'upon Sunday last, your Grace's keeper of Redesdale and Tyndale with 200 horses of the same countrys, entered into Scotland and burnt a town in West Teviotdale called Nether Claveryng and burnt there (as I am informed) about 2000 quarters of corn and took sundry prisoners' (*Ib.*, pp.341-2). Heron was not very popular with his superiors, largely because of his independence. The warden complained, 15 February 1542/3, that when 'the Redesdale men to the number of eight score men, rode a foray into Scotland and raised fire in a town in West Teviotdale called Anckram', the news of the foray was declared to him in the presence of George Heron's servant who told him nothing about it. A little while later he had a letter from Heron 'and yet nothing touching these advertisements mentioned in the same, and whether he was privy to the going in of these men or not I cannot tell, but it maketh me suspect the worst because he wrote nothing to me thereof' (*Ib.*, p.427). The earl of Suffolk writing to the Privy Council, 21 August 1543, says that the king's pleasure shall be followed in proceeding against John Heron and George his son, but thinks himself 'there is no matter against' them 'nor other thing than the misordering of them in their office' (*Ib.*).

On 13 June 1550 John, earl of Warwick, viscount Lyle,

K.G., and master of the king's household, leased to his servant, George Heron of Chipchase, the manor of Birtley and the town of Barrasford, for 21 years, at a rent of £19. 3s. 2d (*NCH*. IV, p.343 with wrong date; *NDD*., p.115). The earl of Northumberland, in November 1552, thought that 'lord Wharton showed himself wise in submitting four or five persons to the Council for choice for the office of deputy warden of the Middle Marches'; if lord Eure were placed in the Middle Marches where he has some of his inheritance, near George Heron and Cuthbert Musgrave, 'one could assist another in need' (*Cal. State Papers*, Domestic, Addenda, 1547-1565, p.417). In 1552 George Heron held Chipchase and Whittle for one third of a knight's fee, and land in West Whelpington for one twentieth of a knight's fee and £1. 1s. 3d. rent, of the barony of Prudhoe (*NCH*. XII, pp.107, 108). The following year he was one of the commissioners for enclosures for the bounds of North Tyndale (*HN*. i, p.361), and at the same time was an overseer of the watches to be kept by the inhabitants of Simonburn and Slaterfield at the Hall Orchard field, by the inhabitants of Chipchase at three places on the North Tyne, and by the inhabitants of Birtley, Buteland and Redesmouth at three other places on the North Tyne (Nicolson, *Leges Marchiarum*, pp.257, 259).

On the death of sir William Heron of Ford in 1535, the Herons of Chipchase laid claim to the manor of Ford as heirs male. So long as the young heiress, sir William Heron's grand daughter, remained unmarried, no special action was taken to establish the claim, as there was always a chance that the heiress might marry one of the Herons of Chipchase. When however she married Thomas Carr of Etal, the dispute developed into a typical family feud and bloodshed ensued. In 1551 the Warden General was advised about 'The title to the lands that were sir William Heron's of Ford, which dependeth in claim and controversy between George Heron of Chipchase, esq., claiming to be heir male, and so heritable to the said lands' (*The History of the Family of Carr*). On 1 April 1557 lord Wharton complained to the sheriff and justices of the peace for Northumberland, 'that you have not taken good sureties for keeping of the King and Queen's Majesty's peace between the parties of Hearons and Carres nor have taken the offenders at the great affray at Ford on Sunday last where the mayor of Berwick was slain' (*Talbot MS* at the College of Arms). On the following day the justices reported to lord Wharton that at their 'sessions at Morpeth came sir John Forster knt, George Heron of Chipchase and Nicholas Errington of Wharmley, esquires, with a band of men to the number of 200 in forcible and warlike array of armour and weapons, claiming that they durst not otherwise come to the sessions for danger of their enemies. The consideration of this matter we have suspended until the sessions at Newcastle on 27 April' (*Ib*.). A few days earlier, on 27 March, John Dixon, one of the constables of Berwick and fourteen garrison men had forcibly taken possession of Ford castle for George Heron. 'On the morrow after, being Sunday in the forenoon Ralph Graye of Chillingham esq., a justice of peace in this country and deputy warden, Gyles Heron, treasurer of Berwick, brother to the said George Heron, and Robert Barrowe, mayor of Berwick aforesaid, accompanied with others to the number of thirty persons or thereupon, the names of so many of whom as we can get knowledge of will appear unto your lordship by the said schedule herein closed, came to the town of Ford aforesaid and minding as we learn to have entered into the said castle of Ford were into the which it chanced them to fall at contention and fray with Robert Carre, brother of the said Thomas Carre, and one of those which were expelled and put out of the said castle of Ford by the said John Dixon and his accomplices. And certain others also being in company with the said Robert Carre to the number of 11 or 12 persons or thereupon as we can in any wise understand. In which fray it chanced the said mayor of Berwick to be wounded to death, and the treasurer of Berwick and one or two more of that company to be somewhat hurt and wounded'. Thus the justices reported to the Lords of the Privy Council (*Ib*.). It was not then known that 'the treasurer had 15 bloody wounds upon him', and had died a few days after the affray.

The Carrs and their friends the Collingwoods demanded protection against lord Wharton the lord warden, Ralph Gray of Chillingham the deputy warden, sir John Forster another deputy warden, George Hearon of Chipchase, Roger Heron his brother, Thomas Heron son to George Heron, Alexander Herron of Meldon, Jarrarde Heron of Riplington, Christopher Heron, John Heron of Bockenfield and his sons, Henry Heron of Alnwick, John Heron of Hallbarns, Gilbert Heron his brother and their sons, John Heron son to John Heron of 'Thernstare' (probably Thirston), William Heron of 'Wawlaw' (probably Wooley) and his sons, P'sevell Shafto of Ingoe and his sons, Nicholas Ridley of Willimontswick and his sons and brother, Oswald Muschance of Lyham hall and his brothers, and several others (*Ib*.). The whole dispute was eventually referred to arbitrators and on 29 June 1559 sir Richard Sackville reported to sir William Cecil, chief secretary to queen Elizabeth, 'if it may please you to understand that wherein my lord of York and my Lord Chief Justice of the King's Bench, my Lord Chief Justice of the Common Pleas and I have agreed upon the award between George Heron and John Carr and they willing to prefer the same' (*State Papers*, Domestic, Eliz. vol.IV, No. 70). The full terms of the award are not known but part of the agreement was that William Carr of Ford should marry within eight years Elizabeth daughter of Giles Heron, or Dorothy daughter of John Heron, George Heron's son (*Acts of Privy Council* VI, p.360). The Carrs retained possession of the Ford estate, but the Herons of Chipchase got the manor of Simonburn which had belonged to the Herons of Ford. The proposed marriage did not take place, as Elizabeth died young, and John Heron would not allow his daughter to marry William Carr (*Hist. of the Family of Carr*, vol.III, p.17).

George Heron, Margaret his wife, and John Heron his son had a fine at Michaelmas 1560 with Cuthbert Ridley for 4 messuages and lands in Whittle, par. Ovingham (*NCH*. XII, p.196). George Heron is a supervisor of the w.d. 18 November 1565 of Reynold Forster of Capheaton (*SS*. 112, p.33). He was a commissioner 12 February 1567/8 to enquire into the lands belonging to the dissolved priory of Hexham (*NCH*. IV, p.207). In (December) 1569 mention is made of two knights made by the earl of Sussex, *viz.* sir George Heron and sir Cuthbert Collingwood (*Cal. State Papers*, Domestic, Addenda 1566-1579, p.173). No favouritism here, because sir Cuthbert Collingwood had been one of the principal supporters of the Carrs in the Heron-Carr feud. As keeper of Redesdale, sir George Heron's principal residence was at Harbottle castle. About this, lord Hunsdon complained that

'Her Majesty is at no small charge with soldiers at Harbottle and as I told her before her face in the orchard at Westminster, I saw no necessity thereof; it is money cast away for no man in the country has his own goods the safer kept, but sir Geo. Heron and some others of his own, and the country is none the better for their lying there; it is more than time it were reformed' (*Ib.*, p.394).

At a wardens' meeting at a place called the Rede Swire on 7 July 1575 an affray broke out with the Scots in which sir George Heron, 'a man much esteemed in both realms', was killed together with 24 other Englishmen (Ridpath, *Border History*, p.651). On 1 December 1575 administration of his goods was granted to his widow Margaret and his sons Thomas and Giles Heron (*Dur. Prob. Reg.*, Act Book 1571-1576, No. 67, p.101). The total value of his goods was £641. 9s. 4d. debts owing to him at his death £29, and his own debts together with the funeral expenses £296. 7s. 11d.; his debts included to Thomas Carlell £106. 13s. 4d., to William Heron, bailiff at Hexham, £5, to John Fenwick of Walker £3. 6s. 8d., and to Roger Heron the younger 25s. The inventory was certified by Thomas Heron and Giles Heron (*SS.* 2, p.411).

Sir George Heron was married twice. His first wife was Marion daughter of George Swinburne of Edlingham (Flower, *Yorks. Vis.* 1563-4). Her brother Gawen Swinburne of Cheeseburn Grange by his w.d. 26 April 1576 leaves his 'right and interest of the Stellinge to one of my nephew John Heron his sonnes of Chipches whome he himself shall think good to bestow it upon' (*SS.*, 2, p.409). Another brother, Thomas Swinburne of Haughton, in his w.d. 7 April 1565, mentions his nieces Isabel Lisle and Annes Heron, who were both daughters of sir George; amongst Thomas Swinburne's debts was one to Mr John Heron of Haughton for wages (Raine, *MS Wills and Inv.*, vol.VI, p.19). Sir George Heron's children by his first wife were his eldest son and heir, John Heron, and three daughters Thomasine, Isabel and Agnes. Thomasine married firstly Lancelot Thirlwall of Thirlwall, and secondly John Whitfield of Randalholme in Alston, co. Cumb. In 1565 Isabel is called Isabel Lisle; she married secondly John Fenwick of Walker, and thirdly James Ogle. Agnes was unmarried in 1565, but by 1576 had a husband called Charlton.

Sir George Heron's second wife was Margaret daughter of sir Thomas Forster of Adderstone and widow of William Heron of Ford (Flower, *Vis. of Nd* 1575—*sub* Forster). After the death of sir George she lived at Pigdon, par. Mitford; the inventory dated 17 June 1592 of John Strother of Lanton, par. Kirknewton, mentions a debt owing to him by 'My lady Heron of Pigdon' (Raine, *MS. Wills and Inv.* vol.I. p.125). Somewhat later she was living at Prudhoe, where her grandson Reynold Heron was tenant of the castle. On 30 April 1596 administration of the goods of dame Margaret Heron, late of Prudhoe, par. Ovingham, was granted to her children Giles Heron, Henry Heron, Thomas Heron, Margery Shafto, Ellinor Muschamp, Elizabeth wife of Percival Paston, and Dorothy Swanne (?) (*Dur. Prob. Reg.* by C.R.H.).

Of these younger sons, Giles Heron is mentioned in the w.d. 1 June 1602 of his half sister Isabel Ogle who leaves him her part of the tithe corn of Burradon, par. Alwinton; she leaves a legacy to his son George Heron (Raine, *MS. Wills and Inv.* vol.II, p.167). Giles Heron died in 1608 and administration of his goods was granted to Margaret Heron his widow; the tuition of his son George aged 17 was given to Percival Shafto of Ingoe (*Dur. Prob. Reg.*—Act Book 1571-1576, No. 67, p.217). The inventory of the goods of Giles Heron, par. Mitford, deceased, signed by Robert Mitford esq., William Heron and others is dated 23 July 1608 (Raine, *MS. Wills and Inv.* vol.II, p.199). Little for certain is known about Henry Heron, but a Henry Heron of Alnwick was concerned in the Carr-Heron feud in 1557-8. In 1584 Henry Heron was one of the appraisers of the goods of Oswald Muschamp of Lyham who had married sir George Heron's daughter Elliner. The next son, Thomas Heron, is also remembered in the will of Isabel Ogle. She leaves the lease of Bedlington corn mill to her nephew Nicholas Heron and his heirs, but Thomas, his father, is to have it until Nicholas comes of age. Thomas Heron and his brother Giles were living at Pigdon 28 May 1606 when they witness the nuncupative will of Thomas Reed of Pigdon (Raine, *MS* with reference *Adm.* ii. 37).

Sir George Heron's daughters by his second marriage were:

1. Margery wife of Edward Shafto of Bavington. When the warden, Hunsdon, complained in 1587 that John Heron had been negligent in his duties as keeper of Tyndale, he reported officially that 'a man of mine called Shaftoe, who is a brother in law of his, called upon him, who had much ado to make him rise, until he told him that he would tell me of it' (*CBP.* vol.I, p.287).

2. Ellinor wife of Oswald Muschamp of Lyham hall. He died in 1584. In 1586 Ellinor Muschamp, widow, held half the demesnes of Lyham. Her w.d. 17 October 1616.

3. Elizabeth second wife of Percival Paston of Wallridge.

4. Dorothy. In the rather illegible administration of the goods of dame Margaret Heron, 30 April 1596 the name of one of her daughters has been read as Dorothy Swindow? The name is perhaps Swanne, as Isabel Ogle in her w.d. 1 June 1602 mentions her sister's son Bertram Swanne. This was the daughter who was to have married William Carr, but her father would not allow it.

It has been mentioned that in a foray into Scotland in 1542 George (afterwards sir George) Heron was accompanied by 'three of his brethren'. Two of the brothers are known; Roger Heron was ancestor of the HERONS OF BIRTLEY, PAR. CHOLLERTON; Giles Heron was the treasurer of Berwick killed during the Carr-Heron feud in 1557. A year earlier he had been living at Lowick (*Hist. of the Family of Carr*, vol.II, p.71) and was in command of 50 horsemen stationed at Horncliff (*Ib.*, p.64). His widow Elizabeth was wife of Thomas Carlell of Newcastle, 10 February 1561/2, when she was given administration of her first husband's goods (Raine, *MS Dur. Adm.*). In 1567/8 special commissioners were appointed to report on the possessions of Elizabeth Carlill wife of Thomas Carlill, but formerly Elizabeth Heron the wife of Giles Heron, a Crown debtor (*AA3.* IV, p.2). She had a town house in Berwick which had belonged to Giles Heron, but the Queen gave instructions in February 1580/1, to lord Eure 'commanding him to place sir Richard Lee and John Brende, while engaged on the fortifications and musters in the North parts, in the town house of the late Giles Heron, letting his widow or others interested know that they must give it up while required for the Queen's service' (*CBP.* vol.I, p.66). Giles Heron seems to have had an only daughter Elizabeth, who died in infancy.

John Heron, the new owner of Chipchase, appears to have

been very dissatisfied with the loss of the manor and castle of Ford, and continued to lay claim to them. On 11 October 1576 he actually conveyed the disputed property to his son and heir Cuthbert Heron, but was quite unable to dislodge the Carrs. His brother-in-law Lancelot Thirlwall appoints him a supervisor of his w.d. 27 December 1582 (SS. 38, p.75) and another brother-in-law John Fenwick by his w.d. 10 October 1580 leaves him his best horse (Ib., p.25). In 1584 the ambassador to Scotland had failed to get any redress for raids made on the Marches, and in retaliation the English warden 'caused a rode to be made, where Mr Fenwick, Mr Herone and others killed 5 or 6 of the Elwetts (Elliotts), and brought off goods' (CBP. vol.I, p.156). Heron was present at the border meeting at Hexpeth gatehead, 27 July 1585 when lord Francis Russell was killed by the Scots (Ib., p.190). In 1586 he held Chipchase and Whittle as of the barony of Prudhoe by ⅓rd of a knight's fee, suit of court, and 4s. 5d. rent (NCH. XII, p.196); at the same time he held lands called Rowchester in the manor of Birtley by fealty, suit of court, and a rent of 12d. (NCH. IV, p.343). He was appointed keeper of Tyndale 31 August 1587 (CBP. vol.I, p.269). Lord Hunsdon reporting on a recent Scots foray to Haydon Bridge states that 'Mr Hearon lying in wait for their home coming with such as he could get, set upon them, rescued the goods, killed 6, took 4, and 16 horses' (Ib., p.284). Shortly after this encounter, tongues began to wag and there were not wanting suggestions that Heron had deliberately allowed the raid to take its course so that he might collect some of the plunder. He was also accused of actually being party to the raid. Lord Hunsdon reported on 8 December 1587 'I have written to Her Majesty touching Mr Heron, whom Her Majesty commanded should remain keeper of Tyndale,—he is not fit for the place, for besides his negligence in that service at the burning of Haydon Bridge which hath been vowed to his face by one that hath married his sister, he is greatly suspected to be acquainted with that journey; for his son by whom he is wholly governed, and a man of his who is one of his bailiffs in Tyndale, and young Ridley, who hath married his daughter, and sundry other of the Ridleys, whom I have here in ward, are directly charged with the bringing in of the Scots to Haydon Bridge' (Ib., p.295).

John Heron was a trustee for Robert Hazelrigg 12 August 1585 (AA3. V, p.119). John Ridley of Wark Eales mentions him in his w.d. 2 February 1589/90 (Raine, MS Wills and Inv. vol.II, p.97). At a Warden's Meeting at the Bells Kyrke on 30 April 1590, John Heron entered six bills for Scottish raids, and with Agnes Heron, his son Cuthbert's widow, he complained against the Croziers of Liddesdale for the losses they had suffered in three recent raids (CBP. vol.I, p.349).

John Heron's will is dated 5 December 1590 and was proved 19 June 1591. To each of his daughters Barbary, Margery and Margaret Heron he leaves 100 marks; his sons Reynold, William and Walter Heron are also to have 100 marks each, and William and Walter are to be in the tuition and keeping of their mother Margery during their minority; to his son John Heron he leaves £66. 13s. 4d. His grandson John son of Cuthbert Heron is to have £10 a year to keep him at school and then for his maintenance for his lifetime. His son George Heron is to have his dun horse, and his grandson Cuthbert Heron £60. To his son Walter he leaves 'the whole farming of Rowchester'. His servant Oswald Heron is to have an annu-ity of £6. 13s. 4d. out of the rents of Whelpington and Ray. Smaller legacies are left to Henry and Robert Raymes, William Ridley the younger, William son of Michael Weldon (all of whom were grandsons), John son of William Vaux, George Thirlwall and Reginald Holland. His servants James Heron, Thomas Ridley, Cuthbert Dodd, Nicholas Thomson and Patrick Watson are not forgotten. He leaves the residue of his goods to his wife Margery and appoints her sole executrix; Ralph Grey of Chillingham and William Ridley of Willimontswick are to be supervisors of the will (SS. 38, p.200).

The editor of Wills and Inventories from the Registry at Durham, part II (SS. 38, p.200n.) states that John Heron married Margery daughter of Roger Swinburne of Edlingham, and this was followed in the pedigree of Swinburne of Edlingham in NCH. VII, p.133. This is incorrect. His wife was in fact Margery daughter and coheiress of sir Thomas Grey of Horton, who is called 'wife to John Heron son of George Heron of Chipchase in Northumberland' in the Grey pedigree registered at Flower's Visitation of Yorks. 1563-4, p.149. The marriage is confirmed in the funeral certificate of sir Thomas Grey dated 10 August 1570, and in the inquisition taken at Alnwick 9 April 1571 after his death (History of the Family of Carr, vol.II, pp.133, 134). In 1571 Margery is stated to have been aged 37 years and more. As 'Margerie Hearon of Chipchase, widow, late wife of John Hearon, esquire', she made her w.d. 3 November 1612, by which she gives all her goods to her son Reynold Heron, except £100 which she gives to Reynold's son Anthony. Administration of her goods was granted 19 March 1613/4 to her son John Heron of Uppertown, par. Simonburn, for the benefit of her children Walter Heron, Margery wife of Thomas Salkeld, Dorothy Raymes widow, Barbara wife of Hugh Ridley and Isabella wife of Michael Weldon (SS. 38, p.200n.). The inventory of her goods is dated 29 March 1613/4 (NCH. IV, p.344).

John Heron's eldest son and heir, George Heron, only survived his father about twelve months and died unmarried on 10 September 1591. Administration of his goods was granted 1591/2 to his brother John Heron. By inquisition dated 22 January 35 Eliz. (1593) he was found to have died seised of the manor of Simonburn and appurtenances in Hallbarns, Uppertown, Sharpley, 'Prestop', Ravensheugh, Mortley and Gofton held of the Queen in capite as one-third of a knight's fee; also the manor of Shitlington, Snabdough and Chirdon with appurtenances in Epplerwoodhope, Hetherington and Harle, and Well Cragge held of the Queen's manor of Wark by the service of one-tenth of a knight's fee; also the manor or castle of Sewingshields castle and appurtenances held of the Queen's manor of Wark by the twentieth part of a knight's fee; also Pigdon in Mitford at the tenth part of a knight's fee. Cuthbert Heron was his cousin (actually nephew) and heir, aged 8 years.

Cuthbert Heron the heir was the eldest son of George Heron's brother Cuthbert Heron. Cuthbert Heron the elder had evidently died in his father's lifetime, as only his two sons Cuthbert and John are mentioned in their grandfather's will. The County History pedigree of Heron of Chipchase (NCH. IV, p.340) calls the elder Cuthbert Heron's wife 'Anne, daughter of Francis Anderson of Newcastle, who remarried Henry Bowes of Newcastle'. Henry Bowes of Newcastle, merchant, who died 29 May 1624 aged about 50 certainly married this Anne Anderson, but the Henry Bowes who married Cuthbert Heron's widow was an entirely different person. Cuthbert Heron's wife Anne (or Agnes) was a daughter of Cuthbert Carnaby of Halton, and she married secondly Henry Bowes, 4th son of sir George Bowes of Streatlam, co. Durham. The *County History* pedigree wrongly makes Anne Carnaby wife of the Cuthbert Heron of the next generation. Lord Eure writing to Burghley 18 February 1595/6 complains of the 'gentlemen of greatest worth who now lie out of the country. . . . In Chipchase, where Mr Hearone lay and kept divers men in aid of Tynedale, his child, an infant in minority, and the widow his mother married to Mr Henry Bowes who lives in the Bishopric' (*CBP*. II, p.107). Henry Bowes was cousin of lord Eure and was acting as his deputy on the marches and keeper of Tyndale in 1579 (*Ib*., pp.309, 314, 334, 339). He was living at Stelling in 1599 and on 26 January 1609/10 sir John Fenwick of Wallington, sold Stelling to Anne Bowes of Newburn hall, widow, and her son Cuthbert Heron of Chipchase (*NCH*. VI, p.139). In 1607 Henry Bowes had a lease of Newburn as assignee of Cuthbert Carnaby (*NCH*. XIII, p.147).

The John Heron who administered the goods of his brother George Heron in 1592 was the third, but eldest surviving, son of John Heron (d.1590-91). He had administration of his mother's goods (*SS*. 38, p.200n.) and as John Heron of Overtown (Uppertown), par. Simonburn, he signed the inventory of her goods 29 March 1613/4. The fourth son of John Heron, Reynold Heron of Prudhoe, had a very turbulent career. He must have been quite a young man when he was charged with march treason. Hunsdon writing to Burghley on 15 March 1587/8 reported that 'both William Ridley of Willimontswick and Renolde Herron refusing to stand to their trial for march treason, hath submitted themselves to Her Majesty's mercy' (*CBP*. I, p.320). In 1589 Reynold Heron took a lease of Prudhoe castle from the earl of Northumberland at an annual rent of £66. 12s. 4d., but in 1598 was deprived of his lease for failing to pay his rent. Before the end of the year the lease was restored to him on his promise to pay the arrears. In 1603 Heron with others was before the assizes for burning and taking the spoil of a house in the Bishop Bank; some of his accomplices were taken and hanged and there was a warrant out for his arrest 'which he flees and will not answer'. In May 1604 pardon was granted to Reynold Heron, gentleman, for burning the house of John Lilburne, gentleman, in county Durham, and carrying away certain goods with divers other. It is evident that Reynold was the ringleader, but two months later there was a pardon to Robert Heron, Robert Ramsay, John Swyneborne and Walter Heron for the same offence (*Privy Seal Dockets*). The earl gave orders that his lease should be withdrawn and that Heron should be turned out of the castle; Heron retaliated by bringing an action in the Court of Star Chamber on 7 July 1604 against Thomas Percy, the earl's agent, alleging that he had used unnecessary violence. No results of these proceedings are recorded, but Heron petitioned the earl for the restoration of his lease, and this was granted in 1606. He was finally deprived of his lease for refusing to pay the arrears of rent which had been standing against him for the last seven years. Heron then brought his case before the Council of the North and on 12 May 1607 the earl wrote a long account of all his dealings with Heron to the President of the Council (*NCH*. XII, p.117). In spite of being the black sheep of the family, or perhaps because

he was, Reynold Heron was his mother's heir and she left him all her goods except £100 which she leaves to her grandson Anthony Heron, Reynold's son (*SS*. 38, p.200).

Reynold Heron had two younger brothers, Walter and William who were both under age when their father John Heron made his w.d. 5 December 1590. He wills that 'Margery, my wyffe, shall have the tuicion of my sonnes, Walter and William, during ther nonage' (*Ib*.).

John Heron's daughters were:

1. Dorothy wife of John Raymes of Bolam. She was married before 26 April 1576 when Gawen Swinburne of Cheeseburn Grange, her great uncle leaves 'to Dorethye Raymes two quyes'; her husband John Raymes is a witness to the will. Her father John Heron does not mention any of his married daughters in his will, presumably because they had been given their portions on marriage. Her two sons Henry and Robert Raymes were, however, given 'to eache three whyes, of two yeres old'. She was granted the administration of her late husband's goods 4 September 1605, and is called 'Dorothy Raymes, widow' in her mother's administration of 19 March 1613/4.

2. Isabella wife of Michael Weldon of Welton. She is not mentioned in her father's will, but her son, 'William sonne unto Michaell Welden' had a legacy of £60.

3. Barbary wife of Hugh Ridley. John Heron leaves to 'Barbary, Margerye and Margarett Hearon, my daughters, to everie of them 100 marks'. It is apparent that they were then unmarried. In the administration of her mother's goods she is called wife of Hugh Ridley. There were many Hugh Ridleys living at this time and Barbary's husband has not been identified.

4. Margerye; unmarried 5 December 1590; she is not mentioned in her mother's administration of 19 March 1613/4, and had perhaps died before then.

5. Margaret: unmarried 5 December 1590; wife of Thomas Salkeld 19 March 1613/4, presumably Thomas Salkeld of Corby, co. Cumberland, who is stated to have married '(blank) dau. of (blank) Heron of Chipchase' (*Cumb. and Wmd Vis. Ped.*, p.112).

6. ——; wife of William Ridley of Willimontswick; Hunsdon writing to Burghley on 14 November 1587 complains that William Ridley and John Heron were concerned with a Scottish raid on Haydon Bridge and states 'Rydley hath marryed with Hearon'. He is more specific in a later letter of 8 December 1587 when he mentions 'young Rydley, who had marryd hys (John Heron's) dawter' (*CBP*. I, pp.286-7, 294-5). William Ridley's wife cannot have been Barbary, Margerye or Margaret as they were unmarried in 1590, neither can it have been Dorothy or Isabella who were then both married. William Ridley was killed 13 May 1599. His wife may have predeceased him as she is not mentioned in the letters of administration of her husband's goods 19 March 1613/4. William Ridley the elder is appointed a supervisor of John Heron's w.d. 5 December 1590 and William Ridley the younger, has a legacy of £40.

Cuthbert Heron the younger was a ward of the Crown in 1604 and held as a freeholder in the barony of Wark, the lands of Shitlington, Simonburn, the North law in Hetherington, and Nunwick; he also held Sewingshields and claimed to be freeholder of Chirdon, Snabdough, Ravensheugh and half of Gofton (*Survey of the Debateable and Border Lands*, 1604.

ed. R. P. Sanderson). In 1608 he was returned as a freeholder in the barony of Styford liable for suit and service; his freehold at this time cannot have been Stelling which was not purchased by his mother until 26 January 1609/10 (*NCH.* VI, p.85). In 1613 he was a tenant of the upper mill at Newburn, which had been held by his grandfather Cuthbert Carnaby (*Ib.*, XIII, p.147). He took a 13 years lease from Michaelmas 1622 of the manor house of Newburn, the over mill, and a house and close called Dewley (*Ib.*, p.148). On 11 November 1622 Cuthbert Heron sold Stelling to Henry Hinde (*NCH.* VI, p.139). He was sheriff of Northumberland in 1625. He is called brother-in-law by Thomas Forster of Adderstone in his w.d. 7 September 1637; Forster had married Heron's wife's sister (*NCH.* I, p.229). He took a lease of Dilston tithes 3 June 1640 (*NCH.* X, p.224).

Shortly before 1 January 1646/7 Cuthbert Heron's eldest surviving son, Cuthbert Heron, had married Elizabeth daughter of sir Richard Graham of Netherby, co. Cumb., baronet. Two elder sons had died previously. The castle, manor and demesnes of Sewingshields, Sewingshields side on the south side of the Picts Wall, the village and demesnes of Hallbarns, messuages called Uppertown, Teppermoor and Sharpley, and the tithes of Newbrough, were now settled on the young couple. On the same day the other Heron estates were settled in tail male on Cuthbert Heron the father and his assigns for his life, remainder to Cuthbert Heron the son in tail male, remainder to any daughters of Cuthbert Heron the son, remainder to Cuthbert Heron of Kirkheaton, gent., remainder to Matthew, George, Thomas and any other sons of said Cuthbert Heron of Kirkheaton in tail male, remainder to John Heron of Simonburn castle, gent., remainder to Cuthbert, Thomas, and any other sons of the said John Heron of Simonburn castle, with final remainder to the right heirs of Cuthbert Heron the father. Cuthbert Heron the son and Elizabeth his wife were to have and enjoy during their lives the lands already settled on them. The estates now settled are detailed as:

The manor, castle and demesne of Simonburn, the township and village of Nunwick, tenements called Burnhouse, Slaterfield, Gofton, Ravensheugh, Mortley, Tecket, a tenement in Haltwhistle, the manor of Shitlington, tenements called Pundershaw, 'Swingenhowse', Hetherington, Blackaburn, Newbiggin, Linshields, Harlow and Harlowside, Mounirees and 'Mospittyerley', the manor of Snabdough and the manor of Chirdon and Chirdonhead, tenements called Roughside, Clintburn, Cairnglassenhope and Dodhill, the lands and waste grounds lying on the north side of the river of Chirdon from the 'Spyecragg' up to the north side of Chirdon to the head of the wester gaire of Bogles gaire, the manor and demesne of Chipchase and tenements called Rochester, Cowdon, Dunley, Mowlaw, Commegan, Warkshaugh, the manor and villages of West Whelpington and Ray, tenements called Blackhall and Ray tongue, the manor of Pigdon, a tenement in Corbridge, two burgages in Morpeth, a burgage in Warkworth, a tenement in Kirkharle, the tithes of corn within the manor and demesne of Chipchase, Rochester, Birtley, 'Birtley Katerend', Carryhouse, Buteland shield, Broomhope, Felling and Calf close.

When Cuthbert Heron the father died in June 1655 (*PRO. Chancery Suit* C.5. 32/59) these estates were almost intact, but within the next fifty years had all been dissipated. Cuthbert

Heron sold his lands in Gofton, 23 June 1619, to William Swinburne of Capheaton (*Allgood Title Deeds*), but purchased lands in Bywell from John and Anne Hodgson. He remained aloof during the civil wars, but complained 19 February 1651 that his purchased lands in Bywell had been wrongly sequestered as belonging to William Fenwick (*SS.* 111, p.204). His lands in Pigdon were mortgaged to Rebecca Salvin, widow, and he owed £300 to Henry Widdrington of Blackheddon (*Ib.*, pp.328, 374).

Cuthbert Heron of Kirkheaton and John Heron of Simonburn castle, the remainder men in the settlement of 1 January 1646/7 were two of the sons of his younger brother John Heron who had died in 1618. *See* HERON OF KIRKHEATON.

Cuthbert Heron the father married Dorothy daughter of sir William Fenwick of Wallington (*Nd.Vis.*1666—Fenwick of Wallington). As their eldest son John Heron was aged 18 in 1632, the marriage of his parents must have taken place before 1614. Cuthbert Heron's widow Dorothy married at St Nicholas, Durham, 18 February 1655/6 Mr Thomas Carnaby of Durham, and on 19 December 1661 'Margaret, dr of Mr Thomas Carnaby and Dorothy his wife' was baptised at St Mary's in the South Bailey, Durham. Cuthbert Heron's widow Dorothy cannot have been his wife Dorothy nèe Fenwick, who would have been much too old in 1661 to have had further children. In a law suit of 10 May 1656 it is clearly stated that Dorothy widow of Cuthbert Heron, married Thomas Carnaby of Durham, but it is nowhere stated that she was the mother of all Cuthbert Heron's children. It must be presumed on this evidence that Heron was married twice, both wives being called Dorothy, the parentage of the second wife being unknown.

It seems evident that Cuthbert Heron by his second wife Dorothy, had a daughter Elizabeth. Elizabeth Heron of the Bailey, Durham, spinster, by her w.d. 2 February 1697/8 leaves everything to her loving sister Mrs Dorothy Carnaby. The bond to perform the will is dated 23 February 1697/8 and was entered into by Dorothy Carnaby of North Bailey, spinster, Thomas Wharton of South Bailey, gent., and Richard Coaleman (Colman) of the city of Durham, gent. (*Dur. Prob. Off.* by C.R.H.). 'Mrs Elizabeth Heron, of ye parish of South Bailye' was buried at St Mary in the South Bailey, Durham, 10 February 1697/8. The compiler of the pedigree of Heron of Chipchase in *NCH.* IV, p.341, not realising that this Elizabeth Heron was a spinster, had suggested that she might have been Elizabeth widow of Cuthbert Heron (d.1684) of Chipchase Park House.

'Madam Dorothy Carnaby, wife of Thomas Carnaby, esq.,' was buried at St Mary's in the South Bailey, Durham on 27 December 1684. Cuthbert and Agnes Heron, besides their sons Cuthbert and John, apparently had a daughter Dorothy. The 1666 Visitation pedigree of Swinburne of Capheaton states that John Swinburne of Capheaton (d.1643/4) married for his first wife 'Dorothy, eldest dau. of Cuthbert Heron of Chipchase, Co. Northumbr.' Hodgson (*HN.* ii. II, pp.231, 232) has Dorothy in this generation, and the County History pedigree of Heron of Chipchase repeats this but, perhaps to be on the safe side, also places her in the next generation.

Cuthbert Heron's eldest son, John Heron, was of Christ Church, Oxford, matriculated 2 June 1632 aged 18, and was admitted to Gray's Inn 29 November 1634. He died unmarried in 1636. The second son, George Heron, was also of Christ

Church, Oxford, matriculated 22 June 1632, and was admitted to Gray's Inn on the same day as his brother and was then aged 16. George Heron died in 1643. The *County History* pedigree states without any reference that he was killed fighting on the king's side at the battle of Marston Moor. If this is correct, he can be identified with colonel George Heron who commanded a regiment of horse for the king during the Civil War (*SS.* vol.111, p. 212n.). Administration of the goods of George Heron of Bywell, esquire, was granted 17 November 1647 to Elizabeth, his widow, for her use and that of Dorothy and Frances, minors, daughters of the deceased (*Dur. Prob. Off.* by C.R.H.). George Heron married at Berwick-on-Tweed 19 January 1636/7 Elizabeth daughter and heiress of Roger Selby of Grindon and widow of John Strother of Kirknewton. In 1656 Dorothy Heron, an infant, by William Strother of Kirknewton 'her uncle and next friend' brought a suit against her uncle Cuthbert Heron for part of the estates of her grandfather Cuthbert Heron. Her sister Frances had died two years earlier. The *County History* pedigree gives George Heron another daughter, Isabella wife of William Errington of Benwell, and this is repeated in the pedigree of Errington of Beaufront (*NCH.* IV, p.188). The dates are completely wrong for Isabella Errington to have been a daughter of this George Heron, as William Errington of Benwell in his w.d. 14 February 1626/7 mentions his three sons George, Anthony and William (Raine, *MS. Wills and Inv.* vol.III, p.53), and George Heron did not marry until ten years later.

Cuthbert Heron the son, on whom the settlement of 1 January 1646/7 had been made, had already received from his father on 20 June 1644 an assignment of a lease of the rectory of Corbridge which his father had taken on 3 June 1630 from the Dean and Chapter of Carlisle for a term of 21 years. Shortly after his father's death in 1655 Cuthbert Heron instituted a chancery suit against his father's widow Dorothy who as administratrix of her husband 'pretends some title to the said rectory and detains the lease and assignment' (*PRO. Chancery Suit*, C.5, 32/57). On 20 November 1662 Cuthbert Heron was created a baronet, and shortly after this mortgages on the estates started to pile up. Before the end of the century the combination of mortgages, provision for widows and the portions for daughters had encumbered the estates inextricably. The first mortgage was quite a small one; on 2 February 1676/7 sir Cuthbert mortgaged Simonburn castle with Sharpley and Hallbarns and the tithes of Newbrough to Richard Bates of Newcastle, merchant, for £300; unpaid interest and further borrowings had by 1 April 1685 increased the mortgage to £1200, and in 1689 it was set over to William Shafto and increased to £1500.

Sir Cuthbert Heron was buried in the chancel of Simonburn church on 27 May 1688, beside his first wife dame Elizabeth Heron who had been buried there on 3 February 1682/3. Sir Cuthbert married secondly at All Saints, Newcastle, 23 November 1684 '(blank) Crome'; she was Elizabeth daughter of Faith Frotheringham, and by her w.d. 6 August 1695, proved 27 November 1697 she makes her mother executrix of her will; she was buried at All Saints, Newcastle, on 17 November 1697. Her mother was sister and devisee by her w.d. 5 March 1687 of Elizabeth, widow of Thomas Crome of Newcastle, merchant. Faith Frotheringham, widow, made her w.d. 13 April 1699, proved 8 July 1703, by which she leaves all her estate to her grandchild Cuthbert Heron and appoints

him executor of her will. She states in her will 'I would that my grandchild Cuthbert Heron do live with my cousin Frances Sanderson until he is put out in the world' —— 'if my said grandchild should die before the age of 21 years, I will that he be interred and buried like a gentleman and that £150 out of the personal estate he hath by his mother be expended in his funeral and a tombstone for that he is the end of my and his mother's issue and that he be buried in All Hallows Church' (*Dur. Prob. Off.* by C.R.H.). We will return later to this Cuthbert Heron.

Sir Cuthbert Heron, first baronet, had two sisters, Ann wife of George Heron of Birtley and Frances wife of Nicholas Errington of Ponteland. Ann Heron of Birtley, widow, by her w.d. 2 January 1669/70 leaves 'To my brother Sir Cuthbert Heron, baronet, my wedding ring which was my mothers. To my nephew Cuthbert Heron esq., my grey gelding. To my nephew Mr John Heron my grey mare. To my niece Mrs Dorothy Heron £5 and to my niece Mrs Marie Heron £5 both of which sums George Heron owes me of Rutchester. To my nephew Mr Charles Heron a cow. To my nephew Mr George Heron a cow. To my niece Mrs Elizabeth Heron a cow. To my niece Mrs Katheren Heron a cow. To my sister the Lady Elizabeth Heron a gold enamelled ring with a green stone' (*Dur. Prob. Off.* by C.R.H.).

Sir Cuthbert Heron had three sons, Cuthbert, John (afterwards sir John, second baronet) and Charles (afterwards sir Charles, third baronet). There may have been another son, the George Heron mentioned in the will of his aunt Ann Heron of Birtley, but it may be that the George Heron mentioned by her amongst the Chipchase Herons was her husband's nephew, George Heron of Birtley. Besides these three (or four) sons there were five daughters Dorothy, Mary, Elizabeth, Catherine and Henrietta Maria.

Cuthbert Heron, the eldest son, after his marriage to Elizabeth daughter and coheiress of sir John Mallory of Studley, Yorks, lived at Chipchase Park House, and was provided for by lands at Chipchase. He died before his father and was buried at Simonburn 28 December 1684. His only surviving child was a daughter Elizabeth who married Ralph Jenison of Elswick; at least seven other children had died in infancy. The lands owned by him at Chipchase passed to his brother John Heron but were already mortgaged, and the half yearly payments of interest were in 'great arrearages'. On 27 February 1684/5 John Heron mortgaged these lands for £750 to Dorothy Milbank, widow. The lands were the Hall Hill, the Millfield, the two Strodders, Snaythesfield, the Townefoote field, Short moore, Burnemouth, Woodcock hole, East Bank, Pacegate, Warkshaugh, Comogan, Standingstone field, the broad Meadows, the West bank, the Cobbles Stobb, the Pit House and colliery, Doddbogg, Espmill, Chipchase Mill, Routchester, Blackhill, and Armstrong's farm. This mortgage, later increased to £1000, came into the hands of Ralph Errington.

John Heron was provided for by his father in his lifetime with the manor, castle and demesne of Simonburn, the tenements of Gofton, Ravensheugh, Mortley and Tecket, the manor of Shitlington, the manor of Snabdough, the manor of Chirdon, the tenements of Roughside, Clintburn, Cairnglassenhope and Doghill, the tenements called Dodbogg, Espmill, Whitehill, Bogles Gaire, the two out quarters, Monneyreys, Hindrigg with Cragg Sheel hope, Sharpley, Hallbarns, Hall-hill and Watsons farm, with the tithes of corn called the Peck tithe or Haydon tithe and Newbrough tithe, and the old rent in Newbrough. On 25 February 1687 John Heron, then living at Chipchase Park House, mortgaged these lands and the lands to which he had succeeded on his brother's death, for £1000 to Charles Hara, esq., and Joseph Embree, gent., both of London. Shortly after succeeding his father as second baronet and to the remaining Heron estates, sir John Heron mortgaged the Shitlington, Snabdough and Chirdon manors and farms to John Shaftoe of Nether Warden, clerk, for £500. Even with all these mortgages, the estates with careful management might have been preserved almost intact, but when sir John died in 1693, he also left an only daughter. At this time there were three 'dowagers' to maintain, sir Cuthbert Heron's second wife Elizabeth (d.1697), Cuthbert Heron the son's widow Elizabeth and sir John's widow Anne (d.1713). Cuthbert the son's only daughter, and sir John's only daughter also had charges on the estate. About this time several outlying properties were sold; these included West Whelpington, Ray, Pigdon, Sewingshields, Uppertown, and the summer pastures of Cairnglassenhope, Clintburn, Whitehill etc.

On 19 May 1692 sir John Heron settled his remaining lands on himself for life, then £200 a year to his widow dame Anne Heron, £2500 to his daughter Henrietta Maria at the age of 21 years, £50 a year to Henrietta Maria Heron during the time she should be under the age of 13 years, and after that £60 a year until she reached the age of 21 years, and finally to such person or persons as sir John Heron should testify.

Sir John Heron by his w.d. 12 March 1692/3, proved 21 March 1692/3, leaves his estates to his younger brother sir Charles Heron, subject to portions of £500 each and £30 a year each for their maintenance until marriage, for his sisters Dorothy, Mary, Elizabeth and Katherine Heron. Sir John was survived by his wife; she was Anne daughter of John Heron of Brampton, Hunts., whose family claimed descent from the Herons of Chipchase. She married secondly George Saffin of the parish of St Margaret's, Westminster, and died 29 October 1713 aged 45 being buried in Bath Abbey. Saffin died in the Fleet Prison; his w.d. 24 July 1694 was proved 30 October 1711.

Sir Charles Heron on succeeding his brother in 1693 found that being only tenant for life he was unable to sell any of the estates and could not raise the portions of £2500 each due to his two nieces. Besides this, dame Anne Heron's annuity was in arrears and also the maintenance payment for her daughter Henrietta Maria. Accordingly he applied for an Act of Parliament to be passed to enable sale of parts of the estate to be made. The Act was passed in 1695 and the estate, with the exception of the Chipchase part of it, was vested in trustees for sale. On 25 December 1696 sir Charles entered into an agreement with Robert Allgood of Newcastle to sell him all the lands specified in the Act of Parliament. The purchase price was to be £9110 subject to all the charges and mortgages which were to be paid off by Allgood within twelve months. Allgood was to have the timber growing on the estate called Nunwick and all arrears of rent due to Heron; if the arrears of rent did not amount to £500, Heron's other lands called Chipchase demesne, Closehouse, Birtley tithes and the lands of Nunwick were to be security to Allgood to make up such sum as the arrears of rent fell short of £500. These other lands were also to be security to Allgood for any other mortgages

or encumbrances not mentioned in the Act, and for the next three years Allgood was to have convenient lodging and apartment in Chipchase house for himself and servant with stabling for his horses, two horses grass and two cows grass winter and summer in Chipchase Park (*Allgood Deeds*).

By 1713 the conveyance to Allgood had not been completed and the whole matter was referred to the Master of Rolls to declare what was owing on either side. Many more debts of sir Charles Heron had been discovered since the agreement of 25 December 1696 had been entered into, and the arrears of rent had not come up to the anticipated £500. Further lands consisting of Shortmoor, Burnmouth foot, Warkshaugh, Pithouse and the ancient rents out of Tecket, Buteland and Steel were thereupon conveyed to Robert Allgood. Sir Charles Heron died in London before 4 August 1718. He had married in Westminster Abbey 15 May 1694 Catherine daughter of sir William Pulteney and she survived him and was buried at St Martin's in the Fields 18 October 1720. Their only son Harry succeeded as 4th baronet; a daughter Catherine married one Panton of Banff in Scotland; two other daughters died in infancy.

The end of the story is soon told. Sir Harry Heron at one time held a lieutenant's commission in the 2nd Regt of Guards. He married at St Bennets, Pauls Wharf, on 18 March 1724/5 Elizabeth Jump of Enfield, Middlesex. All that remained of the vast estates of his ancestors were 'the capital messuage, manor, chapel and demesne lands of Chipchase', and on 8 July 1725 he mortgaged these to George Allgood, brother of the earlier purchaser, Robert Allgood. The amount of the mortgage was £4000 and a further sum of £3976. 9s. 6d. to provide for his wife if she should survive him and for any children they might have. The £4000 lasted no time at all, and on 16 June 1727 he finally parted with Chipchase, George Allgood being the purchaser for £976. 9s. 6d. and an annuity of £166. 13s. 4d. to sir Harry Heron and dame Elizabeth his wife. Even the annuity was not safe, and on 26 September 1729 Heron and his wife mortgaged it for £200 to Martha Parsons of the parish of St James', Westminster, spinster, a life assurance with the London Assurance Office on Heron's life being given as collateral security. Failure to pay the interest on the mortgage caused it to be increased and on 13 April 1730 it was set over to Richard How of the parish of St James', Westminster, breeches maker, now increased to £358. 15s. The last known episode in this pathetic story happened on 25 January 1731/2 when sir Harry Heron, now living in the parish of St Mary le Bone, co. Middlesex, sold £100 a year of his annuity to Joseph Kendall of the parish of St Ann, Westminster, gentleman, for £540. 13s. 7d.

Sir Harry's wife Elizabeth died about 1734, and about 1747 he married for the second time a lady called Sarah, whose surname is unknown. Sir Harry Heron was buried at Acton, Middlesex, on 26 February 1748/9. It seems possible that sir Harry Heron had an illegitimate son who illegally assumed the baronetcy, for capt. sir Harry Heron, RN, from St Pancras, was buried at St James', Piccadilly, 28 June 1817, aged 74.

The representation of the Herons of Chipchase and the baronetcy now passed to the children of Cuthbert Heron of Durham, the only surviving child of sir Cuthbert Heron, 1st baronet, by his second wife Elizabeth Crome. This Cuthbert Heron was of full age in 1703 and then living at Chester-le-Street, co. Durham. He married, articles before marriage

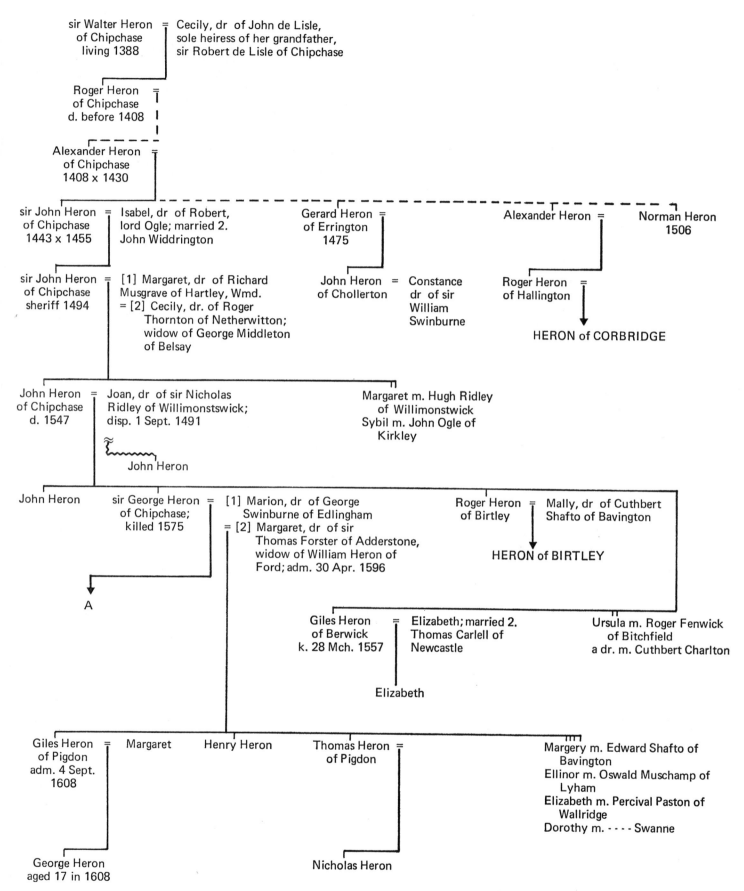

sir Walter Heron = Cecily, dr of John de Lisle,
of Chipchase   sole heiress of her grandfather,
living 1388   sir Robert de Lisle of Chipchase

Roger Heron =
of Chipchase
d. before 1408

Alexander Heron =
of Chipchase
1408 x 1430

sir John Heron = Isabel, dr of Robert,   Gerard Heron =   Alexander Heron =   Norman Heron
of Chipchase   lord Ogle; married 2.   of Errington   1506
1443 x 1455   John Widdrington   1475

sir John Heron = [1] Margaret, dr of Richard   John Heron = Constance   Roger Heron =
of Chipchase   Musgrave of Hartley, Wmd.   of Chollerton   dr of sir   of Hallington
sheriff 1494   = [2] Cecily, dr. of Roger   William
                   Thornton of Netherwitton;   Swinburne
                   widow of George Middleton   HERON of CORBRIDGE
                   of Belsay

John Heron = Joan, dr of sir Nicholas   Margaret m. Hugh Ridley
of Chipchase   Ridley of Willimonstswick;   of Willimonstwick
d. 1547   disp. 1 Sept. 1491   Sybil m. John Ogle of
                                                  Kirkley
              John Heron

John Heron   sir George Heron = [1] Marion, dr of George   Roger Heron = Mally, dr of Cuthbert
             of Chipchase;   Swinburne of Edlingham   of Birtley   Shafto of Bavington
             killed 1575   = [2] Margaret, dr of sir
                                  Thomas Forster of Adderstone,
                                  widow of William Heron of   HERON of BIRTLEY
                                  Ford; adm. 30 Apr. 1596

       A
                          Giles Heron = Elizabeth; married 2.   Ursula m. Roger Fenwick
                          of Berwick   Thomas Carlell of   of Bitchfield
                          k. 28 Mch. 1557 Newcastle   a dr. m. Cuthbert Charlton

                                Elizabeth

Giles Heron = Margaret   Henry Heron   Thomas Heron =   Margery m. Edward Shafto of
of Pigdon   of Pigdon   Bavington
adm. 4 Sept.   Ellinor m. Oswald Muschamp of
1608   Lyham
                                                              Elizabeth m. Percival Paston of
                                                                 Wallridge
                                                              Dorothy m. - - - - Swanne

George Heron   Nicholas Heron
aged 17 in 1608

59

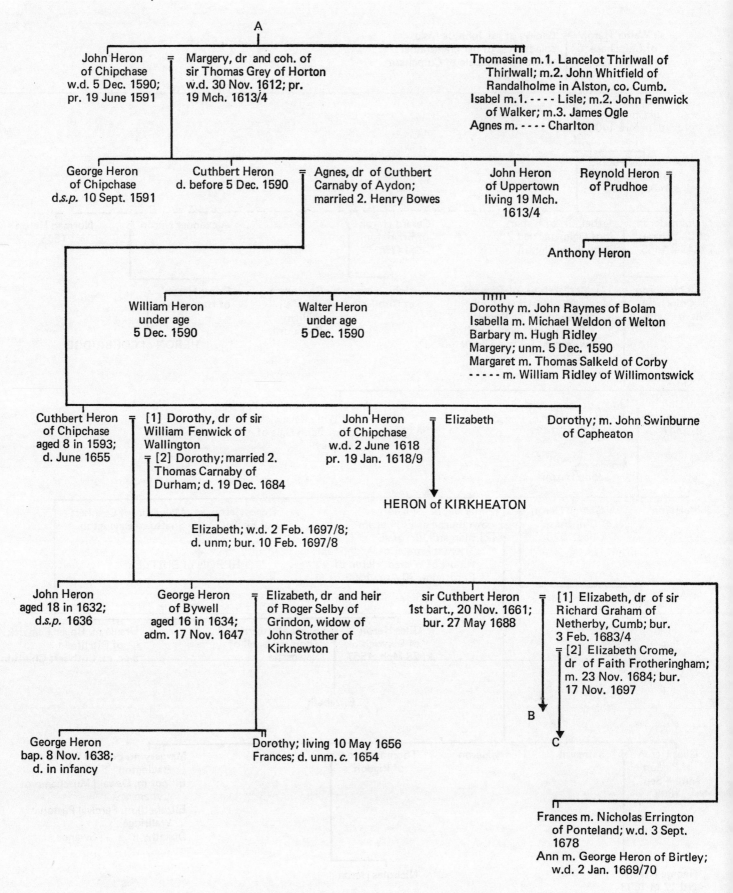

A

John Heron
of Chipchase
w.d. 5 Dec. 1590;
pr. 19 June 1591
= Margery, dr and coh. of
sir Thomas Grey of Horton
w.d. 30 Nov. 1612; pr.
19 Mch. 1613/4

Thomasine m.1. Lancelot Thirlwall of
Thirlwall; m.2. John Whitfield of
Randalholme in Alston, co. Cumb.
Isabel m.1. - - - - Lisle; m.2. John Fenwick
of Walker; m.3. James Ogle
Agnes m. - - - - Charlton

George Heron
of Chipchase
d.s.p. 10 Sept. 1591

Cuthbert Heron
d. before 5 Dec. 1590
= Agnes, dr of Cuthbert
Carnaby of Aydon;
married 2. Henry Bowes

John Heron
of Uppertown
living 19 Mch.
1613/4

Reynold Heron
of Prudhoe
=

Anthony Heron

William Heron
under age
5 Dec. 1590

Walter Heron
under age
5 Dec. 1590

Dorothy m. John Raymes of Bolam
Isabella m. Michael Weldon of Welton
Barbary m. Hugh Ridley
Margery; unm. 5 Dec. 1590
Margaret m. Thomas Salkeld of Corby
- - - - - m. William Ridley of Willimontswick

Cuthbert Heron
of Chipchase
aged 8 in 1593;
d. June 1655
= [1] Dorothy, dr of sir
William Fenwick of
Wallington
= [2] Dorothy; married 2.
Thomas Carnaby of
Durham; d. 19 Dec. 1684

John Heron
of Chipchase
w.d. 2 June 1618
pr. 19 Jan. 1618/9
= Elizabeth

Dorothy; m. John Swinburne
of Capheaton

HERON of KIRKHEATON

Elizabeth; w.d. 2 Feb. 1697/8;
d. unm; bur. 10 Feb. 1697/8

John Heron
aged 18 in 1632;
d.s.p. 1636

George Heron
of Bywell
aged 16 in 1634;
adm. 17 Nov. 1647
= Elizabeth, dr and heir
of Roger Selby of
Grindon, widow of
John Strother of
Kirknewton

sir Cuthbert Heron
1st bart., 20 Nov. 1661;
bur. 27 May 1688
= [1] Elizabeth, dr of sir
Richard Graham of
Netherby, Cumb; bur.
3 Feb. 1683/4
= [2] Elizabeth Crome,
dr of Faith Frotheringham;
m. 23 Nov. 1684; bur.
17 Nov. 1697

B

George Heron
bap. 8 Nov. 1638;
d. in infancy

Dorothy; living 10 May 1656
Frances; d. unm. c. 1654

C

Frances m. Nicholas Errington
of Ponteland; w.d. 3 Sept.
1678
Ann m. George Heron of Birtley;
w.d. 2 Jan. 1669/70

B   C

Cuthbert Heron = Elizabeth, dr and heir   sir John Heron = Anne, dr of John Heron
of Park House;   of sir John Mallory   2nd baronet;   of Brampton, Hunts;
bap. 10 Mch. 1656/7; of Studley, Yorks.   b. 14 May 1677;   married 2. George
bur. 28 Dec. 1684   w.d. 12 Mch.1692/3; Saffin; d. 29 Oct. 1713
                                                  pr. 21 Mch. 1692/3   aged 45

Cuthbert Heron; bap. 7 Sept. 1680;   Elizabeth; bap. 13 Mch.   Elizabeth; bap. 15 Apr. 1686;
bur. 3 Apr. 1681   1679/80; bur. 5 June   bur. 5 June 1686
John Heron; bur. 29 Apr. 1683   1686   Henrietta Maria; bap. 4 Oct.
George Heron; bap. 24 Nov. 1681;   a child; bur. 2 Feb.   1688; m. George Huxley
bur. 5 Mch. 1684/5   1683/4   of London
Cuthbert Heron; bap. 31 Oct. 1686;   Mary; bap. 20 Mch.
bur. 27 May 1688   1683/4; d. young
                                      Elizabeth; bap. 15 Apr.
                                        1686; m. Ralph
                                        Jenison of Elswick

sir Charles Heron = Catherine, dr of   Dorothy; of par. St Andrew, Holburn,
3rd baronet; d.   sir Wm Pulteney;   21 Dec. 1706
before 4 Aug. 1718 m. 15 May 1694;   Mary
                    bur. 18 Oct. 1720   Elizabeth
                                            Catherine m. - - - - Smith of Southampton
                                            Henrietta Maria; bap. 13 Aug. 1670;
                                               living 11 May 1694

sir Harry Heron = [1] Elizabeth Jump   Catherine m. - - - - Panton
4th baronet;   of Enfield; m.   of Banff, Scotland
bur. 26 Feb. 1748/9 18 Mch. 1724/5   2 drs; d. young
                    = [2] Sarah

Cuthbert Heron = Katherine, dr of Richard
of Durham   Middleton of Offerton,
bur. 14 Nov. 1731 co. Durham

Cuthbert Heron   Richard Heron   sir Thomas Heron Middleton = [1] Margaret, dr of rev.
bap. 4 Nov. 1716;   bap. 4 Jan. 1717/8; 5th baronet; bap. 17 Jan. 1722/3;   (Ralph) Finlay of Carrick-
bur. 13 Dec. 1740   d. unm. 1737   w. pr. 8 June 1801   fergus; m. 1749; d. 1753/4
                                                                              = [2] Elizabeth, dr of
                                                                                 Alexander Arbuthnot of
                                                                                 Fortree, Scotland;
                                                                                 m. Aug. 1758

                      Mary; only child; b. 2 Oct. 1750;
                         m. 5 July 1768 capt. Robert Barron
                         of Alnwick; d. 1 June 1804

                                                          Catherine; bap. 19 Jan. 1718/9;
                                                             bur. 10 May 1722
                                                          Elizabeth; bap. 16 Nov. 1720;
                                                             m. Benjamin Raine of Durham;
                                                             d. 31 Mch. 1789 aged 68

dated 20/21 October 1715, Katherine daughter of Richard Middleton of Offerton, co. Durham. Both were buried at St Oswald's, Durham, he on 14 November 1731, and she on 30 September 1738. Their two eldest sons both died unmarried, Cuthbert in 1740 and Richard in 1737. The third, but eldest surviving son was Thomas Heron, who, on the death of sir Harry Heron in 1749, succeeded as 5th baronet. Sir Thomas was in 1745 an ensign in General Handyside's Regt of Foot (*PSAN*3, I, p.180) and assumed the surname of Middleton on succeeding to his mother's estate at Offerton. He died 27 May 1801 when the baronetcy became extinct. By his first wife, Margaret daughter of revd. Ralph Finlay of Carrickfergus in Ireland, he had an only daughter and heiress Mary wife of captain Robert Barron of Alnwick. Sir Thomas Heron-Middleton's second wife was Elizabeth, daughter of Alexander Arbuthnot of Fortree in Scotland, but by her he had no children.

The baronetcy was claimed by Cuthbert Heron of South Shields, co. Durham, butcher, who being well known on Tyneside was usually addressed under the style of a baronet. He claimed to be a grandson of Thomas Heron of Heron's Hill, Corbridge, and further claimed that Thomas Heron was an elder brother of Cuthbert Heron father of sir Thomas Heron-Middleton. The HERONS OF CORBRIDGE were in fact descended from Roger Heron of Hallington who in 1528 had a grant of lands in Corbridge from his 'kinsman', sir John Heron of Chipchase. 'Sir' Cuthbert's claim was naturally never established.

HERON OF KIRKHEATON, PAR. KIRKHEATON

JOHN HERON of Chipchase by his w.d. 5 December 1590 leaves to his grandson, John son of Cuthbert Heron, a legacy of £10 a year to keep him at school and then for his maintenance for life, and a further £6. 13s. 4d. a year. John Heron is described as of Chipchase, gentleman, when he made his own w.d. 2 June 1618, proved 19 January 1618/9. The will has mistakenly been thought to be that of his uncle John Heron of Uppertown (*NCH*. IV, p.341; *SS*. 38, p.200n.). John Heron leaves to his son Cuthbert all his land in Kirkheaton except a house called Blackhall which he gives to his wife Elizabeth; his son Thomas is to have all his lands in Hetherington and his son John a tenement in Barrasford; to his son Ralph he leaves his third part of the Park-end; 'the rest to my son George and daughter Dorothy, whom I make executors, and I make my brother Cuthbert, John Hearon of Birtley hall, and Tristram Fenwick of Kenton, supervisors. I give my son Cuthbert and his goods to my brother Cuthbert, and my daughter Dorothy to my sister in Chipchase'.

After the normal fashion of the times, two of the younger sons were apprenticed to Newcastle merchants. Thomas Hearon, son of John Hearon of Chipchase, gent., decd, was apprenticed 1 June 1623 to Henry Cock of Newcastle, mercer. He can only just have completed his apprenticeship when he died, administration of his goods being granted 18 May 1630 to his brother Cuthbert for the use of John Heron and Dorothy Heron, his brother and sister. Ralph son of John Heron of Chipchase, gent., was apprenticed 2 February 1634 to Henry Cocke of Newcastle, mercer, but did not attain his freedom of the Newcastle Merchant Adventurers until 12 March 1646,

his freedom having been postponed because he was 'an officer in military affairs' in Newcastle before the town was taken by the Scots, and because on the death of his master he had not been set over to another in due time (*SS*. 101, p.254). Ralph Heron was made a freeman of Newcastle 1 April 1647.

On 1 January 1646/7 Cuthbert Heron of Chipchase made a settlement of his estates so that they 'may continue in the said Cuthbert and his issue and in default thereof in the blood and kindred of said Cuthbert Heron'. After his own issue, the estates were to go to Cuthbert Heron of Kirkheaton, gent., and his sons Matthew, George and Thomas and then to John Heron of Simonburn castle, gent., and his sons Cuthbert and Thomas (*Allgood Title Deeds*). Cuthbert Heron of Kirkheaton and John Heron of Simonburn Castle were sons of the John Heron of Chipchase who had died in 1618. The Herons of Kirkheaton were for a long time reckoned as the nearest 'in the blood and kindred' of the Herons of Chipchase, and as late as 6 March 1693/4 Matthew Heron, junior, of the Kirkheaton family was in remainder to the Chipchase estates.

Matthew Heron was rated for lands in Kirkheaton in 1663. Of this family were George Heron of Ingoe and Anthony Heron of Cowpen, guardians of George Shafto of Ingoe in March 1696/7. George Heron of Ingoe married Katherine, sister of Ralph Errington of Newbiggin, par. Hexham. Ralph Errington by his w.d. 31 August 1697 leaves to his 'loving sister, Katherine Heron wife of George Heron of Ingoe', £20 a year for life. George Heron's children have substantial legacies, *viz*., John £100, Mary £200, Elizabeth and Anne, each £100 (*NCH*. IV, p.34n.).

Nothing further is known about John Heron of Simonburn Castle mentioned in the family settlement of 1 January 1646/7 but it seems possible that his younger son Thomas was the Thomas Heron of Simonburn who married Isabel Welden of Dilston. Isabel Welden's sister Mary married George Heron of Rowchester, yeoman, afterwards of Humshaugh. Administration of the goods of Thomas Heron of Simonburn, gent., was granted 19 April 1697 to Isabella Heron his mother, and to Thomas Heron of Hexham (Raine, *MS Hexham Wills and Inv.*).

Simonburn Castle had regularly been used as a residence by younger sons or cadets of the Herons of Chipchase. John Ridley of Wark Eals by his w.d. 2 February 1584/5 leaves 'whatsoever goods of mine are at this present in the hands of George Heron of Simonburn castle I give to the behalf and profit of George Heron, John Heron and Annes Heron his children' (*Dur. Prob. Off.* by C.R.H.).

HERON OF BIRTLEY, PAR. CHOLLERTON

ROGER HERON, brother of sir George Heron of Chipchase, is on the list *circa* 1557-58 of those concerned in the Carr-Heron feud (*Hist. Fam. of Carr*, II, p.78). He was no doubt one of sir George's 'three brethren' who assisted him in the raid on Dolfynstunne on 5 December 1542 (*Hamilton Papers*, I, p.321). Sir George Heron's daughter Isabel Ogle in her w.d. 1 June 1602 mentions her uncle Roger Heron, and her cousins George Heron her servant, Leonard Heron of Whelpington and John Heron of Birtley; although not specifically called sons of Roger, it is probable that they were and that Roger

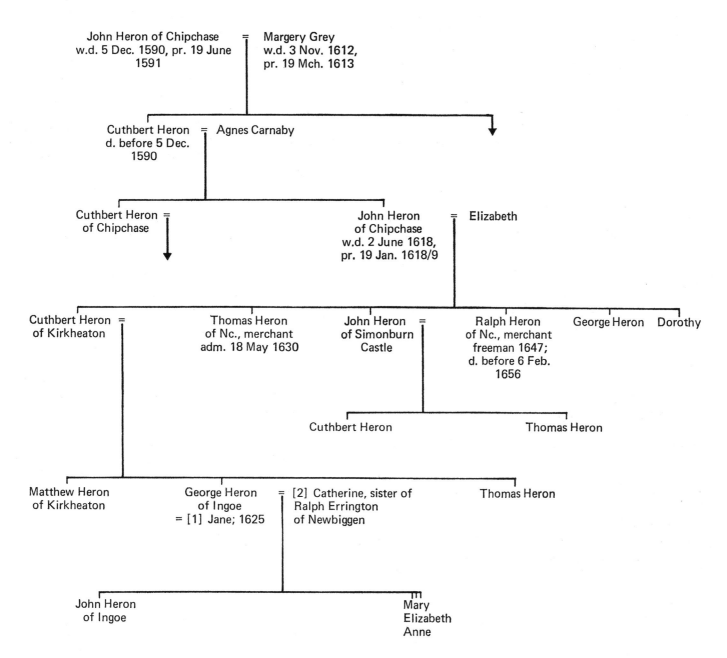

Heron was of Birtley (Raine, *MS Wills and Inv.* II, p.167). In 1553 Roger Heron of Birtley was a setter and searcher of the watch to be kept by the men of Birtley, Buteland and Redesmouth (Nicolson, *Leges Marchiarum,* p.259). He was a supervisor of the w.d. 27 December 1582 of Lancelot Thirlwall of Thirlwall, who had married Thomasine Heron (Raine, *MS Wills and Inv.* II, p.141). Harvey's Visitation pedigree of 1552 records that Mally daughter of Cuthbert Shafto of Bavington was 'maryed to Roger Heron of Byrkley'.

Roger Heron of Birtley seems to have been succeeded by (his son) John Heron of Birtley, gent., called cousin by Isabel Ogle in her w.d. 1 June 1602, and appointed her executor. On 30 May 1611 John Heron of Birtley purchased Shieldhall, par. Slaley, from John Eldred and George Whitmore (*NCH.* VI, p.369; he is called George Heron in error in *NCH.* IV, p.361). On 2 June 1618 he was appointed a supervisor of the

w.d. 2 June 1618 of John Heron of Chipchase. He was a freeholder in 1628 and 1639. John Heron was married twice, as in his will he directs that he shall be buried in Birtley quire 'near my two wives and predecessors and five children'. One of his wives, probably his first, was Alice Farrdon whom he married at St Nicholas', Nc., on 20 October 1591. By his w.d. 10 December 1647, pr. 1650, he leaves his lands in Nether Warden, Warden 'nighe' (?High Warden) and Hexham to his eldest son George Heron with remainder to his second son John Heron; his daughter Elizabeth Horn, widow, is given an annuity of 20 nobles; his son-in-law Mark Ogle of Kirkley has a legacy; his grand children John, Alexander, Isabel and Marjory 'Skot' also have legacies; Cuthbert Heron and Ann Raine, children of his daughter Elizabeth Raine each have £4, and Elizabeth herself has £6. 6s. 8d. a year for life.

The eldest son, George Heron, was a supervisor of the w.d.

31 March 1635 of Cuthbert Ridley, rector of Simonburn; he is called uncle by Cuthbert Ogle of Kirkley in his w.d. 28 November 1667. He made his own will on 9 October 1669, proved 1669, whereby he directs that he is to be buried in the quire of Birtley near his father and his predecessors; he leaves his lands in Nether Warden and Hexham to his wife for life. His wife was a sister of sir Cuthbert Heron of Chipchase, bart. George Heron appoints his brother John Heron of Shield Hall as executor to his will. John Heron's illegitimate son William Heron was George Heron's servant and has £10 by his will; he had previously had a legacy of £10 from his grandfather John Heron. George Heron leaves his lands to his nephew George son of John Heron with remainder to another nephew Cuthbert son of John Heron. John Heron his nephew son of John Heron is appointed executor to his will; he leaves legacies to his 'nieces, daughters of my brother John'. He leaves other legacies to his sister Elizabeth Raine and to her daughters; to Edward Pawtoune and his sisters, children of his sister Margery Pawtoune; to John Ogle and Catherine Nanson, children of his late sister Katherine Ogle; and to his brother-in-law Henry Stokoe of Newbrough (*Dur. Prob. Off.* per C.R.H.).

John Heron of Shieldhall, second son of John Heron of Birtley, paid Hearth Tax at Slaley in 1665, but after his brother's death he lived at Birtley and was buried at Chollerton 8 August 1686. His widow 'Sissely, mother to Mr Cuthbert Heron of Carrihouse' was buried at Chollerton 23 February 1695/6.

George Heron, eldest son of John Heron, was living at Shieldhall in 1669 when he became heir to his uncle George Heron. A year later he married Mary Wilson of Walwick (bond of marriage 16 November 1670), by whom he had an only daughter and heiress Anne (bap. at Chollerton 27 December 1671). George Heron's will is undated but two other documents survive which make the date quite certain; first, there is the inventory of his goods dated 11 April 1672, and then there is the deposition of 27 September 1672 of John Heron of Shield Hall, chap. Slaley, gent., aged 61, father of George; he says he knew him from infancy and knew George's widow Mary Heron for 2 years—that on Friday 5 April last past he and his son William Heron were with his son George, the testator, who was lying sick at his house at Birtley Hall and George told them that he wanted to make his will and would like his cousin Michael Welden to prepare it; Welden came and George got his wife Mary Heron to fetch pen, ink and paper, and the will was duly drawn up. It was proved in 1673 (*Dur. Prob. Off.* by C.R.H.). George Heron leaves £200 each to his wife Mary and his daughter Anne; his widow married secondly (b. of m. 7 October 1672) James Fenwick of Stanton. As the estates were entailed they passed to his brother Cuthbert Heron then living at Hexham where he was acting as coroner. Cuthbert Heron voted as a freeholder in respect of Shieldhall in 1698, 1710, 1715 and 1721. He married at Chollerton 12 August 1680 Elizabeth Shafto; she is called Isabel Shaftoe in her bond of marriage dated 2 July 1680, but in the record of her marriage, and her burial at Birtley on 16 May 1711 she is called Elizabeth. Cuthbert Heron's will is dated 20 July 1731 and he was buried at Birtley on 18 May 1733. To his younger son George Heron he leaves a guinea, and to another son Ralph Heron he leaves the lease of Dinley Hill. Ralph Heron by his w.d. 8 February 1755,

proved 1762, gives all his real and personal estate to his nephew Cuthbert Heron Clifton, and his nieces Hannah and Isabella Clifton. They were the children of his sister Esther who had married Martin Clifton at Corbridge on 26 July 1723.

The eldest son John Heron seems never to have lived at Birtley; in 1721 he was living at Wall when he voted as a freeholder for lands in Warden and he was still there in 1739 when he gave Shieldhall to his eldest son and heir John Heron. Shieldhall had been the appanage of the heir for three generations. Administration of the goods of John Heron of Wall was granted 13 July 1747 to John Heron his son. John Heron the father's wife was Phillis daughter of the revd Henry Guy, vicar of Corbridge, and they were married at Corbridge on 30 March 1709. Their two younger children Cuthbert and Phillis were born at Countesspark near Birtley. Phillis married at Birtley 5 December 1734 William son of Edward Shafto of Bavington, and in her will proved 19 February 1736/7 she is described as 'late wife of William Shafto of Birtley Hall, gent.' (Raine, *MS Prob. and Adm.* II, p.125).

John Heron the son married Elizabeth daughter and heiress of George Robson of Ninebanks, par. Allendale (articles before marriage 7 November 1748), by which marriage he obtained lands in Ninebanks. He was living at Wall in 1748, at Blackhall, par. Hexham in 1750, at Leehall, par. Bellingham in 1774, but was of Hexham when he made his w.d. 31 May 1805.

With the children of John and Elizabeth Heron, the male line of the Herons of Birtley Hall died out. These children were John Robson Heron, a Newcastle barber surgeon (d. *s.p.*); Cuthbert Heron of Shieldhall (d.1812) who had two daughters, Elizabeth wife of John Mason of London and Mary Ann wife of Jonathan Scurr, vicar of Ninebanks; George Heron who served in the Royal Navy; Edward Heron; Matthew Heron (d. Leehall 1781); Betsy (d. in infancy); Elizabeth wife of William Good; Mary wife of —— Wilthew; and Phillis wife of Allan (Shafto) Macdonald of Tone, (m. Bellingham 24 September 1774), both described as of Lee Hall.

HERON OF CORBRIDGE, PAR. CORBRIDGE

IN 1506 Giles Musgrave, Roger Heron, John Heron of Chollerton and Norman Heron were appointed trustees of his estates by John Heron of Chipchase. On 20 March 1516 Giles Musgrave and Roger Heron, the other trustees then being dead, settled the estates on John Heron of Chipchase in tail male with remainders to the heirs male of Gerard Heron, late of Errington, and then to William Heron of Ford. The fact that the Herons of Ford were thus brought into the remainder might suggest that besides the descendants of John Heron of Chipchase himself, the only other male heirs to the Herons of Chipchase were the descendants of Gerard Heron of Errington.

On 12 March 1484 John Swinburne of Capheaton had given lands in Chollerton to John son of Gerard Heron and Constance his wife, sister of the grantor in marriage, for the life of Constance. This John Heron who married Constance Swinburne was no doubt the John Heron of Chollerton who on 13 February 1506 was given by Roger son of Alexander

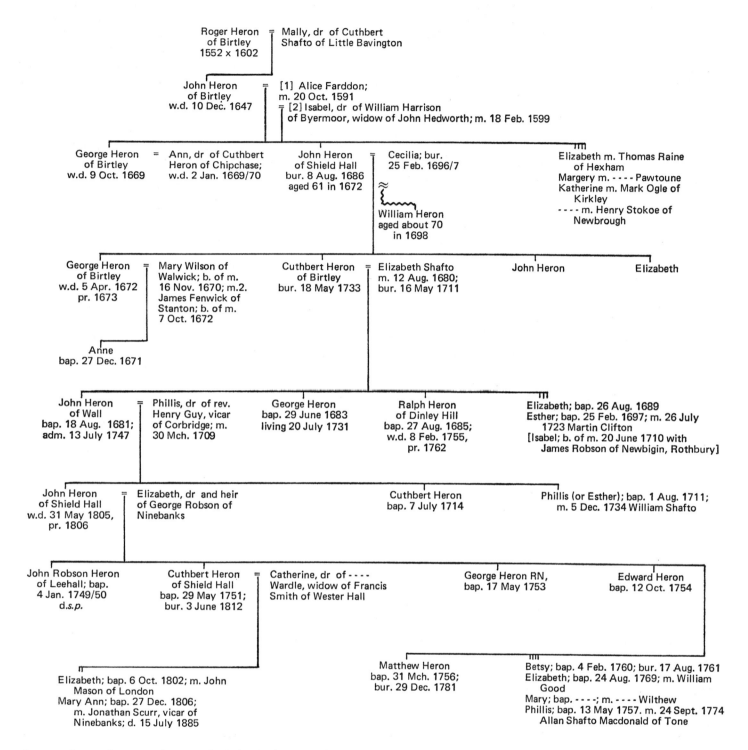

Heron, deceased, a rentcharge which he had received from John Swinburne of Capheaton on 15 June 1490. It is reasonable to assume that this Roger son of Alexander Heron was the same person as the trustee of 1506 and 1516.

In 1495 the archbishop of York granted a 40 years lease of the vill of Hallington at a rent of £7. 13s. 4d. to John Heron of Chipchase, who used it to provide for his 'kinsman' Roger Heron. In 1500 Roger Heron held freehold lands in Corbridge in right of his wife, Margaret daughter and heiress of William Nadall; she had previously been married to a man called Shafto. On 8 July 1517 Roger Heron of Hallington, gentleman, had a perpetual lease from the church of St Margaret's Durham of burgages and lands in Corbridge. It seems likely that there were two Roger Herons of Corbridge, father and son. On 6 August 1529 sir John Heron of Chipchase let lands in Corbridge to Roger Heron of Corbridge, gent. We have already mentioned in the account of the Herons of Chipchase, a royal pardon, perhaps to be dated to 1544 granted to John Heron senior, John Heron junior and George Heron, all of Chipchase, Roger Heron late of Hallington, gent and others.

For about fifty years there was a close contact and no doubt a close relationship between the Herons of Chipchase and those of Corbridge, but the exact connection is not known.

Roger Heron's son was Alexander Heron who on 10 October 1549, for the sum of £12 sold two burgages and certain lands in Corbridge to James Heron of Shieldhall, yeoman; Thomas of 'Moralle' and John Heron of the Hallbarns were to give seisin. On 14 June 1561 he sold a house in Corbridge to David Carnaby of Beaufront. Alexander Heron of Corbridge by his w.d. 24 February 1571/2 directs that he is to be buried in Corbridge church, appoints his wife sole executrix and gives her for life his lease of the Hall Walls in Corbridge; he mentions his sons Anthony and William and his daughters Agnes and Margery Heron (Raine, *MS Wills and Inv.* I, p.93).

A Thomas Heron of Corbridge, whose will is dated 14 April 1596, was probably a relative of Alexander Heron. Thomas Heron directs that he is to be buried in St Thomas' porch in Corbridge; he leaves half of his goods to his wife Dorothy Heron; he gives legacies of 20s., each to Christopher, Isabel, Catherine and Barbara Carr; he leaves legacies to Margaret and Dorothy Heron, natural and lawful children of John Heron and appointed Edmund Heron and Edward Carr as executors. Anthony Heron son and heir of Alexander Heron sold lands in Corbridge in 1579 to Matthew Wilkinson. Administration of his goods was granted on 16 February 1595/6 to his widow Lucy. She was daughter of Thomas Crane of Crawhall who by his w.d. 18 October 1582 leaves to 'either of the two daughters of Luce Heron, my daughter 6s. 8d.'. (SS. 112, p.96). Lucy married secondly a man named Baite and was living as his widow 13 March 1621/2. Thomas Heron son of Anthony, was still a minor in December 1608 when he sold a burgage in Corbridge to Edmund Heron of Dilston. He made a nuncupative will on 13 March 1621/2 (proved 2 April 1622) by which he leaves one third of his lands to his mother Luce Baite, widow; he mentions his base son William Musgrave *alias* Heron, and appoints his two daughters Isabel and Mary executrices; the tuition of his son and heir Alexander is granted to Christopher Welton, Alexander's uncle (Raine, *MS Wills and Inv.* vol.III, p.5). Alexander was still under age on 10 February 1628/9 when his tuition was given to his mother Margaret. In 1665 he conveyed his Corbridge lands to his son reserving a life estate in one half of them. He died on 24 May 1689 and was buried in Corbridge church two days later.

Alexander Heron appears to have been married twice, but the name of neither of his wives is known. His son and heir Thomas Heron married at Corbridge on 3 August 1665 Ann Hudspeth, so can only have been a half-brother to Alexander's other sons and daughters born between 1663 and 1688. Alexander had an illegitimate daughter Margery, bap. 1 October 1663, bur. 29 September 1665. Four sons of his second family died in infancy.

Thomas Heron received a release of his lands in Corbridge from Stephen Heron of Durham 19 June 1694, and voted as a freeholder for these lands in 1698 and 1710. His children appear to have been Thomas (bap. 28 October 1666), Lancelot (bap. 18 July 1671), William, Ann (bap. 2 June 1681, bur. 5 March 1681/2) and Elizabeth (bap. 25 December 1674). Of the younger sons William Heron was a cooper in Newcastle; when he made his w.d. 16 November 1730 he had a messuage in Westgate in Newcastle which he leaves in trust for his daughter Anne and her husband John Latine. They had been married at St John's, Newcastle, on 21 October 1725, and

on 12 October 1726 (one of these dates must be wrong) John Lattine *alias* Letteny made a settlement of lands in Whitburn and Cleadon, co. Durham on his 'intended' marriage with Ann Heron (PSAN3. X, p.332). William Heron had married at St Nicholas', Newcastle, 19 November 1692, Isabel Teasdale, but as she is not mentioned in his will we can presume that she had predeceased him. William mentions in his will his nephew Thomas Heron of Newcastle, butcher, his nephew Ralph Heron, shoemaker, William Heron son of his nephew Thomas Heron (to whom he leaves his leasehold lands in Corbridge) and Elizabeth, daughter of his late brother Thomas Heron deceased (*Dur. Prob. Off.* by C.R.H.). His nephews Thomas the butcher and Ralph the shoemaker were sons of his brother Lancelot. For Lancelot Heron and his descendants *see* HERON OF NEWCASTLE UPON TYNE.

On 2 June 1699 Thomas Heron the elder of Corbridge, gent., in consideration of a marriage to be solemnised between his son and heir Thomas Heron the younger and Elizabeth daughter of Thomas Tindall of West Brenkheugh, yeoman, settled his lands in Corbridge on them and their heirs (PSAN 3. IX, p.108). Thomas Heron and Elizabeth Tindall were married at Longframlington 7 July 1691. He was buried at Corbridge 29 August 1723; by his w.d. three days before, he gives to his wife Elizabeth 'all my real and personal estate paying and discharging all my debts, and as for the remainder as she thinks fit amongst her and my children'. His widow Elizabeth made her w.d. 10 December 1726; she directs that a close in Corbridge Eastfield called Bloody Acre is to be sold and £140 of the proceeds are to be divided between her five children Lancelot, Cuthbert, Elizabeth, Anne and Isabel. The children are to have their money at different ages, Lancelot at 25, Cuthbert at 24, Elizabeth at 29, Anne at 24, and Isabel at 24 years of age. She gives to her eldest son Thomas Heron the sum of half a guinea, to her son William the close bedstead and grates, and to her three daughters all her other household goods. The eldest son, Thomas Heron, thus so casually mentioned in his mother's will, was apprenticed on 13 November 1710 to Thomas Thompson of Newcastle, barber surgeon. Thomas Heron the barber surgeon died before 5 April 1738, when William Heron of North Shields, carpenter, and Cuthbert Heron of Corbridge, mason, 'two of the sons of Thomas Heron, late of Corbridge, gentleman', sold a messuage in Corbridge to John Aynsley of Hexham, gent.; their sisters, Elizabeth wife of John Bell of Newcastle, hostman, Ann Heron and Isabell Heron were parties to the sale.

The other brother, Lancelot Heron, may be identified with a great deal of probability as the Lancelot Heron, 'son of Thomas Heron of Corbridge, yeoman, deceased', who was apprenticed 2 July 1724 to Thomas Heron of Newcastle, butcher, made free of the Newcastle Butchers Company 12 October 1732 and admitted a freeman of Newcastle the same year.

In a pedigree printed in NCH. IV, p.345, and based on a pedigree in the *Hodgson MSS* drawn up about 1819, Thomas Heron the barber surgeon has been identified with Thomas Heron of Newcastle, butcher, the father of 'sir' Cuthbert Heron who claimed the Heron of Chipchase baronetcy. This identification has since been thought doubtful (NCH. X, p.166) and in fact must be entirely discarded. The claimant was son of Thomas Heron of Newcastle,

HERON of CORBRIDGE

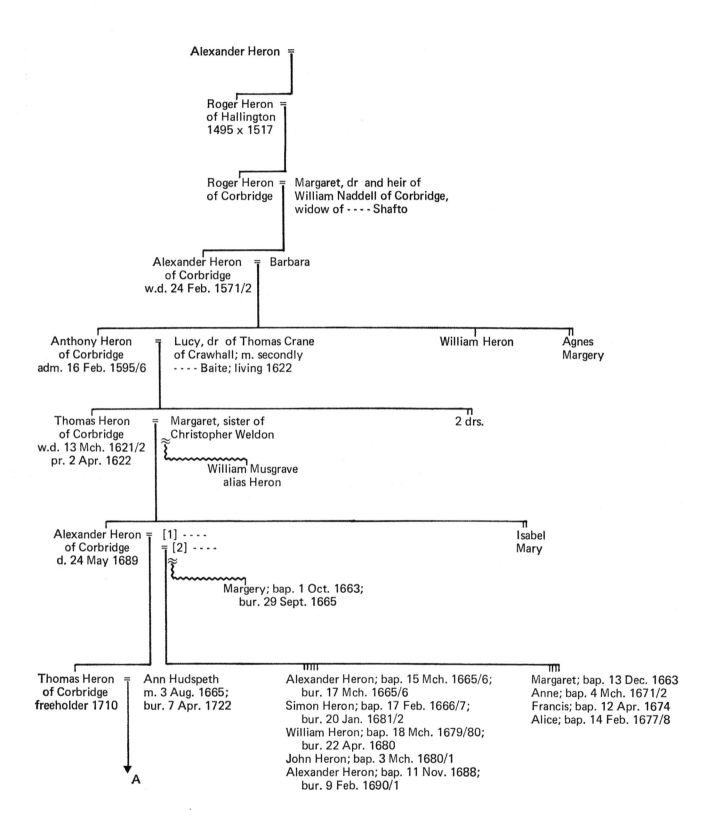

Alexander Heron =

Roger Heron =
of Hallington
1495 x 1517

Roger Heron = Margaret, dr and heir of
of Corbridge | William Naddell of Corbridge,
widow of - - - - Shafto

Alexander Heron = Barbara
of Corbridge
w.d. 24 Feb. 1571/2

Anthony Heron = Lucy, dr of Thomas Crane   William Heron   Agnes
of Corbridge   of Crawhall; m. secondly   Margery
adm. 16 Feb. 1595/6   - - - - Baite; living 1622

Thomas Heron = Margaret, sister of   2 drs.
of Corbridge   Christopher Weldon
w.d. 13 Mch. 1621/2
pr. 2 Apr. 1622
                  William Musgrave
                  alias Heron

Alexander Heron = [1] - - - -   Isabel
of Corbridge   = [2] - - - -   Mary
d. 24 May 1689

                  Margery; bap. 1 Oct. 1663;
                     bur. 29 Sept. 1665

Thomas Heron = Ann Hudspeth   Alexander Heron; bap. 15 Mch. 1665/6;   Margaret; bap. 13 Dec. 1663
of Corbridge   m. 3 Aug. 1665;   bur. 17 Mch. 1665/6   Anne; bap. 4 Mch. 1671/2
freeholder 1710 bur. 7 Apr. 1722   Simon Heron; bap. 17 Feb. 1666/7;   Francis; bap. 12 Apr. 1674
                                       bur. 20 Jan. 1681/2   Alice; bap. 14 Feb. 1677/8
                                    William Heron; bap. 18 Mch. 1679/80;
                                       bur. 22 Apr. 1680
                                    John Heron; bap. 3 Mch. 1680/1
               A   Alexander Heron; bap. 11 Nov. 1688;
                                       bur. 9 Feb. 1690/1

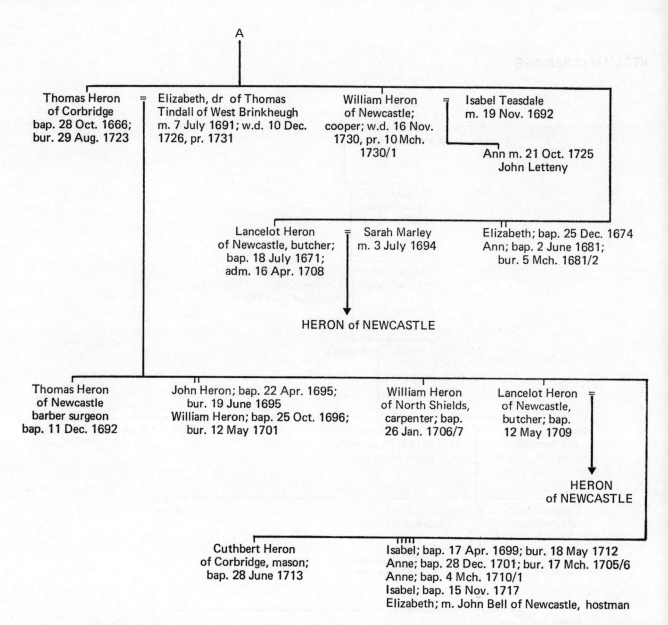

A

Thomas Heron
of Corbridge
bap. 28 Oct. 1666;
bur. 29 Aug. 1723
= Elizabeth, dr of Thomas
Tindall of West Brinkheugh
m. 7 July 1691; w.d. 10 Dec.
1726, pr. 1731

William Heron
of Newcastle;
cooper; w.d. 16 Nov.
1730, pr. 10 Mch.
1730/1
= Isabel Teasdale
m. 19 Nov. 1692

Ann m. 21 Oct. 1725
John Letteny

Lancelot Heron
of Newcastle, butcher;
bap. 18 July 1671;
adm. 16 Apr. 1708
= Sarah Marley
m. 3 July 1694

Elizabeth; bap. 25 Dec. 1674
Ann; bap. 2 June 1681;
bur. 5 Mch. 1681/2

HERON of NEWCASTLE

Thomas Heron
of Newcastle
barber surgeon
bap. 11 Dec. 1692

John Heron; bap. 22 Apr. 1695;
bur. 19 June 1695
William Heron; bap. 25 Oct. 1696;
bur. 12 May 1701

William Heron
of North Shields,
carpenter; bap.
26 Jan. 1706/7

Lancelot Heron =
of Newcastle,
butcher; bap.
12 May 1709

HERON
of NEWCASTLE

Cuthbert Heron
of Corbridge, mason;
bap. 28 June 1713

Isabel; bap. 17 Apr. 1699; bur. 18 May 1712
Anne; bap. 28 Dec. 1701; bur. 17 Mch. 1705/6
Anne; bap. 4 Mch. 1710/1
Isabel; bap. 15 Nov. 1717
Elizabeth; m. John Bell of Newcastle, hostman

butcher, who was an illegitimate son of another Thomas Heron of Newcastle, also a butcher.

HERON OF NEWCASTLE UPON TYNE

LANCELOT HERON, third son of Thomas Heron of Corbridge, senior, by his wife Ann Hudspeth, was apprenticed 11 May 1686 to George Kirkley of Newcastle, butcher, was made free of the Newcastle Butchers' Company 19 April 1694, and became a freeman of Newcastle the same year. Four of his sons became butchers, and another son a cordwainer. The four butcher sons were entered in the books of the Butchers' Company whilst still very young, Thomas and Peter on 2 March 1697/8 and Lancelot and John on 10 February 1702/3. Peter had been baptised at All Saints, Newcastle on 8 June 1697 and Lancelot on 14 December 1699. The two elder sons were probably Thomas Heron, butcher, and Ralph Heron, cordwainer, both mentioned in the w.d. 16 November 1730 of their uncle William Heron of Newcastle, cooper.

Thomas Heron, butcher, had two sons who were entered in the books of the Newcastle Butchers' Company. They were Thomas Heron entered 13 April 1727 and William Heron entered 12 February 1728/9. The latter was probably named after his great uncle William Heron, cooper, who left him his leasehold lands in Corbridge. Besides these two legitimate sons, Thomas Heron appears to have had an illegitimate son Thomas Heron. Thomas, 'natural' son of Thomas Heron, Newcastle, was apprenticed on 24 December 1750 to John Brown of Newcastle, butcher. He was made free of the Newcastle Butchers' Company 13 February 1760 and a freeman of Newcastle on 3 April 1758. The pedigree in *NCH*. IV, p.345 calls him son of Thomas Heron of Heron's Hill, Corbridge, by his wife Elizabeth Hudspeth, and states that he was baptised at Corbridge on 11 September 1692. Thomas Heron of Heron's Hill died in 1723 and his wife Elizabeth Tindall 1726 x 1731. If Thomas Heron the butcher was apprenticed in 1750 at the normal age of 14 he would have been born *circa* 1736 and cannot therefore have been a son of Thomas Heron of Corbridge. There was no Thomas Heron baptised at Corbridge 11 September 1692, although there are two entries in the Registers of 'Thomas son of Thomas Heron, junior, Corbridge', being baptised on 29 November 1692 and again on 11 December 1692. The first of these entries was perhaps a note made by the vicar of the child's birth. In any case this Thomas Heron was Thomas Heron of Newcastle, barber surgeon, eldest son of Thomas Heron, junior, of Corbridge.

Thomas Heron, butcher, married Jane Brown of the par. of All Saints, Newcastle, who married secondly at St John's, Newcastle, 20 February 1759 William Mewburn. Thomas Heron is stated to have made his will on 24 October 1754 and to have died 3 October 1757. The will is not now in the *Durham Probate Office*.

Cuthbert son of Thomas Heron, butcher, was made a freeman of Newcastle 16 January 1775 and sworn 20 February 1777. This was the Cuthbert Heron who after the death of sir Thomas Heron Middleton, 5th baronet, assumed the title. Being well known on Tyneside he was normally addressed as 'Sir' Cuthbert. He died in Gallowgate, Newcastle, 26 May 1825, aged 71. His only son 'Sir' Thomas Heron died 28 October 1830 aged 49. In a letter dated 27 November 1819 to a Mr Petyt of 80 Broad Street, London, 'Sir' Thomas stated:—

'My father always considered that Thomas Heron of Heron's Hill was an elder brother of Cuthbert Heron of Durham, father of the late sir Thomas, and from the strong likeness between the latter and my father must have been a near connection. Sir Thomas was an officer in a foot regiment when he assumed the title and afterwards retired from the army. At his death Mary Baron, his only child, sent by his desire with her complements the original patent, and also said would give up any other papers relative to the family, but being indisposed went to the south, and never saw her afterwards; her only living issue is Mary wife of Major Lunn of Oundle, Northamptonshire, with whom we still occasionally correspond. I take the liberty of sending you a copy of the patent; the original is in Latin, and was deciphered a few years back. I also send some letters for your perusal on family affairs; one was from Mr Lancelot Heron of Morpeth, who was always angry at my father not getting himself righted, but he felt so confident in his mind that the title was in his possession, and undisputed by any rival, that he neglected to pay the heralds' fees, and was of course put out of the Red Book. He has been addressed as a baronet by many of the first people of the land (when chairman of the shipping interest of the port of Tyne), also received thanks for his military services, and bore his majesty's commission as a captain of a volunteer corps raised partly at his own expense in 1797, and also as that of lieut.-colonel in 1803 until the end of the war. He has voted for the county of York as a baronet, also signed the writ for the county of Northumberland, and acted as a grand juryman for the same county.'

'Sir' Thomas Heron had five sisters, Jane wife of Joseph Rennoldson, Ann (d. 12 June 1859 aged 76), Margaret (d. 2 June 1863 aged 75), Elizabeth (d. 4 November 1813 aged 24) and Sarah wife of James Laing. Mrs Rennoldson and Mrs Laing both left descendants.

In 1898 there were exhibited at a meeting of the Society of Antiquaries of Newcastle upon Tyne, a silver patch box with a large garnet set in the centre of the lid, and a small cylindrical rosewood spice-box. These were stated to be relics of the Heron family and were the property of Mr Robert Warden of Gateshead, whose first wife was a descendant of the Herons (*PSAN2*, VIII, p.240).

Ralph Heron the cordwainer married at Eglingham 8 June 1731 Frances Scurfield of Eglingham. Administration of the goods of Ralph Heron, late of St. Nicholas', Newcastle, cordwainer, was granted 13 June 1753 to Frances Heron his widow, the bondsmen being Andrew Scurfield, gent., and Robert Bell, miller, both of St Nicholas' (*Dur. Prob. Off.* by C.R.H.). But according to the published pedigree (*NCH.* IV, p.345) this Ralph Heron, described as of Hexham, 'died owing to fatigue during contested election when Delaval was a candidate', *viz.* 1774.

Ralph Heron's eldest son, Ralph Heron of Hexham afterwards of Clavering Place, Newcastle, attorney, was bailiff of Hexham from 1765 until his death on 13 April 1801 aged 64. He had made a runaway marriage at Gretna Green with Ann daughter of George Cuthbertson, town clerk of Newcastle, and they had a large family of five sons and five daughters. None of the sons married and three of them had tragic endings. The sons were George Heron, lieutenant 52nd regt, who died in India 13 June 1789; Ralph Heron, killed in the Spital, Newcastle, by a fall from Lunardi's balloon 19 September 1786; William Heron, died in infancy 1766; Walter Heron of Newcastle, solicitor, died unmarried 5 July 1811; and Charles Heron, killed at sea 29 July 1803 by an explosion of gunpowder on the *Caledonia* of which he was 2nd officer (*The Calcutta Monthly Journal*, August 1803). The two surviving daughters Frances and Charlotte became coheiresses in 1796 to George Cuthbertson the younger. They were ladies of the manor of Haltwhistle and both died unmarried.

Ralph Heron, cordwainer, and his wife Frances Scurfield had two younger sons. William son of Ralph Heron, cordwainer, was made a freeman of Newcastle by patrimony 18 January 1763; he was of Hexham, cordwainer, 1774 when he voted as a freeman of Newcastle; he is stated to have 'Died on his passage to India' (*NCH.* IV, p.345). Lancelot son of Ralph Heron, cordwainer, was a freeman of Newcastle 20 January 1772; he was living at Alston 1780 when he voted as a freeman of Newcastle. This was Lancelot Heron of Morpeth mentioned in 'Sir' Thomas Heron's letter of 27 November 1819. He died 29 January 1813. His only child Frances died unmarried at Emsworth, Hants., in 1868.

There was a second Lancelot Heron of Newcastle, butcher. He was the third surviving son of Thomas Heron of Corbridge, junior, by his wife Elizabeth Tindall. He was apprenticed 2 July 1724 to Thomas Heron of Newcastle, butcher (his cousin), made free of the Newcastle Butchers' Company 12 October 1732, and admitted a freeman of Newcastle 11 October 1732. Lancelot Heron had two sons Ralph and William both admitted to the Newcastle Butchers' Company by patrimony on 21 January 1741/2.

HERON OF MELDON, PAR. MELDON

By inquisition taken in the castle of Newcastle upon Tyne before John de Scotherskelf, escheator of our lord the king in the county of Northumberland, on Tuesday in the third

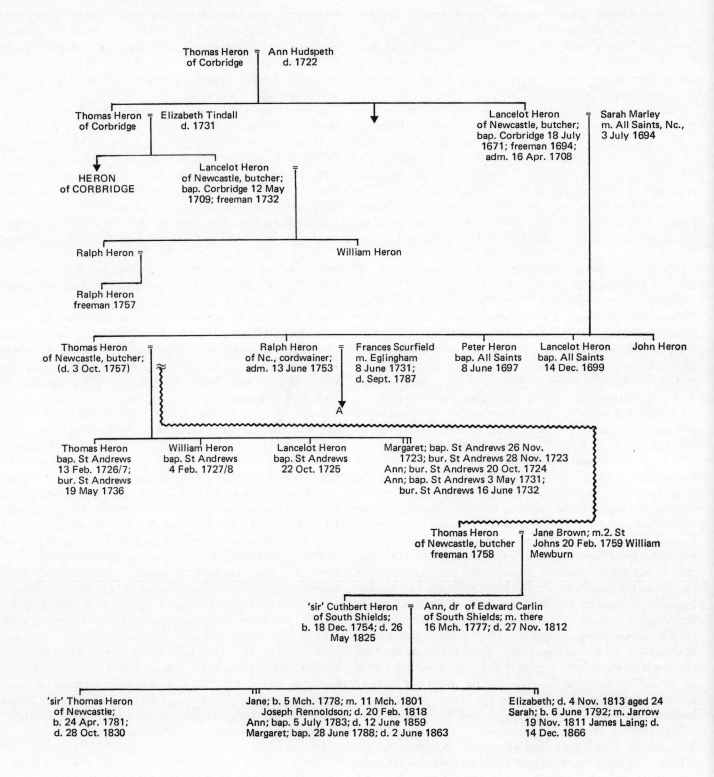

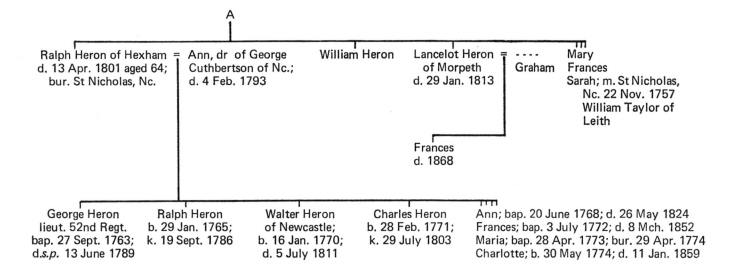

A

| Ralph Heron of Hexham
d. 13 Apr. 1801 aged 64;
bur. St Nicholas, Nc. | = | Ann, dr of George
Cuthbertson of Nc.;
d. 4 Feb. 1793 | William Heron | Lancelot Heron
of Morpeth
d. 29 Jan. 1813 | = | . . . .
Graham | Mary
Frances
Sarah; m. St Nicholas,
Nc. 22 Nov. 1757
William Taylor of
Leith |

Frances
d. 1868

| George Heron
lieut. 52nd Regt.
bap. 27 Sept. 1763;
d.*s.p.* 13 June 1789 | Ralph Heron
b. 29 Jan. 1765;
k. 19 Sept. 1786 | Walter Heron
of Newcastle;
b. 16 Jan. 1770;
d. 5 July 1811 | Charles Heron
b. 28 Feb. 1771;
k. 29 July 1803 | Ann; bap. 20 June 1768; d. 26 May 1824
Frances; bap. 3 July 1772; d. 8 Mch. 1852
Maria; bap. 28 Apr. 1773; bur. 29 Apr. 1774
Charlotte; b. 30 May 1774; d. 11 Jan. 1859 |

week of quadragesima 42 E.III (1368/9) it was found that Isabella de Riggesby, fourth daughter and heir of William and Isabella de Denom, granted by fine to William Heron, *chivaler*, and John Heron, *chivaler*, the reversion of a quarter part of the manors of Meldon and Riplington, which ought to have reverted to them after the death of the said Isabella de Denom, to hold to them and their heirs (*HN.* ii, II, p.6n). The two Herons who thus acquired a quarter of Meldon and Riplington must have been sir William Heron of Ford and his brother sir John Heron of Crawley.

An inquisition taken on 20 September 1404 after the death of Thomas Heron, found that he had died seised of Meldon, one quarter of which was held of the king *in capite* by knight's service, and three quarters of Alan de Fenwick by a rent of 6s. 8d.; he also held a quarter part of Deanham, and lands in Whalton, Rivergreen, Thornton, Fenrother and Titlington (*HN.* iii, II, p.264). Thomas Heron was almost certainly a younger son of sir William Heron. He and other sons of sir William were plaintiffs in 1351 and 1373 (*de Banco Roll* in *AA*3. VI, pp.53, 60). In a settlement made by sir William in June 1377 of the manor of West Whelpington on his son Andrew Heron, his other sons Thomas, Robert and John are remainder men (*NDD.* p.106). It would seem that sir William Heron had acquired Meldon and other lands to make provision for his son Thomas.

Thomas Heron's son and heir was Nicholas Heron who was under age at his father's death. Proof of his age was taken at the king's castle of Newcastle upon Tyne on 4 March 8 H.IV (1406/7) when it was found that Nicholas had been born at Meldon and baptised in Meldon church, and was aged 21 years on the feast of the Conversion of St Paul last past (25 January 1406/7). One of his godfathers was Nicholas Raymes esq. (*AA*2. XXII, p.117). In 1424 Nicholas Heron and Katherine his wife laid claim to the manor of Bockenfield against Liell Heron. Two years earlier he had forcibly entered on to the lands with 30 armed men. He does not appear to have been successful in his claim. His wife Katherine may have been the Katherine Heron who was godmother to Thomas Hesilrig of Eslington at his baptism

in Whittingham church in 1408; she had given her godchild 20s., and a gold ring (*Ib.,* p.125).

Nothing further is recorded about Nicholas Heron except that he owned the *turris de Meldon* in 1415 (*AA*2. XIV, p.16), and was one of the commissioners to receive oaths of allegiance in 1434. For the next 100 years little is known about the Herons of Meldon, though a skeleton pedigree in Vincent's *Northumberland* (*Her. Col.* No. 149, folio 23) fills in the gap with two Thomas Herons, father and son. The elder of these two Thomases was no doubt Thomas Herone of 'Meldowne', aged 66 when at Morpeth on 28 June 1472 he gave evidence at the proof of age of William Bartram of Bothal (*AA*2. XXIV, p.127). The second Thomas Heron is said to have had an elder son Roger who died *s.p.* and to have been succeeded by a younger son Alexander.

With this Alexander Heron we are on sure ground again. On the death of sir William Heron of Ford on 8 July 1535 Alexander was one of those who unsuccessfully claimed the Ford estates as heir male.

Marjory Fenwick of Stanton, widow, 'late wife unto sir Rauffe Fenwik, knight, deceased', made an estate in fee to Thomas Fenwick of Little Harle, John Dent of Byker and Alexander Heron of Meldon, gents, of the manor of Stanton and other lands so that they could carry out the terms of her last will 'as more at length it doth appear in a deed made 7 August 27 H.VIII' (1535). Alexander Heron of Meldon, esquire, is on a list of the gentlemen of the Middle Marches in 1550 (*HN.* iii, II, p.246). He was a commissioner for enclosures in 1552 (Nicolson, *Leges Marchiarum*, p.332). In March 1557 Alexander Heron of Meldon and Gerard Heron of Riplington were trustees for Ralph Fenwick of Stanton. Hodgson suggests that Alexander Heron married Margery sister and coheir of sir Thomas Gray, but he was mistaken in this as Margery Gray's husband was John Heron of Chipchase. Anthony Mitford of Ponteland by his w.d. 18 July 1572 leaves to his father-in-law Alexander Heron, 10s. and his 'black velvet jacket and one quarter of wheat and a quarter of oats'; the inventory of Mitford's goods dated 13 Feb. 1572/3 is signed by Alexander Heron esq., and

Jerrard Heron of Riplington, gent. (Raine, *MS Wills and Inv*. I, p.249 and VII, p.9).

It is uncertain when Alexander Heron died as his eldest son and successor was also called Alexander. The elder Alexander besides his daughter Juliana Mitford had two other daughters—Cecilia wife of Anthony Hedworth, second son of John Hedworth of Harraton, co. Durham (1575 Vis. Ped. of Hedworth), and Isabella wife of Robert Middleton of Belsay. Isabella is called daughter and coheir of Alexander Heron in the 1666 Visitation pedigree of Middleton, but the description coheir is probably inaccurate.

David Taylor, vicar of Bolam, by his w.d. 17 March 1573 appoints 'Mr Alexander Heron of Meldon, gent.' a supervisor of his will (SS. 2, p.393). It is probably the younger Alexander who is referred to in the w.d. 24 February 1587/8 of Lowrance Thorneton of Netherwitton; he leaves a moiety of his lands in Bolam to his son George Thorneton 'after the death of Alexander Heron esq.' (SS. 28, p.313).

On 5 February 1590 Alexander Heron settled his lands in Meldon, Rivergreen, Riplington, Deanham, Whalton, Temple Thornton, Heron's Close, Fenrother, Morpeth and Riding, on himself for life, with remainders to his nephew Alexander son of Roger Heron and to Margaret Middleton his wife and their heirs male, to his nephew Robert Heron, and to his brother Thomas Heron. Hodgson states that this Alexander Heron died 30 September 1598 but this is the date of death of Alexander Heron's nephew and successor, another Alexander Heron.

Alexander Heron the nephew died in Newcastle and was buried at Meldon. For the conveyance of the corpse and for the funeral dinner and other rites his brother Robert Heron paid £7 into the Consistory Court. The inquisition taken on 26 September 1599 found that Alexander Heron had died seised of the manor and vill of Meldon, a messuage called Heron's Close by Fenrother, a messuage called Deanham, half the vill of Riplington, a messuage in Whalton, and a messuage in Thornton; his heir was his brother Robert aged 23 years and more.

Although the settlement of 1590 had passed over Alexander Heron's brother Roger Heron in favour of Roger's son Alexander, Roger was still living. On 12 January 1608/9 James Raymes of South Middleton appoints his father-in-law Roger Heron of Riplington, a supervisor of his will (Raine, *MS Wills and Inv*. II, p.211). On 30 June 1614 Roger Heron made his will whereby he leaves his lands in Riplington to sir William Selby of Shortflatt and Roger Widdrington of Cartington, presumably in trust; he mentions his 'daughters' Margaret Heron and Isabel Errington (*Ib*., I, p.45). Margaret was perhaps his widowed daughter-in-law.

On 31 May 1609 Robert Heron of Meldon made his will. His lands in Meldon were leased to Thomas Lumsden apparently by way of mortgage, and Lumsden is to enjoy these during the residue of the years in his lease, and after that they are to go to the right heirs of the testator. He leaves his lands in Riplington 'after the decease of Roger Hearon my loving father' to 'Catherine my loving wife and to my children to be equally divided amongst them'.

Robert Heron's heir was his son William, aged 12 years and 4 months at his father's death. During the minority, sir William Fenwick of Wallington held a mortgage on Meldon and endeavoured to foreclose, but the Court of Wards and Liveries held that the equity of redemption was held by Thomas Lumsden who had a prior mortgage in the sum of £590. When William Heron came of age he found that his estate was heavily encumbered, and in 1622 he conveyed Meldon to sir William Fenwick.

HERON OF BOCKENFIELD, PAR. FELTON

In the early part of the 13th century, the Herons of Ford held property in Bockenfield, but the holding was a very small one consisting of merely a cottage and half a ploughland. They also held the adjoining property of Helm-on-the-Hill. In 1269 Walter Heron of Ford was defendant in a suit respecting common of pasture in Bockenfield. Again in 1278 there was an action against Walter Heron for common of pasture, apparently in Bockenfield. At his death in 1296 William Heron, Walter's father, held 4 acres in Bockenfield, and a waste place there called Elstrother and Helme.

Nothing further is known about the Heron property in Bockenfield until 21 April 1340 when William Heron of Ford had a grant of free warren in his demesne lands at Bockenfield and elsewhere. By the early 15th century a branch of the Heron family had acquired the whole manor. William Mitford at his death on 7 March 1422/3 held 3 messuages, 80 acres of land, and one acre of meadow in Bockenfield of 'Nicholas Heron, lord of Bockenfield'. Shortly after this John Mitford, son of the same William Mitford, delivered to Nicholas Heron of Meldon certain writings respecting Bockenfield and other lands. From this it appears probable that Nicholas Heron of Meldon was in fact the lord of Bockenfield. There was however a resident family of Herons there, and in 1422 a certain Lyel Heron complained to the bishop of Durham, chancellor of England, that he was possessed of lands and tenements of his own right and inheritance and that Nicholas Heron of Meldon had forcibly entered on to the lands with 30 armed men and expelled the complainant and his wife and children. The result of this appeal is unknown, and not for 120 years have we any information about the owners of Bockenfield.

On 6 October 1549 Margaret Heron of Bockenfield, evidently widow of a cadet of the main family of Heron of Bockenfield, appointed John Heron of Bockenfield, esquire, to be supervisor of her will. Her son John Heron is to be in the custody of his uncle Anthony Heron. She mentions in her will her three daughters Margaret Atkinson, Elenor Atkinson and Isabel Heron (Raine, *MS Wills and Inv*. II, p.33).

In 1552 John Heron of Bockenfield was a commissioner for enclosures in the Middle Marches for the district 'from the sea to the street between Coquet and Wansbeck' (Nicolson, *Leges Marchiarum*, p.222). He was no doubt the John Heron of Bockenfield who with his sons was concerned in the Carr-Heron feud in 1558.

On 29 July 1575 Lionel Heron of East Thickley, co. Durham, registered his pedigree at Flower's Visitation of Durham. He was third son of John Heron of Bockenfield, then living, by his wife Margery daughter of sir William Lisle. His grandfather was another John Heron of Bockenfield, whom he stated was 'descended of a younger brother

HERON of MELDON, par. MELDON

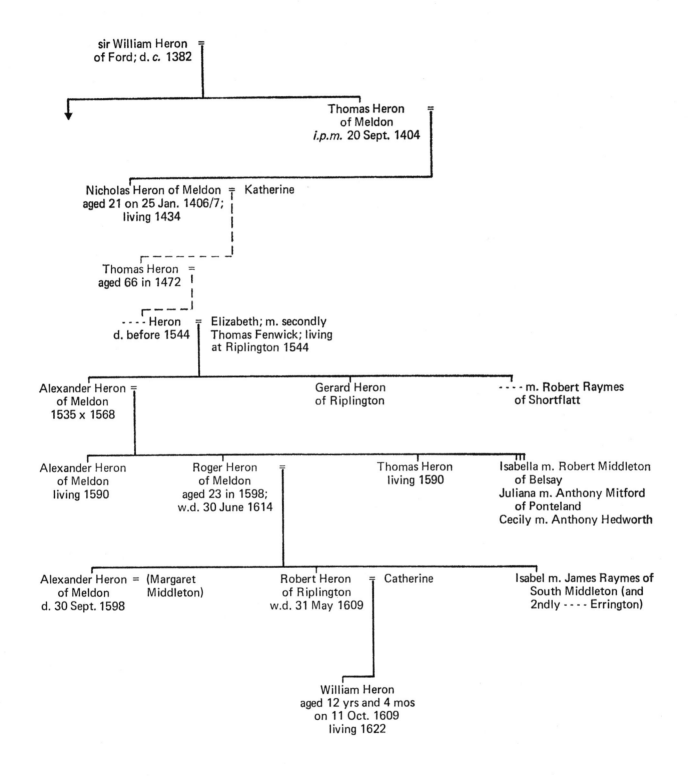

of the house of Ford, Northumberland'. The John Heron of 1558 could have been either the father or grandfather of Lionel Heron. The latter had three brothers, two older and one younger than himself. The eldest brother was Humphrey Heron of Bockenfield, and the second brother Ronian (or Bryan) Heron. He was perhaps Nynion Heron of Killingworth, gent., the inventory of whose goods is dated 23 October 1597. The youngest brother was George Heron who had married Jane daughter of sir William Bulmer, widow of William Wrenne (or Warren). According to the 1575 Visitation pedigree of Grey of Horton, Humphrey Heron of Bockenfield married Ursula one of the six daughters and coheiresses of sir Thomas Grey (d.1571); another of the Grey heiresses married John Heron of Chipchase, which accounts for the fact that Humphrey Heron's younger son Lionel is called cousin of John Heron of Chipchase sometime after 1576. Lionel Heron had been wounded in a fight with the Carrs and in company with several relatives had to flee the country (*Carr Family*, III, p.17). Lionel can have been little more than a boy when this happened, as in 1571 his mother Ursula is stated to have been aged 35 years and more (*Ib.*, II, p.134).

According to the 1666 Visitation pedigree, Humphrey Heron was living at Wintrick, a farm in the manor of Bockenfield, 1 December 1582. He died before 18 March 1585/6 when his son Lionel Heron rendered an account as administrator of his goods. His son and heir was John Heron then aged 22.

On 14 June 1592 John Heron of Bockenfield entered into a bond with Henry, earl of Northumberland, under a penalty of £80 that he would permit the earl's tenants in Thirston to exercise common of pasture on Bockenfield Moor without molestation by him. In a letter dated 31 July 1592 the earl states, 'The injuries offered me and my tenants by Heron of Bockenfield I will according to law reform, and requite to the example of others my oppressors'.

John Heron died at Bockenfield, 6 February 1607, seised of the manor of Bockenfield with the hamlets of Burgham, Wintrick, etc. The inquisition after his death was not taken until 15 August 1622 when his son and heir Richard was aged 36 years. John Heron's wife was Jane daughter of Thomas Norton of Skirningham, co. Durham. About this time the hamlet of Wintrick was occupied by a member of the family, as on 30 March 1610 administration of the personal estate of John Heron of Wintrick was granted to Frances his widow, for the benefit of their children John, Robert, Thomas, Humphrey, Brian and Jane Heron, who were all under age.

These Christian names are nearly all repeated in the children of John Heron of Bockenfield himself whose family was Richard, Arthur, John, Robert, Thomas, Humphrey, Brian, Elizabeth, Anne and Fortune. This would seem to suggest that John Heron of Wintrick was the same person as John Heron of Bockenfield, especially when it is remembered that the latter's father had also lived at Wintrick in his later years. The Christian name of Arthur is so unusual in the Heron family that it is possible to identify Arthur son of John Heron (d.1607) as Ather Herron 'which was killed with a granad' and buried at St Andrew's, Newcastle, 4 October 1644. Umphra Herron buried at the same place 'in the church in the north alley', 22 November 1697, was

also, judging by his Christian name, a scion of the Herons of Bockenfield.

Richard Heron of Bockenfield made his will 18 May 1665 and it was proved at Durham by his son and heir John Heron 12 September 1665. John Heron was his sole executor; Humphrey Heron was one of the witnesses. Richard mentions in his will his eldest daughter Barbara, wife of Robert Johnson of Newcastle and his second daughter Jane, wife of William Carr of Eshot. The two daughters were children of Richard's 3rd wife, Anne daughter of William Barnes of Darlington, co. Durham. His son John was by his second wife, Jane daughter of Anthony Felton of Old Felton. His first wife, Margaret daughter of Robert Hazelrigg of Swarland had died without children.

The year following his father's death, John Herron registered his pedigree at Dugdale's *Visitation of Northumberland*, when he was 52 years of age. He was sheriff of Northumberland in 1669, and was of Beverley, Yorks., on the 8th August 1672 when he sold Bockenfield to Edward Widdrington of Felton. He had two daughters who were his coheiresses, Elizabeth wife of George Dawnay, son of viscount Downe, and Catherine, who married firstly sir John Hotham, bart, and secondly John Moyser of Beverley.

In the Visitation pedigree of 1666 two small scraps of early pedigree are entered as if to suggest that either traditionally they represented early members of the family, or that they were taken from earlier deeds still belonging to the family. These scraps are:—

(a) 'Lyell Heron, esq., living 2 H.V. (1414/5) and 9 H.VI (1431), by his wife Margaret, had three sons, *viz.* John, son and heir, living 9 H.VI (1431) married Agnes daughter of Thomas Burrell, Gerard Heron and William Heron'. This seems to reflect the Lyel Heron who in 1422 had the dispute with Nicholas Heron of Meldon.

(b) 'Agnes de Kirketon and her three sons Lyellus, Odonellas and Jordanus'. These persons were living in the late 14th century, and on 1 February 1377 sir William Heron, son of sir Roger Heron, lord of Ford, granted to Jurdan son of Agnes de Kirketon all lands which the grantor had of the feoffment of John Robinson and Marjorie his wife, daughter of William de Brankeston in the vill of Hetherslaw and the water mill with all the suit thereof; to hold to Jurdan and his heirs male, remainders successively to Odinel son of Agnes and brother of Jurdan, to Liell son of the said Agnes; to the grantor and his heirs male; to the right heirs of Jurdan (*NDD.* p.95). In 1424 Nicholas Heron and Katherine his wife were defendants in a suit by Liellus son of Agnes de Kirton about the manor of Bockenfield which sir William Heron son of sir Roger Heron had given to Jordan son of Agnes de Kirkton, and his heirs. It is evident that the descendants of Agnes de Kirkton took the name of Heron, and founded the family of Heron of Bockenfield.

There is a strong suspicion that this Liell son of Agnes de Kirketon was the same person as the Lyel Heron of 1422 and therefore ancestor of the Herons of Bockenfield.

The male line of the family, after the death of John Heron in 1678, was carried on by the descendants of his uncle Thomas Heron for whom see HERON OF NEWARK-ON-TRENT.

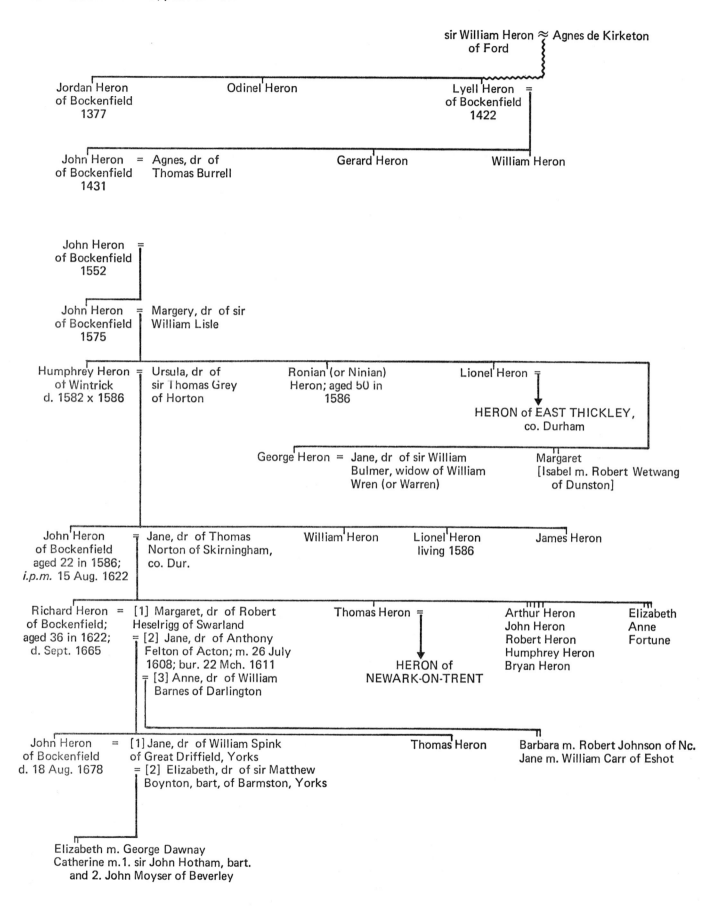

sir William Heron ≈ Agnes de Kirketon
of Ford

Jordan Heron
of Bockenfield
1377

Odinel Heron

Lyell Heron =
of Bockenfield
1422

John Heron = Agnes, dr of
of Bockenfield   Thomas Burrell
1431

Gerard Heron

William Heron

John Heron =
of Bockenfield
1552

John Heron = Margery, dr of sir
of Bockenfield   William Lisle
1575

Humphrey Heron = Ursula, dr of
of Wintrick   sir Thomas Grey
d. 1582 x 1586   of Horton

Ronian (or Ninian)
Heron; aged 50 in
1586

Lionel Heron =

HERON of EAST THICKLEY,
co. Durham

George Heron = Jane, dr of sir William
Bulmer, widow of William
Wren (or Warren)

Margaret
[Isabel m. Robert Wetwang
of Dunston]

John Heron =
of Bockenfield
aged 22 in 1586;
i.p.m. 15 Aug. 1622

Jane, dr of Thomas
Norton of Skirningham,
co. Dur.

William Heron

Lionel Heron
living 1586

James Heron

Richard Heron =
of Bockenfield;
aged 36 in 1622;
d. Sept. 1665

[1] Margaret, dr of Robert
Heselrigg of Swarland
= [2] Jane, dr of Anthony
Felton of Acton; m. 26 July
1608; bur. 22 Mch. 1611
= [3] Anne, dr of William
Barnes of Darlington

Thomas Heron =

HERON of
NEWARK-ON-TRENT

Arthur Heron
John Heron
Robert Heron
Humphrey Heron
Bryan Heron

Elizabeth
Anne
Fortune

John Heron =
of Bockenfield
d. 18 Aug. 1678

[1] Jane, dr of William Spink
of Great Driffield, Yorks
= [2] Elizabeth, dr of sir Matthew
Boynton, bart, of Barmston, Yorks

Thomas Heron

Barbara m. Robert Johnson of Nc.
Jane m. William Carr of Eshot

Elizabeth m. George Dawnay
Catherine m.1. sir John Hotham, bart.
and 2. John Moyser of Beverley

HERON OF CORNHILL, PAR. NORHAM

WILLIAM HERON, younger son of sir William Heron of Ford (d.*circa*1382) is mentioned in the estate settlements made by his father in 1337 and 1340. It was probably his son, also called William, who married Isabel daughter and heiress of Richard Scot of Benwell.

William and Isabel's son, sir William Heron III of Cornhill and Tweedmouth proved himself heir to John Hawkeswell of Elswick in 1422 and died in 1425. It seems probable that Margaret, widow of William Heron III took as her second husband Robert Monceux.

Sir William left two daughters his coheiresses. They were Elizabeth wife of John Heron of Ford, and Isabel wife of John Bertram. Between 1415 and 1418 two parts of half the manor of Benwell and the reversion of the other third after the death of Margaret wife of Robert Monceaux were settled on John and Isabel Bertram (*NCH*. XIII, 218-219, 242).

HERON OF NEWARK-ON-TRENT

THOMAS HERON, younger son of that John Heron of Bockenfield who died in 1607, was a major of horse in the Royalist army and was killed at the battle of Marston Moor on 2 July 1644. He had resided at Stirrup, parish of Blyth, Notts. His eldest son was Robert Heron of Newark-on-Trent, aged 26 in 1666, and admitted to Lincoln's Inn on 1 March 1687/8. Robert made his will on 27 September 1707 and died on 16 May 1709. Pride in his ancestry is very evident in his will and he wishes his son and heir to be quite conversant with this. 'Although I am the lineal heir male of the family of the Herons of Bockenfield in Northumberland, I mention not this of any ostentation, but that my dear son may understand that in case my lady Hotham or madam Dawney, the two only daughters and children of John Heron, esq., of Bockenfield, and after of Beverley, where he died, shall die without issue, that he is the next heir after me (the said John Heron and me being brother's sons) to all such estates as descended to the said lady Hotham and her sister from their said father as by many letters from them, their father, my uncle, and others may appear, which are in a bundle in my desk and worthy to be carefully preserved; and also by the Heralds' Office, for when the said John Heron was high sheriff of Northumberland issued out his patent, etc., and being with him at Newcastle, he introduced me to Norroy King-at-Arms, he then keeping his office there, he caused my name and my son's, being then an infant, to be entered in the said office and paid the fees. Yet I desire no escutcheons or any great pomp or ceremonies to be used at my obsequies, for great charges upon such occasion can be no benefit to the dead but an injury to the living, therefore to be avoided'. His considerable estates at Newark, Farndon, Stirrup Norrey and elsewhere passed to his son and heir John Heron.

John Heron of Newark died 8 December 1727 and his widow Jane (daughter of Daniel Crayle of Newark) on 14 November 1742. Jane is described on her monumental inscription as a woman 'who not only manifested a pious and charitable disposition throughout her life, but did extend the influence of it to posterity by settling an annual charity for ever'. Their only son Robert Heron of Newark was lord of the manors of Westborough and Stubton, Lincs., and was appointed 6 March 1743 one of the deputy lieutenants for the county of Nottingham. He died at Newark 10 August 1753 aged 66; by his wife Elizabeth daughter of Thomas Brecknock, minister of Thorney abbey, Cambs., he had four sons John, Thomas, Robert and Richard, who each attained distinction in his particular walk of life.

John Heron the eldest son was chosen recorder of Newark on 11 February 1748 and died at Villeneuve St George in France on 8 September 1753. He had two daughters Elizabeth wife of Benjamin Fearnley of Oakwell hall, and Margaret.

The second son Thomas Heron succeeded his brother as recorder of Newark and was appointed a deputy lieutenant for Nottingham 7 July 1762. In 1774 he purchased Chilham castle in Kent, and was appointed 5 August 1782 a deputy lieutenant of Kent. Two sons of Thomas Heron died in infancy but his third son, sir Robert Heron of Stubton, bart., was MP for Grimsby in 1812 and for Peterborough 1819-1847. Sir Robert died *s.p.* 29 May 1854.

The third son Robert Heron was rector of Shawell, co. Leicester, and vicar of Basingthorpe, co. Lincoln, and died *s.p.* at Grantham 19 January 1813.

The fourth and youngest son Richard Heron was the most distinguished of the four brothers. He was Lord Treasurer's Remembrancer 1754, and Principal Secretary to the earl of Buckingham when he was lord lieutenant of Ireland. He was made a privy councillor in 1777 and created a baronet 25 July 1778. As sir Richard had no sons, a special limitation in his patent provided that the title, after sir Richard's death, should pass to his nephew Robert.

Sir Richard died 18 January 1805 aged 79 at his house in Grosvenor Square, London, and in accordance with the limitation the baronetcy passed to his nephew Robert. On the death of the latter in 1854 the baronetcy became extinct. So far as is known sir Robert Heron was the last direct male descendant of the Herons of Bockenfield.

HERON OF ESHOT, PAR. FELTON

ON 26 September 1312 sir Roger Heron of Ford purchased lands in Crawley and Hedgeley from Michael de Midelton, and gave these lands to his younger son John. This John Heron of Crawley proceeded to acquire a considerable estate in Northumberland. On 20 April 1339 he had feoffment from sir William de Felton of lands in Hedgeley. On 1 October 1340 he and his wife Elena had a grant from Robert de Helmsley of lands in Beal, and had pardon from the bishop of Durham, 5 November 1340 for acquiring them without licence. He is called John Heron, lord of Hedgeley, 11 May 1344, when he had a release from John son of William Grene of a messuage in 'Boxhill'; this is probably a misreading of Beyhill (Beal). On the Eve of St Matthew Apostle (20 September) 1345 he settled his manors of Crawley, Hedgeley, Beal and Hartside, the trustees being his brother Roger Heron and John de Chilton. In 1344 or 1345 John Heron had a grant from John de Clifford of the reversion of the third part of the manor of Morton which Margaret

HERON of NEWARK-ON-TRENT

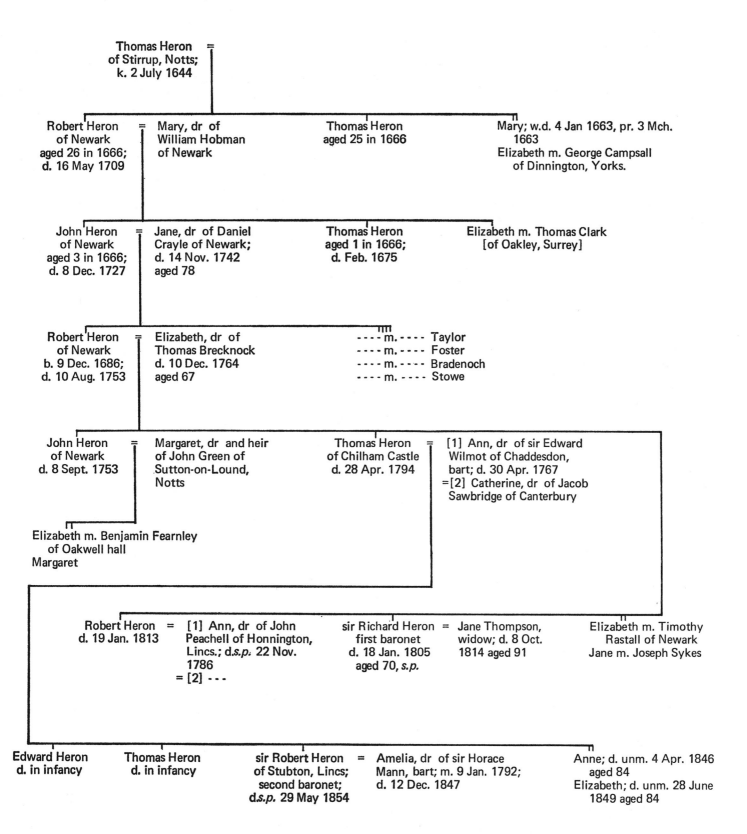

Thomas Heron
of Stirrup, Notts;
k. 2 July 1644
=

Robert Heron
of Newark
aged 26 in 1666;
d. 16 May 1709
= Mary, dr of
William Hobman
of Newark

Thomas Heron
aged 25 in 1666

Mary; w.d. 4 Jan 1663, pr. 3 Mch.
1663
Elizabeth m. George Campsall
of Dinnington, Yorks.

John Heron
of Newark
aged 3 in 1666;
d. 8 Dec. 1727
= Jane, dr of Daniel
Crayle of Newark;
d. 14 Nov. 1742
aged 78

Thomas Heron
aged 1 in 1666;
d. Feb. 1675

Elizabeth m. Thomas Clark
[of Oakley, Surrey]

Robert Heron
of Newark
b. 9 Dec. 1686;
d. 10 Aug. 1753
= Elizabeth, dr of
Thomas Brecknock
d. 10 Dec. 1764
aged 67

- - - - m. - - - - Taylor
- - - - m. - - - - Foster
- - - - m. - - - - Bradenoch
- - - - m. - - - - Stowe

John Heron
of Newark
d. 8 Sept. 1753
= Margaret, dr and heir
of John Green of
Sutton-on-Lound,
Notts

Thomas Heron
of Chilham Castle
d. 28 Apr. 1794
= [1] Ann, dr of sir Edward
Wilmot of Chaddesdon,
bart; d. 30 Apr. 1767
=[2] Catherine, dr of Jacob
Sawbridge of Canterbury

Elizabeth m. Benjamin Fearnley
of Oakwell hall
Margaret

Robert Heron
d. 19 Jan. 1813
= [1] Ann, dr of John
Peachell of Honnington,
Lincs.; d.s.p. 22 Nov.
1786
= [2] - - -

sir Richard Heron
first baronet
d. 18 Jan. 1805
aged 70, s.p.
= Jane Thompson,
widow; d. 8 Oct.
1814 aged 91

Elizabeth m. Timothy
Rastall of Newark
Jane m. Joseph Sykes

Edward Heron
d. in infancy

Thomas Heron
d. in infancy

sir Robert Heron
of Stubton, Lincs;
second baronet;
d.s.p. 29 May 1854
= Amelia, dr of sir Horace
Mann, bart; m. 9 Jan. 1792;
d. 12 Dec. 1847

Anne; d. unm. 4 Apr. 1846
aged 84
Elizabeth; d. unm. 28 June
1849 aged 84

widow of Robert de Clifford held in dower. He is called lord of Morton 28 February 1346 when he had a grant from Thomas de Standen of a moiety of the manor of Emothill. As sir John Heron, he had a grant 30 December 1358 from John de Covintre of land in Briggate and Ravensden, and on 6 January 1362 he acquired lands in the vill of Caldwell by Clifton. He had a quitclaim of the manor and vill of Eshot, 9 July 1375, from Roger Mauduit.

As sir John Heron's son and heir was also called John, it is difficult to decide to which of them certain documents refer. John Heron called *le fitz* in 1379 is obviously the son (*AA*3. XX, p.160). He was member of parliament for Northumberland in 1379. In 1385 sir John Heron made various settlements of his lands, the trustees being Roger del Bothe and William de Meryngton, chaplains. These trustees on 6 January 1385 conveyed the manor of Eshot, the vill of East Duddo, lands in Clifton and Coldwell and the reversion of lands in the vill of Thornton by Hartburn, to sir John Heron with certain remainders. These remainders were on sir William Heron, son of the said John, sir Gerard Heron, brother of the said William, John Heron son of sir John Heron brother of the said Gerard and William, and Nicholas Heron, brother of the said William. Various different interpretations of this have been made, but surely it means that the settlor sir John Heron had three sons, sir William, sir Gerard and sir John Heron, and that the second sir John was now dead, leaving three sons John, William and Nicholas. (The settlement is printed in *HN*. ii, II, p.334 under the date 6 January 1382, 8 R.II, but this regnal year is 1384/5; it is printed in *NCH*. VII, p. 342 with wrong reference; it is noted *HN*. ii, I, p.312 under wrong date 1380; printed in *Nd and Dur. Deeds, NRS*. VII, p.97, No. 20). Sir John Heron, by the same trustees, on 12 April 1385 settled the manor of Twizel and one fourth part of the manor of Tilmouth on sir Gerard Heron with remainders to sir William Heron, brother of sir Gerard; to Nicholas Heron, son of sir John Heron, brother of sirs Gerard and William; to William Heron brother of Nicholas; remainder to the right heirs of sir John Heron father of Gerard and William. In 1387 it was found that Elizabeth, widow of John Heron, had held one third of Eslington and a third of the moieties of Whittingham, Thrunton and Barton as dower of Robert de Eslington, her first husband (*AA*3. VI, p.10n).

Sir John Heron's eldest son and heir, sir William Heron, was steward of the household in 1399, a position he probably owed to the social position of his wife Elizabeth daughter of William lord Say, widow of John de Fallesley. With her he acquired the estate of Sawbridgeworth, Herts., and the courtesy title of lord Say of Sawbridgeworth. He was found heir to his brother sir Gerard Heron on 28 July 1404, but did not long survive him, dying on 20 October 1404. His second wife, Elizabeth Norbury, widow, daughter of Thomas, lord Boteler, survived him and died in 1464; she had married as her third husband, sir John Montgomery. By neither of his wives had sir William Heron any children. His heir was his nephew (not brother) John Heron then aged 23 years and upwards.

Sir Gerard Heron held several important positions on the Border. In 1386 he was a commissioner to execute the Statute of Westminster the second, touching the preservation of salmon in Tyne and Tweed. He was commissioner in 1390

with others from Scotland to prepare for the meeting of ambassadors to arrange a treaty. In 1392, 1397-1399 and 1403 he was a commissioner of array for Northumberland and in 1392 was to enquire about the water supply of Bamburgh. He was chamberlain of Berwick and receiver of the customs there from 1392 until his death, MP for Northumberland 1391-4 and again in 1397, and sheriff of the county in 1400. For his services he was given £20 a year in 1402 from the customs of Newcastle. His wife was Elizabeth daughter and coheiress of Cecily Tailler of Little Usworth, co. Durham; she and her sister Joan Riddell had lands in Little Usworth settled on them by Alice Motherby (*AA*4. XI, p.77).

In 1404 John Heron inherited Eshot and Sawbridgeworth from his uncle sir William Heron and was then aged 23. In 1409 he was heir to his brother Nicholas Heron's lands being the manor of Eppleton and lands in Houghton-le-Spring and North Hart, co. Dur., and the manor of Twizel and land in Tilmouth, Northumberland. Sir John Heron made a settlement of his estates in 1415 and the inquisition after his death is dated 20 March 1420/1. His son and heir was John Heron, then aged 8 years, who in 1460/1 made a settlement of his manors of Crawley and Eshot, a quarter of Whittingham, and Sawbridgeworth in Herts. This John Heron died in 1468, and was succeeded by his son, yet another John Heron, who died in 1478 or 1479. John Heron and his two brothers, Thomas and William, the latter being dean of St Paul's, London, assumed the surname of Say. From John descended the family of Say of Sawbridgeworth (Clutterbuck, *Hist. of Hertfordshire*, vol.iii, pp.193, 195). By some quite unexplained method, the manors of Hedgeley and Crawley became before 1483 the property of Agnes Malpas and her husband David Malpas. In 1500/1 sir William Heron of Ford was found to be cousin and heir of Agnes Malpas. When he died in 1535, sir William Heron held most of the estates in Northumberland which had belonged to the Herons of Eshot, including the manors of Beal and Eshot, with lands in Beal, Eshot, Crawley, Branton, Hedgeley and Twizel.

HERON OF HUMSHAUGH, PAR. SIMONBURN

In the 17th century there were three distinct families of Heron owning property in Humshaugh. They were no doubt connected in some way with the Herons of Chipchase but the connection cannot now be discovered. Edward Heron of Humshaugh was 'sick in body' when he made his will in May 1619. The will is a fine example of the disposition of a yeoman's estate of this time:

'One branded cow and her calf about to my sister Anne Heron her daughter Alice. To my daughter Margaret Heron the red cow and her calf at Sharpley. To George Heron a black haired whye at Sharpley with Wm Burresse in first nolt. To William Heron a black taig'd stot that is about my sister Anne Herons. To John Heron a black stot that stood next the door but one. To Cuthbert Heron 26s., being part of a black hawked stot which John Hutchinson bought of me, for which stot he was to pay me 30s., and for the residue being 4s., I do forgive the said John Hutchinson. To Barbara Heron one red whye that Thomas Usher hath in the first nolt. I give to my father the black cow and her calf that Thomas Usher hath. To Alice Hutchinson a branded cow and

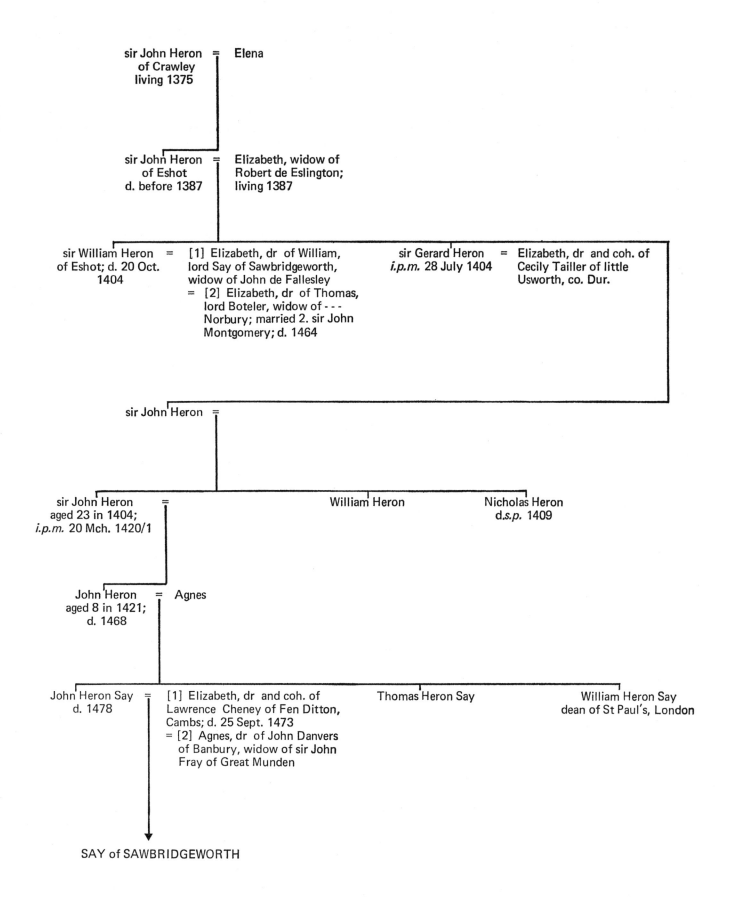

sir John Heron = Elena
of Crawley
living 1375

sir John Heron = Elizabeth, widow of
of Eshot Robert de Eslington;
d. before 1387 living 1387

sir William Heron = [1] Elizabeth, dr of William,
of Eshot; d. 20 Oct. lord Say of Sawbridgeworth,
1404 widow of John de Fallesley
= [2] Elizabeth, dr of Thomas,
lord Boteler, widow of - - -
Norbury; married 2. sir John
Montgomery; d. 1464

sir Gerard Heron = Elizabeth, dr and coh. of
i.p.m. 28 July 1404 Cecily Tailler of little
Usworth, co. Dur.

sir John Heron =

sir John Heron = William Heron Nicholas Heron
aged 23 in 1404; *d.s.p.* 1409
i.p.m. 20 Mch. 1420/1

John Heron = Agnes
aged 8 in 1421;
d. 1468

John Heron Say = [1] Elizabeth, dr and coh. of Thomas Heron Say William Heron Say
d. 1478 Lawrence Cheney of Fen Ditton, dean of St Paul's, London
Cambs; d. 25 Sept. 1473
= [2] Agnes, dr of John Danvers
of Banbury, widow of sir John
Fray of Great Munden

SAY of SAWBRIDGEWORTH

her calf that is about Thomas Ushers. To Eleanor Hutchinson a black taig'd cow and her calf that is about Thomas Ushers. To Margaret Hutchinson a brown cow that is about her fathers. To Annes Heron the cow that is with her father. To my sister Jane a red cow'. There are bequests to Wm Hutchinson, Alice Hutchinson, and Wm Hutchinson's other three children, to William Heron, to his brother Cuthbert Yarrowe's daughter that he had christened, to Geo. Kel's son, to 'my father's children', to 'my sister's children', to Wm Hutchinson's three sons, and to Anne Heron's children. 'To my father one little branded whye stirk. To my brother Oswold Heron 10 sheep. My brother William and my half brother Robert Heron'. The total value of the testator's goods as valued in the inventory dated 19 August 1619, amounted to £26. 16s. 8d. (*Dur. Prob. Off.* by C.R.H.).

In 1625 Oswald Heron and Roger Heron, both of Humshaugh, were recusants; and in 1629 Oswald Heron and Barbara his wife and Roger Heron and Mary his wife are so described.

The brother William Heron was perhaps the person of that name, the administration of whose goods was granted on 19 August 1648 to his widow Mary (Raine, *MS.*). On the division of Humshaugh common fields on 2 January 1666/7 George Heron and Thomas White were occupiers of the East Field and the mill, which were awarded to lord Widdrington; Cuthbert Heron, Joseph Reed and Joseph Dawson were awarded the Mill Field; and Roger Heron and three other freeholders were awarded the West Field. It is possible to some extent to follow the devolution of these properties:

(a) George Heron who was tenant of half the East Field and the mill in 1667 apparently purchased this land from lord Widdrington. He can be identified as George Heron of Rowchester, yeoman, who on 31 October 1670 purchased a half tenement called the Easter House in Humshaugh from Robert Heron of Humshaugh, yeoman; the lands of Cuthbert Heron and other lands of Robert Heron are mentioned in the conveyance and Cuthbert Heron is a witness (*Title Deeds*). George Heron made his will in 1682, proved 1685, in which he mentions his sons George and Michael, his daughters Anne, Isabel and Elizabeth, his wife's sister Anne Weldon, and his wife Mary. His wife was Mary née Weldon who after her husband's death lived at Dilston, par. Corbridge, where she died in 1710. The will of Mary Heron, late of Dilston, was proved by Michael Welden of Newton, esq., 13 June 1710, the bondsmen being Anne Welden of Dilston, spinster, Thomas Shafto of Hexham, gent., and Thos Radcliffe of Dilston, gent. (*Dur. Prob. Off.*, by C.R.H.). Mary had a sister Isabel wife of Thomas Heron of Simonburn, and she also died at Dilston in 1709. The eldest son George Heron on 11 November 1704 sold his Humshaugh property to John Heron of Todsburnshield, gent. (*Title Deeds*).

In his will dated 3 August 1713 this John Heron is described as 'late of Humshaugh, and now of Hexham, gent.'; he mentions his eldest son John Heron of Hexham, merchant, but he leaves his lands in Humshaugh and a house in Hexham called Newhall to his younger son George Heron. The son George Heron died in 1735 and left all his lands to his sister Margery wife of Richard Stokoe of Hexham. There was a bond of marriage dated at York 21 June 1735 between Richard Stokoe of Hexham, gent., bachelor, aged 25, and Mary (sic) Heron of the same, spinster, aged 29, to marry at

St John Lee. George Heron had an illegitimate daughter 'Mary Shaftoe otherwise Heron, infant daughter of Mary Shaftoe, spinster', to whom he leaves 1s. 6d. a week until she reaches the age of 14.

(b) Cuthbert Heron of Humshaugh who was awarded one-third of the Mill Field in 1667, made his will in 1674. In the will he mentions his son William Heron and his daughter Anne Hall (Raine, *MS, Wills and Inv.*). His eldest son Robert Heron had died in 1671. This is the Robert Heron who in 1670 had sold a half tenement in Humshaugh to George Heron of Rowchester. His will is dated 29 May 1671; he directs his 'goods to be sold for paying of my debts according to the discretion of John Downes of Bishop Auckland, gent., George Heron of Rochester, gent., and John Reed of Humshaugh, yeoman, whom I make supervisors for paying all my debts and bringing up of my children. My supervisors to have power to sell, mortgage, or let one house and a garth, a close on the backside thereof and another called the Legitt End being by estimation 3 acres more or less, they also to have power to let one close in the Beat Hill if the land and house aforesaid will not pay the debts, for the year or more till the debts be fully paid. To my eldest daughter Grace Hearon £10. £10 to my second daughter Jane. £10 to my daughter Isabell Hearon and £10 to my daughter Ann. If my wife which is with child shall bear a boy then it shall have the close on the Beate Hill if he live till he come to the age of 21 but if a daughter then she is to have £10, all which money my son George Hearon is to pay out of the land which is due to me by my father Cuthbert Hearon when he shall attain to the age of 21 years but if any one or more shall die before she attain to that age then is he to pay nothing to the rest in regard of her or their £10. My dear wife Francis Hearon sole executrix'.

Both George Heron and his only daughter and heiress Sarah were dead by 6 February 1707/8 when Roger Tweddle of Humshaugh, yeoman, and Jane his wife, and William Hubbuck of the Birks, mason, and Ann his wife, which said Jane and Ann were aunts and coheirs of Sarah Heron, the only daughter and heir of George Heron, deceased, contracted to sell their Humshaugh property to Cuthbert Wilson of Walwick (*Title Deeds*).

(c) Roger Heron of Humshaugh was awarded one quarter of Humshaugh West Field in 1667. The next owner of the property appears to have been William Heron of Lincoln Hill, gent., who on the division of Humshaugh Fell in 1696 was awarded 65 acres being 'the western portion of the Cockplay quarter' and 16 acres being 'the north end and low side of Lancies Doors quarter' (*Title Deeds*). William Heron was living at Smalesmouth 28 April 1707 when he made an indenture of feoffment with John Oliver of Lustrother in Teviotdale, whereby in consideration of his marriage with Christian daughter of the said John Oliver, and a marriage portion of £323 from Oliver, he settled his lands in Humshaugh, Lincoln Hill, Cockplay, Haughton Green, Smalesmouth and Rigend on the issue of the marriage. By his will dated 23 November 1713 when he was 'sick of body but of sound and disposing mind and memory' he divides his lands between his two sons John and William. John is to have his property at Humshaugh and Smalesmouth, and William that at Hillhouse and Rigend. His daughter Elizabeth is to have half of his personal estate. He leaves to 'his dear and loving wife Chris-

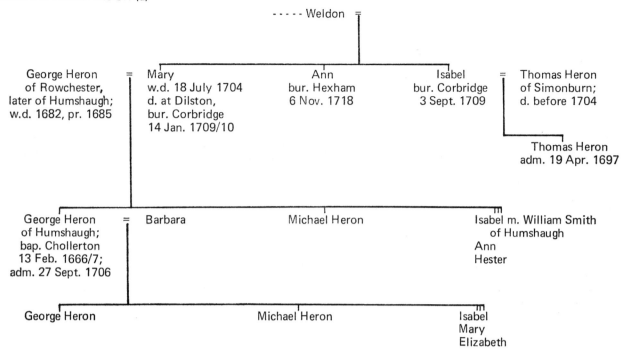

- - - - - Weldon =

George Heron
of Rowchester,
later of Humshaugh;
w.d. 1682, pr. 1685
=
Mary
w.d. 18 July 1704
d. at Dilston,
bur. Corbridge
14 Jan. 1709/10

Ann
bur. Hexham
6 Nov. 1718

Isabel
bur. Corbridge
3 Sept. 1709
=
Thomas Heron
of Simonburn;
d. before 1704

Thomas Heron
adm. 19 Apr. 1697

George Heron
of Humshaugh;
bap. Chollerton
13 Feb. 1666/7;
adm. 27 Sept. 1706
=
Barbara

Michael Heron

Isabel m. William Smith
of Humshaugh
Ann
Hester

George Heron

Michael Heron

Isabel
Mary
Elizabeth

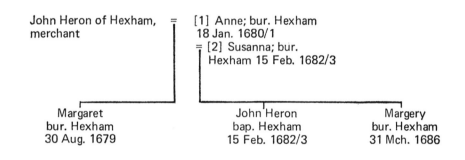

John Heron of Hexham,
merchant
=
[1] Anne; bur. Hexham
18 Jan. 1680/1
= [2] Susanna; bur.
Hexham 15 Feb. 1682/3

Margaret
bur. Hexham
30 Aug. 1679

John Heron
bap. Hexham
15 Feb. 1682/3

Margery
bur. Hexham
31 Mch. 1686

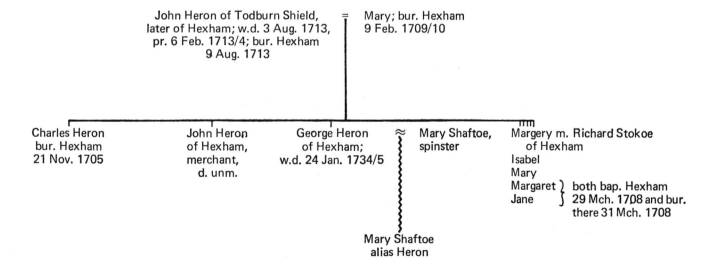

John Heron of Todburn Shield,
later of Hexham; w.d. 3 Aug. 1713,
pr. 6 Feb. 1713/4; bur. Hexham
9 Aug. 1713
=
Mary; bur. Hexham
9 Feb. 1709/10

Charles Heron
bur. Hexham
21 Nov. 1705

John Heron
of Hexham,
merchant,
d. unm.

George Heron
of Hexham;
w.d. 24 Jan. 1734/5
≈
Mary Shaftoe,
spinster

Margery m. Richard Stokoe
of Hexham
Isabel
Mary
Margaret } both bap. Hexham
Jane } 29 Mch. 1708 and bur.
there 31 Mch. 1708

Mary Shaftoe
alias Heron

HERON of HUMSHAUGH (b)

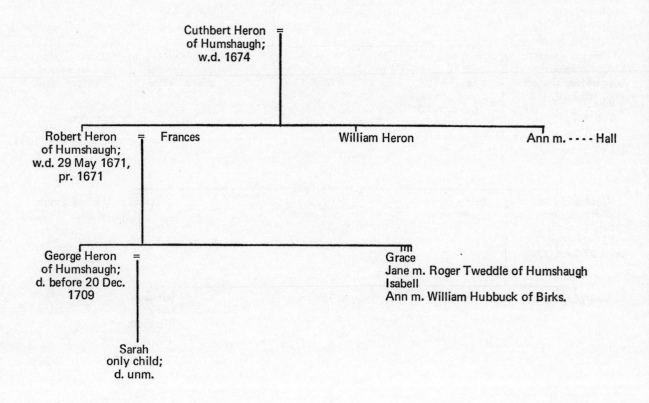

Cuthbert Heron
of Humshaugh;
w.d. 1674
=

Robert Heron   =   Frances
of Humshaugh;
w.d. 29 May 1671,
pr. 1671

William Heron

Ann m. - - - - Hall

George Heron   =
of Humshaugh;
d. before 20 Dec.
1709

Grace
Jane m. Roger Tweddle of Humshaugh
Isabell
Ann m. William Hubbuck of Birks.

Sarah
only child;
d. unm.

HERON of HUMSHAUGH (c)

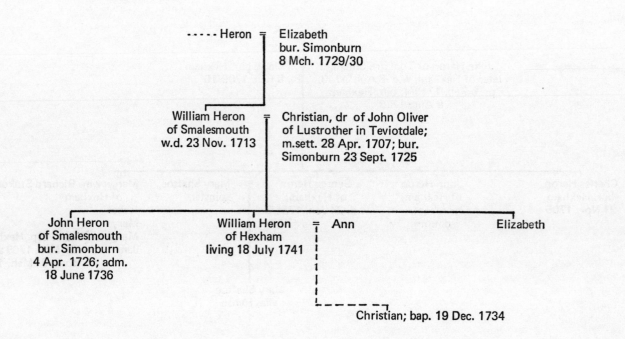

- - - - - Heron   =   Elizabeth
bur. Simonburn
8 Mch. 1729/30

William Heron   =   Christian, dr of John Oliver
of Smalesmouth   of Lustrother in Teviotdale;
w.d. 23 Nov. 1713   m.sett. 28 Apr. 1707; bur.
                        Simonburn 23 Sept. 1725

John Heron
of Smalesmouth
bur. Simonburn
4 Apr. 1726; adm.
18 June 1736

William Heron   =   Ann
of Hexham
living 18 July 1741

Elizabeth

Christian; bap. 19 Dec. 1734

tian £30 a year for life out of Humshaugh and Smalesmouth', and to his 'dear loving mother Elizabeth Heron £10 a year for life out of Humshaugh and a further £10 a year out of Humshaugh if she so require' (*Title Deeds*). Mrs Christian Heron was buried in Simonburn church on 23 September 1725 and her elder son John Heron on 4 April 1726.

The younger son, William Heron, was living at Hexham, 8 February 1736/7 when with his wife Ann he made an agreement to sell Lincoln Hill, Cockplay and Haughton Green to Nicholas Roberts of Hexham, gent. The sale was completed on 3 May 1737.

It is not known if William Heron left any descendants. Christian, daughter of Mr William Heron, baptised at Hexham 19 December 1734 was presumably his daughter.

HERON OF HEXHAM, PAR. HEXHAM

MANY persons of the surname of Heron appear in Hexham from the 16th century onwards and it is reasonable to suggest that their forbears came from Chipchase. A William Heron was bailiff and chief steward of Hexham in 1574 (*NCH*. III, p.65). On 25 May 1595 there was buried at Kendal in Westmorland 'Jenett daughter of Rychard Hearen of Hexham, and dyed at Brigsteare' (*Kendal Registers*). At the time of the survey of the regality of Hexham in 1608 William Heron, tanner, held certain land in Hexham town at a rent of 2s. 2½d., and John Heron held a tenement in Hexham town at a rent of 11d. (*NCH* III, pp.92, 93). The latter was perhaps the 'John Hearun of Hexhame, gent.', who, on 17 March 1630/1 signed the inventory of the goods of 'Johne Hearone of Chipchase decd *alias* Johne the gentilman *alias* White'. The deceased was no doubt a bastard of one of the Herons of Chipchase. Between 1601 and 1609 John Heron of Hexham, tanner, and Janet his wife were convicted as recusants.

Many of the Herons resident in Hexham in the 17th century were tanners and were probably descendants of William Heron the tanner of 1608. Several of them bore the Christian name John so that it is very difficult to identify them separately. The banns of marriage were called for the third and last time on 22 October 1654 for John Heron the elder, tanner, and Agnes Kirsopp, widow (*Hexham Registers*). Shortly after this we have 'John Heron on the bank, tanner', 'John Heron of the Bridge End, tanner, papist', and 'John Heron of Gilligate, tanner', occurring in the Hexham Registers besides 'John Heron, tanner'. In 1682 and again in 1683 Elizabeth Heron, widow, and John Heron and Elizabeth his wife were convicted together as recusants.

On 14 December 1721 sir William Blackett of Wallington, lord of the regality of Hexham, confirmed to John Coatsworth of Hexham, joiner, two seats in the south side of the quire of Hexham church, 'adjoining on galleries lately erected by Cuthbert Heron' (*AA*3, XII, p.30). This Cuthbert Heron was a tanner being either 'Cuthbert son of John Heron, tanner' baptised at Hexham 6 August 1676 or 'Cuthbert son of John Heron of Bank, tanner' baptised 9 January 1677/8. On 9 November 1723 Cuthbert Heron purchased property in Corbridge from Jasper Gibson of Stonecroft. On 6 November 1732 he made his will whereby he leaves his Corbridge property and Parker's house in Pudding Row, Hexham to his son Robert Heron; he leaves a messuage called the Snape, par.

Hexham, to trustees to pay his debts; his son Cuthbert Heron is to have a burgage in Hexham market place and the Intacks which he had bought of the trustees of Benoni Carr; his lands in Knarsdale called Allishill which he had purchased of Joseph Noble of Allenheads are to be sold for the use of his son Robert Heron when he reaches the age of 21 years; he leaves his wife Margaret £20 a year, and his three daughters Ann, Jane and Margaret Heron each £300; his son John is to have £50. The trustees were his brother Richard Heron and Lancelot Allgood of the Riding (Raine, *MS.Test. Ebor.*). On 5 July 1744 'Margaret Heron of Hexham, relict of Cuthbert Heron of same place, tanner, and devisee in the will of Richard Heron of the same place, gent., and Robert Heron of Newcastle upon Tyne, merchant, one of the sons of the said Cuthbert' sold a messuage in Hexham Market Stead to Wilkinson Kirsopp of Hexham, tanner (*AA*3. XII, p.25).

Cuthbert's brother Richard Heron of Hexham, gent., made his w.d. 24 July 1742, pr. 3 February 1742/3, in which he mentions his wife Margaret Heron, his daughters Mary wife of William Hewson, Martha Heron and Margaret Heron; another daughter Frances Johnson was dead but her children Richard, William, Thomas and John Johnson are given legacies; he mentions his sister Margaret Heron, widow, relict of his late brother Cuthbert Heron (Raine, *MS.Test. Ebor.*). Frances Johnson's husband was William Johnson, master of Hexham grammar school 1721-1723, later vicar of Ovingham 1723-1736 where 'he took to drink and other vices'; he was buried at Morpeth 'out of the gaol' 24 April 1742 (C.R.H.).

Margaret, widow of Cuthbert Heron, made her w.d. 25 August 1749 and probate of it was granted 18 June 1753 to her daughters Jane and Margaret Heron, to whom she had left her copyhold houses and lands in Hexham; she leaves £5 for mourning to her son Robert Heron and £10 to her son Cuthbert Heron; she gives legacies to the children of her son-in-law John Johnson of Hexham, and to her sisters Elizabeth Bell, Mary Kirsopp, Eleanor Liddell and Ann Bell (*Ib.*).

Robert son of Cuthbert Heron of Hexham, gent., deceased, was apprenticed 6 July 1737 to Robert Sorsbie of Newcastle, boothman, and admitted to the Newcastle Merchant Adventurers Company on 2 October 1747. By his w.d. 10 June 1745 Robert Heron devises all his lands in Corbridge, Riding Mill, Hexham and Snape to his only child Jane, who became wife of Ralph Sparke of Hexham. Cuthbert Heron's son Cuthbert was a Gateshead merchant, and by his w.d. 26 November 1751, pr. 9 March 1751/2 leaves all his property to his wife Isabel.

A yeoman family of Heron who were Roman Catholics owned the small farmhold of High Shield Rigg, commonly called the Paise in Hexham West Quarter. John Heron of the 'Peas' purchased the farm from John Fenwick of Wallington 29 August 1670. By his w.d. 4 June 1699 he leaves his wife Elizabeth £6. 10s. a year to be paid to her by his son John Heron out of the Paise 'in lieu of her thirds and widow right'; his daughters Ann, Bridget, Mary and Jane Heron are to have £30 each, and his son John Heron the residue. Another daughter, Elizabeth, had died before her father and was buried in Hexham church 9 February 1697/8. 'John Heron of Paise, papist' was buried in the church on 30 June 1699. His son and heir appears to have been married twice as 'Margaret, wife of John Heron of Paise' was buried 27 June 1705, and 'Mary, infant daughter of Mr Jno Heron of Paise, papist'

HERON of HEXHAM

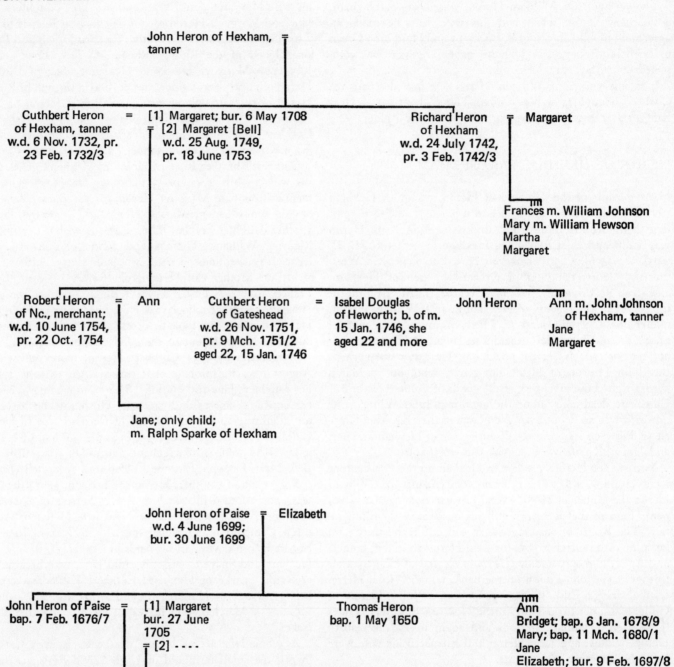

John Heron of Hexham, =
tanner

Cuthbert Heron = [1] Margaret; bur. 6 May 1708
of Hexham, tanner = [2] Margaret [Bell]
w.d. 6 Nov. 1732, pr.   w.d. 25 Aug. 1749,
23 Feb. 1732/3   pr. 18 June 1753

Richard Heron = Margaret
of Hexham
w.d. 24 July 1742,
pr. 3 Feb. 1742/3

Frances m. William **Johnson**
Mary m. William Hewson
Martha
Margaret

Robert Heron = Ann
of Nc., merchant;
w.d. 10 June 1754,
pr. 22 Oct. 1754

Cuthbert Heron = Isabel Douglas
of Gateshead   of Heworth; b. of m.
w.d. 26 Nov. 1751,   15 Jan. 1746, she
pr. 9 Mch. 1751/2   aged 22 and more
aged 22, 15 Jan. 1746

John Heron

Ann m. John **Johnson**
  of Hexham, tanner
Jane
Margaret

Jane; only child;
m. Ralph Sparke of Hexham

John Heron of Paise = Elizabeth
w.d. 4 June 1699;
bur. 30 June 1699

John Heron of Paise = [1] Margaret
bap. 7 Feb. 1676/7   bur. 27 June
                        1705
                      = [2] . . . .

Thomas Heron
bap. 1 May 1650

Ann
Bridget; bap. 6 Jan. 1678/9
Mary; bap. 11 Mch. 1680/1
Jane
Elizabeth; bur. 9 Feb. 1697/8

Mary; bur. 31 May 1715

Elizabeth m. Matthew Leadbitter
of Warden; b. of m. York
3 Jan. 1735

on 31 May 1715. John Heron was living in Hexham in 1739 when he mortgaged the Paise to Matthew Leadbitter of Nether Warden. The Paise was afterwards the property of the Leadbitters and Matthew Leadbitter married John Heron's daughter Elizabeth (*NCH.* IV, pp.21, 22). There was a marriage bond at York on 3 January 1735 between Matthew Leadbitter of Warden, Northumberland, gent., bachelor, aged 25 and Elizabeth Heron, spinster, of Hexham, aged 19, with consent of her father John Heron of Hexham; to be married at St John Lee or Hexham.

Another Roman Catholic family were the Herons of Grundridge. Isabel wife of Robert Heron of Grundridge was buried at Hexham 3 February 1680/1. Administration of the goods of Thomas Heron of Grundridge was granted to his widow Elizabeth 14 March 1690/1, and he was buried at Hexham 1 November 1690. Robert Heron of Grundridge, senior, papist, was buried 8 February 1692/3 and Robert Heron of Grundridge, junior, on 15 February 1692/3. Probate of the wills of both Roberts was granted 19 July 1693 to Margaret wife of Christopher Glendinning (Raine, *MSHexham Wills*).

We get a fleeting glimpse of another yeoman family of Herons in Hexhamshire at the turn of the 17th century. Administration of the goods of Richard Hearon of Ordley was granted at York 5 January 1679 to his widow Elizabeth. An earlier Richard Heron of Ordley (or perhaps the records had not been brought up to date) was convicted as a recusant in 1680/1. On 10 April 1694 John Heron of Ordley, par. Hexham, took a mortgage on lands in Slaley from George Green of Wharmley (*AA*3. XII, p.51). Administration of the goods of Elizabeth Heron of Ordley was granted 31 July 1702 to Richard Heron her son (Raine, *Hexham Adms*. IV, p.22) and it was no doubt the son Richard who as Richard Heron of 'High Street', Nd. yeoman released his rights in a messuage in Slaley 4 January 1708/9 to George Green (*AA*3. XII, p.53). Elizabeth Heron of Ordley, widow, papist, was buried at Hexham 15 June 1702 (*Hexham Registers*).

recommended' (*Ib.* p.262). Perhaps she was a daughter of John Heron of Eshot, par. Felton, who died in 1468, or of his son another John Heron who died in 1478 or 1479.

Mention has already been made of William Heron of Clerkenwell, gent., who in 1580 leaves a messuage in the city of London to his kinsman Thomas Heron of Newcastle and Crawley (*See* HERON OF CRAWLEY).

The families of Heron of Cressy, Lincolnshire, and of Godmanchester, Huntingdonshire, claimed descent from the Herons of Chipchase, and the relationship was perhaps recognised when sir John Heron of Chipchase on 19 May 1692 appointed Charnock Heron of Godmanchester one of the trustees of his estates. These Herons claimed descent from Thomas Heron of Newcastle, merchant, stated to have been a son of sir John Heron of Chipchase, and to have married a daughter of sir William Shafto, 'sometime mayor of Newcastle'. In the pedigree of Heron of Cressy this Thomas Heron the merchant is placed four generations before sir Edward Heron, made K.B. at the coronation of James I—1603 (Le Neve's *Pedigrees of Knights*), and must therefore have been living in the second half of the 15th century.

No Newcastle merchants of the name of Heron are known in the 15th century and there was certainly not a mayor of the name of Shafto at this time. The earliest Shafto to become mayor of Newcastle was Mark Shafto in 1548. The pedigree may be partly traditional, but has the appearance of a fictitious compilation so typical of Tudor times. Thomas Heron the merchant is said to have had a son Robert Heron of Newcastle who by (blank) daughter of (blank) Anderson of Newcastle, merchant, had two sons Richard (or Robert) Heron of Lincolnshire (ancestor of the Herons of Cressy) and John Heron of Yorkshire (ancestor of the Herons of Godmanchester).

Pedigrees of Heron of Burton Coggles, of Cressy Hall and of Lincoln are printed in Lincolnshire Pedigrees (*Harl. Soc.* II, pp.486-490.

HERONS OF THE SOUTH

As EARLY as the 15th century, cadets of the Heron family were seeking their fortunes outside Northumberland. A John Heron of St Dunstan in the East, citizen and mercer of London, remembers his native county in his w.d. 6 February 1515/6 and leaves to the convent of Whitefriars at Hull (Hulne) in the county of Northumberland £5 for a trentall of masses. A trentall is a set of thirty successive daily masses for the dead. The will was proved on 13 March 1515/6 by his son and executor Thomas Heron (*SS.* 116, p.274). John Heron was related to Elizabeth Kyrkeby or a Lathom, who was of London, widow, when she made her w.d. 15 January 1487, proved 20 May 1487. She mentions in her will her sisters Margaret, Kateryn and Isabell, her brothers John, Edmond and William Heron, and her brother's son Roger Heron; John Heron, citizen and mercer, of London, is to have a cup, and he and Thomas Strother are to have the residue of her estate. The testatrix was a native of the parish of Felton, for she leaves 'to the church of Felton in the shire of Northumberland, where the body of John Heron my father lyeth buried, a chalice of silver and a vestment, that the parishioners of the same church have the soul of my father to God in their prayers

OTHER HERONS

A BRANCH of the Heron family having some shadowy connection with the Herons of Birtley owned a small freehold at Mooridge House, par. Elsdon, throughout the 18th century. Roger Heron of Mooridge House, a freeholder in 1698, was buried at Elsdon 12 February 1717/8. Roger Heron of Yatesfield buried 12 July 1731 and Anthony Heron of Yatesfield buried 4 September 1755 were perhaps sons, and Roger Heron of Yatesfield buried 26 May 1794 perhaps a grandson of the first Roger. In 1710 and 1715 Ralph Heron was freeholder of Mooridge House and in 1834 he is specifically called of Birkley (Birtley) when he voted in respect of Dultridge (Durtrees, par. Elsdon). As Mooridge House almost adjoins Durtrees, the latter can easily represent the former. On 12 April 1717 sir Nicholas Shireburne of Stonyhurst, being a Roman Catholic, registered his estates which included a tenement or farm called Cottenshope and Middle Quarter let to Ralph Herne and Mark Headley at £115 a year. Edward Hall of Cottonshope Middle Quarter by his w.d. 7 April 1737 leaves £10 to his niece Sarah, daughter of Ralph Heron of Cottonshopehead. It seems probable that there were two generations of these Herons called Ralph as on 9 June 1761 Ralph Heron and Eleanor Grieve of Mooridge House were married at Elsdon.

In 1774 John Heron of Moor-edge-house and Thomas Heron of Dikehead voted as freeholders.

About this time three persons of the surname of Heron were living at the adjoining farms of Hott Hill, Nook Mill and Shawbush in the chapelry of Bellingham. Nicholas Heron was tenant of Shawbush, Thomas Heron of Hott Hill and John Heron of Nook Mill. The two latter died towards the end of the 18th century and were succeeded in their farms by their brother-in-law William Baty who was rated for the Hole Farm in 1813.

Adjoining Bockenfield lies the township of East Thirston where a yeoman family of Heron was established in the 17th century. The family was no doubt descended from a younger son of the Herons of Bockenfield. Robert Heron of East Thirston entered into a bond of marriage with Barbara Smith on 10 December 1667. He stated that he was aged about 48 when he made a deposition about Felton Moor on 10 October 1692; he made a further deposition on 16 April 1697 when he stated that he was about 57. In 1702 he held a leasehold tenement in Thirston (*NCH*. VII, p.316). He was succeeded by his son Thomas Heron who held 1½ farms in East Thirston in 1727 and gave money in 1759 to build a gallery in Felton church (*Ib*., p.284). This was the Thomas Heron of East Thirston, husbandman, who made his w.d. 14 June 1760, pr. 1766. He leaves his messuage in East Thirston held by lease under the earl and countess of Northumberland to his son John Heron and appoints him sole executor; his grandson and grand daughter John Heron and Jane Heron are each to have £100 at the age of 21 (*Dur. Prob. Off*. by C.R.H.).

Other members of this family were Richard Heron of Thirston and of Whitton, par. Rothbury, who was living at Eshot East House in 1774 when he voted for a freehold in Whitton, and Robert Heron of East Thirston who voted in respect of a freehold at Rothbury in 1826. This Robert Heron died at Thirston 22 November 1843 aged 82. John Heron, son of this Robert, assented in 1870 to the removal of the gallery in Felton church erected by his ancestor, and died at Felton 26 April 1874 aged 75. His brother William Heron died at Rothbury 5 July 1885 aged 84.

Besides the younger sons already mentioned as becoming merchants of Newcastle, there are few other persons of this surname appearing in the book of the Newcastle Merchant Adventurers. Humfrey Heron, an apprentice of Thomas Hanson was admitted 1522-1523, and Peter Heron, an apprentice of George Brandling in 1526-1527, the Christian name of the former suggesting a connection with the Herons of Bockenfield. At the Newcastle muster in 1539 Peter Herone, merchant, with a coat of plate, a bow, and a steel bonnet, was the only one of the surname.

Towards the end of the 17th century Anthony Heron of Newcastle, gentleman, had two sons who became merchants. George son of Anthony Heron was apprenticed 1 November 1648 to John Ellison, mercer, married at St Nicholas', Newcastle 23 October 1701 Rose Lorraine, and was buried at All Saints, Newcastle, 'from St Nicholas' on 28 July 1703. John son of Anthony Heron was apprenticed 20 December 1686 to Joseph Bewicke, boothman. Anthony Heron, the father, was buried at All Saints 4 December 1709.

From the beginning of the 17th century, the lesser trade guilds of Newcastle attracted members of different branches of the Herons. William Heron, joiner, was admitted a freeman of Newcastle in 1619, and his sons John and George were admitted in 1645 and 1646 respectively. Anthony Heron, currier, was a freeman in 1637, and was alive in 1650 when an apprentice of his was made free.

One of the earliest Herons in Newcastle was John Heron, master and mariner, the inventory of whose goods is dated 6 May 1596. Others of this occupation were Robert Heron, freeman 1642—Geo. Hearing 1654—John Heron 1686—Tho. Heron, apprentice of John Heron, 1701—and Geo. Heron, apprentice of Wm Mitford, 1719.

Anthony Heron, baker and brewer, became a freeman of Newcastle in 1655; his wife Ann was buried at All Saints, Newcastle, 1 March 1692/3; and he was buried at All Saints, 'from St Johns', on 23 March 1700/1. His son Michael was baptised at St John's 1 January 1681/2 and was admitted to the freedom of the city on 15 January 1699/1700. He resided in the Bigg Market, and his son John (baptised St John's 1 January 1705/6) was entered as a freeman by patrimony on 17 January 1725/6.

On 25 May 1584 letters of administration of the goods of Tristram Heron, musician, of Newcastle, were granted to his widow Elizabeth. The inventory of his goods includes a lute and case, and four lute books, valued at 16s. together. He had a 'recognisance of scutcheon of silver' worth 2s. 6d. Both he and a child had died of the plague for amongst his debts was the sum of 29s. 1d. 'for dighting and cleansing the house, with the expenses in time of their visitation, and his burial and his child's' (Welford III. p. 23). On 27 October 1613 an inventory of the goods of William Heron of the parish of All Saints, Newcastle, was taken by Jarret Hearon, Ouen Heron and others (Raine, *MSS*). The inventory of Ovin Heron of Newcastle, 'musicioner' was taken in 1623 (Raine, *MS Wills and Inv*. III, p.27).

Administration of the goods of Timothy Robson of Newcastle was granted 22 July 1712 to his widow Mary Robson alias Heron, now wife of George Heron of Newcastle, gent. (*Dur. Prob. Off*. by C.R.H.).

In 1684 there died at Wark, one Giles Heron, said to have been an illegitimate son of one of the Herons of Chipchase. He had been a pedlar and in later life was a shopkeeper in Wark. By his w.d. 23 September 1679 he leaves the whole of his personal estate for charitable purposes. He describes himself in his will as Giles Heron, late of Leehall and now of Wark, yeoman, and then proceeds to state 'I think it a good work of Charity and commendable before God, to distribute the greater part of the same (his temporal estate) to pious and Charitable uses, and it rather is my desire to see some part of it for such uses settled in my lifetime, than to leave it by and according to the discretion and direction of any other person or persons to be done after my death and considering the great necessity of a free school for the education of children of all and every the inhabitants within the said parish (of Simonburn) and the inhabitants of Chipchase, Birtley and Birtley Shields within the parish of Chollerton', he leaves the sum of £200 in the hands of trustees to pay the interest annually for the maintenance of a schoolmaster to reside and teach a free school at Wark. The trustees appointed are George Heron, John Reed, Thomas Dobson, Thomas White and Edward Robson, all of Humshaugh, William Smith of Wester-haughton, Robert Elliot of Haughton Strother, William Liddle of Long-Rigge and Nicholas Ridley of Eals who are to act in conjunction with Christopher Charleton of Heatherington, Reginald Charleton of Motehill, Edward Dodd of Esh, and the Parson of Simonburn for the time being. All the rest and residue of his goods and chattels are to be held by his trustees and the interest thereof distributed half yearly 'among such needy and indigent persons of the said parish of Simonburn as they shall judge most necessiated and proper for it', giving preference to any of the name of Heron. Any 'surplussage' of the interest is to be used towards the binding of one or more of the children of the poor inhabitants of the parish of Simonburn to be apprentices to some trade, again giving preference to any of the name of Heron. In the 18th century the farm of Tecket was purchased by the Giles Heron Trustees and today it remains their property. At the beginning of the 19th century the trustees caused considerable scandal by the amount spent on their annual dinner and the proceedings thereat; in 1811 John Buckbarrow, curate of Simonburn, was said to have died suddenly after one of the dinners. In 1832 archdeacon Singleton reported in his visitation that '130 boys and girls are freely educated by the revenues of Tecket Farm in the principles of the national church'.

In the middle of the 16th century there was a John Heron living at Hall Barns, Simonburn, who must have been a near relative of the Herons of Chipchase, the owners of Hall Barns. In December 1538 a priest from Chichester named Robert More had fled before Henry VIII's commissioners and tried to escape to Scotland. He was arrested at Nunwick and put into Hexham jail. The same day a message was sent to Nunwick by Edward Charlton of Hesleyside with the advice 'Go to John Heron's mother of the Hall Barns and warn her to keep in her cattle, for the outlaws and thieves would come in'. Next day the outlaws and thieves broke into Hexham jail and liberated all the prisoners including the priest, and they escaped to Scotland (*Letters and Papers of H. VIII*, vol. XIII, (2)).

In 1552 the order of the watches specified that the inhabitants of Simonburn and Slaterfield with five men from Nunwick were to watch the Hall-Orchard field with two men in the watch; John Heron of Simonburn and William Ridley of Slaterfield were to be setters and searchers of the watch, the overseers being George Heron, keeper of Tyndale, and John Heron of Hallbarns, bailiff of Simonburn. The inhabitants of the Hallbarns, Uppertown, Teppermoor and Haughton Strother were to watch from the New Meadows in Teppermoor edge to Tecket leas with four men in the watch; John Heron of the Hallbarns and Sandy Armstrong were to be the setters and searchers of this watch (Nicolson, *Leges Marchiarum*, p.257). John Heron of Hall Barns, Gilbert Heron his brother and their sons were concerned in the Carr-Heron feud in 1557.

John Heron of Chipchase in his w.d. 5 December 1590 mentions his servant James Heron. Another James Heron was living at Nunwick in 1680 when his wife Margaret was presented in the Archdeacon's court for entertaining Thomas Ridley and others who were running horse races on a Sunday and having music in her house whereby several were kept from church.

In 1681 Thomas Heron, gent., of 'Castlemaine', was a recusant, and in the following year Isabella Heron, widow,

and Thomas Heron, gent., both of Simonburn castle are similarly described.

It has already been noted that on 10 October 1549 James Heron of Shield Hall, par. Slaley, bought two burgages in Corbridge from Alexander Heron of Corbridge, to whom he was perhaps related. In 1538 James Heron and William Heron are entered on the Muster Roll for Slaley, and in 1552 the latter was one of the setters and searchers at Smart-rake, near Slaley. A 'Wyllm Heron of Wawlaw' and his sons were active in the Carr-Heron feud in 1558 (*Hist. Fam. of Carr*, II, p.78). As Wooley adjoins Shield Hall it seems likely that this refers to William Heron of Shield Hall. It was presumably his son of the same name who in 1570 held a leasehold tenement in Slaley from the Crown at a rent of 19s. 8d. On 15 February 1606/7 the Crown granted a 40 years lease to Thomas Mery of a tenement in Shield Hall in the tenure of William Heron at a rent of 19s. 8d. William Heron was succeeded by a Gawen Heron, one of the churchwardens of Slaley in 1579 who in 1608 held part of a tenement called the Shield Hall late in the occupation of William Heron. On 30 May 1611 the Crown grantees sold Shield Hall to John Heron of Birtley.

In the 16th and 17th centuries there were Herons at Dilston, par. Corbridge, who were probably related to the Herons of Corbridge. Thomas Heron of Corbridge when he made his w.d. 14 April 1596 appoints Edmund Heron as one of the executors. Another Thomas Heron, son of Anthony Heron of Corbridge, sold a burgage in Corbridge in 1608 to Edmund Heron of Dilston. In 1623 Edmund Heron was sworn at Dilston manor court 'that he or his deputy shall carefully look to the woods of the spechells and all other woods belonging to Dilston, the park excepted, and to present all that shall trespass from time to time'. An inventory of the goods of Edmund Hearon of Dilston, deceased, was exhibited at the court of probate on 5 December 1623, and administration was granted to his widow Elizabeth to the use of Barbara, presumably their daughter (Raine, *MSS Wills and Inv.* III, p.21). It would seem that the tenant of one of the Dilston farms had the responsibility of maintaining a bull for the benefit of the other manorial tenants. In 1635 it was laid down at the manor court that the widow of Thomas Heron was to 'provide a sufficient bull for the use of the whole town of Dilston before the 25th day of March next' (*NCH.* X, 273n). Thomas Hearon of Dilston had died quite recently for administration of his goods was granted in 1635 to Isabella, his widow (*Dur. Adm.—Raine MSS*). John Heron of Dilston whose son Edmond was baptised at Corbridge 6 September 1674 was perhaps a descendant of the earlier Edmund 1596 x 1623.

Betham in his *Baronetage of England* mentions a tradition that the ancestor of the Herons of Kirrouchtree, co. Kircudbright, Scotland 'is supposed to have left Northumberland in the 13th century', and to have obtained a grant of Kirrouchtree in the 14th century. In the 17th century they changed the name of their estate to Heron in order to be able to style themselves Heron of Heron. A lot of romantic nonsense was written about the family by Julian C. Rodgers in 1902 in *A History of our Family* part of which is entitled *The Lineage of the Heron Family*. The regular use of the Christian name Andrew in this family might suggest that the family ancestor was Andrew Heron a younger son of sir William Heron of Ford (d.*ante* 1382). The main line of the family died out in the male line early in the 19th century.

Patrick Heron of Heron, M.P., by his wife lady Elizabeth Cochrane, only daughter of the 8th earl of Dundonald, had an only child Mary who married 4 January 1802 sir John Shaw Maxwell, 4th baronet. Their descendants assumed the additional surname of Heron and are now represented by sir Patrick Ivor Heron-Maxwell, 9th baronet, of Spring Kell in Annandale, Scotland.

HERON—NOTE

Since the account of the Herons of Chipchase was wrtten, Mr C. Roy Hudleston has drawn my attention to depositions in Durham Consistory Court in a cause by Elizabeth Heron, spinster, complainant, *versus* Robert Smith, gent., and Ann his wife, taken at Durham 19 March 1677/8. Elizabeth and her mother had been given a rentcharge of £100 a year during their lives by Elizabeth's father, Cuthbert, and her (half) brother sir Cuthbert Heron. Thomas and Dorothy Carnaby had sold the lands which were subject to the rentcharge. Dorothy Carnaby, aged 40 years or thereabouts, deposed that about 26 October 1659 she delivered certain bonds to Mrs Hilda Wright (of the Bailey, Durham, spinster, aged 60). The bonds were in the complainant's name and belonged to her and were delivered to one Mickleton of the city of Durham about 2 years after deponent married Mr Carnaby, when complainant was about 6 or 7 years old (*MS* book of depositions in causes in Durham Consistory Court once in Richard Welford's library and given by sir William Gibson to the Dept. of Palaeography and Diplomatic, University of Durham).

HERON—BIBLIOGRAPHY

(a) *NCH.* IV, pp.332-346 with pedigrees of Heron of Chipchase, Heron of Cressy and Heron of Newcastle.

(b) *NCH.* IV, pp.361-362 with pedigree of Heron of Birtley Hall.

(c) *NCH.* VIII, pp.334-336 (West Chirton and Flatworth).

(d) *NCH.* V, pp.406-410 (Hadston).

(e) *NCH.* VII, pp.357-365 with pedigree of Heron of Bockenfield.

(f) *NCH.* XI, pp.368-393 with pedigree of Heron of Ford.

(g) *NCH.* XIV, pp.410-413 with pedigree of Heron of Crawley.

(h) *HN.* ii. II, pp.13-17 with pedigree of Heron of Meldon.

(i) Publications of the Newcastle upon Tyne Records Committee. vol.VII. *Northumberland and Durham Deeds,* pp.89-118.

(j) *Pedigrees recorded at the Herald's Visitations of the County of Northumberland.* Edited by Joseph Foster. Heron of Bockenfield registered 1666.

(k) *Pedigrees recorded at the Visitations of the County Palatine of Durham.* Edited by Joseph Foster. Heron of East Thickley registered 1575.

(l) Surtees, *History and antiquities of the County Palatine of Durham.* vol. I, p.218, Heron of Eppleton. vol. III, p.288 —Heron of Great Chilton.

(m) Raine's *History and Antiquities of North Durham.* p.304—Heron of Thornton.

(n) J. C. Hodgson's *MS Pedigrees* in Newcastle Public Library.

Heron of Bockenfield and Thirston. I, 100, 69, 428; A. 285.
Heron of Ford and Bockenfield. I, 430.
Heron of Kirrouchtree. III, 396.
Heron of Hexham. IV, 280; VI, 156, 157.
Heron of Newcastle. II, 120, 122; C. 383.
Heron of Chipchase. A, 246, 296.
Heron of Humshaugh. A, 338.
Heron of Crawley. A, 294.
Heron of Plessey. VII, 331.

HERON—FREEHOLDERS

1628. Richard Hearon of Bockenfield esq.; Thomas Hearon of Crawlaw, gent.; John Hearon of Birkley (Birtley), gent.; Cuthb. Hearon of Chipchase esq.

1639. Richard Hearon of Bockenfield gent.; Cuthbert Hearon of Chipchase esq.; Cuthbert Hearon of Kirkheaton gent.; John Hearon of Bircley Hall gent.

1698. Thomas Heron jun. of Corbridge; Cuth. Heron of Sheelehall; William Heron of Humshaugh yeo.; George Heron of Humshaugh; Thomas Heron of Corbridge gent.; Richard Heron of Alneham; Roger Heron of Newrigg (Mooridge, par. Elsdon); John Heron of Todburne Sheell.

1710. Richard Heron of Alnham; Cuthbert Heron of Hexham; John Heron of Ingoe; Thomas Heron of Corbridge; Cuthbert Heron of Sheelehall; Thomas Heron snr. of Corbridge; Thomas Heron of Hexham; Joseph Heron of Hexham; George Heron of Ingoe; John Heron of Netherwarden; Ralph Heron of Moorrigg; William Heron of Smailmouth.

1715. Thomas Harne (*sic*) of Hexham; Cuthbert Heron of Birkley for Sheelhall; Thomas Harne (*sic*) of Whitley for Cullercoates; Richard Heron of Hexham; Joseph Harn of Hexham; Richard Heron of Aledome; George Heron of Ingoe; John Heron of Netherwarden; Cuthbert Heron of Hexham; Tho. Heron of Corbridge; Ralph Heron of Moorrig.

1721. John Heron of Wall for lands in Warden; Cuth. Heron of Birkley; Thomas Heron of Corbridge.

1734. Jno Heron, Wall, for Netherwarden; Richard Heron, Hexham; Wm Heron, Hexham, for Lincoln Hill; Mr George Heron, Hexham; Wm Heron, Corbridge; Ra. Heron, Birkley, for Dultridge (Durtrees, par. Elsdon).

1748. Thomas Heron of Plessey; John Heron of Wall for Sheelhall; Cuthbert Heron of Gateshead for Hexham Intacks; Robert Heron of Newcastle for Snape (par. Hexham).

1774. John Heron of Leehall for Sheelhall; Thomas Heron of Dikehead (par. Elsdon); John Heron of Mooredgehouse; Richard Heron of Eshot east house for Whitton (par. Rothbury).

1826. Sir Thos Heron bart of So. Shields for Broomhaugh; William Heron of Newbiggin for Westgate; John Hearn (*sic*) of No. Shields; James Heron of Morpeth; Robert Heron of East Thirston for Rothbury; John Heron of East Thirston for Rothbury.

KNIGHTS OF 1166

In the 11th century the knights were the professional soldiers who had a full equipment of armour and fought on horseback. They took service under the barons who were the king's military commanders, and either lived in the baron's household or held land in payment for their services. When Henry I succeeded to the kingdom of England he issued a charter of liberties to all his subjects. To knights who did military service for their lands he granted 'the lands of their own domains to be free from all tribute and work; so that being freed from so heavy a burden, they may so fully equip themselves with horses and arms, as to be ready and prepared for my service and the defence of my kingdom' (*Hist. of Richard, prior of Hexham. s.a.* 1135). We have to wait nearly a hundred years after the Norman Conquest before the names of any of the knights of Northumberland are known to us. By then, most of them have acquired surnames from their English lands thus obscuring their family origins.

A few of them betray their native ancestry by use of such Christian names as Gospatric and Liulf. One or two only have retained as a surname the place in Normandy, France or Flanders from whence they came. William de Tubervill and Galfrid de Valloignes, military tenants in the barony of Alnwick in 1166, are obviously of this category.

Even three generations after the conquest, many knights had no surnames. In 1166 Ernulf de Morewic reported that from his one knight's fee in Northumberland (the barony of Chevington), 'a certain David' held half a fee of the old feoffment. At the same time 'a certain knight called Galon' held of the old feoffment a quarter of a knight's fee in the barony of Ellingham. Some knights with less uncommon Christian names had to be distinguished by the addition of their father's Christian name; *e.g.* William son of Adam, John son of Simon.

The holder of a knight's fee was not a knight until he had come of age and had been formally knighted, the ceremony being performed by the new knight's father, or his lord or by another knight. A young man of knightly family entered the household of a baron or nobleman at a very early age as a *vassaletus*, and at the age of about fourteen became an *armiger* (esquire). In much later times the term esquire, originally denoting an apprentice knight became the designation for a lord of a manor or any substantial landowner. In the 20th century it has tended to be applied by courtesy to any male in any class or walk of life. There has been a similar broadening in the use of the term *vassaletus*. In the 16th century any serving man was a varlet. In more modern times the name has been reintroduced from France as the *valet de chambre*.

By the 13th century the military service due to the king from his barons was largely commuted for a money payment, scutage, literally shield money. The feudal levy was replaced by a mercenary army, though on the marches of Wales and Scotland the feudal knight was still needed for garrisoning the king's castles and for defence of the borders.

During the 12th and early 13th centuries many of the original baronies had broken down and become divided amongst coheiresses. The Crown gradually encouraged this disintegration, being aided no doubt by the barons' revolts against king John and Henry III. The breakdown of the baronies increased the advance of the county as an administrative unit. All but the demesne lands of the baronies were brought into the body of the shire for fiscal unity in the first place and gradually the responsibility of the barons was abolished altogether. It becomes obvious in the third quarter of the 13th century that feudal principles are losing hold.

Consequent on this breakdown there was a greater need for knights to carry on the administrative work of the county and for border defence. In the reign of Henry III it was found necessary owing to the splitting up of the tenancies *in capite* to issue general writs to the sheriffs to summon all persons within their county to perform such service as was due under their tenures. It is evident that the increasing burdens placed on the knights became so onerous that many persons of knightly families refrained from taking up knighthood. In an attempt to remedy this Edward I directed that all tenants *in capite* and all holders of 20 librates of land not held *in capite* should tender sureties that they would take upon them the degree of knighthood before Christmas 1278.

Another result of the breakdown of feudal tenure was the need of the Crown to look elsewhere for information and counsel as to county affairs. King John consulted the counties on such matters as forest administration (*Letters Close,* 14 John, p.129) and the rights of the debtors of the Jews (*Ib.,* p.132). Four knights were summoned from every shire to negotiate with the king. More use was made of the knights of the shire by Henry III. In 1254 when the barons could not pledge the counties for an aid for the Gascon war, knights were summoned *vice omnium et singulorum* to make a grant. These knights were not elected by the county but were selected by the sheriff. It is not known if any were sent from Northumberland in this year, but for the parliament of 6 October 1258 four were selected by the sheriff and ordered to enquire with others touching certain trespasses and to bring their inquisitions personally to London.

In later years knights of the shire were selected not only from knightly families, but from those of baronial status. Between 1258 and 1327 members of the families of Fenwick of Fenwick, Widdrington of Widdrington, Halton of Halton, Ogle of Ogle and Vaux of Beaufront were chosen as well as representatives of the Bertrams of Bothal, Herons of Hadston, Mauduits of Eshot, Tailboys of Hepple, Cliffords of Ellingham and Raymes of Shortflatt.

Not until the end of the 14th century were the knights of the shire democratically elected. In 1377 the commons asserted that 'by common right of the Realm there are and ought to be two persons elected from every county of England to be in Parliament for the commune of the said counties' (*Rot. Parl.* ii, 368). In 1430 a statute was passed limiting the right to vote in parliamentary elections to those who held freehold of the annual value of forty shillings, and this became the rule of the constitution until the 19th century.

The descendants of the Norman knights, the knights of the shire of the 14th and 15th century, became the county families of the 17th and 18th centuries. They were augmented by certain merchant and yeoman families of the 17th century, but greatly reduced by the Civil Wars and Jacobite risings of 1715 and 1745.

It has long been recognised that north-country families have been very tenacious of their lands. Grey in his *Chorographia* of 1649 wrote 'The nobility and gentry of the north are of great antiquity, and can produce more ancient families than any other part of England; many of them gentry before the Conquest, the rest came in with the Conqueror. The nobility and gentry of the north have been always employed in their native country in the wars of the kings of England against the Scots'. Here is the idea which even today is not completely dead, that all old families either came in with the Norman Conquest or were already here before 1066. Fuller in his *English Worthies* written in 1799 says 'The English gentry who live southward near London (which for the lustre thereof I may fitly call the sun of our nation), in the warmth of wealth and plenty of pleasure, quickly dissolve themselves of their estates and inheritance, whilst the gentry living in this country in the confines of Scotland, in the wind of war (daily alarmed with their blustering enemies) buckle their estates as their armour the closer to them, and since have no less thriftily defended their patrimony in peace than formerly they valiantly maintained it in war'.

In Northumberland there are still a few families living on estates which have been held by their ancestors for over 700 years.

The first list of knights of Northumberland dates from 1166 though unfortunately it is not complete. In that year Henry II ordered all his tenants in chief to inform him by letters close what service each owed for his barony, the numbers of knights enfeoffed before the death of Henry I, those enfeoffed after that date and the balance of knights' fees to be provided by the demesne lands of the barony. Returns were made then for the baronies of Whalton, Bolam, Styford, Mitford, Chevington, Wooler, Gosforth, Hadston, Embleton, Dilston, Callerton, Warkworth, Bothal, Ellingham, Morpeth and Alnwick. These returns have been printed in the *Black Book of the Exchequer,* (*Liber Niger Scaccarii,* ed. Thomas Hearne, pp.329-339), in Hodgson's *History of Northumberland,* iii. III, and in *Liber Feodorum* or the Book of Fees commonly called *Testa de Nevill,* 3 vols., H.M.S.O. 1920-31.

Only a small minority of the 12th century knights founded families that survived in the male line throughout the Middle Ages and there are even fewer of them surviving at the present day. Pedigrees of many of these families were registered at the various visitations of the North made in the 16th and 17th centuries by heralds from the College of Arms. The accuracy and value of these pedigrees must be carefully considered. *See* HERALDS' VISITATIONS. Many surnames were continued by the descendants of bastard sons. *See* ILLEGITIMACY.

In the pedigrees that illustrate the accounts of each family in the following pages only agnatic kindred are included, that is the descendants through male lines. The only exceptions to this are the pedigrees of descendants in the female line who have adopted the surname of their maternal ancestors. It is, of course, impossible to trace all cadet lines, for many of these after a few generations sank so low in the social scale that they possessed no lands and hence had no family muniments. Parish registers where they survive can be of great value, but only if the family has become fixed in one parish.

HERALDS' VISITATIONS

THE original duty of the king's heralds was to announce war, to proclaim peace, to manage tournaments and combats, to attend on embassies and to officiate at solemnities. They had the right to confirm or sanction the bearing of heraldic arms and to grant them. In the reigns of Henry VII and Henry VIII the power of granting arms was normally granted by letters patent to the three chief heralds, Garter, Clarenceux and Norroy. Garter was the principal king of arms and mainly concerned with the Knights of the Order of the Garter and the higher nobility of the country. Clarenceux was king of arms for the parts of England south of the river Trent; and Norroy for the parts north of that river. A provincial king of arms was expected to register the descents, marriages and issue of the armigerous families residing in his province. In his official capacity he attended the funerals of the magnates in his district. In the schedule of the moneys disbursed for the funeral of sir John Forster (d.1601) of Bamburgh the first item is '*Imprimis* to the herald—£57. 13s. 8d.'.

The College of Arms was incorporated by Richard III in 1483. From then until 1666 the provincial kings of arms made visitations in their districts at irregular intervals. The pedigrees which they then collected were mainly compiled from information given to them by heads of families. The earlier heralds cannot be blamed for any inaccuracies in these for they had no means of checking the information and few of the heralds, if any, were historians. In the time of Elizabeth I the rise of new families produced a demand for new pedigrees. Genuine research was unpopular and few were capable of it. As a result the heralds and others produced spurious pedigrees, many of them sheer fiction. In some cases actual forged documents were concocted for this purpose.

The following visitations for the north of England, the province of Norroy, king of arms, contain pedigrees of Northumberland families:

c.1480-*c*.1500. Visitation of the North of England by an unknown herald. The only pedigrees of families in any way connected with Northumberland are those of Percy, Widdrington, Ogle, Yvers (Eure) and Roos (*SS.* vol.144).

1530. Visitation by Thomas Tonge, Norroy (*SS.* vol.41). Thomas Tonge, 'Norrey Kyng of Armes of the North Cuntrey began hys visitacion at syr Brian Stapultons, knight, of Notynghamshyre, the vijth daie of August, Anno Domini, mcccccxxx'. From Nottinghamshire Tonge's visitation can be traced across Yorkshire into county Durham. It is apparent that he did not enter Northumberland but he recorded the arms and pedigree of Gilbert Middleton, esquire, 'and the said Gilbert was mayor of Newe Castell at the time of our visitation'. He also recorded the arms of the monastery of Tynemouth. He then returned through Durham into Yorkshire and from thence into Cumberland and Westmorland. Although no pedigrees of Northumberland families were recorded in 1530 several marriages of individuals of these families appear in the pedigrees of families from the adjoining counties.

1552. Visitation by William Harvey, Norroy (*SS.* vol.122). Thomas Carr of Ford, Nicholas Ridley of Willimontswick, Ralph Fenwick of Stanton, William Carnaby of Halton, Sir Reynold Carnaby of Hexham, Thomas Carnaby of Langley, Cuthbert Carnaby of Aydon, David Carnaby of Beaufront, Francis Armorer of Ulgham, John Carr of Hetton, sir George Radcliffe of Cartington, William, lord Evre of Witton, co. Dur., John Swinburne of Chopwell, co. Dur., Thomas Swinburne of Edlingham, Christopher Mitford of Newcastle, Christopher Baxter of Newcastle, Matthew Baxter of Newcastle, Henry Anderson of Newcastle, William Carr of Newcastle, Albany Fetherstone of Fetherstonhaugh, John Shaftoe of Bavington.

1558. Visitation by Lawrence Dalton, Norroy (*Ib.*). Thomas Rotherford of Middleton Hall, Bartram Anderson of Newcastle, William Carr of Newcastle, John Roddam of Roddam, sir John Widdrington of Widdrington, Gilbert Swinhoe of Cornhill, William, lord Eure, Thomas Bradford of Bradford, Robert Constable of Wallington, sir Thomas Grey of Horton.

Other pedigrees collected 1560-1561 probably by Lawrence Dalton—Cuthbert Musgrave of Newcastle, sir Robert Brandling of Newcastle, Robert Lewen of Newcastle, Bartram Anderson of Newcastle, Francis Anderson of Newcastle, Henry Anderson of Newcastle, William Dent of Newcastle, Cuthbert Ellison of Newcastle, sir Henry Percy, William Sherwood of Newcastle, John Swinburne of Chopwell, co. Dur., Cuthbert Carnaby of Halton.

1563/4. Visitation by William Flower, Norroy (*Harleian Society* XVI). Although this is described as a Visitation of Yorkshire, it includes many families from Northumberland, Durham, Cumberland, Westmorland and Lancashire. The visitation seems to have been started in 1563 and continued into 1564. The following Northumberland families are included:—

Anderson (of Newcastle).
Armerer of 'Howgham' (Ulgham, par. Bothal).
Baxter of Newcastle.
Bellingham.
Bennet of Newcastle.
Bradford of Bradford.
Brandling (of Newcastle).
Carnaby (of Halton).
Carre (of Newcastle).
Carre (of Horton).
Delaval (of Seaton Delaval).
Dent (of Newcastle).
Ellison (of Newcastle).
Eure (of Kirkley).
Fenwick (of Middleton).
Fetherston (of Fetherstone).
Grey (of Horton).
Lewen (of Newcastle).
Middleton (of Belsay).
Mitford (of Seghill).

Musgrave of Newcastle.
Ogle (of Ogle).
Percy (of Alnwick).
Ratcliff of Dilston.
Ridley (of Willimontswick).
Roddam of Roddam, Northumberland.
Rotherford of Middleton Hall.
Shafto (of Bavington).
Swynborne (of Nafferton).
Swynno (of Cornhill).
Woderyngton (of Widdrington).

1567. Visitation by William Flower, Norroy (*SS.* vol.133). Swinburne of Chopwell, co. Dur., Ridley of Willimontswick.

1575. Visitation by William Flower, Norroy, and Robert Glover (*SS.* vol.146).
De la Vale of Seton de la Vale.
Fenwike de Fenwike.
Forster de Ederston.
Grey de Chillingham.
Lawson of Cramlington.
Ogle de Bothall.
Roper—Robert Roper of Newcastell uppon Tyne one of the Customers theire.
Wodderington de Wodderington.
Wytfeld of the house of Whitfield.

1575. Northumberland Pedigrees taken A.D. 1575, from *Harleian MS.* No. 1554 which are not in *Queen's College MSS.* and not printed by Foster in his *Visitations of Northumberland* (*SS.* vol.146).
Ridley of Willimonteswick.
Collingwood of Eslington.
Baxter of Newcastle.
Riddell of Newcastle.
Salkeld of Hulne Park.

1584/5. Visitation of Yorkshire by Robert Glover, Somerset Herald (Ed. Joseph Forster, London, 1875).
Fowbery of Newbald 'came out of Northumberland into Yorkshire'.
Cresswell of Nunkeeling from George Creswell of Creswell, Nd.
Lawson of Brough from William Lawson of Cramlington, Nd.

1615. Visitation of Northumberland by Richard St George, Norroy (Ed. G. W. Marshall, *The Genealogist*, London 1878; Ed. Joseph Foster, Newcastle upon Tyne n.d.). The pedigrees registered at this visitation were the following:—
Francis Allder of Alnwick.
Roberte Anderson of Newcastle.
Sir Henry Anderson of Newcastle and Haswell.
Thomas Armorer of Belford.
Gawen Ansley of Shaftoe.
George Bedenell of Lemington.
Francis Belgrave of Blaby and now of Newcastle upon Tyne.
John Bell of Bellasis.
Thomas Blenkensop of Blenkinsop.
George Blenkinsop of Bellaster.
Thomas Bradforthe of Bradforthe.
William Burrell of Howtell.
John Carnaby of Langley.

Lancelot Carnaby of Halton.
William Carr of Woodhall.
Roberte Clenhell of Clenhell.
George Collingwood of Eppleton in the Bishoprick (Collingwood of Eslington).
Thomas Collingwood of Little Raile.
Thomas Collingwood of Newsham.
John Crastre of Crastre.
Henry Draper of Newcastle.
John Errington of Errington.
Marke Errington of Pont Eland.
Anthony Errington of Denton.
John Fenwicke of Butterlawe.
George Fenwick of Brinkeburn.
George Fenwicke of Langshawes.
Richard Fenwicke of Stanton.
Aubeny Fetherstonehalghe of Fetherstonehalghe.
Matthew Forster of Etherstone.
John Forster of Tughull Hall and Newham.
Sir Ralfe Grey of Chillingham.
Thomas Gray of Kilay (Kyloe).
Roberte Heslerigg of Swarland.
William Jackson of Newcastle upon Tyne, Town Clerk.
William Jenison of Newcastle, Alderman.
Oliver Killingworth of Killingworth.
Thomas Lawson of Cramlington.
Lancelot Lisle of Newton-in-the-more.
Lionell Maddison of Newcastle, Alderman.
Michael Mitford of Seighall (Seghill).
George Muschampe of Baremore (Barmoor).
Thomas Ogle of Beesyde (Bebside).
Oliver Ogle of Burrowdon.
Thomas Proctor of Shawdon.
Clemente Reade of the Close.
sir Francis Ratcliffe of Darwentwater, co. Cumb., bart.
George Reveley of Angcrofte.
Thomas Ridley of Walltowne.
William Ridley of Westwood.
Edmund Rodham of Rodham and Little Haughton.
John Salkeild of Bassington.
Alexander Selby of Betelsden (Biddleston).
John Strother of Langton and Newton.
John Swynburne of Nafferton and Edlingham.
Richard Thirlewall of Thirlewall.
Nicholas Thornton of Witton.
William Warmouth of Newcastle, Mayor.
Rich. Whitwange of Dunstan.
sir Henry Widdrington (of Widdrington).

1666. Visitation of Northumberland by William Dugdale, Norroy (Ed. Joseph Foster, Newcastle upon Tyne n.d.).
The following pedigrees were registered in 1666:—
Francis Addison of Ovingham.
Peter Astell of Newcastle upon Tyne.
Raphe Bates of Halliwell.
Thomas Bewick of Newcastle upon Tyne and of Close House.
John Buteler, merchant in Newcastle.
Reginald Carnaby of Halton.
Raphe Carre of Cocken in co. pal. Dunelm, now residing in Newcastle upon Tyne.
Radulph Clavering de Callaley.

Cuthbert Collingwood of Dalden in co. pal. Dunelm (Collingwood of Eslington).
Robert Collingwood of Great Ryle.
sir Raphe Delaval of Seaton, bart.
John Dobson of Newcastle upon Tyne.
Robert Ellison, a merchant in Newcastle.
Nicholas Errington of Pont Eland.
Claudius Fenwick of Newcastle upon Tine, esqr. Dr of Phisick, of Brinkeburne.
sir William Fenwick of Wallington, bart.
sir William Forster of Bamborough Castle.
John Greene of Newcastle upon Tyne.
Henry Greye of Bichfield.
Raphe Gray, a merchant in Newcastle super Tine, and William Gray of Newcastle upon Tine.
Raphe Hebburne of Hebburne.
John Heron of Bokinfield.
sir Thomas Horsley of Horsley.
Robert Ile of Newcastle upon Tyne.
Raphe Jenison of Elswick.
Edward Lawson of Brunton near Alnwick.
William Lilburne of Newcastle upon Tine, now a Barrister of Gray's Inne.
sir Thomas Loraine of Kirk Harle, bart.
Miles Man, a Merchant in Newcastle upon Tine.
William Middleton of Belsay Castle.
Marke Milbanke of Newcastle upon Tine, Alderman.
Robert Mitford of Mitford.
Robert Mitford of Newcastle, merchant.
Christopher Nicholson, Merchant in Newcastle.
sir Francis Ratcliffe of Dilston, bart.
Thomas Riddell of Fenham.
John Ridley of Hard Riding, a Justice of the Peace.
John Rogers, a merchant of Newcastle upon Tine.
William Shafto of Babington.
Thomas Sherwood, a Merchant in Newcastle upon Tine.
Richard Stote, a Barrister of Lincoln's Inne, of Jesmond.
sir John Swinburne of Cap Heaton, bart.
John Watson, a Merchant in Newcastle.
Christopher Young, Dr of Phisick, now residing in Newcastle.

In the past too much reliance has been placed on these visitation pedigrees and where errors have been discovered in them the heralds have often been blamed. The truth seems to be that in most cases the head of the family produced his pedigree and this was accepted without question by the herald. Nevertheless there have been pedigrees prepared by the College of Arms and many of these are unreliable. It is generally inadvisable to accept as accurate more than two or three generations of the visitation pedigrees without confirmatory evidence from outside sources. When a man did not know the maiden name of his grandmother it seems unlikely that he had much knowledge of his paternal grandfather. No doubt he could get this information from the family muniments but could he read these?

ILLEGITIMACY

DURING the Middle Ages illegitimacy was little frowned upon and almost ignored except in relation to the descent of land and succession to titles. Henry I of England had set an example that many were prepared to follow. He had many mistresses and at least sixteen bastards of his are known. The church excused this by saying that 'He was led by female blandishments, not for gratification of lust, but for the sake of issue' (William of Malmesbury, II, p.488). His mistresses seem to have been drawn from all walks of life, and included a daughter of one of the Welsh princes, Rhys ap Tydr and a daughter of Forne, lord of Greystoke, a land-owner in Northumberland. The illegitimate daughters were very useful for purposes of diplomacy and were married to neighbouring rulers rather than to his own barons. Amongst Henry's sons-in-law thus honoured were Rotrou, count of Perche, Conan, count of Brittany and Alexander I of Scotland.

A similar form of diplomacy was observed by William the Lion, king of Scots, who married off his illegitimate daughters to Northumbrian barons.

The illegitimacy of William de Vesci of Kildare did not prevent him from being summoned to parliament as a baron in 1313. His father was William de Vesci, lord of Alnwick, and his mother, a daughter of the Irish prince of Desmond. Sir Robert de Umframville, an illegitimate son of sir Thomas de Umframville (d.1387) actually succeeded to the lordship of Redesdale by a special entail which refers to him as 'son of Joanna, daughter of Adam Roddam'. He served with great distinction in the wars against Scotland and France, became vice-admiral of England and was a Knight of the Garter.

There are indeed few Northumberland families that did not have a cadet line descended from an illegitimate son. Perhaps the most remarkable case is that of the Forsters of Adderstone. When Thomas Forster of this family made his will on 4 April 1589 he appoints his grandson Matthew Forster 'base-begotten son to Thomas Forster, late deceased' his full and sole executor. His brother sir John Forster, Mr Nicholas Forster 'base-begotten son to the said sir John Forster', and Hewge Forster 'my base-begotten son' are to be supervisors to the will. It has been said that 'it is not difficult to account for the number of Forsters in Bamboroughshire, without having regard to the legitimate issue of his great grandfather, who is said to have numbered twenty-two sons among his children. The will may truly be called a base one' (SS. 38, p.164n.).

It was the usual custom in the 16th and 17th centuries for a bastard son to take his father's surname, but a daughter born out of wedlock normally took her mother's name.

In the 11th and 12th centuries the Church of Rome had made great efforts to impose clerical celibacy but without very great success. In some cases there is evidence that priests married secretly and so enabled their children to establish legitimacy after their deaths. Instances are also known where the ecclesiastical authorities found it quite remunerative, and they always wanted money, merely to impose a fine on a priest who kept an unofficial wife. The customary 'sin-rent'

was £2 a year. A priest in whose house a child was born could usually compound by a fine of five shillings—a 'cradle crown'.

In 1548 Edward VI gave the clergy freedom to marry. This right was withdrawn by Mary, but restored by Elizabeth I in 1559. Cuthbert Ogle, clerk, parson of Stanhope, co. Durham, and of Ford, by his w.d. 5 June 1530 leaves the manor of Ingram to the use of Isabel Musgrave, 'my servant'. The remainder of his lands, and they were quite extensive, were divided amongst his 'kinsmen', Matthew, Luke, Peter and Mark Ogle. It is clear that these four brothers were Isabel Musgrave's children. The biblical names that he bestowed on his sons are in keeping with the other patriarcal ideas which he evidently possessed. Mark Ogle received a grant of arms in 1535 in which it is stated that he was descended 'of a noble house of Ogle, also of a noble house of Musgrave'. His illegitimacy had very soon been forgotten.

BARONY OF WHALTON—KNIGHTS OF 1166

In 1166 Walter son of William, baron of Whalton, reported in his *carta* that the knights who had been enfeoffed by him of the old feoffment were William de Niweham and Bertram de Woderington. They each held one knight's fee. Out of the demesne lands of the barony Gilbert de Hoggal held half a knight's fee and Otui de Insula a third part of a knight's fee, both of the new feoffment.

The knight's fee held by William de Niweham comprised Newham (par. Whalton), Denton and Newbiggen (par. Newburn), Kenton, Fawdon, and a third part of Gosforth (par. St Nicholas', Newcastle upon Tyne). William was succeeded by his son and grandson both called Robert, and the latter by his daughter Hawise. The surname of Niweham consequently became extinct before the middle of the 13th century.

Bertram de Woderington's fee comprised Widdrington and Druridge (chap. Widdrington) and half of Burradon (par. Earsdon). The Widdringtons retained the manor of Widdrington until it was forfeited for their part in the Jacobite Rising in 1715. The surname has survived until the present day (see WIDDRINGTON OF WIDDRINGTON).

In 1166 Gilbert de Hoggal held Ogle (par. Whalton) and the other half of Burradon (par. Earsdon). The manor of Ogle passed out of the family by marriage in 1597; but cadet lines survive to the present day (see OGLE OF OGLE).

The third part of a knight's fee held by the family of Insula in the barony of Whalton was two thirds of South Gosforth (par. St Nicholas', Newcastle upon Tyne). The family held other lands in Northumberland in the baronies of Prudhoe, Styford and Bywell, and in the lordship of Redesdale. Under the French form of Lisle the surname still survives (see LISLE OF EAST WOODBURN).

WIDDRINGTON

THIS family took its surname from the township and chapelry of Widdrington in the parish of Woodhorn. It ranked from the 14th century as one of the foremost on the Borders. Its origin was no doubt Norman-French. The small estate of Widdrington and half of Burradon was augmented by purchases of land at Ellington, Linton and Druridge in the 13th century. By the marriage of sir John de Widdrington with Christiana one of the daughters and coheiresses of sir Adam de Swinburne of East Swinburne, the family estates were more than doubled by the acquisition of Colwell, Haughton, Humshaugh and Stonecroft. Later marriages with other heiresses brought still more land, and the power and influence that went with it. From the Actons they had the castle and manor of West Swinburne, and from the Radcliffe's the castle and manor of Cartington. When in 1635 William Widdrington married Mary daughter and heiress of Anthony Thorold of Blankney, Lincs., the family obtained extensive estates in Lincolnshire.

The Widdringtons were staunch supporters of the Stuarts and adhered, almost without exception, to the church of Rome. In 1643 sir William Widdrington was created, by Charles I, baron Widdrington of Blankney, and he was killed fighting for his sovereign in 1651. In a list of Northumbrian recusants of 1677 are the names of William, lord Widrington of Widdrington, and Bridget, lady Widrington, Wm Widrington of Buteland gent., Francis Widdrington of Hepple gent., Edward Widdrington of Felton esq., and Dorothy his wife, Henry Widrington of Ritton gent., and (blank) Withrington of Westharle, spinster. Confiscations during the Commonwealth seriously reduced the family fortunes and the family was finally ruined by the participation of the 4th baron in the Jacobite rising of 1715.

Few of the battles on the borders were without a Widdrington participant. The martial qualities of the family are well portrayed in the ballad of 'Chevy Chase' where Richard Widdrington 'a poor squire of land' was killed by the Scots in a border fray after being severely wounded. 'For when his legs were hewn in two. He knelt and fought on his knee'. It is perhaps unfortunate that the poet chose the name of Richard for his hero, for this was about the only common Christian name hardly ever used by the family.

William, 4th baron Widdrington, was attainted in 1716 and his only surviving son, Henry Francis Widdrington, died *s.p.* in 1774.

Amongst the gentlemen of the Middle and East Marches in 1550 were five of the name of Widdrington (Robert Wytherington of Craster, sir John Wetherington knt, Raphe Wetherington, John Wetherington of Mitford, John Wetherington of Hauxley) and in 1639 there were six freeholders of the name (sir Willm Widdrington of Widdrington, knt, Robert Widdrington of Plessey, esq., Robert Widdrington of Hauxley, gent., Henry Widdrington of Blackheddon,

gent., Henry Widdrington of Buteland, gent., and Roger Widdrington of Cartington, esq.). It is doubtful if any direct male descendants survive. The present family of Widdrington of Newton-on-the-Moor is descended in the female line from the Widdringtons of Hauxley, par. Warkworth. The founder of this branch of the family was Roger Widdrington of Chibburn, a younger son of sir Ralph Widdrington of Widdrington (living 1490).

Since the time of the rev. John Hodgson, no really serious attempt has been made to connect the numerous junior branches of the family to the main stem.

WIDDRINGTON OF WIDDRINGTON, CHAP. WIDDRINGTON

THE knight's fee held by Bertram de Woderington in 1166 comprised the vill of Widdrington and half of Burradon. Sometime before 1162 Walter son of William, baron of Whalton, made a grant of these lands to Bertram de Wdringtun to hold of the grantor and his heirs as his father held for one day and one night, and as he has hitherto held, by one knight's service. At the same time notification was made that the claim which William Tasca had against Bertram was defeated by judgment of his lord's court and William lost by fraud and took a day in the court of his chief lord, Walter son of William, to defend himself of the fraud and made default; Alan de Dririg his peer gave his pledge for proving the fraud, and he on his part gave his, and took a day for defending himself by duel but came not; therefore the court adjudged that he had lost by fraud and remitted to Bertram as to the right heir as his proper inheritance. The grantor warrants the judgment which was made and approved at 'Weltun' by Hodenell de Umframville on the appeal of Alan de Dririg and the default of William de Tascha (*NDD*. p.225, No. 1, where it is suggested that Weltun probably means Whalton. It is more likely to be Welton, a manor in the Umframville barony of Prudhoe).

It is evident that Bertram de Wdrington was not the first member of his family to hold the knight's fee in the barony of Whalton, for he held in 1166 of the old feoffment. Hodgson mentions a John de Widdrington as witness to a deed of 1139/40 (*HN*. ii, II, p.230; the reference is apparently from Vincent's pedigree in *Harl. MS*. 5808). Bertram de Wudrinton was charged one mark for a plea in 1171 (*Pipe Roll*).

Bertram's successor was Galfrid de Wudrington who with Randulf Brun was charged one mark for a plea in 1178 (*Ib*.). In 1187 Gaufrid was charged one mark for a forest plea (*Ib*.). Between 1177 and 1182 he witnesses the grant of Gosforth by Walter son of William to Robert de Insula (*NDD*. p.121, No. 4). Galfrid de Wdrintun granted and confirmed to Oelard de Burwindune one half of Burradon which his father had given him. Amongst the witnesses are Randulf brother of Galfrid de Wdrintune and Roger brother of the said Galfrid (*Brumell Charters* No. 2; *NCH.* IX, p.49n.). The grant has been dated *circa* 1200 but may be a little earlier. Galfrid's father who had given the land to Oelard in the first place may have been Bertram de Wdringtun, but it is surprising that the Christian name of Bertram is never afterwards used by the family.

Galfrid had been succeeded before 1209 by Gerard de Wudington who in that year rendered account of 2 marks for 'having his wood' (*Pipe Roll*). In 1219 Gerard owed 10 marks which had been advanced to him by the king in Poitou (*Ib.*). In the following year he owed half a mark for having a *pone* (*Ib.*). This last debt was unpaid in 1221 and 1222 (*Ib.*). On 11 November 1212 Hugh Flandrensis leased to sir Gerald de Wdrington half a toft and 23 acres in Widdrington; the lease was for 16 years and if sir Gerard should die within the term his brother Geoffrey was to have the remainder of the lease (*NDD.* p.226, No. 3).

Gerard de Wodrington, John de Eslington and others were pledges for John son of Waldef in 1241 (*Pipe Roll*). In December 1244 Gerard witnesses a confirmation by Roger Mauduit of a grant made by his father Godfrid to the prior and convent of Brinkburn (*SS.* 90, p.60). We cannot be sure that this Gerard is the same person as Gerard de Wudrington of 1208 x 1222 for it is certain that the latter had a son Gerard as well as two other sons John and Duncan.

John de Woderington was the eldest of these three brothers. He witnesses an agreement in 1245 between William, prior of Brinkburn, and John de Eslington concerning a rent from the mill of Framlington (*Ib.*, p.42). A grant to Brinkburn made during the shrievalty of John de Lythgraynes, 1274-78, is witnessed by sir John de Wodrington and sir Gerard his brother (*Ib.*, p.50). In February 1272 John witnesses a confirmation by John de Kesterne to Brinkburn of lands in Low Trewhitt (*Ib.*, p.119). By an undated grant John, lord of Widdrington, gave to David de Lacel with Joan the grantor's kinswoman, all his land bought by himself and by Duncan his brother in Ellington, and a meadow in Druridge (*NDD.* p.231, No. 33). Duncan de Wuderinton acquired a toft in Ellington from John son of Robert de Gloucestre, and half an acre in Ellington from Edmund de Ellington, son of Ralph de Stokes (*Ib.*, p.230, Nos. 30, 31). Duncan de Wodelington was an attorney for Johanna wife of Thomas Corbet, at the assizes of 1256 (*SS.* 88, p.23). At the assizes of 1269 John de Woderington and Custancia his wife were concerned in a plea of land which had belonged to William de Saint Peter *antecessor* of the said Constance (*Ib.*, p.189). At the same time Dionisia widow of Fulco de Tybenham, gave 20s., for licence to make an agreement with Gerard de Woderyngton and Petronilla his wife (*Ib.*, p.150). The agreement was completed by a fine whereby Dionisia acknowleged the manor of Titlington to be the right of Petronilla, and Gerard and Petronilla agreed that Dionisia should hold it for her lifetime at a rent of 4s. for all services and customs; after the death of Dionisia the manor was to revert to Gerard and Petronilla and the heirs of Petronilla; if the latter should die 'without heir of her body begotten', the manor was to revert to the heirs of Dionisia (*Ib.*, p.417).

Sir Gerard de Woderington and his wife Petronilla left no children, and John de Woderington 1278 x 1281 granted to Geoffrey de Woderington his son ten bovates with tofts and crofts in the vill of Tranwell which had been given by Roger de Merlay III to sir Gerard, and which land the grantor had by hereditary right after the death of sir Gerard his brother (*NDD.* p.227, No. 9). At Hilary term 1277 the prior of the hospital of St John of Jerusalem in England claimed that Gerard de Woderingerim, Geoffrey de Woderington and others should do him service at his mill of Woodhorn; and that John de Woderington had erected a mill at Newbiggen to the nuisance of the prior's free tenement in Woodhorn (*de Banco Roll*). At Easter term 1278 Alan de Holthale claimed 5 messuages and 6 bovates of land in Saltwick from Gerard de Woderington (*Ib.*).

Besides Duncan and sir Gerard, sir John de Woderinton seems to have had another brother, Roger. A Roger de Woderington is mentioned in 1268 as brother of John and must belong to this generation (*HN.* iii. II, p.73). He was presumably the same person as Roger de Woderinton who witnesses c.1265-67 a charter of Roger Bertram, lord of Mitford, another witness being sir Gerard Woderinton (*NDD.* p.75, No. 6). *Circa* 1270 when John de Wudrington demised the vill of Druridge to Gilbert de Wythill and Alice his wife, amongst the witnesses were the same sir Gerard de Wudrungton and Roger de Wudrington (*Ib.*, p.227, No. 8). On Tuesday before the Feast of Philip and James apostles (30 April) 1280, Roger de Widerington was one of the five sureties for Robert son of Roger, lord of Warkworth, in a covenant which he entered into with Thomas de Karliolo (*Ib.*, p.77, No. 13). Roger was distrained for knighthood and Peter de Faudon, Ralph de Essingdon, William de Echewick and Robert Wautlyn became sureties that he would actually take the degree of knighthood before Christmas 1278. In 1287 the sheriff accounted for 40s. for the issues of the lands of Ellen who was the wife of Roger de Woderington forfeited before the barons of exchequer 14th year, *i.e.* 1285/6 (*Pipe Roll*).

Sir John de Woderinton had a son John to whom Richard de Gloucestria son of Robert de Gloucestria conveyed a toft and 3 acres in Ellington (*NDD.* p.231, No. 32). His successor however was another son Gerard who as 'dominus Gerard de Woderington' heads the Subsidy Roll for Widdrington in 1296. On 26 September 1297 Gerard was a juror in a dispute about lands at Gunnerton (*Assize Roll*).

According to a pedigree in *Harl. MS.* (1554, *fol.* 4,5,a,b.) Gerardus de Woderington, *temp.* E.I. (1272-1307) had two sons John, *temp.* E.II (1307-1327) and Gerard. Other evidence confirms this; for Gerard see WIDDRINGTON OF DENTON. On 14 May 1307 John, lord of Widdrington, conveyed to Henry de Thornton, chaplain, the land which Roger de Hartwayton, chaplain, had of the gift of sir John de Wydrington, grantor's grandfather, and 2 marks rent out of Linton mill; Henry was to celebrate throughout his life at St Edmund's altar in Widdrington church or elsewhere in the parish for the souls of the grantor's ancestors (*NDD.* p.228, No. 12). John, lord of Wodryngton, had made a demise of his manor of Linton on 11 November 1304 (*Ib.*, p.227, No. 10; *HN.* ii, II, p.249, evid. 9a. gives the date as 1404 in error). He had a grant of free warren in his demesne lands in 1307.

John de Woderington married Christiana daughter of sir Adam de Swynburne (d.1318) of East Swinburne and sister and coheiress of Henry de Swynburne (d.1326). The Swynburne estates were divided between the coheiresses in 1327 when Gerard de Widdrington, Christiana's son and heir, was aged 24. Widdrington's share of these estates was the manor of Haughton, lands in Colwell and Stonecroft, a third part of a messuage in Newcastle, and Lanerton in Cumberland (*Exchequer Rolls*). Sir Gerard occupied many important positions on the borders. He was a commissioner for array 1335, had protection to go into foreign parts May 1338, a commissioner for punishing violators of the truce 1343. He fought at the battle of Neville's Cross in 1346 and was justice itinerant at the court at Wark in Tyndale 1348. Edward III in the fifteenth year of his reign (1341/2) gave a licence to Gerard de Woderington to crenellate his house (*mansum*) of Widdrington and to have a chantry at Widdrington (*Patent Roll*).

In the list of benefactors to the abbey of Newminster is the entry—*Anno Domini mccclxii, die Jovis proxima post festum Conversionis S. Pauli apostoli, obiit dominus Gerardus de Woderyngton, miles* (*SS*. 66, p.305). Sir Gerard married Joan daughter and coheiress of William Rydell, lord of Tillmouth (*NDD*. p.195, No. 1) but left no issue. His heir was his brother Roger. On 1 May 1335 sir Gerard de Wyderyngstone settled on Roger and on Elizabeth daughter of Richard de Actone of Newcastle and their issue the manor of Colwell and 5 messuages and 38 acres in Gunnerton; if they should die without issue the property was to revert to Gerard and his heirs (*Feet of Fines*). At the same time Richard de Actone and Maud his wife conveyed 12 messuages, 14 acres and 1 rood of land, 74s. rent in Heaton, Jesmond and Newcastle, a moiety of the manor of Wooden, a third of two parts of the manor of Jesmond and two parts of a moiety of the manor of Mindrum to John de Stanyngton, chaplain, in trust for Richard and Maud for life, afterwards to Roger, 'brother of Gerard de Wyderyngtone' and Elizabeth daughter of the said Richard and Maud and their issue, with remainder to the right heirs of Maud (*Ib*.). Besides these lands which he obtained by his marriage, Roger acquired the manor of Plessey with Shotton and Blagdon; in 1345 he purchased from William de Actone of Newcastle, the manor of West Swinburne and a carucate of land in East Swinburne (*Ib*.). He died in 1372 (*SS*. 66, p.305). By his wife Elizabeth Actone he had issue a son John and three daughters Barnaba, Christiana and Alianora. On Thursday in Ascensiontide (27 May) 1367 Roger de Wydryngton gave a letter of attorney for livery of seisin to John his son and to Katherine daughter of sir William de Aton (not Acton) of the manors of Denton and Lanerton in Cumberland and of Bingfield in the liberty of of Hexham (*NDD*. p.232, No. 43).

The young heir John and his mother Elizabeth both died in Roger's lifetime, and Roger married a second wife, called Agnes, by whom he had another son called John, born 2 February 1371. Welford (p.182) has stated that Elizabeth survived her husband Roger de Woderington and married secondly Alexander de Hilton; he is wrong about this for it was Elizabeth's widowed mother Maud who married Hilton. Some earlier historians have not appreciated the fact that there were two brothers called John, both sons of Roger de Woderington; this accounts for the statement made by Hodgson that John was aged about 100 years at his death in 1443; actually he was only 72.

Proof of age of John son and heir of Roger de Wyderington was taken at Morpeth in 1393. Deponents stated that the said John was 21 years old on the Feast of the Purification last past (2 February). William de Swyncburne remembered the day when John was baptised because he came from Roxburgh to Widdrington and on the same day dined with Roger father of the said John. William de Schaftow who was living with Roger at the time, had a different reason for remembering; he was so rejoiced at John's birth that he got drunk on the day of the baptism and fell down in the hall at Widdrington and broke his leg. The child's godparents had been Nicholas Raymes, John Heron and Isabel wife of John Walshe (*AA*1. IV, p.329).

After the death of Roger de Woderington there were disputes about the succession to his estates. Eventually the lands which had come from the Actons were divided between his two surviving daughters Christiana and Alienora. Christiana married sir Bertram Monboucher. Alienora married firstly sir Robert Umframville and secondly Conan Aske of Aske, Yorks. The third daughter Barnaba wife of John de Vaux (m. sett. 11 June 1356) had died *s.p.* before 1362.

A short time before his death Roger de Woderington had conveyed on 3 April 1372 his manors of Widdrington with Druridge, Linton and Gerardlee, East Chevington, Plessey with Shotton and Blagdon, with the castle and manor of West Swinburne to Thomas Surteys, Donald de Hesilrigg, William de Hesylrig and Edmund de Hesellrig in trust (*NDD*. p.233, No. 46). A settlement on the same trustees on the same day of the castle and manor of Haughton, Humshaugh and Stonecroft was alleged to have been made by fraud and collusion to deprive the king of the profits of wardship and marriage of Roger's son and heir John (*Cal. Fine Rolls*, viii, p.209). On 20 October 1386 Edward, duke of York, lord of the manor and liberty of Wark in Tyndale, issued a licence to William de Heselrigg to enfeoff John son and heir of Roger de Wodryngton of the castle and manor of Haughton, the vill of Humshaugh and a piece of land called Stonecroft in Thornton, which Agnes widow of Roger holds in dower, with remainders successively to Thomas son of William de Heselrigg and his heirs male bearing the arms and name of the said Roger; to Roger son of sir Walter Heron with a similar proviso; to Christiana Monboucher and Alianora d'Aske daughters of the said Roger de Wodrington in tail (*NDD*. p.233, No. 47). Two days later William de Heselrigg made the necessary settlement and at the same time conveyed the other Widdrington lands with similar remainders (*Ib*., p.234, Nos. 48, 49). It is not known in what way the Hesilriggs and Herons were related to the Widdringtons.

On 15 July 1418 pope Martin granted to sir John de Wyderyngton and Margaret his wife the right to have a portable altar (*NDD*. p.237, No. 62). Margaret is otherwise unknown. Besides their sons Roger and Gerard, John and Margaret had two daughters. The marriage contract of William de Swinburne and Elizabeth daughter of John de Woderington is dated 7 August 1404. On 18 June 1411 sir John de Wydrington made an agreement for the assignment of dower for Agnes de Lilburn his daughter, and Thomas de Lilburn, brother and heir of Henry de Lilburn, late the husband of Agnes (*NDD*. p.236, No. 61). All that is known about Gerard de Wedrington, John's younger son, is that on 2 April 1419 he gave a bond to sir William de Swynburne and his heirs for quiet enjoyment of the castle of Haughton leased to him by sir John de Wedryngton, father of Gerard (*Ib.*, p.237, No. 63). Sir John was sheriff of Northumberland in 1410, 1426 and 1430.

The extent of the lands held by sir John Wideryngton is given in his *i.p.m.* taken in 22 H.VI. (1443/4). At his death he held the manor of Woodhorn, and vill of Widdrington, the hamlet of Druridge, the manor and vill of West Swinburne, the manor and vill of Colwell, two husbandlands in Little Swinburne, half the vill of East Chevington, two husbandlands and a cottage in Cresswell, three husbandlands and a cottage in Ellington, a rent of 10 marks from the vill of Denton next Newcastle, a waste vill of Gerardlee, two husbandlands in Horsley, a messuage and lands in Capheaton, three husbandlands in Newton next Ellington, two husbandlands in Gunnerton, two husbandlands at Thornton in Glendale, a tenement and 12 acres in 'Aldemore', the vill of Linton next Ellington, a moiety of 40 acres in Jesmond, a rent from Hartford, 5 messuages, 100 acres of land and 20 acres meadow in Cowpen, a messuage, 15 acres of land and an acre of meadow in Shotton, half a husbandland and a cottage in North Horsley (*i.e.* Longhorsley), a messuage, 40 acres of land and 8 acres of meadow in Broomley in the manor of Bywell, the manor of Little Whittington, half of 40 acres of land and 8 acres of meadow in Aydon, the manor of Plessey, the vill of Shotton, and the vill of Blagdon (*HN.* iii, II, p.274). Besides these lands in Northumberland, sir John held property in the liberty of Tyndale and in the county of Cumberland. His son and heir Roger was then aged 40.

With this Roger Wydryngton we come within the scope of the early visitation pedigrees. There are four of these registered before the end of the 16th century, *viz.* Dalton's Visitation in 1558 (*SS.* 122, p.110), Flower's Visitation of Yorkshire 1563/4 (*Harl. Soc.* XVI), a Visitation of *circa* 1480-1500 (*SS.* 144, p.35) and a Visitation in 1575 (*SS.* 146, p.91). The 1558 pedigree commences two generations later than this Roger, but a note states 'One Roger Wydryngton wedyd Margaret, doughtre to sir Thomas Grey and of Alyce Nevell, his wyff, and had issue I think, Gerard Wydryngton, but whether the said Gerard wer his son or no he weded Elizabeth, sustre to Margaret, wyfe to the said Roger, and the said Gerard and Margaret (sic) had issue Gerard, Margaret, Elizabeth, John, Thomas, Isabell, Roger, William, Alyce, Raufe, Alexandre and Robert Wydrington'. There are several obvious errors in this for it is certain that Roger Widdrington married Elizabeth daughter of sir Thomas Grey of Heton (executed 1415) by his wife Alice Nevill daughter of Ralph, first earl of Westmorland. Elizabeth had previously been married to sir William Whitchester (dispensation dated 20 February 1407/8 to marry her kinsman); sir William died *s.p.* before 1424. In an inquisition held at Morpeth 20 April 1428 it is stated that Roger de Woddryngton and Elizabeth his wife, who was wife of William Whitchestre, knight, hold for her life lands in the vills of Black Callerton, Seaton Delaval and Dissington (*NCH.* IX, p.145). Elizabeth died 1454 and her *i.p.m.* records that she held at her death 23 husbandlands and 32 cottages in Woodhorn, 8 messuages and 8 husbandlands in the hamlet of Widdrington, 8 marks rent in Denton, part of 10 marks, the manor of Plessey, the vill of Shotton, and the manor of North Dissington (*HN.* iii, II, p.275). The 1563/4 pedigree still calls Roger's wife Margaret and gives him a brother called Gerard. The children

of Roger and Margaret are given as sir Roger, Thomas (d. young), Ralph (*d.s.p.*), Robert (*d.s.p.*), Roger, William, Alexander, sir John, Margaret (d.young), Alice (d.), Isabell and Elizabeth wife of John Fenwick. The youngest son, sir John, is stated to have married Isabell daughter of lord Ogle and widow of sir John Heron. It is known from other sources that this is correct. There is then a further confusion for the pedigree states that Gerard Widdrington, youngest son of this sir John, married 'Elizabeth, sister to Margaret, wife of said Roger, grandfather to Gerard', their children being given as Gerard (son and heir), John (2nd son), Thomas (3rd son), William (4th son), Ralph (5th son), Alexander (6th son), Roger, Ely, Margaret, Elizabeth, Isabell, Alice and 'Aketh'. With only slight differences these are the children given to Gerard and Elizabeth Wydryngton in the 1558 pedigree. A later scribe, evidently realising that a mistake had been made has added a correction under Gerard 'I think son of Roger' and yet another hand has written 'I doubt this. He was brother to Roger'.

The pedigree of *circa* 1480-1500 correctly gives Roger Wedrington as married to Elizabeth daughter of sir Thomas Gray and omits all reference to Gerard Widdrington and his supposed wife Margaret Gray. Roger and Elizabeth's children are given as sir Roger (m. to a daughter of sir Robert Claxton), Margaret (d.unm.), Isabella, Thomas (d. a boy), Elizabeth (wife of John Fenwick), Ralph (d. without children), Alexander, Roger, Alice (d.), William, Robert (d. a boy), and John (m. Isabella Ogle widow of sir John Heron).

Not until we come to the 1575 pedigree are some of these inconsistencies straightened out. There the children of Roger de Wodderington and his wife Elizabeth daughter of sir Thomas Grey are given as sir Gerard (m. Elizabeth daughter of Christopher Bointon of 'Sadbury'), sir Roger (from whom the later Widdringtons are derived), Elizabeth wife of John Fenwick, John (m. Issabell daughter of Robert, lord Ogle, widow of sir John Heron), and William; a later hand has added the additional names of Isabella, Roger, William and Alexander. That the later Widdringtons are derived from the eldest son, sir Gerard, and not from the second son, sir Roger, is made plain by a bond of sir Henry Wodryngton dated 11 May 1513 whereby he confirms to George Cresswell of Cresswell his rights in lands he occupied by grant from 'my father sir Rafe Wodryngton knt, or that my grandfather, sir Jerret Wodryngton or sir John Wodryngton or sir Roger Wodryngton, knights, had occupied in Cresswell'.

Roger Widdrington was sheriff of Northumberland in 1431, 1435, 1442 and 1449. On 6 April 1438 Walter Tayleboys, lord of Redesdale, appointed 'Roger Wodrington squier his lieutenant in Redesdale and constable of his castle of Harbottle in the county of Northumberland as well for war as for peace, abiding and dwelling in his proper person with his mesnie and household within the dungeon of the said castle' (*NDD.* p.222, No. 8). As a result of this appointment we find Roger living at Harbottle in 1441 when sir William Eure sued him for a debt of £10 (*de Banco Roll*). He died on 2 August 1451.

On 2 September 1454 Thomas Watton and John de Thoresby, chaplain, evidently acting as trustees, conveyed to Gerard Wodryngton esq., son and heir of Roger Wodryngton esq., and Elizabeth his wife, daughter of Christopher Boynton, in tail, the castle, lordship and manor of Haughton in the liberty of Tyndale with the appurtenances in Haughton, Humshaugh, Stonecroft and elsewhere; remainder to the right heirs of Gerard (*NDD.* p.239, No. 72). Gerard was sheriff in 1464. On 7 September 1470 as Gerard Wodryngton, knt, he manumitted his serf William Atkenson and granted him the office of bailiff of his vill and the lordship of Woodhorn (*Ib.*, p.240, No. 74). He died in 1491.

The marriage of sir Gerard Widdrington with Elizabeth daughter of Christopher Boynton of Sedbury, Yorks., is confirmed by the 1584/5 Visitation pedigree of Boynton of Sedbury. Christopher Boynton was twice married, his first wife being a Wandesford, and his second 'Elizabeth' Strangwayes. Elizabeth Widdrington was a daughter of his second marriage. In the 1584/5 pedigree of Barton of Whenby, Yorks., it is stated that Conan (or Richard) Barton of Whenby married Joan daughter of Robert Strangwayes of Sneton, by whom he had, *inter alia*, a daughter (unnamed) who married sir Gerrard Widdrington. This is apparently an error, for Barton's widow married Christopher Boynton and it is evident that Widdrington's wife was a daughter of this second marriage.

The earliest visitation pedigrees are consistent in omitting all reference to sir Gerard and his wife Elizabeth Boynton. That of *circa* 1480-1500 gives Roger Wedrington and his wife Elizabeth Gray an eldest son sir Roger married to a daughter of sir Robert Claxton; the children of this marriage are given as Ralph and Elizabeth. The 1558 pedigree starts with sir Ralph Widdrington and his wife, unnamed, a daughter and one of the heirs of sir Robert Claxton of Horden and Dilston. According to the pedigree of 1563/4 Roger Woderyngton and his wife 'Margaret' Gray had a large family of eight sons and four daughters, of whom the eldest, sir Roger, by his wife, a daughter of sir Robert Claxton, had issue sir Ralph, Robert (no issue) and Elizabeth. The mistake made in the children of Roger and his wife 'Margaret' Grey is quite evident for both the eldest son and the fifth son are here named Roger.

The 1575 pedigree is the first to mention 'sir Gerard de Wodderington maried (to) Elizabeth daughter to Christofer Bointon of Sadbury' and to place him correctly as eldest son of Roger de Wodderington by his wife 'Elizabeth daughter to sir Thomas Grey.' Roger and Elizabeth's second son 'sir Roger de Wodderington knight' is given, by an unnamed wife, a son sir Raffe (married to Felis Claxton) and a daughter Elizabeth.

It has been necessary to consider these visitation pedigrees in great detail, for Hodgson accepted the statement that sir Ralph who married Felicia Claxton was son of Roger Widdrington (born 1427; d. before 1479) a younger brother of sir Gerard who married Elizabeth Boyton. This has also been accepted by the *County History* (XII, p.325). The bond already mentioned of 11 May 1513 in which sir Henry Wodryngton refers to his father sir Rafe and his grandfather sir Jerret must be accepted as correct.

Sir Ralph Widdrington was knighted by the earl of Northumberland in 1482 on the plain of Sefford. Twice he received a royal pardon, on 11 September 1484 from Richard III and on 6 February 1486 from Henry VII. On 7 May 1486 he gave lands in Ellington to his chaplain William Thornton (*NDD.* p.240, No. 78). Robert Wedryngton of Great Swin-

burne, son and heir of sir John Wedrington, on 8 May 1490 conveyed to Ralph Wedryngton the lands in Capheaton which his father had from Roger Thornton (*Ib.*, p.241, No. 79). Sir John Widdrington was sir Ralph's uncle. For his descendants *see* WIDDRINGTON OF COLWELL.

On 6 January 1492 sir Ralph Wedryngton conveyed to George Percy, John Heron of Ford and others, apparently in trust, the castle and manor of Great Swinburne and the vill of Druridge, to hold to the uses expressed in indentures of 4 January between the said Ralph and sir William Evers and Constance his wife, widow of sir Henry Percy (*Ib.*, p.241, No. 80). As sir Ralph's eldest son and heir Henry married Margery daughter of sir Henry Percy, this was apparently in connection with the young couple's marriage settlement.

The visitation pedigrees are agreed that sir Ralph Widdrington was twice married, his first wife being Felicia daughter and coheiress of sir Robert Claxton of Dilston, and his second Mabel Sandford 'of Westmorland'. The children of his first marriage were Henry (son and heir), Roger and Cuthbert (d.*s.p.*). For Roger's descendants *see* WIDDRINGTON OF HAUXLEY, par. Warkworth. Thomas and Margaret, the children of sir Ralph's second marriage both died *s.p.* On the death of sir Robert Claxton on 4 October 1484 his youngest daughter Felice wife of sir Ralph Widdrington, was 26 years of age.

When princess Margaret of England was on her way to marry James IV of Scotland, she was between Alnwick and Berwick on 29 July 1502 when there came to her 'Master Rawff Wodryngton, having in his company many gentlemen well appointed, his folks arrayed in livery, well horsed, to the number of one hundred horses' (Richardson, *Local Historian's Table Book*, I, p.179).

Sir Ralph de Wodrington died before the end of the year and on 11 July 1504 special livery of his lands was granted to Henry de Wodrington, his son and heir (*NDD.* p.241, No. 81). Henry was a knight before 26 July 1514 when he had a royal pardon from Henry VIII (*Ib.*, No. 82). The visitation pedigree of 1558 calls his wife 'Margerye, daughter of sir Henry Percye of Bamburgh, base son of (blank)'. After sir Henry Widdrington's death and before 1 March 1517, his widow married sir William Ellerker. Sir William Ellerker in 1525 with his wife Margery who was administratrix of the goods of Henry Widdrington were sued by Robert Brandling for a debt of £30. According to the 1575 visitation pedigree, sir Henry Widdrington's children were sir John (only son and heir); Dorothy, first wife of Robert, lord Ogle; Constance, married to Walter Fenwik (corrected to Valentine Fenwike) of Walker near Newcastle; Mary, married to John Mitford (or Midcalfe) of Seghill esquire; Margery, married to Roger Fenwick of Bitchfield; and Anne, 'died a virgin'. According to the 1558 and 1563/4 pedigrees, there was another son, Rauphe, who died *s.p.* Hodgson in his pedigree, also gives sir Henry Widdrington a second son Ralph of whom he states 'who was the progenitor of different branches of Widdringtons intended to be noticed under Blackheddon, etc.'. We can however accept the statement of the almost contemporary visitation pedigrees that Ralph died *s.p.*

On 1 March 1517 sir Robert, lord of Ogle and Bothal, conveyed to John Wodrington and others lands in Middleton Morel, Fenrother and Shilvington to the use of Robert Ogle his son and Dorothy daughter of sir Henry de Weddrington, deceased, for the life of Dorothy, with remainder to Robert his son and heirs (*NDD*. p.181, No. 86).

Sir John Widdrington was aged 15 in 1518. A list of such gentlemen as of late retained in the service of Henry VIII, 1526, includes the name of sir John Wetherington of Widdrington, knt, 'deputy warden of the Middle Marches, from Scotland 16 mile and from Redesdale 6 mile, (who) may dispend 300 marks by the year. He may serve the king with 100 men. He is a good housekeeper and a true man'. On 26 January 1537 he had letters patent creating him subwarden of the Middle Marches (*Ib.*, p.241, No. 84). He was knight of the shire for Northumberland in 1552, and sheriff in 1559. Sir John was married twice; his first wife was Agnes daughter of sir James Metcalf of Nappa, Yorks. On 26 July 1548 John Wodrington of Widdrington conveyed to Thomas Gower and others, the manors of Woodhorn, Newbiggen, Plessey with the Brigfeld, Shotton and Denton, in trust to the use of the grantor and his wife Agnes for life (*Ib.*, p.241, No. 85). His children by Agnes Metcalf were sir Henry, Edward, and Dorothy wife of Roger Fenwick of Wallington. Sir John's second wife was Agnes daughter of sir Thomas Gower of Stittenham, Yorks.; on 20 June 1542 sir John Wetheryngton of Widdrington made an indenture with sir Thomas Gower of Stittenham, Yorks., whereby the former covenanted with the latter to marry Agnes his daughter, and the latter agreed to pay 300 marks sterling in three instalments; if the bride or bridegroom died before the payments were complete, the agreement was to be void (*AA4*. XXXIV, p.75, No. 100 where Widdrington is called Thomas in error). The visitation pedigrees of 1558 and 1563/4 state that sir John's second wife Agnes was a daughter of sir 'Edward' Gower.

In 1568 the lands held by sir John Wodrington direct of the Crown were the castle, manor and vill of Widdrington, Druridge, Chibburn, Garretlee, Colwell, Whitesidelaw, Great Swinburne, Shotton, Plessey and Haughton, with half the vill and manor of Humshaugh, and lands in West Chevington, Bingfield, Stonehall, East Chevington, Little Swinburne and Blagdon and in the vill of Woodhorn Newbiggen and lands in Seaton by the Sea (*Liber Feodarii*).

Sir John Widdrington had a large family. By his first wife Agnes Metcalf his children were:—

1. Henry Widdrington.
2. Edward Widdrington.
3. John Widdrington, d.*s.p.*
i. Katheryn, d.*s.p.*
ii. Dorothe wife of sir Roger Fenwick of Wallington.

For his second family, the children of his second wife Agnes Gower *see* WIDDRINGTON OF PLESSEY. 'In the time he was a widower' sir John had cohabited with his maid Alice and by her had two illegitimate sons Hector and Alexander.

Hector Woodrington became one of the constables of horsemen in the garrison of Berwick-on-Tweed. He probably owed his appointment to the fact that sir Henry Widdrington, his eldest half brother, was at that time governor of the town. Hector also had a farm at Chibburn probably as tenant under his brother. By his w.d. 28 April 1593, pr. 15 June 1593, he leaves to Raphe Woodrington the house in Berwick 'wherein I now dwell' and £50 'to be paid him upon the receipt of my goods and debts'. The testator leaves legacies to his sister

Marye Graye, his sister Rebecka Woodrington, and to Robert eldest son of his brother Isacke Woodrington. The residue of his goods is left to his sister-in-law Elizabeth Woodrington, widow of his brother sir Henry.

Sir John Widdrington was succeeded by his eldest son Henry, sheriff of Northumberland in 1579, and made a knight bachelor in 1580 (W. A. Shaw, *Knights of England*, II, p.80). For his service upon the Border with horse and armour, he had a 21 years' lease from the crown, of New Etal from 5 July 1590 (*Survey of the Debateable and Border Lands in 1604*, p.131). In May 1584 when he was marshal of Berwick there were complaints made against him for the way that he administered his office (*CBP*. I, p.138).

A report made on the state of Berwick-on-Tweed in 1587 describes sir Henry Woodrington, marshal there, being deputy governor as 'a man utterly unable for that place, ... He is a man very impatient and furious in all his doings, whereby it cometh to pass that no man of mean calling can have justice at his hands. And by reason of that humour, cannot stay himself, but will commit them to prison; and thereby (amazing the grieved party) decideth his cause as pleaseth himself; and hath beaten divers that had been before him, with great indiscretion. In his life, a right epicure, giving himself wholly to eat, drink and ease, which hath filled him full of diseases and distemperatures, and also so besotted him, that he is almost of no capacity, nor inclined to any goodness. In his religion, an atheist, seldom coming to church, to hear sermons and prayer, but now and then for fashions sake, affirming his diseases are the cause of his absence. When notwithstanding, it is well known he rideth abroad to an alehouse at Scremerston ii miles from the town, and will endure to set at gaming and play' (*AA4*. XLI, p.125). This report was evidently much exaggerated for sir Henry retained the command of Berwick until his death some six years later.

Complaints became so numerous that enquiries as to his conduct were instituted in March 1593. There had been troubles in the town 'this three or four years by the unableness of sir Henry Woddrington's diseased body as having been sick and almost bedridden for that time'. Earlier than this, in 1584/5, it was said of him that 'he suffers his brother William Woddrington, the provost marshal, to misuse, revile and miscall the mayor and townsmen, and intrude on the mayor's office, and do as he list without control'. (*Ib.*, p.139). There were complaints also against lady Widdrington for interfering in her husband's office, but she denied this.

Sir Henry Woddrington's will is dated 15 February 1592/3. He directs that his body is to be buried in the church at Widdrington amongst his ancestors. To his nephew Henry Woddrington he leaves 100 marks a year 'which I will my loving wife, the lady Elyzabeth shall pay unto him for his better maintenance, so long as she shall be possessed and be lady of Widdrington, provided that he use her with all courtesy and kindness as he ought to do or otherwise this my gift to be of no effect or force to him'. His nephew Roger Woddrington is to have £20 a year, and his nephew Raphe Woddrington 20 nobles a year out of the lands and rents of Haughton and Humshaugh. Roger is also to have £100 for the better maintenance of his study and library. The 'three pieces of great ordnance now remaining in my house at Berwick' are to be carried to Widdrington and there to remain. The inventory of his goods is dated 24 April 1593 and their value was estimated at £1013. 2s. 9d. (SS. 38, p.225).

Sir Henry was twice married, firstly to Barbara daughter of Edward Gower of Stittenham, Yorks., and secondly to Elizabeth daughter of sir Hugh Trevanion of Caerhayes in Cornwall. Lady Widdrington survived him and married secondly sir Robert Carey, warden of the marches, afterwards earl of Monmouth. Sir Henry left no issue by either marriage.

Sir Henry's three nephews, the principal legatees under his will, were the sons of his younger brother Edward Widdrington. On 22 January 1565 Edward Woderyngton of Swinburne, gent., made an indenture with Ursula Carnaby daughter and coheiress of sir Reynold Carnaby (of Halton) deceased; sir John Wytherington his father had on 23 July 1554 conveyed the castle and town of Swinburn to him, and Edward now settles it in consideration of a marriage between himself and the said Ursula. This seems to be the purport of a deed seen by Dodsworth in 1639 at Widdrington (NDD. p.242, No. 86). In the visitation pedigree registered in 1575 Edward's children are recorded as Henry (eldest son 8 years old), Roger, Raffe, Dorothe and Agnes (SS. 146, p.93). Within the next two years he had another daughter Katherine. Administration of Edward Woddringtoune's goods was granted to his widow Ursula on 8 June 1577 for the benefit of their children Henry, Roger, Ralph, Dorothy, Agnes and Katherine Woddringtoune (Dur. Prob. Off. by C.R.H.) and the inventory of his goods is dated 11 April 1578.

Edward Widdrington's children, as given in the 1615 visitation pedigree registered by his eldest son sir Henry were:—

1. Sir Henry Widdrington. In 1615 he was already married to Mary daughter of sir Nicholas Curwen of Workington, Cumb., and had issue William (aged 4), Katherine, Mary and Elizabeth. (Sir Henry's wife is incorrectly called daughter of sir Henry Curwen by Hodgson.)

2. Roger Widdrington of Cartington. By 1615 he had issue by his wife, Mary daughter of Francis Radcliffe of Dilston, a son Edward (of the age of one year) and two daughters, Mary and Margaret (see WIDDRINGTON OF CARTINGTON).

3. Raphe Widdrington (see WIDDRINGTON OF STONECROFT).

i. Katherine wife of Roberte, 2nd son of sir John Mallory of Studley, Yorks. (In the 1612 visitation pedigree of Mallory of Studley, Yorks, Robert 4th son of John Mallory is recorded as married to (blank) daughter of (blank) Widdrington).

ii. Dorothy wife of John Errington of Errington (and Beaufront). The daughter Agnes must have died in the interval between 1577 and 1615. There is some evidence that Edward had an illegitimate son Benjamin. (See WIDDRINGTON OF BUTELAND.)

On 27 August 1596 in a Scots raid, sir Robert Kerr broke into Swinburne, 'a house of Henry Woodrington's, and took Roger Widdrington, Henry's brother' (CBP. II, p.184). Sir Robert Carey writing to Burghley on 9 September 1596 complains that Cesford himself came 20 miles into England to Mr Henry Woodrington's house at Swynbourne, taking away a prisoner in his keeping, and some gentlemen in the house prisoners also 'and so sounding his trumpet upon the top of the house, when he had taken his pleasure went his way' (PSAN3. II, p. 232). On 30 November 1596 the warden, lord Eure, complained of 'the disobedience of the race of Woddringtons, their slanders on himself and open bravadoes;

their pride is so high, that now Roger his brother has submitted himself prisoner to sir Robert Kerr and gone to Scotland without leave' (CBP. II, p.226). At a warden court Roger was indicted as an offender to march law for going to Scotland prisoner; his brother Henry disdainfully refused to live on the march (Ib., p.240). Edward Gray writing to Eure on 17 November 1597 mentions that Henry Woodrington has been knighted (Ib., p.453). This seems to be a mistake, for he was knighted by James I at Widdrington on 9 April 1603. On 2 December 1597 Henry Widdrington made a declaration of the principal causes which moved him to withdraw out of the Middle Marches under lord Eure's government. His explanation of the episode at Swinburne when it had been attacked by sir Robert Kerr was that at that time, Raphe Woodrington, Henry's youngest brother, 'to save his life leapt out of his chamber window, being three stories high, upon a pavement where he was almost bruised to death and hardly escaped' (Ib., p.479).

On 2 August 1598 a company of 200 Scots came into England and Mr Woodrington and Mr Fenwick whom sir Robert Carey had sent as leaders, set upon the Scots and overthrew them (Ib., p.551). The Scots king asked that the two principal gentlemen in the field that day should be handed over (Ib., p.553). It was arranged that Widdrington should be tried by an assize of twelve borderers on each side and that in the meantime he was to be kept in durance with the bishop of Durham (Ib., p.584). A duel was arranged between Kerr and Widdrington for 8 September 1599 but the latter did not put in an appearance (Ib., p. 622). On 14 June 1600 the Privy Council sent a letter of commendation to Henry Woodrington, esq., 'to be reconciled to sir Robert Kerr' (Cal. Acts of Privy Council).

Henry Widdrington is referred to as deputy warden of the Middle Marches 8 February 1601/2. He had a lease of Harbottle castle and demesnes in 1604, and in the following year was sheriff of Northumberland. Sir Henry is exhibited to advantage by Taylor the waterpoet in his Penniless Pilgrimage from Scotland by Newcastle, where he arrived on 1 October 1618, and where, he says, 'I found the noble knight sir Henry Witherington; who, because I would have no gold nor silver, gave me a bay mare, in requital of a loaf of bread that I had given him two and twenty years before at the island of Flores' (AA2. III, p.194). It seems evident that Widdrington had been with the abortive attempt under the earl of Essex in 1597 to establish a permanent English base at the Azores and to intercept the Spanish treasure fleet there.

On 2 June 1621 sir Henry Widdrington with sir Robert and dame Elizabeth Cary conveyed to sir Henry Curwen, sir John Fenwick, sir William Lambton and Henry Errington esq., the manors of Widdrington, Woodhorn, Ellington and his lands in Widdrington, Woodhorn, Ellington, Linton, Newbiggen, Druridge, Burradon, Denton near Newcastle, Hirst and Black Callerton, in trust to his own use for life, then to his son William for life, remainder to the first son of William and his heirs male, with several remainders over (SS. III, p.380).

In his w.d. 2 September 1623, sir Henry makes no mention of his only son, no doubt because he had already provided for him. He states in his will that he has already made an estate to his daughter (Katherine) before her marriage, of the manor of Ditchburn and the town of Charlton with the lands thereunto belonging in satisfaction of her portion. Some time afterwards he had agreed with sir Thomas Riddell to give in marriage with his said daughter to Riddell's son the sum of £1000. He now directs 'that my son Riddale and my daughter his wife shall convey and assure the said manor of Ditchburn and town of Charlton to my daughter Elizabeth in satisfaction of her portion which I make no doubt my son and daughter will willingly do as now the estate they have was but in trust for my daughter Elizabeth'. Sir Henry had made a lease of Haughton, Humshaugh and Haughton Green, and another of Swinburne, Colwell and Tone to four of his daughters, Margarett, Dorathy, Annas and Ursuley, and it was his full intent and meaning that his daughter Mary should have her equal share of these leases, her name being forgot to be mentioned in the leases yet for it was his full intent that his daughter Mary should have her equal share and being unwilling to alter the leases his will is that his said daughter Mary's portion shall be made equal with the other of her four sisters out of his personal estate. He had bought the manor of Newcastle and this was to be sold and the money divided amongst his daughters. He appoints his said five daughters executors to his will and their tuition is committed to his brother Roger Widdrington to be brought up and remain with him (*Dur. Prob. Off.* by C.R.H.).

Of sir Henry Widdrington's daughters, Catherine married sir William Riddell of Gateshead, co. Durham, Anne married sir Nicholas Thornton of Netherwitton, Dorothy married sir Charles Howard of Croglin, Cumb., Elizabeth married William Selby of Winlaton, co. Durham, and Mary married sir Francis Howard of Corby, Cumb. Ursula never married; by her w.d. 18 July 1644 she gives to her dearly beloved sisters, the lady Riddall, the lady Mary Howard, the lady Dorothy Howard, Mrs Selby and Mrs Gray, to each of them £50; she leaves to her sister lady Ann Thornton, all her portion, being £1000 and the rentcharge thereof to be paid to her by her brother, the lord William Widdrington (*SS.* 68, p.342n.). The 1615 visitation pedigree of Lambton of Lambton, co. Durham, records that the second wife of sir William Lambton (k.1664) was Catherine daughter of sir Henry Widdrington (Foster, p.207). According to one Widdrington pedigree (Vinc. 149.39) she was illegitimate. She was buried at St Oswald's, Durham, in 1668.

Sir Henry's only son William (aged 4 in 1615) married Mary daughter and heiress of sir Anthony Thorald of Blankney, Lincs., and her father settled Blankney on them on 11 December 1635. He was sheriff of Northumberland in 1636 and was elected MP for the county in 1640 for what was known as the Short Parliament, and again in the same year for the Long Parliament. Shortly after his second election he incurred the disfavour of the House for describing the Scots as 'invading rebels'. He was persuaded to retract this remark, and on 10 November 1640 'sir William in his peace stood up and said he knew them to be the king's subjects, and would no more call them rebels, and with this explanation the House rested satisfied'. The next year he was again in trouble. On 9 June 1641 'There was this morning exceptions taken against Mr Price and sir Wm Widdrington for some carriages of theirs last night concerning the taking away the candles from the serjeant violently, when there was no general command in the House for the bringing of candles in, but a great sense of the House went for rising, it being so

very late. They in their places made explanation with what intentions they did it, and they were commanded to withdraw, which accordingly they did; and then the House fell into debate of the business. Resolved (by 189 to 172 votes) that sir Wm Widdrington and Mr Herbert Price shall, for their offence to this House, be sent to the Tower, there to remain during the pleasure of the House. Sir Wm Widdrington and Mr H. Price were called to the Bar, and there offered to kneel; but because they did not kneel they were caused to withdraw. And after some debate of the House, concerning their coming kneeling they were again called to the Bar, and there, they kneeling all the while, Mr Speaker pronounced the sentence against them of their being committed to the Tower' (*House of Commons Journals*).

Sir William was released from the Tower after a week's detention, but on 26 August 1642 he was expelled the House for raising arms against Parliament. He had joined the armed forces of king Charles. He had already been knighted at Newmarket 18 March 1631, and created a baronet 9 July 1642, and was now rewarded by being created baron Widdrington of Blankney 2 November 1643. Lord Widdrington served throughout the Civil War under the duke of Newcastle, and was present at the fateful battle of Marston Moor in July 1644. After the battle he escaped abroad and in 1649 his name appears in a list of a dozen delinquents who were to be proclaimed traitors and presented for perpetual punishment and confiscation. He ventured back to England with prince Charles and at the battle of Wigan, on 3 September 1651, he was killed. Clarendon in his *History of the Rebellion* calls him 'one of the most goodly persons of that age, being near the head higher than most tall men', and that he was among 'the first who raised both horse and foot at his own charge, and served eminently with them under the marquis of Newcastle, with whom he had a very particular and entire friendship' (*SS.* III, p.379n.).

On 18 July 1651 the estate of sir William Widdrington appears in the first Act for Sale of Lands and Estates forfeited to the Commonwealth for Treason. The Commonwealth consistently ignored the peerage conferred in 1643. Lady Widdrington had already, on 9 July 1650, successfully petitioned for one-fifth of her husband's estates. On 1 January 1652 the widow with William, her eldest son, and her six younger sons, were allowed the benefit of the marriage settlement of 11 December 1635. A little later William Widdrington was allowed a claim to the lands which had been settled in tail male on 2 June 1621. Owing to these settlements most of the family estates were retained.

When, on 1 January 1652, it was agreed that lady Widdrington and her sons should have the benefit of the deed of 11 December 1635, her sons were William, Henry, Edward, Ephraim, Antony, Ralph and Roger. Another son John had died previously (bur. Blankney 7 September 1640). There were also two daughters, Mary wife of major Francis Crane of Woodrising, Norfolk, and Jane wife of sir Charles Stanley. Little is known about the younger sons. Henry was buried at Blankney 5 November 1656. For Edward and his descendants *see* WIDDRINGTON OF FELTON. Ephraim was living in 1680 and was buried at Holy Island 5 February 1683/4. Anthony, born 1644, became a Jesuit in 1665, and died at Ghent en route for Rome in 1682 (Foley, *Records of Society of Jesuits*, VIII, p.841). Ralph lost his sight in the Dutch

War; he married c.1703 Anne daughter of John Thimelby, widow of John Fanning of Sandall; and died 22 June 1718; his w.d. 10 February 1717/8 was proved at London 25 June 1718. Roger was killed at the siege of Maestrict in 1676. When, on 12 June 1667, the Dutch sailed up the Medway and burnt part of the English fleet, a state of considerable unrest spread throughout the whole country, and garrisons were directed to the principal east coast ports. The earl of Carlisle was appointed lieutenant general of all militia forces and of all towns and garrisons of the four northern counties. At that time lord Widdrington was governor of Berwick and the earl of Ogle governor of Newcastle. The latter raised a new regiment of volunteers; Roger Widdrington was one of the captains, Edward Widdrington and Ralph Widdrington being ensigns (*Cal. S.P., Dom.* 1667, p.180). Edward and Ralph were no doubt lord Widdrington's younger brothers; Roger was probably Roger Widdrington of Harbottle.

The eldest son, William, succeeded his father as second lord Widdrington in 1651. He married Elizabeth (Bridget) daughter and heir of sir Peregrine Bertie of Eveden, Lincs. Her will is dated 23 June 1715. They had a family of four sons and eight daughters. They were William, Roger, Henry, Edward, Peregrine; Mary, a nun, Sr Mary Ignatia (d.1713); Elizabeth, abbess of Pontoise (d.1730); Dorothy, a nun, sr Dorothy Agnes (d.1733); Anne wife of John Clavering of Callaly; Bridget (bap. 12 Nov. 1654; d. in infancy); Jane (d.1733); and Catherine wife of Edward Southcote of Blytheborough, Lincs. Of the younger sons Roger died at Blankney in 1715. Henry joined the Society of Jesuits and was personal chaplain at Callaly to his brother-in-law John Clavering; his w.d. 10 December 1727 was proved by John Forster 19 February 1729. Edward was living at St Mary-le-Savoy when he made his w.d. 7 October 1699, pr. 12 October 1699. Two of the second lord Widdrington's children were baptised at Berwick when he was acting as governor, which he had been appointed in 1660:—

26 Jan. 1661/2. Jayne, dr of my lord William Withrington, lord governor of Berwick, bap.

29 May 1663. Peregrine, s. of William Widdrington, sheriff, governor of Berwick, bap.

William, 2nd lord Widdrington, made his will on 30 June 1673 and it was proved 7 September 1676. In the Tynemouth parish registers under the date 15 December 1675 is the entry, 'Md. the Ld Witherington brought on shore at ye low Lights this day and carried in a coach, etc., to Witherington, to be interd there. He died in London and was brought down in one of his Maties Catches'.

On 20 August 1678 William, 3rd lord Widdrington, sold the manor and castle of Swinburne and his lands in Colwell to Thomas Riddell of Fenham. He was appointed governor of Berwick and Holy Island 16 July 1686 which office he retained until the Revolution, 16 December 1688. His w.d. 26 March 1694 was proved in 1695. He married Alathea daughter and heiress of Charles, viscount Fairfax. They had issue William, 4th lord; Charles Widdrington (d. St Omers 1756); Peregrine Widdrington (bap. 20 May 1692), m. Mary dr of sir Nicholas Shireburne of Stonyhurst, widow of Thomas, duke of Norfolk; he died s.p. 4 February 1748/9; Apollonia, a nun; Mary wife of Richard Towneley of Towneley, Lancs, and Elizabeth wife of Marmaduke, lord Langdale of Holme.

William, 4th lord Widdrington, with his two brothers Charles and Peregrine, took an active part in the Jacobite Rising of 1715. They joined the earl of Derwentwater and the other participants at Warkworth on 7 October 1715. After the fiasco at Preston, lord Widdrington was one of those who surrendered and was imprisoned in the Tower of London. On 9 January 1716 with the earls of Derwentwater, Nithsdale, Carnwath and Wintoun, viscount Kenmure and lord Nairn he was impeached of 'high treason, in levying war against His Majesty, and proclaiming a pretender to his Crown to be the king of these realms'. When brought before the House of Lords on 16th January he pleaded guilty. In his answer he declared that he had heard of the rising in Northumberland only the night before it happened; and that being soon afterwards informed that all his neighbours and acquaintances had met in arms, a crowd of confused and mistaken notions hurried him at once into a precipitate resolution of joining them, and he acknowledged that he had thus plunged out of his depth as unprepared for an enterprise as the action itself was unpremeditated (*State Trials*, VI, p.6). Robert Patten who acted as chaplain to the Jacobites and later turned king's evidence, does not appear to have had any high opinion of lord Widdrington. He wrote that 'tho the family of Widdrington be famed in history for their bravery and loyalty to the English crown, yet there is little of it left in this lord, or at least he did not shew it, that ever we could find, unless it consisted in his early persuasions to surrender; for he was never seen at any barrier, or in any action but where there was the least hazard. He was wonderfully esteemed at home by all the gentlemen of the county, and it had been happy for him, and so we thought it would have been better for us (the rebels) if he had stayed at home. I heard a gentleman say "He was vexed to be under the command of an officer that could not travel without strong soup in a bottle; for his officer never wanted (for) strong broth wherever he came, both before and after he was a prisoner"' (*The History of the Rebellion in the year 1715*—3rd edit. pp.97-98). In 1720 his estate at Widdrington was sold by the Crown to a London company of speculators known as the York Buildings Company, but three years later by special Act of Parliament he was given £12,000 from the sale of his lands.

The last lord Widdrington died at Bath in 1743. Roger Gale, his contemporary, described lord Widdrington in 1728 as 'but an infirm sort of a gentlemen and a perfect valetudinarian' (*SS.* I, p.200). By his first wife, Jane daughter of sir Thomas Tempest of Stella, co. Durham, he had issue Henry Francis Widdrington (b. 4 Dec. 1700), Francis Widdrington (bur. Widdrington 23 October 1713), William Tempest Widdrington (b. 21 May 1712), Alathea (b. 21 April 1705, a nun), Mary Gertrude (b. 7 July 1707, bur. 26 September 1708), Elizabeth (b. 8 November, bur. 10 November 1709), Anne bur. 2 February 1711), and Mary (b. 11 October 1713; m. Rowland Eyre of Hassop, Derbyshire).

Lady Widdrington died 9 September 1714, so had not lived to see her husband's downfall. Lord Widdrington married secondly Catherine daughter of Richard Graham, viscount Preston, but had no further issue. The hon. Catherine died s.p. 11 December 1757 aged 80.

The eldest son, Henry Francis Widdrington, married Anne Gatonby 'of Yorkshire' and died s.p. 7 September 1774. By his will he devises his estates to his nephew Thomas Eyre only

WIDDRINGTON of WIDDRINGTON, par. WOODHORN

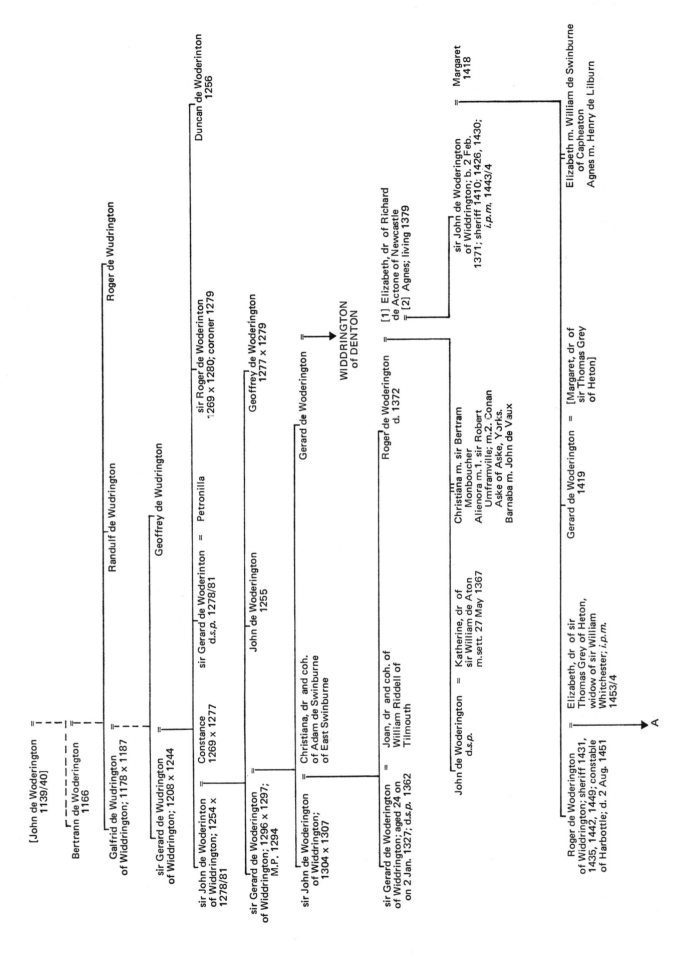

WIDDRINGTON of WIDDRINGTON, cont.

A →

William Wodrington

Robert Wodrington d.s.p.

Ralph Wodrington d.s.p.

Thomas Wodrington d.s.p.

Roger Wodrington aged 48 in 1472 [AA2. XXIV, p. 127]

sir Gerard Wodrington of Widdrington; d. 1491 = Elizabeth, dr of Christopher Boynton of Sadbury, Yorks

Alexander Wodrington

sir John Wodrington sheriff 1472-74 = Isabel, dr of Robert, lord Ogle, widow of John Heron of Chipchase

WIDDRINGTON of COLWELL

Margaret; d. young
Alice
Isabel
Elizabeth m. John Fenwick

sir Ralph Widdrington of Widdrington; d. 1502 = [1] Felicia, dr and coh. of sir Robert Claxton of Dilston = [2] Mabel Sandford

Robert Widdrington d.s.p.

Elizabeth

Thomas Widdrington d.s.p.

Margaret

sir Henry Widdrington of Widdrington; d. before 1 Mch. 1517 = Margery, dr of sir Henry Percy of Bamburgh; m.2. sir William Ellerker

Cuthbert Widdrington d.s.p.

Roger Widdrington of Chibburn = Maud Strother

WIDDRINGTON of HAUXLEY

sir John Widdrington of Widdrington; aged 15 in 1518; MP. 1552; sheriff 1559; d. 10 Aug. 1571 = [1] Agnes, dr of sir James Metcalf of Nappa, Yorks = [2] Agnes, dr of sir Thomas Gower of Stittenham, Yorks; m.sett. 29 June 1542; bur. 29 Mch. 1542; w.d. 23 Mch. 1582/3 ≈ Alice, 'his maid servant'

Ralph Widdrington d.s.p.

Hector Widdrington constable of horsemen at Berwick; w.d. 28 Apr. 1593, pr. 15 June 1593

Alexander Widdrington

Dorothy m. Robert, lord Ogle
Constance m. Valentine Fenwick of Walker
Mary m. John Mitford of Seghill
Margery m. Roger Fenwick of Bitchfield
Anne; d. unm.

WIDDRINGTON of PLESSEY

sir Henry Widdrington of Widdrington; sheriff 1579; marshal of Berwick; w.d. 15 Feb. 1592/3; d.s.p. = [1] Barbara, dr of Edward Gower of Stittenham, Yorks = [2] Elizabeth, dr of Hugh Trevanian of Corriheigh, Cornwall; m.2. sir Robert Carey; (m. Berwick 20 Aug. 1593); bur. Rickmansworth; w.pr. July 1641

Edward Widdrington of Swinburne; adm. 8 June 1577 = Ursula, dr and coh. of sir Reynold Carnaby of Halton; m.2. Thomas Musgrave of Bewcastle, Cumb.

B →

Dorothy m. Roger Fenwick of Wallington (d. 1550)

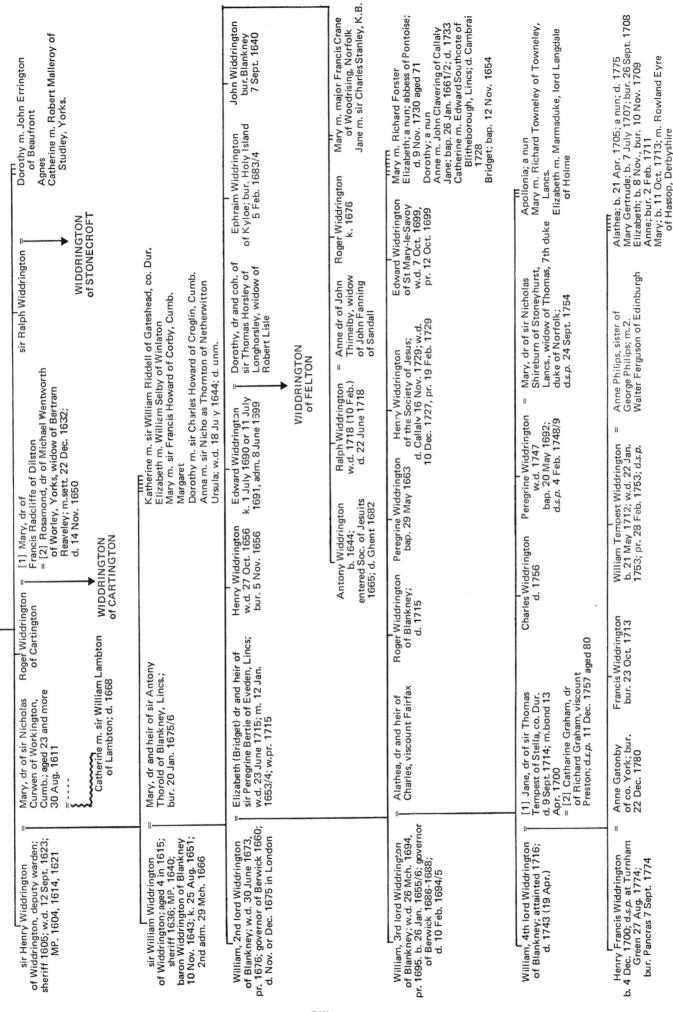

WIDDRINGTON of WIDDRINGTON, cont.

B

sir Henry Widdrington of Widdrington, deputy warden; sheriff 1605; w.d. 12 Sept. 1623; MP. 1604, 1614, 1621 =

Mary, dr of sir Nicholas Curwen of Workington, Cumb.; aged 23 and more 30 Aug. 1611

Roger Widdrington of Cartington =
Catherine m. sir William Lambton of Lambton; d. 1668
WIDDRINGTON of CARTINGTON

[1] Mary, dr of Francis Radcliffe of Dilston = [2] Rosamond, dr of Michael Wentworth of Worley, Yorks, widow of Bertram Reaveley; m.sett. 22 Dec. 1632; d. 14 Nov. 1650

sir Ralph Widdrington =
WIDDRINGTON of STONECROFT

Dorothy m. John Errington of Beaufront
Agnes
Catherine m. Robert Malleroy of Studley, Yorks.

sir William Widdrington of Widdrington; aged 4 in 1615; sheriff 1636; MP. 1640; baron Widdrington of Blankney 10 Nov. 1643; k. 25 Aug. 1651; 2nd adm. 29 Mch. 1666 =

Mary, dr and heir of sir Antony Thorold of Blankney, Lincs.; bur. 20 Jan. 1675/6

Katherine m. sir William Riddell of Gateshead, co. Dur.
Elizabeth m. William Selby of Winlaton
Mary m. sir Francis Howard of Corby, Cumb.
Margaret
Dorothy m. sir Charles Howard of Croglin, Cumb.
Anna m. sir Nicho as Thornton of Netherwitton
Ursula; w.d. 18 Ju y 1644; d. unm.

William, 2nd lord Widdrington of Blankney; w.d. 30 June 1673, pr. 1676; governor of Berwick 1660; d. Nov. or Dec. 1675 in London =

Elizabeth (Bridget) dr and heir of sir Peregrine Bertie of Eveden, Lincs; w.d. 23 June 1715; m. 12 Jan. 1653/4; w.pr. 1715

Henry Widdrington w.d. 27 Oct. 1656 bur. 5 Nov. 1656

Edward Widdrington k. 1 July 1690 or 11 July 1691, adm. 8 June 1399 =
Dorothy, dr and coh. of sir Thomas Horsley of Longhorsley, widow of Robert Lisle

Ephraim Widdrington of Kyloe; bur. Holy Island 5 Feb. 1683/4

John Widdrington bur. Blankney 7 Sept. 1640

WIDDRINGTON of FELTON

Antony Widdrington b. 1644; entered Soc. of Jesuits 1665; d. Ghent 1682

Ralph Widdrington w.d. 1718 (10 Feb.) d. 22 June 1718 =
Anne dr of John Thimelby, widow of John Fanning of Sandall

Roger Widdrington k. 1676

Mary m. major Francis Crane of Woodrising, Norfolk
Jane m. sir Charles Stanley, K.B.

William, 3rd lord Widdrington of Blankney; w.d. 26 Mch. 1694; pr. 1695. b. 26 Jan. 1655/6; governor of Berwick 1686-1688; d. 10 Feb. 1694/5 =
Alathea, dr and heir of Charles, viscount Fairfax

Roger Widdrington of Blankney; d. 1715

Peregrine Widdrington bap. 29 May 1663

Henry Widdrington of the Society of Jesus; d. Callalv 16 Nov. 1729; w.d. 10 Dec. 1727, pr. 19 Feb. 1729

Edward Widdrington of St Mary-le-Savoy w.d. 7 Oct. 1699, pr. 12 Oct. 1699

Mary m. Richard Forster
Elizabeth; a nun; abbess of Pontoise; d. 9 Nov. 1730 aged 71
Dorothy; a nun
Anne m. John Clavering of Callaly
Jane; bap. 26 Jan. 1661/2; d. 1733
Catherine m. Edward Southcote of Blitheborough, Lincs; d. Cambrai 1728
Bridget; bap. 12 Nov. 1654

William, 4th lord Widdrington of Blankney; attainted 1716; d. 1743 (19 Apr.) =
[1] Jane, dr of sir Thomas Tempest of Stella, co. Dur. d. 9 Sept. 1714; m.bond 13 Apr. 1700
= [2] Catharine Graham, dr of Richard Graham, viscount Preston; d.s.p. 11 Dec. 1757 aged 80

Charles Widdrington d. 1756

Peregrine Widdrington w.d. 1747 bap. 20 May 1692; d.s.p. 4 Feb. 1748/9

Mary, dr of sir Nicholas Shireburn of Stoneyhurst, Lancs., widow of Thomas, 7th duke of Norfolk; d.s.p. 24 Sept. 1754

Apollonia; a nun
Mary m. Richard Towneley of Towneley, Lancs.
Elizabeth m. Marmaduke, lord Langdale of Holme

Henry Francis Widdrington b. 4 Dec. 1700; d.s.p. at Turnham Green 27 Aug. 1774; bur. Pancras 7 Sept. 1774 =
Anne Gatonby of co. York; bur. 22 Dec. 1780

Francis Widdrington bur. 23 Oct. 1713

William Tempest Widdrington b. 21 May 1712; w.d. 22 Jan. 1753; pr. 28 Feb. 1753; d.s.p. =
Anne Philips, sister of George Philips; m.2. Walter Ferguson of Edinburgh

Alathea; b. 21 Apr. 1705; a nun; d. 1775
Mary Gertrude; b. 7 July 1707; bur. 26 Sept. 1708
Elizabeth; b. 8 Nov., bur. 10 Nov. 1709
Anne; bur. 2 Feb. 1711
Mary; b. 11 Oct. 1713; m. Rowland Eyre of Hassop, Derbyshire

son of Rowland Eyre and his heirs male, remainder to his cousin Edward Standish and his heirs male, remainder to John Townley for life, remainder to Peregrine Townley and the heirs male of his body, with final remainder to his own right heirs (J. C. Hodgson, *MSS pedigrees*, II, p.27). The younger son William Tempest Widdrington married Anne Philips by whom he had no issue. His will is dated 23 January 1753 and was proved 28 February 1753. It would seem that Anne widow of W. T. Widdrington, married secondly Walter Ferguson, for H. F. Widdrington by a codicil to his will dated 11 April 1774, leaves to 'Mr Walter Ferguson of Edinburgh, who married my brother's widow', £300 (Skeet, p.120).

WIDDRINGTON OF FELTON, PAR. FELTON

EDWARD WIDDRINGTON third son of William, first lord Widdrington of Blankney, was admitted to Gray's Inn 14 May 1656. On 23 February 1660/1 he married Dorothy daughter of sir Thomas Horsley of Longhorsley; she was widow and devisee of Robert Lisle of Felton, and brought the manor of Felton and other property to her second husband. 'That most honourable and most valiant captaine, Mr Edward Widdrington, and the most vertuous and illustrious lady, Mistris Dorothy Lisle, was married the 23 of February, 1660/1' (*Felton Registers*). Sir Thomas Horsley of Longhorsley by his w.d. 12 March 1684/5 leaves the manors of Horsley and Screnwood and lands in Thistleyhaugh and East Brenkheugh to his grandson Edward Widdrington son of Edward, now of Rock, esquire, in tail male; after the death of his grandson his heirs are to take the name of Horsley and not to alienate or sell the lands and also to keep his and their usual and constant abode and residence with their families at or within the manor house of Longhorsley; in case of any breach of this proviso then the lands are to go to his nephew Robert Bewick eldest son of Thomas Bewick of the Close House, esq.; in case of a further breach to his nephew Thomas Bewick, second son of the said Thomas; in case of his death without heirs male all the premises are to go to his six grand-children, Mary, Dorothy, Ellinor, Teresa, Jane and Anne Widdrington daughters of the said Edward Widdrington of Rock; his grand-daughter Elianor now wife of Mr Forster is to have £500 (Neasham, *Wills*, p.420). 'Madam Dorothy Widdrington, wife to the Honourable Captain Edward Widdrington of Felton, departed to the mercy of God the twenty day of July betwixt twelve and one of ye clock at night and was buried about four of ye clocke in ye afternoon of ye 22nd day of July, 1679' (*Felton Registers*). Captain Edward Widdrington is said to have lost his life in king James's service at the battle of the Boyne in Ireland on 11 July 1691. Administration of his personal estate was not however granted until 8 June 1699 (Raine, *Test. Ebor.*).

Edward Widdrington's eldest daughter Mary (bap. Felton 31 October 1662) was educated with the Blue Nuns, entered the Poor Clares at Gravelines, professed 1684 as Sr Mary Francis, and died in 1722. The second daughter, Dorothy, was entered at Cambrai 3 October 1683 aged 17 (*Cath. Rec. Soc.* 13, 54). Eleanor was the only daughter married before 12 March 1684/5; she was wife of Richard Forster of Newham. Teresa married 16 January 1695/6 sir William Wheeler, bart, of Leamington Hastings, Warwickshire. Jane is mentioned in the will of her grandfather, sir Thomas Horsley; she was probably Jane Widdrington, religious of the Poor Clares of Gravelines, professed 1687, aged 17 (*Ib.*, 14, p.104). The youngest daughter Anne married 6 April 1706 William Clavering of Berrington.

Edward Widdrington's only surviving son and heir, a second Edward, received Longhorsley and Screnwood from his grandfather sir Thomas Horsley and took the additional name of Horsley. He married (articles before marriage 24 June 1687) Elizabeth, daughter of Caryll, third viscount Molyneux. She was living in the parish of St Andrew's, Holborn 6 June 1730 when she made her will, proved in the Prerogative Court of Canterbury. She died six days later and was buried in the church of St Paul, Covent Garden. Although professing the Roman Catholic religion, Widdrington took no part in the Jacobite Rising of 1745. In fact he seems to have been a declared pacifist. After the collapse of the Rising, the duke of Cumberland passed through Felton on 29 January 1746 on his way to complete the subjugation of Scotland. Widdrington 'caused the contents of his well-stored cellar to be carted to the street of the village, where he regaled the different corps as they advanced, with bread, beef and beer. His royal highness, in passing through, experienced his hospitality, and at parting expressed his satisfaction at such distinguished liberality. Mr Widdrington replied that he wished well to his illustrious family, and detested internal commotions, as neither plenty nor pleasure could be enjoyed independant of peace' (Richardson, *Local Historians Table Book*, II, p.10).

Edward Horsley Widdrington made his w.d. 31 July 1762 and died at Felton 12 December 1762 aged 67. By his wife Mary daughter of Humphrey Weld of Lulworth castle, Dorset, (articles before marriage 9 August 1728) he had an only daughter and heiress Elizabeth Margaret. Mrs Widdrington died in North Street near Red Lion Square, London, 20 July 1749.

Elizabeth Margaret Widdrington married in August 1760 Thomas Riddell of Swinburne castle, who in right of his wife succeeded to the Horsley estates of Longhorsley and Screnwood, and the Lisle estate of Felton. Mrs Riddell died at Felton 4 April 1798 aged 68.

WIDDRINGTON OF CARTINGTON, PAR. ROTHBURY

ROGER WIDDRINGTON second son of Edward Widdrington (d.1577) of Swinburne by his wife Ursula Carnaby, married Mary daughter of sir Francis Radcliffe of Dilston. On 18 June 1600 his mother Ursula and her second husband Thomas Musgrave gave a third part of Newton Hall, par. Bywell St Peter, to him as a filial portion and in contemplation of his marriage. His father-in-law made several settlements of lands on him and his first wife. On 18 November 1601 Francis Radcliffe conveyed to Roger the manor of Linshields, Loughriggs and Laithough during the lives of Roger and Mary, then to the use of the first son of Roger and his heirs male, and for default to the second, third, fourth, etc., sons with other remainders over (SS. 111, p.370). At the same time Cartington was settled on him, and on 14 November 1615 the town

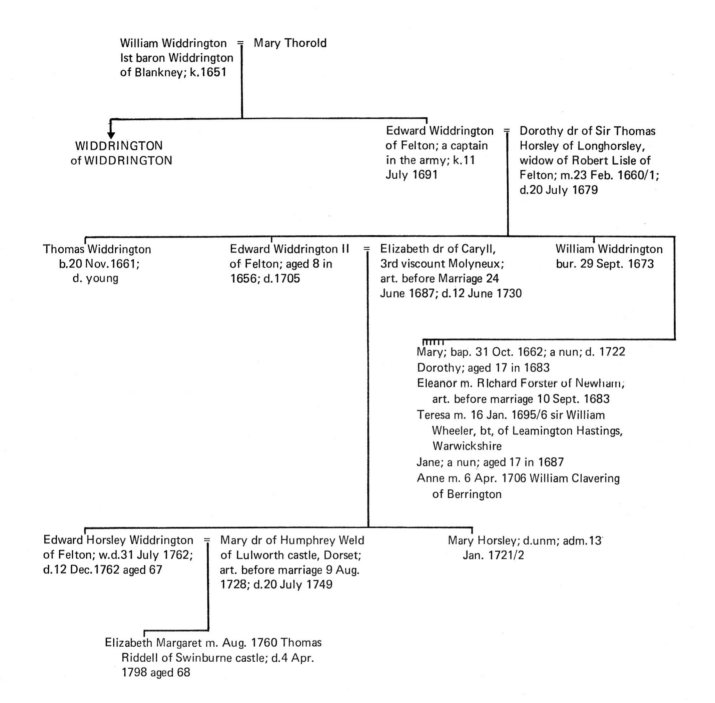

William Widdrington = Mary Thorold
Ist baron Widdrington
of Blankney; k.1651

WIDDRINGTON
of WIDDRINGTON

Edward Widdrington = Dorothy dr of Sir Thomas
of Felton; a captain   Horsley of Longhorsley,
in the army; k.11   widow of Robert Lisle of
July 1691   Felton; m.23 Feb. 1660/1;
                                    d.20 July 1679

Thomas Widdrington
b.20 Nov.1661;
d. young

Edward Widdrington II = Elizabeth dr of Caryll,
of Felton; aged 8 in   3rd viscount Molyneux;
1656; d.1705   art. before Marriage 24
                                         June 1687; d.12 June 1730

William Widdrington
bur. 29 Sept. 1673

Mary; bap. 31 Oct. 1662; a nun; d. 1722
Dorothy; aged 17 in 1683
Eleanor m. Richard Forster of Newham;
    art. before marriage 10 Sept. 1683
Teresa m. 16 Jan. 1695/6 sir William
    Wheeler, bt, of Leamington Hastings,
    Warwickshire
Jane; a nun; aged 17 in 1687
Anne m. 6 Apr. 1706 William Clavering
    of Berrington

Edward Horsley Widdrington = Mary dr of Humphrey Weld
of Felton; w.d.31 July 1762;   of Lulworth castle, Dorset;
d.12 Dec.1762 aged 67   art. before marriage 9 Aug.
                                              1728; d.20 July 1749

Mary Horsley; d.unm; adm.13
Jan. 1721/2

Elizabeth Margaret m. Aug. 1760 Thomas
Riddell of Swinburne castle; d.4 Apr.
1798 aged 68

and lands of Snitter. He acquired Cartington from his father-in-law in exchange for Aydon Shields, par. Hexham, and his lands in Newton Hall.

In 1599 sir Robert Carey calls him 'a very fit man' (*CBP.* II, p.611). In a letter to lord Cecil on 27 October 1600 Carey states that 'Woodrington is an honest and discreet man, and such a borderer as he hath not his fellow; his good services to me since I was placed there have been a great cause of the quiet of this country' (*Ib.*, p.700). It must be remembered that sir Robert Carey had married Roger Widdrington's aunt, so his opinion may have had a certain bias. Richard Lowther also thought highly of him and stated that by his wise service to the warden of the Middle Marches, he has brought that

march to such good order as never the like has been before (*Ib.*, p.709).

Roger Widdrington was a staunch adherent to the Roman Catholic faith. On 1 April 1615/6 sir Henry Anderson, then sheriff of Northumberland, reported that he was expecting a visit from the rev. John Cradocke, vicar of Woodhorn, 'with more ample instructions and informations touching the carriage of the recusants, and certain collections of money which was amongst them, about the time of the Gunpowder treason, wherein I fear me Mr Widdrington will be touched, if it prove true, and some others of greater quality will be occasioned to be enquired after' (*SS.* 68, p.422). It would appear that shortly after this, Widdrington was put under restraint. The rev. William Morton, vicar of Newcastle, in a letter to secretary Winwood on 7 May 1616 says 'I was glad to hear of the restraint of Roger Widdrington as for the country's good so especially for the service of God and his Majesty, both which he hath utterly subverted in Northumberland by his more than false, wicked, seducing inveiglements and tyrannous oppressions' (*Ib.*, p.430). Vicar Morton's words need not be taken too seriously, for he had strong puritan leanings and to him all papists were anathema. Writing to archbishop Abbot on the same day, he is even more outspoken. 'Rodger Withrington has poisoned with Popery all Hexhamshire as since he hath in a manner all Northumberland'; he charges him with spreading many dangerous, seducing books with which he much delights; now, though he is committed he hath in his lodging (or had within these few days) that 'more than pestilent book which a Spaniard writ against his Majesty'. Morton revives the charge that Widdrington was suspected of taking part in Thomas Percy's treason—'they two met in private often before that plot in sundry places, being in deep counsel together'. His own opinion is that Widdrington 'was as false a dissembler, as cunning a hypocrite and as great an equivocator as any Jesuit whatever' (*Ib.*, p.427).

In 1599 Roger Widdrington had been appointed bailiff and steward of Hexhamshire (*NCH.* III, p.65). In a survey of the regality made in 1608 the commissioners recorded that 'Roger Woodrington, gentleman, at this present in banishment, is bailiff there by patent, and is allowed yearly for his fee £13. 6s. 8d.'. He was also steward for which his fee was £6. 13s. 4d. (*Ib.*, p.102). In 1626 he owned the Spital at Hexham, which before the dissolution had been the Hospital of St Giles (*Ib.*, p.311). In 1598 and in 1601 he is described as of Beaufront.

After the death of his first wife, Roger Widdrington eloped with Rosamond daughter of Michael Wentworth of Woolley, Yorks., widow of Bertram Reveley of Newton Underwood. They went through a Scots marriage about Michaelmas 1632 in an open field at Cuthbert-hope in Scotland and Roger was cited before the Court of High Commission at Durham for making a clandestine marriage. It seems evident that the ceremony had been performed by a Romish priest (*SS.* 34, p.68). On 22 December 1632 Roger Widdrington, Oswald Widdrington and others conveyed to Thomas, lord Wentworth, sir George Wentworth and others certain lands in the lordship of Redesdale to the use of Rosamond Revely for life, then to her eldest son and other sons in tail male, with other remainders over, and after their decease to the use of Edward Widdrington, Roger's son (*SS.* 111, p.371).

On 18 June 1635 Roger bought the castle, demesne, park, tithes and water corn mill of Harbottle for £882 from Theophilus, earl of Suffolk, and on 24 June 1637 he bought from the earl twentythree burgages and three closes in Harbottle (*PSAN3*, VIII, p.30).

In the years before the Civil War Roger Widdrington was active in urging the need for better defence of the Border. On 13 August 1638 he wrote to secretary Windebank—'My request is to be held fit to be ranked among the number of his Majesty's most loyal subjects, in which point I will not yield to any subject his Majesty has in any of his kingdoms. — I am in years, but not so decrepid that I will seek after a writ of ease to excuse me in his Majesty's service. . . . I dare

not adventure to advise, yet I crave pardon if to you I advertise to wish that these parts of our country and late borders may be looked into' (*SP.* 16, 397/45). In consequence of this warning, sir Jacob Astley was sent up to make a survey of the Border. On 20 January 1638/9 he reported to Windebank that he had made a tour with Roger Widdrington, visiting Ford, Alnham and Harbottle. 'At Harbottle the bordermen, above 150, came to me to present their services for his Majesty's use, much desiring to have arms for their money to defend themselves. They were all short and broad-shouldered men with broad swords and blue caps: all upon little nags; they are fit for time of war to burn and spoil, and there is good use to be made of them. Mr Roger Widdrington holds them all at his command and is entirely for his Majesty's service' (*Ib.*, 410/99).

After his second marriage, Roger Widdrington seems to have lived at Harbottle and he died there. The inventory of his goods taken after his death is dated 5 March 1641/2. His apparel, sword, horse and furniture with three watches in his pocket, ten bloodstones, two silver seals—a greater and a less, and one gold toothpick, one gold signet on his finger and one hundred and three pounds in his purse, were valued at £200. Even in his young days he had evidently had a leaning for scientific studies, for his uncle sir Henry had left him a legacy of £100 for the better maintenance of his study and library. When he died, his books, certain mathematical instruments, one table with divers drawing boxes, perhaps represented some of the purchases made with his legacy. The appraisers saw some things in the possession of Rosamond, late wife of Roger, deceased, which she would not deliver. At Roger's death there was a trunk containing part of his possessions, at the house of sir George Wentworth of Woolley in Yorkshire, brother to the said Rosamond, but she absolutely refused to give a letter of authority to the administrator for the trunk to be delivered to him. Before his death Roger had recorded in his 'countbooke the said trunk with the parcels of the goods in it'. The trunk had been sent to Yorkshire 'in danger of the Scots'. The appraisers Wm Clennel and Lanc. Thirlwall summed up their valuation:

S'm of his goods	£1446 : 14 : 7
S'm of his debts	£6620 : 0 : 2
The debts surmounts the goods	£5173 : 5 : 7

Administration of his goods was granted 6 March 1641/2 to William Johnson of Cartington on the renunciation, 5 March, of Rosamond Widdrington, widow, relict of deceased (*Dur. Prob. Off.* by C.R.H.).

It has been suggested that Roger Widdrington of Cartington was the writer of a *Humillima Supplicatio* made to Pope Paul V in which the author states that he had been educated at Cambridge and admitted that he was the author of several books published in his name. (*E.H.R.* XVIII, p.116). It seems, however, that the author was Thomas Preston, a Benedictine, who wrote under the pseudonym of Roger Widdrington (*Biographical Studies (later Recusant History)* vol.2, No. 3, pub. Arundel Press, Bognor Regis).

Rosamond Widdrington had no children by her second marriage and died 14 November 1650. The statement that they had issue Dorothy, Ann and Catherine wife of Robert Mallory is incorrect (Clay, *Extinct and Dormant Peerages*, p.250). Catherine wife of Robert Mallory was a daughter of Edward Widdrington of Swinburne (d.1577).

Roger Widdrington by his first wife had an only son Edward (aged 1 in 1615) and three daughters Mary and Margaret (both born before 1615) and Clara. Margaret married Nicholas Errington of Ponteland (1666 Vis. Ped. of Errington). Their eldest son Mark was aged 32 in 1666. Nicholas' grandfather Mark Errington of Ponteland by his w.d. 22 October 1637 leaves to his dear cousin and friend Roger Widdrington of Harbottle, a spur ryal; his god-child Nicholas Errington is to have the best young horse, and Margaret wife of the said god-child, two old angels for a token (*SS*. 111, p.195n.). Clara married William Orde (Vinc. 149, 39). On 13 September 1650 Clara wife of William Orde of Thistlerigg petitioned for a fifth part of her husband's estate for her present maintenance, her husband being a recusant in arms (*SS*. 111, p.306). In the Records of the English Convent at Bruges is the entry that 'In 1676 Mrs Ord, sister of sir Edward Widdrington, brought hither her niece (actually grandniece) Miss Christina Charlton'. Clare Ourd of Crossgate, widow, made her w.d. 17 June 1695, pr. 1696; she leaves to her niece the lady Mary Charleton five guineas, to her niece Mrs Catherine Hammond 2 guineas and the rest of her goods to her friends Nicholas Thornton of Witton castle esq., and John Maire of Gilesgate, gent. Clara Orde died at Cartington and was buried at Rothbury 9 May 1696.

Before his father's death Edward had been created a baronet of Nova Scotia, 26 September 1635. He and his kinsman, lord Widdrington, at their own expense raised 2000 foot and 200 horse to serve the marquis of Newcastle, as well as part of another brigade. He never wavered in his allegiance to king Charles who made him a baronet of England on 8 August 1642.

After the battle of Marston Moor, sir Edward escaped to France. His estates were confiscated by the Commonwealth and appear in the third Act for Sale 18 November 1652. Lady Widdrington was fined £400 for giving information to the king's party and Cartington castle was pulled down. Most of the forfeited estates were purchased by John Rushworth, evidently acting for the family.

Sir Edward died in exile at Bruges and was buried in the church of the Capuchin monks there under a stone bearing this monumental inscription:

Hic jacet dominus Edvardus Widrington eques baronettus Anglus ex illustri familia nobill' dominorum baronum de Widrington qui uxorem duxit Christianum Stuartam neptem comitis de Bothwell ex prosapia Jacobi quinti regis Scotiae. Obiit MLCLXXI 13 Julii aetatis 57.

This serves to identify lady Widdrington as a daughter of John Stewart, commendator of Coldingham, second son of Francis, first earl of Bothwell (G.E.C. *Complete Baronetage*, II, p.118). Her w.d. 17 February 1678/9 and proved at York 8 December 1684 is sealed with the arms of Scotland—a lion within a tressure. She divides her possessions amongst her children, Mary wife of sir Edward Charleton of Hesleyside, and Catherine wife of Gervase Hammond of Scarthingwell, Yorks., and her grandchildren Mary Charleton, Christine Talbott, Catherine Charleton and John Talbott. She was buried

in the church of St Maurice in York.

Besides his two daughters Mary and Catherine, sir Edward Widdrington had a daughter Anne who died unmarried and was buried at Rothbury 28 May 1659, and a son Roger who also died in infancy. 'Roger son of Sr Edward Widdrington of Cartington, knigh. and barr. buried ye 25 day of May 1654' (*Rothbury Registers*). Fr. B. Zimmerman in *Carmel in England* gives the contemporary narrative of the Carmelite priest who attended sir Edward on his death bed in Bruges. 'It was his wish that I should stay with him till death, and see him consigned to his last resting-place, and afterwards proceed to Douai where his son, nineteen years old, was studying, for whom he gave me certain commissions. . . . I found his son at Douai and delivered the message to him, and he showed himself quite willing to conform to the last request of his father'. This son, the 2nd baronet, never returned to England to claim his title. The Records of the Scots College show that he entered the college 19 November 1670, and was drowned 7 April 1672 (*Records of the Scots Colleges*, New Spalding Club, Aberdeen, 1906; I owe this reference to the kindness of Dr A. M. C. Forster of Burradon).

Catherine daughter of sir Edward Widdrington and wife of Gervase Hammond in 1679, had previously been married to a Roger Widdrington. Articles before their marriage are dated 9 April 1670 and Roger died in 1671. An undated petition, perhaps made in 1653, claimed that lands in Shilmore, Soppitt, Dungehope and Peterside had been leased by deed of 30 June 1640 to Henry Widdrington and John Sanderson for a term of 31 years to commence from the birth of the first son of sir Edward Widdrington. In the petition it is stated that 'sir Edward has a son, lately born and now alive'. This presumably was the son Roger who died in May 1654 (*SS*. 111, p.371).

Roger Widdrington and his wife Catherine had an only daughter and heiress Mary who married (articles before marriage 25 November 1687) sir John Gascoigne of Parlington, Yorks., bart. The Gascoigne share of the Widdrington estates was the Harbottle lands and they were sold by sir Edward Gascoigne in 1731 to Luke Clennel of Clennel.

The two Roger Widdringtons, one the son of sir Edward Widdrington, and the other his son-in-law, have often been confused with each other (see *NCH*. VII, p.218n.). It is almost certain that the latter was a younger son of Henry Widdrington of Nether Trewhit and grandson of sir Ephraim Widdrington (*see* WIDDRINGTON OF RITTON). He was buried at Holystone 28 July 1671 (M.I.).

In a Roman Breviary which had apparently belonged to one of the Radcliffe family, there are entries in the calendar of anniversaries some of which are of Widdringtons:

Feb. 10 My uncle Roger Widdrington's anniversary.

Feb. 27 My aunt Widdrington's anniversary.

June 3 Sr Edward Widdrington's anniversary.

Mch 27 Sr Edward Widdrington's junior his anniversary.

Some of these dates might appear to be inaccurate for according to his tombstone sir Edward died 13 July and his son sir Edward is said to have been drowned 7 April (*PSAN*3. VI, p.102). The anonymous author of *Life of sir Edward Widdrington* (1923) after quoting the M.I. at Bruges, says 'the word Julii is evidently an error, (and) should be Junii'. He quotes the entry in the Breviary, but gives no other authority for his emendation. June 3rd (O.S.) would correspond to

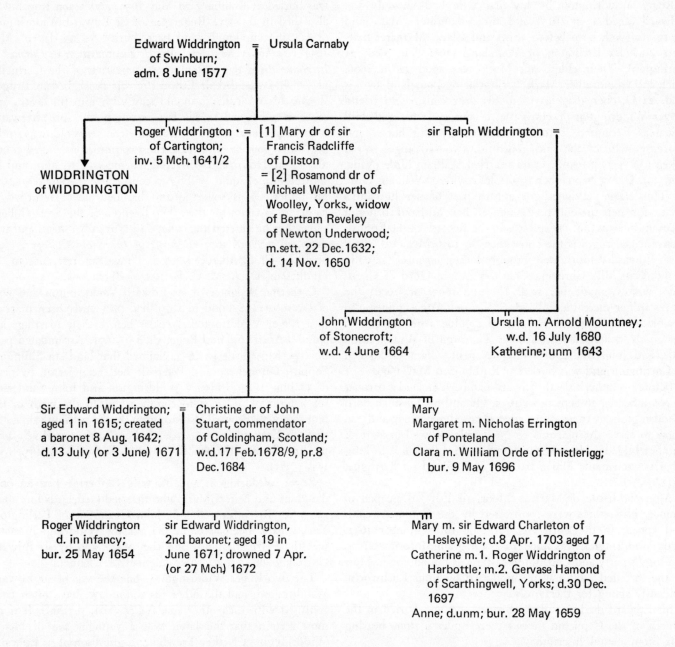

Edward Widdrington = Ursula Carnaby
of Swinburn;
adm. 8 June 1577

Roger Widdrington · = [1] Mary dr of sir   sir Ralph Widdrington =
of Cartington;   Francis Radcliffe
inv. 5 Mch. 1641/2   of Dilston
                            = [2] Rosamond dr of
WIDDRINGTON   Michael Wentworth of
of WIDDRINGTON   Woolley, Yorks., widow
                            of Bertram Reveley
                            of Newton Underwood;
                            m.sett. 22 Dec.1632;
                            d. 14 Nov. 1650

                                                   John Widdrington   Ursula m. Arnold Mountney;
                                                   of Stonecroft;   w.d. 16 July 1680
                                                   w.d. 4 June 1664   Katherine; unm 1643

Sir Edward Widdrington; = Christine dr of John   Mary
aged 1 in 1615; created   Stuart, commendator   Margaret m. Nicholas Errington
a baronet 8 Aug. 1642;   of Coldingham, Scotland;   of Ponteland
d.13 July (or 3 June) 1671 w.d.17 Feb.1678/9, pr.8 Clara m. William Orde of Thistlerigg;
                          Dec.1684   bur. 9 May 1696

Roger Widdrington   sir Edward Widdrington,   Mary m. sir Edward Charleton of
d. in infancy;   2nd baronet; aged 19 in   Hesleyside; d.8 Apr. 1703 aged 71
bur. 25 May 1654   June 1671; drowned 7 Apr. Catherine m.1. Roger Widdrington of
                         (or 27 Mch.) 1672   Harbottle; m.2. Gervase Hamond
                                                        of Scarthingwell, Yorks; d.30 Dec.
                                                        1697
                                                    Anne; d.unm; bur. 28 May 1659

June 13 (N.S. as used on the Continent). Similarly March 27 (O.S.) would be April 3 (N.S.). Possibly the date, April 7, given in the Records of the Scots College, represents the date of burial (Inf. ex Dr A. M. C. Forster).

WIDDRINGTON OF STONECROFT, CHAP. NEWBROUGH

LITTLE is known about sir Ralph Widdrington, third and youngest son of Edward Widdrington (d.1577) of Swinburne. By the w.d. 15 February 1592/3 of his uncle sir Henry Widdrington he is to have 20 nobles a year out of Haughton and Humshaugh. The name of his wife is not known. They had one son, John, and two daughters Ursula and Katherine.

At the time of the Commonwealth, John's lands were seque-

strated for his recusancy. He was living at Stonecroft when, on 11 February 1652 and again on 19 July 1653 he claimed an allowance of one third from Stonecroft and the half of Little Whittington (SS. 111, p.378). By some means or other he managed to retain or recover his lands. He was living in Newcastle in 1663 (not 1643) when by the w.d. 13 September in that year, of his aunt Dorothy widow of John Errington of Beaufront, he succeeded to her estates of Stonecroft, Nunbush, Grottington, Portgate, (Little) Whittington and 'Naickt Eele alias Plankey'. Dorothy Errington directs John Widdrington to pay to the rt hon. William, lord Widdrington, two twenty and two pieces of gold to make him a signet ring 'which I desire his honour will be pleased to wear for my sake' (Dur. Prob. Off. by C.R.H.).

By his w.d. 4 June 1664 John Widdrington of Stonecroft leaves the lands which he had received from his aunt Dorothy to his sister Ursula Mountney of Stonecroft, widow. He also leaves to her lands in Woodhorn and Monkseaton which he had lately purchased from sir Henry Widdrington of Blackheddon and Nicholas Whitehead of Morpeth, and certain lands in Newbrough which he had recently bought from Anthony Stocoe, Wm Urwen, John Glenwright and Henry Stokoe of Newbrough. To his very noble friend the rt hon. William, lord Widdrington, he leaves £100 as a token of his love. Captain Edward Widdrington 'the said lord's brother' is to have a horse for his saddle. His 'cousin' Mr Francis Widdrington of Hepple, his 'nephew' William Widdrington of Buteland, and Arnold Burdett of Unthank, are each to have a colt. His lease of the fourth part of Emblehope which he had from the earl of Northumberland is left to his dear friend, Mr William Charleton, 'now of Moralee'. He leaves a legacy of £20 to Thomas Mountney of Stonecroft, and one of £10 to his 'true friend' John Roggers of Nunbush. The supervisors of the will are to be William, lord Widdrington, capt. Edward Widdrington, sir Edward Charleton, bart, John Thirlwall esq., Wm Charleton of Moralee, esq., and Thomas Errington of Bingfield, gent.

John Widdrington's sister Ursula is said to have married Thomas Mountney, but in fact his Christian name was Arnold. Ursula's aunt, Dorothy Errington in her will mentions her 'cousin Ursula Mountney wife of Arnold Mounteney, gent.', to whom she leaves a legacy of £20. Ursula Mountney by her w.d. 16 July 1680 leaves her estates to William, lord Widdrington, reserving a rentcharge of £32 out of Stonecroft and Nunbush, £20 of which is to be paid to a Roman Catholic priest at Newbrough, the balance of £12 to be distributed amongst the poor of Hexham, Warden, Chollerton, St John Lee and Corbridge (SS. 111, p.378n.).

Dorothy Errington's unmarried daughter Dorothy by her w.d. 19 June 1643 leaves £20 to her cousin Ursula Mountnay, and £20 to Ursula's sister Katherine (Dur. Prob. Off. by C.R.H.).

It has been said that John Widdrington had a brother Henry Widdrington, father of William Widdrington of Buteland. This is incorrect. Henry Widdrington was a son of Benjamin Widdrington, apparently an illegitimate son of Edward Widdrington (d.1577) of Swinburne. Henry's daughter Dorothy married William Widdrington of Buteland.

WIDDRINGTON OF BUTELAND,
PAR. CHOLLERTON

SOMETIME between 1565 and 1573 one Janet Pereson wife of Jenkyn Pereson of Wallsend was charged with witchcraft in the Ecclesiastical Court at Durham. One of the witnesses, Catherine Fenwick, daughter of Constance Fenwicke, generos, aged about 20 years, deposed 'that about 2 years ago her cousin Edward Wyddrington had a child sick, and Jenkyn Pereson's wife asked of Thomas Blackberd, then this deponent's mother's servant, how Byngeman the child did, and bade the said Blackberd bid the child's mother come and speak with her. And upon the same this deponent went unto her; and the said Pereson's wife said the child was taken with the fairy, and bade her (the child's mother) send two (persons) for south-running water, and these two shall not speak by the way, and that the child should be washed in that water, and dip the shirt in the water, and so hang it upon a hedge all that night, and that on the morrow the shirt should be gone and the child should recover health; but the shirt was not gone as she said. And this deponent paid to Pereson's wife 3d. for her pains' (SS. 21, pp.99-100).

It is quite certain that Edward Wyddrington, father of the child Byngeman, was the person of this name, second son of sir John Widdrington (d.1571) of Widdrington, who died at Swinburne in 1577. Sir John had a sister Constance who married Valentine Fenwick of Walker, and the deponent Catherine would be their daughter. The child was no doubt 'Benjamin Wetherington' baptised at St Nicholas', Newcastle, 15 January 1559/60 though the names of the parents are omitted from the register.

Neither in the visitation pedigree of 1575 nor in the administration of Edward Wyddrington's goods in 1577 is a son Benjamin mentioned and it is difficult not to conclude that he was illegitimate. At the time of the alleged witchcraft it seems that Edward Widdrington was living somewhere near Wallsend evidently with Benjamin's mother.

In 1594 Benjamin Widdrington was perhaps living at Little Swinburne when he and Henry Widdrington were defendants in a suit brought by Ralph Errington of Bingfield about pasture rights on the moor between Colwell and Bingfield (NCH. IV, p.294n.). On 18 August 1606 Katherine wife of Benjamin Wotherington of Little Swinburne was convicted of recusancy (Recusant Rolls). On 3 May 1608 Benjamin Widdrington of Little Swinburne, esquire, purchased four farms in Buteland from William Shafto of Bavington. The same year he took a 21 years lease of Barrasford mill (NCH. IV, p.317). A survey of the manor of Hexham made in 1608 records that Benjamin Woodrington was customary tenant at a rent of 16s. 3d. of a tenement and land in Acomb (NCH. III, p.101). He was living at Buteland 15 August 1623 when he bought Hindhaugh, Broomhope, Longlee, Felling Close and Steel, together with Stidley Hill in Corsenside from Percival Reed of Troughen (Ib., p.365).

Benjamin Widdrington's wife has been identified as Katherine daughter of George Lawson of Little Usworth, co. Durham (Surtees, Durham, II, p.47). She was unmarried when her father made his will dated 29 December 1587; he leaves her £300 out of his lease of Barmstone, co. Durham. When Benjamin Widdrington died in 1633 administration of his goods was granted to Edward Lawson of Coastley, par. Hexham; Edward was George Lawson's youngest son.

On 27 August 1625 Beniam Wuddrington of (par. of) Woodhorne, gent., Katherine his wife, and Henry, John, Ursula and Katherine Wuddrington, his children were convicted of recusancy. All the children must have reached the age of 16 for no one under this age could be convicted of recusancy. By 13 January 1629/30 two other children, Dorothy and Mary must have become 16 for they and the others were then convicted of recusancy (Recusant Rolls).

Inventory of the goods of Benjamin Widdrington of Hirst (par. Woodhorn), gent., was made 9 October 1633 by John Heron, William Thirlwall and Andrew Clennell. Administration was granted to Edward Lawson for the use of Katherine the widow, and John, Ursula, Katherine, Dorothy and Mary his children.

An inquest taken at Alnwick on 17 September 1636 found that Benjamin Widdrington had died at Buteland on 9 September 1634 seised of 'lands in Buteland, Seaton Woodhorn late parcel of the possessions of the late monastery of Gisburne als Gisborough in Yorkshire and of Tynemouth monastery. Lands in Hindhaugh, Broumphaugh Whittfeild Skeale Steadlay Hill and Whetsone haugh bought by Benjamin Widdrington of Percival Read gen'. Henry his son and next heir at the time of his death was 30 and more (*PRO. C*, 142 734/39).

On 24 February 1637 Henry Widdrington of Buteland, par. Chollerton, esq., and Katherine Widdrington his mother, convicted recusants, owed £10 p.a. composition on their estate. It was agreed that they were not to be charged with arrears previous to Martinmas 1634 for that the aforesaid lands came to him about that time through the death of his father who died in September 1634 (Inf. from Dr A. M. C. Forster).

Katherine Widdrington seems to have been on very affectionate terms with her late husband Benjamin's half sister Dorothy wife of John Errington of Beaufront, and with Dorothy's daughters. They had of course a closer relationship besides that of marriage, for Dorothy Errington's mother Ursula, and Katherine Widdrington's mother Mabel were both daughters of sir Reynold Carnaby of Halton.

Ursula Errington of Wharmley, a daughter of John and Dorothy Errington, by her w.d. 22 December 1634 leaves legacies to her cousins, Ursula, Catherine, Henry, Dorothy and Mary Widdrington, all of Hirst. Ursula's sister Dorothy Errington of Newcastle by her w.d. 1643 leaves legacies to her aunt Katherine Widdrington and to her cousin Henry Widdrington of St Anthonys. Dorothy, widow of John Errington remembers in her w.d. 13 September 1663, her 'sister' Katherine Widdrington 'sometime wife to Benjamin Widdrington'. She also mentions her cousin Henry Widdrington of St Anthonys and his daughter.

On 20 September 1625 Henry Widdrington bought from Roger Widdrington of Cartington, two farmholds in Buteland, together with a rent of eight groats from two tenements then in the tenure of Benjamin Widdrington, late payable and belonging to the lords of Tecket. He bought two farms called Lee Orchard and White Walls in Buteland, 14 February 1637 from Robert Ord of Birkes, co. Durham.

Henry Widdrington's lands were sequestrated in 1649 and were included in the Third Act for Sale passed 18 November 1652. On 30 October 1650 Isabel wife of Henry Widdrington of Buteland petitioned for a fifth of the estate for maintenance of herself and children, with arrears from 24 December 1649. Henry petitioned for the like allowance on their behalf, 6 November 1650, and this was granted with arrears. There must have been some difficulties in obtaining this allowance for on 17 February 1652 Mary and Catherine, the infant daughters of Henry Widdrington found it necessary to renew the petition of 30 October 1650; it was granted with deduction of taxes and charges. On 10 February 1652 Catherine widow of Benjamin Widdrington, claimed her thirds from Buteland and other lands in Northumberland, allowed already by the County Committee but being sequestrated for the recusancy and delinquency of her son Henry; she claimed that she was 80 years old and very infirm. On 9 November 1653 a messuage and lands in North Seaton, par. Woodhorn, late parcel of the estate of Henry Widdrington was discharged from sequestration as sold by the Treason Trustees to Samuel Foxley, gent. By 1654 Henry's two daughters had still not received the fifth which had first been claimed for them in 1650. Their names are now given as Mary and Dorothy, and their petition was refused, the County Committee stating that they had no power to grant fifths to the wives and children of delinquents. On 25 April 1654 the petition of Catherine Widdrington for her thirds was allowed with arrears from date of petition, and the lands were discharged from sequestration (*SS.* 111, pp.375-376).

Henry Widdrington's wife seems to have been Anne, daughter of Roger Lawson of Heaton (*NCH.* IV, p.369; XII, p.393; Welford, *Men of Mark twixt Tyne and Tweed*, III, p.25; Foster's *Pedigrees of Yorkshire Families*, 1874, vol.III). Roger died in 1613 or 1614 in his father's lifetime; his widow Dorothy died at St Anthony's, Byker in 1632. Henry Widdrington was living at St Anthony's in 1643 and 1663.

At the Restoration, Henry Widdrington recovered his lands, and in 1663 he was rated on the two Butelands, the Steel, Hindhaugh, Broomhope, Calf Close and Felling. He died before 1668 leaving two daughters, Mary who became the wife of Francis Sutton, and Dorothy who became the wife of William Widdrington (*see* WIDDRINGTON OF BULLER'S GREEN).

WIDDRINGTON OF PLESSEY, PAR. STANNINGTON

IN the visitation pedigree of 1558 the children of sir John Widdrington (d.1571) by his second wife Agnes Gower are given as Roberte, Wylliam, Isaac, Abymaer, Jane, Barbara, Margerye, Rebecca, Sara and Marye. These names are repeated in the visitation pedigree of 1563/4 where the fourth son appears as Abynore; in a law suit of 1583 he is Abymeleck.

'Dame Agnes, lady Woddrington, late wife to sir John Woddrington, late of Widdrington, in the county of Northumberland, knight, deceased', made her will on 23 March 1582/3. Her body is to be buried within the parish church of Saint Nicholas, within the town of Newcastle upon Tyne. To her two sons 'Benwell' and Efferam Woddrington she leaves all her right and term of years in the rectory of Kirkwhelpington 'for obtaining of which said lease there is remaining in the hands of Mr John Morley £60'. To her son William Woddrington she leaves £5 and 'the best colt that he will choose'; William's daughter Elizabeth is also to have £5. Her son Isaac Woddrington is left £5 and 'the next best colt he will choose'. Her daughter Jane Carnabye is to have 'my best suit of apparel, that is to say, my French hood, my best gown, doublet, kirtle of velvet and best petticoat'. 'My daughter Sara shall have £45 which was due unto her in full contentment of her child's portion due unto her forth of the goods and chattels of her late father sir John Woddrington, knight, deceased'. She gives to her grandson John Woddrington, son of her eldest son Robert, one bed of downs with all the furniture thereunto belonging, which is remaining within the said town of Newcastle, with the best bedstocks at Plessey, and the chamber as it now standeth, undefaced, together also with her greatest furnish racks and spits at Plessey and Chibburn, the tables in the hall, with all the furniture as it now standeth, the copper, all the brewing vessels as they stand, the buttery with the tonninge vessel and the beef tubs, together also with all her coals lying at the pit and staiths. Robert is appointed sole executor and is to have

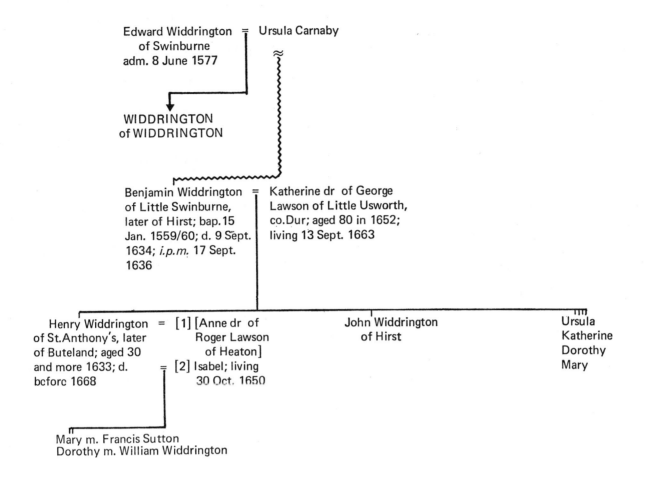

Edward Widdrington = Ursula Carnaby
of Swinburne
adm. 8 June 1577

WIDDRINGTON
of WIDDRINGTON

Benjamin Widdrington = Katherine dr of George
of Little Swinburne, Lawson of Little Usworth,
later of Hirst; bap.15 co.Dur; aged 80 in 1652;
Jan. 1559/60; d. 9 Sept. living 13 Sept. 1663
1634; *i.p.m.* 17 Sept.
1636

Henry Widdrington = [1] [Anne dr of   John Widdrington   Ursula
of St.Anthony's, later   Roger Lawson   of Hirst   Katherine
of Buteland; aged 30   of Heaton]   Dorothy
and more 1633; d. = [2] Isabel; living   Mary
before 1668   30 Oct. 1650

Mary m. Francis Sutton
Dorothy m. William Widdrington

all the rest of her goods to be equally distributed amongst her son Efferam and her three unmarried daughters Rebecca, Marye and Martha. Her servant Barbare Woddrington is given her 'next best cloth gown guarded with velvet, with a tawny taffeta doublet, a feather bed with the furniture thereunto belonging'. Every one of her serving men is to have a quarter's wages (*SS.* 38, p.99; the editor read the name of lady Agnes' son as 'Benwell' but Mr C. Roy Hudleston who has recently examined the will thinks the name is 'Bemivell', apparently a pet form of Abimeleck).

The use of such Old Testament names as Abimeleck, Ephraim, Isaac and Rebecca is unusual at such an early date. It is more to be expected in Puritan families of the next century. In accordance with the directions in her will 'Lady Anne Widerington' was buried at St Nicholas', Newcastle, on 29 March 1583. Her will was proved on 4 August 1584.

A certain amount of information is known about lady Agnes' daughters. Jane was wife of John Carnaby of Langley; upon their marriage in 1564 her husband's uncle, Cuthbert Carnaby, settled Togston and Lyham on them; Jane was buried at St Nicholas', Newcastle, 29 July 1590. Barbara Widdrington, mentioned in the visitation pedigrees, but not in her mother's will, may have died young. Margery Widdrington married Henry Parkinson and was a widow living at Widdrington in 1615 when she conveyed a messuage and a farmhold in Darlington to George Parkinson of Haghouse (Longstaffe, *History of Darlington*, p.115). Rebecca Widdring-

ton never married; she was living at Staindrop, co. Durham 9 November 1625, when she made her will. In it she mentions her nephew Toby Ewbancke, her sister Martha and Martha's daughters Elizabeth Hilton, Martha, Margaret and Dorothy Sanford, her nephew Mr Edward Grey; she leaves a legacy to Rebecca Witherington, daughter of her brother Isaac, 'if she is living and if she be dead' her brother Robert is to have the legacy. Toby Ewbancke had married Mary daughter of Henry Grey of Chillingham, by his wife Mary who was Rebecca's sister. After the death of Henry Grey, Mary married William Jenison of Newcastle.

Martha Widdrington who is not mentioned in the visitation pedigrees of 1558 and 1563/4 but whose name appears in the will of her mother Agnes, lady Widdrington, married Thomas Sandford of Askham, Wmd (1665 visitation pedigree registered by their grandson Thomas Sandford, then aged 35). At the christening at Askham on 14 November 1558 of Ann daughter of Thomas Sandforth, esq., the child's aunt 'Mrs Rebecca Wytherington' was one of the godmothers. When Martha Sandford's property was seized by the Crown in 1609 for recusancy sir Ephraim Widdrington obtained the lease of it, presumably on her behalf.

Besides the four sons, Robert, William, Isaac and Abimeleck, sir John Widdrington by his second wife had another son, Ephraim, not mentioned in the visitation pedigrees. For Abimeleck and Ephraim see WIDDRINGTON OF RITTON. Little is known about William Widdrington except that he was

113

provost marshal of Berwick in 1585 and had a daughter Elizabeth mentioned in the will of her grandmother. Isaac Widdrington was living at Darlington 1 June 1592 when his son James was baptised. James may have died in infancy for he is not mentioned in the will of his aunt Rebecca in 1625 although she leaves legacies to Isaac's son Robert and daughter Rebecca.

Robert Widdrington, eldest son of sir John Widdrington by his second wife Agnes Gower, received from his father the manors of Cowpen and Plessey and lands in Shotton and Chibburn. He was knight of the shire for Northumberland in 1588 and 1597, and sheriff in 1595. On 11 January 1596/7 the Privy Council complained that 'instead of the thankful acceptance' of the sheriffdom he had utterly neglected to execute the same. Ordered to make speedy appearance at the Court within twelve days, he appeared on 23 February and was ordered to attend daily and not depart till dismissed. He apparently made his peace with the Council (*Cal. Acts of Privy Council* vol.26). He seems to have been normally resident at Wearmouth, co. Durham. Hugh Whythead, prior of Durham, had surrendered the monastery of Monkwearmouth to the king 31 December 1540; and on 18 June 1545 it was granted by Henry VIII to Hugh's nephew, Thomas Whythead. Thomas' son William, in 1597 levied a fine of the manor of Monk Wearmouth to Robert Widdrington.

By his w.d. 29 August 1598, pr. 20 January 1598/9 Robert Widdrington leaves to his wife Elizabeth the house, demesne and farmhold in Monk Wearmouth, for her life 'and if she cannot enjoy it freely discharged of all troubles and incumbrances, my salt pans in Cowpen shall be charged to pay her £100 yearly' (*SS*. 38, p.286). Elizabeth was his second wife and has been identified as daughter of sir Thomas Forster of Adderstone and widow of George Craster. In 1550 a Robert Widdrington was living at Craster, but George Craster's wife was called Eleanor, not Elizabeth.

Robert Widdrington of Wearmouth's first wife and the mother of his children was Margaret daughter of Robert, 5th lord Ogle. Their children were an only son, John, and a daughter Katherine wife firstly of Robert Dent of Byker and secondly of John Ogle of Causey Park. 'Mrs Eliz. wife of Mr Robt Widdrington, esq.', was godmother to George son of Robert Dent at his baptism at All Saints, Newcastle, on 16 January 1596/7. Robert leaves to his 'daughter Dent the whole lease of the coal mines of Byker moor, and £100 to be levied out of my cattle and goods'; to her sons Henry and George Dent he leaves the tithe of Newton.

'Robert Dent, gent., of Byker' was buried at All Saints, Newcastle, on 26 April 1602; and on 28 February 1605/6 Katherine Ogle late wife of Robert Dent of Byker, gent., deceased, made a declaration of account of her first husband's affairs.

Robert leaves to his brother Ephraim his two parts of the parsonage of Hartburn. Robert Wodrington, his brother Isaack's son, and perhaps the testator's godson, is to have a legacy of £5. To his son John he leaves all his lands at Chibburn, Plessey and Shotton 'and all such other land as the entail specifies'. The executors are to be 'The right worshipful my nephew, Mr Henry Woodrington, and Mr Robert Woodrington of Hauxley, gent'. Amongst the witnesses to the will are the names of Ephraim Woodrington and Robert Woodrington.

The inventory of Robert's goods, dated 10 October 1598, shews that he lived in a substantial house at Wearmouth, which included the hall, the great chamber, the inner chamber, the privy chamber, Mr John's chamber, the maid's chamber, the brushing chamber, the serving men's chamber, the inner parlour, the fore chamber, the new chamber, the closet and the kitchen. Of outside buildings there was a milk-house, a bolting-house, a brew-house, a buttery and a pantry. His household goods were of the simplest. There was one silver salt and four silver bowls; for general use there were pewter platters, dishes, basons, ewers, potingers, saucers etc. He had sheep, cattle and horses at Monk Wearmouth; cattle at Washington where he had land on lease; cattle and corn at Plessey; and at Cowpen there were three saltpans, the half (share) of a coal keel, cattle, rye and oats. The total value of his goods was £559. 9s. 4d. Robert's house was no doubt part of the monastic buildings converted into a dwelling house.

Robert's son and heir John was 21 years old in 1599 and died three years later on 29 December 1602 (*i.p.m.* in co. Durham, 6 November 1602). On 18 December 1602 Barbara Woddrington of Plessey certified that she had appointed her kinsman Mr Henry Woddrington of Swinburne to take administration for the goods of her late husband, Mr John Woddrington, decd (Raine's *MSS Wills and Inv.* I, p.157). Hodgson states that Barbara was a Whitehead of Tynemouth (*HN.* ii, II, p.297). She was probably daughter and coheiress of that William Whythead from whom Robert Widdrington had acquired the manor of Monk Wearmouth in 1597. William's only son had died in his father's lifetime.

John Widdrington of Plessey left two infant sons, Robert the elder son being aged 4 years and 5 months when his father died. The younger son John had from his brother an annuity of £50 out of his lands in Wearmouth. John married Isabel daughter of sir Ralph Delaval of Seaton Delaval. Isabel had been baptised at Earsdon 27 July 1610 and was living at Whitburn, co. Durham, unmarried, 10 June 1635. The marriage is confirmed by the visitation pedigree of Delaval of 1666, where John is described as 'a younger son of the house of Plessey, in com. Northu'. After John Widdrington's death his widow Isabel married Robert Eden and on 20 February 1651 the Edens claimed and recovered the rentcharge. It had been sequestrated for delinquency of Ralph Pudsey (*SS.* 111, p.312).

Robert Widdrington had a general livery 28 November 1621 of Plessey and Shotton and the other estates of his father. In 1632 he compounded as a recusant and the annual payments were to date back to 1629. He was to pay £6. 13s. 4d. a year with two increments, *viz.* after the death of John Widdrington his brother £16. 13s. 4d. a year more, and after the death of dame Monkton his mother £20 a year more. For several years after Robert's death the unpaid fines on his lands accumulated; in 1649 the position was:

19½ years 1629/30 to 1649 at £ 6. 13. 4.	£130.	0. 0
14 years 1625 to 1649 at	£20.	£280. 0. 0
1 year 1648 to 1649 at	£16. 13. 4.	£ 16. 13. 4
		£426. 13. 4

(*Rec. Roll*, 24 Chas I, E.377/56, It. Dunelm and L.R. 7/87,

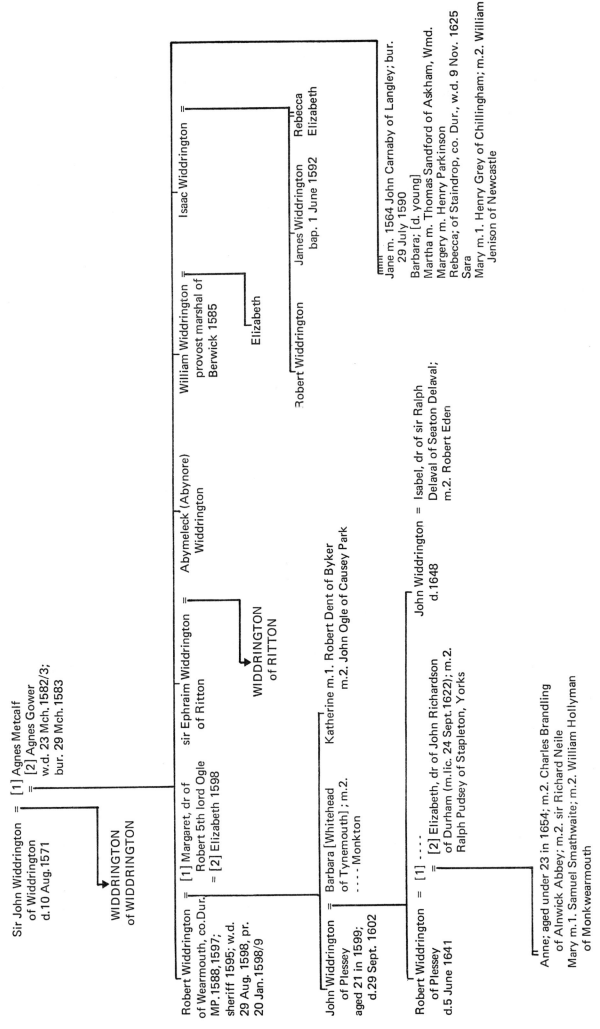

Sir John Widdrington = [1] Agnes Metcalf
of Widdrington = [2] Agnes Gower
d.10 Aug.1571 w.d. 23 Mch. 1582/3;
bur. 29 Mch. 1583

WIDDRINGTON
of WIDDRINGTON

Robert Widdrington = [1] Margaret, dr of   sir Ephraim Widdrington =   Abymeleck (Abynore)   William Widdrington   Isaac Widdrington =
of Wearmouth, co.Dur.   Robert 5th lord Ogle   of Ritton   Widdrington   provost marshal of
MP.1588,1597;   = [2] Elizabeth 1598   Berwick 1585
sheriff 1595; w.d.
29 Aug. 1598, pr.   WIDDRINGTON
20 Jan.1598/9   of RITTON   Elizabeth   James Widdrington   Rebecca
                                                                                                                                           bap. 1 June 1592   Elizabeth

                                                                                                                 Robert Widdrington

John Widdrington = Barbara [Whitehead   Katherine m.1. Robert Dent of Byker
of Plessey   of Tynemouth] ; m.2.   m.2. John Ogle of Causey Park
aged 21 in 1599;   - - - - Monkton
d.29 Sept. 1602

                                                        John Widdrington = Isabel, dr of sir Ralph
                                                        d.1648   Delaval of Seaton Delaval;
                                                                           m.2. Robert Eden

Robert Widdrington = [1] - - -   Jane m. 1564 John Carnaby of Langley; bur.
of Plessey   = [2] Elizabeth, dr of John Richardson   29 July 1590
d.5 June 1641   of Durham (m.lic. 24 Sept.1622); m.2.   Barbara; [d. young]
                       Ralph Pudsey of Stapleton, Yorks   Martha m. Thomas Sandford of Askham, Wmd.
                                                                         Margery m. Henry Parkinson
                                                                         Rebecca; of Staindrop, co. Dur., w.d. 9 Nov. 1625
                                                                         Sara
                                                                         Mary m.1. Henry Grey of Chillingham; m.2. William
                                                                            Jenison of Newcastle

Anne; aged under 23 in 1654; m.2. Charles Brandling
   of Alnwick Abbey; m.2. sir Richard Neile
Mary m.1. Samuel Smathwaite; m.2. William Hollyman
   of Monkwearmouth

115

*f.*47). From this it is evident that Robert Widdrington's mother Barbara had married a second husband, called Monkton, and had died in 1625. His brother John had died in 1648. It does not appear that any of the fine was ever paid.

On 29 May 1641 Widdrington settled his lands in Plessey, Newhouse, Brighouse, Shotton and Shotton Edge in Northumberland and certain other lands in co. Durham to his own use for life and then to the use of Anne Widdrington his daughter and her heirs for ever, provided that if the said Robert should have any heir male of his body after the date of the settlement all the lands should remain to such son. Robert died at York on 5 June 1641 without having had a son. His second wife Elizabeth was daughter of John Richardson; on 24 September 1622 John Richardson of Durham, esq., appeared at Durham Castle and sought a licence for the solemnization of matrimony between Robert Woodrington of Monkwearmouth and Elizabeth Richardson, daughter of the same John and alleged that the same Robert Woodrington is a widower and the same Elizabeth is 21 years or thereabouts and John consents. A licence was issued for the couple to be married in the parish church of Coniscliffe (*Bishop of Durham's Register*, by C.R.H.). His widow Elizabeth married Ralph Pudsey of Stapleton, Yorks., and his daughter Ann married Charles Brandling of Alnwick. Both Pudsey and Brandling had their lands sequestrated for their part in the Civil Wars.

On 20 June 1654 it was reported that Anne was below the age of 23 years and had been married to Charles Brandling about 3 years; in February 1646 the County Committee had decided that Anne had a good title to all her father's lands except what was her mother's jointure and that sequestration as to her ought to be discharged, but care should be taken for her education as she was but thirteen years of age and her mother a papist. On 22 June 1654 the County Committee was asked to certify within a month whether the lands had been sequestrated on account of Anne going to mass between the time of the order in 1647 and the time of her marriage or for any other cause. The County Committee did not report until 12 September 1654 but then had to admit that they could not find anything touching her going to mass, and accordingly the sequestration was absolutely discharged (*SS.* 111, p.134).

Surtees thought that Charles Brandling's wife was Anne, daughter of Ralph Pudsey (*Hist. Dur.* ii, pp.8, 90, 93). Both Surtees and Hodgson assumed that Robert Widdrington had only one daughter, Anne, because he had settled all his lands on her. Actually he had another daughter Mary, married firstly to Samuel Smathwaite, and secondly to William Hollyman of Monkwearmouth. On 7 June 1650 Hollyman claimed a moiety of the manor of Monkwearmouth in right of his wife Mary, the lands having been sequestrated for the delinquency of Ralph Pudsey.

After the death of her husband Charles Brandling (adm. 23 February 1666/7 to his brother Thomas Brandling) and before 2 November 1667 Anne married sir Richard Neile, grandson of archbishop Neile.

WIDDRINGTON OF RITTON, CHAP. NETHERWITTON

EPHRAIM and 'Benwell' (Abimeleck) Widdrington did not obtain undisputed possession of the lease of the parsonage of Kirkwhelpington left to them by their mother's will, for it was claimed by Edward Shaftoe in 1583 (*de Banco Roll* in *AA3.* IV, p.12).

Nothing further is recorded about Abimeleck Widdrington. Ephraim is better known. At the muster of Castle and Morpeth wards on 24 November 1595 the commissioners appointed to hold the muster, one of them being Henry Widdrington, the head of the family, reported that at Woodhorn Demesne Ephraim Woodrington and five others were absent (*CBP.* II, p.79). Included in Middle March bills against England, filed on Henry Woddrington of Swinburne by the commissioners, was one of 16 February 1596/7 by the laird of Mowe against Efram Wodrington (*Ib.*, p.264).

In 1597 tentative arrangements were made by Ephraim with Margaret widow of Hugh Gallon of Trewhit that his son Henry should marry her daughter Katherine then aged about one year. Katherine was Hugh Gallon's only child and it was believed that she was his heiress. The arrangement broke down when it was found that Gallon's lands were subject to a settlement in tail male.

Like many others of his family both before and after these times Ephraim was no great respecter of authority. On 31 December 1597 Edward Gray had apprehended William Hall of Cartington for some misdemeanour, but had not detained him above two hours when Ephraim Wodrington, brother to Harry Wodrington came in dinner time to Gray's house with Ralph Ogle, Andrew Clennel and Luke Errington, servants to Harry Wodrington, and John Smyth, Ephraim's servant armed with long guns, pistols and swords, demanding of the porter that he should open the gates. The porter 'doubting of their pretence' refused. Then the said Wodrington asked for William Hall, and after the said Hall came to him, the said Mr Wodrington asked him if he were in prison or not? who answered he was. Then Mr Wodrington said 'those iron gates shall not hold thee'. And after did revile Edward Gray in the hearing of his servant, first calling him 'dissembling knave', secondly 'cowardly beast', and thirdly 'cowardly dastardly companion' for holding Hall in such sort (*CBP.* II, pp.493, 506).

On 20 January 1597/8 the Privy Council wrote to Henry Widdrington—'You shall understand that complaint hath been made unto us against your uncle Ephraym Woodrington and a servant of his, one Ralfe Smith, and also against divers of your servants, namely Andrewe Clennell, Luke Errington and Roger Oghell, for very great disorders committed by your said uncle and the rest before mentioned in his company in December last at the house of Mr Edward Gray, and for very offensive and outrageous behaviour against the said Edward Gray upon some occasions that concern Her Majesty's service' (*Cal. Acts of Privy Council* vol.27). Those against whom the complaints had been made were ordered to appear at the Court to answer by the 20th February next. Three days after the appointed day Ephraim Woodrington of Earsdon Forest and the four servants put in an appearance, and were ordered to give daily attendance on their lordships at their meeting in Council 'and not to depart until by their honours' order they shall be dismissed'. It seems that they were still in London in May and were concerned in an affray in the City with lord Eure and his brother. On 14 May 1598 the Council ordered that 'the Woodringtons' were to be committed to prison without bail. Whilst in prison they were 'very inconveniencing and noisome' and had to be removed elsewhere. Sir William Eure had been wounded in the affray but on 21 May he was reported to be recovering, and the Woodringtons were to be enlarged on bail of £500 at least. On the following day Eure was 'in dangerous state' and orders were given for the Woodringtons to be further detained (*Ib.*, vol.28).

In 1605 Ephraim Widdrington, gent., and Eleanor his wife, had a conveyance from Giles Gallon, gent., and Juliana his wife, of the manors of Upper Trewhit, Nether Trewhit and Tosson. On 1 October 1618 sir Ephraim Widdrington, dame Eleanor his wife and Henry Widdrington esq., his son and heir, sold lands in Upper and Nether Trewhit to Thomas Orde of Orde and Samshouse, gent. Thomas Orde's wife was that Catherine daughter of Hugh Gallon for whom a marriage had been nearly arranged in 1597 with sir Ephraim's son Henry. Thomas Orde died before 1636 leaving a son and heir George and his widow had married Thomas Richardson of Little Tosson, gent. On 19 January 1636 sir Ephraim Widdrington and Eleanor his wife joined with Thomas Richardson and Catherine his wife, and George Orde and Elizabeth his wife, in conveying lands in Upper and Nether Trewhit and Tosson to sir John Clavering of Callaly (Notes marked R.Sp. in John Hodgson's *MS Rothbury Guard Book*). In 1606 sir Ephraim Woddrington is described as 'not careful of any religion, a great bearer with thieves', his nephews sir Henry Widdrington, Roger Widdrington 'the most dangerous (recusant) in that county', Ralph Widdrington 'a simple man', and their sister married to Mr Herrington of Befront 'both papists' (*Cath. Rec. Soc.* vol.53, p.152).

In 1605 or 1606 Ephraim Widdrington had been knighted, and on 21 March 1609 as sir Ephraim Widdrington of Trewhit, knt, he purchased from the Crown grantees 'Stokershaugh otherwise Carlecrofte' parcel of the possessions of the dissolved monastery of Alnwick. On 12 August 1614 he mortgaged Carlcroft to Arthur Hebburn of Hebburn for £450 (*AA3.* VIII, p.17). It was probably about this time that he purchased from the Crown or from Crown grantees, Coltpark, Ritton and Birkhead formerly part of the possessions of Newminster abbey.

For some unknown reason an inquest was held at Hexham on 11 October 1629 about the extent of sir Ephraim's lands. Robert Thirlwall and the other jurors stated on oath that Ephraim Widdrington of Trewhit, now called sir Ephraim Widdrington of Ritton East House, knight, was seised of one capital messuage called Ritton East House with 50 acres of land (*i.e.* arable), 40 acres of marsh (? meadow), 60 acres of pasture and 200 acres of heath and furze and appurtenances, and one messuage called Birkheads with 20 acres of land, 30 acres of marsh, 20 acres of pasture with appurtenances, which were of the clear annual value above reprisals of £4 (*Hodgson MS, op. cit.*).

On 18 August 1638 it was stated that sir Ephraim was then 83 years of age. This is confirmed in proceedings at Durham Consistory Court in a case of Whitehead *v.* Whitehead on 21 October 1625 when sir Ephraim in making a deposition stated that he was 70 years of age. On 26 July 1654 admini-

stration of the goods of sir Ephraim Widdrington was granted to Henry Widdrington, grandchild and next of kin to sir Ephraim Widdrington, late of Ritton in Northumberland, knight, widower, intestate, deceased (*Somerset House*). The statement made 5 February 1652 by his grandson Ephraim Widdrington that his grandfather had died three years since shows that there had been a good deal of delay in obtaining the administration.

Hodgson has stated that sir Ephraim 'had a brother called Francis, who also had courage to be on the king's side, when the commonwealth was in the height of its glory in 1654' (*HN.* ii, I, p.322n.). This is completely inaccurate for sir Ephraim had been dead for some years in 1654 and there is not the slightest evidence that he had a brother called Francis.

It is certain that sir Ephraim had three wives. He had a young son Henry in 1597 so had married before that date. Hodgson states that his wife, and he only credits him with one, was a sister of George Thirlwell of Rothbury. It is quite clear how Hodgson came to this inaccurate conclusion. Robert Widdrington of West Harle, of the family of WIDDRINGTON OF COLWELL, whom Hodgson thought was a son of sir Ephraim, was a nephew of George Thirlwall. Sir Ephraim's first wife seems to have been Jane daughter of Michael Hebburn of Hebburn, par. Chillingham (1666 vis. ped. Hebburn of Hebburn). Sir Ephraim had business relations with her brother Arthur Hebburn in 1614. His second wife was probably Eleanor living in 1605, but her parentage is not known. On 5 August 1615 he took out a licence to marry Eleanor Strother, and they were married at Gateshead, co. Durham, two days later; she was a daughter of John Conyers of Sockburn, co. Durham, and widow of Lancelot Strother of Kirknewton.

Three sons of sir Ephraim Widdrington are known, his eldest son Henry, a son called William, and 'Edward, son of Sr Ephraim Widdrington, Kt' buried in the quire at Hexham 24 September 1611 (*Hexham Registers*). If sir Ephraim's wife Eleanor came from the Hexham area, it could account for Edward being buried there. He had a daughter Joan who married Alexander Selby of Biddleston; their eldest son Robert was three years old in 1615 (Vis. ped.—Selby of Biddleston). On 10 June 1652 William Widdrington of High Birkhead claimed that his father sir Ephraim had on 26 July 1624 granted him lands in High Birkhead and that these lands had been wrongfully sequestered as the estate of Henry Widdrington, grandchild and heir of sir Ephraim (*SS.* 111, p.377).

When, in 1597, it had been intended to marry sir Ephraim's son Henry to Katherine Gallon it is evident that Henry was quite a young boy for Katherine was only one year old. Thomas Woodrington, a distant kinsman, by his w.d. 2 April 1617 leaves legacies to his 'cousin sir Ephraim Woodrington, knt, and to his eldest son Henry Woodrington'.

On 8 July 1610 Henry Widdrington, described as of the parish of Rothbury, married at Hexham, Margaret widow of John Ridley of Coastley, par. Hexham. Until the marriage of his step-daughter Dorothy Ridley, Henry seems to have lived at Coastley. It appears from the inventory dated 18 October 1621 of Sampson Collingwood of Trewick that he owed money to Henry Widdrington of Coastley. On 10 May 1624 as Henry Widdrington of Coastley, esq., he was party to the marriage settlement of Dorothy Ridley and Richard Carr of Hexham. On 11 December 1630 Richard Carr and Dorothy his wife, and 'Margaret Widdrington, widow, formerly wife of John Ridley' conveyed Coastley to sir Francis Radcliffe of Dilston (*NCH.* IV, pp.14, 15n.).

Henry Widdrington had died on 7 December 1625. This is stated in the inventory of his goods taken on 14 June 1626. On 1 July 1626 administration of the goods of Henry Widdrington of Nether Trewhit was granted to Henry Widdrington, gent., to use of Oswald, Michael, Robert and Roger, children of the deceased with consent of Margaret, the widow (Raine, *MSS. Wills and Inv.* III, p.51). The four sons mentioned in the administration were evidently all under age. In fact Margaret in 1626 cannot have had any children over the age of 21 for she was not married until 1610. Henry Widdrington to whom the administration was granted must have been a son of Henry Widdrington of Nether Trewhit by a previous marriage. He was grandson and heir of sir Ephraim Widdrington in 1654 and we shall see later that he had a brother called Ephraim.

By deed of 22 December 1632 Roger and Oswald Widdrington and others conveyed to Thomas, lord Wentworth, sir George Wentworth and others, certain lands in Redesdale to the use of Rosamond Revely for life (*SS.* 111, p.371). The settlor was Roger Widdrington of Cartington who shortly afterwards married Rosamond Revely. Oswald Widdrington was probably the eldest son of Henry Widdrington of Nether Trewhit by his second marriage. Michael and Roger were perhaps brought up by their aunt Jane Selby at Biddleston. In the declaration of account in 1632 of Joan Selbie, widow, late wife of Alexander Selby of Biddleston is the entry 'To Roger Widdrington, late son of Henry Widdrington of Trewhit for his portion remaining in the said intestate's hands, £43. 10s.' (Raine, *MSS Wills and Inv.* III, p.108). Helen Selby by her w.d. 1 August 1667 leaves '£50 to Roger Widdrington out of that money my lady Widdrington owes me'; her 'friends' Michael Widdrington and Matthew Davison are executors to the will (*Ib.,* VII, p.69).

In 1655 Roger Widdrington of Biddleston, gent., refused to take the Oath of Abjuration (*Recusant Roll* E.377/61). He was present at the muster on Bockenfield Moor on 29 January 1660/1 (*NCH.* VII, p.360). On 31 May 1661 George Pott of Burradon, yeoman, sold a messuage and farmhold in Burradon, par. Alwinton, to Roger Widdrington of Biddleston, gent; on 15 November 1670 Roger sold a messuage, perhaps the same one, in Burradon to Edward Hall (*AA3.* V, p.52). It seems almost certain that it was this Roger Widdrington who married Catherine daughter of sir Edward Widdrington of Cartington, bart, although he must have been quite an elderly bridegroom for such a young bride. The articles before their marriage are dated 9 April 1670. A little over a year later Roger died and was buried at Holystone on 28 July 1671.

His widow Catherine married secondly (b. of m. 3 January 1672/3) Gervase Hamond of Scarthingwell, Yorks. She took out letters of administration of her first husband's estate and was given tuition of their only daughter Mary. In 1673 'Catherine Hamond now the wife of Jarvis Hamond, esq., late the wife and relict of Roger Widdrington, gent., late of Harbottle, par. of Alwinton, decd,' made her declaration of account. Roger's goods were valued at the very considerable sum of £2210; he owed at his death to Michael Widdrington of Morpeth sums of £150, £80 and £80 (*Dur. Prob. Off.* by C.R.H.).

Mary the only child and heiress of Roger and Catherine Widdrington married (articles before marriage 25 November 1687) sir John Gascoigne of Parlington, Yorks., bart, and died 11 June 1723 aged 61.

Sir Ephraim Widdrington's heir was Henry Widdrington his 'grandchild and next of kin' who took out the grant of administration in 1654. On 22 April 1651 Henry was sequestered as a papist and delinquent, and his lands in Ritton, Coltpark and High Birkheads were let by the County Committee to Thomas Horsley at a yearly rent of £45. On 5 February 1652 Ephraim Widdrington of Ritton claimed an annuity of £20 on lands settled on him by his grandfather, sir Ephraim, who had died three years since, but the annuity had been sequestered for the delinquency of his brother Henry. Ephraim's claim was allowed on 9 April 1652 but he was only to have a third of the annuity and of arrears from 24 December 1649 because he had failed to take the Oath of Abjuration. It would seem from this that sir Ephraim had died on 24 December 1649.

On 10 March 1654 information was laid before the County Committee by Edward Trumbel of Morpeth that on Thursday morning two days before, he had been invited to a wedding at Duddo and going thither in the evening he found men there all having pistols to the number of seventy or thereabouts, and that the report was among them that that party would enter upon Sandgate in Newcastle that night, and another party under command of one Delaval was to come in at Westgate, and yet a third party under Willoughby or Cholmley to come in by Gateshead, to take Newcastle; there was one Mr Widdrington of Ritton at this rendezvous. Michael Pratt also gave information about the gathering of 8 March and had heard that Mr Henry Widdrington of Ritton was there (Thurloe, *State Papers,* iii, pp.216, 228).

After the Restoration the estates that had been confiscated and sold by the rebel government were resumed, without compensation to those who had purchased them. In consequence of this Henry Widdrington was rated on Ritton, Colt Park and Birkheads in 1663 on an annual value of £80. On 12 June 1672 he sold Carlcroft to George Potts of Wreighill, his wife Catherine being party to the conveyance. Catherine must have been his second wife for Nicholas Errington of Ponteland when he registered his pedigree on 25 August 1666 recorded that his sister Isabel was wife of Henry Widdrington of Ritton, esq; Isabel was baptised at Ponteland 6 July 1618. Nicholas was a son of Gilbert Errington of Ponteland (d.1644), and in 1666 was 50 years of age.

The name of Henry Widdrington of Ritton, gent., appears in a list of Roman Catholic recusants drawn up in 1677. It seems possible that Henry was still living twenty-four years later if the entry, in the Netherwitton Registers '11 May 1701 —Henry Widdrington, junior, Ritton, bur.' refers to his son.

Two branches of the Widdrington family may have had a descent from sir Ephraim Widdrington of Ritton, but the connections have not been found.

In the second half of the 17th century there were two brothers William Widdrington (d.1667) and Michael Widdrington (d.1680) of Morpeth, merchants. William's only son was called Ephraim. *See* WIDDRINGTON OF MORPETH.

William Widdrington whose parentage is unknown married Dorothy, daughter and coheiress of Henry Widdrington of Buteland; one of their sons Michael Widdrington of Bullers

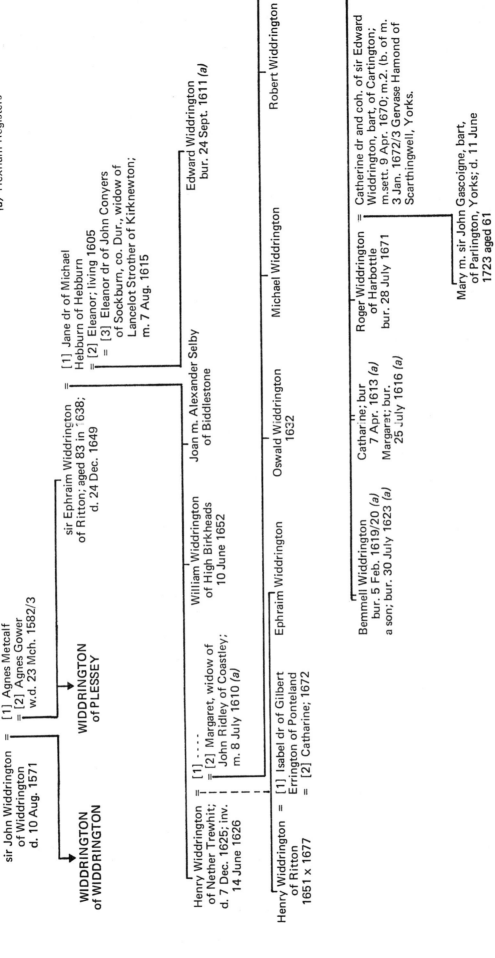

(a) Hexham Registers

sir John Widdrington of Widdrington d. 10 Aug. 1571 = [1] Agnes Metcalf = [2] Agnes Gower w.d. 23 Mch. 1582/3

WIDDRINGTON of WIDDRINGTON

WIDDRINGTON of PLESSEY

sir Ephraim Widdrington of Ritton; aged 83 in 1638; d. 24 Dec. 1649 = [1] Jane dr of Michael Hebburn of Hebburn = [2] Eleanor; living 1605 = [3] Eleanor dr of John Conyers of Sockburn, co. Dur., widow of Lancelot Strother of Kirknewton; m. 7 Aug. 1615

Edward Widdrington bur. 24 Sept. 1611 (a)

Joan m. Alexander Selby of Biddlestone

William Widdrington of High Birkheads 10 June 1652

Henry Widdrington of Nether Trewhit; d. 7 Dec. 1625; inv. 14 June 1626 = [1] - - - - = [2] Margaret, widow of John Ridley of Coastley; m. 8 July 1610 (a)

Henry Widdrington of Ritton 1651 x 1677 = [1] Isabel dr of Gilbert Errington of Ponteland = [2] Catharine; 1672

Robert Widdrington

Michael Widdrington

Oswald Widdrington 1632

Ephraim Widdrington

Roger Widdrington of Harbottle bur. 28 July 1671 = Catherine dr and coh. of sir Edward Widdrington, bart, of Cartington; m.sett. 9 Apr. 1670; m.2. (b. of m. 3 Jan. 1672/3 Gervase Hamond of Scarthingwell, Yorks.

Catharine; bur 7 Apr. 1613 (a) Margaret; bur. 25 July 1616 (a)

Bemmell Widdrington bur. 5 Feb. 1619/20 (a) a son; bur. 30 July 1623 (a)

Mary m. sir John Gascoigne, bart, of Parlington, Yorks; d. 11 June 1723 aged 61

Green, Morpeth, was a papist and died in 1741. *See* WIDDRING-
TON OF BULLERS GREEN.

WIDDRINGTON OF HAUXLEY, PAR. WARKWORTH

ACCORDING to the visitation pedigree of 1558, Roger
Woddryngton 2nd son of sir Rauphe Woddrington of Widdrington married 'Mawlde (or Mabell) dr of (blank) Strother
of Newton in Northumberland'. In the 1563/4 pedigree
Roger's wife is called 'Mabel dr of (blank) Strother of Newton'. She was Matilda daughter of Thomas Strother of Kirknewton, and after Roger's death she married (before 1525)
Robert Fenwick of Chibburn. In 1525 Robert Brandelyng,
executor of John Brandelyng of Newcastle, merchant, claimed
from Robert Fenwyk of Chibburn, gent., and Matilda, his
wife, executors of Roger de Wodryngton of Widdrington,
esq., a sum of £40 which they unjustly detained (*de Banco*
Roll R.76, m.381d, in *AA3*. VI, p.85).

Roger and Matilda Widdrington had two sons John and
Roger and a daughter Dorothie. John Hodgson has changed
the name of the younger son to Ralph and states that he was
'progenitor of different branches of Widdringtons intended to
be noticed under Blackheddon etc'. That his name was Roger
is confirmed by the pedigrees of 1558 and 1563/4. No descendants of Roger have been traced and nothing is known about
him. The elder son John was married three times, the 1558
and the 1563/4 pedigrees being in agreement in naming his
wives:

1. Luce, dr of (blank) Eryngton of Whittington in Nd.

2. Katheryn, dr and one of the heirs of Wylliam Bennett of
Kenton in Nd.

3. Marye, dr of sir William Ogle, 2nd s. of Raufe, lord
Ogle.

The second wife was called Isabel or Elizabeth, not Katheryn. At Michaelmas 1538 she and her sister Margaret were
both unmarried. On 15 May 1540 a declaration was made by
Roger Errington and others that lands in Kenton were to the
use of John Widdrington and Elizabeth his wife and John
Fenwick and Margaret his wife, which Elizabeth and Margaret were daughters of William Bennett, deceased. William
Bennet had died seised of the manor of Kenton, a third of
West Heddon, a tenement in Heddon-on-the-Wall, a tenement
in Cowpen and common of pasture in South Gosforth. His
heirs were Gerard Widdrington and Robert Fenwick as sons
of the said Isabella (*sic*) and Margaret, his daughters (*AA3*.
V, pp.103, 104).

The third marriage took place in 1542. On 13 June 1542
sir John de Wytherington of Widdrington conveyed to John
Wytherington of Hauxley, gent., and Mary Ogle, natural
daughter of William Ogle of Cockle Park, in consideration
of their marriage, three husbandlands in Shotton (*Ridley
Charters* No. 80 in *AA4*. XXXIV, p.72, where the date is
given as 24 H.VIII instead of 34 H.VIII).

John Widdrington was bailiff of Amble and Hauxley in
1539. He was one of the gentlemen of the Middle March in
1550, and an overseer of the watch in 1552 appointed to be
kept from Widdrington Park-nook to the Coquet. (Nicolson,
p.292). By his first wife, Lucy Errington, he had an only
daughter Elizabeth.

By his second wife Elizabeth (or Isabella) Bennett, John
Widdrington had an only son Gerard who died *s.p.* before
1558. John's children by his third wife were three sons Roger,
Robert and James, and six daughters, Isabella, Barbara, Maud,
Anne, Margery and Jane (1558 and 1563/4 pedigrees). The
Christian name James is new to the Widdringtons and was no
doubt acquired from his mother's family, the Ogles. It is
therefore possible that James was the man of this name, late
of Gateshead, co. Dur., administration of whose goods was
granted 22 March 1615/6 to his daughter Mary wife of John
Nixon (*Dur. Prob. Off.* by C.R.H.). In 1575 John Woderyngton is described as of Chibburn and Hauxley, and his eldest
son Roger was then aged 26.

The inventory of Roger's goods is dated 23 March 1587/8
and administration of his personal estate was granted 28
March 1588 to Robert Widdrington the brother, the children
of the deceased, Henry, Claudius, Marcus and Elizabeth
being under age. During the minority of the heir, Robert
acted as head of the family. At the muster on Clifton field on
24 November 1595 he 'rode on a bay horse with two white
feet' and was armed with the 'full furniture of a coat of plate,
a steel cap, sword and dagger and spear or staff' (*CBP*. II,
pp.78-79). Complaint was made against him on 8 June 1597
that being one of the jurors at the manor court at Sturton
Grange he had incited lord Eure's tenants there to complain
of the fines imposed on them (*Ib*., p.244). He had a lease of the
rent-corn of Amble by letters patent dated 7 August 1590 for
21 years at a rent of £6. 2s. 6d. He was a copyhold tenant in
Amble in 1608 his copy being dated 23 April 1602. Lands in
Amble are described 23 November 1630 as formerly in the
occupation of Robert Widdrington.

Debts owed by Roger Widdrington, listed in the inventory
of his goods, 23 March 1587/8 include £30 to his sister Margery for her child's portion and to Jane Woodrington another
sister £17. 1s. 8d. for the last part of her portion. Neither
Margery nor Jane appear in the pedigree of 1563/4 and may
have been born after that date. When sir Thomas Horsley
of Longhorsley registered his pedigree on 25 August 1666
he recorded that he was then aged 54 and that his parents
were Lancelot Horsley of Brenkheugh and Jane daughter of
John Widdrington of Hauxley (Foster, p.69). Administration
of the goods of Lancelot Horsley of Brenkheugh was granted
10 November 1609 to his widow Elizabeth for the benefit
of their children Thomas, Catherine, Florentia and Margaret
who were then under age.

Little is known about Roger Widdrington's younger sons,
Claudius and Marcus. Thomas Widdrington of Newcastle
by his w.d. 2 April 1617 leaves a legacy of £3 'to Claudius
Woodrington my cousin whom I did help to christen'. Marcus
must have been the Marke Wyddrington who was one of the
horsemen allowed to sir Robert Carey, lord warden of the
Middle Marches, and mustered at Five Mile Bridge near
Newcastle, 24 June 1598 (*CBP*. II, p.542).

Roger Widdrington's eldest son and heir Henry held the
office of bailiff of Amble and Hauxley in September 1608 by
letters patent granted to him 'since the king's coming to the
Crown'. At the same time he held two customary tenements
formerly held by Roger his father. Before 22 July 1630 he
had enfranchised his customary lands by grants from the
Crown grantees.

He seems to have married a daughter of Henry Kirton

of Hauxley. They had four sons, Robert, William, Samuel and Thomas. Samuel may have been Mr Samuel Widdrington of Seghill, whose daughter Grace was 'baptised at Seghill by Mr Thomas Dixon, minister of Horton, upon the request of Mr Henderson, September 13th' 1661 (NCH. IX, p.20). Thomas, son of Henry Widdrington of Hauxley, gent., was apprenticed 1 May 1641 to Christopher Nicholson of Newcastle, junior, merchant, and enrolled in the books of the Newcastle Merchant Adventurers 10 March 1642 (SS. 101, p.260).

The eldest son and heir, Robert Widdrington, had administration in 1653 of the goods of his grandfather Henry Kirton of Hauxley. In 1663 he was rated at £30 for his lands in Amble and in Hauxley at £40. He was deputy sheriff of the county in 1664. On 28 May 1684 he settled his estates in Hauxley, Amble, Warkworth, Guyzance, Barnhill, Hartlaw and Hazon on his nephews Robert, Thomas and Henry, sons of his brother William Widdrington, with remainder to Robert, son of his brother Samuel Widdrington; the estates were charged with portions payable to his daughters Elizabeth wife of Cuthbert Karns of Firth House, Isabel wife of Robert Fenwick of Nunriding, and to the children of his other daughters Ann Forster deceased, and Mary wife of Edward Maxwell; certain sums of money were to be paid to Henry, Ralph, Elizabeth and Frances children of his brother William Widdrington.

Robert Widdrington's only son William had died in 1664. William was living at Barnhill when he made his w.d. 17 September 1664. He directs that he is to be buried in the chancel of Warkworth church 'amongst my predecessors'. His wife Barbara is appointed executrix, and the testator divides his possessions between her and his only child Anne. His 'kinsman' sir Ralph Delaval of Seaton Delaval and his father Robert Widdrington of Hauxley, esq., are to be supervisors of the will. There was due to his father £14. 7s. 3d. on his account as under sheriff to sir Thomas Horsley (Raine, MSS Wills and Inv. VII, p.63). By his wife Barbara daughter of Thomas Fenwick of Brenkley whom he married at Stannington 4 May 1658, he had an only child Mary, baptised at Felton 4 December 1662, died in infancy. After her husband's death, Barbara married secondly (b. of m. 24 July 1665) Lionel Fenwick of Blagdon.

Robert Widdrington made his will 28 May 1692 by which he directs that he is to be buried in the parish church of Warkworth. He leaves his leasehold lands in Guyzance to his nephew Robert Widdrington to whom he also leaves his stock, chattels, horses, oxen and sheep, except four kine of the best he had and the mare which he bought and his wife Dorothy is to have these, and is to enjoy two chambers in his dwelling house at Hauxley; his household goods are to be divided between his wife and nephew; to his son-in-law Edward Maxwell he leaves £180 and to his grandson John Fenwick £100. 'Mr Robert Widdrington of Hauxley' was buried at Warkworth 14 November 1696. The name of his first wife, the mother of his children, is unknown. On 30 June 1681 he entered into a bond of marriage with Dorothy Ogle, and in respect of this he made a post-nuptial settlement on 16 June 1693.

Robert Widdrington's heir was his nephew Robert son of his brother William. In 1689 the younger Robert married Frances Humble of the parish of Shilbottle (b. of m. 26 July

1689; bur. Warkworth 5 October 1742). Robert's will is dated 17 January 1716/7 and he was buried at Warkworth 6 October 1719. He had two sons Robert III and John, and three daughters Dorothy, who married firstly Thomas Smith of Togston, and secondly William Carr of Warkworth; Anne wife of Edward Young of Togston; and Frances who died unmarried in 1733.

The third Robert Widdrington enlarged his estate by the purchase of Coquet Island in 1734 and further lands in Hauxley in 1736. He married at Warkworth 5 December 1722 Sarah daughter of rev. Timothy Punshon of Killingworth, minister of Branton. She survived her husband and as 'Sarah Widdrington of Alnwick' was buried at Warkworth 13 July 1775. Robert made his will 5 July 1747 and was buried at Warkworth 20 March 1750/1. He leaves his lands in Hauxley, Amble and Alnwick to his eldest surviving son John, subject to portions of £300 each to his younger children Nathaniel, William, Sarah, Frances, Mary and Elizabeth.

The children of Robert and Sarah Widdrington were:

1. Robert; b. 9 December 1723; bur. 3 November 1743.

2. John Widdrington of Hauxley; b. 19 March 1727/8; an Alnwick attorney; m. at Edlingham 26 May 1767 Isabella dr of John Forster of Adderstone; w.d. 9 December 1779; bur. Warkworth 14 January 1780. By her w.d. 31 March 1780 his widow quit-claims to her husband's heirs and executors all her right to the £1000 settled upon her at her marriage; she leaves the portrait of her husband to Charles Brandling of Gosforth House; she was bur. Warkworth 9 April 1780.

3. Nathaniel Widdrington of Hauxley; heir to his brother John; w.d. 28 April 1783; d. unmarried; bur. Warkworth 9 July 1783.

4. William Widdrington; bur. Warkworth 25 August 1751.

5. Timothy Widdrington; b. 23 November 1729; bur. Warkworth 2 November 1732.

i. Sarah; b. 23 February 1730/1; w.d. 3 July 1775; bur. Warkworth 5 January 1777.

ii. Frances; m. 30 June 1767 Edward Brown of East Chevington (d. 26 January 1785); bur. Warkworth 21 June 1770.

iii. Mary; m. Alnwick 21 January 1762 William Teasdale of Knipe Hall, Wmd. (d. 17 February 1767); she d. before 9 December 1779.

iv. Elizabeth; w.d. 3 July 1775; d. unm. at Alnwick; bur. Warkworth 5 January 1777.

Nathaniel Widdrington of Hauxley by his w.d. 28 April 1783 leaves legacies of £300 each to his nieces Sarah Brown and Sarah Teasdale, £10 to Nathaniel Punshon, £10 to Mr Adams, £10 to Samuel Bell of Hauxley; to his servant Mary Muers he leaves £20 a year and the wearing apparel of his late mother; his real estates at Hauxley, Amble, Guyzance and Alnwick he leaves to his cousin John Widdrington of Newcastle.

John Widdrington of Newcastle was the only child of John Widdrington, younger son of Robert Widdrington (d.1719) of Hauxley. The elder John Widdrington was a Newcastle attorney and resided in Hanover Square. He married at Gateshead 23 July 1728 Jane daughter of John Carr of Dunston Hill, co. Durham. She died at Whickham 14 November 1742 and was buried there. He died 16 October 1769.

In 1771 the younger John Widdrington joined the banking firm of Bell, Cookson, Carr, Airey and Saint, known as 'the Old Bank' that then occupied premises near the end of Silver

WIDDRINGTON of HAUXLEY, par. WARKWORTH

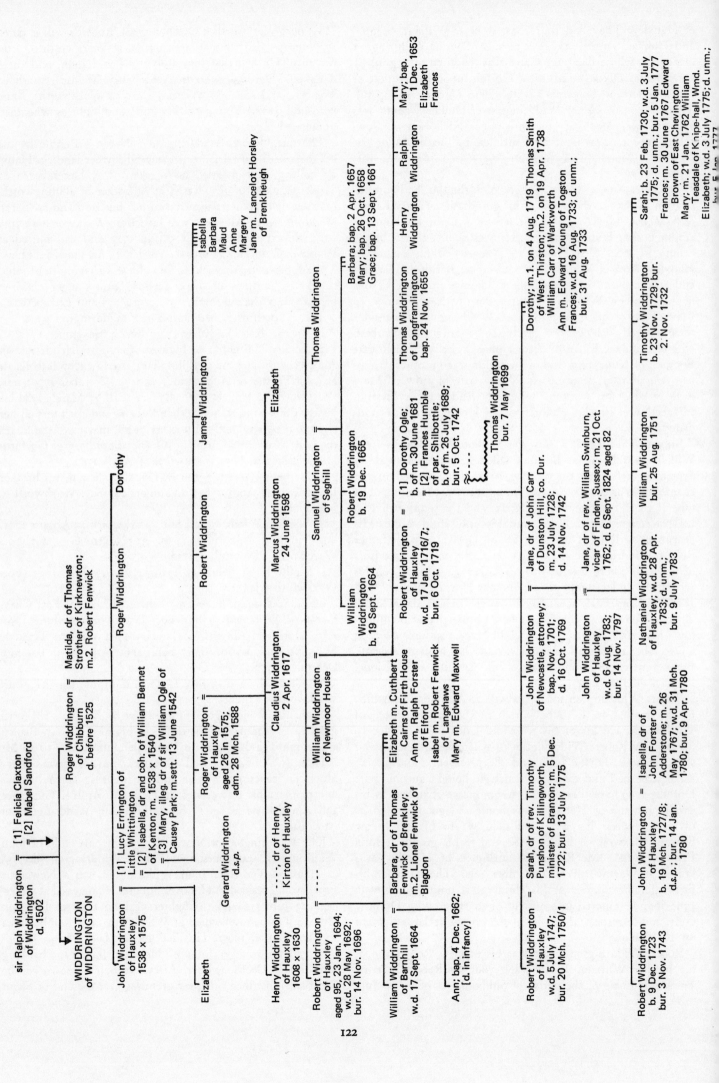

Street in Newcastle. His uncle Ralph Carr had been a founder member of the bank. From 2 January 1771 the firm was to be known as Bell, Cookson, Carr, Widdrington and Saint; the last two each held a sixth share and had to attend to the daily business of the bank 'without extra remuneration'. Early in 1793 Widdrington took part in the foundation of the Literary and Philosophical Society of Newcastle and was elected the first president. He succeeded to Hauxley under the w.d. 28 April 1783 of his cousin Nathaniel Widdrington and made his own will on 6 August 1783. He leaves to his wife Jane £100 a year out of Hauxley, his house in Hanover Square, Newcastle, and his lands in Whickham, co. Durham. He leaves the Widdrington family estates of Hauxley, Amble, Guyzance and Alnwick in equal moieties to his cousins Sarah Brown and Sarah Teasdale. The testator was buried at Warkworth with his ancestors on 14 November 1797. He had married at Midhurst, Sussex, 21 October 1762 Jane daughter of rev. William Swinburn, vicar of Finden, Sussex. She died 6 September 1824 aged 88 and was buried at St Andrew's, Newcastle.

Sarah Brown and Sarah Teasdale were the daughters respectively of Edward Brown (d.1785) of East Chevington by his wife Frances Widdrington; and of William Teasdale (d.1767) by his wife Mary Widdrington. Sarah Brown married lieut.col. David Latimer Tinling who also assumed the surname of Widdrington.

The present representative of Sarah Brown is captain F. N. H. Widdrington of Newton Hall, Newton-on-the-Moor.

WIDDRINGTON OF COLWELL, PAR. CHOLLERTON

LANDS in Colwell had been acquired by the Widdringtons in the early 14th century by the marriage of sir John de Widdrington with Christiana daughter and coheiress of Adam de Swyneburne of East Swinburn. In the 16th century and perhaps earlier these lands had been occupied by a cadet line of the Widdringtons. From this cadet line were derived not only the Widdringtons of Colwell but the WIDDRINGTONS OF CHEESEBURN GRANGE (and Blackheddon). The rev. John Hodgson derived these families from Ralph Widdrington, second son of sir Henry Widdrington of Widdrington by his wife Margaret Percy. Of this Ralph Widdrington he says that he 'was progenitor of different branches of Widdringtons intended to be noticed under Black Heddon, etc.' According to the pedigree registered at the herald's visitation of 1558 Ralph Widdrington died s.p., and this being a contemporary record can be accepted as accurate for the pedigree was registered by Ralph's brother sir John Widdrington (d.1571). Hodgson seems to have realised that he had made a mistake and in his notes (HN. ii, II, p.542n.) adds 'Some manuscript pedigrees state that Sir John Widdrington knight had by his wife Agnes Metcalf a third son Lewis Widdrington who married Catherine, daughter of Gawine Swinburne of Cheeseburn Grange'. These 'manuscript pedigrees' are also inaccurate.

Lewis Widdrington was ancestor of the Widdringtons of Cheeseburn Grange and it is quite certain that he did not marry a daughter of Gawine Swinburne. A pedigree in

Miscellanea Genealogica et Heraldica, 4th series, III, p.158 and another in *AA3*. VI, p.34 did little to clear up the obvious difficulties of the 16th century ancestors of this branch of the Widdringtons. The *County History* (XII, p.325) correctly derived the family from sir John Widdrington, a younger brother of sir Gerard Widdrington (d.1491) of Widdrington.

This sir John Widdrington, as an esquire, witnesses a Haughton deed of 6 June 1454 (*NDD*. p.194) and a Fenwick deed of 23 April 1468 (*Ib.*, p.61). He was knighted before 1471 when he was sheriff of Northumberland, continuing in that office until 1474. He was then resident at Chipchase for he had married Isabel widow of John Heron of Chipchase. She was a daughter of Robert, lord Ogle of Bothal. On 2 January 1478 Widdrington's mother-in-law, lady Ogle, made her will, whereby she leaves lands in Lancashire to her two grandsons John Heron of Chipchase, esq., and Robert Widdrington, esq.; she appoints her son-in-law sir John Widdrington as residuary legatee (*Ib.*, p.179, No. 74).

According to the pedigree registered in 1563/4 sir John Widdrington had four sons, Robert, John, David and Gerard, and three daughters Lucia, Elizabeth and Alice. The eldest son Robert is stated to have died s.p.; he is the Robert Widdrington mentioned by his grandmother lady Ogle in her will in 1478. On 20 January 8 H.VIII (1493) Robert Wetheryngton son and heir of John Wetheryngton, deceased, confirmed to John Cartyngton the fourth part of the vill of Weetslade and all lands, tenements, rents and services with their appurtenances in the same, which were formerly of Ralph Rukby and afterwards of John Hoyp (by C.R.H.). As Robert Widdrington of Swinburne, son and heir of sir John Widdrington, on 8 May 1490, he conveyed to Ralph Widdrington (of Widdrington) the lands in Capheaton which his father had from Roger Thornton (*NDD*. p.241, No. 79).

In each of the visitation pedigrees of 1558 and 1563/4 Gerard, youngest son of sir John Widdrington of Chipchase is given eight sons, in the former named Gerard, John, Thomas, Roger, William, Ralph, Alexander and Robert, and in the latter as Gerard, John, Thomas, William, Ralph, Alexander, Roger and 'Ely'. In both pedigrees the daughters Margaret, Elizabeth, Isabel and Alice are named, the later pedigree adding a fifth called 'Aketh'. Two of the sons can safely be identified with John Widdrington of Mitford and a Ralph Widdrington both named in a list of the gentlemen of the Middle Marches drawn up in 1550.

In 1547 John Widdrington was farmer of Hallington under the archbishop of York (*NCH*. IV, p.240). He was living at Healey 4 February 1570/1 when he made his will. He directs that he should be buried at Bywell St Peter. Annes his wife is to have a third of his lands in Temple Healey; his eldest son James is to have lands in Blagdon and the third part of his lease of the rectory of Hartburn and his lease of the tithes of Hallington, with remainder to his younger son Robert. Robert is to have his lands in Temple Healey and Mitford, the lease of Whitesidelaw and the other two parts of the lease of the rectory of Hartburn, with remainder to the elder son James. Also mentioned in the will are his daughter Dorothy wife of Reynold Shafto, his son-in-law Robert Blaikden, his son-in-law Edward Lawson of Bywell, and his three unmarried daughters Elizabeth, Margaret and Annes. The inventory of John Widdrington's goods is dated

20 February 1570/1 (*SS*. 2, p.320). His eldest son James was at one time living at Whitesidelaw. In his declaration of account of his father's estate he mentions his father's late wife Agnes; his father's daughters Elizabeth, Margaret, Agnes and Isabel; James, William, Grace and Ursula Shaftoe, children of his father's son-in-law Reynold Shaftoe; and his father's son-in-law Robert Blaikden and Blaikden's five children. James Widdrington was of Gateshead when he made his w.d. 2 September 1596. He distributes his property amongst his three sons. John, the eldest, is to have the tithes of Hallington; the second son, Robert, has the nether mill of Hallington and the parsonage of Hartburn; and the youngest son Henry the title to Whitesidelaw. James had two daughters, Annes who has by her father's will the house in Gateshead bought by him, and Mary. The executors of the will are 'Mr Henry Widdrington esq., and Mr Robert Widdrington his brother'.

James Widdrington of Gateshead's brother Robert was living 31 December 1605 when Barbarye Lawson, widow of Edward Lawsonne of Bywell, gent., deceased, by her will of this date leaves 6s. 8d. to her brother Robert Wittherington (*Dur. Prob. Off.* by C.R.H.).

The place of residence of Ralph Widdrington of 1550 is not stated, but his name comes next to that of Thomas Errington of Bingfield. In 1554 he was overseer of no less than four local watches, those to be kept by the men of Birtley, Buteland and Redesmouth, by the men of Little Bavington and Thockrington, by the men of Great Swinburne, Colwell and 'Whitefield' (probably Whitesidelaw) and by the men of Hallington and Little Swinburne (Nicolson, *Leges Marchiarum*, pp.248, 259). The survey of the borders made by sir Robert Bowes and sir Ralph Ellerker in 1541 describes Filton Moor (now Carrycoats) as then divided into four parts or farmholds; one of these four parts was 'in the tenure of one Rauffe Wetheryngton, gent., and occupied in summering for pasture in form aforesaid without any habitation or housing thereupon save a sheil house for his herd in summer. And in winter it lieth waste'. This quarter farmed by Rauffe Wetheryngton was later called Kyllie or Kelly Quarter and is now the farm of Coltcrag.

Ralph Widderington had five sons Roger Widdrington (d.1571) of Bamburgh Friars, Oswin Widdrington (d.1578) of Ryal (from whom the later Widdringtons of Colwell), Robert Widdrington (from whom the Widdringtons of Cheeseburn Grange), Ralph Widdrington and Francis Widdrington. Confirmation that these Widdringtons were in fact descended from sir John Widdrington of Chipchase is found in the title to property at Dukesfield in Slaley and at Horsley, par. Ovingham. On 28 April 1500 Robert Widdrington, described as heir of John Widdrington, exchanged with John Delaval the manor of Newsham for these lands. Newsham had previously belonged to sir John Widdrington. In 1552 Ralph Widdrington was a free tenant in Horsley and in 1562 a John Widdrington had dealings with Dukesfield. These two were surely John of Healey and his brother Ralph.

The w.d. 20 April 1571 of Roger Widdrington of Bamburgh Friars, is one of the main sources of the Widdrington pedigree of this period. Having no children of his own he divides his quite considerable estate between his brothers and nephews. He is to be buried 'where it shall please Jane my now wife' and he leaves 3s. 4d. to 'the parson of Little Swin-

burn for forgotten tithes'. His numerous legacies are:—

to my nephew Thomas Widdrington son of my brother Robert Widdrington, £40;

to my brother Oswyn Widdrington, my best bay horse;

to the children of my said brother Oswyn, £13. 6s. 8d.;

to my nephew Richard the youngest son of my brother Rafe Widdrington, £8;

to my nephew Henry son of my brother Rafe, £3. 6s. 8d.;

to my nephew Gareth Widdrington, £3. 6s. 8d.;

to my brother Francis Widdrington, £3. 6s. 8d.;

to my cousin Thomas Widdrington, servant to Mr Henry Widdrington, 40s.;

He leaves to his wife Jane all his term of years to come in his lands in Little Swinburne and all his term of years in Killiquarter near Little Swinburne. His wife can sell her interest in Killiquarter to his brother Oswyn and to Oswyn's son Roger. He also leaves to his wife the tithe corn of Shoreston and the tithe corn of West Matfen for her lifetime, with remainder to his nephews Thomas and Roger to be equally divided between them. Roger is to have 'that young horse of mine called a stag' (*Dur. Prob. Off.* by C.R.H.).

Roger Widdrington of Bamburgh Friars had held some official position on the Borders, perhaps in the garrison of Berwick, for in the inventory of his goods dated 27 April 1572 there is recorded a debt of £10 due to him 'for his annuity granted by the Queen's Majesty'. On 9 July 1567 he took a 50 years' lease from the Crown of Kellie Quarter and of land called Stelden in Little Swinburne; within six years the tenant was to build a substantial house of stone and timber, commonly called a bastle house, and at the expiration of the lease a new lease was to be granted to his eldest son (*NCH*. IV, p.404).

Further information about these Widdringtons is gained from the w.d. 2 April 1617 of Thomas Woodrington 'of the town of Newcastle upon Tyne, gent., pentioner of H.M.'s town of Barwick upon Tweed'. He was no doubt 'my cousin Thomas Widdrington servant to Mr Henry Widdrington' to whom Roger Widdrington of Bamburgh Friars had left a legacy of 40s. In 1587 Thomas Widdrington was described as 'a very able man and pensioner of Berwick' (*CBP*. I, p.274) where his pay was 10d. a day (*Ib*., p.455). By his will, Thomas leaves to his 'cousins' Roger, Ralph, Benjamin and Lewes Widdrington 'each five angels in gold'. Katheren Woodrington wife to Lewes Woodrington of Cheeseburn Grange is to have 'one twenty-two shillings piece of gold' and Lewes' son Thomas £5. He leaves small legacies to much more distant relations, *viz*. sir Ephraham Woodrington kt, sir Ephraham's eldest son Henry, Elizabeth Horsley late wife of Launcelott Horsley, late of Brenkheugh; Claudeus Woodrington 'whom I did help to christen'; Robert Woodrington of Chibburn who is to have his best cloak. All these he calls 'cousins'. His niece Isabell Bewick wife of Xpofer Bewick of Newcastle, mariner, is to have £40 and 'all implements and furniture as is now in my chamber'. He leaves to Elizabeth Bewick, daughter of the said Xpofer Bewick £20 'and if it shall please God to give to my said niece Isabell any other children of her own body begotten' then the £20 is to be equally divided among them. Other legacies are left to his niece Agnes wife of Mark Potts of Warton, and her five children; his cousin Katheren Ardaile; the 'man child' and 'woman child' of his sister Ellynor. As it was intended that a gallery should be built for the placing of scholars within the parish church of All Saints', Newcastle, he gives towards the building of it £6. 13s. 6d. He appoints as executors to his will sir Henry Woodrington, Robert Woodrington and Lewes Woodrington, gentlemen, Isabell Bewick wife to Xpofer Bewick and Agnes wife to Mark Potts. The inventory of the testator's goods is dated 1 July 1617 and the will was proved on 12 August 1617 (*Dur. Prob. Off.* by C.R.H.).

Of the four brothers of Roger Widdrington (d.1571) of Bamburgh Friars, Oswin became ancestor of the later Widdringtons of Colwell. Robert Widdrington's descendants were the WIDDRINGTONS OF CHEESEBURN GRANGE. Ralph Widdrington had a son called Henry and a 'youngest' son called Richard, but they are otherwise unknown. Roger's brother Francis is also otherwise unknown.

Oswyn Widdrington, described as 'of Ewall, gent' was one of the appraisers of the goods of sir George Heron of Chipchase in 1576. 'Ewall' was evidently Ryal, par. Stamfordham, as on 17 November 1578 Uswane Woodrington of Ryal made his will; he is to be buried in the church of Bothal; his wife Elizabeth is to have 'the farm if Mr Lawson permits', (perhaps a farm at Longhirst, par. Bothal, owned by the family of Lawson); he mentions his two sons Roger and Henry. Oswyn may be further identified with Oswyn Widdrington of Kirkheaton who married Elizabeth daughter of John Fenwick of Wallington. Her brother John Fenwick of Walker by his w.d. 10 October 1580 leaves legacies to 'Roger Wotheryngton's wife of Little Swinburn' and to 'Henry Wotheryngton, son of Oswalld Wotheryngton'.

Oswyn Widdrington's eldest son Roger evidently took over from his aunt Jane the leases of Little Swinburne and Kelley Quarter as provided for in his uncle Roger's will. He was living at Little Swinburne 27 December 1582 when he was appointed a supervisor of the will of his father-in-law Lancelot Thirlwall of Thirlwall; Thirlwall mentions in his will 'my daughter Mallye Woodrington' as being with child. Roger died at Colwell and on 20 December 1597 administration of his goods was granted to Richard Thirlwall and Lewes Widdrington as being 'next in blood', for the benefit of the widow Mally and her children Henry, Robert, Agnes, Margaret and Margery. The eldest son, Henry Widdrington of Colwell, gent., died in 1633. He seems to have farmed the demesne lands in Colwell but owned freehold lands in Bingfield. His will is dated 12 July 1632. He is to be buried in the parish church of Chollerton, where his grave cover still remains with the inscription HIC JACET HENRICVS WIDRINTON DE COLWELL OBITVS XII AVGVSTI ET CLARA VXOR EJUS ORATE PRO EIS. He leaves to his younger sons Ralph and William £100 each. His three daughters Mary wife of Ralph Wilson, and Dorothy and Ann Widdrington are to have £100 each, raised out of the Bingfield lands. Roger Widdrington of Cartington esq., Thomas Widdrington of Gray's Inn, gent., George Thirlwall of Rothbury, gent., together with his brother Robert Widdrington and his son and heir apparent Roger Widdrington are to be executors.

Henry's eldest son Roger did not long survive his father. He was living at Colwell when he made his w.d. 27 August 1633 but died at Cartington. By his will he directs that he is to be buried in the parish church of Chollerton. With the exception of the £100 to his sister Wilson none of his father's legacies had been paid. He appoints his brother Ralph Widdrington as executor; Roger Widdrington of Cartington esq., Thomas Widdrington of Gray's Inn and George Thirlwall of Rothbury, gent., are to be supervisors. His sisters Dorothy and Ann and his brother William are mentioned in the inventory of his goods. His will was proved in 1634.

Ralph Widdrington was admitted to Gray's Inn 16 March 1640/1. At the time of the Civil Wars he was a royalist and his estate was 'declared and adjudged to be justly forfeited by him for his treason against parliament and people of England'. On 2 June 1652 the trustees appointed for the sale of forfeited estates contracted to sell to Gilbert Crouch the manor and certain lands in Colwell as part of the possessions of the late sir William Widdrington (lord Widdrington). Crouch paid the purchase money on 6 September 1652 and the sequestration on the lands was accordingly removed. On 15 March 1653/4 the treason trustees contracted to sell to John Rushworth of Lincoln's Inn and Gilbert Crouch for £980. 9s. 9d., a messuage in Bingfield, the messuage or house called Colwell Hall and the demesne lands of Colwell as parcel of the possessions of Ralph Widdrington, late of Colwell, gent. It was then found out that the Colwell lands had already been sold to Rushworth and Crouch as part of the forfeited estates of William, lord Widdrington, and that Ralph Widdrington had only been farmer thereof (*SS.* 111, pp.381-382).

In 1637 Ralph Widdrington, then of Bingfield, purchased lands in Bingfield from Ralph Errington of Newcastle. In 1640 he settled Bingfield North Side and the water corn mill with custom of grist from the inhabitants of the township of Bingfield. The settlement was on his son Henry with remainder to his other sons in tail, then to William Widdrington his brother, with remainder to Thomas, William and John, sons of Henry Widdrington (*NCH.* IV, p.231). It is difficult to identify these final remainder men, the sons of Henry Widdrington. Ralph Widdrington had a cousin Henry, son of Robert Widdrington (d.1632) of West Harle but he was a Franciscan friar, and therefore childless. Ralph Widdrington's wife was Elizabeth daughter of John Swinburne of Blackheddon. Another daughter of John Swinburne's was Mary wife of sir Henry Widdrington (d.1665) of Blackheddon. In 1664 sir Henry's eldest son was called William and his second son John but it is possible that at the time of the 1640 settlement there was an elder son Thomas who subsequently died. If this supposition is correct, Thomas, William and John Widdrington were nephews of Ralph Widdrington's wife.

Robert Widdrington of West Harle, par. Kirkwhelpington, gent., made a nuncupative will 29 April 1632. He leaves his wife Anne £300, his daughter Mary £200, and his three younger sons Henry, Francis and William Widdrington £100 each to be raised out of his lands in Todridge, Barrasford and Carrycoats. The daughter Mary evidently married Thomas Cotes of Witton Tower, curate of Rothbury, who in his w.d. 29 September 1666 mentions 'my dear wife's three brothers' and made two of them, Francis and William Widdrington, gentlemen, supervisors of his will (*Dur. Prob. Off.* by C.R.H.). Robert's son and heir apparent, John Widdrington, is to have his lands in West Harle. He mentions his brother Henry Widdrington and his uncle George Thirlwall. The inventory of the deceased's goods is dated 11 and 12

May 1632 (*NCH*. IV, p.295). Robert Widdrington was buried in the quire of Kirkwhelpington church where there is a black marble stone with the inscription ROBERT WIDDRINGTON. ANNO DOMINI 1632 AGED 46. ORATE PRO ANIMA EJUS. The estate of his widow was sequestrated in 1653. She had granted a rentcharge of £24 a year out of lands at (Carrycoats) White House to Rowland Robson. On 17 January 1654 she asked to be able to contract for the sequestrated two-thirds of her estate and this was eventually allowed (*SS*. 111, p.368).

Robert Widdrington's eldest son John Widdrington was living at Hepple when he made his w.d. 1 October 1660. He directs that he is to be buried in his parish church of Rothbury. His three daughters Ellenor, Ann and Mary Widdrington are to have his lands in West Harle, charged with a payment of £30 a year to his wife Eleanor. The 'seat house' is to remain to his eldest daughter Eleanor. Eleanor married (m.lic. 20 November 1667) George Potts of Low Trewhit. The witnesses to the will are John Thirlwall, Geo. Ord, Francis Widdrington, Wm Clennel, and Michael Potts. The will was proved in 1663. It is endorsed that the original will was given in 1706 to Mary Potts, widow, of Newtown, his daughter, Edward Potts of Alnwick, merchant, being bondsman (Raine, *MSS. Wills and Inv*. VII, p.25). Mary Potts was John Widdrington's youngest daughter, and widow of William Potts. In the land tax schedule of 1710 lands in West Harle are referred to as 'Popish lands belonging to Mrs Potts' (*HN*. ii, I, p.200n.). In a list of recusants drawn up in 1677 is the name of (blank) Widdrington of West Harle, spinster, and in a list of 1681 Eleanor Widdrington of West Harle, spinster. John Widdrington of West Harle's daughter Eleanor married in 1667 so that either the name 'Eleanor' or the description 'spinster' may be an error in the recusants roll.

Robert Widdrington's second son Henry was brought up as a Franciscan friar. In the *Records of the Scots Colleges* (pub. New Spalding Club, Aberdeen, 1906) is the entry:—
'29 Nov. 1643. *Henricus Withrintonus 16 annorum Northumbr. (patre Dno Roberto Withrintono defuncto, matre Dna Anna Clennel ante nuptias dicta in Westhalla prope Hexim), convictor, ad grammaticam. Dismissus post annum quod pensio non solveretur. Factus est Franciscanus inter recollectos Anglos*'.
This Henry Widdrington, Franciscan friar, died in England in 1685 or 1686.

On 31 August 1654 Francis Widdrington of West Harle and William Widdrington his brother had a conveyance of Filton Quarter *alias* (Carrycoats) White House, in the occupation of Ann Widdrington, widow, from Henry Widdrington of Blackheddon. Francis and William were the two youngest sons of Robert Widdrington (d.1632) of West Harle. On 11 November 1661 they sold Carrycoats and White House to Charles Shafto of Kirkheaton (*NCH*. IV, p.405). Their mother was probably 'Ms Anne Widdrington, Rothbury' buried at Rothbury 28 May 1659. John Widdrington of Stonecroft by his w.d. 4 June 1664 leaves a colt to his 'cousin' Mr Francis Widdrington of Hepple. In a list of recusants in Northumberland drawn up on 20 June 1674 are the names of Francis Withrington of (blank), gent., and his wife. The name of Francis Widdrington of Hepple, gent., is on a similar list of 1677.

On 29 January 1660/1 there was a muster on Bockenfield

moor of 'one hundred and twenty six gentlemen volunteers (besides their servants) all bravely armed and horsed, led by the right honourable and truly loyal William, lord Widdrington, governor of Berwick' (*PSAN*2. V, p.162). Francis Widdrington of Cartington, gent., was one of those present and there is no doubt that this was the younger son of Robert Widdrington (d.1632) of West Harle. Francis was living at Hepple in 1676, 1677 and 1678 when convicted of recusancy (*Recusant rolls*, E.377/71) and in 1680 his name appears in the Papists Removal Bill. In 1681 and 1682 he was living at Cartington and again convicted of recusancy; in the following year he was committed to gaol for refusing the Oath of Allegiance (*SS*. 40, p.238).

On 29 April 1685 Francis Widdrington of Thropton, gent., entered into recognizance in the sum of £200 to appear when required (*Moot Hall MSS*). He died about four years later. 'Mr Francis Widdrington, Thropton', was buried at Rothbury 27 November 1689, and on 30 May 1690 administration of the goods of Francis Widdrington, gent., of (par. of) Rothbury was granted to Dorothy Widdrington of Thropton, his widow (*Dur. Prob. Off*. by C.R.H.). It seems unlikely that Francis Widdrington left any children.

It has already been noted that Francis' younger brother William joined him in the sale of Carrycoats White House in 1661. For William and his descendants *see* WIDDRINGTON OF COLTPARK, CHAP. NETHERWITTON.

WIDDRINGTON OF COLTPARK, CHAP. NETHERWITTON

RICHARD ERRINGTON of Bewclay, par. St John Lee, by his w.d. 11 July 1670 leaves legacies of £10 each to his daughter Catherine Widdrington, to his grandchildren Edward and Henry Widdrington, and to his granddaughter Widdrington (*NCH*. IV, p.213). After the death of Richard Errington's two sons, Edward (d.*s.p. circa* 1721) and Gilbert (d.*s.p.* 1725), the Errington estate of Portgate and Todridge and the tithes of Haydon Bridge descended to Edward Widdrington.

Edward was the son of William Widdrington of Thropton by his wife Catherine Errington. William was almost certainly the youngest son of Robert Widdrington (d.1632) of West Harle. It has not been possible to make this identification before as William is said, erroneously, to have died in 1721 (*Ib*.). In fact the William who died in 1721 was grandson of William Widdrington of Thropton.

It is possible that Catherine wife of William Widdrington of Thropton, died shortly after 1670 and that William married again. 'Dorothy, wife of William Widdrington, Thropton', was buried at Rothbury 1 April 1676 (*Rothbury Registers*). It is not known when William died or where he was buried. His son and heir Edward was living at Thropton in 1689 and 1692. Two infant sons died at Thropton and were buried at Rothbury:—

8 September 1689. Henry, *fil*. Edward Widdrington, esq., Thropton, bur.

15 March 1691/2. Edwd, *fil*. Mr Edwd Widdrington, Thropton, bur.

Either Edward was a great stickler for etiquette, or he had acquired an estate of sufficient extent to justify the title

WIDDRINGTON of COLWELL, par. CHOLLERTON

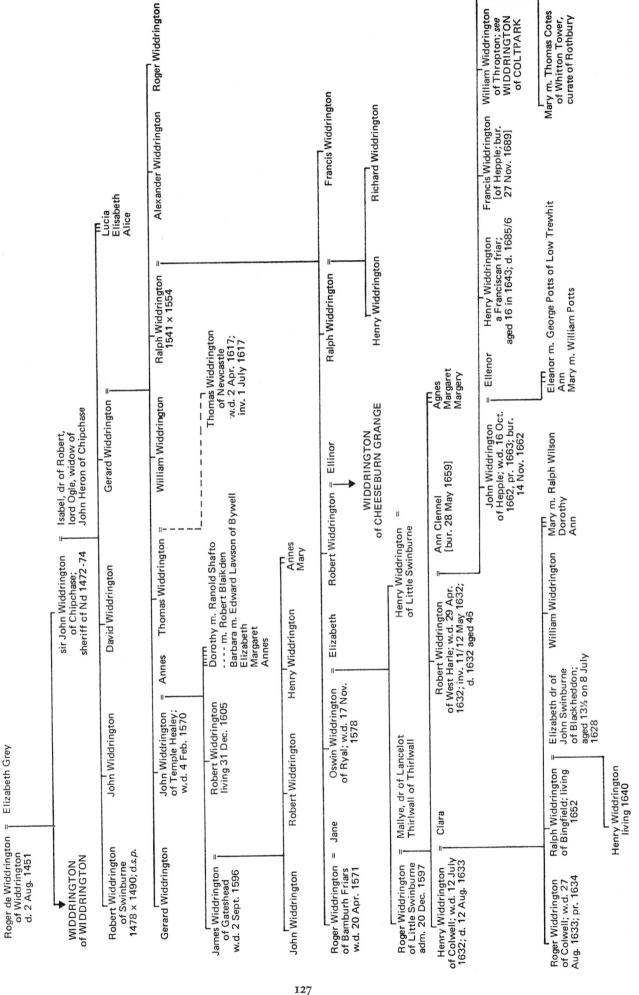

of 'esquire' which is regularly applied to him. He could not have owned sufficient property at Thropton or even in the parish of Rothbury, to justify the designation. He may already have acquired the estate in Ritton, Birkheads and Coltpark, which he registered in 1717; this could have been by purchase or through his wife Mary whose parentage is unknown.

By 1698 Edward had moved to Coltpark. Although a papist he had children baptised and buried in the parish church of Netherwitton and acted as churchwarden several times between 1703 and 1715.

11 August 1698. Robert, son of Edward Widdrington, esq., born, Colt Parke.

11 March 1698/9. Robert, son of Edward Widdrington, Colt Park, bur.

8 April 1700. Richart, son of Edward Widdrington, Colt Park, bap.

27 January 1700/1. Richart, son of Edward Widdrington, Colt Park, bur.

23 June 1703. Eliz. daughter of sqr Waddrington, Colt Park, bap.

25 March 1707. Edward, son of Edward Widdrington, Colt Park, bap.

In a list of non-jurors drawn up in 1715 are the names of Edward Widdrington of Colt Park, esq., and William Widdrington of the same, gent. It is quite clear from these entries that William was not Edward's father, but his son. Wm. Widdrington, Coltpark, was buried at Netherwitton 21 January 1720/1. On 19 April 1717 Edward registered his estate as the mansion house called Ritton and grounds belonging called Ritton and Birkheads, a messuage called Colt-park in his own possession, a messuage and land there let to William Potts, a limestone quarry at Birkheads and a land-sale colliery at Birkheads and Colt-park (*SS.* 131, p.58). Mary, wife of 'Sq, Ed, Widdrington' was buried at Netherwitton 25 June 1712, and 'Edward Widdrington, esq' on 23 May 1749.

Edward Widdrington 'being aged and infirm' had made his will on 4 February 1748/9. Seven sons had predeceased him and none of them had left children. To his daughter Mary wife of Thomas Potts of the Craig he leaves the yearly interest of £50, and six months after her death the £50 is to be paid to his 'grandson' Edward son of Robert Allgood of Hexham, gent. His granddaughter Elizabeth Pringle, daughter of the said Thomas Potts and wife of (blank) Pringle of the Craig is to have £10. His grand daughter Eleanor daughter of Thomas Potts is to have £20, and his grand daughter Mary Rochester of Charlton £26. Other legacies are left to his grand daughter Elizabeth Cuthbertson, his grandchildren William, Henry and Jane Cuthbertson, his sister Elizabeth wife of Thomas Bell of Beaufront and to John Thornton of Netherwitton. The residue of his estate is left to his dear friend Gilbert Park of Warton who is to be sole executor. Gilbert Park proved the will on 25 May 1749.

When his son Henry married Margaret daughter of Major Allgood, rector of Simonburn, Edward Widdrington transferred his estate to the young couple.

The marriage settlement was dated 21 June and enrolled 5 October 1726. As 'Mr Widdrington' he was buried in the quire of Hexham church 14 January 1727/8, and on 1 October 1729 administration was granted to his widow Margaret. His lands had been settled on her in such a manner that after his death intestate, they became hers absolutely.

Margaret Widdrington died at Newcastle 7 December 1777 in her 85th year. By her w.d. 11 August 1777, she leaves her messuages at Haydon Bridge to James Allgood of Nunwick. Her nieces Mrs Mary Rastell, Mrs Esther Hunter and Mrs Mary Bainbridge, and lady Loraine and Isabell Loraine, daughters of her nephew sir Lancelot Allgood, are to have £10 each for mourning. Margaret Allgood daughter of Mr Robert Allgood of Hexham, is to have £5 for mourning. She leaves the residue of her estate to her nephew sir Lancelot Allgood (*Dur. Prob. Off.* by C.R.H.).

Edward Widdrington's two daughters were Elizabeth wife of John Cuthbertson, and Mary wife of Thomas Potts. Elizabeth is said to have eloped from school with Cuthbertson who was an Alnwick periwigmaker (J. C. Hodgson, *MSS. pedigrees*). This can hardly be true for Elizabeth was baptised 23 June 1703 and married at Alnwick 8 June 1729 when she must have been 26 years old. After Margaret Widdrington's death Cuthbertson's son, Henry Cuthbertson, who had been a hairdresser in Newcastle and was now a brewer, unsuccessfully claimed the Widdrington estates from sir Lancelot Allgood. Another claim was made, also unsuccessfully, 7 February 1786, by Robert Potts, only surviving son of Thomas and Mary Potts; he went so far as to take out letters of administration to the personal estate of his uncle Henry Widdrington.

WIDDRINGTON OF CHEESEBURN GRANGE, PAR. STAMFORDHAM

THE founder of this branch of the Widdrington family was Robert Widdrington, brother of Roger Widdrington (d.1571) of Bamburgh Friars and of Oswin Widdrington (d.1578) of Ryal. They were sons of that Ralph Widdrington who had a lease of one quarter of Filton in 1541.

Roger Widdrington of Bamburgh Friars by his w.d. 20 April 1571 leaves a legacy of £40 to his 'nephew Thomas Widdrington son of my brother Robert Widdrington'.

On 15 February 1561/2 sir Henry Percy wrote to the earl of Rutland, lord president in the North, 'on behalf of certain poor inhabitants of Nesbit, co. Northumberland, whom Robert Wothrington, the purchaser, goes about to expel from their tenements, without respect of charity and conscience' (*Belvoir Papers*, I, p.79).

Robert Widdrington's son Thomas was living at Ashington, par. Bothal, 8 January 1589/90 when he made his will. He directs that he is to be buried in the parish church of Bothal. Lewis Mawtlaine, *alias* Widdrington, his base-begotten son is to have all the corn now sown at Nesbit with all the oxen, wains, ploughs etc. 'If it shall please God to send me a son to Dorothie, my wife, I give unto him all my lands and to his heirs male of his body lawfully begotten, and for lack of such, to Lewis Mawtlaine, *alias* Widdrington, and to his heirs male of his body, lawfully begotten, and failing such to Roger Widdrington of Little Swinburne'. To his brother Garrett Widdrington, and to Lewis Widdrington he leaves £10 a year each. After the death of his mother Ellinor Widdrington, his farmhold in Cowpen is to go to his servant, Raphe Wallis, for life. Wallis is also to have his bay mares. His mother Ellinor is to have 'three parts of all my goods' and 'The rest to my wife Dorothie, whom I make executrix'. The witnesses to the will are Henrye Woddrington, Ephraim Woddrington, Robert Coperthwaite and John Errington (*SS*. 38, p.220n.).

Thomas' mother, Ellinor Woddrington of Choppington, par. Bedlington, widow, made her w.d. 3 March 1592/3. She leaves her 'whole goods whatsoever' to Katherine Hobburne, her niece, and makes her sole executrix. She desires her 'well-beloved cousin Mr Henrie Wodrington of Swinburne, esquire', to become supervisor to her will. The will is witnessed by Roger Woddrington, Ephraim Woddrington, Amor Oxley and Thomas Barwick, clerk. The inventory of her goods dated 13 March 1592/3 shows that she had livestock at Choppington, Nesbit and at Hebburn and the White House and corn 'sown upon the ground' at Cowpen. She had 'during one lease of Ashington, for the term of years therein contained, and at yet expired, £21 by year'. Her goods were worth £224. 7s. 4d., 'besides the lease within named, being unvalued' (*SS*. 38, pp. 219-221).

When sir John Forster reported on the killing of lord Francis Russell at a Wardens' meeting on 27 July 1585 a Thomas Woddrington was one of those who signed the report. This was probably Thomas Widdrington of Ashington. Thomas Woodrington was 'a very able man' in the garrison of Berwick in 1587 and in 1593, in the latter year his pay being 10d. a day. He could also be 'my cousin Thomas Woodrengton, servant to Mr Henry Woodrington' who had a legacy of 40s., by the w.d. 20 April 1571 of Roger Widdrington of Bamburgh Friars; Mr Henry Widdrington was marshal of Berwick. Thomas Widdrington of Ashington by his will leaves to 'My Lord Warden' the choice of the first of his three stoned colts, Mr Fenwick getting second choice and Mr Nicholas Forster the third. The lord warden was sir John Forster, Mr (afterwards sir William) Fenwick was sir John's son-in-law and Nicholas Forster was his illegitimate son.

Thomas Widdrington's wife Dorothy was an illegitimate daughter of sir John Forster. Her name of Mawtlaine was no doubt her mother's surname and is perhaps a misreading of Mawclaine, a name that appears in the parish registers of Berwick-on-Tweed in the 16th century. Before marrying Thomas Widdrington, Dorothy had by him an illegitimate son Lewes. After Thomas' death Dorothy gave birth to a posthumous daughter Katherine. She afterwards married Ralph Salkeld, a younger brother of John Salkeld of Hulne abbey. Administration of the goods of Ralph Salkeld, late of Ashington, par. Bothal, deceased, was granted to Dorothee Salkeld his wife to her use and that of Edward Salkeld and posthumous children not yet born of said deceased; Dorothee was to be curator and governor of the said Edward Salkeld, a minor (*Dur. Prob. Off.* by C.R.H.).

In her second widowhood, Dorothy lived at Elvet, par. St Oswald's, Durham. On 16 February 1624/5 there was buried at St Oswald's, Mrs Dorothie Salkield, widow, the scribe adding after this entry in the register, 'a very grave gentlewoman and good to the poor in her lifetime—God send her a joyful resurrection'. The day following Mrs Salkeld's funeral an inventory of her goods was exhibited by William Woodrington, Francis Thompson, John Hall and Henry Dane. William Woodrington was perhaps a relative of her

first husband. He may have been William Widdrington of Shincliffe who had two daughters baptised at St Oswald's, Durham, Mary on 17 July 1625 and Elizabeth on 13 July 1628.

Administration of the goods of Dorothy Salkeld was granted on 22 February 1624 to Lewes Woodrington of Cheeseburn Grange, gent., her next of kin. Before her affairs could be straightened out, her daughter Katherine and her granddaughter Dorothy both died. Kathrine Dakins wife of William Dakins, gent., bur. 30 March 1625 and Dorothy 'daughter of the above named William Dakins and Kathrine Dakins' bur. 1 April 1625. The inventory of the goods of Dorothy Dakins is dated 6 April 1625. Her goods were valued at £74 out of which was to be deducted £20 'the charges of the above named Mrs Katheren Dakins in physic, physicians and other charges in and about the time of her sickness, she languishing long before she died, which with her funerals as particularly appeareth being disbursed and paid by her brother Mr Lewes Woodrington'. Edward Salkeld, only son of Dorothy Salkeld, by reason of his weakness or want of understanding was not well able to govern his own estate much less to undertake the administration of his mother's estate, and Katherine Woodrington *alias* Dakins, the said deceased's only daughter, wife to William Dakins, gent., was also altogether incapable of the said administration, for that her said husband remaineth in the gaol at York, convicted and condemned for felony and judgment of death, his execution respited at his majesty's pleasure (*Dur. Prob. Off.* by C.R.H.).

Lewis Widdrington's illegitimacy was soon forgotten and he has often been accepted as a legitimate son of Thomas and Dorothy. There must have been some special reason why Thomas' brother Gerard was omitted from the settlement of his lands created by Thomas in his will, and passed over in favour of Roger Widdrington of Little Swinburne who was Thomas' cousin. Nicholas Clark, servant to sir John Forster, by his w.d. 26 June 1573 leaves his half tithes of wool and lamb in Embleton parish to Gerard Widdrington, perhaps Thomas' brother, and Thomas Salkeld (Raine, *MSS. Wills and Inv.* III, p.68). Gerard Widdrington had a daughter Mary who married Richard Alder of Alnwick (1615 visitation pedigree of Alder); Richard Alder had a brother Francis Alder of Hobberlaw, who is called 'kinsman' by Lewis Widdrington in his will of 1630.

Cheeseburn Grange had been part of the estates of the dissolved priory of Hexham and was sold by the Crown on 22 June 1554 to Gilbert Langton and Thomas Holmes of London (*Pat. Roll.* 1 Mary, pt 7, m.17 (18)). Margaret Lawson of Cheeseburn Grange, on 27 July 1592, was convicted of recusancy of eleven years standing (*PRO.* E.377/1; *Cath. Rec. Soc.* 18, p.248). In many subsequent years she was convicted and her property at Cheeseburn Grange seized. When her house was raided and searched by sir William Fenwick and others in Jan 1592/3, she is said to have hidden herself in the brick oven, which was still warm, and was ill for a long time in consequence.

In a list of recusants drawn up on 12 February 1595/6 are the following names in the parish of Stamfordham:—

'Mris Lawson of Chesborough Grainge, widow, an householder. Her living worth £20 by year. She is a notorious receipter of seminaries and standeth indicted.

Katherine Lawson daughter to the said Mistrs Lawson.

Anne Shastoe (*sic* for Shaftoe) and Jane Swinburne spinsters resident with the said widow Lawson and maintained by her.

Ambrose Swinburne and William Coke servants to the said Mris Lawson.

James Swinburne gent and Margaret his wife; he hath no living but a wind milne and expecteth to have the said Chesborough grainge after the death of the said Mtres Lawson. They both stand indicted' (*Cath. Rec. Soc.* 53, p.60).

It is almost certain that Mistress Lawson was widow of Gawen Swinburne of Cheeseburn Grange and had taken a second husband called Lawson. In his w.d. 26 April 1576 Gawen makes no specific bequest of Cheeseburn Grange but he leaves to his wife Margaret the residue of all his goods and chattels moveable and unmoveable (*SS.* 2, p.409).

A John Swinburne who made his w.d. 23 November 1613 does not mention his place of residence but directs that he is to be buried in Stamfordham church. He leaves to his uncle Robert Lawson 40s., and to each of his children 20s.; to his sister Anne Strangwish £5; other legacies are given to his cousin James Swinburne and his wife, to his cousin John Swinburne and his wife, to his 'aunt of the Grange', and to Ambrose Swynborn and his wife; to Robert Fletcher and John Fletcher he leaves 'two young quies which I have at Thornley with Robert Lawson'; his cousin Lewis Widdrington is appointed executor (*Dur. Prob. Off.* by C.R.H.).

It would appear certain that John Swinburne's 'aunt of the Grange' was the same person as 'mris Lawson of Chesborough Grainge, widow' living in 1596. Her daughter Katherine, unmarried in 1596, married Lewis Widdrington who eventually became owner of Cheeseburn Grange.

When Lewis Widdrington's younger son Rowland registered his pedigree at St George's Visitation of London in 1634 he stated that his mother was Catherine daughter of William Lawson of Little Usworth, co. Durham. William Lawson was actually of Washington, co. Durham, and was a younger son of William Lawson of Little Usworth; he married Catherine daughter of Rowland Beadnell of Newcastle. No daughter Catherine is recorded in the 1575 visitation pedigree of these Lawsons and it has been suggested (*NCH.* XII, p.324) that she may have been born after 1575. The solution is not as easy as this. William Lawson in his w.d. 20 November 1596 mentions his sons Ralph, John and Francis, and three daughters Dorothy, Margaret and Elizabeth, but no Catherine, nor is she mentioned in the wills, both made in 1590, of her putative brothers Ralph and John.

The elder William Lawson of Usworth, co. Durham, by his wife Isabel daughter of John Hedworth of Harraton, co. Durham, had six sons, Thomas, Robert, William, George, John and Rowland. The youngest son Rowland was 'of Gateside in the b'prick' when he subscribed to the family pedigree at Newcastle on Friday 16 August 1575. The second son, Robert Lawson of Rock, by his w.d. 15 May 1565 left to his two brethren John Lawson and Rowland Lawson his lease of the tithe corn of Cramlington and the tithe corn of Falloden. It may have been this Rowland Lawson who married Margaret widow of Gawen Swinburne of Cheeseburn Grange. Gawen died in 1576. Margaret Lawson's daughter Katherine was convicted of recusancy 12 February 1595/6 and must have been at least sixteen to be described

as a recusant, *i.e.* born after 1579. On 27 July 1592 Mistress Lawson of Cheeseburn Grange was a recusant of eleven years standing—in other words she had been responsible for her own debts from at least 1581. This suggests that Margaret Swinburne married her second husband *circa* 1578 and that he died before 1581. Their only daughter Katherine must have been born *circa* 1578.

There is a strong presumption that John Swinburne's uncle Robert Lawson is the same person as Robert Lawson of Thornley also mentioned in Swinburne's will. An earlier Robert Lawson of Thornley, presumably father of the Robert Lawson of Thornley of 1613, made his will on 2 April 1599; to his son Robert Lawson he leaves his right, interest and title of Thornley; he leaves a legacy to his daughter Annas Stranguishe, and the residue to (his other children) Robert, Grace, Alle and Jane Lawson (*Dur. Prob. Off.* by C.R.H.). Robert Lawson the elder of Thornley was not the husband of Mistress Lawson of Cheeseburn Grange for she was a widow in 1595 and he was living in 1599. All that is known for certain is that Catherine wife of Lewis Widdrington was a Lawson, and that her mother Margaret Lawson was a widow as early as 1595. It is possible that Robert Lawson of Thornley was uncle of John Swinburne's wife, which would account for the elder Robert having a daughter Annas Stranguise and John Swinburne having a sister (actually sister-in-law) Anne Strangwish.

Gawen Swinburne's eldest brother, Roger Swinburne (d.1538) of Edlingham, had a younger son John, and it would appear almost certain that this was the John Swinburne who made his will in 1613. He would accurately describe Gawen's widow Margaret as his 'aunt of the Grange'. His cousins James and John Swinburne were perhaps sons of Gawen's 'base begotten son' John.

On 20 April 1615 a settlement was made of Cheeseburn Grange, the principal party to the settlement being that James Swinburne who in 1595 'expected to have said Cheeseburn Grange after the death of the said Mris Lawson'. His expectations had no doubt been dashed when Mistress Lawson's only daughter had married Lewis Widdrington. The settlement of 20 April 1615 was a tripartite indenture made between James Swinburne of Stamfordham, gent., of the first part; Margaret Lawson of Cheeseburn Grange, widow, Lewis Widdrington of the same, gent., and Katherine his wife, of the second part; and Thomas Swinburne of the city of Durham, esq., Alexander Vasye servant of the said Thomas, Henry Widdrington of Colwell Mains, gent., and Nicholas Forster of Catchburn, gent., of the third part. The terms of the agreement were that James Swinburne, Margaret Lawson, Lewis Widdrington and Katherine his wife, agreed with Thomas Swinburne, Alexander Vasye, Henry Widdrington and Nicholas Forster, that they would before Michaelmas next levy a fine of Cheeseburn Grange to Thomas Swinburne and Alexander Vasye to the use of Margaret Lawson for life, and then to Lewis Widdrington and Katherine his wife, and the heirs and assigns of the said Lewis for ever.

In 1626 the tenants of the two third parts of the lands of Margaret Lawson owed £8. 17s. 9⅓d. a year on the capital messuage called Cheeseburn Grange and 10 acres of land, 20 acres of meadow, 40 acres of pasture and 30 acres of common more or less, in the tenure of Lewis Widdrington of the annual value of £13. 6s. 8d. of which she is seised for life. The lands were taken into the hands of the king 10 November 1626 by Cuthbert Heron, esq., sheriff, and other commissioners (*PRO*. E.377/34). All accounts were squared up by her executors and administrators at Trinity term 1632.

On 10 September 1630 administration of the personal estate of Lewis Widdrington was granted to Thomas Swinburne of Elvet, co. Durham, and Thomas Widdrington of Gray's Inn. He left five sons Thomas, Henry, Rowland, Ralph and Nicholas, and two daughters, Catherine wife of Cuthbert Pepper of Farnton in Silksworth, co. Durham, and Eleanor wife of Anthony Dodsworth of Stranton, co. Durham. An inquest taken at Hexham on 26 July 1631 found that Lewis Widdrington, gent., died at Cheeseburn Grange 20 August 1630 seised of lands in Mattensmore in Nesbit, Cowpen, Dukesfield Hall and Cheeseburn Grange, leaving Katherine then and now his widow, and that Thomas his son and heir was aged 30 (C.142, 475/104, *Public Record Office*).

The eldest son Thomas was educated at Christ's College, Cambridge, where he graduated B.A. in 1621. He adopted the law as a profession being admitted to Gray's Inn 14 February 1618/9. He was recorder of York and knighted 1 April 1639; in the following year he commenced a parliamentary career which lasted until his death. Three of his children were baptised at St Martin's, York, Frances (15 August 1637), Thomas (19 June 1640) and Mary (28 January 1644/5). He was Member of Parliament successively for Berwick (1640), York, Northumberland (1656), York and Berwick (1660, 1661). As a firm supporter of the Commonwealth, he held appointments of Commissioner of the Great Seal 1648, councillor of state 1651-58, Speaker of the House of Commons 1656-58 and Chief Baron of the Exchequer 1658.

Mindful of his mortality and desirous to set his house in order before his death, he made his will 15 September 1663. He is to be buried without the least of funeral pomp by the discretion of his executor, 'and if my departure out of this world be in or near London, then my mind is that my body be interred in the church of St Giles-in-the-Fields as near the bodies of my late dear wife and my dear daughter Dorothy, as conveniently may be'. His wife Frances daughter of Ferdinando, lord Fairfax of Cameron, had died 4 May 1649 aged 36; his daughter Dorothy had died the same year aged 12. 'It having pleased God, the all wise and merciful Lord God, to take to his mercy my only and dear son Thomas, he being then near the age of 20 years,' he confirms a settlement made in July 1663 after his son's death, and confirms certain provision for the maintenance of a schoolmaster at Stamfordham 'where I was born'. The only son, Thomas Widdrington, had died unmarried at the Hague in 1660.

By his will sir Thomas makes ample provision for his surviving daughters, Frances wife of sir John Legard of Ganton, bart, Catherine wife of sir Robert Shafto, and Mary and Ursula, then unmarried. After their father's death, Mary married sir Robert Markham of Sedgebrook, bart, and Ursula married Thomas, earl of Plymouth. He leaves legacies of £5 to his 'late servant and kinsman Thomas Swinburn'; £10 per annum out of the tithe of Chester-le-Street, co. Durham, to his brother Ralph Widdrington; £10 to his nephew

William Widdrington, son of his brother Henry; to his brother Henry £10 and a debt of £100 'due by him to me for stock of mine when he first farmed Nesbit'; £10 to his brother Nicholas; £10 apiece to the children of his brother Rowland, deceased.

Sir Thomas died 13 May 1664 and in accordance with the directions given in his will, he was buried in the chancel of St Giles-in-the-Fields, London.

Lewis Widdrington's third son, Rowland, was of Farringdon Without, London, when he entered his pedigree at St George's Visitation of London in 1634 (*Harl. Soc.* XVII, p.349). Rowland was a draper in London and his two sons Henry and Thomas, were mentioned in the settlement of Cheeseburn Grange made 10 July 1663. 'Frances the daughter of Mr Witherington who lived about Durham had a child died in our parish and was buried at Belfreys', 11 July 1648; seven days later 'Frances daughter of Mr Rowland Widdrington' was buried at St Michael le Belfry, York. The son Henry was born at Hoddesdon, Herts., and was aged about 70 in 1711; he was perhaps the Henry Widdrington of par. St. Martin in the Fields, gent., widower, aged about 36 who took out a licence 26 August 1679 to marry Eleanor Prichard of All Hallows, Hertford, widow, aged about 30 (*Harl. Soc.* XXX, p.4). He and his son Henry were living at Hertford 20 March 1687/8; Henry the son was living 25 August 1705 but died in his minority (*see* Peile, *Christ's College Biographical Reg.*).

Ralph, fourth son of Lewis Widdrington, was fellow of Christ's College, Cambridge and became a Doctor of Divinity. He was admitted to Gray's Inn 16 March 1640/1. At Christ's College he had as his pupils his nine nephews—four of the sons of his brothers and five sons of his sister. The three sons of William, 1st lord Widdrington, were also his pupils, together with William Widdrington of Hauxley and Thomas Widdrington of Morpeth. He was Lady Margaret reader of divinity in Cambridge University 20 March 1687/8, when he made his will. His principle legatees are his nephews Ralph Widdrington of Cheeseburn Grange, son of his brother sir Henry Widdrington, deceased, and Henry Widdrington son of Henry Widdrington of Hertford. His nephew Patricious Widdrington is to have his better chariot; his niece Mary Widdrington of Hertford is to have his Dutch cabinet, his pewter, etc., at Fordham, and his nephews Ralph and Henry Widdrington are to have the pictures in his chambers in the college.

Nicholas youngest son of Lewis Widdrington was apprenticed 24 August 1633 to John Cock of Newcastle, boothman, and was admitted free of the Newcastle Merchants Company 25 November 1641. His name is included in the settlement of 10 July 1663, and he was buried at St Nicholas, Newcastle, 26 June 1676.

Like some other families during the Civil Wars, the Widdringtons of Cheeseburn Grange kept one foot in either camp, for whilst sir Thomas was high in the favour of the Commonwealth leaders, his next brother Henry was an ardent royalist. After his brother's death, Henry succeeded to the paternal estates of Cheeseburn Grange and Nesbit. Sir Thomas had purchased other properties both in Northumberland and Yorkshire and these descended to his daughters.

Henry Widdrington resided at Blackheddon, par. Stamfordham, and at the outbreak of the Civil Wars he became a major (in the train band of Northumberland) of a foot regiment for the king. He continued with the royalist army until March 1643 when he laid down his commission and in August 1644 surrendered to lord Fairfax. He was apprehended in Newcastle, as he complained later, 'through causeless jealousies'. On 27 November 1645 he begged to compound for delinquency, stating that he had taken the National Covenant, and that being a younger brother his chief estate was in horses, corn, cattle and sheep all of which had been taken from him to the value of £1000. His real estate comprised a house and land at Blackheddon, a moiety of Bolton and Broomepark, and a mortgage of the tithes of Stamfordham. On 14 February 1646 the House of Commons passed a resolution to accept a fine of £200 for discharging the delinquency of Henry Widdrington, and on 4 May he received a pardon. He petitioned Cromwell 6 March 1656 for exemption from the decimation tax claiming that he had been a commissioner for trial of offenders against the State, and that therefore he should have the benefit of Cromwell's instructions which extended favour to those who had wholly changed their interest in that party with which they were at first engaged. On producing a certificate signed by Charles Howard and the commissioners of the peace in Northumberland he received a complete discharge (SS. 111, pp.373-375).

After the Restoration Henry Widdrington received knighthood. His will is dated 13 September 1664 and he was buried in the chancel of Stamfordham church 5 December 1665. His wife Mary, a daughter of John Swinburne of Blackheddon, had predeceased him. He states in his will that 'If my departure out of this world be in, or near, Northumberland, then my mind is that my body be interred in the church of Stannerton (Stamfordham) where my dear wife is interred'. Their family was eight sons and two daughters:—

1. William Widdrington; eldest son and heir.

2. John Widdrington. He was now or lately in the East Indies when his father made his will, by which he is to have £400. Adm. 5 January 1674/5.

3. Ralph Widdrington; heir to his brother William.

4. Edward Widdrington; he is to have £400 when 22 years of age by his father's will. He was probably Edward Widdrington of Blackheddon whose will is dated 20 July 1674. His wife Eleanor survived him but he died s.p. and was buried St Paul's, Covent Garden, 22 July 1674. Sir Nicholas Thornton of Netherwitton had a daughter Elenor (Hellen) Widdrington; she was probably wife of this Edward Widdrington.

5. Thomas Widdrington; by his father's will is to have £400 when 22 years of age.

6. Robert Widdrington; is to have £400 when 22 years of age; living at Cheeseburn Grange when he made his will 7 March 1676. He was 22 years old when he took out a marriage licence 12 December 1668, to marry Martha Nicholson, aged 25, of the parish of St Saviour's, Southwark. She died at Hawkwell 1708. They had a son Henry named in his father's will (and buried at Stamfordham 4 June 1700).

7. Lewis Widdrington; by his father's will he is to have £400 at the age of 22; he died at Cheeseburn Grange and was buried at Stamfordham 25 April 1702.

8. Patrick Widdrington; by his father's will is to have £400 when he was 22 years of age. He was living in London

25 January 1715.

i. Mary, married firstly George Ramsay of Bewick (m.sett. 28 October 1652), and secondly William Delaval of Dissington.

ii. Margaret, married Nicholas Whitehead of Boulmer, par. Longhoughton.

There may have been an older son, Thomas, living 1640, who died young.

William Widdrington, the heir, married Barbara daughter of sir Ralph Jenison of Elswick (b. of m. 1663). Three sons and two daughters died in infancy and when William died in 1681 (bur. 7 January 1680/1) he was survived by four daughters, Mary, unmarried; Elizabeth wife of Richard Darby of Gray's Inn (m.lic. 22 Sept. 1691); Jane, unmarried; and Catherine wife of sir Thomas Aston (m.lic. 22 October 1703).

Cheeseburn Grange passed to William's next surviving brother Ralph. Ralph was twice married; his first wife Elizabeth died at Blackheddon and was buried at Stamfordham 3 February 1666/7; his second wife Margaret is named in his will, (and was buried at Stamfordham 7 March 1701/2). Ralph's will is dated 24 July 1688; he was living 2 August 1704 but dead before 25 April 1708. He leaves to Margaret 'my now wife' certain rooms at Cheeseburn Grange for her life, his lesser silver tankard, six silver spoons, six silver forks, two silver porringers and two silver salts, 4 pillow beers, 4 table cloths, 4 side board cloths, 4 dozen napkins, and a horse with grazing and hay for the same. Martha Widdrington, widow of his brother Robert, is to have £10 a year. He leaves to his nephew Henry Widdrington, son and heir of his said brother Robert, £250 'in satisfaction of the like sum left him by his late father and deposited in my hands for his use'. Each of ten priests are to have 20s.

Ralph Widdrington's eldest son John had died s.p., in his father's lifetime. The heir to Cheeseburn Grange was the second but eldest surviving son, William. Ralph had a daughter Mary Anne who professed at the English convent at Bruges in 1687 and died there in 1745 aged 77.

William Widdrington of Cheeseburn Grange died between 1 May 1708 and 25 January 1715. By his wife Anne daughter of Caryl, viscount Molyneux, (articles before marriage 14 June 1693) he had an only son Ralph and two daughters Mary and Elizabeth.

Ralph Widdrington was under age 25 January 1715 but of full age 1 September 1718. He died 'respected by all ranks of people' and was buried at Stamfordham 21 December 1752. By his wife Anne daughter of Martin Woolascott of Woolhampton, Berks., he had no issue. (She died Hammersmith, Sept. 1764). His coheiresses were his sisters Mary wife of Thomas Riddell of Swinburne (m.lic. 5 June 1726) and Elizabeth wife of George Sanderson of Healey (m.lic. 23 October 1725), but by his w.d. 7 May 1748 he leaves Cheeseburn Grange to such son of his sister Mary as should not succeed to Swinburne Castle. In consequence of this the heir to Cheeseburn Grange was Ralph, second son of Thomas Riddell of Swinburne. The property now (1966) belongs to Ralph's direct descendant Mr Philip Oswald Riddell.

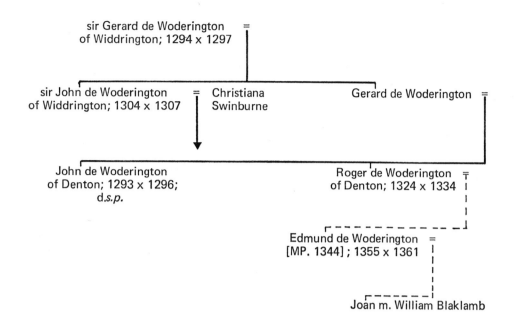

sir Gerard de Woderington =
of Widdrington; 1294 x 1297

sir John de Woderington = Christiana   Gerard de Woderington =
of Widdrington; 1304 x 1307   Swinburne

John de Woderington   Roger de Woderington =
of Denton; 1293 x 1296;   of Denton; 1324 x 1334
d.*s.p.*

Edmund de Woderington =
[MP. 1344] ; 1355 x 1361

Joan m. William Blaklamb

WIDDRINGTON OF DENTON, PAR. NEWBURN

ON 8 May 1293 there was a fine between John de Woderington and Richard de Scouland and Ellen his wife for the
manor of Denton by Newcastle and another fine on 1 July
1304 between the same parties for a moiety of the manor of
Newham. In this second fine John is described as 'of Denton'.
In 1296 the name of John de Woderington heads the Subsidy
Roll for Denton. He was son of Gerard de Widdrington
who was a younger brother of sir John de Widdrington of
Widdrington. Ellen wife of Richard de Scouland was
daughter and heiress of Robert de Newham. In 1242 Hawise
de Neuham held Newham, Denton, Newbiggen, Kenton,
Fawdon and a third part of Gosforth as one knight's fee of
the barony of Whalton.

On 24 May 1324 Roger de Widdrington, brother and
heir of John de Widdrington, formerly lord of Denton, had
a grant from John de Denton of a yearly rent of five marks
(*NDD.* p.250). On 5 March 1328 Roger de Widdrington
had confirmation of lands in Denton from Geoffrey le Scrope,
baron of Whalton (*Ib.*, p.228). In 1334 Roger de Wyderyngton is described as son of Gerard de Wyderyngton and
brother and heir of John de Wyderyngton who had died *s.p.*
(*de Banco Roll*, R.297, m.160). In 1337 he is again described
as brother and heir of John de Widdrington, who had died
s.p. temp.Ed.II (*Ib.*, R.310, m.158). John was still alive in
1312 when his name appears on a subsidy roll for Denton.

Long after the event Roger was charged with complicity
of Gilbert de Middleton's rebellion of 1317 and his lands
were forfeited. It seems likely that they were then acquired
by the Widdringtons of Widdrington.

On Sunday in All Saints (1 November) 1355 sir Gerard
de Wodryngton of Widdrington and Roger his brother gave
to Edmund de Wodrington an annual rent of ten marks in
Denton which Edmund had granted to them. An *inspeximus*
of this grant was given on 22 February 1361 and the rentcharge was settled on Edmund for life with successive

remainders to Joan widow of William Blaklamb, burgess of
Newcastle, for life; to John Blaklamb and Joan his wife and
the heirs of the body of John; final remainder to sir Gerard
and his heirs (*NDD.* p.250, Nos. 131, 132). It seems probable that Edmund was a son of Roger de Widdrington of
Denton, and had a daughter Joan wife of William Blaklamb.
Edmund was probably the person of that name who represented Newcastle in the parliament convened for 7 June 1344.

Joan widow of William Blaklamb, was living 7 June 1393
when it is stated that she had a rent of ten marks out of the
manor of Denton, of which the reversion lay with John de
Woderington, heir to sir Gerard and to Roger de Woderington (*Ib.*, p.251, No. 133).

WIDDRINGTON OF BULLER'S GREEN, PAR. MORPETH

JOHN WIDDRINGTON of Stonecroft, son of Sir Ralph Widd-
rington, by his w.d. 4 June 1664 leaves a colt to his 'nephew'
William Widdrington of Buteland. This William Widding-
ton had married Dorothy daughter and coheiress of Henry
Widdrington of Buteland (*see* WIDDRINGTON OF BUTELAND).
In right of his wife he had recently succeeded to lands at
Buteland, Broomhope, Steel, Hindhaugh and Calf Close. In
order to justify John Widdrington's use of the designation
'nephew' as applied by him to William Widdrington,
Hodgson thought that William's father-in-law Henry Widd-
rington was John Widdrington's brother (*HN.* ii, II, p.237).
This was qualified in the *County History* where Henry
Widdrington 'is said to be second son of sir Ralph Widd-
rington' (*NCH.* IV, p.369).

It is quite certain that Henry Widdrington was not a
brother of John Widdrington of Stonecroft and equally
certain that he was a son of Benjamin Widdrington originally
of Little Swinburne, but later of Buteland. The designations
of 'cousin' and 'nephew' as used in the 17th century should

not be taken too literally.

William Widdrington's parentage is unknown. He had some connection with the parish of Kirkwhelpington, for 'Edward, son of Mr William Widderington Buteland', was buried there on 9 June 1692.

In a list of Roman Catholic recusants in Northumberland drawn up in 1677 is the name of Wm Widrington of Buteland, gent. He was convicted of recusancy in 1678, 1681 and 1682. A messuage, 3 cottages, 1 acre of land and 10 acres of moor belonging to him were seised 6 October 1679 for a debt of £6. 13s. 4d. per annum charged on the land. His name occurs in the Removal of Papists Bill 1680. As William Widdrington of Colwell is also included in the Bill it is evident that William of Buteland could not have been a son of Henry Widdrington of Colwell. He was indicted at the Quarter Sessions at Alnwick 3 October 1683 and in the same year was imprisoned for refusing the Oath of Allegiance. Two years later he entered into recognizance in the sum of £200 to render himself when required (*Session Records, Q.S.*, 29 April 1685). He was living 18 May 1687 but at the Quarter Sessions of 5 October 1687 it was ordered that Mr Robert Widdrington, son of Mr William Widdrington, decd, be made treasurer of this county (*Sessions Order Books*).

William's widow Dorothy was living 31 August 1702. Their eldest son and heir was Henry Widdrington, against whom and his brother Robert a warrant was issued in March 1696/7 for interrupting the vicar of Whelpington at a burial (*Ib.*). As a non-juror he entered into recognizance in £100 on 30 March 1708 and in £500 on 13 July 1709.

On 21 February 1710/1 Henry Widdrington and his neighbour William Charlton of Redesmouth quarrelled about a horse on the occasion of a horse race held that day on the Doddheaps near Bellingham. Deciding to fight it out they retired to a small hollow at Redeswood Scroggs. William Laidley of Emblehope saw the two men fighting and raised the alarm amongst those present at the horse race. Charlton had however killed his opponent and fled; he was pursued and taken. He had many powerful friends who arranged for the case against him to be dismissed. Widdrington's widow was very dissatisfied with the verdict, and brought a charge against Charlton that he had wilfully and of malice aforethought assaulted and murdered her husband at the hour of 3 p.m. on the 21st day of February 1710/1. By a certain amount of legal manipulation, the case against Charlton was again dismissed (*Allgood MSS.*). Charlton subsequently received a royal pardon on 21 July 1713 (*AA1.* VI, p.30).

It is said that Widdrington's body was buried before Charlton's pew door in Bellingham church under a stone inscribed:—

'The burial place of Henry Widdrington of Butland, gentleman, who was killed by M. William Charlton of Reedsmouth, February 23rd in the year of our Lord, 1711' (*NCH.* IV, p.372).

The date on the stone was presumably that of Widdrington's burial, unless he had survived his wounds for two days. The inscription is now hidden by pew-work.

Henry's heir was his brother Robert Widdrington, then living at Buller's Green. He was of Plessey 15 April 1717 when as a Roman Catholic he registered his estate. He had messuages and lands in the parishes of Chollerton and Corsenside, let for £120. 12s. a year in which he was seised in an estate of inheritance in fee simple. Debts charged against the estate by his predecessors included £200 to his younger brother Michael Widdrington, £150 each to his sisters Barbara and Margaret Widdrington, and £20 a year for life to the widow of his elder brother Mr Henry Widdrington (*SS.* 131, p.56).

By his w.d. 10 February 1731/2 Robert Widdrington devises his lands at Broomhope, Steel, Hindhaugh and Buteland to his 'dear brother' Michael Widdrington; he leaves legacies to his sister Ann Hewitt and his brother-in-law James Robinson of Whitley (*Dur. Prob. Off.* by C.R.H.). Like his two brothers, Michael was a papist. He was a non-juror in 1708 and 1715; twice in 1709 on 10 April and on 13 July he entered into recognizance in the sum of £100.

Michael's will is dated 16 July 1741 and by it he nominates his nephew John Hewitt of Buller's Green as his heir and devisee. His niece Elizabeth Hewitt is to have the house in Buller's Green and £30 a year out of the residue to his real estate; he leaves legacies to his nephews and niece, Widd-

WIDDRINGTON of BULLER'S GREEN, par. MORPETH

William Widdrington of Buteland; d. 18 May x 5 Oct. 1687 = Dorothy, dr and coh. of Henry Widdrington of Buteland

- Henry Widdrington of Buteland; k. 21 Feb. 1709/10 = Elizabeth; living 15 Apr. 1717
- Robert Widdrington of Buller's Green; w.d. 10 Feb. 1731/2
- Edward Widdrington bur. Kirkwhelpington 9 June 1692

- Michael Widdrington of Buller's Green; w.d. 16 July 1741
- Ann m. ---- Hewitt
- Margaret m. James Robinson of Whitley
- ---- m. ---- Bourne

rington, John, Joseph and Dorothy Bourne. 'Michael Withrington, papist,' was buried at Morpeth 4 September 1741. He had failed to administer the will of his brother Robert and on 21 April 1748 administration was granted to their niece Elizabeth Hewit, spinster; Frances Lesley, fuller, and Widdrington Burn, silk dyer, both of Morpeth, were co-bondsmen (Ib.).

In 1745 John Hewit of Morpeth and John Bourne of Morpeth were both papist non-jurors. Widdrington Bourne had changed his occupation of silk dyer. The rev. J. Sharp reported to the bishop of Durham that Bourne was 'a popish schoolmaster, who has a great number of scholars and brings them on extremely well'.

WIDDRINGTON OF MORPETH, PAR. MORPETH

Two brothers, Michael and William Widdrington, living at Morpeth in the second half of the 17th century, were almost certainly descended from sir Ephraim Widdrington (d.1649) of Ritton but the intervening link has not been found.

When Alexander Selby of Biddleston registered his pedigree in 1615, he recorded that his wife was 'Joane, dau. of Sr Ephraim Widdrington, of Trewhit'. Their eldest son Robert was of the age of three years, and they had a second son William. The second son married Helen daughter of sir Thomas Haggerston, bart.

Helen Selby of Biddleston, widow, by her w.d. 1 August 1667 leaves to her daughter Mary Selby 'all those bondes which is writen on for here and one moare of Sr Edward Charleton's which Roger Widdrington in Biddleston hath which will make up to £500'. She leaves to Roger Widdrington £50 'to be aresed out of the money my lady Widdrington ous me'. As executors to her will she appoints her sons Thomas and Charles Selby and her friends Michell Widdrington and Mathew Davison of Hardon. Thomas and Charles proved the will, power reserved to Widdrington and Davison (Dur. Prob. Off. by C.R.H.). Roger Widdrington 'in Bittleston' was the youngest son of Henry Widdrington (d.1625) of Nether Trewhit by his second wife Margaret Ridley, Henry being sir Ephraim Widdrington's eldest son. Henry's other sons by his second wife were Oswald, Michael and Robert, and there can be little doubt that Helen Selby's friend Michell Widdrington was a son of one of these three brothers.

Michael Widdrington was living at Morpeth as early as 1650 and between then and 1667 had eleven children born, many of whom died in infancy. He witnesses the w.d. 2 December 1667 of Roger Raymes of Morpeth, gent., and he is mentioned in the w.d. 1 September 1668 of Robert Ridley of Birling, gent.

On 18 April 1668 Arthur Fenwick of Morpeth, merchant, leased a brewhouse in Morpeth for a term of 51 years to Michaell Widdrington of the same, merchant (Howard MSS. per C.R.H.). On 5 October 1689 Michael's eldest son and heir, Thomas Widdrington of Morpeth, conveyed the brewhouse to George Fenwick of Morpeth, merchant (Ib.).

In the inventory taken in 1673 of the goods of Roger Widdrington (d.1671) of Harbottle, gent., whom we have presumed was Michael's uncle, are entries of three separate debts of £150, £80, and £80 which he owed to Michael

Widdrington of Morpeth, gent. Mrs Ann Widdrington wife of Mr Michael Widdrington was buried at Morpeth 3 March 1678/9, and Mr Michaell Widdrington, merchant, was buried there 6 August 1680.

Michael Widdrington the elder of Morpeth, gent., had made his w.d. 3 August 1680. He leaves to his eldest son Thomas his messuage, burgage or tenement in Morpeth and failing him and his heirs to his son Michael and his heirs and in default to his daughters Mary wife of William Fenwick, Ann wife of Thomas Acton, gent., Margaret Widdrington, Elizabeth Widdrington and Martha Widdrington, spinsters. The inventory of his goods taken on 10 August 1680 found that they were worth £60 but £406 was owing to him (Dur. Prob. Off. by C.R.H.).

Michael Widdrington's eldest son Thomas was educated at Morpeth under Mr Lumsden; he was admitted pensioner under Dr Widdrington at Christ's College, Cambridge, 13 June 1670 aged 16, and became B.A. 1673/4. He married at St Andrew's, Newcastle, 10 May 1683 Ann Widdrington and they had two daughters baptised at Morpeth A . . . (3 April 1684) and Mary (24 February 1684/5).

Michael Widdrington had a brother William who also lived at Morpeth. On 2 September 1661 Isabell daughter of William Widdrington was baptised at Morpeth. Her mother must have died about this time, for on 16 September 1662 William Widdrington of Morpeth, gent., entered into a bond of marriage with Frances Richardson of (blank), North'd, spinster. For some unexplained reason the tuition of Isabella Widdrington was granted to her father on 11 December 1662 and after his death to her uncle Michael Widdrington, 27 August 1667.

Mr William Widdrington was buried at Morpeth 28 April 1667 and administration of his goods was granted 14 October 1667 to his widow Frances. Frances made her will 29 May 1686. To her daughter Margaret Widdrington she leaves £80 and her son Ephraim Widdrington is to find for Margaret until the day of her marriage, sufficient maintenance of meat, drink and clothes suitable to her quality and then pay her the said legacy; 'but if it shall happen that my said daughter Margaret shall dislike such maintenance as shall be given her by my said son after my death and before her marriage then my will is that my said son do presently pay her in the said legacy of £80 and she shall maintain herself therewith at her pleasure'. Margaret is to have half of her father's stuff, and Ephraim, who is appointed sole executor, is to have the residue. Frances signs the will with her mark, Thomas Widdrington, presumably her late husband's nephew, being one of the witnesses. When the inventory of her goods was taken on 8 November 1686, they were found to be worth £37. 9s. 10d. (Dur. Prob. Off. by C.R.H.).

WIDDRINGTON OF NEWCASTLE UPON TYNE

At the south side of St John's church, Newcastle, there is a tombstone bearing the inscription: 'The burial place of Robert and Jane Widdrington, cordwainer, Newcastle. Jane, their daughter, departed this life July 10th 1806, aged 12 years. The above-named Robert Widdrington departed this life July 21st, 1806, aged 60 years. Also two of their children died in infancy. Michael Widdrington, son of the above

WIDDRINGTON of MORPETH, par. MORPETH

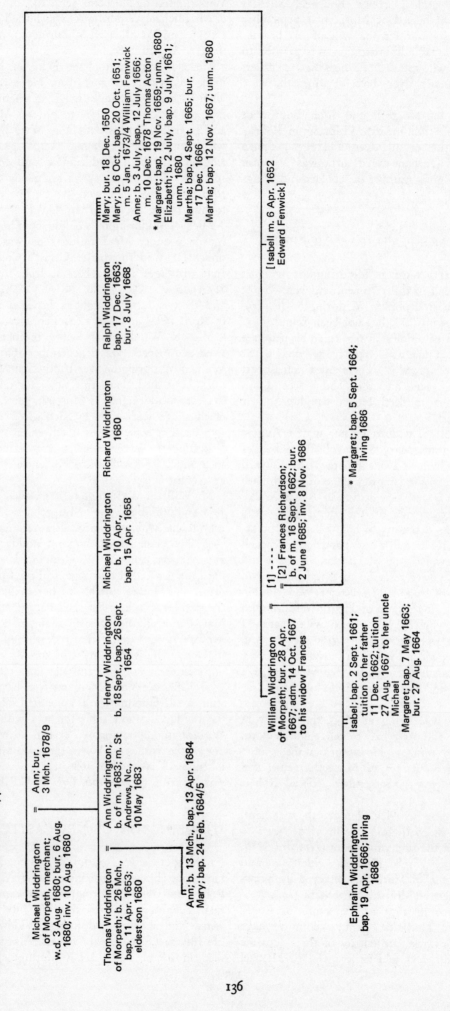

Michael Widdrington of Morpeth, merchant; w.d. 3 Aug. 1680; bur. 6 Aug. 1680; inv. 10 Aug. 1680 = Ann; bur. 3 Mch. 1678/9

Thomas Widdrington of Morpeth; b. 26 Mch., bap. 11 Apr. 1653; eldest son 1680 = Ann Widdrington; b. of m. 1683; m. St Andrews, Nc., 10 May 1683

Ann; b. 13 Mch., bap. 13 Apr. 1684
Mary; bap. 24 Feb. 1684/5

Henry Widdrington b. 18 Sept., bap. 26 Sept. 1654

Michael Widdrington b. 10 Apr., bap. 15 Apr. 1658

Richard Widdrington 1680

Ralph Widdrington bap. 17 Dec. 1663; bur. 8 July 1668

Mary; bur. 18 Dec. 1650
Mary; b. 6 Oct., bap. 20 Oct. 1651; m. 5 Jan. 1673/4 William Fenwick
Anne; b. 3 July, bap. 12 July 1656; m. 10 Dec. 1678 Thomas Acton
* Margaret; bap. 19 Nov. 1659; unm. 1680
Elizabeth; b. 2 July, bap. 9 July 1661; unm. 1680
Martha; bap. 4 Sept. 1665; bur. 17 Dec. 1666
Martha; bap. 12 Nov. 1667; unm. 1680

William Widdrington of Morpeth; bur. 28 Apr. 1667; adm. 14 Oct. 1667 to his widow Frances
[1] ----
= [2] Frances Richardson; b. of m. 16 Sept. 1662; bur. 2 June 1685; inv. 8 Nov. 1686

[Isabell m. 6 Apr. 1652 Edward Fenwick]

Isabel; bap. 2 Sept. 1661; tuition to her father 11 Dec. 1662; tuition 27 Aug. 1667 to her uncle Michael
Margaret; bap. 7 May 1663; bur. 27 Aug. 1664

* Margaret; bap. 5 Sept. 1664; living 1686

Ephraim Widdrington bap. 19 Apr. 1666; living 1686

4 Sept. 1684 Mr. Thomas Bowhey and Mrs. Margaret Widdrington m. at Morpeth
2 Sept. 1686 Mr. Robert King and Mrs. Margaret Widdrington m. at Morpeth

136

Robert Widdrington, departed this life June 1st, 1826, aged 21 years.'

It has been stated that 'These persons were descended from a certain Robert Widdrington, an officer of the Life Guards, who, after spending his patrimony, returned to Northumberland and resided at Quarry-house, Westgate— . . . He is asserted to have been a cadet of the Hauxley family; if that were so, he may perhaps be identified with Robert, son of Samuel Widdrington, whose name occurs in a deed of entail made in 1684' (NCH. V, p.307).

Samuel Widdrington was the third of four sons of Henry Widdrington of Hauxley (1610 x 1630). The youngest of these four was Thomas Widdrington apprenticed 1 May 1641 to Christopher Nicholson of Newcastle, merchant. If Thomas had been apprenticed at the normal age of fourteen years he would have been born about 1627. It may be suggested that Samuel was two or three years older and perhaps born about 1625. Robert, son of Mr Samuel Widdrington of Seghill was born 19 December 1666 and was baptised at Earsdon on 8 January 1666/7.

Robert Widdrington of Quarry House's first child to be baptised at St John's church was a daughter Esther on 15 May 1709. The word 'twin' is entered against her name and on the same day 'Robert son to Robert Widdrington, West-gate' was buried at St John's; he was presumably Esther's twin brother. Robert Widdrington of Westgate can hardly be the same person as Robert son of Samuel Widdrington for there is more than a generation between them.

Robert Widdrington had a daughter Jane baptised at St John's 20 January 1716/7, his daughter Esther was buried 28 February 1719/20, and a son, a second Robert baptised 20 December 1724. There were other children besides these.

The eldest surviving son, Thomas Widdrington, married, 4 November 1744, at St John's, Dorothy Richardson, and was buried at the same church on 22 July 1770. He had at least three sons, Robert, a shoemaker in Middle Street, Newcastle; Thomas, baptised at St John's, 13 December 1747, a publican in Gateshead; and Michael, baptised at St John's, 18 February 1749/50, a shoemaker in Newcastle. The eldest of these three brothers, Robert, was the owner of the burial place at St John's mentioned above. His first wife was Margaret daughter of John Anderson of Wylam, and widow of Thomas Brown of Newcastle (m. St Nicholas', Newcastle, 1 August 1775; d.s.p. 8 July 1791). By his second wife Jane daughter of Thomas Johnson (m. St Nicholas', Newcastle, 24 December 1792) he had at least eight children:—

1. Robert Widdrington.
2. Thomas Widdrington; m. 13 November 1820 Jane daughter of John Dobson of Newcastle, upholsterer.
3. Hugh Widdrington.
4. Michael Widdrington; d. unmarried 1 June 1826 aged 21 years.
5. Dorothy; m. 12 June 1815 James Horsley of Newcastle, linen draper.
6. Jane; d. 10 July 1806 aged 12.
7 & 8. Two children; died in infancy.

Robert Widdrington's will is dated 21 July 1806. He directs his executors Mr Charles Charlton of Lisle Street, Mr Ralph Shevell, cordwainer at the Head of the Side, Mr John Bell of Newcastle, tide surveyor, and 'my now wife' Jane Widdrington, to sell the house which Mr John Bell, stationer,

was living in. They were to sell to the Corporation the house which Mr Robinson occupied. The other three houses in St Nicholas' Churchyard were to remain in the hands of the executors during his wife's lifetime or until his youngest child was 21. Besides this house property, the testator had a share in the business of pawnbroker of John Johnson and Co. (Dur. Prob. Off. by C.R.H.).

Thomas Widdrington, the Gateshead publican, married Elizabeth Hedley and had issue. Michael Widdrington the shoemaker was living in the Flesh Market, Newcastle in 1790. He obviously got on in the world and became a man of property. In his w.d. 23 February 1828 he is described as 'gentleman'. His 'dear wife' mentioned in the will was Jane daughter of Robert Green. To his son Michael he leaves all his estate at Stoney Gate, and all his lands at Newbottle Colliery with the messuage and premises at Newbottle. His daughter Elizabeth Dernole is to have £50 and his granddaughter Charlotte Hodgson £5. He leaves to his daughter Isabella wife of Edward Robson Mark, surgeon, his land at Murton Hill, par. of Houghton le Spring, co. Durham, and his messuage in Percy Court in Newcastle then in his own occupation. His daughter Jane wife of Matthew Renwick of Newcastle, draper, is to have the messuage, shop and premises in the Old Flesh Market, par. of St Nicholas', Newcastle, then in the occupation of the said Matthew Renwick, but subject to a rentcharge of £20 apiece yearly to the testator's daughters Maria Widdrington and Matilda Widdrington. Matilda is also to have the dwelling house in Fenkle Street, par. of St John, Newcastle. The executors to the will are the testator's son Michael Widdrington and his sons-in-law Edward Robson Mark and Matthew Renwick. Michael Widdrington the elder died 27 June 1831 aged 81 and the executors proved his will on 26 August 1831 (Dur. Prob. Off. by C.R.H.).

It seems possible that there are male descendants of these Newcastle Widdringtons living at the present time. If this should be so, and if the generations preceeding Robert Widdrington of Westgate can be discovered, such present day Widdringtons may have the unique distinction of being direct male representatives of Bertram de Woderington of 1166.

John Widdrington of Sunderland, shoemaker, who died 27 November 1910, aged 83 (M.I. Bishop Wearmouth Cemetery) may have been of this family. He left grandchildren now living in Sunderland.

OTHER WIDDRINGTONS

THERE are only a few persons of the name of Widdrington that cannot be connected with one or other of the known branches of the family.

On 1 January 1858 a remarkable and eccentric antiquary claimed, by the name of 'George Henry de Strabolgie Neville Plantagenet-Harrison, a General Officer in the armies of Peru, Uruguay, Corrientes, Denmark and the Germanic Confederation etc., etc.,' a summons to parliament as duke of Lancaster. He claimed descent from two of the daughters and coheiresses of Charles Nevill, 6th earl of Westmorland. Of the youngest of the coheiresses, Anne, he claimed that she married David Ingleby of Ripley, York., and that their daughter Ursula, coheiress of her mother, married Robert

WIDDRINGTON of NEWCASTLE UPON TYNE

Robert Widdrington
'an officer of the Life Guards';
of Westgate, Nc.

Robert Widdrington
bur. 15 May 1709 (a)

Thomas Widdrington
bur. 22 July 1770 (a) = Dorothy Richardson;
m. 4 Nov. 1744 (a);
bur. 14 Aug. 1765 (a)

Robert Widdrington
bap. 20 Dec. 1724 (a)

Esther (a twin); bap. 15 May 1709 (a);
bur. 28 Feb. 1719/20 (a);
Jane; bap. 20 Jan. 1716/7 (a)

Robert Widdrington
of Newcastle, cordwainer
and pawnbroker; w.d. 21
July 1806; d. 21 July 1806
aged 60
= [1] Margaret, dr of John
Anderson of Wylam, widow
of Thomas Brown of Nc. m.
1 Aug. 1775 (b); d.s.p.
8 July 1791
= [2] Jane dr of Thomas Johnson;
m. 24 Dec. 1792 (b)

Thomas Widdrington
of Gateshead, publican;
bap. 13 Dec. 1747 (a) = Elizabeth Hedley

Michael Widdrington
of Newcastle, cordwainer;
bap. 18 Feb. 1749/50 (a);
d. 27 June 1831 aged 81
= Jane, dr of Robert
Green of Newcastle

Robert Widdrington

Thomas Widdrington = Jane, dr of John
Dobson of Newcastle,
upholsterer; m.
13 Nov. 1820

Hugh Widdrington

Michael Widdrington
d. unm. 1 June 1826
aged 21

Jane; d. 10 July 1806
aged 12
Dorothy m. 12 June 1815
James Horsley of
Newcastle, linen
draper

Michael Widdrington

Elizabeth m. - - - - Dernole
Isabella m. Edward Robson Mark,
surgeon
Jane m. Matthew Renwick of
Newcastle, draper
Maria
Matilda

(a) Registers of St John's, Newcastle
(b) Registers of St Nicholas', Newcastle

Widdrington of Widdrington, co. Northumberland, esq. According to Plantagenet-Harrison, Robert and Ursula Widdrington's only daughter and heiress Margaret married Francis Woodruffe of Woolley, Yorks., from whom the claimant imagined he was descended. There was no Robert Widdrington of Widdrington about this time and there is no need to take much notice of the claimant's pedigree which seems to be mainly a product of his own imagination. He had also decided that he was 'heir male of the blood of king Canute the Great'! David Ingleby was younger brother of sir William Ingleby (d.*s.p.* 1617) and according to Dugdale's visitation of Yorkshire, his only daughter Mary married sir Peter Middleton of Stokeld, Yorks. (*AA2.* III, p.51).

On 13 September 1732 Mark Milbank of Barningham, Yorks., as owner of West Whelpington common, made an agreement with Charles Francis Howard of Overacres, esq., Robert Widdrington of Morpeth, gent., and Archibald Forster of Monkridge, gent., for themselves and on behalf of the several other freeholders of land adjoining to West Whelpington common. Michael Widdrington was a witness (*AA3.* V, p.122).

A Robert Widdrington was among a group transported beyond the seas for recusancy in 1630, the warrant being dated 25 June (*S.P.* 16/169/37).

Henry Widdrington of Bellasis, par. Stannington, had an only daughter Margaret who married Robert Fenwick of Ovingham (b.ofm. 4 November 1703). Fenwick was buried at St John's, Newcastle, 22 September 1706. The following year his widow married John Mackay of Netherwitton. As Roman Catholics John Mackay of Newbiggin, gent., and Margaret his wife, late Margaret Fenwick, widow and relict of Robert Fenwick of Newcastle, registered their estate on 20 April 1717 as a rentcharge of £20 out of a farmhold in Ovingham of which Mackay was seised in right of his said wife (*SS.* 131, p.53). John Mackay was tenant of Newbiggen, par. Hexham, and his wife was buried at Hexham 6 February 1717/8 (*NCH.* XIII, p.363).

On 13 January 1667/8 administration of the goods of John Widdrington, late of Berwick-on-Tweed, gent., was granted to Henry Gibbs, gent., brother uterine of the deceased (*Dur. Prob. Off.* by C.R.H.). The two following references may have some connection.

20 September 1666. Margaret dr of John Widdrington, soldier, bap. (*Berwick-on-Tweed Registers*).

9 September 1672. William, s. of capt. John Widdrington, deceased, bur. (*Registers of St Nicholas, Newcastle*).

On 19 January 1654 John Widdrington of Bedlington petitioned the County Committee for Compounding that two-thirds of his estate being under sequestration for recusancy he might be permitted to contract according to particulars annexed. Unfortunately the particulars are now missing. On 8 August 1654 Matthew Currey asked the Committee to discharge him from his lease of Bedlington Mill which he held for seven years at a rent of £48; it had been sequestrated for the recusancy of John Widdrington, gent. (*SS.* 111, p.377). This may have been John Widdrington of Hirst, son of Benjamin Widdrington (d.1633) of Buteland.

Margaret, dr. of Lionel Fenwick of Blagdon, was three times married. Her first husband was Robert Rymer of Newcastle, vintner, and on 24 July 1696 Margaret Rymer, widow, was granted administration of the goods of her late husband Robert Rymer, gent. In 1697 Margaret married her second husband Henry Raine of Bedlington. Her third husband was a Widdrington and as Mrs Margaret Widdrington she was buried at Bedlington in 1706. She had a son Robert Widdrington who had a legacy by the w.d. 24 September 1699 of his aunt Isabel Fenwick of Blagdon, spinster.

WIDDRINGTON—NOTES

1. I am greatly indebted to Dr A. M. C. Forster of Burradon, Thropton, whose knowledge of Northumberland recusant families of the 17th and 18th centuries is unrivalled. Not only has she allowed me to draw from her fund of information but by reading the proofs of this account of the Widdrington family has prevented me from perpetuating the mistakes of others, and making too many new ones myself.

2. Three burials at St Nicholas', Newcastle, between 1643 and 1649 perhaps refer to Widdringtons of Cheeseburn Grange:—

Mrs Mary Woodrington, bur. 21 December 1643, was perhaps a daughter of Henry Widdrington of Blackheddon.

Elizabeth dr of Henry Woodrington, bur. 10 August 1644, was perhaps another daughter.

Thomas Widdrington, d. 9 January, bur. 10 January 1648/9, was perhaps the eldest son of the same Henry Widdrington. Thomas, William and John Widdrington, sons of Henry Widdrington are mentioned in the settlement made in 1640 by Ralph Widdrington of Bingfield (*see* WIDDRINGTON OF COLWELL).

3. A roll of arms transcribed by the herald, Robert Glover, in the 16th century, contains the shields of men living in the first half of the 15th century. Two of the shields are attributed to Th. de Woderington and sir Willm Woderington (*SS.* 146, pp.152, 167). They were perhaps two of the younger sons of Roger de Widdrington (d.1451) of Widdrington.

4. Sir Ephraim Widdrington (d.1649) of Ritton evidently had a daughter who married George Wallis of Coupland, par. Kirknewton. Administration of the goods of George Wallace, deceased, on renunciation of Robert Lisle, husband of Martha Lisle *alias* Wallace, natural and lawful daughter of the deceased, was granted 31 July 1622 to sir Ephraim Widdrington, knight, *socero* of deceased, to use of James Wallace, natural and lawful son of the deceased (*Dur. Prob. Off.* by C.R.H.).

5. Robert Carey, baron Carey of Lepington, Yorks. (1622), earl of Monmouth (1626) m. at Berwick-on-Tweed 20 August 1593 Elizabeth widow of sir Henry Widdrington of Widdrington. Carey, in his Memoirs relates how Charles I, then duke of York and a child of 4 (1604) was in the charge of his wife, and, being in advance of age in surgical matters, she successfully resisted after many a battle, the suggestions of king James that 'the string under his tongue should be cut' and his feet cased in iron boots, the little prince being slow to speak and having weak ankles (G.E.C. *The Complete Peerage*, IX, p.59, from *Memoirs*, pp.167, 168).

WIDDRINGTON—FREEHOLDERS

1628—Sr Ephraim Widrington, of Birkheads, kt; Robert

Widrington, of Plessy, esq; Henry Widrington, of Hawxley, gent; Robert Widrington, of Cartington, esq; Lewes Widrington, of Chesburne Graing, esq; Robte Widrington, of West Harle, gent; Beniamin Widrington, of Buteland, gent; Henry Widrington, of Collwell, gent.

1639—Robert Widdrington, of Plessey, esq; Sr Willm Widdrington, of Widdrington, gent; Robert Widdrington, of Hauxley, gent; Henry Widdrington, of Blackheddon, gent; Henry Widdrington, of Booteland, gent; Roger Widrington, of Cartington, esq.

1698—none.

1710—Robt Widdrington of Hauxley.

1715—Robert Widdrington of Hauxley.

1721—Robert Widdrington, high constable for Morpeth Ward, East Division.

1734—none.

1748—John Widdrington, Newcastle, for Warkworth; Rbt Widdrington, Hauxley, for Hauxley.

1774—John Widdrington, Hauxley, for Hauxley.

1826—none.

WIDDRINGTON—BIBLIOGRAPHY

Hodgson, *History of Northumberland*, pt. ii, vol.II, Widdrington of Widdrington, pp.230-238, 248-258 with pedigree; Widdrington of Plessey, *ib.*, p.297; of West Harle, ii, I, p.200. F. J. A. Skeet, *A history of the families of Skeet, Somerscales, Widdrington etc.* pp.89-141 (1906). The B.M. copy contains author's additions (1922) reproduced from *MS.* Skeet prints two Widdrington pedigrees from the College of Arms being Vinc.149, 39 and 39(2). Neither of these is very accurate.

F. J. A. Skeet, *Life of sir Edward Widdrington and notices of his family.*

G.E.C., The *Complete Peerage*, vol.XII, pt. ii. Widdrington of Blankney, pp. 625-630.

J. W. Clay, *The extinct and dormant peerages of the Northern Counties of England* (1913). Widdrington, lords Widdrington, pp.248-252. This repeats many of Hodgson's inaccuracies and adds others.

W. Percy Hedley, *The Widdringtons of Widdrington. AA*4. XXXV, pp.1-6 with pedigree.

Somes Notes on Widdrington and the Widdringtons by W. H. D. Longstaffe in *AA*2. III, pp.189-196.

NCH. IV. Widdrington of West Swinburne pp.279-281; Widdrington of Colwell pp.294-296 with pedigree; Widdrington of Buteland pp.365-367 and Widdrington of Bullers Green with pedigree; Widdrington of Colt Park pp.213-214 with pedigree.

NCH. V. Widdrington of Hauxley pp.302-308 with pedigree.

NCH. VII. Widdrington of Felton pp.262-264 with pedigree.

NCH. XII. Widdrington of Cheeseburn Grange pp.323-328 with pedigree.

Miscellanea Genealogica et Heraldica (4th series), vol.iii, pp.158-161.

J. C. Hodgson, *A pedigree of Widdrington of Cheeseburn Grange* in *AA*3. VI, pp.34-40 with pedigree.

J. C. Hodgson's *MS pedigrees* in Newcastle Public Library: of Coltpark I, 140-143: of Hauxley I, 8; of Newcastle I, 10; pedigree by Radcliffe the herald II, 26, 30; of Hauxley II, 29, 103; of Cheeseburne Grange II, 433-434; of Cartington II, 436-439; of Cartington III, 132; of Newton-on-the-Moor (formerly Tinling) III, 1; of Cheeseburn Grange, A.184, 186; of Newcastle A.156, 158.

W. Percy Hedley, *Denton in Cumberland and Denton in Northumberland.* CW2. LIX, pp.151-152.

OGLE

THE family of Ogle, taking its name from the township and manor of Ogle in the parish of Whalton, can be traced from the middle of the 12th century to the present day. It has been the subject of a history entitled *Ogle and Bothal* by sir Henry Asgill Ogle, 7th baronet, printed privately, Newcastle upon Tyne, 1902.

About 1640 sir William Cavendish, 9th lord Ogle, 1st earl of Ogle and duke of Newcastle, instructed Roger Dodsworth of York, a well known antiquary, to prepare an account of his Ogle ancestors. Dodsworth entitled his work *The Ogle tree, or the descent of the very ancient family of the Barons Ogle of Northumberland, from a certain Humphrey—a very distinguished man, who lived and flourished about the time of William the Conqueror—properly extended and brought down in an unbroken succession to the time of our fathers.* An earlier pedigree was at one time inscribed in red characters on the south wall of the chancel of Bothal church. It was apparently based on the pedigree prepared for Cuthbert, lord Ogle, in 1575 by Flower, Norroy and Glover, Somerset Herald. It was nearly obliterated at the time of the Commonwealth, the church being mutilated by the Scots when they occupied Northumberland. A new copy of the pedigree was put up shortly after 1664 and this survived until repairs to the church were made in 1845-1850. A copy of the pedigree taken in 1725 has fortunately survived. It commences: 'The Genealogie or descent of the Noble Family of the Ogles. Humphrey Ogle Esquire lived at Ogle castle at the Conquest, to whom William the Conqueror by his deed without date did confirm unto him all his Liberties and Royalties of his Manoer and estate of Ogle; in as ample manner as any of his ancestors enjoyed the same before the time of the Normans, and from Humphrey Ogle Esquire did descend seven Lords and thirtie Knights'.

These early pedigrees were of course prepared for the prime purpose of extolling the great antiquity of the family and the merits of its members. It was therefore necessary for the manufacturer to have a powerful imagination. The fictitious charter ascribed to William the Conqueror was probably invented from the authentic charter of Walter son of William, baron of Whalton, who made a grant to Umfrid de Hoggel about the middle of the 12th century. The mention of 'Liberties and Royalties' suggests an invention of the 13th century to satisfy the requirements of *Quo Warranto* proceedings.

Dugdale (1676) states 'Of this family, which hath been of great antiquity in Northumberland, taking its surname from the lordship of Oggil, their principal seat there, was John de Oggil, whose lands were extended in 49 H.3 for his adherence to the rebellious barons of that age' (II, p.262). He had no further information about early members until the grant of free warren to Robert de Oggle in 1341.

Sir Henry Ogle's family history did not carefully distin-

guish fact from fiction, but it did collect together all references to members of the family from both public and private records. The amount of research work done by and for the author was truly stupendous. The introduction to *Ogle and Bothal* is largely concerned with attempting to arrive at a derivation of the name of Ogle and to prove an Anglo-Saxon origin for the family.

The first member of the family on record is Umfrid de Hoggel and he had been succeeded before 1166 by his son Gilbert de Hoggal. The use of such Christian names as Umfrid and Gilbert in the 12th century is a clear indication that the family was of Norman or French extraction. Most Christian names used by the Norman were either gallicized forms of old German names or else gallicized forms of Norse names. Umfrid is Old German Hunfrith, a compound of the folk name *Huni* and *frith* 'peace'. Similarly Gilbert is the Old German *gisil* 'pledge' and *berhta* 'bright'. Neither of these names appear in England before the Conquest, although there was an Old English Hunfrith, a cognate of the Old German name.

The inventor of the Anglo-Saxon origin of the Ogles was probably some Tudor herald. The fact that the pedigree formerly in Bothal church and that compiled by Roger Dodsworth both commence with Humphrey Ogle 'who lived and flourished about the time of William the Conqueror' and to whom William the Conqueror 'did confirm' the manor of Ogle, suggests that both are derived from the same original source.

OGLE OF OGLE, PAR. WHALTON

By an undated charter, Walter son of William, baron of Whalton, notified all his friends both present and future 'French and English that he concedes to Umfrid de Hoggel the making of his mill and all the multure of his lands in fee and inheritance to him and his heirs of the grantor and his heirs to hold freely and quietly with the remainder of his fee, dame I(sabella) grantor's wife assenting and witnessing'. The witnesses include Gilbert de Umfranvill, who was constable to the Scots earls of Northumberland *c*.1141 x *c*.1152; four Northumberland barons, William de Merlay (of Morpeth), John vicecomes (of Embleton), Richard Bertram (of Bothal) and William de Grenvill (of Ellingham); and three knights of the barony of Whalton, William de Insula, Robert de Newham and Bertram de Wuderinton (*NDD.* p.166, No. 1; also printed in *HN.* ii. I, p.387, No. 1 and in *Ogle and Bothal*, app.p.iv). William de Merlay, William de Grenvill and William de Insula were all dead in 1166 and it is possible that Grenvill had died before 1158. The date of the charter is probably between 1150 and 1158, and it is evident that Umfrid de Hoggel was already in possession of the manor of Ogle and is now getting authority for having his own manorial mill with the valuable right of multure for it.

The charter whereby Walter son of William confirmed to Bertram de Wuderinton the vill of Widdrington and half of Burradon is witnessed by many of the same persons as his charter to Umfrid de Hoggel. It is still before 1166 but perhaps shortly after the Ogle charter, say c.1155 x c.1158 (*NDD*. p.225, No. 1; it is also printed, rather inaccurately in *HN*. ii. II, p.248 evid.1). Sir Henry Ogle suggested that the earlier of these charters could be dated to *circa* 1125 and the later one to *circa* 1145 but he was very anxious to make it possible for Umfrid de Hoggel to be living in the time of William the Conqueror.

In 1166 Walter son of William reported to the king that Gilbert de Hoggel held half a knight's fee in his barony of the new feoffment. The Ogle family had therefore acquired Ogle since the death of Henry I in 1135. So much for the claim made on their behalf that they had lived at Ogle castle at the Conquest.

In 1170 Gilbert de Hoggel is charged one mark in the sheriff's roll for a concealed plea. His fine was carried forward to 1171 and then paid (*Pipe Roll*). Sometime between 1177 and 1182 Walter son of William, baron of Whalton made a grant of Gosforth to Robert de Insula, and his charter is witnessed by Gilbert de Ogel (*NDD*. p.121, No. 4). In 1181 Robert de Ogle was fined half a mark 'for not having him whom he had pledged'; *i.e.* he had failed to produce before the sheriff's court a person for whom he had given his name as a pledge. Robert is called son of Gilbert by Collins in his *Historical and Genealogical Collections of the families of Cavendish . . . and Ogle*, and Collins has presumably taken this from an early pedigree by Vincent (*Harl. MS*. 1554 *f.* 132b). Except where Collins or Vincent can be corroborated by contemporary documents their statements must be accepted with considerable caution. In another *Harleian MS*. (No. 1363) is the statement that 'In his Maties Rolles of the Pipe office it is recorded in the 27th year of king Henry the Second, and that amongst them of Northumberland, that Robert de Ogle was to bring fower pledges to be bound to the King that he should continue his true and loyall subject for defence of his Castle of Ogle against the Scotts'. The 27th year of Henry II is 1181 and the only mention of Robert de Ogle in the Pipe Roll for that year is his fine of half a mark mentioned above. The whole statement is suspect as it is quite unthinkable that the holder of half a knight's fee in the 12th century could have been the owner of a castle suitable for defence against the Scots.

It seems possible that the first Gilbert de Hoggel had died between 1171 and 1181 and had been succeeded by a Robert de Hoggel, but it cannot be taken as certain that Robert, living in 1181 was the head of the family. It is certain, however, that the owner of the manor of Ogle about 1204 was called Gilbert.

Walter son of William, baron of Whalton, seems to have died in 1188 leaving two daughters as his coheiresses, Constance wife of Ralph de Crammavill and Helewys wife of Richard de Camvill, the former succeeding to the Northumberland lands and the latter to lands in Leicestershire. Ralph de Crammavill died in 1198 and his widow survived until 1202. Sometime between these years, the widow Constance

gave half of Burradon to Gilbert de Oggell and when her son Robert de Cramavill succeeded to the barony he confirmed his mother's grant (*Brumell Charters* in *AA2*. XXIV, p.115). This confirmation must have been made about 1204; the name of Robert de Oggell appears as one of the witnesses to this confirmation.

Between 1203 and 1212 Gilbert Oggel witnesses an agreement between Alan son of William de Milleburne and Thomas de Divelestone (*Dur. Treas. Misc. Chart.* 5227). The jurors at an assize in 1208 found that William de Dauton had wrongfully and without judgment disseised John de Dauton of his free tenement in Dalton; the damage and the amercement were assessed at 2 marks 6 shillings by pledge of William de Coniers and Gilbert Oggel (*Nd Pleas*, No. 121). A charter, witnessed by Gilbert de Oggell, whereby Richard de Umframvill granted the vill of Ray to Peter de Insula and Margery his wife, can be dated to about this time (*NDD*. p.110, No. 77).

In 1219 Thomas Doggell was fined half a mark for a transgression. The debt remained charged against him in 1220 and 1221, and in the latter year Roger de Hogghill was charged half a mark by summons of Thomas de Hogghill (*Pipe Roll*). In 1221 Agnes widow of Gillebert de Hogghill, agreed to pay half a mark for having a *pone* with Reginald de Hogghill concerning land in Burradon. A *pone* was a writ to remove a cause from a lower court to the King's Bench at Westminster. Both Thomas Doggel's fine of ½m. and Agnes' ½m. for the *pone* were accounted for by the sheriff in his accounts for the year ended at Michaelmas 1222 (*Ib.*). At Trinity term 1222 Agnes Dogel at the *curia regis* claimed from Thomas de Oggel, guardian of the land and heir of Hugh de Oggel, 84 acres with the appurtenances in Burradon as appertaining to her dower which she holds of the free tenement which was sometime of the said Gilbert, her late husband. A compromise was arrived at whereby she remitted her claim and for this received from Thomas de Oggel 20s., of rent in his mill of Ogle to hold to her for the whole of her life by name of dower (*Cur. Reg. Roll*).

It is evident that at this time the heir to the manor of Ogle was under age and Thomas was his guardian. The latter was perhaps Thomas de Hoggel of Neu(ham) who with two other 'electors' essoined themselves a month from Hilary term 1229/30 in a suit concerning lands at Waskerley (*NRS*. II, p.100).

The Thomas and Roger de Hogghill of 1221 were apparently brothers. An undated deed relating to Stickley in Horton is witnessed by Thomas de Hogil and another deed also undated is witnessed by Thomas and by Roger his brother. It is difficult to arrive at any close dating of these two deeds but they cannot have been made much before or after 1230 (*Waterford Charters*, Nos. 14 and 69).

We are on surer ground in the second half of the 13th century. It is said that Thomas de Oggel had respite concerning the bearing of arms to Hilary term 25 H.III (1241) (*Close Roll* quoted in *Ogle and Bothal*, app.22). In 1242 it was reported by the heirs of John son of Robert, baron of Whalton, that Thomas de Oggill held of them Ogle and half of Burradon as 1½ knights' fees of old feoffment (*Book of Fees*). The statement that the holding was of old feoffment must be incorrect as in 1166 Gilbert de Hoggal had held of new feoffment.

Thomas de Oggell was one of four knights at Easter 1249

directed to make a view of land in the case of John Baard *versus* Waleran de Horton (*Assize Roll*). The four knights failed to put in an appearance and Thomas de Moggell (*sic*) was mainperned by Alexander de Morgel s. of Avice, William Neuery and Robert s. of Richard. The name 'Adam' has evidently been omitted before the words 's. of Avice'. In 1250 Thomas Oggel was fined 2 marks 'for not coming', and Alexander Oggel ½ m. 'for not having him whom he had pledged'. Both charges were carried forward for some years. In 1259 Thomas Oggel and Simon de Dyveston were charged 2m. 'for not having'. The latter debt was still unpaid in 1269 but was probably paid the next year (*Pipe Roll*).

The last mention of Thomas de Oggel is on 23 September 1263 when John de Midelton, Walter his son, Richard de Midelton and William his son made an agreement with him about the boundaries of Belsay (*NDD*. p.226, No. 4).

There were other persons of the name of Oggill about this time who were probably members of the family. In 1256 William de Madle (*recte* le Masle) was summoned by Roger son of Richard in a plea that he should hold to the agreement made between Simon son of William, kinsman of the said William de Madle whose heir he is, and Richard de Oggel father of the said Roger of a toft and 12 acres in Riplington (*SS*. 88, p.32). In 1241 Adam de Replinton quitclaimed to Gilbert de Ogle all right to a fourth part of the manor of Burradon and to 8s., rent issuing from the vill (*Feet of Fines* II.III, No. 108 in *NCH*. IX, p.45). Gilbert de Oggill occurs as a pledge in 1256 (*Ib*., p.22) and was a commissioner for the river Wansbeck in 1269 (*Ib*., p.208). In 1279 the executors of Alan Wodeman claimed a debt of 19s. 4d. from him (*Ib*., p.293). Gilbert forfeited his lands and in 1286 the sheriff was charged 100s. for issues of Gilbert's lands (*Pipe Roll*).

Sir Thomas de Oggel's heir was his son John. In 1269 John was one of four knights in a plea of service in Edlingham; they chose twelve others to form a jury, one of them being another John de Oggylle (*NRS*. II, p.137). At Hilary term 1271/2 John Oggel and William his brother were charged by Hugh de Eure that with force and arms they came to Hugh's manor of Kirkley and beat and evil entreated his men whom they found there, doing damage to the extent of 100s.; the sheriff was instructed to distrain John by his lands and to take William into custody and to have both of them before the king three weeks from Easter (*Ib*., p.306). This sounds more like an escapade of the young son than of the father who after all was a knight and a man of some standing in the county. It was probably also the younger John who in 1279 was arrested for the death of Isabella daughter of Alan son of Martin de Corbrigge; twelve jurors from Corbridge found him not guilty (*SS*. 88, p.340). By a deed dated when sir John de Kirkby was sheriff, 1296/7, John son of Thomas de Oggill settled a carucate of land in his demesnes of Ogle on his son Robert and the heirs of his body (*NDD*. p.166, No. 3). John is presumably called 'son of Thomas' to distinguish him from this John. At Whalton, on the Friday next after the nativity of St John the Baptist, 26 June 1304, John son of John de Oggell recorded that he owed his father sir John 100 marks (*Ib*., p.167, No. 5).

The younger John de Oggle was probably the man of this name, who with Agnes his wife, Simon Warde and Alicia his wife and Thomas de Belsowe and Maria his wife, was plaintiff in 1315 against Ralph Buteturt and Johanna his wife, about

lands in Shilvington (*de Banco Roll*). This might suggest that John's wife was one of the heiresses to Shilvington, a place that long remained a possession of the Ogles.

In 30 E.I. (1301/2) Robert son of John de Oggle settled six messuages, one carucate and 50 acres of land and 3 acres of meadow with appurtenances in Ogle on John de Denum and John de Oggle (*Ib*., p.166, No. 4). On 29 December 1304 sir John de Oggill confirmed to Robert his son, and his own heirs lawfully begotten all the land of Northstrother in his field of Ogle (*Ib*., p.167, No. 6). The Ogles had further dealings with the family of Denum of Deanham which might suggest some marriage connection between the two families. On 18 September 1309, sir John gave to William de Denum all the meadow in Ogle called Milnefordhagh, to hold for life (*Ib*., p.167, No. 7). Sir John gave to Isabel his daughter lands in Newham which he had of the gift and feoffment of the lady Elen de Newham, which land had formerly belonged to Roger son of Roger Steyward (*Ib*., p.167, No. 10). He gave his son Robert six acres in the fields of Ogle in 1312/3.

After sir John's death, his widow Annabel released and quitclaimed to her son Robert all the right which she had in the way of dowry; the release is witnessed by sir John de Fenwike whilst he was sheriff 1319-1323 or 1325-1326. Still whilst sir John de Fenwike was sheriff, Annabel quitclaimed to her son Robert all the manor of Ogle, reserving for the term of her life the chapel of the manor (*Ib*., p.167, No. 12). According to Glover, Annabel was a daughter of sir Walter Selby, but no confirmation of this has been found.

Hodgson in the introduction to his pedigree of Ogle admits that he has largely used Glover's pedigree of 1575 but is careful to state that the earlier part of Glover's pedigree is at variance with the evidences which Hodgson himself had consulted. In correlating Glover's pedigree with that compiled by Dugdale he found that the latter was confused and contradictory in the 14th century but thought that this period was the most interesting part of the pedigree. Throughout the 14th century and well into the 15th century the eldest son in each generation was called Robert and genealogists have found it difficult to attribute to each Robert his own proper actions. In this connection Hodgson made a great improvement on earlier pedigrees.

Robert de Oggil I acquired lands in Fowberry from John de Malton at Martinmas 1327 (*NDD*. p.168, No. 15). On 3 August 1328 by indenture he released to sir John de Lilleburn all actions etc (*Ib*., No. 16). He received a royal pardon for all homicides, felonies, etc., on 28 March 1329 (*Pat. Rolls*, 3 E.III, 1327-30, p.475). By a charter dated at Westminster on 11 May 1341 Edward III gave to Robert de Ogle for his good services in the march of Scotland, free warren in all his demesne lands in Ogle, Aydonshields, Rowley, Shilvington, Hazelrigg and Fowberry, Thirston and Hurworth; at the same time he had licence to crenellate his house at Ogle. (*Cal. Charter Rolls* V, p.4; the original charter is now *B.M. Cott.* Ch. xvii, 13). The lands in Hurworth, co. Durham, had been acquired by the marriage of Robert de Ogle and Joan daughter of Robert de Heppale. This marriage had taken place before 10 May 1331 when Robert de Heppale had received royal licence to settle lands in Great Tosson and Nether Trewhit, a moiety of the manor of Hepple, a knight's fee in Little Tosson, Flotterton, Warton and Upper Trewhit, and the advowson of a moiety of the hospital of St Leonard of Alriborn;

the settlement was on Thomas Styward, chaplain, in trust for Robert de Heppale for life, remainder to Robert de Ogle and Joan his wife in tail (*Cal. Pat. Rolls*, 1330-34, p.112; *NDD*. p.171, No. 24).

It would seem that we have here two distinct persons, father and son. The elder Robert de Ogle was old enough in 1296/7 for his father sir John to settle lands on him, and in 1301/2 to make a settlement himself. Sir John was still alive in 1312/3 and the date of his death is not known. Robert de Ogle I was presumably the person of this name who had dealings with John de Malton in 1327 and with sir John de Lilleburn in 1328. It must have been his son, Robert de Ogle II who married Joan de Hephale. When her father settled lands on them in 1331 they may have been married for some time, for their grandson Robert de Ogle IV was three years old in 1355. Hodgson, following Brand (*Hist. Newc.* II, p.399) states that Robert de Ogle I married Margaret daughter and heir of sir Hugh Gubium, and 'By this match the estates of North Middleton, Longwitton and Shilvington, therefore, probably came to the Ogle family'. There does not appear to be any evidence for this marriage. On 24 January 1323 Richard de Ogle of Wutton (Longwitton) granted to Roger de Redesdale a toft, 16 acres of land and 2 acres of meadow in Longwitton, and on the same day there was a release of the same by Richard's son John, and confirmations by his daughters Joan and Elizabeth (*NDD*. p.168, Nos. 13 and 14; the originals are now *B.M. Cott.* Ch.xxviii, Nos. 26-29). When Robert de Ogle II died in 1362 he held lands in North Middleton, Longwitton and Shilvington.

In 1338/9 Christiana de Acton widow of Hugh de Acton gave to Robert de Ogle, lord of Ogle, a messuage and lands in the vill of Whalton (*NDD*. p.171, No. 26). This was probably Robert de Ogle II. He continued to acquire lands in various parts of the county. On 11 August 1341 he had from Thomas de Burneton a quitclaim to him and his heirs of all right and claim which he had in Seaton next Woodhorn and a fishery in the water of Wansbeck (*Ib.*, p.172, No. 28). Adam Vaus of Beaufront on 21 December 1341 gave him all his lands in Twizel, and in 1349 Mary daughter and one of the heirs of Thomas Thorald of Newcastle quitclaimed to him all the rights which she had in the manor of Twizel (*Ib.*, Nos. 29 and 34). On 22 November 1342 Richard de Saltwyke gave and confirmed to Robert de Ogle all his manor of Saltwick (*Ib.*, No. 30). On 16 March 1343 William son of William de Denum remitted to Robert de Ogle all the right which he had in all the lands which Adam Multinge and Robert de Mydsted held in the vill of Ogle of sir John de Ogle (*Ib.*, No. 31).

Robert de Oggle 'senior' gave a letter of attorney on 15 August 1351 to William Byset and Robert de Oggle 'junior' to take seisin of the manor of 'Thirneham' (Farnham) and the following day he had a conveyance of the manor from William de Aketon of Newcastle (*Ib.*, p.172, No. 35, and p.173, No. 36). On the feast of St Luke Evangelist (18 October) 1351 sir John de Ogle gave to Robert de Oggle 'senior' all his lands in Shilvington; this sir John was probably son of that Richard de Ogle who had dealings in lands at Longwitton in 1323 (*Ib.*, p.173, No. 37). Robert de Ogle acquired other lands in Shilvington, being a twelfth part of the manor, from Thomas de Fenwyke and Joan his wife; the Fenwicks confirmed the conveyance on Monday before SS. Simon and Jude (26 October) 1360, one of the witnesses to the confirma-

tion being Thomas de Oggle (*Ib.*, No. 41). Thomas de Oggle was Robert's younger son. At Michaelmas 1352 Robert gave to Thomas his son, and to Robert [de] Harun chaplain, John de Wauton and John son of Richard de Fallowfield all his lands and tenements in the vills of Ogle, Shilvington, Saltwick, Twizel, Seaton by Woodhorn, Longwitton and Farnham; William de Heppescotes was appointed to deliver seisin. This is evidently a settlement and the grantees were to pay to Robert £1000 a year (*Ib.*, p.173, No. 38).

So far we have only dealt with the land transactions of Robert de Ogle I and II. The evidences for these are mainly taken from the *Dodsworth MSS* and Dodsworth found them 'Among the charters of the nobleman William, earl of Newcastle, 30 September 1641'. In none of these charters is either of the Ogles referred to as 'knight' although both of them were prominent in border affairs.

In 1335 Robert Oggle and others were instructed to array the militia at Newcastle, but the instructions were cancelled on 13 May. In the same year as bailiff of the lordship of Tyndale, he was deputed, 25 November, to raise all men capable of bearing arms in Hexhamshire (*Rot. Scot.* I, pp.327, 289). When David Bruce laid siege to Newcastle in 1341 'some gentlemen of the neighbourhood, who were in the town, made a sally out of one of the gates, in a secret manner, with about 200 lances, to make an attack upon the Scots army. They fell upon one of the wings of the army, directly on the quarters of the earl of Moray', whom they took prisoner. This is Froissart's account of the episode (*Chron.* I, chap. LXXII). It is known that at this time king David's headquarters were at Heddon Laws, for John de Denton, a Newcastle burgess, was accused of having arranged to supply the Scots army with provisions 'the time when David le Bruys lay upon Heddon-laws with his army, on Sunday after the feast of St Bartholomew Apostle' (26 August), 1341. Wyntoun in his *Chronicle of Scotland* may be referring to the same episode when he mentions that five knights were taken prisoner through the strategy of sir Robert Ogle, but it sounds more like what happened at Neville's Cross a few years later.

On 10 May 1344 and again on 10 April 1345 Robert de Ogle was appointed a commissioner of array (*Rot. Scot.* I, pp.649, 660). In 1345 'upon that great incursion by the Scots, the Scots were opposed by a chosen body of men collected by the bishop of Carlisle, sir Thomas Lucy and sir Robert Ogle'. Ogle accompanied the bishop 'in a charge which he made upon a strong party of those bold invaders: and encountering with Alexander Stragan, their chief commander (spurring on a horse) ran him into the side with his lance; but was sore wounded himself also, the bishop being likewise unhorsed, but valiantly recovering his saddle, escaped the danger' (Dugdale II, p.262).

We cannot be certain whether it was Robert de Ogle I or his son Robert de Ogle II who, as seneschal of Annandale, was ordered on 9 May 1346 to keep Lochmaben castle for one year. The dates would, however, suggest that it was the son, and it seems likely that it was also the younger Robert who was present at the battle of Neville's Cross, fought on 17 October 1346. Ridpath in his account of the battle (*Border History*, p.337), after describing the four divisions that comprised the English army goes on to say 'Besides the forces above related, a strong and gallant party under the command of lords Deincourt and Ogle, guarded queen Philippa'. Ridpath admits that the statement that queen Philippa assembled the army 'depends entire upon the credit of Froissard' (*Ib.*, p.337n.). It is certain that queen Philippa was not present at Neville's Cross and it is known that Robert Ogle was not a lord. Froissart's account of the battle (vol.I, chap. CXXXVII) mentions the four divisions of the English army and the divisional commanders; he says nothing about the party guarding the queen. He relates how after the battle John Copeland, who had captured David Bruce, conveyed the captive king to 'Ogle castle, on the river Blythe, and there declared that he would not surrender his prisoner, the king of Scotland, to man or woman except to his lord the king of England'. The statement made by Ridpath that Copeland was governor of the castle of Ogle is obviously inaccurate. Rymer (V,533) tells us that Ogle took prisoner John Douglas, brother to the earl, the earl of Fife, Henry de Ramsay and Thomas Boyd. Robert de Ogle was one of the principal men of the north who had special letters of thanks addressed by the regent and on 8 December 1346 he and Robert Bertram had a royal writ concerning the conducting of John Douglas, prisoner, to the Tower.

It would seem that Robert de Ogle and others who had taken prisoners at Neville's Cross were very tardy in handing over their captives, no doubt expecting to receive ransom for them. On 28 January 1347 the king wrote to the sheriffs of Northumberland and of other northern counties complaining that although the prisoners should have been delivered to the Tower before Wednesday in the Epiphany this had not been done. The sheriffs were to take Robert Ogle and others and keep them in the prison of the castle of Newcastle until the king should otherwise ordain.

Robert de Oggle had a daughter Joan who married William de Swynburn of Capheaton. William's father William de Swynburn settled the manor of Capheaton on them on 10 January 1352/3, the settlement being witnessed by Robert de Oggle senior, Robert de Oggle junior and others. At this time neither of the Oggles were knights (*Swinburn Charters* 4/22).

By writ dated 28 July 1356 Edward III informed Robert de Ogele that he had appointed Henry de Percy and Ralph de Nevile jointly and separately as Wardens of the Marches of the kingdom of England in the borders of the county of Northumberland. He commanded Ogle to support, help and obey the wardens and their deputies in everything pertaining to the safety and secure guardianship of the county, in his own person with men at arms, hobelars and archers as many as he can to repulse the enemies and for the defence of security of the kingdom (*Ib.*, 1/68).

The writ for the *i.p.m.* of Robert de Ogle II is dated 18 July 1362 on which day the escheator was commanded to take his lands into the king's hands. The inquisition cannot now be read, except that he died on Thursday, the feast of Corpus Christi, 36th year (16 June 1362), and Robert, the heir will be nine years old at the feast of the Nativity of the Lord. According to the escheator's accounts, Ogle was seised of lands in Saltwick, Ogle, Twizel, Shilvington, 'Aldeworthe', Longwitton, Seaton Woodhorn, Farnham, Fowberry, North Middleton, Dissington, 'Aldesheles', 'Roulay' and the 'Wall-felde'. On 22 October custody of the lands was granted to John Philippot and Joan his wife. Other *i.p.m.*'s were taken at Doncaster on 9 May 1363 and at Carlisle on 7 January

1364/5. The former records that sir Richard de Denton held the manor of Thursby in Cumberland of Robert Ogle, lately deceased, and the right of reversion descended to Robert son of Robert son of the said Robert. At Carlisle the jurors found that Robert Ogle had been seised of Thoresby after marriage with Joan his wife, and the manor was demised to sir Richard de Denton, except 98 acres.

By writ dated 13 November 1364 the widow Joan was to have dower out of Thoresby. She died 19 March 1364/5 seised of half the manor of Hepple by enfeoffment of Thomas Styward, chaplain; she held in dower a messuage in Saltwick.

Robert de Ogle III, son of Robert de Ogle II, died in 1355 in his father's lifetime. An *i.p.m.* taken at Sadberge, co. Durham, 4 July 1355, found that he held of the bishop jointly with Elena his wife, a moiety of the manor of Hurworth-on-Tees, except one rood and the advowson of the church, to her and her heirs, by gift of Robert de Oggell the elder. Robert, son of the said Robert, was his next heir and aged three years. Robert de Ogle III married Elena daughter and heiress of sir Robert Bertram, baron of Bothal. Elena made her will 29 July 1403 in which she mentions her sons sir Robert Ogle and John Bertram.

The elder son, sir Robert Ogle IV, did not become of age until 48 E.III (1374/5) when an inquisition was taken at Newcastle for proof of his age. Geoffrey Faule deposed that Robert had been born at Callerton on the Feast of the Conception of the Virgin 27 E.III (1353/4) and baptised in the parish church of Ponteland; he remembered the day because he was in the church when the said Robert was baptised, and William his brother was buried that day. Robert de Eland recollected the day because in going towards Ponteland, he met Alice the wife of Robert Short, godmother of the baby carrying him from the church to Callerton. John de Brampton, Robert de Belingham, William de Hedwyn and John de Ogle had been in Newcastle in the company of Robert, father of the child, when news was brought to him of the birth of his son, and he gave the messenger a horse for his labour. Thomas Ayre was at Bothal with sir Robert Bertram, the child's grandfather, when a messenger arrived with news of the birth of the said Robert son of Robert de Ogle; the grandfather was so pleased with the news that he gave the bearer of the good tidings a husbandland in 'Staunton' to hold for his life (*AA1. IV, p.327*).

On 27 May 1360 William Acton of Newcastle, merchant, founded the monastery of the house of Trinitarians in Newcastle for the repose of the souls of lord Edward, by the Grace of God, king of England and France, and for his progenitors and heirs; for the health of his own body and soul and those of Mary his wife, Robert de Oggell, William del Strother and Robert de Angerton; and for the health of the souls of William [de] Thorald and Dionisia his wife, and those of William de Aketon his father, Isolda wife of William de Aketon and mother of the founder, of John, Thomas, Walter, 'Edae', 'Adae', Edmund, William, Peter and all the founder's antecessors, benefactors and friends and their successors and all the faithful dead (Welford I. p.158). There may have been some family relationship between the Aketons, Thoralds and Ogles for the Ogles acquired the manor of Twisel from the Thoralds in 1349 and the manor of Farnham in 1351 from the Actons.

By deed poll given at Ogle on the feast of St Michael (29

September) 1352 Robert de Ogle II declared that he had appointed William de Heppescotes as attorney to deliver seisin in his name to Thomas Ogle his son, Robert Harun chaplain, and others, of all his lands, tenements, rents and services in the vills of Ogle, Shilvington, Saltwick, Twizel, Seaton by Woodhorn, Witton and Farnham. The grantees were to render to Robert the grantor, the sum of £1000 a year. The reserved rent must have been very much more than the total rents of the property so it would seem that the figure is being used to cover all the income up to £1000 a year.

Robert de Ogle's younger son Thomas occupied the Cumberland manor of Thursby from his father's death in 1362 but in 1366 it was found by inquisition that it should be the property of Robert son of Robert son of Robert de Ogle.

Sir Robert de Ogle IV is the first of his name that we can be sure was a knight. Although proof of his age was taken in 1374/5 the date of his birth is by no means certain. At the inquisition for the proof of his age it was deposed that he was born on the Feast of the Conception of the Virgin 27 E.III (1353/4); this should be 8 December 1353. When his father died in 1355 he was said to have been three years old (*i.e.* born 1352). When his grandfather died it was stated that he would be nine years old at Christmas 1362 (*i.e.* born 1353). He was aged 14 in 1368 (born 1354). The most detailed statement is that which says he was aged 21 years and 16 days on 24 December 1372, in which case he would have been born on 8 December 1351.

Sir Robert de Ogle IV married Joan youngest of the three daughters and coheiresses of sir Alan Heton (d.1387) of Chillingham. By this marriage the Ogles acquired lands in Lowick, Ingram, Tritlington and Unthank. A partition of the Heton lands was made on 24 May 1389. In 1399 Sir Robert Ogle and Joan his wife entailed lands in Lowick on their sons Alexander, Robert and John successively. These lands eventually came into the possession of John Ogle—see OGLE OF WHISTON, Lancs. On 10 July 1386 sir Robert was appointed conservator of the truce between England and Scotland. In February 1387 Walter Tayleboys conveyed to sir Robert Ogle and William Thymelby four husbandlands in Hepple in exchange for a moiety of the manor of Hurworth-on-Tees, except the advowson of Hurworth church (*NDD*. p.221, No. 6). His mother's fourth husband David Holgrave, died in 1405, and he did homage for the castle and barony of Bothal which were of her inheritance. On 2 January 1407 he settled on his second son, John, who had assumed the surname Bertram, a rent of £200 a year out of the castle and manor of Ogle, the manor of Shilvington, Saltwick, the vill of Twisel, Seaton by Woodhorn, Longwitton, North Middleton, Hepple, Great Tosson, Flotterton and Lorbottle (*Ib.*, p.176, No. 55). Sir Robert de Ogle, senior, leased the manor and castle of Bothal for a term of 20 years at a rent of £80 a year to his younger son John Bertram, and shortly afterwards, on 21 March 1409, he settled the Bothal lands on him in tail male (*Ib.*, No. 56).

Sir Robert Ogle IV died on 31 October 1410. The date of his will has been wrongly transcribed as 7 February 1410 (*SS*. 2, p.47), but must have been made a year earlier. By his will he directs that he is to be buried in the parish church of Whalton in the porch of the Blessed Mary, and he leaves to the rector of the said church for tithes and oblations 40s. Two honest and upright chaplains are, for twelve years, to pray for his soul, that of his wife Johanna, and those of all their par-

ents and benefactors, and their salaries are to be paid out of the rents of his lands in North Middleton, Deanham, Hartington and Fernylaw. The friars mendicant of Newcastle upon Tyne are to have 20s. He leaves to William Karre all his lands and tenements in the vill of Heaton by Newcastle, for the term of his life, and William Scryvane for his lifetime is to have all the lands and tenements which he had in Fowberry. His son Robert Ogill is given a horse 'in English called Gray gelding' and two mares with their followers, whilst his other son John Barthram is left a sword and two mares with their followers. Sir John Clavering, John Blenkensoppe, Alexander Heron, Robert Raymus and Thomas son of Robert Hibburn of Newcastle are each to have two mares and their followers to be distributed by Johanna his wife. The executors of his will, sir John Clavering, John Barthram, John Blenkensop and sir William Thymylby, rector of Bothal, are each to have a colt and 40s., for their trouble. Administration was granted on 26 August (1411) to his two sons, sir Robert Ogle and John Barthram, the other executors renouncing.

Sir Robert was buried in Hexham Priory church in a chapel that was destroyed during the church alterations of 1858-60.

His tomb slab with a portion of the brass and parts of the wooden lattices remains in the church. The inscription on the slab runs *Hic jacet Robertus Ogle, filius Elene Bertram, filie Roberti Bertram militis, qui obiit in vigilia omnium, sanctorum, anno domini mccccx., cujus anime propicietur Deus. Amen* (*NCH*. III, p.193n., where the date is wrongly transcribed).

On 4 November 1400 Robert Ogle, esquire, had a grant of 100 marks out of the customs of Newcastle in aid of his ransom when taken prisoner by the Scots. He was only a little over twenty years old when this happened, and the particular encounter with the Scots has not been identified. The following year he was summoned with his father to attend the king's council at Westminster. On 2 February 1403 he is described as son of sir Robert Ogle when he was appointed constable of Norham castle and sheriff of Norhamshire and Islandshire for seven years; later in the year, on 6 September his appointment was extended for life. When his father died in 1410 he was aged 30 years and more, and received livery of his father's lands on 12 May 1410 (*NDD*. p.177, No. 57).

Robert Ogle was greatly incensed that his younger brother John had been given the barony of Bothal and the valuable estates that went with it. On 13 February 1410 John presented a petition to parliament complaining that his brother Robert with two hundred armed men and archers laid siege to Bothal castle and forcibly took, occupied and held it, notwithstanding that at the time of the siege and assault, sir John de Wedrington and Sampson Hardyng, justices of the peace in the county, had commanded them to cease (*Rot. Parl.* iii, p.629; *NDD*. p.178, No. 65). In May 1410 with others he was appointed a commissioner with the duke of Albany on matters between England and Scotland, and later in the year, on 5 July, he was made a commissioner for array.

He was a commissioner to treat for a truce with Scotland in 1411. With others he was to treat with the duke of Albany on 19 July 1413 and again on 5 August 1413. In 1415 Robert Ogill, *chevalier*, held the castles of Ogle and Sewingshields, the 'fortalice' of Flotterton and the towers of North Middleton, Newstead and Hepple. Sir Robert was knight of the shire for Northumberland in 1416, 1420, 1421 and 1425; he was sheriff in 1417. He was constable of Wark castle in 1419 when it was taken by the Scots but he recovered it before the end of the year. On 28 March 1424 sir Robert was one of the embassy to conduct king James of Scotland from Durham into Scotland. He was made warden of Roxburgh castle 17 July 1424 for three years at a salary of £1000 a year in time of peace and £2000 in time of war.

Sir Robert died on 13 August 1436.

In the herald's visitation of *circa* 1480-1500 a later hand has entered the wife of sir Robert de Ogle V as Matilda daughter of sir John Gray; the pedigree of 1563/4 calls him sir John Grey, earl of Tankervyle and lord Powes. Hodgson calls her daughter of sir Robert Grey of Horton. All these identifications are incorrect. In *Ogle and Bothal* sir Robert de Ogle's wife is called Matilda daughter of sir Thomas Grey of Heton, and this is confirmed by a charter of 21 May 1399 whereby sir Thomas Gray granted to Robert de Ogle, son and heir of sir Robert de Ogle, and to Maud his daughter, wife of the said Robert, lands in Lowick called Sammesland (*Brumell Charters* in *AA2*. XXIV, p.118). Sir John Gray was a younger son of sir Thomas and had the foreign title of count of Tankerville.

The family of sir Robert de Ogle V by his wife Matilda was three sons and seven daughters. The sons were Robert, his eldest son and heir, John (*see* OGLE OF WHISTON, Lancs), and William (*see* OGLE OF CHOPPINGTON). The daughters are given in the pedigrees of *circa* 1480-1500 and 1563/4 as:

i. Margaret; wife firstly of sir Robert Herbottell (corrected from Gray) and secondly of (blank) Bellingham. On 14 June 1424 sir Robert de Ogle and sir John Bertram made an agreement with dame Isabel, widow of Robert Herbottel, esquire, and Robert Herbottell son and heir of the said Robert, for the marriage of the said Robert Herbotell the son and Margery daughter of the said Robert de Ogle (*NDD*. p.152, No. 39). On 20 August 1424 sir Robert de Ogle gave to Robert Herbotell son and heir of Robert Herbotell, esquire, deceased, and Margery, grantor's daughter, wife of the said Robert the son, lands in the fields of Ellingham (*Ib.*, p.153, No. 40).

ii. (blank); wife firstly of sir William Heron of Ford, and secondly of sir John de Mydelton. In the 1563/4 pedigree she is called Ann, but in fact her name was Elizabeth, for on 13 January 1411/2 sir William Heron of Ford had dispensation to marry Elizabeth daughter of sir Robert Ogle to whom he was related in the 4th degree (*SS*. 45, p.321). Heron was killed 20 January 1428, and his widow married sir John de Middleton of Belsay.

iii. (blank); called Johanna in the 1563/4 pedigree; wife of Robert Manners, esquire, who was living in 1462.

iv. Constance wife of John, son of sir John Mydford.

v. (blank) wife of John Lilburne. John de Lilburn, son and heir of Thomas de Lilburn (d.1438) of West Lilburn was aged 23 in 1438.

vi. (blank) wife of Thomas Lille. This is presumably Thomas Lisle of Felton, aged 13 in 1426 and 21 in 1434. In 17 H.VI (1438/9) Thomas Lyle, *armiger*, conveyed the manor and vill of Felton to sir Robert Ogle and John Swinburne, presumably as trustees for a settlement; the deed is witnessed by sir John Bartram, John Ogle esq., and William Muscham (*NDD*. p.132, No. 35).

vii. (blank) wife of Matthew Whitfield. Sir Matthew Whitfield owned a tower at Whitfield in 1415 and was sheriff of Northumberland in 1433.

Sir Robert Ogle VI had started his military career on the Border in his father's lifetime. In 1434 he and his father were appointed commissioners to prevent violations of the truce with Scotland (*Rot. Scot.* II, p.286). The following year he is described as sir Robert Ogle the younger, captain of Berwick, when he was defeated in an engagement with the Scots at Piperden and taken prisoner (Ridpath, p.400). Three years later there was a dispute about the compensation due to him for being held to ransom for 750 marks; it was agreed that he should be indemnified with a Scottish ship seized at Newcastle, but this had already been sold and as late as 1442 sir Robert was in dispute with the admiral's lieutenant who had made the sale.

When his father died in 1436 sir Robert Ogle was said to have been aged thirty years and more. Immediately after his father's death he was appointed, 24 August 1436, constable of Norham castle, seneschal, sheriff and escheator in Norhamshire and Islandshire for 20 years. On 2 November 1439 the appointment was extended for his lifetime. He was on numerous commissions for conserving truces with Scotland and arraying the forces of Northumberland when invasion by the Scots was threatened. In 1438 he was appointed captain of Roxburgh castle and in that year and the year following he was warden ot the East Marches.

In the Wars of the Roses sir Robert was a Yorkist and was rewarded with a grant of the forfeited lordship of Redesdale. He was summoned on 26 July 1461 to the first parliament of Edward IV as baron Ogle. On 8 August 1461 he had a grant for life in the offices of seneschal and constable of the lordships and castles of Alnwick, Warkworth, Prudhoe, Rothbury and Newburn which had been forfeited by the earl of Northumberland. The same year he was made Warden-general of the East Marches and was ordered to take into the king's hands various castles which had been held by Lancastrians and 'to crush any of the county of Northumberland who may resist'.

On 20 April 1467 'Robert, lord of Ogle and Redesdale' and Owin his son leased a tenement in Morpeth to Thomas Spire for a term of 100 years (*NDD*. p.179, No. 71). Under the same description he gave a letter of attorney 26 May 1467 for livery of seisin of the manor of North Middleton to Evan his son and heir and Alianor his wife.

Robert, 1st lord Ogle, married Isabel daughter and heiress of sir Alexander Kirkby of Kirkby Ireleth in Lancashire. 'On the second day of the month of January' 1477/8 lady Ogle made her will. She is 'to be buried in the monastery of St Andrew of Hexham, with my due and accustomed rights'. All her lands in Lancashire she bequeaths 'to John Wedryngton, esquire, and Isabel, my daughter and his wife, and to John Heron of Chipchase, esquire, son of the said Isabel'. The will was proved by the commissary of the lord bishop of Durham in the church of Gateshead on 5 February 1477/8 (*Ib.*, No. 74).

The children of lord Ogle and his wife Isabel were three sons, Robert, Thomas and Owen and a daughter Isabel. The daughter married firstly sir John Heron of Chipchase and secondly sir John Widdrington. An inquisition taken at Bedlington on 24 July 1449 found that sir Robert Ogle and his brother Thomas had on 24 June by force of arms taken oxen, sheep and other goods from the bishop of Durham's liberty of West Sleekburn and Cambois. For this episode sir Robert was outlawed, and if Thomas was the man of this name who was living with Andrew Crawford at Edinburgh in 1456, he also may have been outlawed. Sir Henry Percy and Robert Manners had a joint grant of the goods and chattels of the outlawed sir Robert Ogle. Sir Robert was soon pardoned for in 1459 he and his father were ambassadors to Scotland.

The visitation pedigree of *circa* 1480-1500 of Greystoke states that Elizabeth daughter of Roger Thornton of Newcastle married sir Robert Ogle and died *s.p.* (*SS.* 144, p.111). Hodgson accepted this marriage as a fact but changed Elizabeth's name to Johanna. No doubt he made this change because on 14 January 1460 Robert Ogle, senior, knight, settled in tail on Robert Ogle, knight, his son and Joan his wife, a rent out of a messuage in the Close in Newcastle (*NDD.* p.179, No. 69). In *Ogle and Bothal* it is inferred that Johanna was daughter of sir William Eure of Kirkley. In the pedigree of *circa* 1480-1500 of Eure (Yvers) it is stated that Johanna daughter of sir Ralph Yvers first married sir Robert de Ogle and afterwards John de Pennyngton. Actually Johanna's father was sir William de Eure. On 15 October 1472 John Pennington had a dispensation to marry Joan widow of sir Robert Ogle (*SS.* 45, p.341). Matilda widow of sir William Evers by her w.d. 12 February 1466/7 left a piece of silver plate to her daughter Johan Ogle (*SS.* 30. p.284). It is evident therefore that sir Robert Ogle junior married firstly Elizabeth Thornton who died *s.p.*, and secondly Johanna Eure; in 1472 after sir Robert's death his widow married John Pennington.

When Robert, 1st lord Ogle, died in 1469 he was succeeded by his eldest surviving son Owen. Inquisitions after his death were taken at Carlisle on 5 February 1469/70 and at Newbiggen three days later. In Cumberland he held Thursby and the jurors recorded that he died 1 November last and Ewin Ogle is his son and heir, aged 30 years. In Northumberland he held in fee the manors of Hepple and Ogle, Twizel, the manor of Shilvington, half the manor of Thirnham, Fowberry, one third of Ingram, Horsley, twelve burgages in Bamburgh, Newhall, Clifton, East Hartington and Morpeth; he held in fee tail heirs male the lordship and liberty of Redesdale and the castle, manor and borough of Harbottle by grant dated 16 April 1465 worth only £20 a year by reason of destruction by the Scots. The jurors at Newbiggen also recorded that Robert, lord Ogle, died 1 November 1469 and that Ewin Ogle, his son and next heir, was aged 30 years and more.

The Christian name of the 2nd lord Ogle appears in many different forms—Owen, Owin, Ewan, Ewyn and Ewin. On 9 March 1470 Owin Ogle, lord of Ogle, settled on his uncle John Ogle for his lifetime the manor of North Middleton (*NDD.* p.179, No. 73). On 21 January 1485 he made a settlement of the castle of Ogle with the demesne lands, the trustees being sir Guy Fairfax, justice of the king's bench, sir Robert Constable, sir John Pekering, sir Christopher Ward and sir Robert Plumpton (*Ib.*, p.180, No. 75). Ewin Ogle, baron, son and heir of sir Robert Ogle, and John Swinburne, released to Humfrey Lile, esq., all right in the manor and vill of Felton which they had of the gift of Thomas Lyle, esq., grandfather of Humfrey. This is evidently a release of the trusteeship created in 17 H.VI (1438/9); the date is uncertain, Hodgson printing it with date 3 H.VII (from *Harl. MSS.*

2101; *HN.* ii, I, p.169, evid. 11) but in Dodsworth it is dated 2 R.III (1484/5) (*NDD.* p.132, No. 36).

According to Dugdale (*Baronage* II, p.263) this Owen is the same person whom Polydorus Virgil, by mistake, calls George, who was in the battle of Stoke *juxta* Newark in 2 H.VII (16 June 1486) on behalf of that king against John, earl of Lincoln, and his adherents. As lord Ogle died 1 September that same year, it is possible that he had been wounded in the battle. His wife was Aleonora daughter of sir William Hilton of Hilton, co. Durham; the marriage probably took place shortly before 26 May 1467 when Robert, lord of Ogle and Redesdale, gave a letter of attorney to John Whitfield, senior, esq., and Robert Whitfield to deliver seisin to Ewan, his son and heir, and Alianore his wife of the manor of North Middleton (*NDD.* p.179, No. 72).

After her first husband's death, Alianore, lady Ogle, married George Percy, third son of sir Ralph Percy, seventh son of Henry, second earl of Northumberland. On 4 July 1491 George Percy and lady Eleanor his wife, late wife to Ewyn, lord Ogle, released to Ralph, lord Ogle, all right in the lands which Eleanor had in the name of a dowry throughout the whole kingdom of England (*Ogle and Bothal*, app. 90). On 1 July 1513 dame Eleanor, widow, and Robert, lord Ogle, gave lands in Alnwick fields to Thomas Tood (?), prior of Brinkburn (*Ogle and Bothal* has the date 1518 but Dodsworth is probably right in dating it to 1513.—*NDD.* p.181, No. 83).

Owen, 2nd lord Ogle, was succeeded by his eldest son Ralph as 3rd lord Ogle, who was aged 18 in 1486. According to the visitation pedigree of 1563/4 there was a younger son Robert and a daughter Johanna wife of Robert Clavering. There is no confirmation of this marriage in the Clavering pedigree. Hodgson has omitted Robert Ogle from his pedigree of Ogle of Ogle, but there seems to be some independent evidence for his existence. On 4 May 7 H.VII (1491) sir Thomas Burrow, lord of Gainborough, gave and confirmed to Robert, abbot of Newminster, and the monks serving God there, a certain waste chapel formerly called the chapel of St Leonard next Mitford; the witnesses are John, lord of Greystock, Ralph, lord of Ogle, sir Ralph Wodryngton, George Percy esq., Robert Ogle and 'many others' (*SS.* 66, pp.252-254). Robert, 4th lord Ogle, was not born until 1489 so that Robert Ogle the witness of 1491 may have been the 2nd lord's younger son. On 6 July 1515 sir William Gascoigne, Robert Ogle and William Ogle, esquires, Robert Wenslow, clerk, Thomas Forster and John Heron of Chipchase esquires with the consent of dame Margaret, lady Ogle, demised the manor of Horton to Thomas Lile (*NDD.* p.181, No. 84). Robert Ogle, esquire, cannot represent Robert, eldest son of Ralph lord Ogle because he had already succeeded his father as lord Ogle more than two years earlier. Presumably therefore he was Ralph lord Ogle's younger brother.

No inquisition was taken after the death of Owen, lord Ogle, until 1506 when one was taken 30 September at Haltwhistle. 'He died 1 September 1486, and Ralph Ogle of Ogle, his son and next heir, was then aged 18 years'.

Ralph, 3rd lord Ogle, had a general pardon in 1509 to include all offences before 23 April 1486, and a pardon granted in 1494 for all offences before 7 November 1489. This latter date is probably the date of his coming of age. In 1503 lord Ogle was one of the Northumbrian magnates who conducted princess Margaret to Scotland for her marriage with James IV.

In 1509 his towers at Ingram and Hepple were uninhabited (*AA2.* XIV, p.24). On 10 October 1510 he gave to his younger son William the manor of the Hirst by Woodhorn (*NDD.* p.180, No. 78), and on 3 June 1511 he settled on 'master Roberte Ogle his son and heir' his demesne belonging to his castle of Ogle for ten years with remainder to Margaret Ogle, mother of the said Robert (*Ib.*, No. 79). The surviving trustees of the settlement made on 21 January 1485 reconveyed to him on 3 January 1512 the castle and demesnes of Ogle (*Ib.*, No. 80).

An inquisition taken at Morpeth 16 March 1512/3 found that Ralph, lord Ogle, had died on 16 January last and Robert Ogle was his next heir aged 22 years and more. The jurors also recorded that he had given to his son William, Twizel and the fourth part of South Dissington, for life, and to his son John another fourth part of South Dissington for life (*Ogle and Bothal*, app.201). The inquisition for his Durham lands gives the date of his death as 27 January 1512/3 (*Ib.*, app.202).

The fine alabaster tomb of Ralph, lord Ogle, and his wife Margaret still remains in the east end of the nave of St Andrew's Church, Bothal. His wife was a daughter of sir William Gascoigne.

The 1563/4 visitation pedigree only credits Ralph, lord Ogle, with one child, a son Robert, but the 1575 pedigree gives him two other sons William and John, and three daughters Dorothy wife of Thomas Forster, Anne wife of Humfrey, son and heir to sir William Lisle, and Margaret wife of George Harbottle. For William and his descendants *see* OGLE OF CAUSEY PARK.

Sir Thomas Forster of Adderstone 'marshal of the king's town of Berwick upon Tweed' made his will 4 March 1526/7 but in it makes no mention of his wife. His widow married sir Thomas Grey (d.1570) of Horton. In the Forster pedigree of 1575 Dorothy is called daughter of Robert, lord Ogle, but it is clear that she was Ralph, 3rd lord Ogle's daughter; sir Thomas Forster had a son Thomas who in his will dated 1589 mentions his 'nephew' sir Thomas Grey. Sir Humphrey Lisle of Felton, who married Anne Ogle, died before 1542 and his widow married sir John Delaval (d.1572) of Seaton Delaval. George Harbottle was of Horton, chap. Horton, and his two sisters who were his coheiresses, Eleanor wife of sir Thomas Percy and Mary wife of sir Edward Fitton, divided his estates 3 November 1538. George Harbottle died *s.p.* 20 January 1527/8; before 1530 his widow Margaret married Thomas Middleton of Belsay; Thomas Middleton died 8 March 1545/6 and Margaret took for her third husband Richard Dacre, constable of Morpeth.

Shortly after succeeding to his father's estates, Robert, 4th lord Ogle, made provision for his mother. On 10 June 1513 he conveyed to her for her lifetime the lands in Hirst by Woodhorn which his father had acquired from John Wedell, with reversion to William Ogle, the grantor's brother (*NDD.* p.81, No. 82). On 7 August 1522 lord Ogle mortgaged to his brothers William and John, the manors and towers of Great Tosson, Hepple and Lorbottle, to secure £100. He gave power of attorney to Thomas Ogle and Robert (*sic*) to deliver possession (*Ib.*, p.182, No. 88).

By reason of his affection towards his dearly-beloved kinsman John Ogle son of Gilbert Ogle, he conveyed on 4 March 1529 all his lands in the vill of Oldmoor by Longhirst, to

George Ogle of Bothal and Oswin Ogle, gentlemen, presumably in trust for the grantee (*Ib.*, p.183, No. 92). John Ogle made a conveyance of lands in Oldmoor in 28 H.VIII (1536/7) (*Ib.*, No. 94). This John Ogle is otherwise unknown, but his mother was probably Isabel the 'kinswoman' of Margaret, widow of Ralph, lord Ogle, to whom on 6 May 1513 she gave a rent in Farnham (*Ib.*, p.181, No. 81). Isabel was presumably Bell Ogle of Bothal par. who made her will on 24 January 1539/40. She directs that her body is to be buried in the church of St Andrew at Bothal before the rood-loft. Her eldest son George is to be her 'full-executor for to dispone her goods and chattels moveable and immovable for the health of my soul as hereafter followeth'. George is to have a counter and chest, a counterpoint, a pair of linen sheets, a feather bed, a bolster and pillow and two cushions, a brazen mortar, a longspit, two silver spoons, a board cloth and towel. Her other sons John and Uswyn are 'every one of them' to have a silver spoon. She leaves her daughter An a mantle, Beyll Horsle a pair of silver crucks; her daughter Margat is to have her best gown and kirtle, her best belt, a chest, an aumory, a caldron, two blankets, two pair of sheets, two coverlets, two happings, a boardcloth, two candlesticks, a towel, an old feather bed, a brass pot, 4 pewter vessels, a little brazen mortar, an old basin. William Cramlyngton's daughter is to have three kine, Bayll Dixson a quey, dame Mawyng a quey, Beyll Horsle a quey, and her daughter Margaret 8 ewes and 7 hoggs. She evidently had a lease of certain tithes including those of Thrunton. Her sons John and Uswyn are to have her part of the tithes 'for their money payment saving the half of Thrunton tithe to William Cramlynton for 10 years paying yearly the ferm'. Her 'forth bringing' is to be taken off her goods together with a ryal gold which she had. Her son George is to have the rest of her goods. The will was proved in 1549 (*SS.* 2. p.114).

When Robert, 6th lord Ogle, made his w.d. 27 July 1562 he gives to his sister's sons Thomas and Robert Ogle, the reversion of Ralph Elleker's lease of the Oldmoor after the decease of John Ogle, brother to George Ogle. It is evident that Gilbert Ogle, his wife Isabel, and their sons George, John and Uswyn were closely related to the lords Ogle, but the exact relationship has not been discovered.

When James IV of Scotland invaded England in 1513 he occupied Flodden Hill whilst the earl of Surrey with the English army was encamped on Wooler Haugh. On 7 September Surrey sent by a herald a letter to the Scottish king subscribed by himself, his son Thomas, and the rest of the lords and principal captains of his army desiring the king to come down from his heights to be with his army on the day following on the side of Millfield plain nearest to his present situation, promising for his part to be in readiness with his own army to join battle. The name of R. Ogle is given by Stowe as one of the subscribers to the letter (Ridpath, p.489) and he was one of the forty knighted by the earl of Surrey after the battle.

In 1515 with his wife and lady Musgrave, lord Ogle met the queen of Scotland, widow of James IV and conducted her on her journey south. The same year he was charged with some misdemeanour before the Star Chamber but there is no record of him being punished in any way. The following year he was captain of Norham.

In 1519 lord Ogle received a reward of £13. 6s. 8d. for

casting down Blackadder, Cessford and other fortresses in Scotland. He was on another expedition in 1522 when with P. Dacre and sir William Percy and 2000 men from Berwick they killed Lance Carr and forty other persons, with the loss of only one man on their side. In 1523 he was with lord Dacre in Teviotdale burning villages and returning with 4000 head of cattle; for this he received the king's thanks.

On 7 October 1523 he was captain of the garrison of Wark castle, with 'sir William Lisle, deputy, John Ogle brother to the lord, W. Lisle, T. Lisle, Thomas Ogle, George Ogle, John Ogle, William Ogle—with 100 spearmen, 6 gunners, 14 archers and 12 more. The number of all the soldiers of the retinue of lord Ogle, 113' (*Letters and Papers, Foreign and Domestic*, H.VIII, III, 3410). 'The names of those gentlemen to whom the king's patents of annuities are delivered within Northumberland with a declaration of what ability they are to do the king's highness service and of other their qualities' was drawn up in 1526. Included in this list are:

'The lord Ogle may dispend £100 land by year in possession and £100 in reversion.

Sir William Ogle may dispend for the term of (his) life 40 marks.

John Ogle of Kirkley may dispend £6 by year.

George Ogle of Ogle Castle a younger brother and hath no lands.

John Ogle of Ogle Castle may dispend 20 marks by year.

Which men be well minded to justice and may serve the king with themselves and friends (to) the number of 60 or 70 horsemen' (*Cott. MS. Caligula B. vi. f.432*).

Robert, 4th lord Ogle, died shortly before 26 January 1531/2 when a commission was issued to sir Thomas Hilton and others to make *i.p.m.* on the lands and heir of sir Robert Ogle, lord Bothal and Ogle.

Robert, 4th lord Ogle, married Anne daughter of sir Thomas Lumley of Lumley, co. Durham by whom he had two sons, Robert who succeeded as 5th lord Ogle, and Oswin Ogle. He also had a bastard son Lewes Ogle.

Oswin Ogle is mentioned in the w.d. 5 May 1543 of his brother lord Ogle, who gives him 'all and singular my lands and tenements that belong to the town of Twizel and the stone house with all manner of commodities (and) profits thereto belonging during his life natural; and after the decease of the said Uswyne then to remain to my heirs'. By his w.d. 27 July 1562 Robert, 6th lord Ogle, leaves to 'my uncle Oswyne Ogle the Ridding until he enters Twizel, and to have timber necessary delivered for building an house there to dwell upon'. 'To Robert Ogle, my uncle Oswin's son' he leaves the manor and tenement of Twizel after the years of the lease of John Ogle.

Lewes Ogle is also mentioned in the wills of his brother and nephew. The former left to 'my brother Lewes Ogle, bastard, the whole town of Hepple with all commodities and profits thereunto belonging during his life natural saving £4 which is now in the hands of George Ogle, now of Hepple'.

Shortly after the death of the 4th lord Ogle another schedule was prepared of the principal gentlemen in Northumberland who could be of service to the Crown. The following Ogles are included:

The lord Ogle of Bothal—may dispend 300 marks in possession and reversion. He may serve the king with 100 horsemen; he is a true young man and a good housekeeper.

George Ogle hath married the lord Ogle's mother, and is both in house with the said lord Ogle; what he hath in right of his wife we know not; he is a true sharp forward man.

John Ogle of Ogle castle—he may dispend 20 marks by the year; he may serve the king with 10 horsemen, and is a sharp, forward man.

John Ogle of Kirkley—may dispend £10 by the year, and may serve with 8 men, and is a sharp, forward man.

Sir William Ogle, uncle of the lord Ogle, of Cockle Park—he may dispend during his life 40 marks by the year; he may serve the king with five or six household servants, and is a true man (*HN*. i. p.346).

A list of 1537 includes the same names and adds the amount of their fees—The lord Ogle £100; sir William Ogle, knight, £20; John Ogle of Kirkley, gent., £13. 6s. 8d.; George Ogle, gent., £13. 6s. 8d.; John Ogle of Ogle Castle, £13. 6s. 8d. (*Cott. MS. Caligula B. ii, f.257 and iii 60203*). With the exception of George Ogle, gent., all these persons can easily be identified in the Ogle pedigree. They are Robert, 5th lord Ogle, his uncles sir William Ogle and John Ogle of Kirkley, and his distant cousin John Ogle of Ogle castle. George Ogle is not so easy to identify, and there may have been more than one person of this name living in the first half of the 16th century.

In the 1526 list of the names of those gentlemen to whom the king's patents of annuities are delivered within Northumberland, John Ogle of Kirkley is followed by George Ogle of Ogle castle 'a younger brother and hath no lands'. On the strength of this, the author of *Ogle and Bothal*, decided that George Ogle was a younger brother of John Ogle of Kirkley and in consequence a younger son of Robert, 3rd lord Ogle. This identification must be discarded.

William and John, the younger sons of the 3rd lord Ogle were amply provided with lands by their father, their elder brother and their nephew. No such provision was made for George Ogle until the 6th lord Ogle on 22 April 1536 gave him lands in Newhall near Harbottle, the Hirst and Newintone, Gallow-field and close, Newclose and Wheit Northmore, without any payment.

Robert, 5th lord Ogle, in his w.d. 5 May 1543 appointed 'my cousin George Ogle of the Hirst' to see his will executed; he would hardly have referred to George as his cousin if in fact he had been his uncle. It is possible that John Ogle of Ogle castle had a younger brother George living in 1526, but if so there is no further mention of him.

There seems little doubt that the George Ogle who married the widow of the 4th lord Ogle was the eldest son of Gilbert Ogle and his wife Isabel. Isabel was 'kinswoman' of Margaret, lady Ogle, in 1513 and made her will in 1540. She had three sons George, John and Uswyn. The eldest son is described as 'George Ogle of Bothal, gentleman', in 1529. For his faithful service he had a grant of the water mill of Bothal for life from Robert, 4th lord Ogle, on 5 March 1529/30. By 1536 George Ogle had married the widow of the 5th lord. He was living at Bothal 24 May 1537 when he with 'lady Anne Ogle his wife, late wife of the late lord Ogle' and lord Ogle granted an annuity out of Shilvington to George Lumley. After this time he seems to have resided at Hirst which had been given to him in 1536. He was a trustee for lord Ogle on 15 September 1542 and 4 April 1544. In 1549 he was in charge of the beacon on Hirst Tower Head. In the inquisition taken on 30 May

1546 of the lands of Robert, 5th lord Ogle, the conveyance of Newhall, Hirst and other lands made in 1536 to George Ogle is mentioned with a note 'George being still alive'. For George's descendants *see* OGLE OF HIRST, PAR. WOODHORN.

The early visitation pedigrees of the Ogle family are very inconsistent about the sons of the 4th baron and his wife Anne Lumley. The pedigree of 1563/4 has internal evidence that it was very out of date at the time of this visitation. *Robertus Dominus de Ogle* by his wife *Annam filiam Thome Lomley* is given two sons, Robert and William. Actually Robert the 4th baron had died over 30 years before and his eldest son Robert had died in 1545 leaving children by his two wives. The 1575 pedigree, on the other hand, is completely up to date for it states that Edward Talbot who married Jane daughter of the 7th lord Ogle was aged 9 years in 1575.

This pedigree can therefore be taken as reasonably accurate in respect of the children of the 4th lord. These are given as:

1. Rauf, eldest son, died young.
2. Robert, the 5th lord Ogle, slaine at Panierhough in Scotland (his two wives and five children are detailed).
3. Thomas, 3rd son, died young.
4. Owin, 4th son.
i. Agnes.

Hodgson's pedigree (*HN.* ii, II, p.384) replaces the 3rd son Thomas, by John stated to have died young, and adds a second daughter Dorothy. A good deal is known about the 4th son Owin. (*See* OGLE OF SHILVINGTON.)

On 1 March 1527 'Robert lord of Ogle and Bothal, knight' conveyed to John de Woddrington, John Ogle of Hirst and John Mitford of Seghill, North Middleton, Fenrother and Shilvington for the use of Robert Ogle his son and Dorothy daughter of sir Henry de Weddrington for the life of Dorothy, with remainder to Robert the son and his heirs (*NDD.* p.181, No. 86; in *Ogle and Bothal*, app.98 this settlement is dated 8 H.VIII, but a note states that it is mis-dated by ten years and should read 18 H.VIII). In 1537 lord Ogle was one of the pensioners upon the marches of England foranenst Scotland with a fee of £100. On 8 July 1537 his wife Dorothy having died, he covenanted to marry Jane Radcliffe eldest daughter of sir Cuthbert Radcliffe of Dilston, 'before the asumption of our Lady next' (*NDD.* p.183, No. 95). On 14 September 1537 he covenanted with sir Edward Radcliffe of Cartington to make a sure estate to sir Edward and to the grantor's kinswoman Margaret Ogle of his manor and town of Flotterton in Coquetdale (*Ib.*, p.184, Nos. 96, 97; some confusion has arisen by sir Edward Radcliffe being termed, incorrectly, father-in-law of lord Ogle).

In September 1538 sir Reynold Carnaby reported to the Council of the North the names of those appointed to meet at midnight on 13 September for a rode into Tyndale; included are lord Ogle with 20 men, sir William Ogle with 10 men, Parson Ogle with 10 men, John Ogle of Ogle with 10 men and John Ogle of Twizel with 20 men.

On 24 August 1542 lord Ogle was one of 3000 men who invaded Scotland and having burnt many places in Teviotdale were routed by the Scots at Hadden Rig and there lost four or five hundred prisoners, including Parson Ogle. This episode may have made an impression on lord Ogle's nerves for on 5 May 1543 being 'commanded to invade the realm of Scotland in the king's majesty's wars if the case be I slain by

chance of war' he made his will. He gives his 'soul to God omnipotent and my body to be buried in the church of Bothal dedicated in the honour of God and St Andrew the apostle'. He leaves to his wife Jane all his goods and chattels moveable and unmoveable to the profit use and nourishment of his children. She is also to have for her lifetime Cockle Park and tower and all lands and tenements in the towns of Tritlington, Earsdon and Earsdon Forest, Fenrother, Hebburn and the tenement in Seaton next to Woodhorn, Saltwick, Ogle castle with the demesnes and all lands within the town of Ogle and the park with the water mill. His son Cuthbert Ogle is to have all the lands and tenements in the town and fields of North Middleton for his lifetime; Cuthbert is also to have, after the death of the testator's wife, Cockle Park with the tower and the fourth part of Hebburn 'which I have now in occupation'; after the death of Jane and Cuthbert these lands are 'to remain to my heirs'. His son Thomas Ogle is to have for life the lands and tenements in the town of Lorbottle for his native life, paying therefore to Thomas Ogle, now of Lorbottle, £7. 6s. 8d. a year. To his 'young son' John Ogle he leaves the lands and tenements in 'my town' of Flotterton 'during his life native'. His daughters Margerie, Jeyne and Margaret are to have 300 marks out of the town of Great Tosson. The bequest to his brother Oswyn Ogle has already been mentioned. The testator gives to sir John Widdrington and his father-in-law sir Cuthbert Ratcliffe his lands in Pegswood and Shilvington for the next three years until £60 is paid that he owes for liverage for which sir John and Cuthbert were bound by writing. His brother Lewes Ogle, bastard, is to have £4 a year out of the town of Hepple, and he directs that his wife Jane 'shall give to my daughter Annas Ogle, bastard, to her marriage twenty head of kine and oxen'.

The executors of lord Ogle's will are his wife Jane and his two sons Cuthbert and Thomas. He appoints as supervisors his cousin sir Thomas Hylton, his brother-in-law sir John Widdrington, his father-in-law sir Cuthbert Radcliffe, his 'cousin' George Ogle of the Hirst, and sir Thomas Burton, clerk and commissary who are 'to see my will executed according this my deed and will and my soul's health' (*SS.* 2, p.119).

Lord Ogle, in spite of his fears, returned safely from the expedition into Scotland, but in a later inroad over the border in 1545 he was killed at the battle of Ancrum Moor or Penielheugh on 6 March. His body was taken home from the battlefield and in accordance with his last wishes was buried at Bothal.

Lord Ogle had children by both of his wives. By his first wife, Dorothy Widdrington, he had a son Robert who succeeded as 6th lord Ogle, and a daughter Margery. His children by his second wife, Jane Radcliffe, were three sons, Cuthbert, Thomas and John, and two daughters Jane and Margaret; these are the only children mentioned in his will but there was another son Ralph apparently born after the date of his father's will. On 8 May 1566 Ralph Ogle of Bothal gave a bond for £200 to Cuthbert, lord Ogle, his brother; and on 14 November 1567 when he is described as of Alnwick he gave another bond for £200 to his brother.

An inquisition taken at Alnwick on 30 May 1546 found that lord Ogle's heir was his son Robert then aged 18. During his minority Robert was a ward of sir Robert Bowes. He had livery of his lands on 1 November 1550 and was appointed deputy warden of the Middle Marches on 6 May 1551, a very important post for a young man only 22 years of age. On 14 August 1553 and every year subsequently in the reign of queen Mary up to 5 November 1558 he was summoned to parliament.

In consideration of a marriage with Joan daughter and heiress of sir Thomas Mauleverer, of Allerton, Yorks., widow of sir Henry Wharton, (d.c.1550) he made a settlement of his lands on 17 September 1552. He died s.p. at Allerton Maulerever on 1 August 1562. By his w.d. 27 July 1562 he commends and bequeaths his soul into the hands of Almighty God and to all the blessed company of heaven, and his body is to be buried within the church of Bothal beside his father and mother without pomp or solemnity. Portions of the will are in a mutilated state but there is mention of his brothers Cuthbert and Thomas. He leaves to his brother Rauff Ogle the advowson of the parsonage of Bothal at the next avoidance. His sisters Anne and Jane Ogle are both mentioned in the will; the former is to have £30 to her marriage; she was presumably his father's bastard daughter Annas. He leaves to his sister Meriall Ogle a ring in token of remembrance; this was probably his sister Margery for his sister's sons Cuthbert, Thomas and Robert are mentioned. Cuthbert is to have his young stoned horse, and Thomas and Robert are to have the reversion of Rauff Elleker's lease of the Oldmoor after the decease of John Ogle, brother to George Ogle. The testator also remembers his uncle Oswyne Ogle, his 'cousin' George Ogle and his uncle Lewes Ogle. William Clarke is to have the advowson of the parsonage of Sheepwash after the death of sir Thomas Ogle, now incumbent of the same. Probate of the will was granted on 28 August 1562. When the inquisition as to his lands was taken at Newcastle on 20 October 1564 his brother and heir Cuthbert was 24 years old. His widow Joan had by then taken sir Richard Mauleverer of Allerton, Yorks., for her third husband (m. 19 November 1562).

Cuthbert, 7th lord Ogle, paid £10 for his relief for the castle and manor of Bothal and divers other lands in 1567 (Pipe Roll). In 1574 he was a member of the Council of the North. The name of lord Ogle heads a list of the principal men and officers on the Middle Marches, 29 September 1595, who were to enquire how Harbottle castle had been repaired (CBP. II, p.56).

In 1596 the laird of Buccleugh claimed that as his office of keeper of Liddlesdale was an hereditary one he was of much higher standing than the keepers of Redesdale and Tyndale, and should therefore treat on all border matters direct with the English warden. The latter made strong objections to this, stating that as to Buccleugh's exemption by inheritance the like may be said for the earl of Northumberland, lord Ogle, myself and many others who have lands chartered in this march, and estates equal if not some better, than Buccleugh. It would seem from this statement that lord Ogle's estates were considered to be second only in extent to those of the earl of Northumberland (Ib., p.116).

On 17 April 1596 lord Eure, warden of the Middle March, reported direct to queen Elizabeth about the great scarcity of horses. The light horse fit for service on this march was 71 including 'the whole stable' of the best gentlemen, viz. the lord Ogell, Mr Dallavaile, Mr Woodrington and Mr Fenwick, and some of these would not be allowed in other countries, but

they had to do it in hope of better amends. The Scots borderers had been enriched with English sheep and cattle for some time, and the poor Englishmen could not steal from them again for want of horse! (Ib., p.125).

Lord Ogle died on 20 November 1597 at Cockle Park, bur. Bothal, and the inquisition taken at Morpeth on 21 October 1598 found that he had on 20 September 1583 in consideration of a marriage between Edward Talbot and Jane his eldest daughter settled the bulk of his lands on them, except some to the use of Katherine, lady Ogle, his wife, for her lifetime. The marriage of his daughter Jane had taken place on 11 December 1583. The jurors found that the said Jane was aged 30, and her sister Katherine wife of sir Charles Cavendish, was 28.

Lord Ogle's wife was Katherine, one of the three daughters and coheiresses of sir Reynold Carnaby of Halton. By his w.d. 8 July 1543 sir Reynold leaves the sum of 1000 marks 'to be employed and delivered by even portions to the marriage of my daughters Katheryne Carnaby, Ursula Carnaby and Mabell Carnabye and to the longer liver of them not married'. The inquisition taken 20 June 1545 of the extent of sir Reynold's estates found that his daughter Katherine was aged 5, Ursula aged 4 and Mabel aged 3 (NDD. p.12, No. 36). Administration of the goods of the honourable lady Catherine, baroness Ogle, widow, of Bothal, was committed 10 January 1622/3 to Jane, countess of Shrewsbury, her daughter, for her own use and for the use of the honourable lady Catherine Cavendish, widow, late wife of sir Charles Cavendish, deceased. Her goods were worth £1616. 17s. 6d.

Cuthbert, lord Ogle, had been predeceased by his three younger brothers Thomas, John and Ralph. John had still been in his infancy when he died on 20 November 1545. Thomas can have been little more than a year old when on 15 September 1542 his father granted to him the reversion of Lorbottle after the death of Thomas Ogle of Lorbottle. By 20 October 1564 Thomas Ogle of Lorbottle had died and Thomas, the son of Robert, lord Ogle, had 'entered and was seized in freehold for life'; this is mentioned in the i.p.m. of Robert, lord Ogle. Thomas was living on 9 April 1571 but died before 10 November in the same year. He married Isabel daughter and coheiress of sir Thomas Grey of Horton, widow of sir Ralph Grey (d.1564) of Chillingham; they had a daughter Grace who died in infancy. After the death of her husband Thomas Ogle, Isabel reverted to the surname of Grey and as dame Isabel Gray of Ogle Castle, widow, made her will on 6 October 1581. She leaves small legacies to 'the right honourable the lady Ogle, my mother-in-law' and to her 'cousins, either of the lady Ogle's daughters'. Her servant Henry Ogle is to have one year's wages. To the poor of Ogle and parts adjoining she leaves £6. 13s. 4d., and to Frances Ogle 40s. When she died she had a lease of Ogle demesnes and Shilvington fields (SS. 38, p.49).

Ralph Ogle is not mentioned in the w.d. 5 May 1543 of his father Robert, 5th lord Ogle, but may have been born before his father died in 1545. By the will of the 6th lord Ogle, 'my brother Rauff Ogle' is to have the advowson of the parsonage of Bothal at the next avoidance. As Ralph Ogle of Alnwick, esquire, brother to Robert, late lord Ogle, he presented to the church of Bothal on 4 February 1563/4 (Bishop Pilkington's Reg.). He was presumably the R. Ogle who held a burgage in Alnwick in 1569 (Tate, Hist. of Aln-

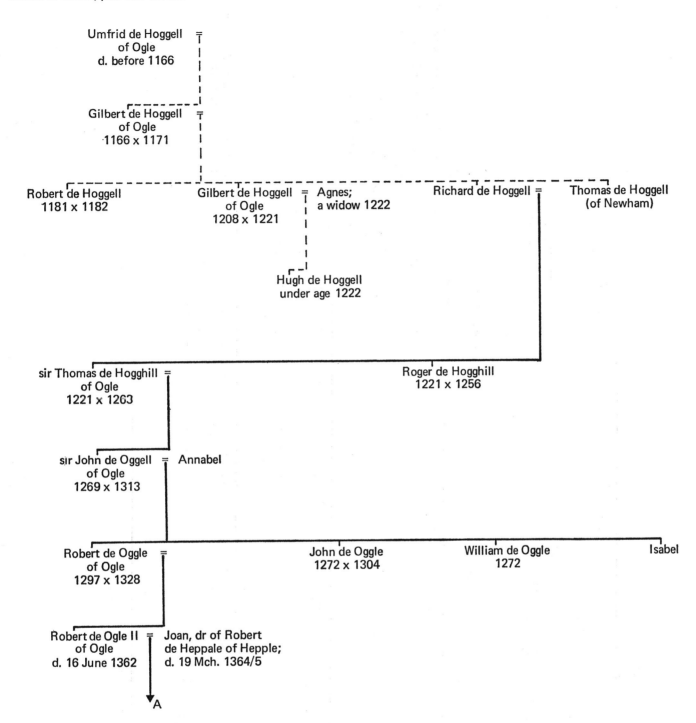

wick, I, p.259). He must have died s.p.

By his first wife, Dorothy Widdrington, Robert, 5th lord Ogle, had a daughter Margery who married her distant kinsman, Gregory Ogle of Choppington. (See OGLE OF CHOPPINGTON). By his second wife, Jane Radcliffe, he had two other daughters Jane and Margaret. By the will of her half brother Robert, Jane is to have £200 and be under the tuition of sir John Widdrington; there is no further record of her. Margaret married Robert Widdrington of Wearmouth, co. Durham, a younger son of sir John Widdrington (d.1571) of Widdrington.

Edward Talbot, husband of Jane Ogle, succeeded his brother in 1615 as 8th earl of Shrewsbury, and died s.p. at

Bothal on 8 February 1617/8. Jane's sister Katherine wife of sir Charles Cavendish of Welbeck, Notts., then became sole heir to the Ogle estates. On 4 December 1628 she was by letters patent declared to be baroness Ogle. She was succeeded in 1619 as 9th lord Ogle by her son William Cavendish, created baron Ogle of Bothal and viscount Mansfield 1620; baron Cavendish of Bolsover and earl of Newcastle upon Tyne 1628; marquis of Newcastle 1643; earl of Ogle and duke of Newcastle upon Tyne 1665.

Henry Cavendish, 10th lord Ogle, 2nd duke of Newcastle upon Tyne died in 1691, survived by three daughters, Margaret wife of John Holles, earl of Clare; Catherine wife of the earl of Thanet; and Arabella wife of lord Spencer, after-

OGLE of OGLE, par. WHALTON [cont.]

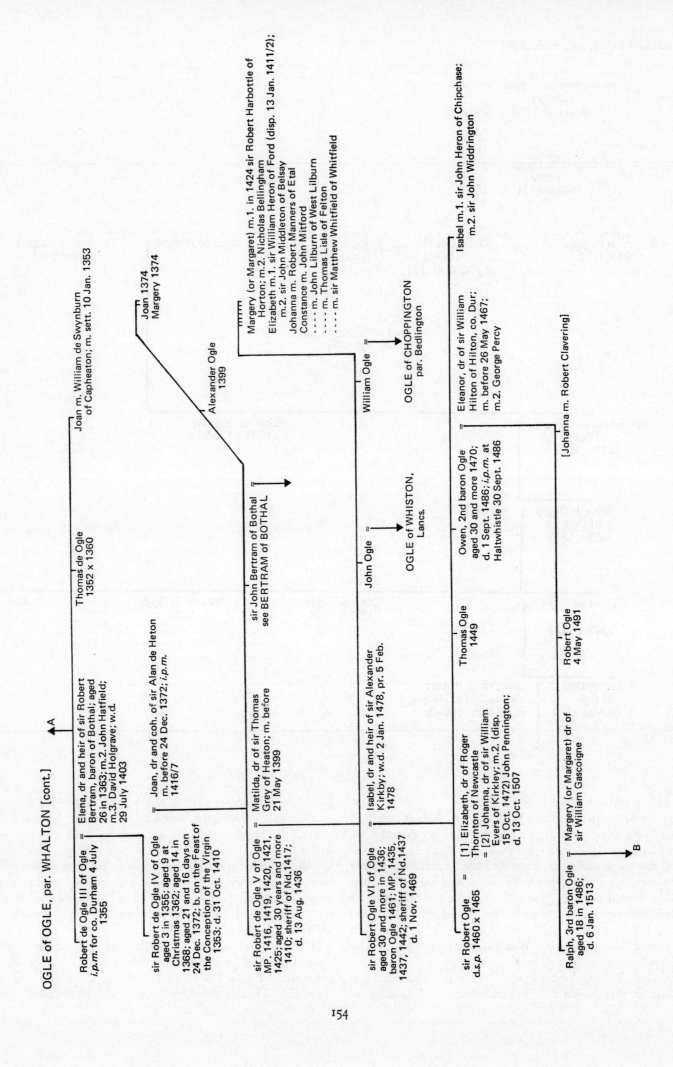

OGLE of OGLE, cont.

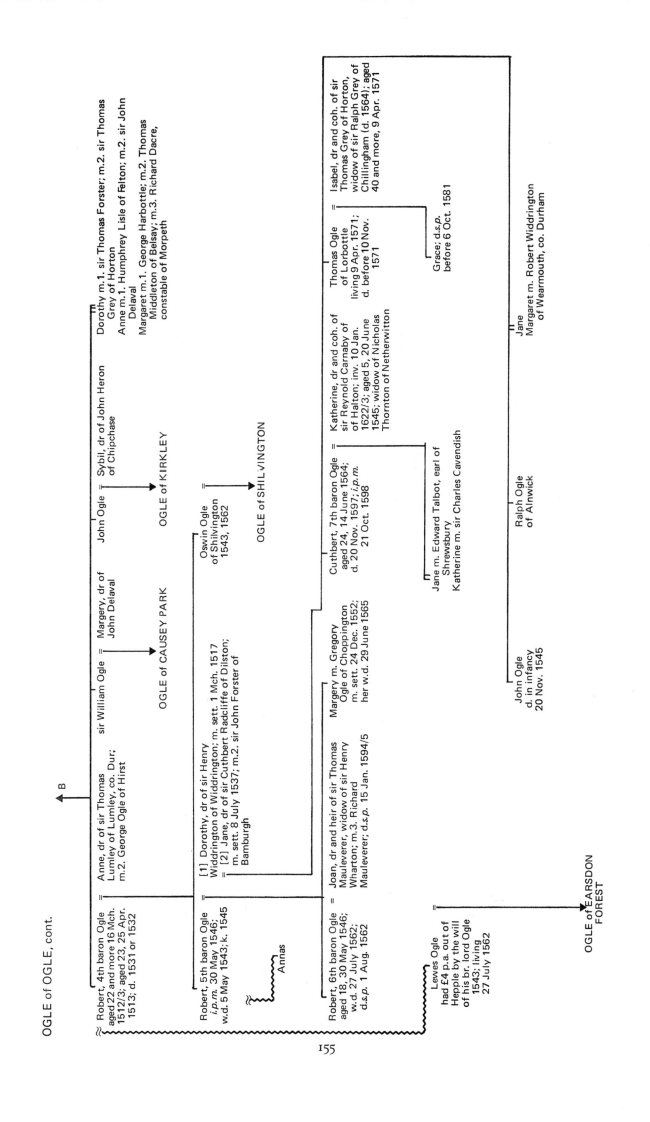

wards earl of Sunderland. Amongst the descendants of these three coheiresses, the barony of Ogle remains in abeyance. From the eldest daughter is descended the present duke of Portland.

After the death of Cuthbert, 7th lord Ogle, in 1597, the male representation of the Ogle family passed to the descendants of Oswin Ogle of Shilvington, younger brother of the 5th lord. (*See* OGLE OF SHILVINGTON.)

OGLE OF EARSDON FOREST, CHAP. HEBRON

IT has already been noted that Robert, 5th lord Ogle, left to his brother Lewes Ogle 'bastard' £4 a year for life out of the town of Hepple. Lewes is also mentioned in the w.d. 27 July 1562 of Robert, 6th lord Ogle, who calls him 'my uncle Lewes Ogle'. In the *i.p.m.* dated 30 May 1546 of the 5th lord Ogle is the statement that on 6 June 1541 he had granted to Louis Ogle an annuity of £3 out of Earsdon. In the *i.p.m.* of the 6th lord Ogle it is recorded that Lewes Ogle was then in possession of some land in Hepple.

In *Ogle and Bothal* it is presumed that Lewes Ogle was a son of Robert Ogle, illegitimate son of sir William Ogle of Cockle Park, but this can be nothing more than a guess and all the evidence is against it. When Luke Ogle of Edlingham made his w.d. 5 July 1596 he gave a legacy of 20 nobles to his sister Julyan Ogle and mentions her son Lewes Ogle.

The will of Lewes Ogle of Earsdon Forest, par. Hebburn, is dated 14 March 1585/6. He is to be buried in the parish churchyard of Hebburn, and leaves all his goods to his wife Jellien and his two sons Alexander and Lewes. His wife and

his son Alexander Ogle are to be executors. The inventory of his goods is dated 14 July 1586 and shews that he owed Roger Foberil £5. 15s., other creditors being Mistress Carr of F - - - arle, George Forster, John Fenwicke, Alexander Ogle (*Dur. Prob. Off.* by C.R.H.). The elder son Alexander did not long survive his father. He made his w.d. 23 November (1587) pr. 19 June 1588, by which he leaves to his son and heir Arther his right of his living in Earsdon Forest and bequeaths him 'with the commodity of the said living' to Mr Martin Ogle of Tritlington until he be of age; if Martin should die then to Mr George Ogle son of Mr James Ogle; remainder to the rest of his children. He desires his good master Sir Thomas Graye to be a good friend to his wife and children and especially to his son Arthur. Mr Christopher Ogle is to be guardian to his daughter Jane Ogle. His wife Elizabeth was pregnant. His son Arthur is to be sole executor of the will, and he appoints as supervisors Cuthbert Ogle, sir Thomas Graye, knt, Mr James Ogle esquire and John Heron, gent. (*Ib.*).

No other members of this branch of the Ogle family have been traced, and it is possible that Alexander's son Arthur did not live long after his father's death.

OGLE OF SHILVINGTON, PAR. MORPETH

AFTER the death of Cuthbert, 7th lord Ogle, the male representation of the family passed to his uncle Oswin Ogle.

On 15 September 1542 Robert, 5th lord Ogle, gave to Oswin his brother, to George Ogle of Hirst and to Cuthbert Horsley of Horsley the reversion of the tenements which his kinsman Thomas Ogle of Lorbottle then held for life

OGLE of EARSDON FOREST, par. HEBBURN

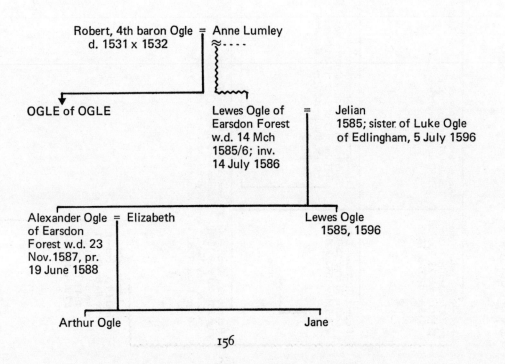

(*NDD.* p.184, No. 98). On 4 April 1544 lord Ogle appointed Oswin his brother, and others, trustees of a settlement of lands to the use of the grantor and Joan his wife, with remainder to Cuthbert Ogle his son (*Ib.*, p.99). When lord Ogle made his will on 5 May 1543 he gives and bequeathes 'to my brother Oswyne Ogle all and singular the lands (and) tenements that belongeth to the town of Twizel and the stone house with all manner of commodities (and) profits thereto belonging during his life native, and after the decease of the said Oswyne then to remain to my heirs'.

Oswin was at the battle of Penielheugh or Ancrum Moor on 6 March 1545 and was there taken prisoner. On 27 July 1562 the 6th lord Ogle by his will gives to 'my uncle Oswyne Ogle, the Ridding unto such time as he shall enter Twizel and to have timber necessary delivered for building an house there to dwell upon (*SS.* 2, p.202). In 1583 Oswin Ogle was living at Shilvington. At that time Cuthbert, lord Ogle, having no sons had a licence from the Crown to alienate his property to Jane his daughter and her husband Edward Talbot (*Pat. Roll* 2 Sept. 1583).

Oswin Ogle thereupon complained to the queen stating that 'whereas the house of the lord Ogle being of great antiquity hath for many years done true service to your majesty and your progenitors since and before the memory of man, as sundry of your highness's council can testify. It is so that the lord Cuthbert Ogle now living and having no heirs male goeth about to cut off your poor suppliant and his children from the benefit of that whereby he is now lord Ogle, for he the said lord Cuthbert continued the entail which was like to be cut off and yet would he do the like to your said suppliant and his children being the next of blood in the entail. Wherefore, for that chief house is in danger of utter ruin which hath always done your majesty and your progenitors special service against the Scots who slew your said suppliant's brother and took him prisoner at Pamer-Heugh; these are most humbly to beseech your most gracious majesty to consider this case to maintain the entail in the heirs male and to will your right honourable council to take order herein. Then shall your majesty do a thing to God acceptable your poor orator and all the name of the Ogles shall be bound in double duty to your highness and great quietness may hereby be maintained which otherwise would in time grow to great grudge and dissension. Your majesty's poor and daily suppliant, Oswen Ogle' (*Lands. MS.* No. 106, *f.*51).

As might have been expected this appeal was unavailing. Cuthbert, lord Ogle's sons-in-law belonged to two families better known in the south of England, and no doubt at court, than the Ogles. Oswin Ogle had also been rather meanly provided with landed property by successive heads of the family.

Oswin Ogle is said to have married Jane daughter of John Horsley of Milbourne Grange, but this seems doubtful. John Horsley by his w.d. 17 March 1582/3 appoints Oswin Ogle of Shilvington, gent., to be supervisor; his son Lamroch Horsley purchased lands in Newham from Oswin Ogle on 4 October 1578 (*NCH.* XII, p.539). Oswald Ogle of Shilvington, gentleman, aged 82, gave evidence on 16 September 1596 about the tenant right in Tynemouthshire (*NCH.* VIII, p.234). He was no doubt the Uswald Ogle buried at Morpeth 15 March 1596/7.

Oswin Ogle had a son Robert. Robert, 6th lord Ogle, by his w.d. 27 July 1563 leaves to Robert Ogle, his uncle Oswen's son, the manor and tenements of Twizel in reversion after the lease which John Ogle held. In the *i.p.m.* dated 20 October 1564 of Robert, 6th lord Ogle, it is stated that on 26 April 1530 lord Ogle had given Shilvington to Robert Ogle of Shilvington, 'who is yet alive'. About 1561-1571 Robert Ogle of Shilvington, gent., aged about 30, deposed in a matrimonial cause brought by Agnes Foster, single-woman, against Gabriel Anderson, who was Ogle's servant (*SS.* 21, p.71). Administration of the goods of Robert Ogle of Shilvington, gent., was granted on 11 July 1569; he left a widow Janet and two sons James and Ralph; his daughter and heir (*sic*) Anne was under age. 'Daughter' is perhaps a mistake for grand daughter, but the administration cannot now be found (C.R.H.).

James Ogle of Shilvington died in 1627, administration of his goods being granted on 9 May 1627 to Robert his son; he left a widow Isabel; the inventory of his goods is dated 19 April 1627. (James?) Ogle and Isbell Smyth had been married at Morpeth on 14 December 1600 and Robert son of James Ogle was baptised there on 1 August 1602. James' widow was no doubt Issabella Ogle of Shilvington bur. 28 January 1627/8. The son Robert had two daughters baptised at Morpeth, Issabella (31 January 1629/30) and Jane (26 August 1632).

No other member of this branch of the family has been identified, but Brian Ogle of Shilvington whose inventory is dated 15 September 1588 may have been one. A later Bryan Ogle, perhaps of this family, married at Morpeth 12 July 1618 Elizabeth Rydley; a son George was baptised 30 October 1619 and was bur. 19 July 1620.

OGLE OF CAUSEY PARK, CHAP. HEBRON

WILLIAM OGLE, ancestor of the Ogles of Causey Park, was second son of Ralph, 3rd lord Ogle (d.1513). In spite of the statement in the 1575 pedigree that William was *sans issu*, there is overwhelming evidence that he married and had children. Some later pedigrees suggest that William was lord Ogle's third son but if this is correct he must have been the second surviving son. The evidence that there was an intervening brother between him and his elder brother Robert is not very satisfactory and can be rejected.

On 10 October 1510 Ralph Ogle, lord of Ogle, gave the manor of Hirst by Woodhorn to William Ogle, esquire, his son; and on 10 June 1513 Robert Ogle, lord Ogle and Bothal, gave to Margaret Ogle his mother for life, with remainder to William Ogle, grantor's brother, lands in Hirst which his father had of John Wedell (*NDD.* p. 180, No. 78 and p.181, No. 2). In the *i.p.m.* of his father taken 16 March 1612/3 it is recorded that his father had given him for life, Twizel, the fourth part of South Dissington, and Tosson (*Ogle and Bothal*, app.201). In 1515 with sir William Gascoigne, Robert Ogle his brother, and others, he was a trustee for the manor of Horton (*NDD.* p.181, No. 84).

William Ogle and (his brother) John Ogle lent £100 to their brother Robert, lord Ogle, and on 7 August 1522 lord Ogle conveyed to them the manors and towers of Great Tosson, Hepple and Lorbottle, until they shall have received

OGLE of SHILVINGTON, par. MORPETH

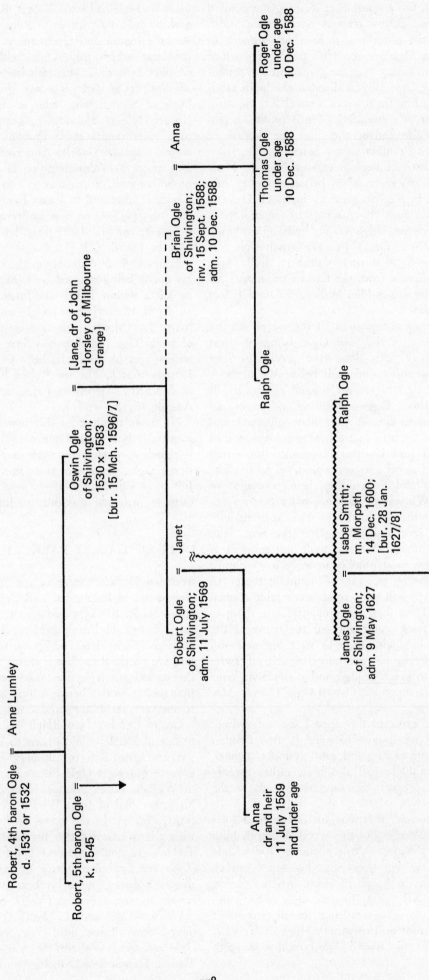

Robert, 4th baron Ogle = Anne Lumley
d. 1531 or 1532

Robert, 5th baron Ogle =
k. 1545

Oswin Ogle = [Jane, dr of John
of Shilvington;   Horsley of Milbourne
1530 x 1583   Grange]
[bur. 15 Mch. 1596/7]

Brian Ogle
of Shilvington;
inv. 15 Sept. 1588;
adm. 10 Dec. 1588

= Anna

Thomas Ogle
under age
10 Dec. 1588

Roger Ogle
under age
10 Dec. 1588

Ralph Ogle

Anna
dr and heir
11 July 1569
and under age

Robert Ogle
of Shilvington;
adm. 11 July 1569

= Janet

James Ogle
of Shilvington;
adm. 9 May 1627

= Isabel Smith;
m. Morpeth
14 Dec. 1600;
[bur. 28 Jan.
1627/8]

Ralph Ogle

Robert Ogle
bap. 1 Aug. 1602

158

£100; Thomas Ogle and Robert (*sic*) were appointed attorneys to deliver possession. Thomas Ogle was probably William Ogle's youngest son, and Robert was no doubt his illegitimate son (*Ib.*, p.182, No. 88).

Sometime in the next three or four years William Ogle was knighted, and in 1526 he was one 'of those gentlemen to whom the king's patents of annuities are delivered within Northumberland'; it was then reported that 'Sir William Ogle may dispend for the term of life 40 marks' (*Cott. MS. Caligula* B.vi, *f.*432). Shortly after 1532 it was again reported that sir William Ogle, uncle of the lord Ogle, of Cockle Park could dispend 40 marks by the year during his life; 'he may serve the king with five or six household servants, and is a true man' (*HN.* i, p.346). In 1537 he was a pensioner on the marches with a fee of £20, and in September 1538 he joined sir Reynold Carnaby with ten men for a 'rode' into Tyndale.

We have seen that about 1532 sir William was living at Cockle Park. On 10 May 1526 his brother, lord Ogle, released to him the park of Causey Park with the enclosures of Southfield and Baronsfield. It is with Causey Park that sir William's descendants became closely connected for the next three hundred years. Sir William died before 30 June 1542 and it is possible that he had lost his life in the inroad into Scotland earlier in the year. He married Margery daughter of John Delaval (d.1498) of Seaton Delaval. She is wrongly called Margaret in the 1666 Delaval pedigree. They had four sons James, John, Matthew and Thomas, and two daughters, Elinor wife of Christopher Selby of Biddleston and Elizabeth wife of Martin Fenwick of East Heddon. For the second son John and his descendants *see* OGLE OF BEBSIDE. From Thomas Ogle came the OGLES OF TRITLINGTON.

Matthew Ogle, third son of sir William Ogle, apparently died unmarried. He purchased the manor of Axwell and a tenement in Swalwell, co. Durham, in 1574. By his w.d. 28 September 1598 he directs that he is to be buried in the church of Bothal. He leaves to his 'cousin' John Ogle of Causey Park his lands in the bishopric of Durham, and to his 'cousin' Anne Ogle, daughter of his brother James Ogle, late of Causey Park, ground called Foxholes which he had in mortgage of John Horsley (Raine, *MSS. Wills and Inv.* VI, 27). In the later years of his life Matthew Ogle had been living at Causey Park; Thomas Reed of Houghton, who had a lease of two farmholds in North Dissington, mentions Matthew Ogle of Causey Park, gent., in his w.d. 13 July 1578 (*Ib.*, VII, p.183).

Sir William Ogle had two illegitimate children, a son Robert and a daughter Mary. On 20 November 1525 Robert, lord Ogle, and sir William Ogle, demised to Robert Ogle, bastard son of sir William, all the lands and tenements in the town of Hebburn to have to the end of fourscore years (*NDD.* p.183, No. 90). On 4 April 1530 these lands in Hebburn were conveyed by lord Ogle to William his brother, to Marjory, William's wife and to Robert, bastard son of William (*Ib.*, No. 93). John Widdrington of Hauxley 'wedded to his 3d wife, Marye, daughter of sir William Ogle, 2d son to Raufe, lorde Ogle' (Widdrington pedigree of 1558); in their marriage settlement of 13 June 1532 Mary is called 'natural' daughter of William Ogle (*AA4.* XXXIV, p.72).

Sir William's property at Causey Park passed to his eldest son James. In 1568 (blank) Ogle held of the Crown a (*sic*) site of a capital messuage called Causey Park with the park of the same and certain lands in Horsley (*Liber Feodarii, HN.* iii, III, p.lxiii). It is apparent that at this time the pele tower at Causey Park was not habitable, which accounts for it being rebuilt by James Ogle in 1589. At this time his initials and those of his wife and the date were cut on two shields on the east end of the house. This end of the house fell down in the early 19th century and was rebuilt more to the west and the shields refixed. Henry Ogle of Kirkley in his w.d. 2 January 1580/1 calls James Ogle his 'loving cousin' and appoints him a supervisor of the will. James was present at Hexpeth gatehead on 27 July 1595 when lord Francis Russell was killed. On 17 March 1592/3 he and others were appointed to enquire into abuses at Berwick, and on 16 October 1593 he was complaining about the outrageous foraging of the Scots in Northumberland (*CBP.* I, pp.190, 440, 506).

James Ogle was sheriff of Northumberland in 1584. After his death, an inquisition was taken at Morpeth on 1 September 1619 to find out the extent of his lands. The jurors found that he was seised in fee of Causey and Causey Park and lands in Horsley, Horsley forest, Earsdon forest, Felton, Tritlington and Fenrother, of which he had enfeoffed James Lysley and Martin Ogle to himself for life and then to John his son and heir, and to his heirs. He also held lands in Bothal called Earsdon Hill, closes in Felton called Ladyclose and Gallowclose, and Bridgham, Lee and Horsley. They found that James Ogle died 1 March 1612/3 and John his son and heir was aged 40 years. John Ogle and Isabella Ogle, now deceased, late wife and relict of said James, had occupied the lands from the date of James' death. The jurors were very much astray in the date which they gave for James' death, for he was certainly dead by 28 September 1598 when his brother Matthew in his will refers to him as late of Causey Park. On 14 December 1598 Isabel Ogle, widow, of Causey Park, was reported for refusing to contribute to the church. James Ogle's wife was Isabel daughter of John Clavering of Callaly; she is incorrectly called Elizabeth in the 1615 Ogle pedigree. James Ogle's brother, John Ogle of Newsham, by his w.d. 18 January 1585/6 leaves £100 to his daughter Margaret 'to be delivered to my sister-in-law Isabell, wife to my brother Jaymes Ogle for the use of my said daughter'. Probate of the will of James Ogle of Causey Park was granted on 5 April 1600 to John Ogle, his son and sole executor; the will does not seem to have survived.

In the 1615 Ogle pedigree the only son of James Ogle who is recorded is his eldest son John. In fact he also had four younger sons. Gawine Claveringe of Callaly, a relative of James Ogle's wife, by his w.d. 19 November 1580 leaves to John son of James Ogle of Causey Park two angels of gold, the same to George, Cuthbert, Robert and Charles his brothers and Jane and Agnes his sisters. One of James Ogle's daughters seems to have been the first wife of Ralph Carr of Howburn, par. Lowick; Ralph Carr died before 1 September 1615 leaving a widow Jane and an only daughter and heiress Jane. The widow agreed to take half of Ralph's goods in lieu of her dower and agreed that John Ogle of Causey Park, the younger Jane's uncle should administer the other half; on 19 August 1615 Jane the daughter chose her uncle as her guardian; his sureties were Thomas Bradfurth and Thomas Ogle, gents (*Dur. Prob. Off.* by C.R.H.).

James Ogle's brother, John Ogle of Newsham, leaves 'to my brother James' sons, John, George, Cuthbert, Robert and Charles Ogle, to every of them an old angel'. The two elder sons were concerned in a quarrel in which Philip Grene of Morpeth received mortal injuries. In his w.d. 20 July 1583 Grene requests that Mr Franncis Dacres and Mr Nycholas Rydlye 'will see my said wife and children maintained in law, for reformation of this cruel murder, committed upon me by George Ogle (and) John Ogle, sons to Jaymes Ogle of Causey' with others, 'whom I fully charge with my death, having no cause against me, but that I compared the Dacres blood to be as good as the Ogles' (SS. 38, p.82).

On 14 June 1578 there was a lease of the Crown of the rectory and church of Longhorsley for 21 years to Matthew Ogle and John Howlands; and on 11 May 1594 it was leased to Matthew, Charles and John Ogle for their lives paying yearly £15. These three were John Ogle of Causey Park, his uncle Matthew and his younger brother Charles. In 1601 John Ogle was presented as farmer of Longhorsley rectory because the choir was in great decay. On 4 December 1630 he paid to the king's commissioners the sum of £13. 6s. 8d. in discharge of a composition made with them for compounding the fines for not attending and receiving knighthood at the coronation of Charles I (AA2, XXIV, p.121). His will is dated 27 September 1634; he desires to be buried in the chancel of Hebburn under the same stone as his father. He leaves to his daughter Katherine wife of Henry Milbourne of Bedlington £300 out of Causey Park, and smaller legacies to his grandchildren Barbara and Mary Milbourne. James Ogle, his younger son, is also to have £300 out of Causey Park. The remainder of his lands including the rectory of Longhorsley is left to his son and heir Edward. Sir Matthew Palmer and Mr Gervase Palmer, parson of Staunton, Notts., are two of the supervisors of the will, which was proved in 1635. The stone under which John Ogle wished to be buried was no doubt the black stone now under the altar on which was the inscription.—'Anno 15—. Here lyeth the body of James Ogle of Causey Park esqr sonne and heir of William second sonne of Ralphe the 3 Lord Ogle. He left issue 5 sonnes'.

According to the Ogle pedigree of 1615 John Ogle was twice married. By his first wife Catherine daughter of Robert Widdrington he had a daughter Catherine already married to Henry Milbourne of Bedlington. His second wife was Alice daughter of (blank) Palmer of York., by whom he had a son and heir Edward then aged 1 year. Catherine Ogle's tomb still remains in Bothal church with the inscription—'Here Lyeth Catherine the wife of John Ogle of Causey Park, esqr., daughter of Robert Woodrington, esqr., by Margaret his wife, which Margaret was sister to Robert the 6th and Cuthbert the 7th Lord Ogle. She died May 23rd, 1609'. Catherine was widow of Robert Dent (d.1602) of Byker.

Edward Ogle of Causey Park was admitted to Gray's Inn 23 January 1637, and then disappears from history. It is possible that he was killed in the Civil Wars and he may have been the Edward Ogle who served in sir William Ogle's regiment. His brother and heir James Ogle was a staunch royalist. He was major of the regiment of foot commanded by William, lord Widdrington, until the storming of Newcastle. Before then he was dangerously wounded in the thigh, 'so that most men conceived it impossible for him to recover'.

On 31 March 1646 James Ogle petitioned to be allowed to compound for his delinquency. He explained the delay as caused by 'the great storms, frost and snow, beginning in November, continued so sore that the like was not for many years before nor since; that in respect of the extraordinariness of the weather and many of the members being employed in taking the Scots' account for cess and billet the Committee (for Compounding) seldom met that winter, and that he could not attend but in great danger of his life'. His estate comprised Causey Park, Earsdon Hills, Langdickes and certain tithes in the parish of Longhorsley; in right of his wife he had lands and tenements in Burradon. His elder brother Edward Ogle had granted a rentcharge of £15 for 5 years on 18 April 1634 out of Earsdon Hills and 2½ years rent was unpaid; Edward had granted another rentcharge of £15 out of Langdickes alias Foxholes, 17 May 1639, and 2½ years of this was not paid. On 23 January 1647 James Ogle gave further particulars of his estate. He had a lease of the rectory of Longhorsley for a term of seven years to come; this had originally been his father's but was mortgaged to sir Matthew Palmer for £350 from 9 July 1632. His lands were charged with an annuity of £5 to Margaret Miller, who was yet living; this had been bequeathed to her by Launcelot Ogle in 1640. Launcelot Ogle was James' father-in-law; he had left a legacy of £50 to his base daughter Jane Ogle to be paid to her when she reached 21 or married and she was now 14 (SS. 111, p.301).

After the Restoration James Ogle was a deputy lieutenant and a commissioner of subsidies for Northumberland. On 4 May 1663 he was appointed captain of a troop of horse to be raised in the county. By his w.d. 30 July 1664 he leaves the rents of his lands to trustees for ten years to pay his debts, with remainder to his son William Ogle at the age of 21, remainder to Edward Ogle of Welbeck, Notts., remainder to David Shevill of Newcastle, chirurgeon and his children. James Ogle died on 4 December 1664 and was buried in the chancel of St Andrew's church, Newcastle. There was a latin inscription on his tombstone which recorded that, 'Here lies James Ogle of Causey park in the county of Northumberland, esquire, truly distinguished by the antiquity of his house, as being sprung by race in the direct line from the most noble barony of Ogle of Ogle, but much more illustrious for his great and indomitable courage against the rebels during the wicked fury of the late civil wars, for his constancy to the king, for his fidelity even in the most sad falling away of authority, for his obedience to his superiors, for his courtesy in peace, for his kindness to his inferiors, all which qualities by most just title he could call his own' (Brand, *Newcastle*, I, p.189).

The mention of Edward Ogle of Welbeck in James Ogle's will is a reminder that John Ogle (d.1635) of Causey Park had four younger brothers, George, Cuthbert, Robert and Charles. The last mention of George Ogle is in 1597 and there is no evidence that he ever married. Cuthbert Ogle has been identified with Cuthbert Ogle of Longhorsley who by his w.d. 1 December 1603 directs that he is to be buried in the church of Hebburn, and leaves to his son Samuel all his title to two farmholds in Lorbottle. The fact that he wishes to be buried at Hebburn certainly suggests that this Cuthbert Ogle was closely related to the family of Causey Park. Administration of the goods of Samuel Ogle of the parish of (Long)

Horsley was granted on 28 May 1608 to Nicholas Forster, husband of Janet Forster, sister of the deceased, and to Dorothy Ogle his widow. Samuel Ogle's wife Dorothy was a daughter of Stephen Fenwick of Langshaws (1615 vis. ped. Fenwick of Langshaws).

Robert Ogle, 3rd brother of John Ogle (d.1635), may have left a widow Elizabeth, for on 25 July 1627 inventory of the goods of Elizabeth Ogle, late of Ogle, widow, was exhibited, and two days later Robert Ogle of Rufford, Notts., gent., son of Elizabeth, gave up administration to Nicholas Hudson, husband of Catherine his sister, daughter of the deceased. Robert Ogle of Rufford, can be identified as the Robert Ogle of Welbeck whose will is dated 10 December 1660. He leaves his sister Katherine Hutton £150 and his nephew John Hutton £150; by a codicil dated 20 December he leaves 'to my lady Jane' the gold watch which she had given him. John Hutton of Earsdon Forest proved the will in September 1662. 'My lady Jane' was probably a daughter of William, duke of Newcastle, who died at Welbeck 25 December 1676, and Robert Ogle's residence at Welbeck denotes that he was in the duke's service. Edward Ogle of Welbeck mentioned in the will of James Ogle (1664) was perhaps Robert's brother, and was apparently next male heir to the Ogles of Causey Park failing James' son William.

Charles Ogle, youngest brother of John Ogle (d.1635) can be identified with the man of this name who in 1600/1 was a prisoner in the White Lion, Southwark, as a result of the earl of Essex's rebellion. On 12 September 1604 Charles Ogle of the par. of St Clement Danes, Temple Bar, made his will. He leaves to Mr Ralph Burgoyne his black nag and silver rapier that he took from Wallington; and to Mr Richard Ogle his damascus sword and dagger. The will was proved in 1607.

James Ogle's only son and heir William was born at Burradon, and baptised at Earsdon on 29 September 1653. His mother Jane died two years later and was buried at Earsdon 30 March 1655. It is possible that James Ogle had a daughter who married David Shevill of Newcastle, chirurgeon; he and his children are mentioned in James Ogle's will. William may have been the man of this name who on 19 June 1673 is mentioned as an ensign in the earl of Ogle's regiment. Three years later he was appointed lieutenant in his father-in-law, colonel Strother's regiment of dragoons because he had 'ability suitable to his loyalty'. He eventually became a lieutenant colonel. James II, on 20 June 1685, appointed him captain of a troop of horse. His wife was Elizabeth daughter of colonel William Strother of Fowberry; she had been baptised at St John's, Newcastle, 10 May 1658, and was buried at Hebburn 4 November 1699. Elizabeth has been called second wife of William Ogle (PSAN3 X, p.61) but this seems unlikely. Robert Strother of Fowberry, gent., by his w.d. 29 May 1723 leaves his new-erected messuage called the Newhall and his lands in the parish of Chatton to his wife for life with remainder to William Ogle, late of Causey Park, esq., and his heirs male; he mentions in his will Katherine Ogle of Causey Park, spinster.

William Ogle was buried at Hebburn on 15 December 1718. He left two sons Henry and William, and five daughters, Mary wife of William Orde of Felkington, Jane wife of Gawen Aynsley of Little Harle, Elizabeth wife of Ralph Wallis of Coupland, Catherine wife of William Carr of Eshot, and Dorothy who probably died unmarried. Henry Ogle was sheriff of Northumberland in 1737. His will is dated 16 December 1761; to his wife Anne he leaves Ogleborough which he had lately purchased from his brother William, together with lands in Norham and Sandy bank, co. Durham. To his brother William he leaves Longdike, Earsdon Hill, Tritlington and the tithes of Longhorsley. Dorothy Ogle, spinster, daughter of the rev. Thomas Ogle vicar of Carham, is to have £50. This Thomas Ogle must have been a near relative. 'On the 28th November 1808, in Chancery Lane, died Lucy, wife of Francis Vaughan, esq., and daughter of the late Thomas Ogle, vicar of Carham, the last in the female line of the Ogles of Causey Park' (Gent. Mag.).

Thomas Ogle was instituted perpetual curate of Carham on 28 October 1701, and died as incumbent in January 1748 (NCH. XI, p.22). In an account of the deanery of Bamburgh drawn up in 1725 it is stated that 'The revd mr Ogle is the curate, who after the first year cou'd get nothing of his patron (Mr Forster of Adderstone) for supplying the cure. This exasperated him, and put him upon methods of righting himself: upon which the patron raised a persecution against him, drew him thro' all the courts and starv'd him. Which hard and unjust usage together with the concern for a starving family, for some time disorder'd his head. . . . Mr Forster in the persecution pull'd down the house: which now the curate at his own expense has rebuilt' (PSAN2. IV, p.274). Of the 'numerous family' in 1725 only Lucy and Dorothy seem to have survived. Records of the baptisms of six daughters of the rev. mr Thomas Ogle, Carham, are recorded in the parish registers of Carham, viz. Jean (28 March 1722), Dorothy (2 December 1724), Mary (21 March 1726), Margaret (12 July 1729), Elizabeth (1 March 1729) and Catherine (4 September 1731). None of these daughters was buried at Carham. Rev. Mr Thos Ogle was buried there 24 January 1748 (new style).

Henry Ogle made his w.d. 16 December 1760, and died without issue on 27 February 1761. He seems to have been married twice, his first wife is called Mrs Elizabeth Manners in Felton registers, but Raine (North Durham, p.230) calls her Mary Anna daughter of (blank) Carr, widow of Thomas Manners. This Thomas Manners, however, lived two hundred years earlier. He was of Cheswick, chap. Ancroft, and died 1551; his widow Maryane married secondly Henry Ogle. Henry's second wife was Anne daughter of William Orde of Felkington. After Henry's death she married William Carr of Etal, and died in 1766.

William Ogle who succeeded to Causey Park in 1761 on the death of his brother Henry, had been a captain in the 1st regiment of dragoons. His will is dated 2 September 1774. He calls his wife 'Margaret Ogle alias Rutter', daughter of the late William Rutter of Newcastle, gent., the reason for thus describing her, he states, being to prevent disputes on account of relation before marriage and being married in Scotland. His lands are left in trust for Margaret his wife, then to William Ogle, late major 34th regiment of foot, for life, then in trust for entailing on William Ogle Wallis, son of the testator's nephew, James Wallis, deceased; in default to William Ogle Wallis, son of Ogle Wallis of Newcastle; in default to John Wallis, another son of Ogle Wallis; in default to Henry Wallis, another son; in default to the eldest son of Major William Ogle; in default to the daughters of William Ogle Wallis, son of Ogle Wallis; in default to the daughters of Henry Wallis, the heir to take the name and arms of Ogle. He leaves a legacy to Mary Ogle, daughter of Jane Wrangham, sister to William Rutter.

William Ogle had been married three times. His first wife whom he had married at Felton 3 or 13 November 1698 was Mary daughter of William Carr of Eshot, widow of William Carr of Etal. He married in Scotland in 1725 Elizabeth daughter of John Maier (or Earl) of Yorkshire; she may have been related to Thomas Maire, governor of Berwick, who had been William's godfather and who by his w.d. 20 March 1710/1 had left him his best laced coat.

Elizabeth was buried at Chatton 5 May 1755. His third wife was Margaret daughter of William Rutter of Newcastle; their marriage took place in Scotland, and there seems to have been some irregularity about it. William Rutter of Newcastle, gent., by his w.d. 23 July 1762 gives his messuage in Pudding chare, Newcastle, to trustees for his daughter Jane wife of Henry Ogle, for life with remainder to her son William Ogle. He gives to William Ogle of Causey Park, esq., £100, to put him and his wife, 'my dear daughter' into mourning (AA2. XVIII, p.256). After William Ogle's death, his widow married at Bothal 2 September 1777 Bernard Shaw, captain Queen's Regt.

William, son of captain William Ogle of Ogleborough, was baptised at Chatton 31 December 1730. He was in the army in 1751, became a captain in 1759 and a major in the 34rd Regt in 1768. In March 1783 he went out to India as major of the 52nd Regt and on his arrival was promoted to major-general. He died in Calcutta in 1786. Administration of his goods was granted 21 April 1797 to Frances Courtenay, the only child, Mary Garway the relict having died without taking out letters of administration. Major-general Ogle's wife was Frances Mary Garway, daughter of governor Stockwell of Cape Coast Castle, Africa, and she had died at Hampton in 1796.

The daughter Frances married firstly captain Courtenay, RN., nephew of the earl of Bute, and secondly, in 1800, William Brune Prideaux. There were two other daughters, Sarah wife of Arthur Henry Daly of Galway, Ireland; and Catherine, who died unmarried at Kingston-on-Thames on 25 August 1790.

In 1786 William Ogle Wallis succeeded to Causey Park and took the name of Ogle as required by the will of his great uncle William Ogle. William Ogle Wallis Ogle died 10 August 1844 and was succeeded by his son of the same name. The younger William Ogle Wallis Ogle sold Causey Park and died without male heirs.

In the 19th century a Thomas James Ogle claimed that he was the rightful heir to the Causey Park estate. He claimed that he was a direct descendant of Edward Ogle, eldest son of John Ogle (d.1636) of Causey Park. According to his story this Edward Ogle married Mary Fenwick and had a son Thomas born in 1638. When Thomas came of age he had mortgaged Causey Park to his uncle James. Actually James had undisputed ownership long before this, and there can be no doubt that his elder brother Edward died without children, perhaps killed in the Civil Wars. Thomas Ogle is said to have married Mary Grey and to have had a son Edward baptised at Rothbury in 1662. There is no record of this

baptism in the Rothbury Parish Registers. Edward married in 1678, aged sixteen, Anna Dawson, and his son John, a lieutenant in the 28th regiment died at Flotterton aged 110. There was in fact an Edward Ogle of Flotterton who married at Rothbury 21 May 1678 Anne Davison (not Dawson) of Snitter.

The story continues that lieut. colonel Ogle was twice married, his first wife being Mary Barber, widow, and the second 'a lady who destroyed her husband's will'. A son Thomas, by his first wife, was in the navy 'and destroyed all the deeds of Causey Park'. He married at Whittingham 1 June 1754 Jane Swan. They were the parents of Henry Ogle, a well-known local worthy. He was born in Whittingham pele in 1765/6 and as a young man went to sea, where he gained some knowledge of navigation, but was lamed. Leaving the sea he became a schoolmaster at Newsham and later at Rennington. In 1822 he invented a reaping machine which never worked; he had a scheme for curing smoky chimneys and was a searcher after perpetual motion. Later in life he taught school in Alnwick and died there in the workhouse on 10 February 1848 in his 84th year.

Henry Ogle married in 1783 Jane Chrisp and they had three sons Henry, Thomas (born 1790) and George. Thomas James Ogle the claimant was son of Thomas. His pedigree is inserted in pencil in a copy of Hodgson's *Northumberland* belonging to the Society of Antiquaries of Newcastle upon Tyne. The early part is a complete fabrication.

There were Ogles at Flotterton in the 17th century, but nothing is known of their origins. George Ogle of Flotterton and (blank) of Shilmoor were married at Rothbury 18 May 1654. Ellen wife of George Ogle, Flotterton, was buried 12 May 1669. Their children were Samuel (d. in infancy) and Michael. George Ogle was buried 12 March 1692/3.

Edward Ogle of Flotterton and his wife Anne Davison had a numerous family, at least fifteen children, many of whom died in infancy. There is no record in the parish registers of a son called John.

OGLE OF BEBSIDE, CHAP. HORTON

ON 20 November 1540 lord Ogle gave Tritlington to John and Matthew Ogle, sons of sir William Ogle, for their lives. John was sir William's second son and lived at Newsham, chap. Earsdon, two thirds of that place belonging to his wife Phillis in right of her first husband, George Cramlington. On 11 August 1565 John Ogle purchased Bebside, part of the confiscated lands of Tynemouth priory. In 1568 he was returned as owner of 'a vill called Bebside'. His will is dated 18 January 1585/6. His body is to be buried within the chapel of Seaton Delaval, and he leaves 40s., to be distributed amongst the poor.

To his eldest son William Ogle he leaves all his lands in Bebside 'to him and his heirs male lawfully begotten, and in default of such to my son Thomas and his heirs, and in default of such to my son Raphe, then to my son Launcelote, then to my brother Jaymes Ogle, and then to my right heirs'. His son Thomas is to have £100 'in full contentation of his child's portion'; the legacy is to be delivered to the testator's son-in-law (*i.e.* step-son) Peter Delavall to be employed for Thomas' use. William's younger sons Raphe and Launce-

OGLE of CAUSEY PARK, chap. Hebron

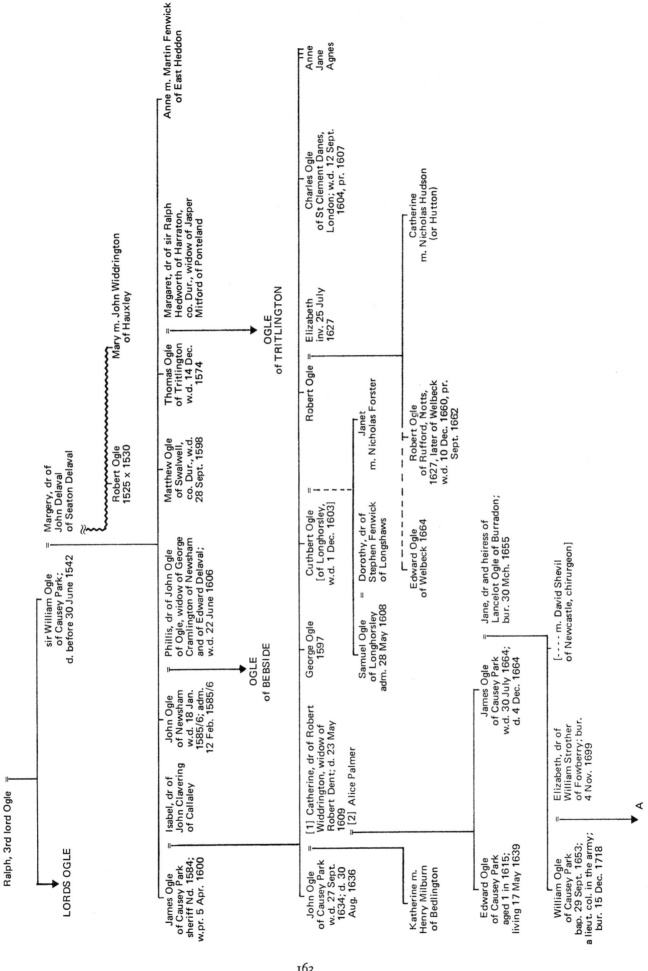

OGLE of CAUSEY PARK, cont.

A →

William Ogle
of Ogleborough;
capt. 1st dragoons;
w.d. 2 Sept. 1774;
d. 29 Nov. 1774;
bur. Hebburn

= [1] Mary Carr, widow;
b. of m. 24 Nov. 1721; d. 1725
= [2] Elizabeth, dr of John
Maier (or Earl) of Yorks;
m. 1725; bur. 5 May 1755
= [3] Margaret, dr of William
Rutter of Nc; m.2. 2 Sept.
1777 Bernard Shaw, capt.
2nd foot

Mary; bap. 11 May 1679; m. 10 Nov. 1698
William Orde of Felkington
Jane; bap. 7 Dec. 1680; m. Gawen
Aynsley of Little Harle

Henry Ogle
of Causey Park;
bap. 12 Oct. 1685;
sheriff Nd.1737;
d.s.p. 27 Feb. 1761

= [1] 'Mrs Elizabeth Manners'
= [2] Anne, dr of William
Orde of Felkington; m. 1736;
m.2. 26 May 1761 William Carr
of Etal; d. 7 Mch. 1766

Catharine; bap. 28 Aug. 1692; m. (lic. 18 Jan. 1723/4)
William Carr of Eshot
Dorothy; bap. 29 Nov. 1696; [d. 1713]

Elizabeth m. Ralph Wallis
of Coupland; bap. 26 June
1683

William Ogle
bap. 31 Dec. 1730;
major 34th foot;
maj. gen. 7 Jan. 1783;
d. 1786

= Frances Mary, dr of
- - - - Stockwell,
governor of Cape Coast Castle;
m.2. - - - - Garway; d. Hampton,
Glos. Oct. 1796

Frances; bap. Alnwick 9 July 1766;
m.1. capt. Courtenay, RN;
m.2. William Bruno Prideaux
Sarah; bap. Alnwick 13 Sept. 1767
Arthur Henry Daly of Galway,
Ireland

Catherine; d. unm. 25 Aug. 1790

164

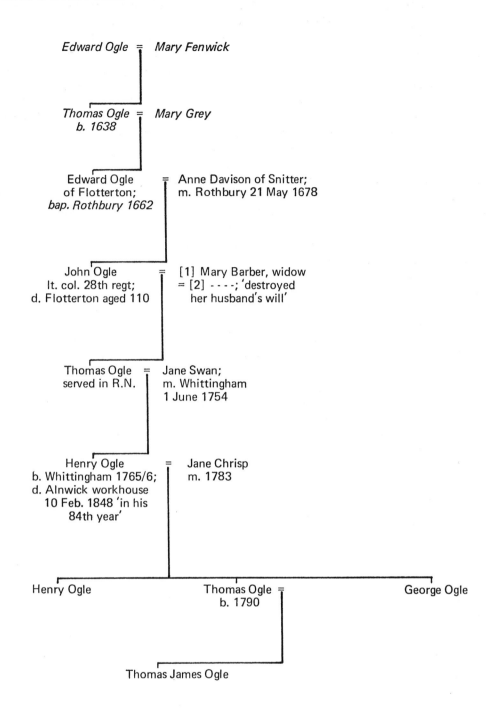

Edward Ogle = Mary Fenwick

Thomas Ogle = Mary Grey
b. 1638

Edward Ogle = Anne Davison of Snitter;
of Flotterton;   m. Rothbury 21 May 1678
bap. Rothbury 1662

John Ogle = [1] Mary Barber, widow
lt. col. 28th regt;   = [2] - - - -; 'destroyed
d. Flotterton aged 110   her husband's will'

Thomas Ogle = Jane Swan;
served in R.N.   m. Whittingham
                  1 June 1754

Henry Ogle = Jane Chrisp
b. Whittingham 1765/6;   m. 1783
d. Alnwick workhouse
10 Feb. 1848 'in his
84th year'

Henry Ogle   Thomas Ogle =   George Ogle
                    b. 1790

Thomas James Ogle

lote are each to have 100 marks for their portions and are to be in the custody of their uncle Jaymes Ogle. His son-in-law Launcelote Cramlington is to have £40 in full payment of 200 marks 'which I gave in marriage with my daughter Marye'. His daughters Elizabeth and Margaret Ogle have legacies of £100 each, and his daughters Barbara and Dorytye Ogle each 100 marks. If any of the children should die 'before they accomplish their full age, then his or her portion to be divided equally amongst the rest'. James Ogle of Hebburn and Brian Ogle of Shilvington are each to have a young quye of two year old. His brother Jaymes and Jaymes' sons John, George, Cuthbert, Robert and Charles Ogle 'to every of them an old angel'.

His son Launcelote is to be sole executor to the will. Robert Delavall, esq., James Ogle esq., Edward Graye,

Matthew Ogle, Ollyver Ogle and Jaymes Lyle, gentlemen, are to act as supervisors. The will was proved on 9 May 1586. An inventory of his goods had been exhibited on 20 January 1585/6, his principal possessions being farming stock at Newsham and Bebside and household goods at Newsham. Robert Ogle of Newcastle owed him 23s. 4d. (SS. 38, p.129).

John Ogle of Newsham's wife was Phillis daughter of John Ogle of Ogle, widow of George Cramlington (d.1551) of Newsham and of Edward Delaval. Phillis Ogle, late of Newsham, co. North'd, widow, now being at Lemington made her w.d. 22 June 1606. She leaves to her daughters Barbarie Harbottle £20, Dorrytye Swynborne £15 and Margaret Beddnell £10. Phillis remembers in her will two of her Delaval sons, Peter and Ralph, and her youngest Ogle son Lance (Raine, MSS. Wills and Inv. II, p.179). The inventory of Phillis Ogle's goods is dated 10 January 1606/7.

The children of John Ogle of Newsham were four sons, William, Thomas, Ralph and Lancelot; and five daughters, Mary wife of Lancelot Cramlington of Newsham; Elizabeth married firstly Cuthbert Bates of Halliwell and secondly (on 18 August 1608) Thomas Smelt of Gray's Inn; Margaret wife of George Beadnell of Lemington; Barbara whose husband was called Harbottle; and Dorothy wife of John Swinburne of Wylam. Margaret Beadnell had a daughter called Jane Ogle, for her mother in her will leaves a legacy of £10 to 'Jane Ogle of Causey Park, daughter to my daughter Beadnell'. Margaret may have been married to one of the younger sons of James Ogle of Causey Park before she married George Beadnell.

The eldest son, William Ogle, in 1586 conveyed a quarter of the manor of Swalwell, co. Durham, to William Shafto. In 1587 administration of his goods was granted to his brothers Ralph and Thomas Ogle; mention is made of Constance Middleton of Newcastle, 'pretended wife' of the deceased. The second son, Thomas, is called 'my brother' Thomas Ogle in the w.d. 23 January 1601/2 of his brother-in-law Cuthbert Bates. He was probably 'Master Thomas Ogell, steward of Bedlingtonshire' who is a witness to the w.d. 10 March 1607/8 of William Watson of Bedlington. He registered his pedigree at the 1615 visitation. On 9 March 1615/6 administration of the goods of Thomas Ogle, late of Bebside, was granted to Dorothy his widow. On 25 January 1616/7 Mrs Dorothy Ogle, widow, rendered an account into the Consistory Court of Durham. She was a daughter of George Whitfield of Newcastle and married secondly, before 26 June 1618, Edward Delaval of Cowpen. She died in 1647, retaining until her death an interest in Bebside.

John Ogle's third son Ralph, living in 1606, had predeceased his brother Thomas. When Thomas registered his pedigree in 1615 he calls himself eldest son and his brother Lancelot 2nd son. Ralph may have been the Ralph Ogle of par. Bothal, administration of whose goods was granted 22 February 1613/4 to his widow Frances.

Lancelot, the youngest son of John Ogle of Newsham, outlived his three elder brothers and was the only one to leave issue. In 1618 Lancelot Ogle sold his interest in Bebside to John Ogle of Causey Park for £400 in hand and £700 to be paid to him within two years of the death of Dorothy Delaval (*Brumell Deeds*). John Ogle assigned his rights in 1633 to Thomas Ogle of Tritlington, and on the death of the latter they passed to his brother George. On 18 July 1643 Lancelot Ogle confirmed the manor of Bebside to George Ogle. When Dorothy Delaval died *circa* 1647 the balance of £700 of the purchase money was due to be paid and the right to it passed to Lancelot's son Thomas. He died about 1644. His wife was Dorothy daughter of Thomas Watson of Ellingham; she is mentioned in the w.d. 10 March 1607/8 of her brother William Watson of Bedlington. Their children were two sons, Thomas and Robert, and a daughter (probably called Dorothy) who married George Ogle of Tritlington; there may also have been a daughter Isabel for Daniel Brader of Bedlington, gent., by his w.d. 22 October 1620 leaves legacies to Isabel Ogle daughter of Lancelot Ogle, gent., and to Edward Delaval, gent., of Bebside. William Watson of Bedlington in his w.d. 10 March 1607/8 mentions his sister Dorothy Ogle and her daughter

Dorothy. The younger son Robert, a Newcastle mariner, died before 1661, leaving a widow Mable. Mabell Ogle of Newcastle, widow, made her will on 20 September 1669. In the will she mentions her late husband Robert Ogle mariner, deceased, son of Lancelot Ogle of Bedlington, gent.; she leaves £100 to her son William Barnett (Raine, *MSS. Wills and Inv.* VII, p.85).

In his w.d. 2 November 1651 (pr. 1 December 1651) Thomas Ogle directs that he is to be buried in Horton chapel; to his wife Jane he leaves his lands and the tuition of her children. The £700 owing on Bebside is bequeathed to his children, of which his eldest son Thomas is to have £200. The widow married secondly James Bell of Bothal Barns.

'This Thomas, returning from sea, where he was bred, and wanting his £200, he married, and, having no place to live in, George Ogle allowed him a room or two in Bebside house, and £12 per annum for the interest of the £200'. This was stated in a law suit many years later, in 1709. The younger Thomas' wife was Barbara daughter of Ralph Anderson, widow of Cuthbert Ogle of Kirkley. Thomas Ogle seems to have regained possession of Bebside which he sold on 6 October 1702 for £2200 to John Johnson of Newcastle, hostman. He was then living in London.

He is described in his w.d. 11 July 1725 as late of Bebside. £500 due to him by Ralph Anderson of South Shields and a house and lands in Bedlington, he bequeaths to his daughters Isabella wife of William Fletcher, Sarah wife of John Bailiffe and Elizabeth wife of George Kirkley.

Thomas Ogle's son Humphrey was living at Cullercoats in 1706 but afterwards lived at North Blyth, par. Bedlington, where he was salt officer. He married 8 May 1706 Margaret Clark of the parish of Tynemouth. They had children baptised at Tynemouth and others at Bedlington, of whom nothing further is known.

OGLE OF TRITLINGTON, CHAP. HEBRON

ON 4 February 1563/4 Richard Robson conveyed to Thomas Ogle of Tritlington two tenements and 27 acres of land in Tritlington, together with other lands which Thomas already held by lease. This Thomas Ogle was a younger son of sir William Ogle of Cockle Park. He made his will 14 December 1574. His son James Ogle is to have all his lands in Tritlington to him and his heirs male for ever, and failing such they are to go to his other son Martyn and his heirs male for ever. If neither of the sons should have heirs male, the testator's right heirs are to succeed. It would seem that the eldest son James was perhaps mentally retarded for his father goes on to state in his will that if James 'be proved to lack natural wit and reason to govern himself', the lands at Tritlington are to go to the other son Martyn in such manner and sort as though James has died without heirs male. Nevertheless James is to have out of the lands yearly sufficient to find himself during his lifetime; this is to be done by the sight of the testator's brother James Ogle and Martyng Fenwick, Mathoo Ogle and John Ogle, his brethren. Thomas leaves to his wife the purchased lands in Tritlington according to the condition of an obligation wherein his brother James Ogle and himself stood bound to Mr Hedworth of Harraton for performance of the same. The testator's two daughters Annes and Juliane

OGLE of BEBSIDE, chap. HORTON

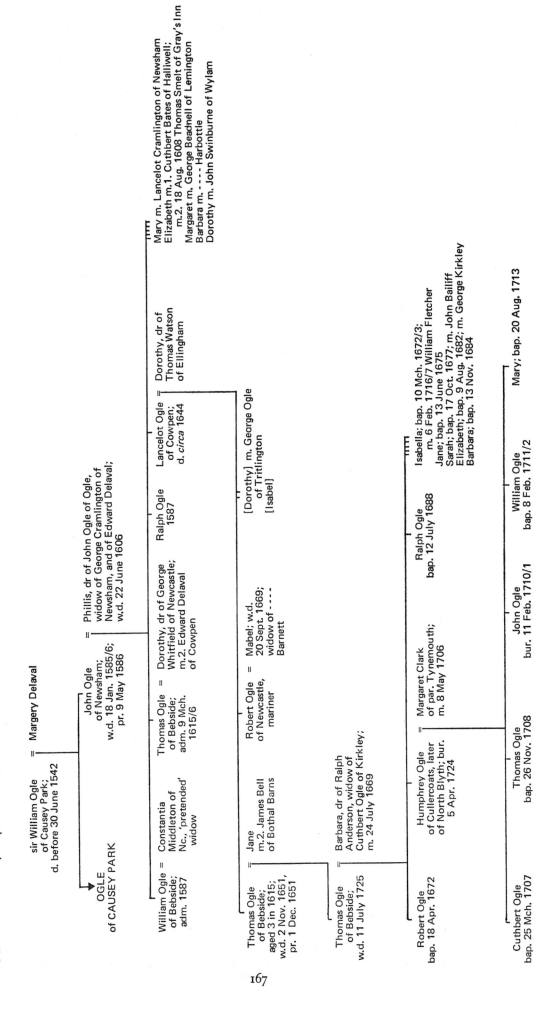

sir William Ogle
of Causey Park;
d. before 30 June 1542

= Margery Delaval

OGLE
of CAUSEY PARK

John Ogle
of Newsham;
w.d. 18 Jan. 1585/6;
pr. 9 May 1586

= Phillis, dr of John Ogle of Ogle,
widow of George Cramlington of
Newsham, and of Edward Delaval;
w.d. 22 June 1606

Mary m. Lancelot Cramlington of Newsham
Elizabeth m.1. Cuthbert Bates of Halliwell;
m.2. 18 Aug. 1608 Thomas Smelt of Gray's Inn
Margaret m. George Beadnell of Lemington
Barbara m. - - - - Harbottle
Dorothy m. John Swinburne of Wylam

William Ogle =
of Bebside;
adm. 1587

Constantia
Middleton of
Nc., 'pretended'
widow

Thomas Ogle =
of Bebside;
adm. 9 Mch.
1615/6

Dorothy, dr of George
Whitfield of Newcastle;
m.2. Edward Delaval
of Cowpen

Ralph Ogle
1587

Lancelot Ogle =
of Cowpen;
d. circa 1644

Dorothy, dr of
Thomas Watson
of Ellingham

[Dorothy] m. George Ogle
of Tritlington
[Isabel]

Thomas Ogle =
of Bebside;
aged 3 in 1615;
w.d. 2 Nov. 1651,
pr. 1 Dec. 1651

Jane
m.2. James Bell
of Bothal Barns

Robert Ogle =
of Newcastle,
mariner

Mabel; w.d.
20 Sept. 1669;
widow of - - - -
Barnett

Thomas Ogle =
of Bebside;
w.d. 11 July 1725

Barbara, dr of Ralph
Anderson, widow of
Cuthbert Ogle of Kirkley;
m. 24 July 1669

Humphrey Ogle =
of Cullercoats, later
of North Blyth; bur.
5 Apr. 1724

Margaret Clark
of par. Tynemouth;
m. 8 May 1706

Robert Ogle
bap. 18 Apr. 1672

Ralph Ogle
bap. 12 July 1688

Isabella; bap. 10 Mch. 1672/3;
m. 6 Feb. 1716/7 William Fletcher
Jane; bap. 13 June 1675
Sarah; bap. 17 Oct. 1677; m. John Bailiff
Elizabeth; bap. 9 Aug. 1682; m. George Kirkley
Barbara; bap. 13 Nov. 1684

Cuthbert Ogle
bap. 25 Mch. 1707

Thomas Ogle
bap. 26 Nov. 1708

John Ogle
bur. 11 Feb. 1710/1

William Ogle
bap. 8 Feb. 1711/2

Mary; bap. 20 Aug. 1713

are each to have £60 to their marriage. His wife Margaret and his two daughters are to have the leasehold term of years in the tithe corn of Prestwick, and his two sons are to have the lease of the tithe corn of Benridge. He desires the right honourable my lord Ogle to be good to his wife and children, and he, John Hedworth of Harraton esq., James Ogle, Martin Fenwick, Matho Ogle and John Ogle are to be the supervisors. The will was proved 21 June 1575 and the inventory of the deceased's goods is dated 17 January 1574/5.

Thomas Ogle's wife was Margaret daughter of sir Ralph Hedworth of Harraton, co. Durham, widow of Jasper Mitford of Ponteland (1575 Vis. ped. of Hedworth where Thomas is called of 'Kirklington' in error). Administration of the goods of Jasper Mitford of Ponteland was granted 21 August 1572 to Margaret Ogle wife of Thomas Ogle of Tritlington, late wife of the said Jasper.

There is no evidence that Thomas Ogle's eldest son James ever succeeded to his father's lands in Tritlington. He certainly survived his father, for when Martin Ogle proved his father's will, power was reserved to James Ogle, the other executor. In *Ogle and Bothal* references to James Ogle of Causey Park and to James Ogle of Shilvington have been wrongly attributed to the eldest son of Thomas Ogle of Tritlington.

Patrike and Martyne Ogle of Tritlington were two of the men whom Philloppe Grene of Morpeth in his w.d. 20 July 1583 charged with his murder. In *Ogle and Bothal* 'Patrick Ogle of Tritlington is assumed to be the eldest son of Thomas Ogle', but there is not the slightest evidence for such an assumption, and the fact that there is no mention of Patrick in Thomas' will should be enough to reject it. On 23 November 1587 Alexander Ogle appointed Mr Martin Ogle of Tritlington guardian of his infant son Arthur. At the view and muster of the horsemen within the Castle ward and Morpeth ward of the Middle Marches taken at Clifton field on 24 November 1595, there were only two persons from Tritlington, Matthew Cockson and Martin Ogle, the latter being fully furnished with petronel, coat of plate, steel cap, sword and dagger, and riding a gray horse (*CBP*. II, p.78). Martin Ogle of Tritlington, gent., was one of the jurors charged and sworn at Hexham on 9 April 1596 to inquire into the decays of the Middle Marches (*Ib*., p.132). He was no doubt the Martin Ogell, one of the jury, a follower of Woodrington, with whom Robert Shaftooe of 'Stannerton', a notable offender, was reset in 1597 (*Ib*., p.340).

Later in the year, Edward Gray, deputy warden, had to complain that the gentlemen of his ward refused to stand watches 'by the reason of my lord Ogell his strict directions to his deputy Merting Ogell of Tritlington, utterly to refuse the same for him and his tenants', saying it was impossible for them to do it, though both his deputy and the assembled gentlemen thought it most easy, and no watch more necessary (*Ib*., p.452).

Martyn Ogle's will is dated 28 April 1601; he was 'sick in body but yet strong in mind', and directs that he is to be buried in the parish church of Hebburn. He bequeathes his eldest son Thomas Ogle to his 'true and assured good friend and cousin M'tres Talbot whom my hope and confidence is in who with the help of God will be careful for the standing of my posterity'. The name of his good friend and cousin

has previously been read as 'Mrs Tallent' but it is evident that the person referred to is the head of the Ogle family—Jane, daughter and coheiress of Cuthbert, 7th lord Ogle, and wife of Edward Talbot. Martyn Ogle leaves all his lands, his best horse, his furniture, a bedstead with a feather bed and all the furniture that belonged to it, six silver spoons that he had bought at London and the table in the hall to his son Thomas. The rest of his goods unbequeathed are to go to his wife and his other four children Margaret Ogle, Mathew Ogle, Georg Ogle and Luck Ogle. His son Mathew is to have 40 marks in consideration of his filial portion and £40 that 'my uncle Mathew gave him which my cousin John Ogle standeth bound for me for the payment'. His daughter Margret Ogle is to have £100 for her filial portion if his goods will go so far, and Georg and Luck are to have £50 apiece with the same qualification. The four younger children are left one each to the care of his cousin John Ogle of Causey Park, his cousin Thomas Ogle of Bebside, his cousin Lanclote Ogle of Darras Hall, and his wife. The supervisors are to be Mrs Talbut, Mr Hennerye Wotherington, Mr Fenwick of Wallington and the testator's cousin John Ogle of Causey Park; the will is witnessed by John Ogle and Lancelote Ogle (*Dur. Prob. Off.* by C.R.H.; the will is vilely written and until recently repaired was in two pieces and part is missing).

Thomas Ogle, son and heir of Martin Ogle, late of Tritlington, matriculated BA from University college, Oxford, 8 July 1614. On 12 October 1621 Thomas Ogle, esq., Matthew and Luke Ogle, gentlemen, all of Tritlington, bound themselves to Gregory Ogle of Choppington for an annual payment by Thomas to Gregory in the south church porch of Bothal, until Thomas received possession of the manor house and demesne of Choppington, Cleaswell Hill, and a water corn mill and Slackhouses by right of tenant right of Gregory, and by lease from the bishop of Durham.

On 12 June 1628 Thomas Ogle of Tritlington conveyed (or mortgaged) to Thomas Middleton of Belsay for £3,050 all his estate in Tritlington and the manor of Choppington; on 18 December 1633 he bought the manor of Bebside from John Ogle of Cawsey Park; on 8 November 1637 Thomas Middleton took a lease for three lives from the bishop of Durham of the manor of Choppington and Cleaswell Hill. A story told very much later was that Thomas Ogle being greatly in debt had to go abroad to Ireland and made arrangements concerning his property with Thomas Middleton, who was a creditor (*PSAN2*, X, p.140).

Thomas was living at Dublin when he made his w.d. 10 October 1641. He appoints his 'cousin Thomas Ogle of Darrashall co. N, esq., one of the gentlemen of H.M. Privy Chamber' executor, and leaves to him all his lands in co. Northumberland and bishopric of Durham (Tritlington excepted), viz. Choppington, Bedlington, East Sleekburn, Spittle land, Cleaswell hill and the Mill, Bebside, Ellington and the farms and rectory of Heddon-on-the-Wall. As for Tritlington he gives it to his brother George Ogle and his heirs male for ever, and in default of heirs male to Thomas Ogle of Darrashall and his heirs for ever except heirs general if George happen to intermarry with an Ogle. The testator had acquired considerable estates in Ireland and these also he leaves to Thomas Ogle of Darrashall. Every one of his brother George's children are to have £100 to be paid at 21 or day of marriage. The will was proved at London 11 October 1648 by oath of Thomas

Ogle *consobrini* of the deceased (*Ib.*).

Although under his brother's will, George Ogle was only to have Tritlington, he may have obtained the other lands of Choppington, Bedlington, Bebside, etc., and it could be that there was some trust implied when these lands had been willed to Thomas Ogle of Darrashall.

George Ogle is said to have married 'the eldest daughter' of Lancelot Ogle of Cowpen and to have died about 1654. His wife's name was probably Dorothy. George Ogle was succeeded by his son Martin Ogle.

Martin Ogle lived in Virginia for 30 years, returning to England in 1682. On 21 February 1682/3 Martin Ogle of Tritlington gave letters of attorney to William Ogle of Causey Park to recover lands in Bebside, Choppington and Ellington, co. Northumberland, and in Bedlington, Cleaswell Hill, East Sleekburn and West Sleekburn, co. Durham. On the following day Martin released the lands to William and made an agreement with him that whereas Martin had appointed William his attorney to recover the said lands, William's expences were to be repaid out of the first profits of the lands, and the lands were to be conveyed to such person as William should appoint (*Brumell Charters* 43, 44, 45). It would seem from these documents that Martin was endeavouring to recover the lands that his uncle Thomas had bequeathed to Thomas Ogle of Darrashall. On 20 October 1691 William Ogle of Causey Park strengthened his hold on these lands by obtaining a release from Thomas Ogle of Bishop Wearmouth 'nephew and heir-at-law to Martin Ogle, late of Tritlington, deceased', of the lands conveyed to William on 22 February 1682/3. The lands are detailed as all those tenements and lands in Bebside, all tenements and lands in Choppington, two tenements in Ellington, a tenement in Bedlington, a tenement called Cleaswell hill, and two tenements in East Sleekburn and West Sleekburn; Thomas was to receive ten shillings (*Ib.*, No. 49).

About this time sir William Middleton, bart, issued a bill of complaint against John Ogle and Dorothy his wife, heir at law of Thomas Ogle, late of Titlington (*sic* for Tritlington) deceased, and Robert Clark, administrator of the goods and chattels, rights and credits of the said Thomas Ogle. Dorothy Ogle for herself answers that she believes to be true and hopes to prove that Thomas Ogle, deceased, died about 50 or 60 years ago without leaving any issue of his body and only two brothers named Matthew Ogle and George Ogle and that the said Matthew Ogle also died without leaving any issue of his body and that the said George Ogle is also dead and had issue only two sons named Martin and William and one daughter to witt this defendant Dorothy; and that the said Martin Ogle and William Ogle did both of them also die without leaving any issue of their or either of their bodies so that this defendant is heir at law to the said Thomas Ogle, she being the only sister and heir at law to her late brothers Martin Ogle and William Ogle. This statement was sworn at Bishop Auckland 19 January 1691 (*Ib.*, No. 46).

If Dorothy Ogle's statement is accepted as fact, there seems no place in the pedigree for Thomas Ogle of Bishop Auckland. Dorothy's first husband was John Browne of East Chevington, their bond of marriage being dated 25 April 1664. Administration of the goods of John Brown, late of Chevington Moorhouse, par. Warkworth, deceased, was granted 7 January 1667/8 to Dorothy Browne, widow and relict of the deceased, together with tuition of Thomas and Dorothy their children (*Dur. Prob. Off.* by C.R.H.). Dorothy Browne, widow, married at Bolam 24 May 1670 John Ogle of Bradford. *See* OGLE OF BRADFORD, PAR. BOLAM.

OGLE OF DARRAS HALL, PAR. PONTELAND

AT the muster of Castle and Morpeth wards on 24 November 1595 there came from Darras Hall, Gawin Ogle with a petronel, coat of plate, steel cap, sword and dagger riding a grey nag, and Lancelot Ogle, also furnished, on a bay horse (*CBP.* II, p.78). These two were father and son and were probably closely related to the Ogles of Tritlington, but the exact connection is not known. Martin Ogle of Tritlington in his w.d. 28 April 1602 calls Lancelot Ogle 'cousin' and appoints him a supervisor of his will. Of course the term 'cousin' at this time often denotes no closer relationship than kinsman. In the next generation however Martin's son Thomas appointed his 'cousin' Thomas Ogle of Darras Hall (Lancelot's son) executor to his will, a trustee of his estates, and his residuary legatee.

On 15 May 1676 Gawen Ogle of Darrashall owed 16s. 8d. to William Fenwick. Gawen Ogle was brother of a George Ogle who held a lease of Darras Hall from Robert Brandling. Their father, whose name is unknown, had previously had a lease of Darras Hall from the Brandlings, for sir Robert Brandling of Newcastle, in his w.d. 1 January 1562/3 states that Gawen Ogle is to 'have the farm hall of Darras hall, now in the tenure of his father' (*SS.* 121, p.36).

In his w.d. 1 November 1594 George mentions his well beloved wife Isabell Ogle and her son Hughe Collingwood. His nephew Robert Ogle, son of his late brother Robert is to have a gray horse. Robert Ogle's daughter Margaret Ogle is to have a young heifer and her sister Elizabeth Ogle two goats. He leaves to his brother Roger one rigg of his wheat land, to his sister Margerie Ogle one young branded cow, and to his brother John any one of the five eastmost riggs of his faughe or wheat land. He also remembers his brother John Ogle's two children. The residue of his estate is to go to his well beloved nephew Lancelot Ogle, son of his brother Gawayne Ogle, and Lancelot is to be sole executor. 'If the said Lancelot Ogle shall claim any lease or grant of my landlord Mr Robert Brandlyn, gent., of that messuage which I now occupy in Darrashall he shall suffer the said Isabell my wife to have her dwelling in my said messuage'. The will is witnessed by Gawen Ogle, Charles Gofton, Ambros Foster, Nicholas Hall and Richard Handcock (*Dur. Prob. Off.* by C.R.H.).

George Ogle's brother Roger was perhaps the man of that name who was buried at Ponteland 28 August 1612. 'The wife of Roger Ogle of High Callerton' was buried there between 4 September and 29 September 1612.

'Gawinus Ogle de Darishal' was buried at Ponteland 6 March 1612/3. His son Lancelot was probably the man of that name who married at Ponteland 30 August 1602 Anna Ogle. In *Ogle and Bothal* it is suggested that the connection between the Ogles of Tritlington and the Ogles of Darras Hall was through Lancelot Ogle's wife Anna, further suggesting that Anna could be the same person as Annes, daughter of Thomas Ogle (d.1574/5) of Tritlington. This completely ignores the fact that Annes was apparently of age in 1574 and

OGLE of TRITLINGTON, chap. HEBRON

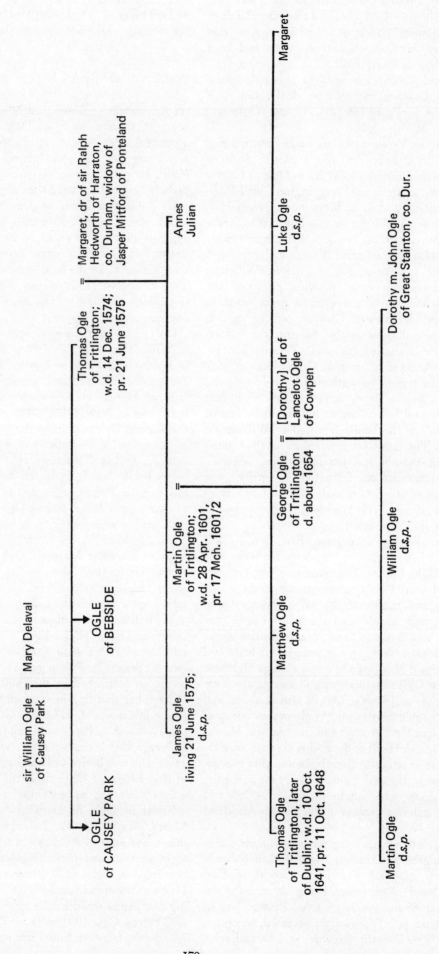

sir William Ogle = Mary Delaval
of Causey Park

OGLE
of CAUSEY PARK

OGLE
of BEBSIDE

Thomas Ogle = Margaret, dr of sir Ralph
of Tritlington;   Hedworth of Harraton,
w.d. 14 Dec. 1574;   co. Durham, widow of
pr. 21 June 1575   Jasper Mitford of Ponteland

James Ogle
living 21 June 1575;
d.s.p.

Annes
Julian

Martin Ogle
of Tritlington;
w.d. 28 Apr. 1601,
pr. 17 Mch. 1601/2

George Ogle = [Dorothy] dr of
of Tritlington   Lancelot Ogle
d. about 1654   of Cowpen

Luke Ogle
d.s.p.

Margaret

Matthew Ogle
d.s.p.

Thomas Ogle
of Tritlington, later
of Dublin; w.d. 10 Oct.
1641, pr. 11 Oct. 1648

William Ogle
d.s.p.

Dorothy m. John Ogle
of Great Stainton, co. Dur.

Martin Ogle
d.s.p.

so must have been over 40 years old in 1602. Lancelot and Anna had at least six sons baptised between 1603 and 1612, the four eldest Mark, William, Robert and John dying in infancy. The youngest son Gerard (bap. 10 May 1612) was apprenticed 28 June 1631 with the London Drapers Company (*PSAN*4. III, p.250).

Mark Errington of Ponteland by his w.d. 22 October 1637 leaves to his 'cousin' Lanc Ogle of Darras Hall and his wife, an old angel each. On 4 April 1628 Robert Brandling gave a lease of Darras Hall, then in the occupation of Lancelot Ogle, to Thomas Ogle, son of Lancelot, and Thomas' wife Susan. In 1636 the Ogles agreed to purchase Darras Hall, which was then mortgaged to Mark Errington of West Denton for £1230.

Lancelot Ogle's heir was his fifth, but eldest surviving son, Thomas, who was admitted to Gray's Inn 2 February 1629/30. On 11 May 1642 Thomas Ogle, as son and heir of Lancelot Ogle, deceased, and one of the gentlemen of his majesty's privy chamber, and Gerard Ogle of Darras Hall, filed a bill of complaint about the lease of Darras Hall and the purchase of the estate and the question was referred to the arbitration of sir John Fenwick, sir William Widdrington and sir William Carnaby. On 10 May 1654 this question was still unsettled, for Thomas and his wife filed another bill, and also again on 24 October 1655 when his wife is described as a daughter of Peter Smart, of the county of Durham, clerk, deceased. The answers were given on 20 November 1655.

In the meantime Thomas Ogle as a royalist had petitioned on 17 January 1645/6 to compound for his estates. On 6 April 1646 he deposed that about two years ago he departed from Oxford into France with his wife and children, resolving not to return until a final end was made to these unhappy wars, but falling desperately sick at Flushing he returned home about October 1644 where he has remained not intermeddling in the affairs of this kingdom. In a case before the House of Lords concerning Thomas Ogle's father-in-law, Peter Smart, prebendary of Durham, the gentleman usher was directed on 18 November 1646 to apprehend captain Ogle who had been present at the hearing; it appears that Ogle had been formerly committed for treason and other offences against the state, but escaped prison. On the following day captain Thomas Ogle petitioned to be released but it was decided that he should stand committed to the custody of the gentleman usher until the particulars of the charge against him should be produced. Sometime later Ogle asked for bail or liberty to go into the country with a keeper to procure money to pay his fine and perfect his composition; on 19 June 1647 bail was allowed to him, the sureties being Mr Witherington of Broome, co. Durham, and Wm Stevens of Drury Lane, co. Middlesex, cutler. Two years later he was fined at a sixth, £240, in respect of the capital messuage and lands called Darras Hall (*SS.* 111, p.302).

Under the w.d. 10 October 1641 of Thomas Ogle of Dublin, Thomas Ogle of Darras Hall is to have his estates in Ireland and the farm and rectory of Heddon-on-the-Wall (*NCH.* XIII, p.60). Thomas Ogle had a son William described as of Gray's Inn, Middlesex, esq., 3 November 1674 when he made a statement that Thomas Ogle of Darras Hall, his father, was seized of manors and lands of very great value in Ireland which came to him from Thomas Ogle of Tritlington, the orator's father being so seised and having raised forces for king Charles I was sequestered and died about the year 1658,

leaving William his son and heir a minor and unable to prosecute his right for recovery, he therefore made arrangements with one Edward Gittings who offered to allow William £200 a year and in recompense he should receive half the property. On 29 April 1659 Gittings became his guardian and William went over to Ireland. Somewhat later William Ogle was a prisoner in custody of the Warden of the Fleet. His debts seem to have been considerable. He was living 28 November 1695. It is not known when he died or if he left any descendants.

OGLE OF KIRKLEY, PAR. PONTELAND

In the inquisition taken on 16 March 1512/3 after the death of Ralph, 3rd lord Ogle, it is recorded that 'he gave to John Ogle, his son (as by his writing sealed with his own seal more plainly appears) a fourth part of South Dissington for life'. According to the visitation pedigree of 1575, John Ogle was the third and youngest son, and married Sibell daughter to John Heron. On 7 August 1522 Robert, 4th lord Ogle, gave to (his brothers) William Ogle and John Ogle the manors and castles of Great Tosson, Hepple, and Lorbottle to hold until they shall have received £100 (*NDD.* p.182, No. 88).

On 7 October 1523 'John Ogle, brother to the lord', was in the garrison of Wark. He is first described as 'of Kirkley' about 1526 when it is stated that he may dispend £6 by the year in the defence of the borders. A few years later he 'may dispend £10 by the year and may serve with 8 men, and is a sharp forward man'. At this time Kirkley belonged to the Eures of Witton, co. Durham, and John Ogle was both tenant and steward. Sir Ralph Eure of Witton in his w.d. 6 May 1533 directs that all his officers, both receivers and bailiffs, are to be clearly discharged for and of their accounts of and for all and every sum accounted before the day of his death, except John Ogle (*SS.* 106, p.183).

On 10 December 1528 Ralph, lord Ogle, demised to John Ogle of Kirkley, gent., the town and territory of Twizel to him and his heirs for 31 years for an annual payment of £10. In 1537 and again in 1540 John Ogle of Kirkley, gent., is described as a pensioner upon the Middle and West Marches with a fee of £13. 6s. 8d. About this time he seems to have moved to Twizel.

Sir Reynold Carnaby sent to the Council of the North a list of names of those appointed to meet for a 'rode' in Tynedale, 13 September 1538, which includes lord Ogle with 20 men, sir William Ogle with 10 men, Parson Ogle with 10 men, John Ogle of Ogle with 10 men, John Ogle of Twysell with 20 men. In *Ogle and Bothal* it has been accepted that John Ogle of Twysell was son of John Ogle of Kirkley and 'took his father's place'. This is hardly possible. As Robert, 4th lord Ogle, was born in 1490 or 1491 it is unlikely that his youngest brother John could have been born before 1495 and his birth may have been a few years later, for he had three sisters. In any case he can hardly have been the father of a man old enough in 1538 to be a junior commander. It must also have been the elder John Ogle who in November 1544 was stationed by sir Ralph Eure at Fernihurst with a few men. On 2 December 1544 the earl of Shrewsbury writing to the Privy Council states that he is enclosing 'such letters as presently arrived here from the wardens of the East and West Marches, and

OGLE of DARRAS HALL, par. PONTELAND

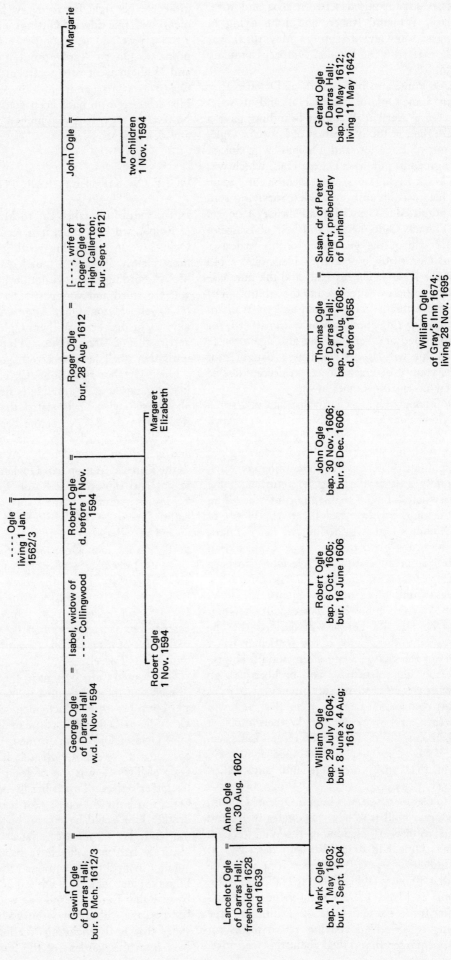

a letter from the laird of Fernihurst and John Ogle to the Warden of the Middle Marches. The said John Ogle is an English man appointed by the said lord Warden to be with the said Fernihurst, as before this hath been advertised,—with a small company of Englishmen' (*Hamilton Papers*, II. p.522). In the *State Papers* is a letter from the laird of Fernihurst and John Ogle to the warden of the Middle Marches, and also a letter from the laird of Bonjedworth to Ogle.

On 15 September 1545 John Ogle of Ogle castle, John Ogle of Twizel, with 8 or 9 evil disposed persons with force and arms and arrayed with weapons came to Newton Thropple and Nunriding fields within the parish of Mitford and by force carried away the tithe corn belonging to the vicar, and Ralph Ogle of Twizel with others lying in wait 'sore wounded and hurt'. The parties concerned were commanded to appear before the king and council in the Star Chamber at Westminster.

The name of John Ogle of Twizel, esq., appears in a list drawn up in 1550 of the gentlemen inhabitants within the Middle Marches. On the death of John Carr, captain of Wark, in 1551 he owed 'to Johne Oggyll of Twyssill iiij old crowns of gold, xxs' (*SS.* 2, p.139).

All these references to John Ogle of Kirkley and John Ogle of Twizel can and probably do refer to one and the same person. The lease of Twizel originally taken for 31 years from 10 December 1528 should have expired in 1559 but seems to have been renewed for a further term. Robert, 6th lord Ogle, by his w.d. 27 July 1562 leaves to Robert Ogle, his uncle Oswen's son, the manor and tenement of Twissle in reversion after the years of the lease of John Ogle (*Ib.*, p.203; Hodgson has wrongly transcribed this as the manor of Hepple). The wording of this might suggest that the original lessee was still living. In 1568 it is recorded that a John Ogle had died seised of half of South Dissington and lands in Bradford, but this was John Ogle of Ogle castle who by his w.d. 4 April 1565 left all his lands and tenements in South Dissington to three of his sons and a grandson. From this it seems probable that John Ogle of Twizel was dead for he had had a lease of a quarter of South Dissington for his lifetime, and in 1565 this quarter was undoubtedly part of the half then held by John Ogle of Ogle castle.

According to Hodgson, John Ogle (of Kirkley) by his wife Sibell Heron 'had issue one son, Robert' (*HN.* ii. I, p.385). It is admitted in *Ogle and Bothal* that from the entire absence of Robert's name in documents 'it is doubtful whether he lived long' (p.108). Nevertheless it is there 'assumed' that Robert was father of another Robert Ogle, ancestor of the Ogles of Darras Hall. This method of making a pedigree can hardly inspire confidence.

About 1580 two brothers, Henry Ogle of Kirkley and John Ogle of Saltwick each held farmholds in Kirkley under William, lord Eure. It has generally been accepted that they were sons of John Ogle of Kirkley, later of Twizel. It is not known for certain if Henry or John was the elder brother. For John and his descendants *see* OGLE OF SALTWICK.

Henry Ogle of Kirkley, par. Ponteland, gentleman, made his will on 2 January 1580/1. He gives to his son Marke Ogle all his interest in the water corn mill and farmhold in Kirkley, in his own occupation, 'trusting that my singular good lord and master William lord Ewrye will stand and be good lord unto my wife and children, as heretofore he hath

been unto me'. His son Mark is also to have £40. To his son Luke Ogle he leaves a tenement or farmhold in Newham 'during the term of years my son Marke hath in the same'; besides this, Luke is to have £20. His son Roberte Ogle is to have a tenement in Newham and 20 marks. His wife Margaret Ogle is to have his right in two tenements in Coldcoats. Small legacies of livestock are left to Cuthbert Ogle of Edington, his godson Henry Ogle of Saltwick, his brother Jasper Ogle, Alice Ogle and Dorathe Ogle of Edington. The rest of his goods are left to his wife Margaret and his son Marke 'and they to have the custody of my four youngest sons, Lancelot, Henrye, Myghell and Cuthbert Ogle during their minorities'. He leaves his son Mygell Ogle to 'my brother Cuthbert Forster, and he to have the rule of him'. The supervisors of the will are to be his loving cousins and friends James Ogle of Causey, esq., Clement Ogle of South Dissington, gent., Oliver Ogle of Burradon, gent., and his 'brother' Cuthbert Forster (*SS.* 38, p.32).

In a footnote, the editor of *SS.* 38, states of this Henry Ogle, 'A member of a numerous clan at Kirkley and Saltwick. It is almost impossible to construct a satisfactory pedigree of this family. This will, and the notes appended to it, will give occupation and interest to any one, who wishes to disentangle the ravelled skein of the genealogy of the Ogles'. The 'ravelled skein' has not proved too difficult. Henry's will was proved 2 August 1581 by Margaret his widow and Mark Ogle his son, and to them was granted tuition of Lancelot, Henry, Michael and Cuthbert, children of the deceased (*Dur. Prob. Off.* by C.R.H.).

The will of Margaret widow of Henry Ogle of Kirkley, is dated 7 February 1587/8 and was proved 10 December 1588. To her son Cuthbert, in payment of his filial portion of his late father's goods, she leaves all the right she has in the half of one farm in Newham, four oxen, and all the wheat and oats, sown and unsown, with all the implements of husbandry, all the wheat sown on the farm at Coldcoats, one mare of colour grey, one branded cut ox, and two kine, one black and one branded. Her son Lancelot is to pay £8 to his brother Cuthbert, and on his paying it, she forgives him all he owed her. Her 'nephew' Mark Ogle, her son's son, is to have a great brass pot, and a brown stott. Her 'niece' Mary Ogle, daughter of her son Mark is to have 'a brown hawked why in Newham'. She leaves smaller legacies, mainly of livestock, to her son Mark Ogle, to Jane sister of the said Mark, to Cuthbert Ogle of Edington, to her sons Robert, Henry, Michael and Cuthbert Ogle, and to her brother Cuthbert Forster. The rest of her possessions are to go to her sons Michael and Cuthbert and they to be executors. Her son Mark is to have the tuition of Cuthbert, and Cuthbert Forster that of Michael.

The Cuthbert Forster mentioned in Margaret Ogle's will was her brother. Having no children of his own, he leaves the greater part of his possessions to the family of his brother-in-law Henry Ogle. By his w.d. 12 September 1587 Cuthbert Forster of the parish of Ponteland, gentleman, leaves:

'To my cousin Marke, the son of Marke Ogle of Kirkley, one quarter of all the tithe corn and sheaves of the town of Ryall in the parish of Stamfordham, during all such time as I have in the same. To Marie, the daughter of the forenamed Marke Ogle, senior, one brown qwhie that is now in Caldcotes, and 40s. To Jane Ogle sister of the said Marie, 13s. 4d. To my cousin Marie Ogle wife of the said Marke Ogle, senior, one foal of colour dun, and one great Dansick chest. To my forenamed cousin, Marke Ogle, senior, one old rial of gold, and one year-old filly of colour gray, now in Kirkley. To Henrie Ogle of Saltwick £10, and to Jasper Ogle, brother of the same Henrie, 10s. To Thomas Ogle their brother 4s. To Marie the daughter of Cuthbert Ogle of Saltwick, one qwhie now in Saltwick. To my cousin Lancelot Ogle's wife 10s. To my cousin Robert Ogle, one ox now in his own custody. To my cousin Cuthbert Ogle, brother of the said Robert, 40s., out of that £5 his mother oweth to me, for Michael Ogle's filial portion'. The rest of his goods are left to his nephew Michael Ogle, whom he makes executor (*SS.* 38, p.288).

The combined information contained in this series of wills gives us the following details. There were three brothers:

1. Henry Ogle of Kirkley; w.d. 2 January 1580/1, pr. 2 August 1581; wife Margaret (sister of Cuthbert Forster), w.d. 7 February 1587/8, pr. 10 December 1588; children Mark, Luke, Lancelot, Robert, Henry, Michael and Cuthbert.

2. John Ogle of Saltwick. *See* OGLE OF SALTWICK.

3. Jasper Ogle; brother of John and Henry; his children were probably Cuthbert Ogle and Dorothy Ogle, both of Edington, and mentioned in Henry Ogle's will. 'Little Cuthbert Ogle of Edington' who had a legacy by the w.d. 17 April 1613 of Henry Ogle of Huntlaw was presumably Jasper's grandson.

Henry Ogle (d.1581) of Kirkley had seven sons. These were:

1. Mark Ogle; eldest son and heir.

2. Luke Ogle; mentioned in his father's will of 1581; as no mention of him is made in his mother's will of 1588 he probably predeceased her.

3. Robert Ogle; aged 24 in 1589 and then living at Kirkley; he had a cow and calf by the w.d. 17 April 1613 of his brother Henry, and everyone of his children is to have 10s. 'My nephew Lancloat Ogle' also mentioned in Henry's will was perhaps a son of this Robert. The baptisms of two of his daughters are recorded in the Ponteland parish registers— Dorothea (17 November 1605) and Katherine (19 May 1608).

4. Lancelot Ogle. He was of Berwick on the Hill, co. Northumberland, and sick in body when he made his w.d. 1 April 1588. He is to be buried in the quire or chancel of the parish church of Ponteland. His right and interest in his farmhold in Berwick on the Hill is to go to his well beloved wife Jane Ogle and to the son or daughter 'she is now great withal' and failing them to his brother Henry Ogle. His brother Mark Ogle is to have the tuition of the said son or daughter. 'My said child if any such shall be born' is to have three oxen and other farm stock. Other legacies of cattle are left to his brothers Mark, Henry, Cuthbert and Robert Ogle. His brother Michael Ogle is to have his steel cap. Lancelot Ogle died before the end of the year as the inventory of his goods is dated 1588. The expected child was a posthumous daughter Juliana, of whom nothing further is known.

5. Henry Ogle. On 4 November 1611 he purchased lands in Newham and Huntlaw from John and Peter Ward; the conveyance is 'endorsed' by Michael Ogle, presumably Henry's brother. Henry Ogle was living at the Huntlaw in the parish of Whalton when he made his w.d. 17 April 1613. He leaves his land of the Huntlaw to his wife for life and then to his brother Cuthbert Ogle and his heirs. His legacies are his gray colt to sir John Fenwyck, a black colt to Mr Williame Fenwyck, a black gray mare to his brother Cuthbert Ogle, his best gray horse to his nephew Lancloat Ogle, one grey filly to his nephew Marke Ogle, his brown mare and her foal to his nephew Henry Ogle, one black colt foal and one black filly foal to his brother Michall, one brown filly at Newham to little Cuthbert Ogle of Edington, one little grey colt at Newham to Jane, Mary and Isabell the daughters of Mark Ogle of Kirkley, to his brother Mark one cow and one calf, to his brother Robart Ogle one cow and one calf, to everyone of his brother Robart's children 10s., and to his nephew Lansloat Ogle one ewe and one lamb. The inventory of Henry Ogle's goods is dated 9 May 1613. He was buried in the north aisle of Whalton church, where on a broken marble bearing the arms of Ogle differenced with a mullet, could still be read in 1902 the inscription 'Here Lyeth Henry Ogle who died 1613'. 'The writings in my custody belonging to Cuthbert Ogle of Kirkley, gent., and Dorothy Ogle, widow, of a place called Huntlaw' are mentioned in the w.d. 6 February 1617/8 of Robert Lorraine of Choppington, esq. Henry's widow Dorothy was still in occupation of Huntlaw in March 1621.

6. Michael Ogle. He was under age on 2 January 1580/1 when his father left him to the guardianship of Cuthbert Forster. In March 1621 he witnesses a conveyance of Newham and Huntlaw by his brother Mark Ogle to his brother Cuthbert Ogle. In the parish registers of Ponteland are the records of the baptisms between 1622 and 1628 of John, Henry, Margaret and Dorothea, children of a Michael Ogle.

7. Cuthbert Ogle from whom the later Ogles of Kirkley were descended.

At a muster of the horsemen within the Castle ward and Morpeth ward of the Middle Marches taken at Clifton Field on 24 November 1595, three of these brothers appeared for Kirkley, *viz.*, Marke Ogle with a gray horse, Michaell Ogle with a 'frayned' horse and Robert Ogle with a black nag (*CBP.* II, p.78).

On 5 August 1611 lord Eure and sir William Eure leased to Mark Ogle senior, Mark Ogle junior and Henry Ogle, the manor house, water corn mill, three farmholds and a fourth part of the town of Kirkley. The following year the Eures sold their lands in Kirkley to their tenants Mark Ogle and Cuthbert Ogle and to Nicholas Thornton of Netherwitton. On 10 August 1612 Ralph, lord Eure, sir William Eure his son and heir, lady Lucie his wife, sir Francis Eure, sir William Eure and Charles Eure for £1100 conveyed to Mark Ogle of Kirkley, their dwelling house, messuages, etc., known by the name of the Hall house of Kirkley, half the township, a water corn mill and 932 acres in Kirkley, together with rents from Milbourne, Dinnington, Brenkley, etc., excepting Berwick (Hill), Callerton, etc., and that half of the township conveyed to Nicholas Thornton and Cuthbert Ogle of Bothal. It would seem that the Eures had already mortgaged their lands to the Ogles for on 8 August 1611 there was a statute merchant bond in £2000 from Mark Ogle senior and Mark Ogle junior to sir William Eure, who states he is satisfied and that Mark's brother, Cuthbert, did pay the money to his father who has also an agreement with Cuthbert.

Mark Ogle senior was buried at Ponteland 20 January 1624/5 and an inquisition taken at Newcastle on 16 April 1630 found that he had died seised in fee of a fourth part of the village and hamlets of Kirkley. In *Ogle and Bothal* the administration of Mark Ogle of Kirkley is said to be dated 14 December 1635 and the author suggests that this is 'probably a mistake for 1625'; the Act Book (*Dur. Prob. Off.*) is quite clear and reads *Die Lune vizt decimo sexto die mensis Nouembris 1635*; it was not at all unusual for administrations to be granted many years after death. Mark's wife Mary had died shortly before her husband and was buried at Ponteland on 7 November 1624.

The children of Mark Ogle were a son Mark and two daughters Jane and Mary, the two daughters being mentioned in the wills of their grandmother Margaret Ogle (1588) and their great uncle Cuthbert Forster (1587); a third daughter Isabel may have been born subsequently. Jane Ogle married 27 February 1618/9 Thomas Ogle of North Seaton (*See* OGLE OF HIRST). Isabel married 3 February 1624/5 Anthony Rea. (*Ogle and Bothal* gives his name as Ogle instead of Rea). A daughter of Mark Ogle married Thomas Holborne of Whitchester (C2. 2 Jas. I. F8/29).

On 25 August 1621 Mark Ogle in consideration of the marriage of Mark, his son and heir, with Catherine daughter of John Heron of Birtley Hall, conveyed to John Heron and John Hedworth the manor house and capital messuage of Kirkley in trust, one moiety to the use of Mark Ogle the father and the other to the use of Mark Ogle junior and his wife.

The inventory of the goods of Mark Ogle of Kirkley is dated 27 March 1660 and administration of his goods was granted on 17 December 1660 to Katherine his widow. His eldest son John was baptised 8 October 1622 but must have died in infancy for his heir was a son Cuthbert, baptised 30 October 1627; a third son John must have been born after this. Their uncle George Heron of Birtley by his w.d. 9 October 1699 leaves legacies to John Ogle and Catherine Nanson, children of his late sister Katherine Ogle. The b. of m. of Robert Nanson and Katherine Ogle, spinster, is dated 12 July 1664; Nanson was instituted vicar of Ponteland 25 February 1662/3 and died in 1675. Mark Ogle had two other daughters Jane and Elizabeth one of whom may have married Thomas Gofton who is called brother-in-law by Cuthbert Ogle in his w.d. 28 November 1667.

Cuthbert Ogle, the eldest surviving son of Mark Ogle (d.1660) seems to have been living at Shortflatt in 1666. He married at South Shields 9 July 1667 Barbara daughter of Ralph Anderson. His will is dated 28 November 1667 and by it he declares that his wife's settlement shall stand good. His wife was expecting a child; if it was a daughter she is to have £100; if a son he is to have all his father's estate to be enjoyed at 13 years of age. Failing the birth of a son the estate is to revert to the family of the Ogles of Kirkley. If his own issue should die in their infancy his estate is to be entailed on his brother John and failing him to John Ogle of Carter Moor. The executors to the will are his brother John Ogle of Kirkley, his uncle George Heron of Birtley, his kinsman John Ogle of Carter Moor, and his brother-in-law Thomas Gofton. Cuthbert Ogle was buried at South Shields 3 December 1667 and his widow Barbara married at Stamfordham 24 July 1669 Thomas Ogle of Bebside.

The expected child was a son, named Cuthbert after his father and born posthumously. On 27 May 1699 administration of Cuthbert Ogle of Kirkley was granted to John Erring-

ton, the principal creditor; his next of kin was George Ogle (his cousin).

After Cuthbert's death, his mother and his step-father, Thomas Ogle, leased her life interest in the manor house and moiety of the township of Kirkley, the Mill and half of Benridge to John Errington of Beaufront for £65 a year. When George Ogle the heir succeeded to Kirkley he had considerable difficulty in ousting the Erringtons, but established his claim in 1722. By then the estate was heavily mortgaged and on 30 May 1730 he sold it to Joshua Douglas of Newcastle who already held a mortgage of £4000.

John Ogle youngest son of Mark Ogle (d.1660), married at Bolam 30 August 1668 Jane daughter of Thomas Winckles of Harnham. He seems to have died at Harnham and administration of his goods was granted on 14 May 1699 to Jane his widow. Their son and heir George Ogle was next of kin in 1699 to Cuthbert Ogle of Kirkley. He married his cousin Mary daughter of Thomas Winckles of Harnham; she was buried at Ford 29 September 1693; their only son Thomas Ogle died in infancy in 1693; their two daughters Catherine wife of Daniel Whitton of Ford, and Eleanor wife of William Thew of Denwick, were coheiresses to their mother. George Ogle took a second wife whose name is unknown, and by her had two sons, John and Mark, and three daughters, Jane, Isabel and Mary. This second family has not been traced further.

The lands in Kirkley sold by George Ogle of Harnham in 1730 were eventually purchased by the branch of the Ogle family already owning the remainder of the township. These other Ogles were descended from Cuthbert Ogle youngest son of Henry Ogle (d.1581) of Kirkley. Cuthbert was probably the person of this name of Queen's college, Oxford, who matriculated 9 November 1582 aged 13 and became BA on 14 December 1586.

Cuthbert Ogle was living at Bothal 10 August 1612, when with Nicholas Thornton of Netherwitton he purchased from the Eures for £980 half the town of Kirkley known as the east and west quarters and part of the south quarter of Alderhaugh. A year later, on 7 August 1613, he bought from his brother four messuages in the south quarter for £700 and made arrangements with Nicholas Thornton to divide Alderhaugh, he taking the east quarter and Thornton the west quarter. From 1619 he is described as of Kirkley and a few years later built or rebuilt the house there; there still remains, but not in its original setting, a stone with the initials C.O. and D.O. with a coat of arms of Ogle impaling Fenwick and the date 1632. Cuthbert Ogle's wife was Dorothy daughter of Roger Fenwick of Bitchfield.

Sir Henry Ogle found a w.d. 24 May 1654 of Cuthbert Ogle of Kirkley amongst the Kirkley deeds. No probate of the will can now be found either at Durham or at Somerset House, so sir Henry's extract must be accepted. It purports to leave to the testator's eldest son Henry all his lands in Kirkley not already granted, and it would appear that other lands there had already been given to his second son John and were now confirmed to him and his heirs, with remainders to the testator's son William, and then to his youngest son Cuthbert (*Ogle and Bothal*, app.466).

The eldest son Henry was living at Newcastle, 1 June 1659, when for £100 he conveyed certain lands in Kirkley to his brother John. On 27 October 1659 John Ogle settled on his brother Henry an annuity of £40 out of Kirkley. Henry still retained part of the estate, for on 3 April 1664 he conveyed lands in Kirkley to his nephew Ralph son of John Ogle for an annuity of £50. He was living 25 April 1673 when Henry and William Thornton released all their estate in Kirkley to John and Henry Ogle.

William Ogle, Cuthbert's third son, was probably William Ogle of Newcastle who by his w.d. 25 August 1680 leaves all his goods to his children William and Elleanor. Cuthbert Ogle, whom Cuthbert Ogle in his w.d. 24 May 1654 calls his youngest son, married Mary one of the five daughters and coheiresses of Cuthbert Fenwick of Great Bavington; their one fifth of a moiety of Great Bavington was purchased by John Ogle of Kirkley in the name of his 2nd son Cuthbert. Cuthbert Ogle, gent., of Great Bavington was buried at Kirkwhelpington 20 January 1696/7.

John Ogle, second son of Cuthbert Ogle (w.d.1654), was apprenticed 1 August 1633 to Marke Milbank of Newcastle, mercer, and admitted free of the Newcastle Merchant Adventurers Company on 20 June 1645. He was living in Newcastle 19 November 1645 when he settled his lands in trust on his marriage with Elizabeth daughter of Ralph Fewler (or Fowler) of Newcastle, merchant; these lands were presumably Newham and Huntlaw which his father had given him on 24 July 1640. Ralph Fowler owned Sandyford Stone in Jesmond and leaves it by will to his only daughter Elizabeth Ogle. In 1672/3 John Ogle's house was licensed as a presbyterian meeting house, and he was buried at Ponteland 6 July 1699. His widow 'Mrs Elizabeth Ogle, widow, of Apperley' was buried at Bywell St Peter on 31 December 1708; she had apparently been living with her daughter Dorothy wife of Nathaniel Boutflower of Apperley.

John and Elizabeth Ogle had four sons Ralph, Cuthbert, John and Thomas, and five daughters, Dorothy wife of Nathaniel Boutflower of Apperley (m. Bolam 22 February 1676/7), Sarah wife of Francis Paston of Wallridge, Isabel wife of William Rutherford, Elizabeth wife of John Newton of Eltringham and Jane wife of Thomas Morrison of Morpeth (m. Ponteland 3 March 1698). The second son Cuthbert is mentioned in the w.d. 3 July 1658 of his grandfather Ralph Fowler, but apparently died s.p. before 28 July 1671. The third (but second surviving) son John was admitted barrister at Gray's Inn 28 July 1671. He seems to have been living in Cowgate, Newcastle in 1699, and on 25 September 1705 was appointed judge at the court of admiralty at Newcastle. On 27 September 1723 he was admitted by patrimony to the freedom of the Newcastle Merchant Adventurers Company. On a tombstone in the nave of St Nicholas' church, Newcastle, is the inscription—'John Ogle esq., Mary his wife and their issue. Underneath lies Mary Lisle relict of Robert Lisle of Hazon esq., deceased, and daughter of the above named John Ogle and Mary who died the 19th December 1728 aged 44. He departed this life the 28th of March 1740 aged 90 years. Mary his wife died Novr 16 1744 aged 81. And left issue only one son sir Chaloner Ogle kt, admiral etc'. John Ogle's wife Mary was daughter of Richard Braithwaite of Warcop, Wmd, by Mariana his wife, daughter of James Chaloner of Gisburn, Yorks.

Thomas Ogle, youngest son of John Ogle (d.1699), was presented 11 January 1682 for preaching at his father's house in Kirkley (*Quarter Sessions Order Books*, vol.1, p.72). He

was living in Newcastle 22 February 1722/3 when he made his will; his lands in Westoe and Jarrow, co. Durham, and a rent of £18 a year out of the lands in Kirkley west quarter are left to his brother John Ogle of Newcastle, esq. (*Dur. Prob. Off.* by C.R.H.).

Chaloner Ogle, the only son of John Ogle of Newcastle, was so called from his maternal grandmother Mariana Chaloner. He had a very distinguished naval career, entering the navy in July 1697. At the age of twenty one he was promoted to be lieutenant on the *Royal Oak* on 2 April 1702 and received his first command on the *St Antonio* on 24 November 1703. On 3 July he commanded the *Deal Castle* when she was taken off Ostend by three French ships; at the subsequent court martial he was acquitted of all blame. In 1716 he commanded the *Plymouth* in the Baltic under sir John Norris, and in 1717 the *Worcester*, a fourth rate of 50 guns under sir George Byng, also in the Baltic. Two years later he was appointed to the 60 gun ship *Swallow*, and after convoying the trade to Newfoundland and thence to the Mediterranean was sent early in 1721 to the coast of Africa. It was here that his most famous exploit occurred. In September his ship was temporarily disabled by sickness; he had buried 50 men and still had 100 sick. At Cape Coast Castle in November he learnt that the pirate Bartholomew Roberts was plundering the coast. This Roberts had been a passenger on a vessel captured by pirates and to save his life joined his captors. By his outstanding character—he was a strict teetotaller and a great disciplinarian, he soon rose to be the leader of the pirates, a position he maintained for four years and, it is said, read prayers regularly every day to his crew. In February 1722 Roberts was in command of three ships of 40, 32 and 24 guns and his men numbered 374. Captain Ogle discovered the pirates at anchor under Cape Lopez where two of the ships, the largest and the smallest were careened for cleaning. Drawing his lower deck guns, Ogle lay off at some distance where he could be mistaken for a merchantman. The ruse was successful and the 32-gun pirate ship gave chase. When out of sight of the remaining pirate ships the *Swallow* turned on her pursuer and after a short encounter captured her. Ogle then hoisted the pirate's black flag with death's head, hour glass and human heart, above the King's colour and returned to the anchorage where the other two pirate ships lay. Early in the ensuing encounter Roberts was killed and his men surrendered.

On his return to England in April 1723 captain Ogle was knighted. On 17 May 1731 he commanded the *Edinburgh* of 70 guns in the Mediterranean, and in 1732 he was commodore of a squadron in the West Indies. He became rear admiral of the blue 11 July 1739 and led the attack on Cartagena on 9 March 1741. Regular promotion followed, rear admiral of the red in March 1742, vice admiral of the blue 9 August 1743, vice-admiral of the white 7 December 1743, admiral of the blue April 1745 and admiral of the fleet 28 June 1749.

On 13 November 1713 his father had purchased for him the estate of Coupland and Akeld. He was returned MP for Rochester 24 November 1745 and again on 18 July 1747. He died 11 April 1750 aged 70 and was buried in St Mary's parish church at Twickenham. Although married twice he had no children; his first wife, Henrietta daughter of Anthony Isaacson of Newcastle died in 1737 and on 30 October 1737 he married his cousin Isabel daughter of Nathaniel Ogle of

Kirkley; after sir Chaloner's death she married James, lord Kingston.

Ralph Ogle, eldest son and heir of John Ogle (d.1699) of Kirkley, was admitted to Gray's Inn on 21 November 1666, but there is no evidence that he ever practiced as a barrister. Ralph Ogle's wife was Martha daughter of the rev. John Thompson, rector of Bothal and vicar of Morpeth. Thompson had 'married a great fortune and kept his coach, and having but one daughter she was married to the eldest son of Mr Barnes's old friend, Mr John Ogle of Kirkley, who was bred a merchant' (*Memoir of Ambrose Barnes, SS*. 50, p.146). There is no other evidence that Ralph was 'bred a merchant'. On his marriage, his father on 5 August 1670 settled Kirkley and Huntlaw for their use; he made provision for his wife Elizabeth and his brother Henry Ogle of Newcastle. On the same date, and in consideration of £1500 paid by John Thompson, John Ogle and Elizabeth his wife gave lands in Jesmond and Carter Moor in trust for the use of Ralph and Martha with provision for Isabel Fowler, Ralph's grandmother. On 5 February 1671 Ralph Ogle for £1150 bought the west quarter of Kirkley and Alderhaugh from Henry Blackett of Kirkley; two days later he conveyed half of his purchase to his father, John Ogle. Ralph's wife Martha had an only brother Nathaniel Thompson and when he died without issue she was his heiress. The Christian name Nathaniel was afterwards used regularly in the Ogle family. Ralph was admitted to the freedom of the Newcastle Merchant Adventurers by patrimony on 2 July 1692. By his w.d. 10 March 1704 he leaves his lands in the west quarter of Kirkley, lately purchased from Henry Blackett, lands in Jesmond and a tenement in Pilgrim Street, Newcastle, to his brother Thomas Ogle and his brother-in-law Nathaniel Boutflower upon trust for his children, Nathaniel, Henry, Martha, Catherine, Anne and Jane; after his mother's death his lands in Huntlaw were to go to the same trustees for certain uses. He leaves £70 to his nephew Wolstan Paston and his lands in Huntlaw to his eldest son Cuthbert. Ralph Ogle was buried at Ponteland 29 May 1705. His wife had pre-deceased him.

On 1 October 1685 Ralph Ogle, then living at Sandiford, and Martha his wife, sister and heir of Nathaniel Thompson, deceased, released West Newham to John Ogle of Kirkley for the use of themselves, then for John, son and heir of Ralph, the other children to have arrangements made out of lands in Newham and Huntlaw to certain uses. This eldest son John died unmarried before 12 May 1691. The second, but eldest surviving son, is described as son and heir of Ralph Ogle of Kirkley when on 12 May 1691 he was admitted to Gray's Inn. He died unmarried before 13 October 1707 when administration of his goods was granted to his brother Nathaniel.

Nathaniel Ogle, who became his father's heir, studied medicine, took his degree as M.D. and served as a physician to the forces under the command of the duke of Marlborough. He married at St James', London, on 22 April 1708 Elizabeth only daughter and eventual heiress of Jonathan Newton of Newcastle. Their two elder sons Nathaniel Ogle (b.29 Sept. 1715; d.1762) and Ralph Ogle (b.1717; d.1737) died without issue. From the third son, Newton Ogle (d.4 January 1804) the later Ogles of Kirkley are descended. The fourth son Chaloner Ogle was created a baronet 12 March 1816; for his descendants *see* OGLE OF WORTHY, Hants.

Many of the descendants of Newton Ogle (d.1804) served with distinction in the Royal Navy, and others obtained high preferment in the church. The estate of Kirkley, Benridge and North Carter Moor was sold by John Francis Chaloner Ogle in 1922. He is believed to be the sole direct male descendant of Newton Ogle (d.1804).

OGLE OF WORTHY, HANTS.

CHALONER OGLE, 4th and youngest son of dr Nathaniel Ogle (d.1739) of Kirkley, entered the Royal Navy as a young man and became lieutenant on 31 January 1747 at the age of eighteen. He was promoted to be commander of the *Swan* on 17 June 1755, and captain of the *Yarmouth* on 30 June 1756. Early in January 1761 in command of the *Aquilon* he captured the *Santa Theresa*, privateer of 10 guns, together with a smaller privateer. Before the middle of August he had taken the *Compte de Grammont* of 20 guns, the *Zephire* of 12 guns, the *Aurora* of 10 guns and the *Subtile* of 16 guns. He was back home on 7 September 1761 when he married Hester youngest daughter and coheiress of the rt. rev. John Thomas, bishop of Peterborough. About this time he succeeded to Worthy Park in Hampshire under the will of his sister lady Kingston. He was knighted at St James' on 20 November 1768. From 1775 to 1779 he seems to have served at sea in the wars with America, France and Spain. Late in 1779 he was under the command of sir George Rodney at the relief of Gibraltar, and was promoted rear admiral of the blue, 26 September 1780. He was vice admiral of the blue 24 September 1787 and of the red on 1 February 1793; admiral of the blue 12 April 1794, admiral of the white 14 February 1799, admiral of the red 9 November 1805. Created a baronet on 12 March 1816, he died on 28 August 1816 aged 87 and was buried in the vault of the church of Martyr Worthy.

Sir Chaloner Ogle's two elder sons predeceased their father; they were George Chaloner Ogle and Edward Henry Ogle, who both served in the Royal Navy and both died at sea. The third son, sir Charles Ogle, 2nd baronet, also served with distinction at sea and became admiral of the fleet on 8 December 1857. The succeeding baronets were:

Sir Chaloner Ogle, 3rd baronet, eldest son of the second baronet by his first wife Charlotte Margaret daughter of general the hon. Thomas Gage. Died 3 February 1859.

Sir Chaloner Roe Majendie Ogle, 4th baronet, eldest son of the 3rd baronet, by his wife Elizabeth Sophia Frances daughter and heiress of William Roe of Withdean Court, Sussex. Died 29 November 1861.

Sir William Ogle, 5th baronet, only son of the second baronet by his second wife Letitia daughter of sir William Burroughs. Died 2 December 1885.

Sir Edmund Ogle, 6th baronet, eldest surviving son of James Ogle (d.1833) who was youngest son of the 1st baronet. Died 14 June 1887.

Sir Henry Asgill Ogle, 7th baronet, eldest surviving son of the 6th baronet by his wife Catherine Beverley daughter of Henry St Hill of Bradrinch manor, Collompton, Devonshire. In 1902 he had privately printed a volume entitled *Ogle and Bothal*, being a history of the families of Ogle and Bertram and their landed estates. Died 5 March 1921.

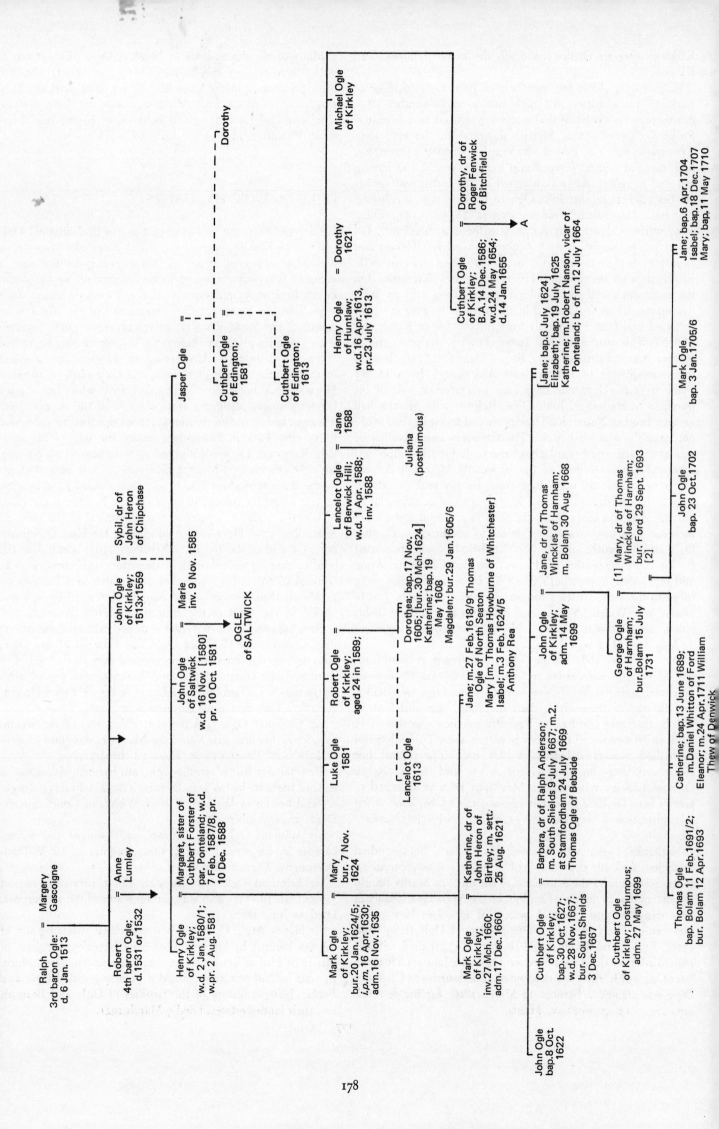

OGLE of KIRKLEY, par. PONTELAND

178

OGLE OF KIRKLEY, cont.

↑A

Henry Ogle
of Newcastle;
1659x1673
[Henry Ogle gent.,
bur. All Saints,
Nc., 9 Feb.1671/2]

= Elizabeth, dr of Ralph
Fowler of Sandiford Stone,
Jesmond; m.25 Nov.1645;
[bur.31 Dec.1708]

John Ogle
of Kirkley;
bur.6 July 1699

[Charles Ogle
bap.12 Feb.
1621/2]

William Ogle = Susan Bishop
of Newcastle   m.1656; bur.
bap.11 Mch.   20 Dec.1677
1622/3; w.d. 25
Aug.1680; inv.
6 Sept.1680;
bur.2 Sept.1680

Cuthbert Ogle = Mary, dr & coh. of
of Great Bavington   Cuthbert Fenwick
bur.20 Jan.1696/7   of Great Bavington

Francis Ogle
bap.29 Apr.1624;
bur.1 Feb.1624/5

Thomas Ogle
bap.11 Jan.1629/30

Katherine: bap.22 Aug.1620; bur.23 Dec.1622
Dorothy: bap.30 Nov.1626
Joan; bap.8 Oct.1625; m.25 Oct.1655
    Thomas Boutflower of Apperley

Thomas Ogle
bap.14 Feb.
1658/9: bur.
16 Jan.1666/7
Cuthbert Ogle
bap.17 Feb.1669/
70: bur.28 Dec.
1672

William Ogle
bap.16 July
1661; living
1680

Charles Ogle
bap.8 Jan.
1662/3
John Ogle
bap.23 Aug.
1666; bur.29
Jan.1666/7

Eleanor; bap.13 Feb.
1657/8; living 1680
Susanna; bap.28 July
1665; bur.10 Feb.
1666/7
Dorothie; bur.17 Apr.
1673

Ralph Ogle = Martha, dr of John
of Kirkley   Thompson, rector of
w.d.10 Mch.1704; Bothal; m.16 Aug.
bur.29 May 1705   1670; [d.1687]

Cuthbert Ogle
d.before 28 July
1671

John Ogle
of Newcastle
d.28 Mch.1740
aged 90

= Mary, dr of Richard
  Braithwaite of Warcop,
  Wmd; d.16 Nov.1744
  aged 81

Thomas Ogle
of Newcastle:
w.d.22 Feb.1722/3,
pr.15 Jan.1736/7

Dorothy; m.22 Feb.1676/7 Nathaniel Boutflower of Apperley
Sarah; m. Francis Paston of Wallridge
Isabel; m.26 Dec.1698 William Rutherford
Elizabeth; m.1 Jan.1698/9 John Newton of Eltringham
Jane; m.3 Mch.1697/8 Thomas Morrison of Morpeth

sir Chaloner Ogle = [1] Henrietta, dr of
of Copeland; admiral   Anthony Isaacson
RN; M.P.1745,1747;   of Newcastle
d.11 Apr.1750 aged 70 = [2] Isabella, dr of
                             Nathaniel Ogle
                             of Kirkley; m.30
                             Oct.1737;
                             m.2. James, lord
                             Kingston

Mary m.17 May 1704 Robert
    Lisle of Hazon
Elizabeth; b.11 Mch; bap.
    Warcop 17 Mch.1679 or 1681

Cuthbert Ogle
of Kirkley;
d.s.p. adm. 13
Oct.1707

Nathaniel Ogle
of Kirkley, M.D.;
w.d. 9 Mch.1738;
bur.19 June 1739

Henry Ogle = Isabella Baxter
of Newcastle   m.2 June 1709
w.d.5 Jan.1731;
pr.30 Dec.1737

Martha; unm.6 Mch.1705
Katherine; unm. 6 Mch.1705
Ann m. 1 Nov.1705 George Headlam
Jane m. 16 May 1714 William Sowerby
    of Newcastle

Chaloner Ogle
b.1725; captain R.N;
d.12 June 1814 aged
89

= Catherine, dr of
  Joseph Solley,
  prebendary of
  Winchester; m.22 May
  1764; d.16 Jan.1820
  aged 82

Jane; living unm.1737

John Ogle
d.unm. before
12 May 1691

= Elizabeth, dr of
  Jonathan Newton;
  m.22 Apr.1708; w.d.
  5 Oct.1750, pr.5
  May 1751

Nathaniel Ogle
aged 18 in 1733

Thomas Ogle

Chaloner Blake Ogle
of Southampton;
d.11 Nov.1857 aged 92

= Frances Jane
  Courtenay;
  d.20 June 1864

Joseph Blake Ogle
of Southampton, clerk
in holy orders; d.19
Mch.1849

Isabella Catherine; b.1766; bur.12 Jan.1775
Catherine Elizabeth; b.1782; d.30 Jan.1852
Charlotte Anne; w.pr.3 May 1869

Ralph Ogle
R.N; adm.24
Mch.1736/7

Newton Ogle = Susannah, dr & coh.
of Kirkley,   of John Thomas, bishop
b.29 Sept.1715;   of Peterborough; m.21
bur.10 Jan.1763/4; Apr.1757; d.1820
adm.24 Jan.1763/4

Newton Ogle
of Kirkley, D.D;
dean of Win-
chester; bap.18
Oct.1726; d.4
Jan.1804

sir Chaloner Ogle

Jonathan Ogle
bap. 1 Mch.1723/4;
bur.3 Mch.1723/4

Isabella; b.1709; m(1) 30 Oct.1737 sir Chaloner
    Ogle of Copeland; m (2) James, lord Kingston
Anne; bap.1711; d.1726
Elizabeth; bap.29 June 1714; m.1740 George Grey
    of Southwick, co.Dur.
Martha; bap.13 May 1719; m.Charles Sigismund,
    baron de Starck
Mary; bap.14 Mch.1722/3; bur.24 Mch.1722/3

OGLE
of WORTHY,
Hants.

→B

179

OGLE of KIRKLEY, cont.

180

→ B

Nathaniel Ogle of Kirkley; b. 7 Oct. 1765; w.d. 7 Feb. 1813 = **Anna Maria Cowlam**; m. 1787

John Savile Ogle M.A., of Kirkley; b. 24 Aug. 1767; prebendary of Durham; d. 1 Apr. 1853 = **Catherine Hannah** dr of Edward Sneyd of Testwood, Ireland; m. 14 Oct. 1794; d. 18 Mch. 1853

Richard Newton Ogle b. 1769; capt. 70th regt; adm. 5 July 1795

Henry Bertram Ogle of London, M.A.; b. 1774; d. 11 Mch. 1835 = **Anna Maria, dr of Edward Raphael** of Fort St George, Madras; m. 1802; d. 21 Dec. 1851

Susannah; b. 1762; d. unm. 19 Feb. 1825
Elizabeth Catherine; m. 6 June 1782 Henry Streatfield of Chiddingstone, Kent
Isabella Newton; b. 1764; d. unm. 1780
Anne; m. 3 Jan. 1798 Henry Scott, capt. Light Infantry of South Hants.
Hester Jane; m. 27 Apr. 1795 rt hon. Richard Brinsley Sheridan, M.P.

Charles Ogle b. 7 July 1799; d. unm. 13 Aug. 1820
Nathaniel Ogle b. 12 July 1801; d. 9 May 1813

John Ogle M.A.; b. 5 Mch. 1796; d. 14 July 1831 = **Sarah Agatha, dr of Philip John Miles** of Leigh Court, Som.; m. 25 Aug. 1828; d. 4 Apr. 1830

Henry Ogle b. 1797; lieut. R.N.; d.s.p. 17 Oct. 1841 = **Harriet Anna, dr of Walter Bracebridge** of Atherston Hall, Warw.; m. 13 Mch. 1827

Edward Chaloner Ogle b. 7 Aug. 1798; M.A. 1823; prebendary of Durham; d. 7 Nov. 1869 = **Sophia, dr of vice adm. sir Charles Ogle**; m. 17 Aug. 1830; d. 23 Apr. 1896

Anne Charlotte; b. 19 Jan. 1832
Sophia Henrietta; b. 28 May 1833; m. 24 June 1879 rev. Hugh W. Jermyn, D.D., bishop of Brechin
Mary; b. 1 Oct. 1837; d. 17 Jan. 1873
Isabel; b. 1 Sept. 1840; m. 12 Dec. 1860 Nathaniel George Clayton of Chesters
Alice; d. in inf. 1 June 1842
Alice Katherine; b. 16 May 1844; m. 21 Feb. 1874 capt. George A. Fenwick

Sarah Kate Elizabeth; b. 1830; d. 10 July 1846, at Cadiz

Charles Edward Ogle b. 1848; d. 9 June 1851

John Savile Ogle of Kirkley; b. 21 Jan. 1836; d. unm. 18 Jan. 1892

Newton Charles Ogle b. 19 Feb. 1850; d. 23 July 1912 = [1] **Lilian Katherine Selina** dr of William Henry Forester Denison, 1st earl of Londesborough, m. 28 Nov. 1895; d. 1899 = [2] **Beatrice Ann, dr of sir John William Cradock Hartopp**; m. 1903

Hester Mary
Bridget Catherine

Marjorie Edith Sophia; b. 4 Feb. 1897; d. 23 June 1897

John Francis Chaloner Ogle b. 1 Dec. 1898; sold Kirkley in 1922

Arthur Ogle b. 19 Jan. 1805; capt. 9th regt.; d. 28 Dec. 1878 = **Caroline Amelia, dr of William Lechmere**, vice admiral; m. 10 Sept. 1844; d. 21 May 1880

Savile Craven Henry Ogle b. 4 June 1811; d.s.p. 11 Mch. 1854 = **Mary Anne Wilson**; d. 21 Aug. 1854

Catherine Elizabeth; b. 1 July 1800; m. 15 Nov. 1831 Charles Ogle Streatfield
Anne Charlotte; b. 18 Nov. 1802; m. 20 Mch. 1826 sir James Macdonald, bart, M.P.

Bertram Newton Ogle b. 7 Mch. 1804; capt. 4th Queen's Own Dragoons; d. 29 Nov. 1840 = **Maria Jane, dr of George Simpson** of Bombay; m. 1834

Bertram Savile Ogle b. 24 Dec. 1846 = **Edith, dr of Arthur Edward Somerset**

Caroline Anna Mary; m. 15 Dec. 1881 lieut. col. Robert Henry Maude
Adela; m. 19 Oct. 1886 rev. Constantine Francis Dillon, rector of Tubney, Berks

Augusta Kate; m. 1863 Edward Ward

OGLE of WORTHY, Hants.

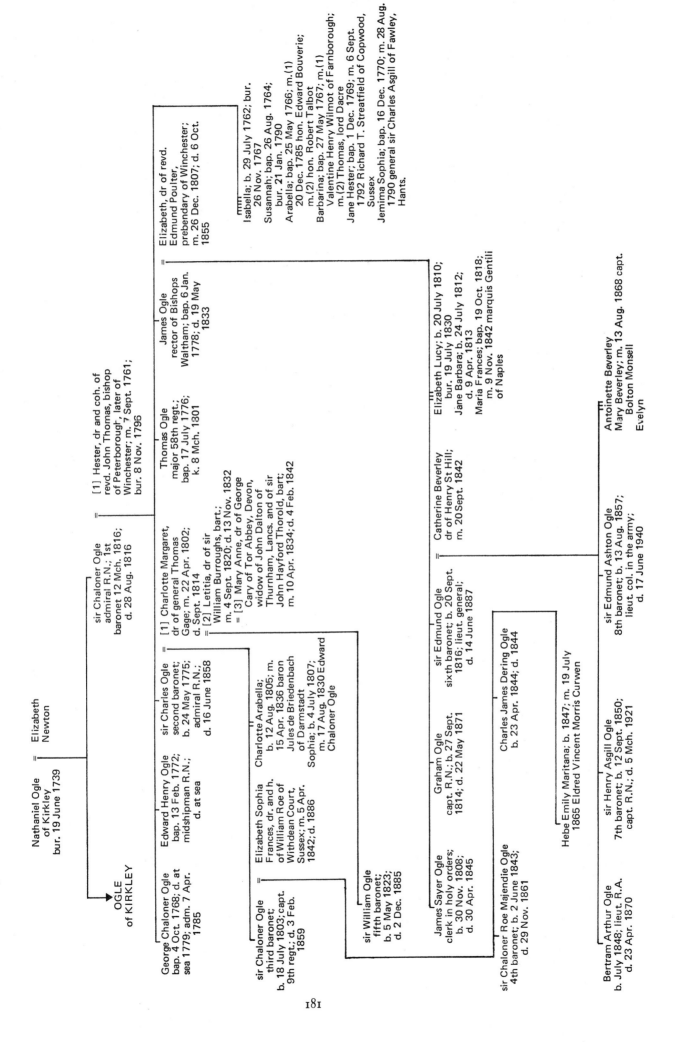

Nathaniel Ogle = Elizabeth
of Kirkley   Newton
bur. 19 June 1739

→ OGLE
  of KIRKLEY

sir Chaloner Ogle
admiral R.N.; 1st
baronet 12 Mch. 1816;
d. 28 Aug. 1816

= [1] Hester, dr and coh. of
revd. John Thomas, bishop
of Peterborough, later of
Winchester; m. 7 Sept. 1761;
bur. 8 Nov. 1796

George Chaloner Ogle
bap. 4 Oct. 1768; d. at
sea 1779; adm. 7 Apr.
1785

Edward Henry Ogle
bap. 13 Feb. 1772;
midshipman R.N.;
d. at sea

sir Charles Ogle
second baronet;
b. 24 May 1775;
admiral R.N.;
d. 16 June 1858

Thomas Ogle
major 58th regt.;
bap. 17 July 1776;
k. 8 Mch. 1801

James Ogle
rector of Bishops
Waltham; bap. 6 Jan.
1778; d. 19 May
1833

Elizabeth, dr of revd.
Edmund Poulter,
prebendary of Winchester;
m. 26 Dec. 1807; d. 6 Oct.
1855

Isabella; b. 29 July 1762; bur.
26 Nov. 1767
Susannah; bap. 26 Aug. 1764;
bur. 21 Jan. 1790
Arabella; bap. 25 May 1766; m.(1)
20 Dec. 1785 hon. Edward Bouverie;
m.(2) hon. Robert Talbot
Barbarina; bap. 27 May 1767; m.(1)
Valentine Henry Wilmot of Farnborough;
m.(2) Thomas, lord Dacre
Jane Hester; bap. 1 Dec. 1769; m. 6 Sept.
1792 Richard T. Streatfield of Copwood,
Sussex
Jemima Sophia; bap. 16 Dec. 1770; m. 28 Aug.
1790 general sir Charles Asgill of Fawley,
Hants.

= [1] Charlotte Margaret,
dr of general Thomas
Gage; m. 22 Apr. 1802;
d. Sept. 1814
= [2] Letitia, dr of sir
William Burroughs, bart.;
m. 4 Sept. 1820; d. 13 Nov. 1832
= [3] Mary Anne, dr of George
Cary of Tor Abbey, Devon,
widow of John Dalton of
Thurnham, Lancs. and of sir
John Hayford Thorold, bart;
m. 10 Apr. 1834; d. 4 Feb. 1842

sir Chaloner Ogle
third baronet;
b. 18 July 1803; capt.
9th regt.; d. 3 Feb.
1859

Elizabeth Sophia
Frances, dr. and h.
of William Roe of
Withdean Court,
Sussex; m. 5 Apr.
1842; d. 1886

Charlotte Arabella;
b. 12 Aug. 1805; m.
15 Apr. 1836 baron
Jules de Briedenbach
of Darmstadt
Sophia; b. 4 July 1807;
m. 17 Aug. 1830 Edward
Chaloner Ogle

sir Edmund Ogle
sixth baronet; b. 20 Sept.
1816; lieut. general;
d. 14 June 1887

Catherine Beverley
dr of Henry St Hill;
m. 20 Sept. 1842

Elizabeth Lucy; b. 20 July 1810;
bur. 19 July 1830
Jane Barbara; b. 24 July 1812;
d. 9 Apr. 1813
Maria Frances; bap. 19 Oct. 1818;
m. 9 Nov. 1842 marquis Gentili
of Naples

sir William Ogle
fifth baronet;
b. 5 May 1823;
d. 2 Dec. 1885

James Sayer Ogle
clerk in holy orders;
b. 30 Nov. 1808;
d. 30 Apr. 1845

Graham Ogle
capt. R.N.; b. 27 Sept.
1814; d. 22 May 1871

Charles James Dering Ogle
b. 23 Apr. 1844; d. 1844

sir Edmund Ashton Ogle
8th baronet; b. 13 Aug. 1857;
lieut. col. in the army;
d. 17 June 1940

Antoinette Beverley
Mary Beverley; m. 13 Aug. 1868 capt.
Bolton Monsell
Evelyn

sir Chaloner Roe Majendie Ogle
4th baronet; b. 2 June 1843;
d. 29 Nov. 1861

Hebe Emily Maritana; b. 1847; m. 19 July
1865 Eldred Vincent Morris Curwen

sir Henry Asgill Ogle
7th baronet; b. 12 Sept. 1850;
capt. R.N.; d. 5 Mch. 1921

Bertram Arthur Ogle
b. July 1848; lieut. R.A.
d. 23 Apr. 1870

Sir Edmund Ashton Ogle, 8th baronet, brother of the 7th baronet. Died 17 June 1940.

OGLE OF CARTER MOOR, PAR. PONTELAND

THIS branch of the Ogle family had some close connection with the Ogles of Kirkley, for Cuthbert Ogle of Kirkley in his w.d. 28 November 1667 states that if his own issue should die in their infancy his estate is to be entailed on his brother John and failing him to John Ogle of Carter Moor.

On 30 November 1613 an earlier Cuthbert Ogle of Kirkley conveyed to Mark Ogle of Eland Hall a plot of ground in the east quarter of Kirkley, occupied by Gawen Ogle near Carter Moor; the copy of the conveyance amongst the Kirkley deeds is signed by Mark Ogle of Carter Moor and witnessed by Michael Ogle and Cuthbert Ogle of Edington. It would appear that Mark Ogle was son of Gawen Ogle for Spearmen in his notes refers to '1628 Gawen Ogle of Kirkley and Mark Ogle his son and heir of New Kirkley'. Gawen Ogle of Eland Hall had a son William baptised at Ponteland 2 December 1604, and a daughter Dorothy on 7 February 1607/8. Mark must have been born many years before but the surviving registers do not commence until 1602. Gawen Ogle of Carter Moor was buried 21 September 1627.

On 5 August 1619 Cuthbert Ogle of Kirkley and Hugh Gofton conveyed to Mark Ogle a cottage, mill, etc. Mark Ogle voted as a freeholder in respect of Carter Moor in 1628 and 1639. He married at Ponteland 8 January 1615/6 Elizabeth Hedworth. A son Cuthbert was baptised 13 December 1621, but died in infancy. A second son, John, who became his father's heir was baptised 8 October 1622.

James Ogle of Causey Park by his w.d. 30 July 1664 leaves to John Ogle of Carter Moor 20s., for a mourning ring. It has already been mentioned that Cuthbert Ogle of Kirkley in 1667 called him 'kinsman' and placed him in remainder to his estate. Marke Ogle of Whinney Hill, par. Stannington, may have been even a closer kinsman. In his w.d. 8 February (presumably 1681/2 for the inventory of his goods is dated 16 February 1681/2) he mentions his five children, and appoints Mr John Ogle of Carter Moor and Mr John Fenwick of West Duddo as executors (*Dur. Prob. Off.* by C.R.H.). Lancelot Ogle is a witness to the will, and the inventory is signed by James Ogle, Edward Ogle and others; his goods were valued at £119. John Ogle of Carter Moor was buried at Ponteland 13 September 1696.

His son and heir Mark Ogle married at Felton 2 July 1713 Elizabeth daughter of Edward Manners of Framlington. Mark had been living at Carter Moor in 1698 and 1710 when he voted as a freeholder, but after his marriage he lived at Ashington where his children John, Mark and Jane were born. John and Jane are both mentioned in the w.d. 29 May 1727 of their grandfather Edward Manners.

Mark Ogle of Ashington made his will 23 February 1719/20 leaving his lands at Carter Moor and Horton Grange in Ponteland in trust for the use of his son John. His son Mark is to have £200 and his daughter Jane £100, and he leaves Horton Grange for his wife's jointure. His widow may have been the Elizabeth Ogle who married at Morpeth 22 April 1725 Cuthbert Alder, who already, in 1721 owned property in Horton Grange (*Poll Book*).

OGLE OF SALTWICK, PAR. STANNINGTON

JOHN OGLE of Saltwick, younger brother of Henry Ogle (d.1581) of Kirkley, made his will 16 November (no year given, but it was proved on 10 October 1581). He was 'sick in body' and desires to be buried in the church of Stannington. He leaves to Allesin Ogle his daughter a young cow; to Dorothie Ogle his brother's daughter a young cow. His son Henrie Ogle the younger is to have his farmhold in Kirkley which he had of his good lord Eures. He appoints as executors his wife Marie Ogle and his son Cuthbert Ogle and they are to have the residue and to bring up his children 'in the fear of God and to give them their portions when they come to lawful age'. His son Henrie is to be under the guardianship of Cuthbert Foster. Henry Ogle of Kirkley and Cuthbert are to be supervisors. The will was proved by Marie *als* Male Ogle late wife of deceased and Cuthbert Ogle his son (*Dur. Prob. Off.* by C.R.H.).

The inventory of Marye Ogle, late wife of John Ogle of Saltwick, deceased, is dated 9 November 1585; her goods were worth £30. 10s. She owed Cuthbert Foster of Kirkley 20s., her son Cuthbert Ogle 7s., and Thomas Ogle for his portion £10 (*Ib.*).

John Ogle's eldest son was no doubt Cuthbert Ogle of Saltwick, administration of whose goods was granted 1 April 1618 to his widow Debbora, his children Edward, John, Cuthbert, William, Henry, Barbara and Debbora, being under age. An elder son Thomas was evidently of age.

Thomas Ogle of Saltwick's will is dated 24 September 1632. He leaves the third part of his goods to his wife, to his mother four kine, and the residue to be divided amongst his children. His brothers Cuthbert and Henry Ogle are each to have a whie stirk, and he gives to the poor of the parish £3. 6s. 8d. The inventory of his goods is dated 20 October 1632 and the will was proved 12 April 1633 by Isabella Ogle, widow, of Saltwick, to whom was granted tuition of Cuthbert, Dorothy, Mary, Elizabeth and Katherine Ogle (*Ib.*).

No later descendants of these Ogles have been traced.

OGLE OF CHOPPINGTON, PAR. WOODHORN

THE visitation pedigree of the Ogles of c.1480-1500 does not mention any younger sons of sir Robert Ogle (d.1436), but seems to have been primarily concerned with his seven daughters and their children. The pedigree of 1575 only commences with Robert, 1st lord Ogle (d.1469). It is quite clear however that sir Robert Ogle had two younger sons, William and John. On 22 August 29 H.VI (1451) Robert Ogle senior gave to William Ogle his brother the reversion of lands in Longwitton which Matilda de Ogle, formerly wife of Robert de Ogle his father then held (*NDD.* p.178, No. 67). John de Ogle made settlements of his lands on 12 March 1457 and 12 May 1461, the first trustee being 'William Ogle my brother'.

Before June 1444 William Ogle had married Margaret daughter and coheiress of sir Henry de Heton of Chillingham, widow of Thomas Middleton of Silksworth co. Durham; she was born 13 January 1394/5 and had married Thomas Middleton before 10 April 1422. There is a record of a settlement in June 1444 of one third of the manor of Chillingham, one third of a moiety of the vill of Hartley and one third of

OGLE of CARTER MOOR, par. PONTELAND

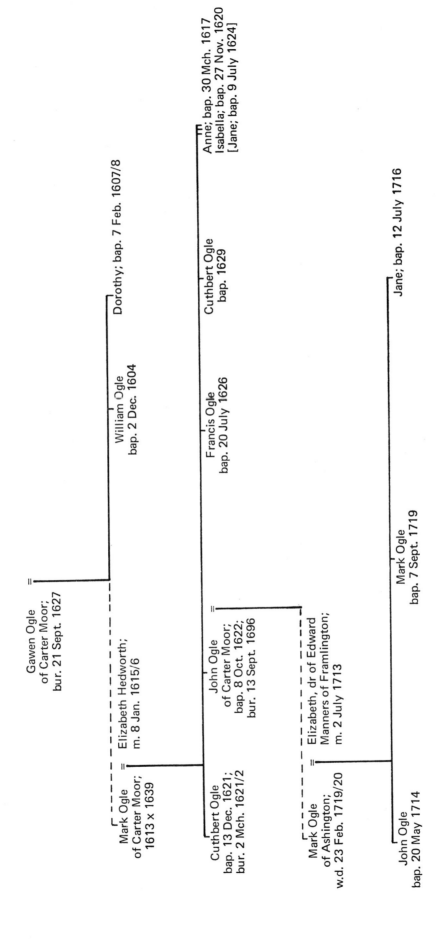

Gawen Ogle
of Carter Moor;
bur. 21 Sept. 1627

= Elizabeth Hedworth;
m. 8 Jan. 1615/6

William Ogle
bap. 2 Dec. 1604

Dorothy; bap. 7 Feb. 1607/8

Mark Ogle
of Carter Moor;
1613 x 1639

John Ogle
of Carter Moor;
bap. 8 Oct. 1622;
bur. 13 Sept. 1696

Francis Ogle
bap. 20 July 1626

Cuthbert Ogle
bap. 1629

Anne; bap. 30 Mch. 1617
Isabella; bap. 27 Nov. 1620
[Jane; bap. 9 July 1624]

Cuthbert Ogle
bap. 13 Dec. 1621;
bur. 2 Mch. 1621/2

= Elizabeth, dr of Edward
Manners of Framlington;
m. 2 July 1713

Mark Ogle
of Ashington;
w.d. 23 Feb. 1719/20

John Ogle
bap. 20 May 1714

Mark Ogle
bap. 7 Sept. 1719

Jane; bap. 12 July 1716

OGLE of SALTWICK, par. STANNINGTON

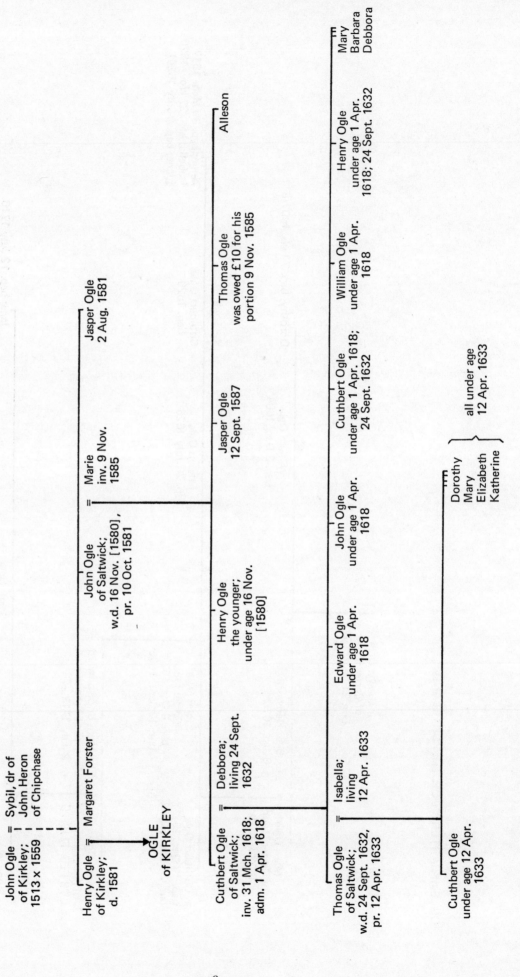

John Ogle of Kirkley; 1513 x 1559 = Sybil, dr of John Heron of Chipchase

Henry Ogle of Kirkley; d. 1581 = Margaret Forster

OGLE of KIRKLEY

John Ogle of Saltwick; w.d. 16 Nov. [1580], pr. 10 Oct. 1581 = Marie inv. 9 Nov. 1585

Jasper Ogle 2 Aug. 1581

Alleson

Thomas Ogle was owed £10 for his portion 9 Nov. 1585

Jasper Ogle 12 Sept. 1587

Henry Ogle the younger; under age 16 Nov. [1580]

Cuthbert Ogle of Saltwick; inv. 31 Mch. 1618; adm. 1 Apr. 1618 = Debbora; living 24 Sept. 1632

Thomas Ogle of Saltwick; w.d. 24 Sept. 1632, pr. 12 Apr. 1633 = Isabella; living 12 Apr. 1633

Edward Ogle under age 1 Apr. 1618

John Ogle under age 1 Apr. 1618

Cuthbert Ogle under age 1 Apr. 1618; 24 Sept. 1632

William Ogle under age 1 Apr. 1618

Henry Ogle under age 1 Apr. 1618; 24 Sept. 1632

Mary
Barbara
Debbora

Cuthbert Ogle under age 12 Apr. 1633

Dorothy
Mary
Elizabeth
Katherine
all under age 12 Apr. 1633

lands in Bamburgh and elsewhere, upon William Ogle and Margaret his wife, with reversion to Margaret's right heirs (*Feet of Fines*, 22 H.VI, Trinity). Thomas Middleton, the eldest son of her first marriage, claimed this third against his step-father William Ogle in 1455 after his mother's death (*de Banco R.* C.P. 40, roll 778, m.298d.). William Ogle retained some of the Heton lands until his death on 12 September 1479; an inquisition taken at Alnwick on 12 June 1480 found that he had died seised of 5 messuages and 60 acres in Hartley held by knight's service and that his heir was Thomas Middleton aged eleven (*i.p.m.* 20 E.IV, No. 26). William Ogle also held lands of the bishop of Durham, and an *i.p.m.* taken at Bedlington 28 July 1495 found that he had held lands in Choppington, had died 10 August (perhaps 1479) and that Gawin Ogle, his son and next heir, is aged 34 years. It is evident that Gawen, not born until 1461, cannot have been a son of William Ogle by his wife Margaret Heton, for she was dead in 1455. After her death William must have taken a second wife who was mother of Gawen.

Hodgson in his pedigree of the Ogles (*HN.* ii, I, p.384) states that William Ogle 'had issue two sons, *viz.*: 1stly, Gawen, from whose eldest son Ralph, the Ogles of Choppington descended; and from his second son John Ogle, were the Ogles of Ogle Castle and Burradon: and 2ndly, Henry, this William's 2nd son, who does not appear to have had issue'. There are at least two errors in this statement; the Ogles of Choppington were in fact descended from Gawen Ogle's son Cuthbert; and it seems reasonably certain that William Ogle's younger son Henry left descendants (*see* OGLE OF EGLINGHAM). William Ogle also had a daughter Margaret wife of Jasper Bradford of Bradford (1558 Vis. ped. of Bradford).

In a law suit of 1563 John Ogle of Ogle castle deposed that Gawen Ogle was 'great-grandfather' of Gregory Ogle and purchased John Anderson's lands in Choppington about 60 years past and built the tower there; Gregory, lately attainted, was 'cousin' and heir of the said Gawen, being son and heir of Cuthbert, who was son and heir to the said Gawen, the which Gawen was father to the deponent. It was not unusual in those times for a grandson to be referred to as 'cousin' but it is evident that 'great-grandfather' is a mistake for grandfather. Raine and others, not realising this error have endeavoured to fit another generation into their pedigrees.

On 4 July 1516 a Gawen Ogle with lord Ogle and John Ogle witnesses a settlement made by Cuthbert Ogle, rector of Ford, of the manors of Kirknewton, West Newton and Lanton (*Laing Charters*, p.79).

When Oliver Ogle of Burradon registered his pedigree in 1615 he stated that his grandfather, John Ogle of Ogle castle, was younger son of Gawen Ogle, and that Gawen's 1st son was Cuthberte Ogle of Choppington. He further stated that John Ogle of Ogle castle's wife was (blank) daughter and heir of William Bernaby of Gunerby, co. Lancs. (Lancs is a mistake for Lincs.). It is possible that the Bernaby heiress is placed in the wrong generation for the lands in Lincolnshire derived through her were later held by the Ogles of Choppington. Perhaps she was Gawen Ogle's wife.

Cuthbert Ogle had livery of his lands on 18 April 4th year of bishop Wolsey (1525). In 1528 his name appears in a list of the gentlemen of the Middle Marches. On 15 December 1533 he took a 41 years lease of the rectory of Eglingham and on 12 March 1533/4 he divided it with his brother John Ogle

who was to pay half the rent. Cuthbert Ogle's wife was called Joan and after his death she became second wife of George Fenwick of Brinkburn. Her son Gregory Ogle may have been godfather to George Fenwick's grandson Gregory Fenwick (w.d. 25 Nov. 1615).

Cuthbert Ogle died before (perhaps shortly before) 24 December 1552 on which date his son and heir Gregory Ogle entered into an indenture to marry Margery Ogle sister to Robert, lord Ogle, before Childermass (28 December) (*NDD.* p.184, No. 100). On 28 December 1552 Gregory Ogle granted to Oswin Ogle of Bothal, Launcelot Ogle of Ogle, George Ogle of Hirst and Matthew Ogle of Saltwick, gentlemen, an annuity of £6. 13s. 4d. out of his tenement in Choppington for the life of Margaret Ogle, widow, his grandmother; after her death the rent was to issue out of his lands in Gonerby, Grantham, Manthorp, Kirkby and Bilton in Lincolnshire, and the grantees were to re-enfeoff Gregory and Marjory his wife (*Ib.*, p.185, No. 101). The true import of this document is uncertain as nothing is said about the purpose for which the annuity was intended. It would appear however that Gregory was unable to charge the Lincolnshire lands during the lifetime of his grandmother Margaret, suggesting that she was the Bernaby heiress.

Robert, 6th lord Ogle, in his w.d. 27 July 1562 mentions his sister Meriall Ogle, to whom he leaves a ring, and Cuthbert Ogle, his sister's son; Thomas and Robert Ogle, his sister's sons, are to have the reversion of Rauff Elleker's lease of the Old Moor after the decease of John Ogle, brother to George Ogle. Meriall was a pet name for Margery at this time. Margery Ogle's husband Gregory was no longer alive. An *i.p.m.* of Gregory Ogle of Choppington, taken at Tattersall, Lincs., on 15 January 1604/5 found that about 26 March, 4 Eliz. (1562) at Newcastle, Gregory had been attainted and adjudged for felony and murder of a man unknown, to be hanged; he was seised of lands in Gonerby, Manthorp, Hartby, Belton near Grantham, Kirkby, Laythorpe and Houghton.

On 2 August it was reported that Gregory Ogle, Roger Heron and one Wilson, Ogle's servant, had been detected of coining, murder and other felonies; they were the persons who had murdered Thomas Carr. On 10 July 1562 Francis and Brian Ogle were examined. Roger Heron asserted that 'our friend Gregory Ogle is gone and Robert Wetherington was one of the procurers of his death'. Brian Ogle, brother to Francis and servant to Mistress Ogle of Choppington examined about the taking down of Gregory Ogle from the gallows on Easter eve last admitted that he was at Causey Park on the Saturday night (*Cal. S.P. Foreign* 1561 and 1562).

On 1 March 1563/4 Margery Ogle, widow, having annulled the interest she had in the rectory of Eglingham formerly granted to Cuthbert Ogle of Choppington, a new lease for 21 years from 29 September 1563 was granted of the rectory, lately in the tenure of George (*recte* Gregory) Ogle, to Margery Ogle (*Patent Roll*).

Gregory Ogle's widow Margerye made her will on 25 June 1565 and directs that she is to be buried in Bedlington quire. Her children who were all under age she gives them 'to dame Dorethy Fenwicke and Johan Fenwicke my mother, in Brinkburn'. Johan Fenwick was her mother-in-law who had married for her second husband George Fenwick of Brinkburn. The third part of her lease is left to her two daughters, 'whiles either of them have £40 to their marriage', and then it to come to Cuthbert, Robert and Thomas Ogle. If Johan Fenwicke should die, the testator's brother Thomas Ogle is to 'have the charge she had'. Thomas Oggle, the bastard, was to have the tithe corn of Beanley 'when it comes to my hands'. Her eldest son Cuthbert Ogle is to have her horse that George Heron hath in hands. The three sons Cuthbert, Robert and Thomas Oggle are to be executors; and her two brethren my lord Oggle and Thomas Oggle, supervisors. The will is witnessed by Cuthbert Watson, clerk, Lyonell and Thomas Ogle, Marmeduke Fenwycke and Thomas Harle, and was proved 22 May 1566 (*SS.* 102, p.32).

Thomas Ogle 'the bastard' who was to have the tithes of Beanley, may have been an illegitimate son of Gregory, and perhaps founded a line of tenant farmers that remained at Beanley until the 17th century. In 1586 a Gawen Ogle held a farm at Beanley and in 1612 John Ogle was a farmer there.

One of Margery Ogle's unnamed daughters may have been Agnes married firstly to William Lorrane of Kirkharle and after his death in 1594, to John Lisle of Acton. Her son Robert Lorrane was living at Choppington when he made his w.d. 6 February 1617/8.

The lease mentioned in Margery Ogle's will was undoubtedly the lease of the rectory of Eglingham. Her two sons Cuthbert and Thomas surrendered the lease and on 20 December 1581 the Crown gave them a lease for 21 years from 29 September 1581 (*Patent Roll*). The other son Robert had perhaps died before this. Thomas Ogle married Anne daughter of sir Ralph Grey of Chillingham, widow of Thomas Collingwood of Eslington. On 29 June 1612 Thomas Ogle, now of Choppington but late of Morpeth, made a complaint that by his obligation dated 20 July (1599) he had become bound to John Salkeld of Hulne Park in the sum of £80. Thomas Ogle was of Bedlington 5 February 1615/6 and is mentioned in a bill of complaint as uncle of Robert Lorraine of Kirkharle on the mother's side.

Cuthbert, the eldest son of Gregory Ogle, married Isabel daughter of Cuthbert Mitford of Mitford. By his w.d. 18 January 1593/4 Cuthbert Mitford leaves 'To Mr Cuthbert Ogle, my son-in-law, my viij oxen which I have in the custody of my servant William Pott, together with £4. 13s. 4d. which he is indebted unto me for one year, upon condition that the said Cuthbert Ogle shall not hereafter molest nor trouble Isabell, my wife, for the sum of £20 which he alleges to be behind and unpaid of his marriage goods' (*SS.* 38, p.242).

On 12 October 1621 Thomas Ogle, esquire, Matthew Ogle and Luke Ogle, gentlemen, all of Tritlington, bound themselves to Gregory Ogle of Choppington, esquire, for the annual payment of £30 by Thomas to Gregory 'in the south church porch of Bothal' until Thomas should recover possession of the manor house and demesne of Choppington, Clifwell Hill, a water corn mill and Slackhouses by right of the tenant right of Gregory and by lease from the bishop of Durham (*AA2.* I, p.24). This Gregory Ogle was probably son and heir of Cuthbert Ogle of Choppington.

On 23 November 1629 inventory was taken of the goods of Gregorie Ogle, gentleman, of the parish of Woodhorn; Mr Thomas Ogle of Choppington owed him £300. On 16 January 1629/30 administration of his goods was granted to Margarie alias Mabell Ogle, widow, for John, Ralph, Thomazin, Katherine and Agnes Ogle, his children who were

under age; his goods were valued at £340. Nothing further is known about any later descendants of the Ogles of Choppington.

OGLE OF BURRADON, PAR. EARSDON

THE services of John Ogle of Ogle castle, younger son of Gawen Ogle of Chippington, on the Marches and to the lords Ogle have already been mentioned. He was amply rewarded by the head of the family, when on 20 January 1525 Robert, 4th lord Ogle, gave him 'for his faithful services' lands in Ogle and the office of constable of Ogle castle; and on 12 January 1526/7 demised to the said John and to Lancelot Ogle, his son and heir, Saltwick for 41 years for £5 a year. Two days later he leased to John Ogle the manor and castle of Ogle for 41 years at the yearly rent of £14.

It seems clear that John Ogle was married more than once, one of his wives being Anne daughter of Edward Shafto of Little Bavington. It has been suggested that his second wife was Barbara Fenwick; this is doubtful but he had a daughter Barbara or Dorothy who married Ralph Fenwick of Stanton. On 26 April 1530 Shilvington and Whalton were granted to sir Ralph Fenwick, Roger Heron and others 'for the wife of John Ogle'. If this was a marriage settlement it cannot have been for John Ogle's first wife as he already had a son and heir Lancelot in 1527. In 1563 John Ogle was aged 86.

John Ogle's will is dated 4 April 1565. He was then 'whole of mind and of good memory', and commends his soul unto Almighty God and his body to be buried in his parish church of Whalton within the porch commonly called Our Lady porch within the said church with duties due and accustomed. He gives to his son Clement Ogle all his whole lease, interest, right, title and term of years yet to come in and to Ogle castle and the tithes and half tithes in Eglingham parish and the lease of the same, provided that his son Mathe Ogle shall have the whole tithe of West Lilburn, and his son Olyver Ogle shall have the half tithe of Old Beanley and Eglingham paying the parsonal rent thereof. His son Olyver is also to have the half tithe of Beanley. He gives the wardship and marriage of Marion Redley to Olyver Ogle son to his son Lancelot Ogle. His lands and tenements in Bradford, Mitford and Newbiggen are bequeathed to his sons Mathe and Gaberill Ogle, 'according to the true meaning of two several deeds as more at large it doth appear'. His three sons Clemet Ogle, Cuthbert Ogle and Lewes Ogle and his grandson Lyonell Ogle son to his son Alexandre Ogle are to have his lands and tenements in South Dissington, according to four several deeds of gift thereof, three of them dated 12 August 5 E.VI and the fourth on (blank) day in 2 Eliz. If his son Gaberill Ogle should like Dissington better than Bradford then he is to have it and Lionell is to have Bradford 'making sufficient assurance either to other for exchange of the same'. It was the testator's will and mind and intent that his son Clamet should have the keeping, order, and rule and governance of his son Cuthbert Ogle and his brother during his life natural. John Ogle bequeaths to each of his sons Cuthbert and Lewes, 8 oxen, 8 kine and 20 ewes. He declares that such reckonings as there have been between himself and his son Clamet before the making of his will should be void 'and at no time hereafter to the hindrance or trouble of the said

OGLE of CHOPPINGTON, par. WOODHORN

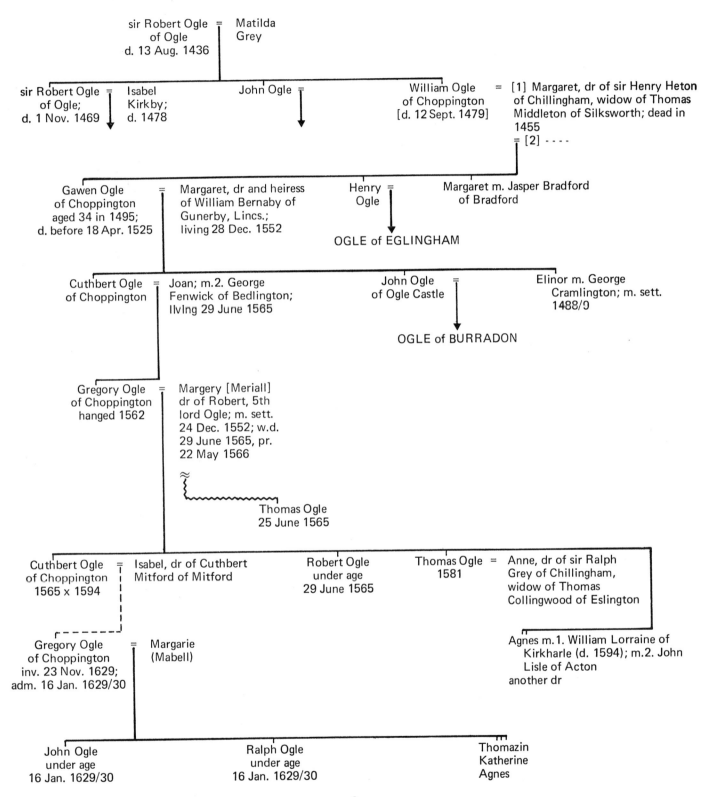

Clemet by any person'. The rest of his goods unbequeathed, his debts being paid, he leaves to his sons Clemet and Gaberell and he appoints them executors. He appoints as supervisors of his will Robert Medilton of Belsay, esq., Roger Heron of Abshield, gent., John Ogle of Newsham and Olyver Ogle (*SS.* 2, p.247).

None of John Ogle's daughters are mentioned in his will, but two of his sons-in-law are to be supervisors. Robert Middleton of Belsay married for his second wife John Ogle's daughter Mabel; they were married before September 1574; Robert Middleton died 31 August 1590 and his widow Mabel was returned as a recusant in 1603 and in 10 Jas I (1613/4). Phillis daughter of John Ogle married firstly George Cramlington, secondly Edward Delaval, and thirdly John Ogle of Newsham. According to the 1563/4 visitation pedigree of Fenwick of Stanton, Raff Fenwyke of Stanton married 'Barbara, dau. to sir John Ogle of Ogle castle'; John Ogle was not in fact a knight. In the 1615 pedigree of Fenwick of Stanton, Raphe Fenwicke's wife is called Dorothie.

John Ogle's eldest son Lancelot died in his father's lifetime, leaving an only son Oliver; at least no other children are mentioned in John's will. Lancelot Ogle was buried in Whalton church where his tombstone still records that 'Here lyeth Lancelot Ogle sone and heire to John Ogle of Ogle castle, esqr., who died 18 Feb. 1564'. According to the 1615 pedigree, Lancelot Ogle married one of the daughters and coheiresses of sir Thomas Grey of Horton. This cannot be correct, for the six daughters of sir Thomas Grey (d.1570) are all mentioned in his will and were all married before 1571 and none of them to Lancelot Ogle. Lancelot had an illegitimate daughter Fillis Ogle.

In 1570 Oliver Ogle purchased four messuages and lands in Burradon from Ralph Harding (*Feet of Fines*). He made his will on 24 October 1614 and was buried at Earsdon 27 October 1616. He leaves directions that he is to be buried in the parish church of Earsdon under a broad through stone within the choir there beside 'my brother Mitford of Seghill'. His lands in Burradon are settled on his eldest son Lancelot and his heirs male, remainder to his son Harcules Ogle, remainder to Ollyver son of Hector Ogle his late son, remainder to Matthew Ogle, Hector's second son with final remainder to the testator's right heirs. Lancelot is to pay £100 to Harcules. Olliver son of Hector Ogle is to have his lands in Whalton for ever. He leaves legacies to Fillis his base sister, to his 'son' George Ord's eldest daughter, to Lancelot Newtone and to Ralph Ogle. The witnesses to the will are Matthew Newtone, Oliver Killingworth, Charles Ogle, Phillipp Ogle etc. The will was proved on 5 May 1620 and an *i.p.m.* was taken at Morpeth on 30 August 1626. The jurors found that Oliver died on 26 October 1616 and Lancelot his son and heir was then aged 34 years; Magdalen late wife of Oliver was alive and dowable out of Burradon. On 17 March 1619/20 Magdalen widow of Oliver Ogle appears to have been at variance with Lancelot Ogle son of the deceased, over the administration of the will (*Act Book, Durham*, by C.R.H.).

Oliver Ogle's wife was Magdalen daughter of John Mitford of Seghill. They had three sons Lancelot, Hercules and Hector, and three daughters Catherine wife of George Ord, Barbara wife of Matthew Newton of Stocksfield and Fortune wife of Oliver Killingworth of Killingworth.

The eldest son Lancelot Ogle was aged 33 when his father

registered his pedigree in 1615. He was buried at Earsdon on 5 January 1640/1. By his wife Mary sister of Robert Ogle of Bothal, he had a son William and a daughter Jane. Jane became her father's heiress and carried the manor of Burradon by marriage to her husband James Ogle of Causey Park.

Lancelot Ogle made a will in 1640 but it was never proved. This is stated in the particulars of the estate of James Ogle of Causey Park drawn up for his sequestration in 1647. Lancelot had bequeathed an annuity of £5 to Margaret Miller, and a legacy of £50 to his base daughter Jane Ogle, to be paid when she was 21 or married and £4 yearly to be paid her in the interim; Jane was aged 14 in 1647 (*SS.* 111, p.302).

Hercules Ogle son of Olliver Ogle of Burradon, gent., was apprenticed on 25 September 1611 to Stephan Maddison of Newcastle, boothman (*SS.* 101, p.233). He apparently never married. His will is dated 29 December 1620 and was proved on 26 February 1620/1. He leaves legacies to the nine children of Oliver Killingworth; to the seven children of Mathew Newton; to Oliver son of Hector Ogle, deceased, and his two sisters; to his sister Barbara wife of Mathew Newton and to Fortune wife of Oliver Killingworth; to Mary daughter of Robert Killingworth, merchant; to William Ogle son of his brother Lancelot Ogle of Burradon; and to his sister Margaret Ogle and her three children. His mother Magdalen Ogle is appointed sole executrix. Hercules Ogle had directed in his will that he was to be buried in St Nicholas', Newcastle, but there is no confirmation in the parish registers that his wishes were carried out.

Hector, the youngest son of Oliver Ogle (d.1616), was buried at Earsdon on 13 September 1613 and administration of his goods was granted on 28 September 1614 to Margaret his widow, for their children Oliver, Matthew, Isabel and Grace Ogle who were under age. Hector Ogle's wife was Margaret daughter and coheiress of Robert Fenwick of Kenton; as a widow she lived in Newcastle and an inventory of her goods was exhibited on 24 November 1626.

Oliver Ogle, eldest son and heir of Hector Ogle, was baptised on 23 October 1604. He married on 21 April 1645 Mary daughter of John Cramlington of the parish of Tynemouth. Oliver Ogle had lands in Whalton by his grandfather's will, and also held lands in Backworth. He died in 1670. His widow survived him for nearly 40 years and in 1708 being in extreme poverty applied to Quarter Sessions for relief:

'To the worshipful the justices to hold the Quarter Sessions for the county of Northumberland, the humble petition of Mary Ogle of Backworth in the county of Northumberland aforesaid. Humbly sheweth that your petitioner (who was born in Tynemouth, being daughter to John Cramlington who lived in the said place and died in the parish) lived all along in the said parish of Tynemouth, residing in Backworth with her husband, Oliver Ogle, for many years, till it pleased God to take him from her, and since falling into adverse fortune, and being very ancient, and consequently uncapable of keeping herself or preventing her falling into extreme poverty, too much of which (God knows) she already feels. These are, therefore, humbly to implore your worships seriously to consider and piously to redress these her present circumstances by assigning her either a place and relief in her own parish, or otherwise by causing some to come yearly to her here. And your petitioner shall ever pray, etc.' (*AA*2. XIX, p.5).

The petitioner was ordered to have a shilling a week from

the chapelry of Earsdon. Although Oliver Ogle had a son Lancelot (d.1675) and five daughters, there is no evidence that any of them had children. At the court of the manor of Tynemouth on 6 April 1684 it was found that John Ogle of Bradford was heir to Lancelot Ogle and Oliver Ogle, both deceased. It has been suggested that this John Ogle was perhaps a younger son of Oliver, but this is very unlikely. He was probably a descendant of Gabriel Ogle (d.1580), a younger son of John Ogle (d.1565) of Ogle castle.

It is now necessary to consider these younger sons of John Ogle of Ogle castle. Seven of them are mentioned in their father's will:

1. Clement Ogle. John Ogle of Ogle castle by his w.d. 4 April 1565 leaves his lands and tenements in South Dissington to his sons Clement, Cuthbert and Lewes and his grandson Lyonell son to his son Alexander Ogle. It has been stated that 'by 1527 all the Ogle property in South Dissington seems to have been in the possession of John Ogle, third son of Ralph, lord Ogle' (NCH. XIII, p.181). This is incorrect for the John Ogle who held the South Dissington lands was John Ogle of Ogle castle who was a grandson of William Ogle of Choppington, a younger son of sir Robert Ogle (d.1436). He had acquired 14 messuages and 820 acres of land in South Dissington from Robert, 4th lord Ogle in 1529 (de Banco Roll 21 H.VIII).

There is no question of an entail mentioned in John Ogle's will but in 1573 two messuages and lands in South Dissington were settled by fine upon Clement Ogle and his heirs with remainder successively to Gabriel, Lewes and Cuthbert Ogle (Feet of Fines).

Clement Ogle was apprenticed to Edward Baxter and became free of the Newcastle Merchants Company on 19 January 1552; as a mercer he took apprentices in 1553 and 1560. He married a daughter of James Hodgson of Newcastle. Her brother, alderman Richard Hodgson of Newcastle, by his w.d. 1 March 1581/2 gives 'unto Clement Ogle and his wife, my sister, and to either of them an old ryall for a token and more I do forgive them all such money as they are owing me at the day of my death'; Richard Ogle, Clement's son is to have £3. 6s. 8d., 'and to all the residue of his brethren and sisters 40s., apiece' (SS. 38, p.117). Another brother, Lancelot Hodschon of Lanchester, co. Dur., by his w.d. 23 February 1558/9 leaves legacies to 'everyone of my sister Oggell's children' (SS. 112, p.18).

The Hodgsons were Roman Catholics and Clement Ogle and his sons became ardent followers of that religion. In a list of recusants in the parish of Newburn drawn up on 11 February 1595 are the names of 'Clement Ogle of South Dissington, gent.; Richard Ogle of the same, son to the said Clement a most obstinate and dangerous young man; they keep there together and have the demesnes of Dissington worth xxli by year and a tithe in Northumberland and goods worth xli; they both stand indicted; Thomas Ogle and Willm Ogle sons to the said Clement and by him maintained, having no living' (Cath. Rec. Soc. vol.53, p.61).

In 1581 amongst those who had any children or others belonging unto them 'that now remain in the parts beyond the seas', was Clement (Ogle) of Dissing(ton) whose son Richard was abroad 'with the privity of his father' (State Papers. Dom. Eliz. 12/150/95).

William Ogle, apparently Clement Ogle's youngest son,

was admitted to the English College at Rheims 12 June 1592 but was sent home ill in November 1592 (Knox, Douay Diaries, 246, 248). The president of the north brought with him to York a youth new come from beyond sea, taken at his father's house, called Mr William Ogill, and committed him to Outlaw's the pursuivant, for that he would not go to church nor confer with ministers (Fr. Chr. Grene's MSS. printed in Foley, Records of the English Province S.J. III, 759). In January 1593/4 Ogle was in prison at York. He was again abroad in 1598 when he was ordained priest (Douay Diaries). In 1599 and in 1601 he was living at Dissington when he was convicted as a recusant. In 1615 he was 'maintained at Beamish and had his dwelling amongst the two sisters called Hodgson' his mother's relatives (S.P. 14/81/54 IV). William Ogle, priest, was cited by the Court of High Commission at Durham in 1616.

Administration of the goods of Clement Ogle of Dissington in the parish of Newburn was granted 18 March 1597/8 to Thomas Ogle his son who agreed to pay the other children of the deceased; an inventory of Clement Ogle's goods was exhibited on 18 March 1597/8.

In 1601/2 Thomas Ogle of South Dissington was plaintiff in a writ against Ralph Grey of Chillingham; his father had held a lease of certain tithes in the parish of Eglingham from 29 September 1590 to which Thomas had succeeded. On 7 September 1601 Ralph Grey by force carried away the tithes of Old Bewick with the assistance of about thirty persons armed with bows, bills, guns and other weapons. Two days later other men incited by Grey assembled at East Lilburn to take the tithes from there and violently assaulted Thomas and his brother Richard. Thomas Ogle of Dissington, aged 40 or thereabouts, gave his deposition about the affair, at Felton 1602. In the affray at East Lilburn Richard Ogle had been wounded in three places (Star Chamber Proc.).

Thomas Ogle of Dissington, gent., was convicted of recusancy on 18 August 1607. In 1616 and again in 1620 he is described as of the parish of Stamfordham when he and his wife were convicted. His wife was Eleanor daughter of Thomas Swinburne of Capheaton. On 27 April 1629 the mayor and aldermen of Newcastle sent to the Privy Council a list of all recusants who were to be indicted at the Easter Sessions. On the list are the names of Thomas Ogle, gentleman, Ellinor his wife, and Clement Ogle, gentleman. A Clement Ogle, mercer, was admitted to the freedom of Newcastle in 1639 (NRS. III, p.21); he was not a member of the Newcastle Merchant Adventurers.

William Ogle alias Swinburne, ordained priest at Lisbon and sent to England in 1644 was perhaps a son of Thomas Ogle and his wife Eleanor Swinburne (Hist. of Lisbon Coll., p.235).

Richard Ogle of Dissington was regularly convicted of recusancy between 1599 and 1607. In 1608 Richard and his wife Adelina sold 'their manor' of South Dissington to John Delaval. He was living at Bavington 9 January 1608/9 when he owed £20 for goods seized for his recusancy in 1606. On 12 July 1626 there were convictions recorded against two Richard Ogles in co. Durham, viz., Richard Ogle, gent., of Beamish, and Richard Ogle, gent., of Manor House, Lanchester. As both these places belonged to the Hodgsons, it is likely that these two Ogles were Richard, formerly of Dissington, and a son of the same name.

Richard Ogle, gent., and Mary Ogle of Elvet, Durham, were convicted recusants on 11 April 1632 and on 11 October 1632 Richard Ogle of Durham, gent., and his wife were prosecuted in the archbishop's court at York.

2. Gabriel Ogle. *See* OGLE OF BRADFORD, PAR. BOLAM.

3. Matthew Ogle. He was probably the person of this name apprenticed 5 December 1534 to Edward Baxter of Newcastle, mercer. He may have been Matthew Ogle of Saltwick who for £50 on 7 August 1569 sold his lands in Bradford to Gabriel Ogle of Bradford; the transaction was completed in 1570 by a fine, in which Margaret wife of Matthew Ogle was included. Between 1565 and 1573 Matthew Ogle of Saltwick, gent., aged about 60, and his son Raiff Ogle, gent., aged 22, were charged at Durham Ecclesiastical Court with quarreling and fighting in the church and churchyard of Stannington (*SS.* 21, pp.259-260).

The will of Raphe Ogle of the parish of Stannington was proved in 1629. He leaves to his wife Isabel Ogle £5 out of his lands in Saltwick and his house in Stannington for life. To his son Edward Ogle he leaves 40s., and to his daughter Margerye Ogle, 6s. 8d. Mr Edward son of Mr Cuthbert Ogle of Ogle is to have all his tenant right for a certain sum of money already given.

4. Oliver Ogle. By his father's will he is to have the lease of the half tithe of Old Beanley and Eglingham.

5. Cuthbert Ogle. With his brothers Clement and Lewes Ogle and his nephew Lionel son of Alexander Ogle he is to have lands in South Dissington by his father's will. He was perhaps the Cuthbert Ogle appointed a supervisor of the w.d. 23 November 1587 of Alexander Ogle of Earsdon Forest. Alexander Ogle's father Lewes Ogle (d.1586) may have been godfather to Cuthbert's younger brothers Lewes and Alexander.

6. Lewes Ogle. Administration of the goods of Ludevic Ogle of Dissington was granted 10 March 1605/6 to his widow Elizabeth; his daughters Edith, Margaret, Agnes and Maria were under age.

7. Alexander Ogle. He had apparently died before 4 April 1565 leaving a son Lyonell who is mentioned in his grandfather's will. A Lionel Ogle witnesses the w.d. 29 June 1565 of Margery Ogle of Choppington, but probably died before 1573 for he is not mentioned in a settlement of the South Dissington lands made in that year.

OGLE OF BRADFORD, PAR. BOLAM

ON 7 August 1569 Matthew Ogle of Saltwick sold for £50 his lands in Bradford to Gabriel Ogle of Bradford, and in 1570 Matthew Ogle and Margaret his wife conveyed a messuage and lands to Gabriel Ogle, gent. (*HN.* ii, I, p.351n.). Matthew Ogle was Gabriel's brother.

Gabriel Ogle witnesses the w.d. 21 July 1579 of Clare Forster of Capheaton; she leaves to her son-in-law's children Robert, Cuthbert and John Musgrave and John and Margerie Ogle, 15 young neat. Clare was a daughter of William Carnaby of Halton and married firstly William Swinburne of Capheaton and after his death on 7 April 1550, Reynold Forster. By her first husband she had two sons Thomas and Reynold and two daughters Jane and Margaret. Jane was unmarried in 1579 for Clare calls her 'my daughter Jane Swinburne', and she was still unmarried on 10 April 1585, when Ranolde Swynborne of Bothal calls her 'my sister Jane Swynborne' in his will. William Swinburne's other daughter Margaret seems to have married Thomas Musgrave whom Reynold Swinburne calls 'my brother'. By an earlier marriage Musgrave had three sons Robert, Cuthbert and John, and apparently a daughter Jane who married Gabriel Ogle of Bradford. Ranolde Swynborne by his will leaves 'To Mergerie Ogle, my cousin, 20 bolls of oats' and 'To my cousin John Ogle 20s.' (*SS.* 38, p.108).

Probate of the will of Gabriel Ogle, par. Whalton, was granted on 7 December 1580 and mentions his wife Jane, the supervisor of his will Tristram Fenwick, his brother Clement Ogle and his children John and Margerie.

John Ogle of Bradford was a trustee for a settlement of the manor of Edlingham made on 20 October 1617 by John Swinburne of Edlingham (*Swinburne Deeds*, 3/65). Depositions taken at Stamfordham on 8 May 1638 on behalf of William Swinburne concerning the manor of Hawkwell include one by John Ogle of Bradford, gent., aged 64 (*Ib.,* 5/72). It must have been the son and grandson of this John Ogle, who as John Ogle the elder, and John Ogle the younger, both of Bradford, on 8 January 1670 sold their third part of Bradford to sir John Swinburne for £300; in exchange, the Ogles were to have a farmhold in the manor of Hawkwell (*HN.* ii, I, p.351).

John Ogle the elder of Bradford can be identified as the Mr Ogle, a neighbour of sir John Swinburne of Capheaton, for whose son sir John applied to lord Ogle for employment. Lord Ogle replied on 29 May 1673—'Since my coming here, I have thought of what you was pleased to desire me, which was that I would take Mr Ogle, your neighbour's son. I am sure I would not now be willing to take him, but you did desire me to do it: and I find I must take no servant, but such a one as will be very useful to me: my condition will not permit other: I am a poor man. If Mr Ogle is willing to have his son bred up to my butler and go of messages here in the town (not to be foot boy, God forbid!) I will take him, much for your sake. If he likes of this I would have him send his son up here to me, spending as little by the way as he can. I will pay for his journey, and let him buy no clothes'. Sir John drafted a reply on the back of this original letter to the effect that 'your so very ready acceptance of my cousin Ogle's son, upon my account from your own hand, has so infinitely obliged me, that I want words to express the favours. Yet I hope you will find him worthy your service. He is a gentleman both by father and mother, always great loyalists, and professors of the church of England; and have suffered by the late rebellion, as much as any, according to their ability, for they lost all they had. Now for the boy himself you will find him very honest and apt enough; but he never was (away) from his father, so you can expect nothing of garb. He intends to take the journey within a day or two; but whether by sea or land, they as yet cannot tell; but which way soever the charge will be little; for the boy can drink nothing, as yet, but small beer' (*HN.* ii, I, p.224n.).

The boy, Thomas Ogle, when he grew up, was of St Martin in the Fields, London, a bachelor aged 32, when he took out a licence 11 June 1683 to marry Anne Chaytor of St Paul, Covent Garden, spinster, aged about 30, at St Mary

OGLE of BURRADON, par. EARSDON

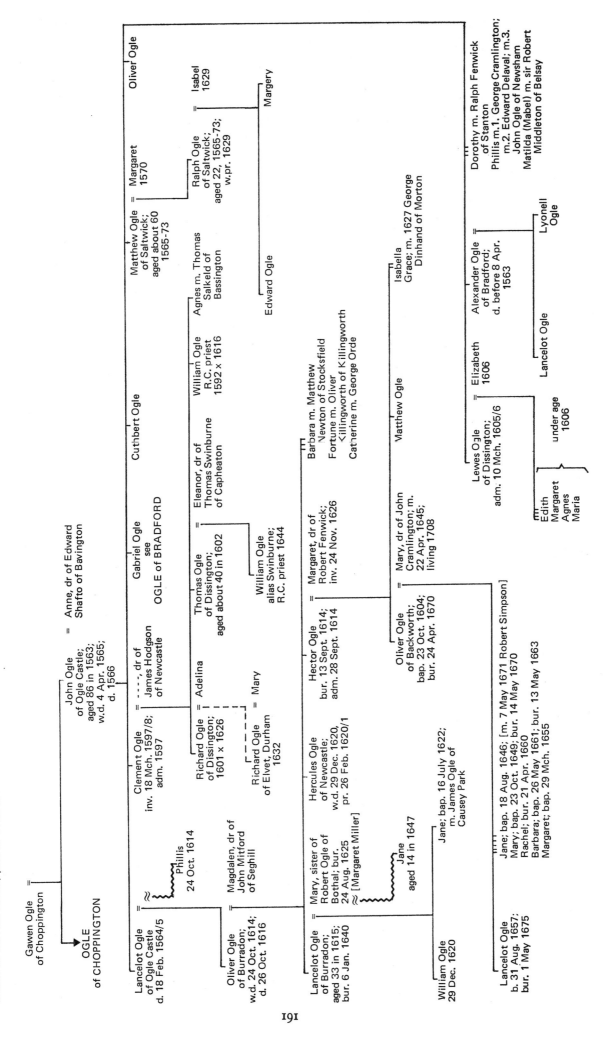

191

Somerset, London. His bride was a daughter of sir Nicholas Chaytor of Croft, Yorks. Thomas was living at Blackburn, Lancs., when he and Anne his wife were plaintiffs in 1688 in a writ against sir William Chaytor, bart., and his brother Henry Chaytor. They claimed that sir Nicholas by his w.d. 8 February 1685/6 had settled the manor of Butterby, co. Durham, on his son William, subject to a payment of £500 to Anne Ogle. Anne had been unable to get her legacy, Henry Chaytor in his reply to the writ stating that the £500 was a provision for Anne's children. Letters from Thomas Ogle to sir William Chaytor 1682-1687 are amongst the Chaytor papers in Durham Record Office.

About 1695 Thomas Ogle purchased half the manor of Great Stainton, co. Durham from William Killinghall, his wife's cousin. Killinghall's steward noted about this—'Mr Thomas Ogle bought all Mr Killinghall's moiety of Stainton at £1650 but baffled him out of £25 on account of a gentlewoman Mr Ogle proposed as a match for Mr Killinghall, which, if he had married the purchase was to be £1600 only, but was to pay £1625' (AA2, II, p.98). Ogle apparently made the purchase on behalf of his elder brother John.

Thomas Ogle was living at Northstreet, par. St Andrew's, Holborn, when he made his w.d. 20 March 1712/3. As for 'the estate and wordly goods God Almighty hath been graciously pleased to endow me with' he gives it all to his wife 'for and during her natural life to be disposed of as she think fit and convenient' desiring her to pay to his nephew John Ogle, £30 a year out of Bland Close (Yorks) and £10 a year out of Ashholm (Yorks) to his nephew Wentworth Ogle. To his 'unnatural' brother Luke Ogle—this was Wentworth's father—he leaves one shilling. Four days after making his will Thomas Ogle added a codicil to it. By this he directs that £10 is to be given towards the teaching four or five poor children of the Glebe in the township of Blackburn, 'to learn them to read, knit and sew'. Probate of the will was granted on 16 July 1714.

We shall return later to Luke Ogle the 'unnatural' brother and his descendants. Thomas Ogle's widow Anne was still living in the parish of St Andrew, Holborn, 12 March 1716 when she made her will. She desires her funeral to be performed in a plain, decent manner without escutcheons or rings, and she mentions her brother Henry Chaytor, her cousin Henry Stockar and a picture of her husband. She survived the making of her will for many years and the inventory of her goods is dated 14 January 1728; amongst her effects was a family seal of the Ogles.

Thomas Ogle's elder brother John Ogle was living at Bradford 24 May 1670 when he married at Bolam, Dorothy Browne, widow. For their marriage bond of 18 April 1670 Thomas Ogle of 'Hallewell', Durham, gent., was bondsman. She was daughter of George Ogle of Tritlington and sister and heir of Martin Ogle of the same place. Her first husband was John Browne of East Chevington, gent., their marriage bond being dated 25 April 1664. Administration of the goods of John Browne, late of Chevington Moorhouse, par. Warkworth, deceased, was granted on 7 January 1667/8 to Dorothy Browne widow and relict of deceased, together with the tuition of Thomas Browne and Dorothy Browne, their children (Dur. Prob. Off. by C.R.H.).

In 1690 sir William Middleton of Belsay, bart, who seems to have had a mortgage on the Tritlington estate, entered a bill of complaint against John Ogle and Dorothy his wife, 'heir-at-law of Thomas Ogle, late of Tritlington, deceased' and Robert Clark. John Ogle's legal advisor seems to have been Lancelot Allgood of Newcastle, to whom he wrote from Blencow on 5 November 1690 (Brumell Charters, No. 46). The answer of John and Dorothy Ogle was sworn at Bishop Auckland, 19 January 1691 (Ib., No. 48).

The fact that the letter of 5 November 1690 was addressed from Blencowe serves to identify John Ogle with the man of that name who was appointed master of the free grammar school in Great Blencowe, Cumb., on 5 October 1688. One of his receipts for 'table and learning' of Gervase and Thomas Birkbeck, dated 7 November 1693 has survived (CW2. LXIV, p.215). Sir Daniel Fleming writing to sir John Lowther, 24 June 1692, reported that 'Mr Ogle (schoolmaster of Blencow) came lately hither to desire my vote for one of his sons, a Batchelor of Arts in Scotland, to be schoolmaster of Barton, upon the resignation of Mr William Airay the present schoolmaster there' (J. R. Magrath, The Flemings in Oxford iii.). It seems likely that John Ogle was the man of this name who on 3 March 1676/7 was licensed as schoolmaster of Hartforth Free School, par. Gilling, Yorks. (by C.R.H.). John Ogle was ordained deacon 3 June 1694 and became curate of Hutton-in-the-Forest; he became priest 5 June 1696. He was probably the John Ogle who became master of the Free Grammar School at Hexham in 1701; bur. Hexham 19 March 1701/2.

Before leaving Bradford, John Ogle had two sons baptised at Bolam, viz. John, 30 March 1671 and George, 16 January 1672/3. He had a younger son Benjamin and a daughter Dorothy who married a man called Snowden. George was apparently the Scottish graduate of 1692. He became curate of Wolsingham, co. Durham, 1 July 1695.

The Blencowe schoolmaster's eldest son John became vicar of Holme Cultram, Cumb., 2 February 1694/5 and resigned 25 June 1715. He afterwards lived at Stockton, co. Durham, where he made his w.d. 31 March 1719 and added a codicil on 23 May 1719. He leaves to Thomas Ogle of Durham 'now clerk to Mr Maskall' all his estate at Great Stainton, subject to an annuity of £20 to his brother Benjamin Ogle, £12 a year to his mother Dorathy Ogle and £30 a year to his aunt Ann Ogle. His sister Dorathy Snowden's eldest son is to have Bland Close in the West Riding of Yorkshire after the death of his aunt Ann Ogle, and Dorathy's second son is to have Ashholm in the East Riding after Ann Ogle's death. His 'dear cousin and kind friend' John Ogle of Stockton is to have £20 a year out of Stainton. The revd John Ogle was buried at Stockton 26 May 1719.

As John Ogle's trustee, William Woodburne, Jurat, of Knaresborough, was directed to take care of John's brother Benjamin's affairs during life, it seems likely that Benjamin was not quite normal. His other brother George is not mentioned in the will, although we shall see later that he married and had a daughter.

Thomas Ogle of Durham, who was appointed by John Ogle of Stockton as his principal heir, was son of another Thomas Ogle who had been curate of Bishop Wearmouth 1694-1701.

Thomas Ogle became curate of Bishop Wearmouth 1 October 1694 and died 1 September 1701. About this time there were two Thomas Ogles who graduated at Edinburgh, and both were Northumbrians. Thomas Ogle *e Northumbria Angliae* graduated 1690/1, and Thomas Ogle *anglus*, graduated MA, at Edinburgh 7 July 1698. A Thomas Ogle was ordained deacon 21 September 1690 by the bishop of Durham and priest exactly twelve months later. He must have been 23 years of age before he could have been ordained so he could not have been a son of John and Dorothy Ogle of Blencowe. He could however have been the curate of Bishop Wearmouth. By his wife Anne Ettrick (m.11 September 1698) the curate had an only son Thomas Ogle. It was this second Thomas who was clerk to Mr Maskall and heir to John Ogle of Stockton in 1719.

Thomas Ogle of the city of Durham, gent., made his will 25 July 1725 and added codicils on 25 August and 16 September 1725. He leaves his moiety of the manor of Great Stainton to his mother Ann Ogle for life, then to his uncle John Ogle for life and then as to one half to his cousin Margaret wife of Thos Robinson the younger of Sunderland for life and then to his cousin lady Ann Myddleton wife of sir William Myddleton, bart; after the death of Margaret Robinson her half also was to go to lady Ann Myddleton. Thomas leaves to the trustees for the charity of the late rev. dr Bowes an annuity of £5 charged upon the moiety of Great Stainton 'after all the annuities charged upon the said premises by the last will and testament of my cousin John Ogle shall be determined'. The first codicil to the will dealt with a new almshouse at Bishop Wearmouth. In the second the testator mentions that his mother Mrs Ann Ogle of Sunderland, widow, stands bound to Dorothy Ogle, late spinster, and now Dorothy Mohill by bond dated October 1719 or 1720; elsewhere she is called 'my cousin Dorothy wife of John Mole of or near Shotley Bridge'. Also in the second codicil there is mention of 'my kinswoman Mrs Ann Ogle of London, widow'. The will was proved 31 January 1725/6 by Thomas Robinson, jun., of Sunderland, fitter, and Anne Ogle of Sunderland, widow, and the testator is described as late of Silksworth.

Mrs Robinson and lady Middleton, to whom Thomas Ogle left his lands in Great Stainton were relatives of his mother.

'Dorothy Ogle, late spinster, and now Dorothy Mohill' was Dorothy Ogle of Wolsingham who married at Durham Cathedral 26 March 1721 John Mall of Lanchester. She was daughter of George Ogle, gent., baptised at Wolsingham 24 May 1698, and her father was presumably John Ogle of Stockton's younger brother. George Ogle BA was licensed to teach at Wolsingham on 1 July 1695. He had married at St Giles', Durham, 11 December 1696 Mary Maugham of Wolsingham. It seems strange that John mentions neither of them in his will.

The relationship between John Ogle of Stockton (w.d. 1719) and Thomas Ogle of Durham (w.d. 1725) must, until further evidence is found, remain uncertain.

We must now return to the descendants of Luke Ogle, the 'unnatural' brother of Thomas Ogle (d.1713-14) of London. On 24 November 1713 Wentworth son of Luke Ogle of Royston, Yorks., was admitted to Gray's Inn; he must be the Wentworth Ogle who was to have an annuity of £10 out of Ashholme, Yorks, by his uncle Thomas' will; 'my niece Elizabeth' mentioned in Thomas Ogle's will in 1713 may have been Wentworth's sister. Administration of the estate of a Wentworth Ogle of Hertfordshire was granted

22 June 1730 to Elinor or Eliza Ogle.

Later Ogles with the unusual name of Wentworth can be presumed to belong to this same branch of the family. Administration of the goods of Harriott Ogle, late of the parish of St Stephen Walbrook, London, was granted 24 December 1768 to her husband Wentworth Ogle. In the next generation the administration of Jane Ogle of the parish of St Stephen Walbrook was given in February 1787/8 to her husband Wentworth Ogle. He was living in Cannon Street, London, apparently a surgeon, 13 February 1796, when he made his will and it was proved 13 March 1796. He mentions in his will his wife Martha, his poor nephew Thomas Aves and Aves' wife and children. His two sons were Robert Ogle, a captain in the army, and George Ogle who was in holy orders (*Ogle and Bothal*, pp.239-240).

OGLE OF EGLINGHAM, PAR. EGLINGHAM

A BRANCH of the Ogles held the manor of Eglingham from the early 16th century until 1890 but their connection with the main line of the family is uncertain. An early pedigree (*Harl. MS.* 1554) states that William Ogle (d.1479) of Choppington had a younger son Henry and it was thought that he was the progenitor of the Ogles of Eglingham. In a law suit of 1776 x 1781 mention was made of a deed of gift of lands in Eglingham and Bewick on 23 March 1514 to Henry Ogle. This statement is difficult to understand, for the manor of Bewick and lands in Eglingham belonged to Tynemouth priory which was not dissolved until 12 January 1539. In 31 H.VIII (1539/40) a Cuthbert Ogle is mentioned as owing rent to the king for land and tenements he had lately purchased in Eglingham.

It is possible that this Cuthbert Ogle was a son of Henry Ogle (1514) but the latter seems to have made no mark on local history. For over 30 years Cuthbert Ogle was well known on the Borders. Although a churchman holding a plurality of benefices he had sporting tastes and martial qualities. In 1518 he was reported as having the finest pair of greyhounds in all the country and a cast of good falcons, and he served on expeditions into Scotland in 1523, 1524 and 1545.

In a law suit of 1678 relating to the tithes of Ford it was stated that Cuthbert Ogle had been rector of Ford in 1497. The date is impossible—Lawrence Heron was rector in 1496 and Thomas Tindin was presented on 16 November 1503. Ogle is first mentioned as rector on 4 July 1516 (*Laing Charters*, p.79). In 1523 he was rector of Ilderton and in the same year he was one of those ordered to join the expedition under lords Dacre and Ogle into Scotland to burn Kelso and other places. In 1526 he held the rectory of Stanhope, co. Durham, and on 4 March he witnesses the will of sir Thomas Forster of Adderstone as 'sir Cuthb't Ogle, parson of Stanhope'.

That he was a near relative of the lords Ogle is suggested by the fact that on 12 June 1526 he had a conveyance from Robert, lord Ogle, of (one-third) of the manor and vill of Ingram with Huntlaw and Greenshields and the advowson of the church of Ingram. Eight days later he exchanged with lord Ogle lands in Oldmoor, Newmoor, Longhirst and Earsdon for lands in Fowberry.

OGLE of BRADFORD, par. BOLAM

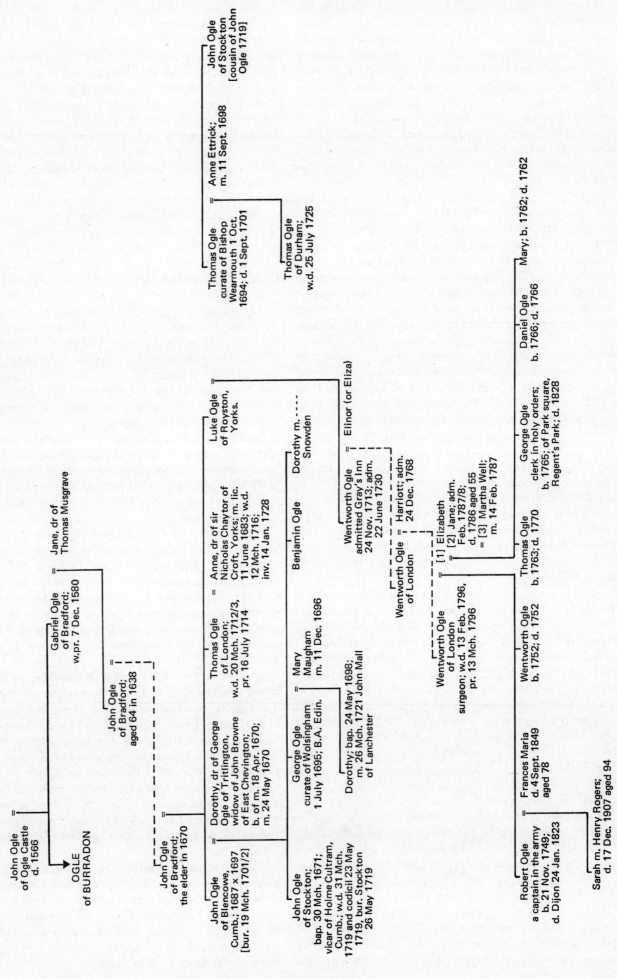

Cuthbert Ogle, clerk, parson of Stanhope and Ford made his will 5 June 1530. He leaves the manor of Ingram to his 'servant' Isabel Musgrave; his lands in Aydonshields and Hexham to his 'kinsman' Matthew Ogle of Eglingham; his lands in Fowberry, Bolton and Reaveley to Luke Ogle, brother of Matthew; his lands in South Middleton, Ilderton and Akeld, and the corn tithe of Bolton and Alnham to Peter Ogle, brother of Matthew and Luke; his lands in Downham and West Lilburn to Mark Ogle, brother of Matthew, Luke and Peter. All these bequests are for the life-time of the recipients, and after their deaths the lands are settled on the heirs male of Mark Ogle, with successive remainders to the heirs of Matthew, Luke and Peter. The lands in Fowberry were called Newhall or Ogleburgh and were later acquired by the family of Strother.

It is evident that the four brothers, named after the evangelists, were the rector's illegitimate sons by his 'servant' Isabel Musgrave. On 18 August 1535 Mark Ogle, who seems to have been the eldest son, had a grant of arms 'for the good services that the said Mark Ogle hath at sundry times done in Scotland against the king our sovereign lord's enemies there, manly and valiently using himself'; the grant refers to him as 'descended of a noble house of Ogle also of a noble house of Musgrave in the said county'.

Cuthbert Ogle long survived the making of his will. On 4 March 1532 he had licence to absent himself from his benefice of Ford, and to receive to farm during his life or a term of years, lands, tenements, etc., or rectories and other benefices, not exceeding the annual value of 100m., notwith-standing the statute of 21 H. VIII (*Letters and Papers*, H.VIII, V, p.427). Perhaps in pursuance of this licence he was presented by the king to the church of Ingram on 30 June 1532 (*Ib.*, No. 1207 (19)), and about the same time he was appointed king's chaplain with an annuity of £40. On 28 March 1533 he wrote from Eglingham to Richard Cromwell claiming that he could get nothing out of the patent the king had given him and hoped that if he got promotion that it would be without cure. Objections to his promotion came from the earl of Northumberland who informed Richard Cromwell on 23 August 1533 that parson Ogle never came to any raid into Scotland and had served the king as ill as any man. In 1534 he got an annuity of £5 from the barony of Bolam during the minority of Mary Ridley with her wardship and marriage.

At the time of the 1536 rising known as the Pilgrimage of Grace, sir Thomas Percy, the leader of the malcontents in Northumberland 'spake with parson Ogle and first after loving manner moved him that he would deliver a casket with money of sir Raynold Carnaby's, which he supposed was in the said parson's keeping; and the same being to him denied by the said parson, the said sir Thomas gave him great words and menaced him to do him displeasure; and likewise he moved one John Ogle of Ogle castle to deliver him such plate of sir Raynold Carnaby's as was in his custody; and because he said nay, in like manner he departed with him at open defiance, with such cruel words as he thought good' (*SS*. 44, p.cxxxii).

Parson Ogle's loyalty was well rewarded. On 15 August 1537 the bishop of Carlisle was asked in the king's name to appoint him to the vicarage of St Michael's, Appleby, Wmd. Although no longer a young man he still continued his border service. On a list of those appointed to meet for a rode into Tyndale on 13 September 1538 is the name of Parson Ogle with 10 men.

In 1541 it was reported that when the township of Down-ham lay waste by occasion of war, sir Cuthbert Ogle, clerk, purchased it, and was now engaged in building a new tower there but it was not fully finished. At Ford he was also rebuilding the little tower which was the mansion of the parsonage of the same (*AA2*. XIV, pp.31, 39). He was at the battle of Hadden Rig in Scotland in 1542 where his servant John Wilson was killed and he was taken prisoner. On 14 June 1543 he asked for the life of his former captor, Pringle, who had been captured in a raid. Ogle was again taken prisoner by the Scots at the battle of Ancrum Moor in 1545 and was exchanged for James Pringle.

It has been stated that Cuthbert Ogle was sometime rector of Bothal, but this seems to be a mistake. In 1549 Cuthbert Ogle and John Ogle, executors to Mark Ogle of Eglingham claimed against William Harryson, clerk, the right of presentation to the church of Bothal; it was claimed that sir Robert Ogle, lord Ogle, was seised of the manor of Bothal and the advowson of the church there in the time of Henry VIII and by deed dated 31 July 1528 gave an acre of land and the said advowson to George Lawson; William Harryson had been presented to the church by George Lawson son and heir of the said George (*de Banco Roll*, R.912, m.356).

The two executors to Mark Ogle's will cannot be clearly identified. On the strength of the fact that a new rector of Bothal was appointed on 14 March 1546 and the apparently erroneous belief that Cuthbert Ogle was the previous rector, it has been stated that Cuthbert died in 1546.

By letters patent of 6 October 1541 Mark and Luke Ogle had a lease for their lives of Burton, par. Bamburgh, it being specified that in the event of the death of either of the lessees his half share should revert to the Crown; Mark died and his half was leased to Luke Ogle on 15 November 1550. It is probable that Mark had died *s.p.* The lands in South Middleton, Ilderton and Akeld which were to have been the inheritance of Peter Ogle are not again mentioned as belonging to the Ogles. The corn tithes of Alnham had belonged to Alnwick abbey and in 1525 were leased by abbot Robert for 41 years to 'our brother of our chapter, sir Cuth-bert Ogle, clerk, for the good and faithful counsel he had given in times past and may hereafter give' (Tate, *History of Alnwick*, II, p.29).

Matthew Ogle who was to have lands in Aydonshields (in Hexhamshire) and Hexham from his father, may have left descendants. On 19 October 1534 George Ogle was admitted copyhold tenant of the water corn mill called Whitley Mill in Hexhamshire to hold at an annual rent of 26s. 8d. In 1547 he held Aydonshields, whilst Whitley Mill was held by Henry Ogle and George Ogle and divers burgages in Hex-ham are described as 'lately Geo. Ogle, now his widow'. By October 1547 George Ogle was dead and his son Henry was admitted to Whitley Mill, his mother's dower excepted. Henry Ogle in 1591 surrendered to John Ogle lands in Hexham and Whitley Mill and seven years later John Ogle surrendered Whitley Mill to Frances his wife. When the survey of the manor of Hexham was made in 1608 Aydon-shields was a freehold held by Edward Radcliffe; Whitley Mill and other lands were held by John Ogle and his wife

Frances Ogle, whilst John Ogle held Nether Mirehouse and George Ogle two tenements called Winter house and Eshells. In 1620 John Ogle sold Whitley Mill to sir Ralph and sir John Delaval. The following entries about these Ogles appear in the Hexham parish registers—

10 Sept. 1587 Reginald Ogle bur.
24 Nov. 1587 Wife of Henry Ogle bur.
20 Aug. 1591 Cuth^bt. Ogle bur.
22 Feb. 1607/8 Catharine wife of George Ogle, ch., bur.
18 Mch 1607/8 Henry Ogle, gent., ch. bur.
3 June 1612 Thomas s. of George Ogle, bur.
27 Sept. 1612 George Ogle, gent., and Agnes Carnabie m.
27 Aug. 1616 Mary dr of George Ogle, bur.
11 Mch 1617/8 Agnes wife of Cuth^bt. Ogle, bur.
8 May 1623 Elizabeth wife of Henry Ogle de Whitley Mill, bur.
19 June 1633 George Ogle, ch., bur.
9 Oct. 1634 William s. of George Ogill, ch., bur.
16 Oct. 1637 John Ogle, ch., bur.
6 Feb. 1639 Agnes Ogle, ch., bur.

In 1549 the name of Lucas Ogle of Eglingham appears in a list of the gentlemen of Northumberland, and in 1550 Luke Ogle was one of the gentlemen inhabitants within the Middle Marches. He was one of four overseers appointed in 1553 for the night watches between Bolton and Titlington and between Titlington and Harehopeswire (*Leges Marchiarum*, p.285). At the same time he was appointed a commissioner for enclosures from the water of Aln to Hetton Burn on the east side of Till with Bamburghshire (*HN.* i, p.362). He was still holding the lease of Burton in 1579 when he was in dispute with John Selbie and Richard Burrill. The latter complained that on 17 June 1579 Luke Ogle with 17 persons did by force of arms eject him from his tenement in Burton.

At the Muster of the East Marches on 10 March 1579/80, Downham is described as a village of Lewke Ogills of Eglingham, esquire, with four tenants, two only furnished; West Lilburn was a village of Roger Parttrers and Lewke Ogilles gentlemen, with 22 tenants, 3 furnished; Shipley and Burton were villages of her Majestys, under the rule of Lewke Ogill. He was present on 27 July 1585 when lord Francis Russell was killed at a wardens' meeting (*CBP.* I, p.189).

The will of Luke Ogle of Eglingham, gentleman, is dated 5 July 1596. He leaves to his three 'reputed daughters', Isabell, Myrryell and Beile Ogle, every of them £10. His son's daughter Myrryell Ogle is to have £20 besides her portion. The sons of his late son Christofer Ogle are to have his right and title of the mill of Eglingham and the tithe corn of Alnham. He leaves to his sister Jullyan Ogle 20 nobles, to her son Lewes Ogle 40s., and to Thomas Ilderton 20s. He had purchased a house in Baileygate, Alnwick, from John Spence, and leaves it to Marke Ogle's son Lewes. His 'reputed sons' Lennard and Robert Ogle are to have 20 nobles. Luke Ogle son of the testator's son Robert Ogle is to have one yoke of oxen with the heirlooms of the house 'that is to say, the tables, boards and forms, the great cauldron, the great pot, with the brasen mortar, the best bed in the house, the racks and spits'. He leaves the farmhold in Framlington, after the expiry of Lainge's lease with the freehold there to Trestrom son of his late son Christofer Ogle, and after the said Trestrom to come to his brother Cuthbert, and the longer liver of them. 'I make Thomas and Trestrom, the sons of my late

son Christofer, executors, and Mr Raffe Gray of Chillingham and Mr William Lawson of Rock, supervisors' (*SS.* 112, p.160). In the extract of the will in *Ogle and Bothal* (app.381) the legacy to 'my son Robt Ogle's son Luke Ogle' is incorrectly given as 'Sir Robert Ogle's first son Luke Ogle'.

Luke Ogle died before 23 November 1597 for on that day Samuel Fox wrote to sir Robert Cecil saying that a lease of the moiety of Burton and Shipley had been conferred upon him but he had never received profit from it, his especial hindrance being Luke Ogle who had the other moiety given him by king Henry. Ogle now being dead, Fox asks for a lease of his moiety. This Luke Ogle who had recently died was obviously not the same Luke Ogle as the one who had been given a lease on 15 November 1550 of the moiety of Burton formerly held by his recently deceased brother Mark Ogle. Sometime between 1550 and 1597 the first Luke Ogle must have died, and one half of Burton must then have been leased to the second Luke Ogle and the other half to Samuel Fox.

According to his will Luke Ogle had two sons Christopher and Mark, both of whom had predeceased him. They may have been legitimate. He also had two 'reputed' sons Lennard and Robert, and three 'reputed' daughters Isabel, Myrryell and Beile. According to a pedigree registered at the College of Arms in 1715 Luke also had a son Luke who had predeceased him, leaving a son and heir, also called Luke, who succeeded to the estates of Eglingham, Ingram and Downham. There is no mention of these properties in the 1596 will and the presumption is that either there was an entail or the heir had received them during his father's lifetime.

It is certain that the heir was a grandson Luke Ogle, but his parentage is uncertain. The only Luke Ogle mentioned in the will of 1596 is the son of the testator's 'reputed' son Robert Ogle and to him were left the heirlooms of the house.

Mark Ogle is referred to as 'a natural son' in *Ogle and Bothal* (p.195) but there is no evidence from his father's will that he was illegitimate. Mark's will is dated 2 September 1575. He is to be buried in Alnwick church and leaves the goodwill of his farm in Shipley to his son Lewis. He mentions in his will his brothers Leonard and Robert and his mother. His son Lewis and his wife Annes are to be executors and his father Luke Ogle and his father Richard Bennet are supervisors. Richard Bennet was presumably his father-in-law. (The will appears to be no longer extant—C.R.H.)

In the muster of horse on the East Marches on 30 September 1584, Leonard Ogle attended from Shipley (*CBP.* I, p.161). On 14 April 1597 administration of the goods of Leonard Ogle, late of par. of Eglingham, was granted to Elizabeth his wife for her use and that of Thomas, Oliver, Luke, Margaret and Dorothy his children (*Dur. Prob. Off.* by C.R.H.; in *Ogle and Bothal*, app.383, the name of the deceased is given as Luke in error).

In 1567 Luke Ogle had purchased the manor of Harehope from James, lord Mountjoy, and Katherine his wife (*Feet of Fines*, Trinity Term, 9 Eliz.). He seems to have transferred this to his son Christopher. According to the Act Book at Durham, administration of the goods of Christopher Ogle was granted on 'Sabbat 14 June 1597', but Saturday fell on 11 June in 1597 so either the clerk wrote xiiii instead of xi or wrote it so badly that it looks like 14 (*Dur. Prob. Off.* by C.R.H.). The administration was given to the widow

Thomasine to her use and use of Thomas, Tristram, Cuthbert, Elizabeth, Juliana and Dorothy, children of the deceased. On the same day there was the business of assigning tutors 'to Thomas and Tristram Ogle, children of Christofer Ogle of Eglingham, deceased, executors of the will of Luke Ogle late of said parish, deceased'. Thomasine Ogle, mother of the said children, minors, was appointed tutrix and also tutrix of Cuthbert, Elizabeth, Juliana and Dorothy Ogle, children of the said Christofer Ogle, deceased (*Ib.*). In the inventory of his goods Christopher is designated as of Harehope. His eldest son Thomas was of Harehope in 1629 when he voted as a freeholder; on 17 February 1635 he witnesses the will of Thomas Salkeld of Rock. Thomas Collingwood of Buckton by his w.d. November 1638 leaves £10 to Dorothy Ogle daughter of Thomas Ogle of Harehope, gent. One of Thomas Ogle's sisters may have married Henry Harbottle of Beanley, gent., who in his w.pr. 1629 calls Henry Ogle of Eglingham 'cousin' and Thomas Ogle of Harehope 'brother-in-law'.

Christopher Ogle of Harehope, a freeholder in 1638, was presumably Thomas' son. He married Mary Chapman of the parish of Eglingham (b.of m. 2 February 1634/5). Ogle was tenant of five farms in Eglingham, sold on 20 August 1649 by John Ramsay of Old Bewick to John Ogle of Eglingham. The conveyance is witnessed by Henry Ogle and Christopher Ogle and an endorsement that quiet possession has been given is signed by Henry Ogle, Christopher Ogle, Thomas Ogle, another Henry Ogle and others. There is no evidence that Thomas Ogle or either of the Henry Ogles belonged to the Harehope branch of the family. In 1653 the crown rent of 20s., in respect of Alnham tithes and then payable by Chris. Ogle was with other crown rents acquired by trustees for the benefit of the minister and schoolmaster of Alnwick (Tate, *Alnwick*, II, p.79).

In 1663 Christopher was rated for Harehope, Alnham, Alnham moor and half the rectory of Alnham. His successor was Henry Ogle who in 1672 mortgaged half of Harehope to John Storey to secure £448. Apparently unable to redeem he sold the half on 16 April 1677 to John Storey for £100. He sold Eglingham mill on 8 October 1691 to Henry Ogle of Eglingham and with his wife Eleanor covenanted to levy a fine. His wife was Eleanor Proctor of Shawdon whom he had married at Whittingham on 3 February 1664. The name of Henry Ogle of Harehope appears in a list of Northumbrian recusants dated 20 June 1674. The list contains a large proportion of dissenters, presbyterians and quakers as well as papists, and Henry Ogle's name not appearing in any other lists, we can presume that he was a dissenter. At the Easter Sessions for Northumberland, 9 October 1686, information was laid that on 5 September last, Robert Ogle of Eglingham, gen., Henry Ogle of 'Harrupp' and others had assembled at the house of Clement Gourley in Brocksfield under the colour of exercise of religion other than the Church of England (by C.R.H.).

Henry Ogle of Harehope voted as a freeholder in 1715, presumably for the half of Harehope which the family still retained. Henry son of Mr Henry Ogle of Harehope was buried at Eglingham 14 March 1709/10. Shortly after this Harehope passed from the family (*AA3*. XIX, pp.79-81). At the Quarter Sessions at Morpeth at Easter 1717 a letter was considered from Henry Ogle of Harehope, gent., aged 60; his house had been burnt down and he pleaded poverty

(*Session Papers*, vol.46, p.96). The Ogles lingered on at Harehope although no longer as landowners. At the bishop of Durham's visitation for the parish of Eglingham in 1732 John Ogle of 'Harup' was presented 'for turning papist' (by C.R.H.).

It has already been stated that the heir of Luke Ogle (w.d. 1596) was a grandson also called Luke Ogle. After the death of the latter no less than three *i.p.m.*'s were taken about his lands. The first, taken at Alnwick 19 January 1604/5, states that he died seised of West Lilburn, Downham, Eglingham, one third of Ingram and the advowson of the church, and West Ditchburn; West Lilburn was held of sir Ralph Grey, also Downham; Eglingham was held of the king in free socage of his manor of Tynemouth; Henry Ogle was son and heir of Luke and aged 4½ years. In consequence of the insufficiency of this inquisition another was taken at Alnwick on 2 April 1607 which found that Luke had on 6 May 1600 sold Downham to Ralph Carr, esquire, for £400; Luke had died on 29 October 1604. The third inquisition taken at Alnwick on 24 October 1618 found that Ingram was held of the earl of Northumberland, and West Ditchburn of sir Henry Widdrington.

On 31 May 1605 administration of the goods of Luke Ogle was granted to Isabella Ogle his wife, to her use and that of Nicholas and Anne Ogle, children of the deceased, minors. Debts owing by Mr Luck Ogle were 'To my servant Thomas Ogle 40s., to my niece Jean Halidaa 7s., to my cousin Luck Ogle of Bradburie (?) 14s., to Henrye Collingwood of Ryle £6; to my sister Marian Ogle £20'. 'Lucke Ogle of Eglingham, gent' was buried at St Nicholas, Newcastle, 30 October 1604.

Luke Ogle's wife was Isabella daughter of Edmund Craster of Craster. Her mother, Alice Craster of Dunstanburgh, by her w.d. 23 September 1597 leaves to her daughter Isabel Ogle, £20, 'to buy her a gown, petticoat and forekirtle which I did promise her'. The widow married Edward Ogle before 1607.

Henry Ogle was a strong parliamentarian and as such became one of the sequestrators for Northumberland and a deputy lieutenant. He sat in Cromwell's first two parliaments of 1653 and 1654. On 21 August 1650 fourteen witches and one wizard of Newcastle were burnt on the Town Moor there; they had been 'found' by Hopkins, the infamous Scottish witch finder. When Hopkins had finished his work in Newcastle 'he went into Northumberland to try women there, where he got of some three pounds apiece. But Hen. Ogle, esquire, a late member of Parlt, laid hold on him and required bond of him to answer the sessions, but he got away for Scotland, and it was conceived that if he had stayed he would have made most of the women in the north witches for money'. When Hopkins was finally captured, he admitted before his execution that he had caused the death of over 220 women in England and Scotland. Ogle is said to have entertained Oliver Cromwell at Eglingham in 1650; this must have been between 17 July when he was at Alnwick, and 22 July when he crossed the Tweed at Berwick for his advance into Scotland. In 1659 he was arrested as the result of a claim against him by sir Robert Collingwood for payment of a debt of £1500 incurred when Ogle was one of the commissioners for raising forces for the Parliament in 1645. The house of Commons ordered his release and directed that the County Committee should examine into the matter further and report. Henry Ogle died about 1669 for in a dispute between the Carrs and Ogles 1718-1721 it was stated that he had died about 50 years earlier.

On 20 June 1668 Henry Ogle the elder of Eglingham made a settlement of all his estate in Ingram, Eglingham etc., the trustees being Ralph Salkeld and Roger Pearson of Titlington. The lands were settled to the use of Henry Ogle the elder, with successive remainders to Henry Ogle the younger (grandson of Henry Ogle the elder) and his heirs male; to Robert Ogle, brother to Henry Ogle the younger and his heirs male; to the heirs male of John Ogle, eldest son of Henry the elder; to Nicholas, second son of Henry the elder; to Thomas, third son of Henry the elder; to Henry, fourth son of Henry the elder; and to Ralph, fifth son of Henry the elder. In this settlement of 1668 five sons of Henry Ogle the elder are mentioned, John, Nicholas, Thomas, Henry and Ralph. Nicholas son of Henry Ogle of Eglingham, North'd, *arm.*, was apprenticed in the London Draper's Company on 26 March 1640. Henry Ogle, aged 17, was admitted 31 August 1654 to Magdalene College, Cambridge. Ralph Ogle, aged 15, was admitted on the same day to the same college. Another son, Richard, had died before 1668; he had been fatally wounded at Newcastle by Ralph Salkeld in August 1664. Mary daughter of Henry Ogle, married John Carr of Lesbury.

In his father's lifetime John Ogle, the eldest son, had enlarged the family estates by the purchase on 5 March 1646 from George Denton of Cardew, Cumb., of another third of the manor of Ingram and of the advowson of Ingram church. He was one of the commissioners for sequestration for Northumberland in 1650 and in that year he received a commission as captain of militia for the four northern counties. In April 1651 it was proposed to replace him as a commissioner for he 'is now commander of a troop of horse in Scotland', but he was back in Newcastle by 1 October 1651. John Ogle's wife was Eleanor daughter of Robert Pringle of Stichell in Scotland. They had two sons, Henry and Robert, and three daughters, Jane wife of William Reed of Beadnell, Anne wife of Thomas Weems (m.22 September 1684) and Margaret wife of Robert Manners of Newmoor House (m.28 September 1697). Administration of the goods of Henry Ogle was not taken out until many years after his death. On 18 August 1697 Henry Ogle of Edlingham, esq., as administrator of Henry Ogle, esq., his late grandfather, late of Eglingham, signed a bond to pay his grandfather's debts, Thomas Ogle of Shipley being a witness.

Thomas Ogle of Shipley was probably a near relative and perhaps a son of Leonard Ogle (d.1597) of Shipley.

On 21 December 1685 Thomas Ogle of Shipley, gent., entered into a bond of marriage with Frances Forster of the parish of Chatton. Their children Thomas, Elizabeth, Mary and Frances were baptised at Eglingham between 1687 and 1697. Frances Forster must have been a near relative of Marmaduke Forster of Lyham who by his w.d. 23 April 1713 leaves £5 to 'young Thomas Ogell' and half a guinea for mourning to 'old Thomas Ogell'. On 23 July 1719 he made a second will leaving to Tho. Ogle half a guinea, to Fannie Ogle, junior, half a guinea, to Tho. Ogle jun., £5 and to his mother Fannie Ogle £4.

Frances Ogle of Haughhead was buried at Eglingham

20 December 1731 and Thomas Ogle of Eglingham buried there 16 April 1731.

The younger Thomas probably left the parish, but he and his immediate descendants seem to have retained a burial plot there. The following entries in Eglingham parish registers probably refer to members of the family:—

27 May 1745. Frances, dr of Thomas Ogle, Alnham, bur.
18 Jan. 1758. Frances, dr of Thomas Ogle, Lesbury, bur.
3 Sept. 1760. Thos. Ogle, Bilton in Lesbury, bur.
In Lesbury parish registers are the following entries:—
15 Sept. 1766. Joshua Donkin and Dorothy Ogle, both of this par. m. by licence; witnesses, Thomas Ogle and Wm Lough.
29 June 1768. Mrs Dorithy Ogle, Lesbury, bur.
21 May 1773. Mr Thomas Ogle, Lesbury, bur.
For Nicholas Ogle, younger son of Luke Ogle (d.1604) *see* OGLE OF BERWICK-ON-TWEED.

Henry Ogle of Eglingham made his will 17 January 1700/1. He leaves his wife Grace £20 over and above her jointure. His son James by his now wife Grace is to have £1000 with interest during his minority charged on Eglingham, Greenside Hill, Grieves Ash, Linhope etc. He leaves annuities of £6 to his sister Margaret Manners and to his uncle Ralph Ogle. His 'kinsman' William Salkeld of Falloden is to have £20, and he appoints as executors Henry and James Ogle 'sons of my now wife'. Henry Ogle was buried at Eglingham 4 May 1711. He had married in 1664 Apollina daughter of sir Charles Howard of Overacres, but by her had no issue. 'Aqualina, wife of Henry Ogle, esq.', was buried at St Nicholas', Newcastle, 4 July 1689. After her death, Henry Ogle lived with Grace Widdrington and by her had two illegitimate sons Henry and James. About November 1692 he married his mistress and had further children, John, Frances, Christiana and Diana; of these only Frances survived infancy; she married Thomas Robinson of Newcastle, surgeon.

After Henry Ogle's death, his son Henry attempted to obtain possession of the family estates, but his uncle Robert Ogle of North Shields was able to prove that both Henry (born about February 1690/1) and James (born about 1691) had been born before the marriage of their parents. On 17 April 1714 articles of agreement were entered into between Grace Ogle widow of Henry Ogle, of the first part; Robert Ogle, brother of the said Henry, and Henry Ogle, eldest son of Robert, of the second part; and Thomas Robinson and Frances his wife, of the third part. It was agreed that Grace Ogle should have an annuity of £120 in full settlement of all her right in the real estate of her late husband; Robert and Henry Ogle were to release their right to lands in Beadnell to Thomas and Frances Robinson; Grace Ogle and the Robinsons were to release all their right to all other real estate of the said Henry. Robert Ogle originally intended to settle his estates on his eldest son Henry, but Henry having incurred his displeasure, he settled everything, 19 August 1724 on John, his second son. Henry complained to the lord chancellor about this and on 21 May 1729 it was arranged that John should pay Henry £1300 upon which he was to confirm the premises to the said John. Robert Ogle married Dorothy daughter of John Grey of Howick, and was buried at Eglingham 21 February 1736/7.

John Ogle, the second son, who became his father's heir,

made a settlement of his estates by his w.d. 7 January 1737/8. His elder brother Henry is to have the estates for life with remainders in succession to Henry's son, William Henry Ogle; to John, son of the testator's late brother Robert, deceased; to Benjamin, another son of the testator's late brother Robert; to Ralph Ogle, the testator's brother. John Ogle directs in his will that his nephew William Henry Ogle is to be called to the bar and if he refuses, the estates are to go to the next in the entail; the nephew is to have £100 a year for his studies. John Ogle died at Bath 13 February 1737/8 aged 48. He had married Sarah daughter of Robert Bell of Bellasis, widow of Jonathan Pilsbury and of Ralph Scourfield of Eachwick. By her w.d. 8 October 1754 Sarah Ogle of Alnwick, widow, leaves everything to her nephew Robert Bell. She had no children.

John Ogle left considerable debts behind him, and his brother Henry had to sell part of the estates to pay them off. Henry was nicknamed 'the count' because of his wife Ann Ker daughter of William, 2nd marquis of Lothian, widow of Alexander, 7th earl of Home; she died in 1727. Henry Ogle was buried at Eglingham 1 April 1757. His only son William Henry Ogle had carried out his uncle's instructions to adopt the legal profession for he was admitted to Gray's Inn 18 April 1749. Somewhat later he seems to have joined the army where he served under his half brother the earl of Home, and he was probably the captain Ogle who died in 1756. He certainly predeceased his father.

Next in the entail of 1738 were John and Benjamin Ogle, sons of Robert Ogle, but they seem to have been lost at sea. Ann, an old servant of Mr Henry Ogle, used to relate a story of two young men, brothers, heirs to the estate, being drowned at sea. In 1757 the heir of Eglingham was Ralph Ogle of Morpeth, the youngest brother of Henry Ogle (d.1757). Ralph had been a soldier in India or elsewhere abroad and returned to Newcastle after his brother's death with a wife and four or five children. He had married at Stoke Damoral, Devon, 11 May 1752, Mary Terry. They lived for several years at Heworth, co. Durham, where most of their children were baptised. He made his will at Heworth 18 April 1771 whereby he leaves all his goods in trust for his wife Mary. He died at Benwell and was buried at Eglingham 25 January 1772.

The children of Ralph and Mary Ogle were:—

1. Robert Ogle; his son and heir.

2. Charles Ogle, born 17 December 1756; bap. 21 January 1756/7 from Middleton hall from the parish church, Rothwell; as a young man he served in the American war where he lost an arm; he evidently brought back with him to England, a negro servant, for 'Charles, son of Francis Reed of Virginia, servant to capt. Charles Ogle, a negro, aged 15' was buried at Eglingham 17 April 1778; he was collector of customs at Newcastle in 1791 and retained the post until superannuated in May 1825; he died at his home in Savill row, Newcastle, on 5 June 1826 aged 70, and was buried at Eglingham 16 June 1826. Charles Ogle's will is dated 15 September 1824 and was proved at Durham 25 November 1826. He leaves £200 to Mrs Hannah Melvin for her tender care of his two natural children, Charles Ogle *alias* Melvin and Jane Melvin, both minors. The son Charles Ogle was an auctioneer in the Groat Market, Newcastle, and died 12 September 1850 aged 34 (by C.R.H.).

3. John Ogle; bap. Heworth, co. Durham, 31 March 1758; he joined the army and became a captain in the 61st regiment; he married firstly at Bath on 7 April 1791 Julia Eliza only daughter of Susanna Barton, sister and heiress of Richard Jackson of Forkhill, co. Armagh, Ireland. Her will is dated 29 January 1825 and a codicil is dated 31 October 1828 when she was living at Carrick Edmond, co. Louth; the will was proved 14 April 1830. By Elizabeth Croft, John Ogle had eight illegitimate children; she died 22 January 1867 aged 82. John Ogle, formerly of Carrick Edmond, but now of Brighton, Sussex, made his w.d. 29 November 1825; his wife Julia Eliza being independant, he leaves all his property to Elizabeth Croft, late of London Road, St George's-in-the-Fields, Surrey, for his natural children Elizabeth, Charles, John, Matthew, Mark, Julia, Anne and Charlotte; he added codicils to his will on 14 August 1827 and 8 February 1830 and the will was proved 20 November 1830. Colonel Ogle was living at Brixtible lodge, Mortlake, in 1830 when one day out driving in his phaeton the front axle broke and the horse becoming restive, he jumped out of the carriage and was killed.

4. Ralph Ogle; born at Heworth 2 March 1762; he matriculated at University college, Oxford on 17 March 1780 aged 18 and became BA in 1784. He was rector of Ingram in 1787 and was buried at Eglingham 15 September 1790 aged 25.

i. Dorothy; born at Heworth 19 February 1760; m. William Augustus Cane, rector of St Mary at Hill, London, curate of Doddington.

Ralph Ogle's eldest son and heir Robert was born 'near Newcastle' in 1753. He was living at Alnwick in 1774 when he voted in respect of his freehold at Eglingham. He married at Berwick 23 November 1780 Hannah daughter and heiress of William Compton, recorder of Berwick. He lived on his wife's property at Gainslaw near Berwick where he made his w.d. 7 January 1807/8. His estate is left in trust to Charles Ogle of Newcastle; his eldest son Robert is to have Broomhouse and Langraw, which were let with Eglingham; his lands of Gainslaw, and the tithes from Lesbury and Alnwick and all his other real estate are left in trust for his younger children.

Robert Ogle died at Gainslaw 8 January 1807 aged 53; his widow Hannah, survived him until July 1821. They had eight sons and six daughters, several of whom died in infancy. The fifth son, John, entered the army and became a captain in the 9th regiment; he served in the Peninsular War where he was severely wounded at the fall of San Sebastian on 31 August 1813; he was in Canada in 1814; he was invalided out of the army and died at sea, 11 November 1821 during the journey home. Another son, Henry, became a lieutenant in the royal navy on 6 March 1815 and died in 1840.

Robert Ogle's great grandson Robert Bertram Ogle, sold the estate of Eglingham in 1890.

OGLE OF BERWICK-ON-TWEED

Administration of the goods of Luke Ogle of Eglingham was granted on 31 May 1605 to his widow Isabella Ogle, his children Nicholas and Anne Ogle being under age. Luke's

OGLE of EGLINGHAM, par. EGLINGHAM

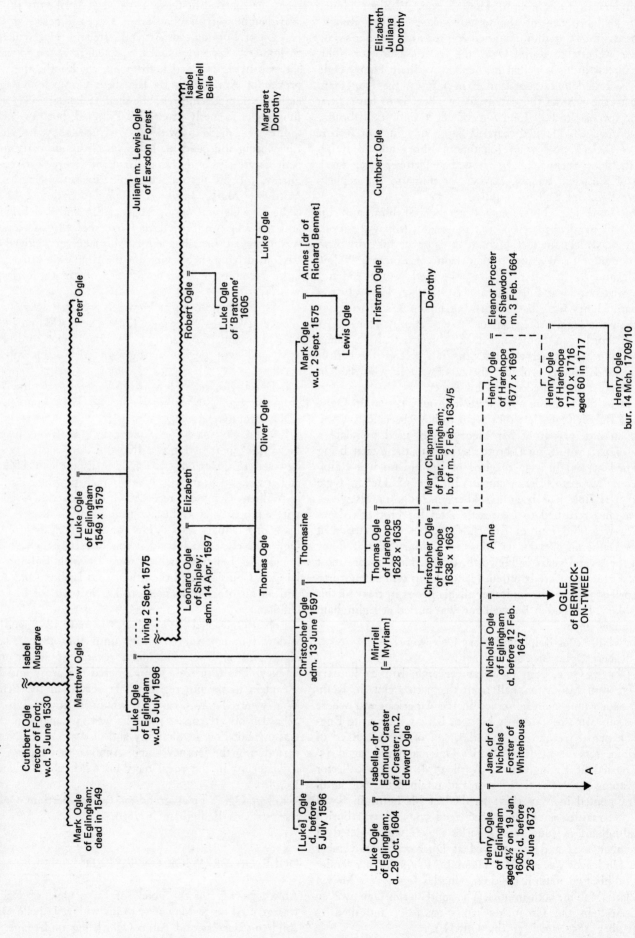

200

OGLE of EGLINGHAM, cont.

A ◄

Mary m. John Carr of Lesbury

Richard Ogle of Eglingham

Ralph Ogle 5th son, 20 June 1668; living 17 Jan. 1700/1

Henry Ogle 4th son, 20 June 1668

Jane m. William Reed of Beadnell; Anne m. 22 Sept. 1684 Thomas Weems; Margaret m. 28 Sept. 1697 Robert Manners of Newmoor House

Robert Ogle [of Eslington, 1657]

Thomas Ogle 20 June 1668

Nicholas Ogle [of Eslington, 1654]

John Ogle of Eglingham d. before 11 June 1686

= Eleanor, dr of Robert Pringle of Stichell, Scotland; [bur. 1 May 1736]

Henry Ogle w.d. 17 Jan. 1700/1; bur. 4 May 1711

= [1] Appolina, dr of sir Charles Howard of Overacres, par. Elsdon; bur. 4 July 1689

≈ [2] Grace Widdrington; m. Nov. 1692

Robert Ogle of Eglingham bur. 21 Feb. 1736/7

= Dorothy, dr of John Grey of Howick; m.2 Aug. 1687; living 29 Dec. 1714

Henry Ogle b. about Feb. 1690/1; bur. 27 Dec. 1713

James Ogle bap. 28 Sept. 1692 d.s.p. before 2 July 1715

Frances m. Thomas Robinson of Newcastle, surgeon; Christiana; bap. 15 Nov. 1693; bur. 1 May 1697; Diana; bap. 25 Jan. 1694; bur. 18 Apr. 1697

John Ogle bap. 4 Apr. 1700; bur. 29 June 1700

Henry Ogle of Eglingham bur. 1 Apr. 1757

= Ann Ker, dr of William, 2nd marquis of Lothian, widow of Alexander, 7th earl of Home; d. 1727

John Ogle of Eglingham sheriff of Nd. 1734; d. 13 Feb. 1737/8 aged 48

= Sarah, dr of Robert Bell of Bellasis, widow of Jonathan Pilsbury and of Ralph Scourfield; bur. Alnwick 1755/6; m. Felton 11 May 1731

Robert Ogle d. before 7 Jan. 1737/8

Charles Ogle d. before 7 Jan. 1737/8

Mary Terry m. 11 May 1752; bur. 4 Aug. 1808 aged 86

Ralph Ogle of Morpeth; w.d. 18 Apr. 1771; bur. 25 Jan. 1772

Eleanor; m. 21 Aug. 1727 Ralph Brandling of Felling Margaret; living 1746

William Henry Ogle d. before 1757

John Ogle drowned at sea before 1757

Benjamin Ogle drowned at sea before 1757

Dorothy; b. 19 Feb. 1760; m. 1777 William Augustus Cane, rector of St Mary at Hill, London, curate of Doddington

Robert Ogle of Eglingham d. 8 Jan. 1807 aged 53

= Hannah, dr and heir of William Compton of Gainslaw; m. 23 Nov. 1780; d. July 1821

Charles Ogle of Newcastle b. 17 Dec. 1756; d. 5 June 1826

≈ Hannah Melvin

Charles Ogle of Newcastle, auctioneer; d. 12 Sept. 1850 aged 34

Jane

John Ogle a colonel in the army; bap. 31 Mch. 1758; k. 1830

= Julia Eliza Barton; m. 7 Apr. 1791; w.d. 29 Jan. 1825, pr. 14 Apr. 1830; ≈ Elizabeth C. Croft d. 22 Jan. 1867 aged 82

Charles

John

Matthew

Mark

Elizabeth Anne Charlotte

Ralph Ogle b. 2 Mch. 1762; rector of Ingram; bur. 15 Sept. 1790 aged 25

Robert Ogle of Eglingham b. 14 Sept. 1781; d. 5 Dec. 1857

= Jane, dr of John Burgess of Brook farm, Hants; m. 1815; d. 4 July 1867 aged 83

Ralph William Ogle bap. 3 Sept. 1782; bur. 7 Sept. 1782

Charles Ogle b. 27 July 1786

Ralph William Ogle bap. 18 Sept. 1784; bur. 19 Nov. 1789

John Ogle bap. 1 Apr. 1789; capt. 9th regt.; d. at sea 11 Nov. 1821

Ralph William Ogle bap. 1 June 1794

Henry Ogle bap. 9 Dec. 1795; lieut. R.N.; d. 1840

William Ogle bap. 16 Apr. 1798; living 29 Jan. 1825

Frances Ann; bap. 20 Dec. 1796; m. Sept. 1820

Hannah; bap. 19 Sept. 1790; m. 6 Mch. 1845 rear adm. W. Browne of Walmer, Kent

Mary, bap. 25 Oct. 1791; d. 1833

Elizabeth; bap. 1 Jan. 1793; bur. 23 July 1798 aged 5

William Hay of Hopes Elizabeth; bap. 28 July 1799

Ann Eliza; bap. 9 Nov. 1800; bur. 12 Feb. 1810 aged 9

B ►

OGLE of EGLINGHAM, cont.

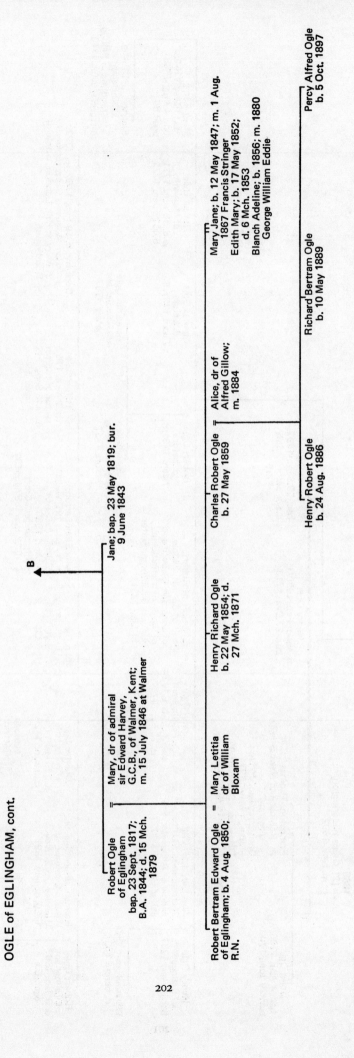

Robert Ogle
of Eglingham
bap. 23 Sept. 1817;
B.A. 1844; d. 15 Mch.
1879
= Mary, dr of admiral
sir Edward Harvey,
G.C.B., of Walmer, Kent;
m. 15 July 1846 at Walmer

Jane; bap. 23 May 1819; bur.
9 June 1843

B →

Robert Bertram Edward Ogle
of Eglingham; b. 4 Aug. 1850;
R.N.
= Mary Letitia
dr of William
Bloxam

Henry Richard Ogle
b. 22 May 1854; d.
27 Mch. 1871

Charles Robert Ogle
b. 27 May 1859
= Alice, dr of
Alfred Gillow;
m. 1884

Mary Jane; b. 12 May 1847; m. 1 Aug.
1867 Francis Stringer
Edith Mary; b. 17 May 1852;
d. 6 Mch. 1853
Blanch Adeline; b. 1856; m. 1880
George William Eddie

Henry Robert Ogle
b. 24 Aug. 1886

Richard Bertram Ogle
b. 10 May 1889

Percy Alfred Ogle
b. 5 Oct. 1897

202

eldest son and heir was Henry Ogle, from whom were descended the later Ogles of Eglingham. We are here concerned with the descendants of the younger son Nicholas.

In a settlement made by Henry Ogle of Eglingham on 20 June 1668 mention is made of his brother Nicholas and the latter's children Luke and Thomas. Nicholas had died many years before, for on 12 February 1647 Thomas son of Nicholas Ogle of Eglingham, gent., deceased, was apprenticed to Henry Dawson of Newcastle, mercer; he 'departed his master's service' and never became a freeman of the Merchants Company (SS. 101, p.265).

Nicholas Ogle's eldest son Luke is said to have been born in 1630 and to have at one time been rector of Ingram. In 1655 he was appointed vicar of Berwick at a salary of £120 a year. During the Commonwealth his puritanical leanings made him very popular with his congregation, but at the Restoration he came under suspicion for his anti-papal views. Lord Widdrington, the papist governor of Berwick, employed an agent to take notes of his sermons, and as a result of this, accused the vicar of preaching treason. On 26 December 1661 the governor took action, sent a guard of soldiers to take possession of the church and lock the doors. The burgess guild of Berwick who had kindly feelings towards the vicar suggested that he should be allowed to preach only with someone else to read the prayers but the governor would not agree. When the Act of Uniformity came into force Ogle was formally ejected from his church. After this he preached at Ancroft, many of his former parishioners going there to hear him. Arrested by Widdrington he was in prison for six weeks, and shortly after his release was again imprisoned for preaching in Scotland. A personal appeal to general Monk in London was of no avail, and returning to Berwick he was again put in prison. On the coming into force of the Five Mile Act in 1665 he moved to Bowsdon, par. Lowick, where he had purchased a small property. Here he preached privately although constantly molested by the authorities.

On 2 May 1672 Charles II issued a licence to Luke Ogle of Berwick to be a general presbyterian teacher, and on 5 September the same year his house at Bowsdon was licensed as a meeting place.

The will of Luke Ogle of Berwick, gent., is dated 1 July 1690. His lands in Bowsdon are left to his wife Mary for her widowhood, and to pay legacies of £100 to his daughter Ellinor at the age of 21; to his son Arthur £100 at the end of his apprenticeship; to his son William £80 when 21; and to his youngest son Luke £80. His lands are then settled on his eldest son Samuel and his heirs male with remainder to his other sons. His wife Mary is appointed executrix and his friends Henry Ogle of Eglingham, esq., and Samuel Salkeld of Falloden, gent., are to be supervisors. His son William having died he added a codicil to his will on 17 April 1696, in which he mentions his daughter Mary Nealson and her son Luke Nealson.

Luke Ogle died in 1696. His first wife was Katherine Graham, and administration of her goods was granted on 21 June 1659 to her husband.

Luke Ogle's second wife was Mary daughter of Arthur Foster of Stonegarthside, Cumb. According to *Ogle and Bothal* the banns for their marriage were called 'three times at Berwick on the 15th February 1667/8'; presumably for 'three times' we must read 'a third time'. Arthur Foster by his w.d. 15 December 1669 leaves to 'my daughter Mary in legacy twenty pounds and to her son Samwell thirty pounds and to each one of her children ten pounds apiece' (*CW*2. LXI, p.190).

Joseph eldest son of Luke Ogle, was living 10 November 1677 for Samuel, 'second' son of Luke Ogle of Bowsdon was admitted to Gray's Inn on that date. Joseph is not mentioned in his father's will so had apparently died before 1 July 1690. Luke and Mary Ogle had at least six other sons and two daughters, viz., Samuel (bap. Berwick 25 March 1659), Theophilus (bap. Berwick Oct. 1660), Arthur, Nicholas, William, Luke, Mary and Ellinor.

Arthur Ogle was an apprentice in 1690. The unusual Christian name derived from the Fosters of Stonegarthside, makes it possible to identify him with Arthur Ogle of co. Middlesex whose will was proved in London in September 1741. Theophilus apparently died before 1 July 1690 as he is not mentioned in his father's will. Nicholas son of Luke Ogle of Bowsdon, clerk, was apprenticed 11 November 1687 to Richard Wall of Newcastle, boothman, and became free of the Newcastle Merchants Company on 17 August 1698. He was Nicholas Ogle of Stepney, late of Berwick-on-Tweed, who made his will 25 May 1722, proved 3 June 1727; he mentions his wife Elizabeth and leaves £1000 to his daughter Elizabeth. William Ogle, living 1 July 1690, died before 17 April 1696 as mentioned in the codicil to his father's will. The youngest son, Luke, died at Youghal, co. Cork, Ireland, and administration of his goods was granted 16 April 1706 to Samuel Ogle of Dublin, his brother.

Samuel Ogle was a graduate of Edinburgh university and after being at Gray's Inn, was recorder for Berwick 1689-1698. He first entered parliament as MP for Berwick on 20 March 1690 and was re-elected in 1695, 1698, 1701, 1702, 1705 and 1708. In July 1699 he was a commissioner for the revenue in Ireland, a position he still held in July 1712. He was also a commissioner for the colony of Maryland and died at Dublin on 10 March 1718. By his w.d. 4 March 1718 he leaves his purchased lands in Ireland to his wife Ursula, baroness dowager Altham, having already made provision for his children.

By his first wife, Samuel Ogle had an only daughter Mary wife of John Broughton of Maidstone, Kent. His second wife gave him five sons and a daughter.

Samuel, the eldest son, became a captain of cavalry and served in America. On 21 August 1731 a warrant was issued to take security in the sum of £2000 of Samuel Ogle as lieutgovernor of Maryland. He was in Maryland as governor in 1737 but returned to England in 1742. After a second term as governor, he made his will on 11 February 1752 and it was proved in London on 1 September 1756.

The second son, George Ogle, was BA of Cambridge in 1722, and MA in 1728. In 1736 he published a book on *Antiquities explained, Being a Collection of figured Gems, illustrated by similar descriptions taken from the classics*. Other books of his were *Basia or the Kisses* published in 1731 and *Epistles of Horace imitated* in 1735. He was living in Audley street, Hanover square, London, 2 February 1744, when he made his will. His only son, also called George, lived at Bellevue, co. Wexford, Ireland, and represented Wexford county in the Irish Parliament 1768-1796. On 26

OGLE of BERWICK-ON-TWEED

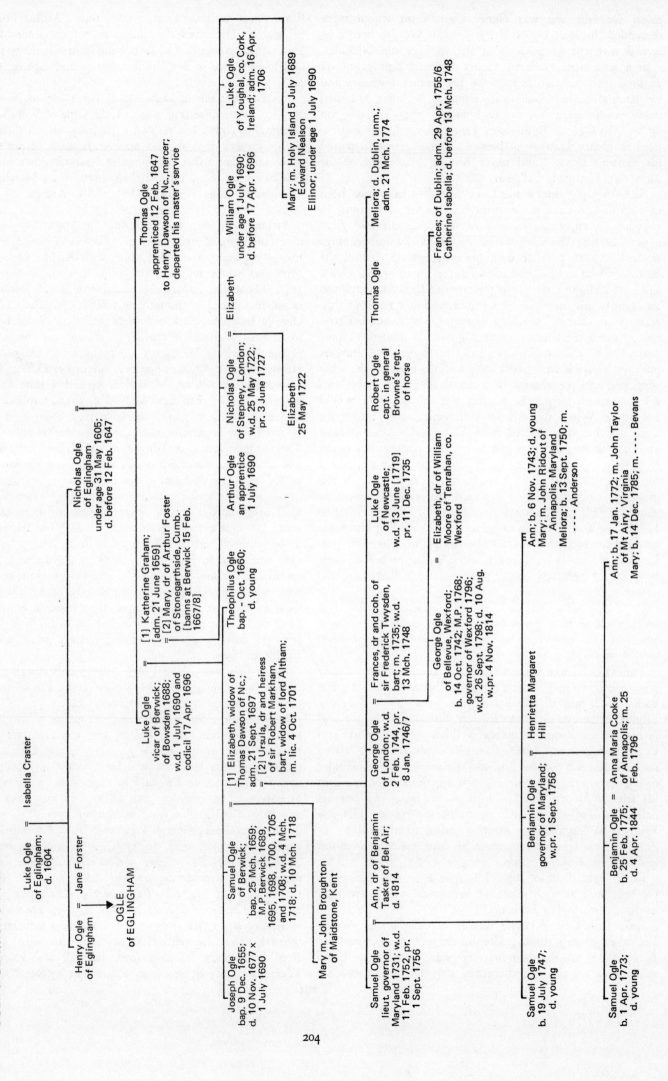

204

August 1783 he was admitted to the Irish privy council, and in 1784 was appointed registrar of deeds at Dublin at a salary of £1300 a year. In 1796 he became governor of Wexford, and died 10 August 1814 aged 75. By his wife Elizabeth daughter of William Moore of Tenrahan, co. Wexford, he had no children.

Luke Ogle of Newcastle by his w.d. 13 June 1719 leaves all his goods to his brother Samuel Ogle of Newcastle and appoints him executor; the will was proved 11 December 1735 by John Broughton of par. St Margaret's, Westminster, as attorney for Samuel Ogle who was abroad. Robert Ogle became a captain in general Browne's regiment of horse in Ireland; he may have been the Robert Ogle, esq., of Dysart lodge, whose will was proved in Ireland in 1791.

Benjamin Ogle, second but eldest surviving son of Samuel Ogle, was, like his father, governor of Maryland for a time. His father had left him a house and lands in Prince George's county and his slaves. His will was proved in London 1 September 1756. His only surviving son, a second Benjamin Ogle, died at Prince George's, Maryland, on 4 April 1844.

OGLE OF ROTHBURY, PAR. ROTHBURY

IN 1654 Thomas Ogle 'of the parish of Eglingham' was married at Rothbury to Margaret Maving of that place. Thomas' connection with the Ogles of Eglingham, if any, has not been traced. He made his will on 13 June 1694 and it was proved by Henry Ogle of Egremont, Cumberland, clerk, and John Ogle of Rothbury, gent., on 9 August 1694. An inventory of his goods was exhibited three days earlier, and he was buried at Rothbury on 4 August 1694.

He leaves to his eldest son William Ogle, the burgage in Rothbury and lands which he had by marriage with his wife Margaret and £20. His second son Thomas is to have £50 now in the hands of Charles Selby of Biddleston, esq. He leaves to his fourth son, John Ogle, his now dwelling house and all his household goods, whilst his youngest son Edward is to have four riggs of land lying in the North Croft of Rothbury and £70 at the age of 21 years. If the eldest son should be not now living the £20 left to him is to be distributed among the other sons and daughters. The daughters were Blanch wife of Tristram Fenwick, and Grace wife of Oliver Nichols. His brother Lewis Ogle, his sister Anne James and his sister Elinor Clennell are left small legacies. The residue of his estate is to be divided between his sons Henry and John, who are to be executors.

The brother Lewis is named Lewis Ogle of Eglingham when he married at Rothbury on 26 February 1659 Elizabeth Urpeth. Isabel (sic) wife of Lewis Ogle of Rothbury was buried 20 March 1666/7 and Lewis married secondly on 19 January 1667/8 Margaret Clark of Rothbury Forest. Lewis Ogle married as his third wife Jane Spurnam of Rothley, par. Hartburn, and by her had a son Roland.

Henry, third son of Thomas Ogle, was ordained priest 25 September 1692, became rector of Egremont in Cumberland 30 September 1692, which living he resigned in 1700. The fourth son, John, died at Bonus Hill, otherwise known as Ogle demesne, par. Whalton, and was buried at Whalton 23 March 1697/8; administration of his goods was granted 17 June 1698 to his sister Blanch Fenwick.

The youngest son, Edward, voted in respect of his freehold at Rothbury in 1715 and made his will on 29 May 1730. His loving wife Sarah Ogle is to have the house in which he is now living and the eight ridges in the North Crofts. His eldest son Thomas is to have all his other lands, his second son James £30, his third son Fenwick £60, and his daughter Mary Ogle £50 (Dur. Prob. Off. by C.R.H.).

Thomas Ogle was a Sunderland surgeon and voted for a freehold at Rothbury in 1734; James Ogle voted in 1747. The two sons of the latter, James and Edward, moved to London. James' descendants are shown in the attached pedigree, but they died out in the male line. It is interesting that one of his granddaughters renewed the family's connection with Northumberland when she married on 24 July 1859 Charles Selby Bigge, only son of Charles John Bigge (d.1846) of Linden, par. Longhorsley.

Rowland Ogle of Whitton, par. Rothbury, by his will leaves all his land and tenements whatsoever and leasehold under the duke of Somerset, and all his personal estate, to James Ogle of Rothbury who proved the will on 27 May 1747 (Dur. Prob. Off. by C.R.H.). This was no doubt the Rowl'd Ogle of Hartlepool whose vote at the elections of 1715 for 'Nigh Rothbury' was rejected because the land belonged to the duke of Somerset. He was son of Lewis Ogle of Whitburn by his third wife.

OGLE OF HIRST, PAR. WOODHORN

THE origin of this branch of the Ogle family has already been discussed in the account of the Ogles of Ogle, because George Ogle who had been given Hirst and other lands by the 6th lord Ogle in 1536, married Anne widow of the 5th lord.

When the i.p.m. of Robert, 6th lord Ogle, was taken on 20 October 1564 George Ogle of Hirst was in possession of Shilvington and Newhall, and of lands in North Middleton and Hirst. George Ogle was succeeded in his estates by his son, also called George. It is not known if the second George Ogle was a son of Anne, lady Ogle, or of some other wife. He married Anne daughter of Lancelot Middleton of Silksworth, co. Durham.

The later history of the family is detailed in chancery suits of 1626 and 1628. On 21 June 1626 Jane Ogle of Woodhorn Seaton, widow, exhibited a bill against Margaret Ogle, widow, concerning Woodhorn Seaton which after Margaret's death would have reverted to Jane who was widow of Margaret's son Thomas. When Thomas contracted to marry the said Jane daughter of Mark Ogle, late of Kirkley, arrangements had been made for Margaret's lodging and keep. After the marriage had taken place Thomas Ogle fell sick and in February 1618/9 in the time of his sickness, Margaret with her brother Anthony Errington, had, according to the claimant, purloined the deeds out of Jane's house at Woodhorn Seaton, and had afterwards disturbed her in her possession. In September 1623 she complained to the President and Council of the North; they examined a deed of feoffment dated 17 September 1599 by Henry Ogle to Anthony Errington and William Hudspeth in trust, and decreed that so long as Margaret widow of Henry Ogle, should remain unmarried, Jane was to enjoy the premises for her life saving the west house for Margaret. Jane now states that Anthony Errington

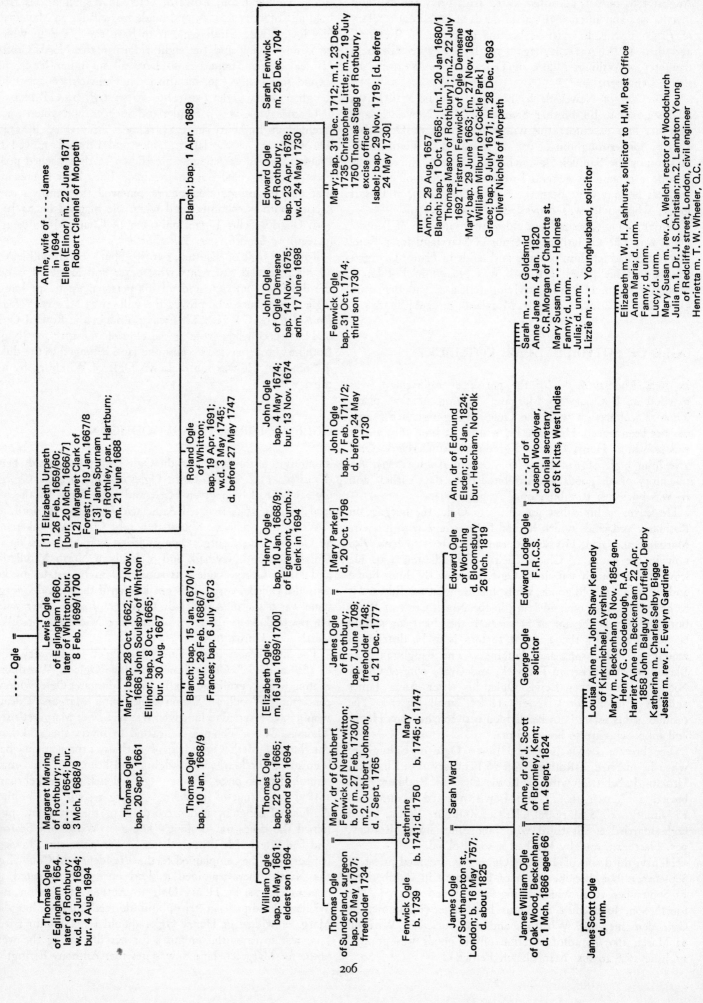

OGLE of HIRST, par. WOODHORN

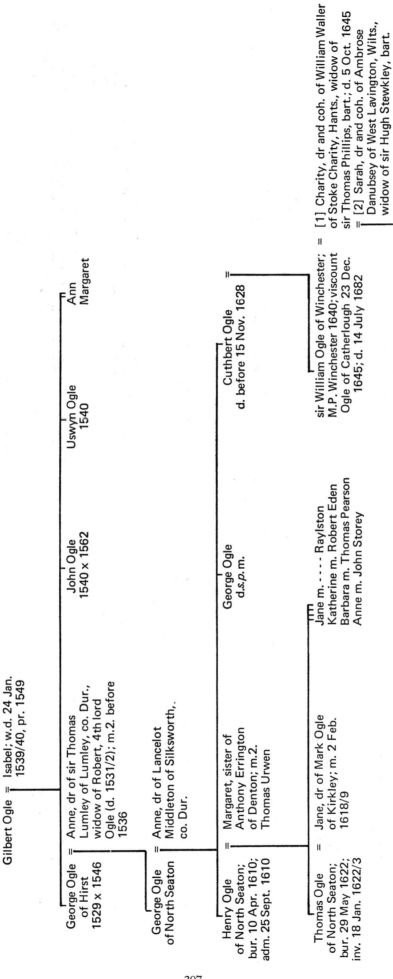

OGLE of WHISTON, Lancs.

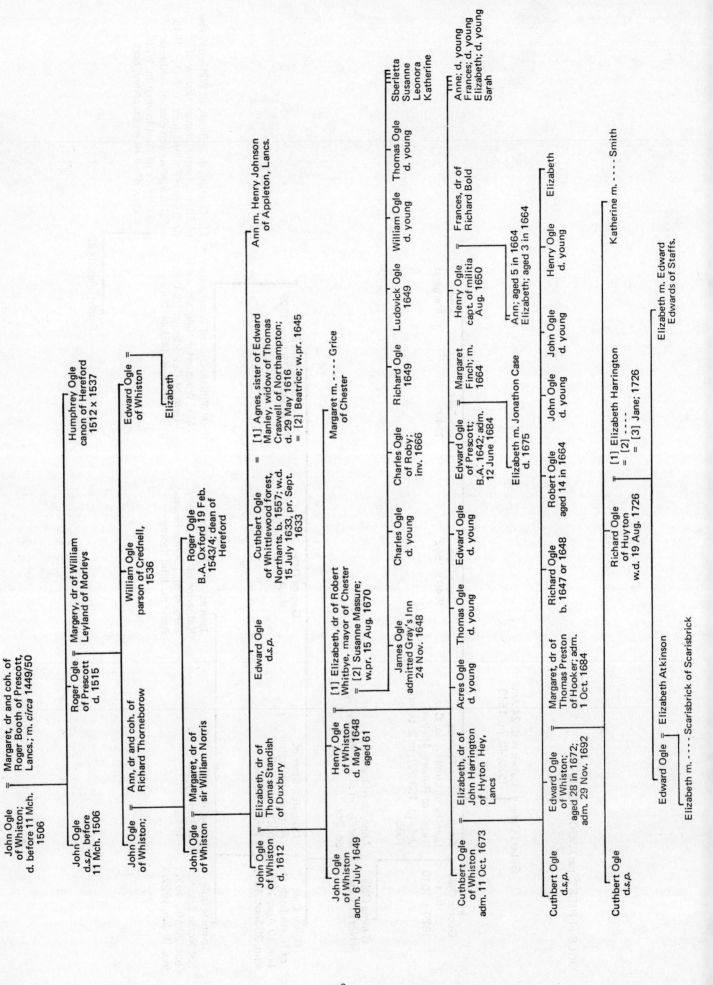

claims the premises as purchased by him from John Storey and Anne his wife, Robert Eden and Katherine his wife, Thomas Pearson and Barbara his wife, and Isabel daughter of Jane Raylston, deceased.

On 17 January 1627/8 Anthony Errington answered Jane Ogle's claim. He stated that Margaret widow of Henry Ogle, had married Thomas Urwen, and Thomas Ogle dying without issue, the inheritance descended to his sisters Anne Storey, Katherine Eden, Barbara Pearson and Jane Raylston from whom he had bought the property on 9 September 1622 and 20 June 1626. He further stated that there had been no jointure for Jane, Thomas Ogle's wife, and denied that there had been any assurance made in February 1618/9 to Thomas and Jane for their lives.

A further statement by Jane Ogle was to the effect that Thomas Ogle, her late husband, formerly lived with his uncle Anthony Errington at Denton, who with his wife Dorothy tried to get the estate and tendered to Thomas a deed of conveyance, but he left the house and 'went on service'; his mother Margaret being poor, with the assistance of Ralph Ogle of Saltwick, deceased, and Stephen Ogle assisted to marry Thomas Ogle to Jane daughter of Mark Ogle of Kirkley. At first Mark Ogle had objected to the marriage as the young couple were 'nigh kinsmen' but eventually consenting he gave Margaret £100 with the promise of a further £40 at his death.

Later in 1628, on 15 November, another claimant came forward in the person of sir William Ogle of Winchester. According to his claim George Ogle of Hirst being seised of lands in North Seaton had entailed them on his three sons Henry, George and Cuthbert and their heirs male. Henry entered and about twenty years ago died and the premises descended to Thomas his son who died seven or eight years ago without issue male, and George died without issue male, and Cuthbert, sir William's father was dead. When Thomas died, sir William was employed in war beyond the seas in His Majesty's service and the late king, and he had not heard of Thomas' death until now.

Henry Ogle had died in 1610 (bur. Woodhorn 10 April 1610). On 25 September 1610 administration of the goods of Henry Ogle of the parish of Woodhorn was granted to his widow Margaret, their children Thomas, Jane, Katherine, Barbara and Anne being under age. Thomas Ogle and Jane Ogle were married at Ponteland 2 February 1618/9; Thomas was buried at Woodhorn 29 May 1622. Administration of his goods was granted 19 July 1622 to Jane his widow; in the administration there is mention of Lewis Ogle, illegitimate son of Henry Ogle of Kirkley, junior.

Nothing is known about the early life of sir William Ogle, except for his own statement that he had been employed in war beyond the seas. He purchased lands at Stoke Charity near Winchester, and became a freeman of the merchant's guild of Winchester. In 1640 he was member of parliament for Winchester but three years later was disabled for sitting for being a royalist. On 23 April 1642 the House of Commons resolved 'of sir William Ogle that this house doth approve of sir William Ogle nominated by the lord lieutenant to be colonel of one regiment'. He assisted in the reduction of the castles of the rebels in Munster for which he received the thanks of the Commons. King Charles created him Viscount Ogle of Catherlough in the peerage of Ireland on 23

December 1645. He died on 14 July 1682 and was buried at Michelmersh, Hants.

Lord Ogle's first wife was Charity daughter and coheiress of William Waller of Stoke Charity, widow of sir Thomas Phillips, first baronet. She died 5 October 1645 and he married secondly about 1647 Sarah daughter and coheiress of Ambrose Danubsey of West Lavington, Wilts, widow of sir Hugh Stewkley, bart. By her he had an only daughter Sarah, who was living unmarried in 1682.

OGLE OF WHISTON, LANCS.

THE Ogles of Whiston in Lancashire claimed descent from John Ogle, younger son of sir Robert Ogle V (d.1436). On Friday next after the feast of Saint John Baptist 1427 sir Robert Ogle acquired from Thomas de Denome the manor of Unthank with lands in Belford and Easington. At Unthank on 1 May 13 H.VI (1436) sir Robert executed a deed poll by which he gave to John Ogle 'my lawfully begotten son' the manor of Unthank, a tenement and husbandland in Howtel and two tenements and husbandlands in Mindrum. These two deeds were taken by Dodsworth 'From the original charters in the custody of Henry de Ogle of Whistan by Prestcote, co. Lancs., esquire. 6 July 1643'. This John Ogle was apparently in the service of Henry, earl of Northumberland, who on 12 October 28 H.VI (1450) for his good and faithful service gave him the whole lordship and manor of Fawdon 'to have to him without any rent or service to us or our heirs therefore to be yielded for the term of his life'.

John Ogle of Unthank received from his brother sir Robert Ogle VI (d.1469) on 11 September 1455 the manor of North Middleton near Angerton. On 12 May 1460 he settled Unthank and his lands in Belford, Easington, Detchant and Lowick in the hands of trustees, one of them being his brother William Ogle. Three days later the trustees appointed attorneys to deliver these lands to Robert Bothe, John Bothe, Thomas Bothe and Christopher Worthington.

This settlement serves to identify John Ogle of Unthank with the John Ogle who married Margaret daughter and coheiress of Roger Booth of Prescott, Lancs., and founded the family of Ogle of Whiston and Prescott which continued in the direct male line until the beginning of the 18th century. The pedigree of the family was compiled by sir Henry Ogle chiefly from one in the possession of the late Richard Ogle (d.1899) 'and is apparently similar to the one in Harleian manuscript No. 2042, and is proved more or less by Dugdale's Visitation of Lancashire (*Chetham Soc.* vol.65, p.223) and by Gregson, *Portfolio of Fragments Lancashire* p.176 etc.'. (*Ogle and Bothal*, p.168).

OGLE OF PINCHBECK, LINCS.

A RICHARD OGLE owned lands in Pinchbeck, Lincolnshire, 1504 x 1540, and it was no doubt a natural wish of his descendants to have a descent from the Ogles of Ogle and Bothal. In various pedigrees Richard Ogle is described as son of sir Robert Ogle (*Harl. MSS.* Nos. 1097, 1190, 1408, 1484, 1550) or as 'descended from a younger brother of the lord Ogle'. In a grant of arms to sir John Ogle in 1614 he is stated to have

OGLE of PINCHBECK, Lincs.

sir Robert Ogle =

Richard Ogle
of Pinchbeck;
1528 x 1540

= Mary, dr of John fitz William
of Gaynspark hall, Essex,
widow of Thomas Waddington

---- m. William Percy
of Spalding (d. 1536)

Richard Ogle
of Pinchbeck;
w.d. 8 Sept. 1555;
d. 25 Nov. 1555

= Beatrice, dr of John Cooke
of Gildea hall, Essex; w.d.
13 June 1561

Elizabeth m. ---- Sergeant
of Whaplode, Lincs.

Thomas Ogle
of Pinchbeck;
aged 30 in 1556;
d. 3 May 1574

= Jane, dr of Adlard Welby
of Gedney; d. 2 Sept. 1574

Nicholas Ogle
of Bolingbroke;
w.d. 1 Sept. 1582;
d. 6 Sept. 1582

= Anne, dr and coh. of
John Freeman of
Collier row, Essex

B

Audrey m. 1. John Man of Bolingbroke,
m.2. sir Vincent Skynner of Thornton
college, Lincs.
----; unm. 1555 and 1561

sir Richard Ogle
aged 20 in 1574;
knighted 23 Apr. 1603;
adm. 27 Nov. 1627

= Dorothy, dr of
Robert Ashfield
of Stowland toft,
Suffolk; d.
10 Dec. 1627

Robert Ogle
of Pinchbeck
bap. 1 Apr. 1566;
bur. 27 July 1627

= Jane, dr of ----
Laughton, widow of
Robert Leaves; m.2.
May 1602; bur. 18 Nov.
1637

Thomas Ogle
of Pinchbeck
bur. 29 June 1618

[1] Ann, dr of William
Bryan of Bolingbroke,
widow of rev. Robert
Bendish; d. 1598
= [2] Frances Blackburne
of Lincoln; w.d. 7 Feb.
1632, pr. 3 Nov. 1634

[1] Dorothy, dr of William Hunston
of Boston; m. 23 Sept. 1590
= [2] Mary; bur. 4 Oct. 1604
= [3] Anne Rose; m. 30 Oct.
1610; bur. 8 Feb. 1610/1

Clinton Ogle
bap. 18 Oct. 1604;
bur. 3 May 1606

Frances; bap. 2 Oct.
1606; bur.
10 June 1615

Jane; bap. 1609

Thomas Ogle
bap. 23 Dec. 1593

Bridget;
bap. 1 July 1596

Thomas Ogle
bap. 27 Dec. 1603;
a capt. in the army;
bur. 20 Aug. 1638

Thomas Ogle
1638

William Ogle
bap. 30 Sept. 1604

Mary
bap. 17 Nov. 1602

Elizabeth; bap. 3 Nov. 1610

Valentine Ogle
of Pinchbeck;
bap. 12 Mch. 1600/1;
bur. 28 Feb. 1669/70

= Bridget, dr of
Richard Browne
of Saltfleetby,
lincs.; m. 28 Apr.
1625

John Ogle
of Immingham;
bap. 21 Dec. 1609;
w.d. 20 Sept. 1690

= Frances, dr of
Nicholas Evington;
m. Aug. 1644

Margaret; bap.
1 Jan. 1603/4;
d. young

Bridget; bap. 9 Mch.
1604/5; bur.
15 May 1605

Dorothy; bap. 20 Feb.
1605/6; m. 10 May
1625 Matthew Read

Robert Ogle
bap. 2 Dec. 1637;
bur. 5 Jan. 1637/8

Frances; bap.
20 Mch. 1627/8;
bur. 7 May 1644

John Ogle
bap. 21 Jan. 1607/8;
bur. 14 Oct. 1608

John Ogle
d. 1687 x 1690

William Ogle
bap. 9 July 1636;
bur. 22 Sept. 1636

Bryan Ogle
bap. 23 Nov. 1633;
bur. 25 May 1644

Richard Ogle
of Gedney;
bap. 25 Nov. 1629;
w.d. 3 Feb. 1689,
pr. 1693

= Anne

John Ogle
bap. 2 Dec. 1631

Thomas Ogle
bap. 4 Aug. 1626;
living 3 Feb. 1689

Henry Ogle
bap. 28 May 1570

sir John Ogle
of Pinchbeck
bap. 25 Feb. 1568/9;
bur. 17 Mch. 1639/40

= Elizabeth, dr of
Cornelius de Vries
of Dordrecht

Beatrix; bap. 11 June 1560;
m.1. Leonard Pury of
Kirton in Holland, Lincs.;
m.2. William Walcot of
Walcot

Mary; bap. 19 Dec. 1563

Cassandra; bap. 7 Jan. 1564/5;
m.1. Robert Lacy of
Stamford, Lincs.; m.2. sir
Francis Beaumont of
Washingborough

Helen; bap. 21 Sept. 1567

Jane; bap. 8 Apr. 1571;
m. 31 Mch. 1605 Anthony
Doughty of Boston

A

C

OGLE of PINCHBECK, cont.

A →
B →

sir John Ogle = ?
of Pinchbeck;
bur. 26 Mch. 1663

sir Thomas Ogle = Sence, dr of John
governor of Chelsea   Whatton of Newark
hospital 1689;
d. 23 Nov. 1702

Thomas Ogle = Henrietta Bruce, dr of the
of Pinchbeck   2nd earl of Elgin and Aylesbury

Henrietta; of Windsor w.d. 29 Feb. 1772;
d. 25 Nov. 1774
Hariot; d. in infancy aged 14 days
Catherine; m. rev. Robert Aylmer

Lavinia; m. 11 Dec. 1627 sir John Manwood,
chief justice of the common pleas;
d. 19 Feb. 1641/2 aged 36
Elizabeth
Utricia; m. 18 Dec. 1645 sir William Swan of
Southfleet, Kent
Trajectina
Henrica
Sophia
Susanna; m. Onslow Gardiner
Dorothy

Cornelius Ogle   Julius Ogle

Anthony Ogle = [1] Alice, dr of rev. Robert
of Keddington;   Doughty, vicar of Louth;
aged 10 and more 1582;   m. 18 Oct. 1596
w.d. 24 Aug. 1606,   = [2] Anne Pape; m. 3 Aug.
pr. 4 Dec. 1606   1598

Clinton Ogle
1582 × 1606

Hastings Ogle
1582

Thomas Ogle
1582 × 1606

Leonard Ogle
bur. 11 Mch. 1590

Richard Ogle
1582

Elizabeth; 1582
Frances; 1582

Dorothy; bap. 5 Mch. 1597/8

Jane; bap. 1599; d. in infancy
Anne
Mary
Frances
Audrey

C →
D →

Richard Ogle
bap. 6 Jan. 1588/9;
d. before 25 June
1618

Thomas Ogle = [1] Alethea, dr of Roger
of Pinchbeck   Smith of Edmondthorpe,
bap. 1 Mch. 1589/90;   Leics.; bur. 15 July 1627
w.d. 19 Apr. 1656; = [2] Millicent, dr of sir
bur. 8 June 1656   Thomas Temple of
                       Stowe, Bucks

Robert Ogle
bap. 4 Apr. 1591
bur. 15 June 1591

Anthony Ogle
bap. 10 Sept. 1592;
d. young

John Ogle
bap. 10 Sept. 1592;
bur. 10 Mch. 1594/5

Jane; m. 12 Dec. 1608 Dymock Walpole of
Pinchbeck
Cassandra; bap. 4 Nov. 1593; bur. 28 July 1596
Frances; bap. 6 Oct. 1594; m. 24 July 1619 rev.
Christopher Humphery, vicar of Pinchbeck
Rachel; bap. 6 Oct. 1594; bur. 28 July 1596
Anne; bap. 4 Jan. 1597/8; m. 5 Oct. 1618
Leonard Brown of Pinchbeck

Edward Ogle
bap. 7 July 1627;
bur. 6 Aug. 1627

Anne; bap. 1 Apr.
1624; w.d. 11 Feb.
1663

Thomas Ogle = Mary
of Kingston-upon
Hull; bur. 17 Apr.
1636

Temple Ogle
bap. 3 Dec. 1640;
bur. 2 Feb. 1641/2

Temple Ogle
of Rathwell;
ba. 27 Sept. 1646;
M.A. 1673

Charles Ogle
bap. 7 Nov. 1647;
bur. 25 Oct. 1649

Charles Ogle = Lydia
of St Martins-in-
the-fields; bap. 23
Apr. 1650; adm.
16 Nov. 1680

John Ogle
1690

Anne; 1670
Elizabeth; 1670

Thomas Ogle
1690

Hester; m. rev. Robert Haslewood,
rector of Fleet
Millicent; bap. 12 Apr. 1632; bur.
2 June 1669
Rachel; bap. 13 Aug. 1637; of Rathwell
in 1690
Beatrice; bap. 2 May 1642; d. unm.

Robert Ogle
d.s.p. before 1628

Thomas Ogle = Anne, dr of sir John Reade
of Wicken, Suffolk;   of Wrangle, Lincs.
w.d. 10 June 1659,
pr. 14 July 1660

Frances; bap. 26 Sept. 1594;
m. - - - - Dearsley of Essex
Jane; bap. 23 May 1596; m.
Francis Plumbe
Anne; bap. 22 Jan. 1597/8;
m. sir John Hales

Magdalene
Dorothy m. John Windham of Felbrigg, Norfolk
Anne; m. 29 July 1673 Craven Howard of
Ravesby abbey, Lincs.

sir Thomas Ogle = Anna, dr of sir Anthony Haselwood
of Wicken; adm.   of Maidwell, widow of sir William
16 Mch. 1671   Kingsmill; m.lic. 7 Oct. 1662

Dorothy; of Maydwell, Northants.,
w.d. 8 Aug. 1692

John Ogle
of Spalding

Elizabeth; bap. 24 Mch. 1646/7;
bur. 1 Jan. 1647/8

Ashfield Ogle
1651

211

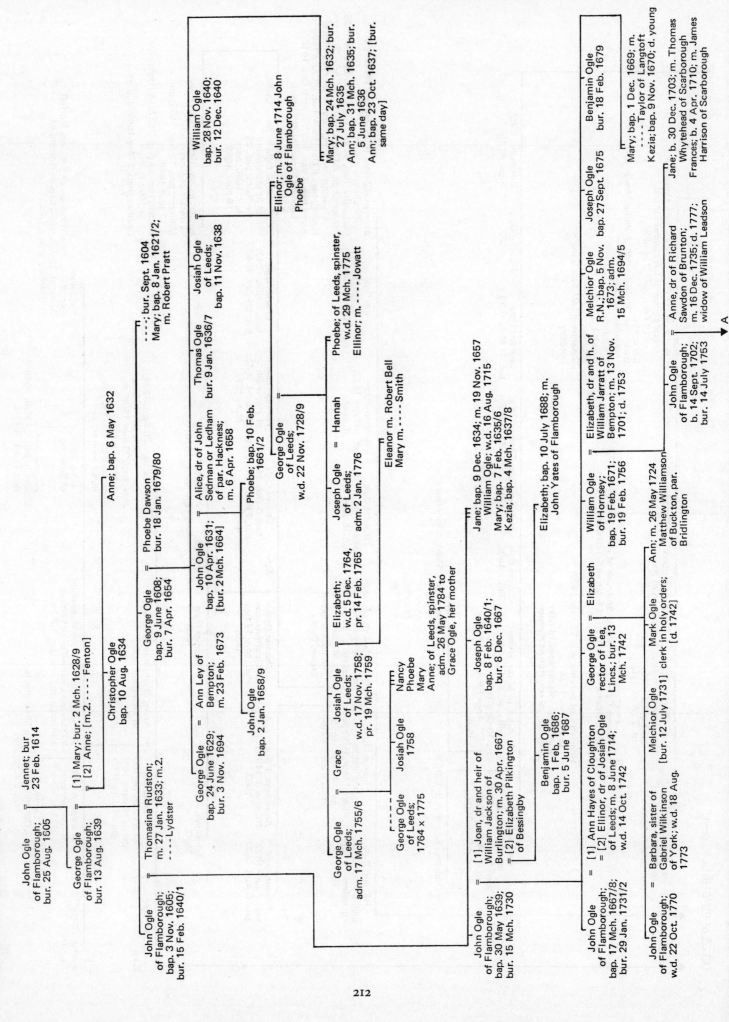

descended from lord Ogle and Bothal.

The first lord Ogle was sir Robert Ogle VI who was summoned to parliament on 26 July 1461 and died 1 November 1469, but Richard Ogle of Pinchbeck who was living in 1540, over seventy years later, can hardly have been his son. Owen, 2nd lord Ogle, was aged 30 and more in 1470 and died 1 September 1486; and Ralph, 3rd lord Ogle, was aged 18 in 1486 and died 6 January 1513. We can be reasonably certain that neither of these had a son called Richard. The presumption is that if the Ogles of Pinchbeck had in fact a descent from the Ogles of Ogle it was from much further back than the 15th century.

Of this family was sir Richard Ogle, knighted at Belvoir castle on the coronation of James I on 23 April 1603 and sheriff of Lincolnshire in 1608. Sir Richard's younger brother, John, entered the army and became in 1591 a sergeant major general under sir Francis Vere in the Low Countries; he was knighted at Woodstock on 16 December 1603 and buried in Westminster abbey on 17 March 1639/40. Sir John's wife was a Dutch lady and some of their children were born abroad. In May 1622 a denization order was granted to lady Elizabeth Ogle now wife of sir John Ogle, knight, and to John, Thomas, Cornelius and Dorothie Ogle, his children, born in the Low Countries (*Privy Seal Dockets*). When sir John received a grant of arms on 11 January 1614/5 it seems to have been recognised that he was descended from the Ogles of Ogle for his arms were Argent, on a fess, between three crescents, gules, a lion passant or.

The Ogles of Pinchbeck can be traced to a Thomas Ogle who died about 1711 leaving only daughters. A cadet line of the family was living at Kingston-upon-Hull, Yorks., at the end of the 17th century.

The attached pedigree is taken from *Ogle and Bothal* and was based on one drawn up by Everard Green, Rouge Dragon Herald. It has not been checked.

OGLE OF FLAMBOROUGH, YORKS.

A family of Ogle that held lands in Flamborough, Yorks., from the late 16th century until it died out in the male line in 1772, claimed that they were descended from a John Ogle who left Northumberland *circa* 1565 and settled at Flamborough. This claim first appears in a pedigree at the Heralds' College dated 1778 and can only be accepted as a family tradition of doubtful historical accuracy.

The pedigree is taken from *Ogle and Bothal*, and has not been confirmed.

OGLE OF STAFFORDSHIRE

On 27 December 1722 John Ogle of Chapel Cholton, par. Eccleshall, Staffs., yeoman, married at Trentham, Lydia Hargreaves of Trentham, spinster. She was sister of the rev. John Hargreaves of Trentham, and surviving her husband, was buried at Kynnersley on 9 October 1777 in her eighty-first year.

A tradition extant with the descendants of this couple in the 19th century was that John Ogle who married in 1722 was son of an Ogle of Causey Park 'that his brothers—both married—without children, lived at Causey Park and would have left the property to John's son (also a John) but that he having objections to becoming either a clergyman or a barrister was cut off by his two uncles, whereupon he took some office in the excise'. The pedigree of the Ogles of Causey Park in the early part of the 18th century is so well known in considerable detail that this tradition must be rejected as historically inaccurate. This was realised by the author of *Ogle and Bothal* but his suggestion that this branch of the Ogles was descended from a Cuthbert Ogle, who held a lease of lands in Ogle and died in 1632, can be nothing more than a guess. Other suggestions have been made as to the origin of this branch of the Ogle family, but they are not convincing. The description of John Ogle as 'yeoman' when he married might suggest that he sprang from quite a junior branch of the Northumberland Ogles.

One distinguished member of this family was admiral Thomas Ogle RN (1794-1886), and another was James Adey Ogle, MA, MB, MD, FRS. (1792-1857) who became regius professor of medicine in Oxford University in 1851.

By the end of the 19th century the known descendants of John and Lydia Ogle (m.1722) were very numerous, and some of them were using the Christian names of Chaloner, Savile and Bertram, no doubt on account of a presumed connection with the Ogles of Kirkley in Northumberland, then the most prominent branch of the family.

The pedigree has been taken from *Ogle and Bothal* and has not been checked.

OGLES OF SCOTLAND

Throughout the greater part of the 15th, 16th and 17th centuries a family, whose name is usually written Ogill were lairds of Hartremwood and Popple near Haddington in Scotland. Their coat of arms differs completely from that of the Northumberland Ogles and the family does not appear to have ever claimed any connection. Notices of the family are collected together in *Ogle and Bothal* (pp.273-275) and it does not seem necessary to repeat them here.

Shortly after the middle of the 18th century John Ogle was appointed to the office of clerk of the commissariat of Lanark, in succession to Alan Ogle, who was probably his father. Descendants of John Ogle in the 19th century moved to the south of England. John Ogle of Sevenoaks had one of his younger sons christened Charles Chaloner Ogle thus 'borrowing' from the Ogles of Kirkley one of their regular Christian names.

OGLES OF IRELAND

When Thomas Ogle of Tritlington made his will at Dublin 10 October 1641 he left to Thomas Ogle of Darrashall and his heirs forever all his lands in cos. Dublin, Wicklow, Wexford, Kilkenny, Cotterlagh, Tipperary, the Queen's County, Longford, Sligo and Kildare in Ireland. The lands are specified as the house of Banemore, the manor of Kilmorey, manor of Dangen within the borough of Thomas towne; the castle, manor and lands of Kinleston, the castle, manor and lands af Ballingander, Ballginder, Dilgenry *alias* Temple Dilgenny,

OGLE of STAFFORDSHIRE, etc.

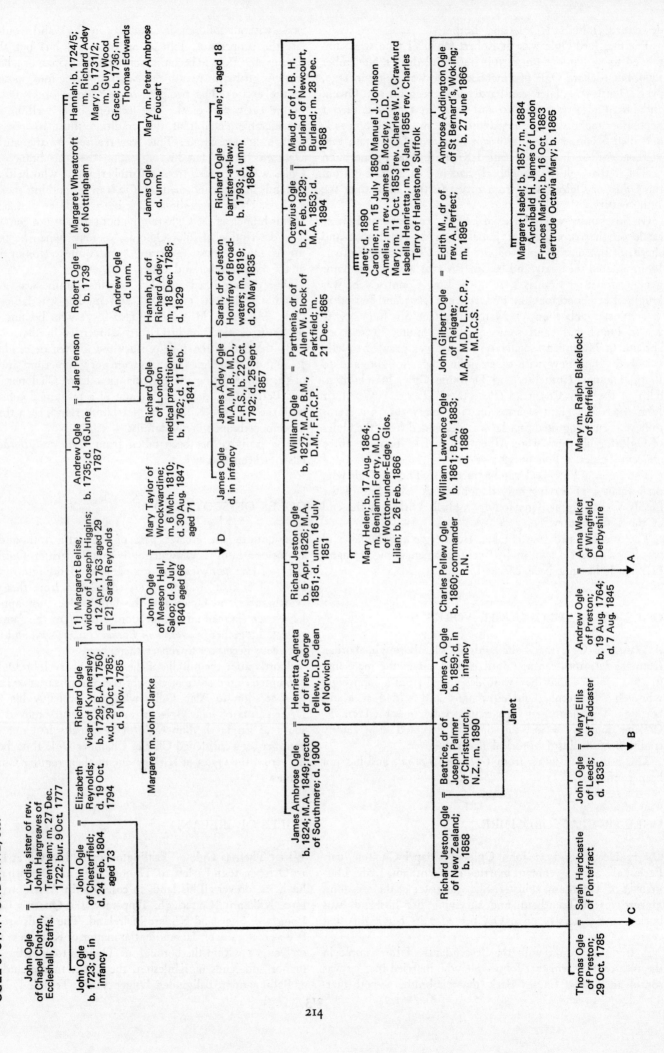

OGLE OF STAFFORDSHIRE, cont.

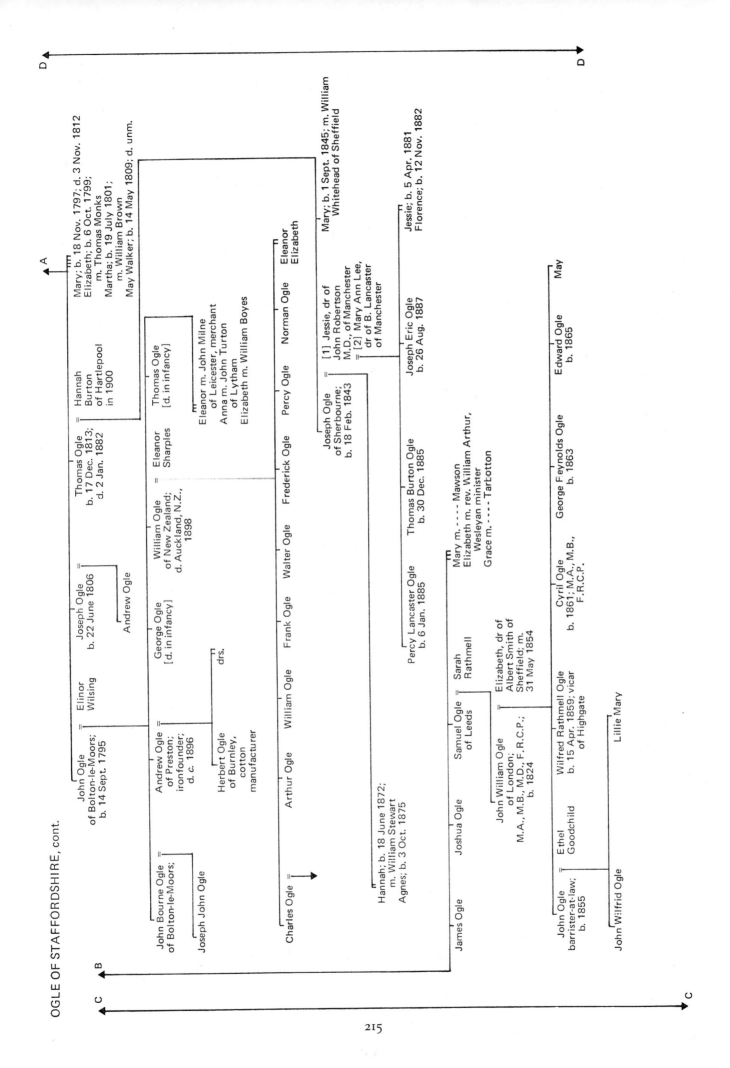

OGLE of STAFFORDSHIRE, etc.

John Ogle b. 14 Feb. 1793; d. 12 July 1881 = Alice, dr of Thomas Bray; m. 31 Oct. 1817

Thomas Ogle b. 14 Mch. 1794; admiral R.N.; d. 27 Dec. 1886 = Mary, dr of John Garth of Preston, Lancs.

Richard Ogle b. 12 May 1797 = Emily Gallop

William Ogle b. 6 May 1801

Anne Eliza; b. 31 May 1803; d. unm. 26 Mch. 1883

Mary; b. 11 Nov. 1806; m. David Jones

Frederick Amelius Ogle b. 1841; a major general in the army, C.B. = Agnes Richmond, dr of James Reid; m. 1876

Anne Eliza; b. 1831; m. 22 Aug. 1855 Thomas Owen of Trefeiler, Anglesey

Mary; d. unm. before 1855

Thomas Frederick Garth Ogle b. 24 July 1877; lieut. Royal Fusiliers; d. 1901

Mary; b. 1882; d. 1893 two children; d. young

Thomas Bray Ogle b. 28 Aug. 1818; d. Upper Norwood 4 June 1868

Richard Ogle of Altrincham; b. 29 Apr. 1824; d. 2 Jan. 1899 = [1] --- Gill, widow d. 1871 = [2] Emily Hansard

Sarah Anne; b. 10 Sept. 1820; d. unm. 27 Oct. 1888

Betsy; b. 18 May 1822; d. in infancy

Alice Hardcastle; b. 22 Apr. 1826; d. young

Mary Hannah Maria; b. 20 June 1828; m. 5 June 1883 Thomas Payne

Emily; b. 20 June 1832

John Ogle b. 3 May 1830; d. 3 May 1900 = Amelia Matilda Nichol; m. Calcutta 10 Dec. 1857

Cecil Herbert Ogle b. 26 Apr. 1871

Ernest Chaloner Ogle b. 21 Feb. 1869; d. 16 May 1900

Alice Maude; b. 5 Sept. 1862

Edith Emily; b. 23 Dec. 1864

Lilian Amelia; b. 26 Mch. 1866; m. 11 Feb. 1893 Walter N. Morrison

Joseph Taylor Reynolds Ogle of Meeson hall; b. 1818; d. 4 Oct. 1883 = Mary, dr of John Heatley

Katherine Mary Anne; b. 1814; m. 1841 James Evett

Sarah Maria; b. 1821; m. 1850 Samuel Holmes Leigh

Hugh Gilbert Lloyd Ogle b. 1876; d. 1877

St John Chaloner Ogle of Farleigh View, Batheaston, Bath; b. 1873

William Hall Ogle b. 19 Dec. 1870

Florence Hall; b. 27 Aug. 1863

Mildred; b. 8 Mch. 1866; m. 31 July 1890 Arthur Edghill

Frank Bray Ogle b. 6 Oct. 1859

Percy John Ogle b. 7 Apr. 1861; civil engineer

William Reynolds Ogle b. 1815; M.A. 1842; vicar of Luton, Devon; d. 6 Jan. 1886 = [1] Julia, dr of major Tallmadge of New York; m. 7 Feb. 1850; d. 1862 = [2] Mary Anne Elizabeth, dr. of rev. J. M. Downes, vicar of Llanspyddid; d. 12 Nov. 1901

Grace Margaret; b. 1852; d. 1855

Mary Josephine; m. John Sadler

Sally Helen; m. J.H.Seagram, lieut. col. 95th regt.

Charles Robert Ogle b. 1858

Frank Cecil Ogle b. 1857

Joseph Godfrey Ogle b. 1856; lieut. Nd. Fusiliers; d. 10 Apr. 1879 in Afghanistan

John Reynolds Ogle of Meeson hall; b. 1811; bur. 10 Nov. 1856 = [1] --- Matthews = [2] Eliza Margaret, dr of The Gungrog, Morris Jones of Welshpool; living 1863

Herbert Moss Ogle b. 1841; d. unm. 1870

Alice Rose; b. 1843; d. 3 May 1863

Arthur Joseph Saville Ogle b. 1850; B.A. 1875; vicar of Bishop's Teignton, Devon = Helen, dr of W. H. Phillips of Penn, Staffs.; m. 1880

Richard Pelham Reynolds Ogle b. 1852; d. 1863 or 1864

Mary Julia Helen; b. 1849

Richard William Savile Ogle b. 1882

Arthur Bertram Ogle b. 1883; lieut. R.E.

Helen Florence b. 1887

Pelham Moss Ogle b. 1881

Ponsonby Dugmore Ogle b. 1853; M.A. 1879; vicar of Mackworth, Derby

William Pomeroy Ogle b. 1859; curate of Brentwood; Essex; d. 1 Aug. 1884 = Kate Angeline, dr of Alonzo Cooper Rand of Minneapolis, U.S.A.

Lucie Elizabeth, dr of Charles W. Elkington; m. 1879 = John Reynolds Ogle of Lutterworth, Leics.; b. 1851; L.R.C.P.,M.R.C.S.

William Moss Ogle b. 1853; rector of St Bride's, Magor, Mon. = Elizabeth Flora, dr of Frederick A. Malcolmson; m. 1882

Richard Ogle b. 1812; d. 1889 = Louisa Amy, dr of Joseph Taylor Phillips; m. 1848

Nina Marion; b. 1882

Lucie Doris; b. 1892

Joseph Godfrey Ogle b. 1884

216

and the castle, manor and lands of Bray and Little Bray; and also the castles, manors and lands of and in Bally Keppoke, Betagh Keppocke, Landestone, Barrestone, Babrayne, Stablertowne, Courtduffe; one water mill in Clane and one water mill in Lady Castle in co. Kildare (*PSAN2*, X, p.141).

Thomas Ogle's son and heir, William, raised forces for Charles I at the time of the civil wars and his lands were sequestered. It is not known if he left any descendants.

Sir William Ogle of Winchester, of the family of Ogle of Hirst, owned lands in Ireland from which he took his title of viscount Ogle of Catherlough in the peerage of Ireland in 1645. Catherlough is now Carlow and seems to be the same place as Cotterlagh owned by Thomas Ogle of Tritlington in 1641. Lord Ogle had no male descendants.

A Henry Ogle of Drogheda, alderman, made his w.d. 11 January 1712, pr. August 1712. His descendants were connected with Drogheda for the next 100 years. There is a pedigree in *Ogle and Bothal* (p.279).

OGLES OF AMERICA

OGLES of Northumberland had connections with America from at least the middle of the 17th century. Martin Ogle of Tritlington lived in Virginia for nearly 30 years returning to England about 1682; he seems to have been greatly in debt when he went abroad and there is little evidence that he had improved his finances in Virginia.

A much longer connection with America was started in 1731 when Samuel Ogle, of the family of Ogle of Berwick-on-Tweed was appointed lieut-governor of Maryland. His son Benjamin Ogle succeeded him in this office and his family settled in America. The last of the family was Ann daughter of Benjamin Ogle (d.*c*.1756) who married John Taylor of Mt Airy, Virginia. A descendant of this marriage was Mrs Ogle Taylor who compiled a book about the Ogles entitled *In Memoriam Benjamin Ogle Taylor*—Washington, 1872.

A 'sir' John Ogle is said to have come from Somersetshire and to have landed at Newcastle, Delaware, in 1664. From him in succession descended (2) Thomas Ogle, (3) Thomas Ogle, (4) James Ogle, (5) Thomas B. Ogle, and (6) Henry K. B. Ogle. Two sons of H. K. B. Ogle, Harry L. Ogle and Frank Ogle were living in 1902. Sir Henry Ogle obtained this information from their sister, Miss Maria L. Ogle, living at Philadelphia in 1902 (*Ogle and Bothal*, p.217).

Another Ogle is said to have come from London to Delaware shortly after that province had been wrested from the Dutch in 1664. Ogle had large grants of land from the duke of York to whom the colony had been granted by Charles II. Ogle county, Illinois, was so named to perpetuate the name of captain Ogle, 'whose coolness, courage and daring were so conspicuous in the long and bloody conflict attending the siege of Fort Henry'.

OTHER OGLES

Brotherwick.

In 1585 a Gabriel Ogle held a mansion house and lands in Nether Buston (*NCH.* V, p.239). It seems that he married Agnes daughter of George Hunter of Acklington. The Hunt-ers were Roman Catholics and in 1595 a list of popish recusants includes the names of 'Mabell Hunter of Acklington, widow, an householder; she hath a farmhold and a milne of the yearly value of £13; George Hunter, Agnes Hunter, Agnes Ogle wife of Gabriell Ogle; they dwell in household with the said Mabell and are maintained by her' (*Cath. Rec. Soc.* 53, p.56).

Agnes wife of Gabriel Ogle of Acklington was convicted of recusancy 20 August 1599; she was again convicted 27 August 1601 when her husband is described as of Warkworth, and on 21 July 1619 when he was living at Brotherwick. In 1602 John Wilkinson of Over Buston complained that Thomas Percy, the earl of Northumberland's commissioner, had received £30 for renewing Wilkinson's customary tenancy, besides £4 he gave to sir John Ladyman and Gabriel Ogle for procuring the bargain at Mr Percy's hands (*NCH.* V, p.210).

A Launcellot Ogle, gent., held both freehold and copyhold lands in Brotherwick. The copyhold had been taken in the name of his son, and in 1616 Lancelot Ogle's son 'is lately drowned, being of the age of fourteen years'. Eventually Lancelot had to compound for these lands for a lease at treble rent (*Ib.*, pp.259, 260). Gabriel Ogle, living at Brotherwick in 1619, and Lancelot Ogle, living there in 1616 were perhaps father and son.

Stephen Ogle of Morpeth.

In the account of the Ogles of Hirst it has been mentioned that one of the complaints made in 1628 by Jane widow of Thomas Ogle of North Seaton, was that her mother Margaret with the assistance of Ralph Ogle of Saltwick and Stephen Ogle had arranged Jane's marriage with Thomas Ogle. Steven Ogle witnesses the w.pr. 1629 of Raphe Ogle of par. Stannington; Raphe had lands in Saltwick and a house in Stannington out of which he leaves by will to his wife Isabel £5 a year for life. As the name Stephen is rarely used by the Ogles it is safe to identify him with Stephen Ogle of Morpeth, a papist in 1601, and Stephen Ogle of Shilvington, a papist in 1606.

Robert son of Stephan Ogle was baptised at Morpeth 29 October 1592, his godparents being Mr Robert Dalivell, Mr Henry Gray and Mrs Katherine Gray.

Hadston Linkhouse.

Administration of the goods of William Ogle, late of the Linkhouse, chap. of Chevington, gent., was granted on 17 June 1685 to Jane Ogle his widow, who was to have tuition of his children Thomas, William, Martin and Dorothy Ogle (*Dur. Prob. Off.* by C.R.H.). The youngest son, Martin, was living at Linkhouse on Monday 20 March 1714/5 when he made a nuncupative will, leaving to his brother the rev. Thomas Ogle all his goods and declaring that neither his brother William nor his brother William's wife should have any part thereof. The will was proved by Thomas Ogle, clerk, of Longhorsley, on 21 April 1715 (*Ib.*).

Martin's brother William, with whom he was on such un-friendly terms, was tenant of the farm of Hadston Linkhouse at a rent of £63. 10s., under sir Carnaby Haggerston in 1719 (*NCH.* V, p.414). Mr William Ogle of 'Cheburn' (*sic*) Linkhouse in the parish of Warkworth, and Mrs Margaret Greene of Holywell were married at Earsdon 24 June 1711. He had children baptised at Warkworth between 1712 and 1722—a child (3 June 1712), a daughter Jane (20 Nov. 1713; bur. 26 December 1725), a son William (26 April 1716), and a daughter Margaret (13 February 1721/2).

There was also a Thomas Ogle of Linkhouse at this time, who had a son Thomas baptised 25 August 1720. He may have been the same person as Thomas Ogle of Hauxley whose son Bartholomew was baptised 23 September 1718.

Longhorsley.

William Ogle of Longhorsley, gent., 'sick in body but perfect in memory (thanks be to God)' made his will on 25 May 1655. He directs that his body is to be buried in the chancel of the parish church of Longhorsley 'in hope of a joyfull resurrection'. As for the worldly goods with which God had been pleased to bless him, he leaves to his wife Dorothy during her natural life the lease of a moiety of Hedleywood and the house and tenement in Longhorsley in which he lives. His daughter Barbara Ogle is to have £30 out of his house in Berwick now in the possession of widow Faneside; the Berwick house is to be sold and anything realised over and above the £30 is to be equally divided amongst the children of his daughter and of Thomas Soppett. He leaves to his daughter Anne wife of Thomas Dickson 'seven head of beasts' for her portion. After the death of his wife everything is to go to William Earsden, the son of Humphrey Earsden. The will was proved on 16 February 1655/6 (*PPR.*).

Holy Island.

On 24 February 1570/1 Margaret Ogle, widow, made her will, appointing as executors Richard Bell and Margaret Johnson her daughter; she mentions that Oswald Ogle of Holy Island was indebted to her. There had been Ogles connected with Holy Island long before this, for in 1495 Oswald Ogle had a conveyance of a messuage on the island (Raine, *North Durham*, p.159). In 1528 bishop Wolsey granted to Oswald Ogle of Holy Island, gent., and Henry his son, a lease for 12 years of the rabbit warren at a yearly rent of £4, and the borough of Holy Island for £3 a year. Henry Ogle's name occurs in 1539.

Another Oswald Ogle had a lease of the warren of Holy Island by indenture dated 23 March 1555, and he was perhaps the Oswald Ogle mentioned in Margaret Ogle's will in 1571. Thomas Ogle of Holy Island, gent., by his w.d. 1581 (?) directs that he is to be buried in the church of Holy Island, and appoints his son Henry Ogle as executor to his will; the will is witnessed by Oswald Ogle and Thos Mannars. The inventory of Thomas Ogle's goods is dated 1 October 1590. In 1592 Oswin (? Oswald) Ogle owned lands in Holy Island (*Ib.*, p.157). Henry Ogle who was tenant of lands in Goswick in 1595/6 may have had some connections with Holy Island.

William Ogle, 'indweller' in Holy Island, by his w.d. 20 February 1605/6 leaves all his goods to his wife Isabel, and mentions his son Francis Ogle and his daughter Anne Ogle; his 'cousin' Harie Ogle of Holy Island was a debtor to him; the will was proved 16 March 1606/7 and his children were then under age.

On 14 February 1613/4 an inventory of the goods of Henry Ogle, late of Holy Island, deceased, was made by Edward Muschampe and Olyver Selby. Administration of Henry Ogle's goods was granted 25 February 1613/4 to his widow Anne for their children Henry, Christopher, Lucy, Margaret,

Phillis and Anne, who were all under age.

Henry Ogle of Newcastle took a 99 years lease of lands in Holy Island in 1635, and was perhaps the same person as Henry Ogle mentioned in 1658 as 'now of Holy Island' who sold lands there to J. Bowden (*Ib.*, p.158).

Liverpool.

Margaret daughter of William Rutter of Newcastle, attorney-at-law, and wife of William Ogle (d.1774) of Causey Park, had a sister Jane who married a Henry Ogle. In their b. of m. of 19 March 1754 he is described as of North Shields, a bachelor, and aged 23. They were married at Tynemouth on 24 March 1754. Henry Ogle's will is dated 9 April 1754 and by it he appoints his wife Jane as executrix, the witnesses to the will being W. Rutter junior and W. Rutter (his wife's brother and father). Probate of the will of Henry Ogle of Liverpool, but late of St Ann's, Westminster, was granted to W. Rutter, attorney of Jane Ogle, widow, residing at Newcastle. Jane Ogle married secondly at All Saints', Newcastle, 30 March 1766 William Wrangham of Newcastle, shipwright.

The children of Henry and Jane Ogle were a son William and a daughter Mary. Mary married at St John's, Newcastle, 11 August 1787, Stephen Humble of par. All Saints, Newcastle, hat manufacturer. William Ogle was an ensign in the 6th foot 3 April 1776 but retired from the army 23 June 1779. He died at Glasshouse Bridge, par. All Saints', Newcastle, 9 April 1819 aged 64. He had been twice married, firstly to Elizabeth Harvey, and secondly to Jane Hoppat. A son William Rutter Ogle was born in 1777 and died 1789. His daughters were Jane Elizabeth (b.27 July 1779; m.12 October 1820 rev. Christopher Love of Ashtone, Devonshire), Margaretta (m. before 1813 John Bell Irving), Mary Humble (m.13 January 1814 John Armstrong of the Cut, Newcastle, grocer), Lowther, (bap.Holy Trinity, Whitehaven, Cumb., 29 October 1781; bur. Berwick 1 May 1782), and Jane Rutter (m. at Annan, Dumfriesshire 3 August 1816 David Wright, MD., RN.).

Henry Ogle may have had a brother Cuthbert, for in November 1755 administration of the goods of Cuthbert Ogle of St Ann's, Westminster, who died at Williamsberg, Virginia, was granted to Mary, his widow.

It has been suggested (*Ogle and Bothal*, p.256) that the family tradition of the Ogles of Staffordshire that they were descended from the Ogles of Causey Park may have had its roots in the fact that William Ogle of Causey Park and Henry Ogle of Liverpool married two sisters. If John Ogle, the earliest known ancestor of the Staffordshire Ogles was a brother of Henry Ogle of Liverpool, it could have become a tradition of the Staffordshire branch that they were descended from the Causey Park branch.

Old Felton.

Edward Lisle (d.1676) of Acton, par. Felton, left three daughters his coheiresses. The eldest daughter, Katherine, married Thomas Ogle and had Old Felton secured to her by deed dated 19 April 1675. Katherine died at Old Felton and was buried at Felton 19 March 1692/3. She was survived by her husband who died in 1704 (bur. Felton 3 August 1704). Their eldest son, Thomas, voted in respect of his freehold at Old Felton in 1715 but sold it before 18 April 1720. He was apparently married twice; 'Mr Thos Ogle jun's wife of Old Felton' was buried 4 April 1699; on 6 May 1709 he entered into a bond of marriage with Sarah Knewstob, widow, and married her at Durham cathedral the same day.

Thomas Ogle, junior, had three younger brothers and two sisters:

1. Henry Ogle; b. at Acton; bap. Felton 4 November 1654/5.

2. Robert Ogle; b. at Acton; bap. Felton 4 November 1662; d. at Old Felton; bur. 15 August 1696.

3. Ralph Ogle; b. at Acton; bap. Felton 16 May 1672.

i. Maudlen; d. at Acton 8 November 1661.

ii. Elizabeth; b. at Old Felton; bap. Felton 27 August 1674 (*NCH.* VII, p.379).

Mrs Appelina Ogle of Old Felton, bur. 8 July 1710, may have been a member of this family. The Christian name is so unusual that there might have been a connection with the Ogles of Eglingham; Henry Ogle (d.1711) married for his first wife Appolina daughter of sir Charles Howard of Over-acres; she died 1689. Henry Ogle of Eglingham had an uncle Thomas, living 20 June 1668, who might have been the elder Thomas Ogle of Old Felton.

Snookbank.

Edward Ogle, master and mariner, was buried at St Nicholas', Newcastle, 23 May 1658. He can be identified with Edward Ogle, apprentice of George Shafto, master and mariner, who became a freeman of Newcastle 15 January 1648/9. On 17 January 1659 administration of the goods of Edward Ogle late of Newcastle upon Tyne was granted to John, Richard, Metcalfe, Lancelot, Mary, and Frances Ogle, his children who were under age. Christian 'dr of Edw. Ogle, deceased' was buried at St Nicholas 25 March 1659; and 'Mitcaffe son of Thos Ogle, master and mar. decd' was buried there 14 October 1663; here Thos is surely a mistake for Edward.

The name Metcalf used as a Christian name suggests an Ogle-Metcalf marriage about this time. A much later marriage connection between these two families was in 1729 when Cuthbert Ogle of Newcastle, eldest son of Cuthbert Ogle of the same place, married Mary daughter of Richard Metcalf of Newcastle, tinsmith, by his wife Dorothy Curry. Dorothy Curry's mother Hannah was widow and devisee of Robert Heselrigg of Blyth. On 24 June 1729 Hannah Heselrigg made a settlement of lands in Framlington on her grand-daughter Mary Metcalf before her marriage with Cuthbert Ogle.

Cuthbert Ogle voted in respect of the freehold lands at Snookbank in Framlington in 1734 and 1748. On 13 June 1752 he sold Snookbank to Samuel Cook of Newton-on-the-Moor. His widow was living at Newcastle in 1768 when she released all her claims for dower (*NCH.* VII, p.442).

Longhirst.

In the early years of the 17th century, a Cuthbert Ogle had a lease of a farm (or farms) at Ogle. The inventory dated 17 May 1613 of the goods of Raphe Ogle, late of Bothal, deceased, records that he owed money to Cuthbert Ogle of Ogle. On 22 February 1613/4 administration of the goods of Ralph Ogle of par. Bothal, was granted to Frances, his widow.

Cuthbert Ogle of Ogle may have been the Cuthbert Ogle mentioned in the nuncupative will of Robert Ogle of Bothal. On Tuesday the 29th day of December 1618 Robert Ogle of Bothal within the county of Northumberland, gentleman, by word of mouth did declare and make his last will as followeth. 'First he said that he had six score pounds in gold which he willed should be given to the countess of Shrewsbury. And he also said that he had £200 in money which he left undisposed. And for his goods which he did estimate worth an hundred pounds and better he did give the same to his brother Henrie Ogle. Then he did give his two farms in Longhirst to his brother Cuthbert Ogle if the ladies thought him worthy thereof and were so pleased and contented'. An inventory of Robert Ogle's goods was taken on 14 January 1618/9.

Raphe Ogle of the par. of Stannington, by his will proved 1629 leaves all his tenant right to Mr Edward son of Mr Cuthbert Ogle of Ogle for a certain sum of money already given.

Cuthbert Ogle by his w.d. 24 January 1631/2 directs that he is to be buried in the church of Whalton. His sons Thomas, John, Christopher and Henry are each to have £10; and his son William and daughter Catherine each £20. He leaves all his other goods and his lease to his eldest son Edward, whom he appoints sole executor. He had the reversion of a lease in Ogle worth £150. On 20 June 1633 administration was granted to Edward Ogle of Coven, par. Breewood, Staffordshire.

Edward was not the only son of Cuthbert Ogle to move south, for on 7 January 1634/5 Henry son of Cuthbert Ogle of Ogle, Nd, gent., decd was apprenticed in the London Drapers Company (*PSAN*4. III, p.250).

Nearly a hundred years later, an Edward Ogle was tenant of a farm at Ogle belonging to the duke and duchess of Somerset. His will was proved in 1724 by his widow Ann and his sons James Ogle of Morpeth and Francis Ogle of Lanshot, par. Elsdon. Edward Ogle of Ogle had voted in respect of a freehold in Longhirst in 1715 and was therefore the same person as Edward Ogle of Longhirst who had voted in 1710. Edward Ogle and Judith Rey were married at Whalton 24 April 1673, and Judith wife of Edward Ogle was buried there 31 December 1676. The parentage of Edward Ogle's second wife Ann is not known; Anne Ogle of Longhirst was buried at Bothal 2 July 1735.

James son of Edward Ogle was baptised at Whalton 12 March 1673/4. He was living at Morpeth in 1724 but may have moved to Ogle after his father's death, for Ellinor wife of James Oglle, Ogle, was buried Whalton 2 November 1725.

Edward Ogle's younger son Francis married Isabel sister of Mark Bowman, widow of William Hedley of Lanshot, par. Elsdon. Francis Ogle voted for the freeholds held by his wife during the minority of her son William Hedley; he voted in respect of Grasslees in 1710 and Lanshot in 1715. Isable wife of Frances (*sic*) Ogle of Ogle was buried at Whalton 3 September 1730. In 1734 Francis Ogle of Ogle voted in respect of a freehold in Glanton.

Francis Ogle died at Harwood Head, par. Hartburn, and was buried at Elsdon 22 February 1744/5; his widow was buried there 22 January 1764. Francis' w.d. 11 February 1744/5 was proved by William Hedley (his step-son) 9 July 1745; in the will he mentions his brother James Ogle.

Most of the landowning families of Northumberland at one time or another sent their younger sons into trade in one of the towns. The Ogles were no exception and towards the end of the 13th century we find William de Oggill holding a prominent position in Newcastle. It is possible that he was a younger son of sir John de Oggell (1269 x 1313).

For the lay subsidy of 1296 there were only three persons of the name of Oggill who paid tax in Northumberland. Besides sir John de Oggill of Ogle, these were Richard de Oggill, one of the twelve jurors for the ward of Inter Wansbeck and Coquet, and William de Oggill, one of the twelve jurors for Newcastle.

In 1292 William de Oggill witnesses a gift to St Mary's Hospital in Newcastle (Brand, *Newcastle*, I, p.31) and a deed of 25 April 1300 contains the signatures of the chief bailiff (or mayor) and four bailiffs, William Ogle being one of the latter. He was bailiff many times between 1283 and 1306 but the exact years are uncertain as most of the early lists of bailiffs are unreliable. It seems probable that William de Oggill had two sons Henry and Gilbert.

On 3 January 1319 Henry de Oggill, formerly a burgess of Newcastle, gave to Gilbert Ogle, burgess, all his land and tenements in Newcastle for ever (Welford, I, p.49). In 1344 John son of Gilbert de Oggill and Alice his wife (daughter of Nicholas Wyght) were plaintiffs against Eva wife of John Crag of Newcastle, about a messuage in Newcastle that had been given in marriage by William de Oggill to the said Gilbert (*de Banco Roll*).

On 7 January 1355 a piece of land in Newcastle held by Peter Ogle was released by John Castle to William Strother (Welford, I, p.145).

When the able bodied men of Newcastle were mustered in 1539 there was only one person of the name of Ogyll—Crystoffe who for himself and 2 servants had 3 jacks, 3 salletts, a bow and 2 halberts. In later years almost every branch of the Ogles sent some of their younger sons to Newcastle, but none of them seem to have been established there for more than one or two generations.

Cuthbert Ogle occurs as a grammar-school master of St Nicholas on 27 December 1596. A Roger Ogle of Newcastle by his w.d. 10 December 1622 directs that he is to be buried in St Andrew's church. To his eldest son Ralph he leaves '10s., and no more for he can work for himself'. Roger had a wife Grace whom he mentions in his will; his three youngest children Margaret, Roger and Timothy are to have £10 each. The will was proved on 17 January 1622/3.

As an example of the different walks of life into which the Ogles spread we may take the parish of All Saints, Newcastle, in the second half of the 17th century. At this time there were living in the parish, William Ogle, gentleman, (younger son of Cuthbert Ogle of Kirkley, d.1655); John Ogle, gentleman; Henry Ogle, gentleman; Thomas Ogle, shipwright; Robert Ogle, barber chirurgeon; and Ralf Ogle, smith.

On 15 May 1713 the Newcastle Merchant Adventurers took proceedings against Cuthbert Ogle, confectioner, for presuming to keep open shop and sell divers wares and merchandise, as well groceries as mercers goods by retail, having only a glass window before the shop. Ogle gave the answer: 'That if he could make a profit, he would not only sell figs, but sugars also, and that after the figs he had were sold, he would order to London for twenty barrels more'. The Merchants Court was so incensed at this that it ordered that no brother of their fellowship should buy of the said Cuthbert Ogle, his wife, servant, or agent, 'any wet or dry sweetmeats, comfits, or other confectionary goods whatsoever, until the said Cuthbert Ogle shall first make his submission to the satisfaction of the Company' (SS. 93, pp.xlii, 248, 249).

OGLE—FREEHOLDERS.

1628. Lancelot Ogle of Burrodon, gent; Lancelot Ogle of Darrishall, gent; Cuthbert Ogle of Kirkley, gent; Marke Ogle of Kirkley, gent; Marke Ogle of Carter Moore, gent; Thomas Ogle of Tritlington, esq; John Ogle of Cawsey Park, esq; Henry Ogle of Eglingham, gent; Thomas Ogle of Hareopp, gent.

1639. Marke Ogle of Kirkley, gent; Lancelott Ogle of Burroden, gent; Lancelott Ogle of Darreshall, gent; Marke Ogle of Kirkley, gent; Marke Ogle of Cartermoore, gent; Henry Ogle of Eglingham, gent; Christopher Ogle of Harup, gent.

1698. Mark Ogle of Carter Moore, gent.

1710. Edwd Ogle of Longhurst; Henry Ogle of Eglingham, esq; Mark Ogle of Carter Moor; Francis Ogle of Grislee; Tho. Ogle of Carham, clerk; Geo. Ogle of Farnham; Edwd Ogle of Rothbury; Henry Ogle of Burradon; James Ogle of Beadnell; Wm Ogle of Earsdon Hill; Wm Ogle of Wooler; Tho. Ogle of Kirkleywesthall; John Ogle of Bavington, esq.

1715. Tho. Ogle of Old Felton; Edw. Ogle of Ogle; Robt Ogle, esq., of Eglingham; Wm Ogle of Bullers Green; Wm Ogle of Wooler for Humbleton; Henry Ogle of Hareup; John Ogle, esq., of Newcastle for Bavington; Nath. Ogle, esq., of Kirkley; Wm Ogle, esq., of Causey Park; Geo. Ogle of Harnham; Franc. Ogle of Lancet; Edward Ogle of Rothbury.

1721. Nath. Ogle, esq., for Lonbenton; Nath. Ogle of Kirkley, esq; Henry Ogle of Cawsey Park, esq; Robert Ogle of Eglingham, esq.

1734. Francis Ogle, Ogle, for Glanton.

1748. Thomas Ogle, clerk, Carham, for tithes of Carham; Cuthbert Ogle, Newcastle, for Snukebank; James Ogle, Rothbury; Mark Ogle, Sandyford.

1774. Mark Ogle, Sandyford; Newton Ogle, D.D., Kirkleyhouse; Robert Ogle, esq., Alnwick, for Eglingham.

1826. John Saville Ogle, clerk, Kirkley; James Ogle, North Seaton, for Morpeth; Robert Ogle, esq., Eglingham.

OGLE—BIBLIOGRAPHY

Ogle and Bothal or 'a History of the Baronies of Ogle, Bothal and Hepple, and of The Families of Ogle and Bertram, who held possession of those baronies and other property in the County of Northumberland and elsewhere; showing also how the property descended into other hands; to which is added Accounts of Several Branches of Families bearing the name of Ogle settled in other Counties and Countries; with appendices and illustrations compiled from ancient records and other sources'. By sir Henry A. Ogle, baronet. Privately printed, Newcastle upon Tyne 1902.

Ogle of Ogle and Bothal. *HN.* ii, I, pp.378-394 with pedigree; Dugdale, *Baronage of England,* II, pp.262-264; Visitation of *circa* A.D.1480-1500, *SS.* 144, p.55; Visitation of A.D.1575, *SS.* 146, pp.88-89.

Complete Peerage, vol.X. Barons Ogle.

Lord Ogle and Ogle of Causey Park; *Visitation of Northumberland 1615,* ed. Joseph Foster, Newcastle upon Tyne, n.d., p.94.

Ogle of Causey Park; *HN.* ii, II, p.135 with pedigree; *J. C. Hodgson's MS pedigrees* I, 77; IV, 24; B. 68, 218.

Ogle of Bebside; *HN.* ii, II, p.276 with pedigree; *NCH.* IX, p.294 with pedigree; *J. C. Hodgson's MS pedigrees* VII, 47.

Ogle of Burradon; *NCH.* IX, p.52 with pedigree; *J. C. Hodgson's MS pedigrees* III, 138; VII, 45; *Visitation of Northumberland 1615,* ed. Joseph Foster p.95.

Ogle of Choppington; *HN.* ii, II, p.365 with pedigree.

Ogle of Kirkley; *NCH.* XII, p.501 with pedigree; *J. C. Hodgson's MS pedigrees* I, 213; II, 114.

Ogle of Old Felton; *NCH.* VII, p.379 with pedigree.

Ogle of Eglingham; *NCH.* XIV, p.395 with pedigree; *J. C. Hodgson's MS pedigrees* I, 255, lxiv, lxxi.

Ogle of Berwick-on-Tweed; *J. C. Hodgson's MS pedigrees* A.216.

Ogle of Newcastle upon Tyne; *J. C. Hodgson's MS pedigrees* C.580; VII, 49.

Newcastle upon Tyne Records Committee, vol.VII. pp.163-190 Ogle Charters.

The Brumell Collection of Charters in *AA2.* XXIV, pp.115-123; there is a considerable number of charters in this collection which deal with the Ogles of Causey Park, Tritlington and Bebside.

OGLE—NOTES

1. In the compilation of this account of the Ogle family, sir Henry Ogle's book on *Ogle and Bothal* has been of considerable use but almost every item of information taken from that source has had to be carefully checked. Many of the dates have been wrongly transcribed, some perhaps by inadequate proof reading, and too much has been taken for granted of the early pedigrees of the 16th century.

2. Some account has been given of all branches of the family that are known or presumed to have been descended from the Ogles of Northumberland. As can be seen from the long section on OTHER OGLES there are many Ogles that cannot be firmly attached to any of the known branches of the family. This section could have been made very much longer if every known person of the name of Ogle had been included. Many have been omitted where they had no known relatives. Such is Emmeric Ogle, litster, buried at St John's, Newcastle, 7 September 1595; he had both an unusual Christian name and an unusual occupation, for a lister was a reader, no doubt a useful occupation at a time when few could read or write.

3. Dr A. M. C. Forster of Burradon has again proved herself to be a mine of information about Roman Catholic families, and the section on the Ogles of Dissington is largely made up of information she has collected from many sources.

LISLE

THE family of Lisle first appears in Northumberland in the middle of the 12th century. In Latin documents of that time the name appears as de Insula, but when the French language took the place of Latin the name became de l'Isle, later anglicised to Lisle. We cannot say for certain from what island the name is derived but the probability is that it was the Isle of Wight. By a charter probably of the time of William II, Hugh de Insula son of William son of Stur of the Isle of Wight, gave to the abbey of Marmoutier the tithe of Torlavilla which he held by hereditary right (*Harl. Soc.* 103, p.99). The immediate ancestors of the Northumberland family came from Lincolnshire. At the time of the Lindsay survey 1115 x 1118 a Robert de Insula held lands in Ludborough and Fotherby in Lincolnshire. This Robert de Insula married shortly after 1116 Albreda widow of Berenger de Toeny, and between 1122 and *c.*1137 with his wife gave lands in Scrampston in Yorkshire to the abbey of St Mary's at York.

LISLE OF EAST WOODBURN, PAR. CORSENSIDE

IN Northumberland the family held Woodburn in the Umframville lordship of Redesdale; Chipchase and Whittle in the Umframville barony of Prudhoe; East Matfen, Fenwick, Thornton, Angerton, Heddon and Brunton in the Bolbec barony of Styford; Newton Hall in the Bailliol barony of Bywell; and South Gosforth in the barony of Whalton.

The first member of the Northumberland family on record is William de Insula who is recorded in the *Pipe Roll* for 1159 as rendering an account for £40 which was accounted for by Robert son of Sawin. *Circa* 1142 x 1165 Walter de Bolebeck, baron of Styford, 'restored and granted and confirmed in fee and inheritance to William de Insula my man and to his heirs, to hold of me and my heirs, that land that my father gave to him for his service'; the lands so confirmed were East Matfen, Fenwick, Angerton, Thornton, Heddon and Brunton, and the service of Ernald son of Adelin with Hawkwell and Bearl, and Insula is described as a knight (*NDD.* p.120, No. 1; *NCH.* VI, p.222 and p.250 with some errors and omissions and with wrong reference; *HN.* ii.I. p.167, 2b).

Between 1153 and 1165 William de Insula notified all his 'lords and friends French and English and men' that with 'my heir William and my wife Cecilia and my sons' he granted 'to the church of Christ of Lund and the canons therein serving God' a knight's fee in Becham. Amongst the witnesses are 'Cecelia my wife and my sons Robert de Insula and Thomas de Insula' and 'Ralph my kinsman' (*NDD.* p.133). Another monastic grant by William de Insula was to St Mary of Blida (Blyth); this was a grant of 'all his tithe in Apelbia and in Swalecliva and in Ingeham in his crops and cattle and in horses and calves and sheep and lambs and in wool and swine and cheeses with the consent of his wife Cecelia and of all his sons whose names are these—William, Othuel, Robert, Richard, the poor' (? *puer*, the boy, later named Henry).

William de Insula died before 1166, having been predeceased by his eldest son William. His heir was his second son Othuel, who confirmed the grant to Blyth 'as his father William de Insula gave the same in frankelmoin, namely all the demesne tithes in Apelbeia and in Salecliva and in Ingeham, his sons Robert, Othewel, William, Richard, Henry, assenting'. It has been assumed that the expression 'his sons —assenting' refers to the sons of Othuel, but it must be taken as a recital of the assent of the sons of William de Insula, the original grantor (*NDD.* p.134, No. 42; *HN.* ii. I, p.167; *NCH.* VII, p.255).

In 1166 Walter de Bolebec, baron of Styford, reported to the king that Ot. de Insula held of him of the new feoffment, 1½ knights' fees. In the barony of Whalton, Otui de Insula held a third part of a knight's fee of the new feoffment from Walter son of William. No returns were made at this time for the baronies of Prudhoe and Bywell, and Redesdale being a regality no return was expected in respect of it. It is not even certain that the Insulas held Woodburn in Redesdale as early as this. *Circa* 1163-1165 Walter son of William granted South Gosforth to Othewir de Insula 'as his right' (*NDD.* p.121, No. 3; *HN.* ii, I, p.168, No. 3b). Bernard de Bailliol confirmed to Othewer de Insula and his heirs East Newton and 40 acres of demesne lands in Overton (? Ovington) in exchange for Blackheddon, to hold as half a knight's fee. This deed has been assigned to Bernard de Bailliol I, but it is more likely to have been given by Bernard de Bailliol II *circa* 1167 x 1182. One of the witnesses, Joel de Corbridge, occurs as reeve of Corbridge in 1158, 1163 and 1170 and had been succeeded before 1198 by his son John. Another witness, Odinel de Umfranville, if he can be identified as the second of that name, died in 1181. Other witnesses are Walter de Insula and William son of Walter (*NDD.* p.120, No. 20; *NCH.* VI, p.122, note 4 with some small inaccuracies; *HN.* ii. I, p.168, No. 3c). Otuwi de Insula accounts for one mark in the *Pipe Roll* for 1178. He was dead by 1187 when Robert de Insula rendered account to the sheriff of 40s. for having recognition after the death of his uncle of the vills of Angerton and Heddon against Walter de Bolebec; the entry is carried forward to 1188 where a statement is added that he is dead (*i.e.* the uncle) and his heir (*i.e.* Robert) under age; the fine is entered as unpaid in the *Pipe Roll* for 1190, 1191, 1195 and 1196 and was finally paid in 1197.

Robert de Insula was heir to his brother William who had held the manor of Angerton in demesne of the enfeoffment of Walter de Bolebeck 'the old'. In 1248 Hugh de Veer, earl of Oxford, claimed the manor of Angerton against Hugh de Bolebeck and then stated that after William de Insula's death 'because he died without an heir of himself' the manor had been seised by Walter de Bolebeck; and afterwards came one Robert de Insula, William's brother and heir, and impleaded Walter de Bolebeck of the said manor in the court of king Richard so that by fine made between the parties the manor remained to Walter and his heirs for ever for an exchange which Walter made to Robert in other his lands (*Nd Pleas, Assize Roll* No. 871). The entry *Rodbertus de Insula et uxor ejus Agnes* in the Durham *Liber Vitae* probably refers to this Robert de Insula. Robert de Insula confirmed the grant of William de Insula his brother of one carucate of land in Thornton to God and the blessed Mary and the master of the Knights of the Temple of Solomon of Jerusalem in England in pure alms for one priest to celebrate daily in the chapel of Thornton, as the charter of the said William testified (*NDD.* p.124, No. 8). This was the land later called Temple Thornton. It was probably this William de Insula who gave a toft and land in Thornton to the prior and convent of Hexham (*HN.* iii, II, p.167). Walter son of William, baron of Whalton *c.*1174-82 granted to Robert de Insula and his heirs, Gosforth by its right bounds together with the monastery and mill except the portion of Rodbert de Neuham which Ernisius had held; he was to hold in fee and by hereditary right in consideration of the grantee's homage and for the performance of a third part of the service of a knight within the county and ward of fifteen days in the New Castle (*NDD.* p.121, No. 4). Walter de Insula and Hugh de Insula who were two of the witnesses were perhaps cousins of the grantee.

Walter de Insula held lands at Newtown in Coquetdale and his lord Robert de Umframville, after the death of his father, had given him a further 25 acres of land. This must have been shortly after 1181 when Robert de Umframville's father Odinel died. Walter de Insula gave the 25 acres to the prior and monks of Durham. Sometime after this Thomas, prior of Durham, gave a perpetual lease of the land to Thomas de Insula for an annual rent of one mark silver for all services. Robert son of Roger, baron of Warkworth (d.1214), gave to Durham Priory the chapel of St Mary Magdalene outside the vill of Warkworth with certain lands and as an endowment to the chapel Reginald son of Thomas de Insula gave all the lands which they held in Newtown next Harbottle (*SS.* 58, p.3n.; *NCH.* XV, p.445; *NCH.* V, p.121).

Richard de Camvill and his wife Helewys who was one of the daughters and coheiresses of Walter son of William granted (or confirmed) to Robert de Insula about 1185, Gosforth except a half carucate held by Robert de Newham; the lands were to be held by Robert as freely as his ancestors had held of Walter son of William (*NDD.* p.122, No. 5). The grant was confirmed by Henry II when the service for Gosforth was stated to be a third of a knight's fee (*Ib.*, No. 6). This grant and confirmation have been taken to imply that Robert de Insula married a daughter of Richard de Camvill, but there is no evidence for this. This vill of South Gosforth was later, about 1197, given by Robert de Insula to Otuel his son in free marriage with Isabel Fauconberg. This must have been a child marriage as Robert himself was still under age in 1188. Isabel Fauconberg may have been the person of that name on whom William Foliot by fine dated 28 January 1197 settled in free dower the manor of Albury in Oxfordshire (*NDD.* p.123n.).

Robert de Insula must have died 1206 x 1208, as before

1208 his son and heir Otuel was a witness to a grant of lands by Thomas de Oviggeham, parson, to the chantry of St Mary in Ovingham (*NCH.* XII, p.73). Before 1214 Otuel de Insula witnesses a grant by Hugh de Bolebek to Blanchland abbey (*NCH.* VI, p.314n.). In 1219 he was charged 10 marks in the *Nova Oblata* (*Pipe Roll*). As Otterwer de Insula *c.*1200-1227 he witnesses a confirmation by Richard de Umfranvill to Gilbert Batail of land in Hartside (*NDD.* p.210, No. 75). Between 1214 and 1240 he had a quit claim from John son of Robert, baron of Whalton, of scutage of Gosforth, which Othuer held of him, and of suit of court of Whalton, except that if the king's writ be brought in the said court and the proceedings carried to a verdict, Othuer, his heirs or assigns were to be of the verdict, and similarly in proceedings carried to a verdict concerning any robber (*NDD.* p.124, No. 9). He is described as lord of Gosforth in an undated covenant which he made with Robert de Newham (*Ib.*, No. 10). As sir Otower de Insula, knight, on 21 January 1241 he settled on his daughter Juliana and her husband Michael de Bayfeld a carucate of land in Gosforth and Troughen. The latter place is in Redesdale and this is the earliest record of lands held by the Insulas in that regality (*NDD.* p.124, No. 11). In 1242 the lands which he held in the barony of Styford were Bearl, Thornton, Brunton, Fenwick, East Matfen, Hawkwell and two carucates in Kirkharle by the service of 1¼ knights' fees of the old feoffment (*NCH.* VI, p.250; *SS.* 66, p.286). The inquisition taken after his death, and dated 14 October 1250, records that he had died seised of nothing held in *capite*; he held Gosforth of the heirs of Egii son of John; Newton of sir John de Bayllol; Bearl, Thornton, Brunton, Fenwick and Matfen of Hugh de Bollebec; his heir was Robert de Insula aged 28 years (*HN.* ii. I, p.168, No. 4b).

Otuel de Insula had an uncle called Otuel for at Hilary Term 1202/3, a day was given to the master of the knighthood of the Temple and Otuel de Insula in a plea of service which Otuel brings against the same master concerning the fourth part of the town of Thornton; Otuel appointed his uncle Otuel as his attorney (*Nd Pleas*). Otwel died shortly before 1269 for at the assizes held in that year it is recorded that 'from Robert himself the right of possessing the aforesaid lands (of South Gosforth) in his own separate estate descended to a certain Otuel as his son and heir, and from Otuel to a certain Hugh as his son and heir, and from Hugh who died without an heir of his body to the Robert who is now the complainant, as brother and heir' (*SS.* 88, p.191). Sometime about 1240-1250 Robert de Insula married Ada sister of Nicholas Corbet, her dower being eight bovates of land in Lanton, par. Kirknewton (Hodgson *MSS notebook S.* p.171).

Before the middle of the 13th century the senior line of the Insulas descended from sir Otwel de Insula are particularly identified with East Woodburn in the lordship of Redesdale, whilst a cadet line deriving from sir Otwel's younger brother sir Peter held the manor of Chipchase in the Umframville barony of Prudhoe until the middle of the 14th century when it passed by marriage to the Herons (*See* LISLE OF CHIPCHASE).

In the return made for Redesdale in 1242 there is no mention of any lands being held by the Insulas in that lordship (*Book of Fees*).

Circa 1272-1283 Robert de Insula of Woodburn granted to John son of Nicholas de Insula, his son, and the heirs of Ida his wife in free marriage, the annual rent of £16 out of the lands which Richard del Hay then held of the grantor in South Gosforth, the witnesses to the grant being sir Robert de Insula of Chipchase, sir Robert de Insula of Welton and sir Peter de Fauden (*NDD*. p.125, No. 12). The date suggested for this grant is perhaps too late, for the grandson John de Insula was aged 26 in 1300 and therefore born about 1274. By a deed dated when Robert de Hampton was sheriff of Northumberland, November 1272-1274, sir Robert de Insula made a covenant with his sister Juliana widow of Michael Bayfelt, whereby Juliana released to Robert and his heirs all her right in the vills of South Gosforth and Troughen (*Ib*. Nos. 13 and 14). In 1292 John de Herle had a cause against Robert de Insula about a messuage in Troughen (*HN*. ii, I, p.27n.). In 1293 Robert claimed at the assizes at Newcastle certain privileges under the Statute *Quo Warranto* (*Ib*., p.173). Before 1296 Robert de Insula of Chipchase granted to Robert de Insula of Woodburn, his 'kinsman', for himself and his heirs and their tenants of Woodburn, of marl in his moor of Ray to be taken at their pleasure and will (*Ib*., p.126, No. 15). About 1299 sir Robert de Insula, 'lord of Woodburn', granted to John de Insula son of Nicholas de Insula his heir, all his lands in Northumberland and Redesdale, rendering 40 marks yearly to the grantor during his life (*Ib*., No. 16). Hodgson in his pedigree of the Lisles of Woodburn makes John son of Nicholas nephew of sir Robert, instead of grandson. Sir Robert may have resided at times on his manor of East Newton for he had a licence from Hugh, prior of Durham, to have an oratory there (*NCH*. VI, p.123), and for the 1296 Subsidy he was assessed on goods at Newton. He served as sheriff of Northumberland in 1264 and died about 1300 when his grandson and heir, John de Lisle was aged 26. John was constable of Newcastle 1303/4 (*HN*. iii, II, p.301). He was already a knight as he is described as such when he witnesses a deed of Simon de Welteden (*NCH*. X, p.317n.). He is described as sir John del Isle of Woodburn, knight, as a witness to a conveyance of 2 May 1321 (*Ib*., p.421n.). Sir John died 30 March 1350 (*Genealogist* NS. XXVI, p.194), and an inquisition taken after his death found that he held in his demesne as of fee on the day he died, tenements in Salcliff and Appleby, co. Lincoln, in chief, and in Thornton, Gosforth, East Newton, Bearl, Broomhope, Woodburn and Hawkwell in Northumberland; Robert de Lyle his son and heir forthwith after his death entered upon the same (*NDD*. p.127, No. 17).

Sir John de Lisle had a younger brother Peter de Lisle, a canon of Bole, sub dean of York, archdeacon of Carlisle and Coventry; on 19 June 1311 this Peter de Lisle had a grant of the right of hunting in Hexhamshire from archbishop Greenfield (*NCH*. III, p.24).

The son and heir, Robert, was aged 50 at his father's death. On 25 April 1367 Robert de Insula of Woodburn gave to Robert his 'kinsman', son and heir of Robert de Insula the grantor's son, and to Mary his wife, all his lands in the vill of Kirkharle and Broomhope (*NDD*. p.127, No. 18). The heir's wife was Mary daughter and coheiress of sir Aymer de Athol, and through this marriage the Lisles eventually acquired the manor of Felton. Robert de Lisle the grandfather died 29 June 1367. His younger son Thomas de Lisle succeeded to the Lincolnshire manor of Salcliff, but when he died *s.p.* in 1392 his heir was his nephew sir Robert Lisle aged 30 years and more; actually the heir was 37 years old. In 1417/8 Robert Johnson of Redesdale released to sir Robert his rights

in the lands, vill and territory of Temple Thornton (*NDD*. p.127, No. 19). Sir Robert was sheriff of Northumberland in 1414. Hodgson makes the statement that he died *s.p.* but 'before his death passed his manor of Felton to Thomas Lisle his younger brother's son, who was his cousin and heir'. This statement is inaccurate; sir Robert Lisle succeeded to the manor of Felton on the death of his wife's brother-in-law sir Ralph de Eure, and when he himself died 19 March 1425/6 it was found that Thomas Lisle was his kinsman and heir, being 'son of John de Lisle, son of the said Robert, aged 13 years on the feast of St Barnabas, the apostle, last past'. John Lisle the son had died 8 October 1422 in his father's lifetime, seised of the manor of Salcliff. Proof of age of 'Thomas Lisle, son and heir of John Lisle, son of Robert Lisle, knight, deceased, and kinsman and heir of the said Robert', was taken in the king's castle of Newcastle upon Tyne on 1 February 1434/5. The jurors found that Thomas was born at Nafferton and baptised in the parish church of Ovingham, and was aged 21 years on the feast of St Barnabas, apostle, last past—11 June 1434 (*AA*2. XXII, p.126).

On 12 March 1450/1 John Swynburn evidently acting as trustee conveyed to Thomas Lisle, esquire, for life, the manor and lordship of Newtonhall, and all lands which he had of the gift of the said Thomas in the vills of Bearl, East Matfen, Thornton, Callerton, Hawkwell and Kirkharle and in Woodburn and Woodburnhead with remainders successively to Robert Lyle, esquire, in tail male; William Lysle brother of Robert and his heirs male; Roger Lysle brother of William and his heirs male; Thomas Lysle brother of Robert, William and Roger and his heirs male; with final remainder to Thomas Lysle father of Robert, William, Roger and Thomas. The conveyance was made at Newtonhall which appears to have been the chief residence of the Lisles at this time (*NDD*. p.128, No. 21; *NCH*. VI, p.124n; *HN*. ii, I, p.169, evid. 10a). On 2 June 1472 Thomas Lyel, lord of Felton, with his son and heir Robert and Robert's son and heir Humphrey granted part of the forest of Weldon to the prior and convent of Brinkburn (*NCH*. VII, p.244n.).

Thomas Lisle's son and heir Robert died in his father's lifetime and Thomas was succeeded by his grandson Humphrey, who was knighted in Scotland in 1497 and became sheriff of Northumberland in 1506. On 30 April 1509 he was in prison in London for misdemeanours in the late reign and was exempted by name from a general pardon given on that date. He was released from imprisonment before the end of the year on being able to find sureties. In November 1512 he was a debtor to the Crown. He was taken prisoner by the Scots at the battle of Flodden on 9 September 1513 and after his release was appointed to the commission of the peace for Northumberland, 14 March 1515/6. It is probable that he was the Humphrey Lisle appointed gentleman usher to the king in 1516. Thomas, lord Dacre, complained to the king's council that sir Humphrey had committed many 'injuries, wrongs and misdemeanours' against the prior of Brinkburn and his brethren 'as well as taking their goods and chattels as imprisoning of their servants and tenants setting them in the stocks wrongfully, as also putting the vicar of Felton, being a canon of Brinkburn, from his cure'. Dacre asked that sir Humphrey and his sons should appear before a commission and find sureties, or else that they may be proclaimed the king's rebels for their disobedience, and further punished

LISLE of EAST WOODBURN, par. CORSENSIDE

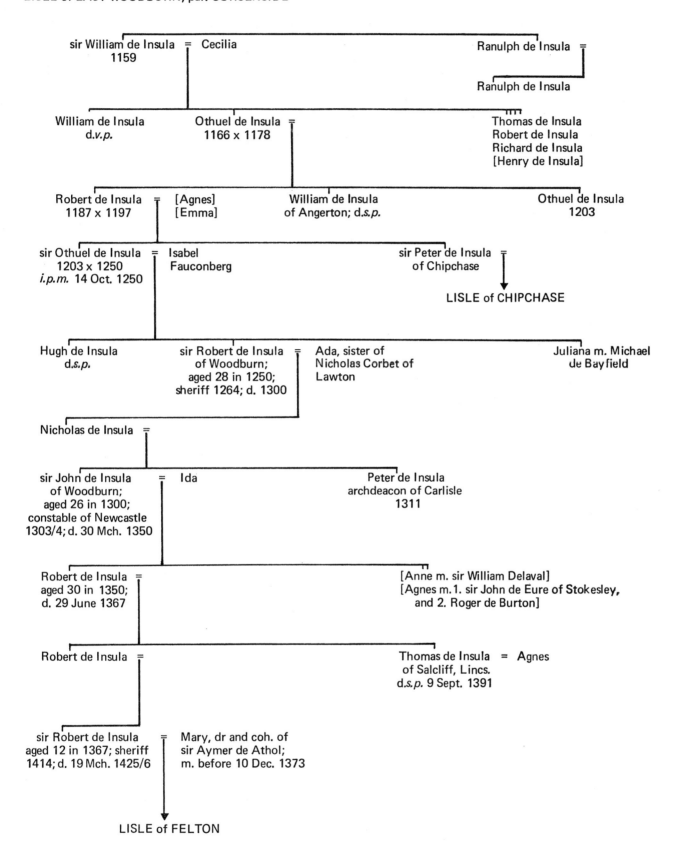

so as may be an example to others in these parts'.

The inquisition taken at Rothbury 17 November 1516 after the death of sir Humphrey Lisle found that he died seised of the manor of Felton, held of Edward Burro, knt, as of his manor of Mitford; the manors of Bearl, Hawkwell, Thornton, Buteland, Redesmouth, South Gosforth, East Newton, Matfen and Kirkharle held of the earl of Westmoreland and not of the king, as of his manor of Bywell; lands in Broomhope and Woodburn in the liberty of Redesdale held of George Taylboys, knt, as of his manor of Harbottle; he died 30 July then last past; William Lyle, knt, is son and heir, aged 30 years and more (*NDD*. p.129, No. 28). The jurors were wrong in stating that Buteland and Redesmouth were in the manor (*i.e.* barony) of Bywell as they were in fact in the barony of Prudhoe but adjoining Redesdale.

Besides his eldest son, William, sir Humphrey seems to have had several younger sons. One of these was probably the Thomas Lisle to whom Margaret, lady Ogle, leased the manor of Horton on 6 July 1515 (*NCH*. IX, p.268). In the following year Margaret Delaval, widow, charged William Lysle of Ogle, *miles*, Thomas Lisle of Ogle, gent., and Otewell Lisle of Temple Thornton, gent., with forcibly entering a close at Horton and depasturing cattle thereon (*de Banco Roll. AA*3. VI, p.85). The description of William Lisle as *miles* serves clearly to identify him as sir Humphrey's eldest son and heir, sir William Lisle. Surely Thomas and Otewell were younger sons of sir Humphrey. Thomas was probably the ancestor of the Lisles of Elyhaugh and the Lisles of Hazon. Another son of sir Humphrey was probably Percival Lisle of Burradon (*see* LISLE OF BARMSTON).

Sir William Lisle, like his father, is mainly known from his services on the Borders against the Scots in war time, and his unruly behaviour at home in times of peace. He was rewarded in 1519 for his services in Scotland, and a few years later, when he was deputy captain of Wark castle, with only 100 soldiers he repulsed an attack made on the castle, 2 November 1253, by the duke of Albany with 3000 Frenchmen and 500 Scots. In 1527 with his son Humphrey and about 40 armed men, sir William seised the gaol at Newcastle and liberated nine prisoners. On their way home they raided sir William Ellerker at Widdrington and carried off from thence 40 head of young cattle. Ellerker was at this time sheriff of Northumberland and had indicted Lisle for unlawful distress. Sir William Lisle and his son were apprehended and committed in ward to Pontefract castle but before the end of the year they had given bond and obtained their release. No sooner had they returned to Northumberland than they committed further offences and were sent to gaol in Newcastle. On 8 July 1527 it was reported that they had 'not only broken the prison wherein they were themselves, but also other prisons there, wherein was divers outlaws kept, some for felony, some for murder and treason. They fled and escaped into Scotland; and with them, at their issuing out of Newcastle, joined twenty other outlaws'. For some time the outlaws haunted the borders plundering at will, one of their largest raids being the burning of Humshaugh with 140 men. Rewards were offered for their apprehension, 100 marks for sir William and £40 for his son. Sir William Eure, the warden, writing from Harbottle castle on 27 October, stated that 'of late I did certify your grace of the demeanour of the county, and how oft I have demanded justice and redress

of the Scots for such offences and attempts as are committed and done by the surnames Armstrongs, Nixons and Crosiers, with whom sir William Lisle, and all other his adherents, are reset, and daily ride together, and commit burnings, murders, and hardships within the realm of England'. On 28 January 1527/8 the earl of Northumberland, warden general of the marches, reported that 'upon Sunday the 26th day of this present month of January, came William Lisle, Humphrey Lysle, William Shaftowe and other their adherents, in all the number of 18 persons, without any composition, covenant or comfort of me or any other to my knowledge, in my way coming from the high mass at the parish church of Alnwick in their linen clothes and halters about their necks, kneeling upon their knees in very humble and lowly manner submitted their selves to the king's highness mercy and your grace, knowledging their offences and requiring of his highness mercy and pardon, and if not they were ready to bide his execution of his most dread laws'. William and Humphrey Lisle, John Ogle, William Shaftowe and Thomas Fenwike, 'gentlemen of name and chief leaders of all the said rebels' were attainted of high treason. The earl of Northumberland writing to Henry VIII on 2 April 1528 states that he had 'proceeded in execution of justice against William Lyle and his other complices then remaining here in ward';—'the said William Lisle, Humfrey Lisle his son, John Ogle, William Shaftowe and Thomas Fenwike, gentlemen of name, and chief leaders of all the said rebels, for their deserts been attainted of high treason and had the judgment by me given to be hanged, drawn and quartered according to their demerits, and so was executed accordingly. The said Humfrey Lisle only reserved after his judgment was given, whom according to your most gracious pleasure I have sent by this bearer to your Tower of London, and the heads and quarters of them so executed. I have done to be set up in sundry most eminent and open places and where most assembly and recourse of people is, to the terrible and dreadful example of all other such like offenders' (*HN*. ii, III, p.380). In another letter of the same date he says 'And the other young son of the said William Lysle I detain here with me to such time as I shall be advertised of the further mind and pleasure of the king's highness and your graces concerning the said young Lysle'. Humphrey and apparently his younger brother were pardoned on account of their youth. Humphrey's pardon is all the more surprising for whilst about thirteen years old he had been concerned in the murder of Richard Lighton, a canon of Brinkburn. At this time the tithe corn of Acton was held by the prior and convent of Brinkburn, but sir William Lisle had taken possession for two years illegally against the will of the canons. In 1521 the canons asserted themselves and occupied the tithe corn and when sir William heard of this 'he sent his son and servant (called Jowsey) to turn them out; on which they killed him (the canon) with their swords (Welford II, p.64). The Lisles' estates were confiscated by the Crown but were later, 23 August 1536, restored to sir Humphrey. Even before the restoration of his estates sir Humphrey was in trouble with the authorities; at a wardens' court held at Newcastle on 28 July 1535 he was indicted for divers march treasons; hearing of the indictment the accused had fled and the earl of Northumberland had issued a proclamation against him (*Ib.*, II, p.148). 'Syr Vmffry Lyell, knight, Jarret Lyele, Thomas Lyle' head the Muster Roll for Felton in 1538.

Sir Humphrey Lisle died without legitimate children before 1542, and his widow Anne, who was a daughter of Ralph, 3rd lord Ogle, was in possession of her dower 28 April 1558. He had an illegitimate son Humphrey Lisle, who was father of William, George and Humphrey Lisle of Barnhill. Sir Humphrey's illegitimate son Humphrey was living at Dunstanburgh when he made his w.d. 27 November 1575. He is to be buried in the parish church of Embleton and leaves all his 'goods and chattels to be divided into three equal parts, whereof my wife Elizabeth shall have one equal part to her own proper use, the second part to my sons Willm, George and Umpheril equally divided among them at their lawful age. The other part of my goods I bequeath to myne executors to be divided equally among them for payment of my debts and the discharge of my funeral expenses'. His wife Elizabeth is to have the house in Warkworth which he had bought. Mr John Horslye of Screnwood and Mr John Weighall in the county of York, esq., are 'to be tutors and have the governance and bringing up of my children and supervisors of my will during the nonage of my said children' (*Dur. Prob. Off.* by C.R.H.).

Sir Humphrey's heir, his brother Robert Lisle, on 20 February 1545/6 settled on himself in tail male, the manor of Felton and five-sixths of the manor of South Gosforth. When he died on 25 April 1554 he was in possession of these same lands, the remaining sixth part of South Gosforth together with an annuity of £8 out of Felton being held by his sister-in-law, Anne widow of sir Humphrey Lisle. Two brothers of Robert Lisle's, Lancelot and John, also had charges on the estates (*PSAN*3. VII, p.170). Lancelot was living at Gosforth 8 November 1559 when he and five others signed a bond to the earl of Northumberland for the personal appearance of Jarret Charlton of Howe Hill at Newcastle on 15 January next (Welford II, p.347). In 1562 he was one of the overseers of the watch to be held from the river Tyne to Hartford Bridge (Nicolson, *Leges Marchiarum*, p.290). It would seem that Newton Hall, Woodburn and all the other Lisle estates had by now been disposed of. Robert Lisle's son and heir, also named Robert 'was aged six years at Christmas last', 1553.

In 1562 Robert Lysle was one of the overseers of the three watches to be kept between Thistleyhaugh and Barton to be kept by the men of Felton and elsewhere (Nicolson, *Leges Marchiarum*, p.285). At the same time he was a commissioner for enclosures on the Middle Marches for the area 'between the waters of Coquet and Aln from Learchild to the sea' (*Ib.*, p.330). At a muster of horsemen of the Middle Marches taken on 26 March 1580 at the Mootlaw, six of 'Robert Lisle's tenants of Felton' were present (*CBP*. I, p.21). On 21 October 1583 sir John Forster, the lord warden, requested on behalf of Robert Lislie of Felton, esquire, a defendant in a suit before the Court of Wards and Liveries, that a commission may be appointed to receive Lislie's answer to his adversary's bill, or to hear and determine the suit (*Ib.*, p.112). He was presumably the Robert Lysley who was present at the Border meeting in July 1585 when lord Francis Russell was killed (*Ib.*, p.190). Among Mr Lysle's tenants from Felton who attended the muster of light horsemen from Coquetdale and Redesdale wards at Abberwick edge on 24 November 1595 were Lanc. Lysley and John Lisle (*CBP*. II, p.75).

On 17 January 1595/6 Robert Lisle for the continuance of his estates in the name of the Lisles and for the better promotion of his name, house and blood, made an elaborate entail of the manors of Felton and South Gosforth. Subject to his wife Catherine's life interest in the demesne lands, houses and mills of Felton, the manors were to be held by himself for life, with successive remainders to:

William Lisle, his son and heir apparent, in tail male.
Robert Lisle, his second son, in tail male.
John Lisle, his third son, in tail male.
John Lisle of Acton, his brother, in tail male.
James Lisle of Barmston, co. Durham, gent., in tail male.
John Lisle, brother of said James Lisle, in tail male.
Robert Lisle, another brother of said James Lisle, in tail male.
Ralph Lisle of Felton, gent.
William Lisle of Felton, gent.
William Lisle of Barnhill, gent.
George Lisle of Barnhill, gent.
Humphrey Lisle of Barnhill, gent.
Lancelot Lisle of Felton.

Robert Lisle obtained a licence 1 May 1609 to alienate the manor of South Gosforth with Coxlodge, which he had already mortgaged 1 April 1602, to Robert Brandling of Felling. He died about 1617 having been predeceased by his wife Catherine and his eldest son William. Catherine was a daughter of Cuthbert Carnaby of Halton (Harvey's vis. 1552). The heir was their second son, another Robert Lisle.

In 1629 the attorney-general brought a suit against Robert Lisle calling into question his title to the manor of Felton on account of the attainder of sir William Lisle a hundred years before. Depositions were taken in this suit from John Lisley of Acton, esquire, aged 75, Edward Lisley of Acton, gent., aged about 30 years, and many others; and on 19 April 1630 the defendant obtained a verdict.

Robert Lisle remained unmarried until he was not less than 65 years of age, and in 1655 he married Dorothy daughter of sir Thomas Horsley of Longhorsley. On 1 November 1655 'in consideration of a marriage recently solemnized' he settled on his wife the manor and lands of Felton, Elihaugh, Shothaugh, Turnerstead, Todstead, Catheugh etc. 'Robert Lisle, esq. of Felton, departed to the mercy of God, the 6th day of June, and was buried the 8th of the same instant June, in the year of God, 1659' (*Felton Registers*). He had no children, and notwithstanding the settlement of 17 January 1595/6 which had entailed his estates on his male heirs, he left them absolutely to his wife. Robert Lisle's will is dated 4 November 1657 'being old, yet of good and perfect mind and memory, God be thanked, considering the frailties and the uncertainty of the time of death, for the preventing of all suits and controversies that may arise touching my estate after my death'. He gives to his 'loving cousin Robert Lisle of Weldon in the said county of Northumberland, gentleman', the yearly rent of £40 out of the colliery and coal mine of Coxlodge so long as the rents, issues and clear profits of the colliery shall amount to £100; his cousin Robert is also to have the farmholds of Catheugh, Turnerstead and Todstead; another cousin, John Ripley of Pethfoot, gent., is to have the farmhold called Shothaugh; his servant Robert Walles is to have two closes adjoining to a place called Longdyke. Everything else he possessed is to go to his wife Dorothy. She married 23 February 1660/1 captain Edward Widdrington and their great grand daughter carried the manor of Felton by marriage to Thomas Riddell of Swinburne castle.

It has been accepted that the male representation of the family after the death of Robert Lisle in 1659 passed to Edward Lisle of Acton, son of John Lisle of Acton, Robert's uncle. This presupposes that Robert Lisle's younger brother John, mentioned in the settlement of 17 January 1595/6 had died without male issue. This cannot be taken as certain and it has been suggested that the Lisles of Elyhaugh were descended from this John Lisle (*see* LISLE OF ELYHAUGH, PAR. FELTON).

On 8 March 1578/9 a lease of the rectory of Felton was granted to Francis Harvey of Cressing Temple, Essex, esquire, for the use of William Ellerker son of Ralph Ellerker, deceased, and John Lysley son of Ann Ellerker, widow, late wife of the said Ralph Ellerker. Robert Lisle (d.1554) of Felton had married Anne daughter of John Hervey of Ickworth, Suffolk, and after Robert's death she married Ralph Ellerker. John Lysley was Robert Lisle's younger son, and was living at Acton, 31 January 1589/90 when he bought half of Acton from Anthony Felton. He made a settlement of his lands in Acton, 18 August 1629 and died in April 1640 (w.d. 26 March 1640). By his wife Agnes daughter of Gregory Ogle of Choppington, he had a son and heir Edward Lisle and a daughter Anne wife of William Carr of Eshot. Agnes Lysle wife of John Lysle of Acton, gent., by her w.d. 1 October 1601 appoints her 'well-beloved husband' John and her son Edward as executors and gives them all her goods and chattels; the inventory of her goods dated 19 November 1616 mentions that she died possessed of a lease for 21 years of the demesnes of Kirkharle, Greatlaw, Trewick and Offerton 'after the value of 100 marks a year' (*Dur. Prob. Off.* by C.R.H.). Robert Lorane of Choppington in his w.d. 6 February 1617/8 refers to John Lisle of Acton as his step father, and appoints John's son Edward Lisle, whom he calls brother as sole executor to his will; Robert Lisle of Weldon is a witness to the will (*Ib.*, p.234). Edward Lisle's name appears in the freeholder's lists of 1628 and 1639. By a deed dated 9 March 1660 he settled his lands in North Acton and Old Felton on his daughter Jane wife of Robert Manners of Longframlington. He had two other daughters, Catherine wife of Thomas Ogle and Dorothy wife of John Grey of Howick.

LISLE OF HAZON, PAR. SHILBOTTLE

BEFORE the middle of the 16th century a branch of the Lisle family was settled at Hazon, par. Shilbottle. In the Muster Roll for 1538 the only men from Hazon who were able in horse and harness were Thomas Lessell and Lancelot Lyle. When Robert Lisle of Hazon registered his pedigree at the herald's visitation in 1615 he claimed that his grandfather Thomas Lisle of Elyhaugh was son of (blank) Lisle, 2nd son of sir Humfrey Lisle, knight, the eldest son being sir John Lisle who married (blank) Harvy. He probably named his grandfather correctly but he was inaccurate in the earlier generations, for it was Robert Lisle of Felton, brother and heir of sir Humphrey Lisle (d. before 1554) who married Anne Hervey. When in 1596 Robert Lisle of Felton made the settlement of his estates with successive remainders to no less than thirteen relatives and kinsmen of the name of Lisle none of the Lisles of Elyhaugh or Hazon are mentioned. The

presumption is that they were very distant relatives. Now an earlier sir Humphrey Lisle (d.1516) had a younger son Thomas Lisle who was living 25 November 1529 in enjoyment of a rentcharge out of Newton Hall secured by a deed dated 4 January 1513/4 (*NCH.* VI, p.125). On 17 August 1549 Thomas Lisle of Elyhaugh purchased lands in Hazon, North Charlton and South Charlton from Roger Tocket of Tocket, Yorks. In 1550 Thomas Lisle was one of the 'gentlemen inhabitants within the Middle Marches'. A Thomas Lisle of Elyhaugh on 17 February 1559/60 took a 40 years' lease of lands in Hazon from Marmaduke Thirkeld at a rent of £10. 11s. 8d. per annum. According to the 1615 visitation pedigree Thomas Lisle's wife was Margaret daughter of Thomas Heron of Bockenfield. By his w.d. 3 June 1551 after directing that he is to be buried in the church of Felton, he leaves his office and farmhold lease in Hazon to his son Thomas, also mentioning his younger son John Lyell and other children. The younger son John Lyslie made his w.d. 18 September 1571 by which he gives the custody of his daughter Allison to his brother Umfrey Lisly. This must have been Umferay Lesley of Shilbottle who made his w.d. 7 July 1589; he is to be buried in the quire of the parish church of Shilbottle; Yssaibell Allesson and Ysaibell Cowlman (?) are each to have a quye; the rest of his goods he gives 'unto my wife and my daughter Elsaybeth, which two I make executrixes'; he was indebted to his daughter ten ewes and a hogg; the supervisors are to be the testators cousin George Alder of Hobberlaw and Wm Mydcalf. The inventory of Humferay Lisle's goods was exhibited 16 February 1589/90 and mentions 'my nephew Robert Lyle of Hazon is bound for them' (*Dur. Prob. Off.* by C.R.H.).

About 1561 the eldest son Thomas Lisle of Hazon killed his kinsman Richard Heron of Bockenfield for which crime he forfeited his lands being two husbandlands in Hazon. It was perhaps a tradition of this crime that sir David Smith mentions—'The common people have a tradition that the Lisles were very wicked people, and in the days of superstition they relate, that one of them dying, the horses which came with the hearse to take the corpse from Hazon, could not be forced by any means to draw the body, which at length was moved by the deceased's own coach horses. One other time one of this family murdered a person coming out of Felton church, and having fled, hid himself among the whins on Guyzance Moor, then unenclosed. A woman having been observed regularly to go that way was suspected of carrying him food, and being watched more closely, the place of his concealment was discovered by the friends of the man who had been killed, and they immediately resorting to the spot cut him to pieces there to avenge the death of their friend; the place is remembered to this day'.

In spite of the forfeiture, Thomas Lisle's descendants continued to own freehold lands in Hazon. Thomas Lisle had three sons Robert, John and Lancelot. During the early years of the 17th century, the earl of Northumberland, being the principal landowner in Hazon, was anxious that the common lands there should be divided. The earl's agent found that Robert Lisle was the principal objector to the enclosure. Writing to the earl on 22 January 1616/7 he complains that Lisle was 'a very wilful old man now he is lately dead, and the living come to his brother John Lysley, who is a plain honest man, and one that doth much desire your lordship's favour'. The 'wilful old man' had made a nuncupative will on 11

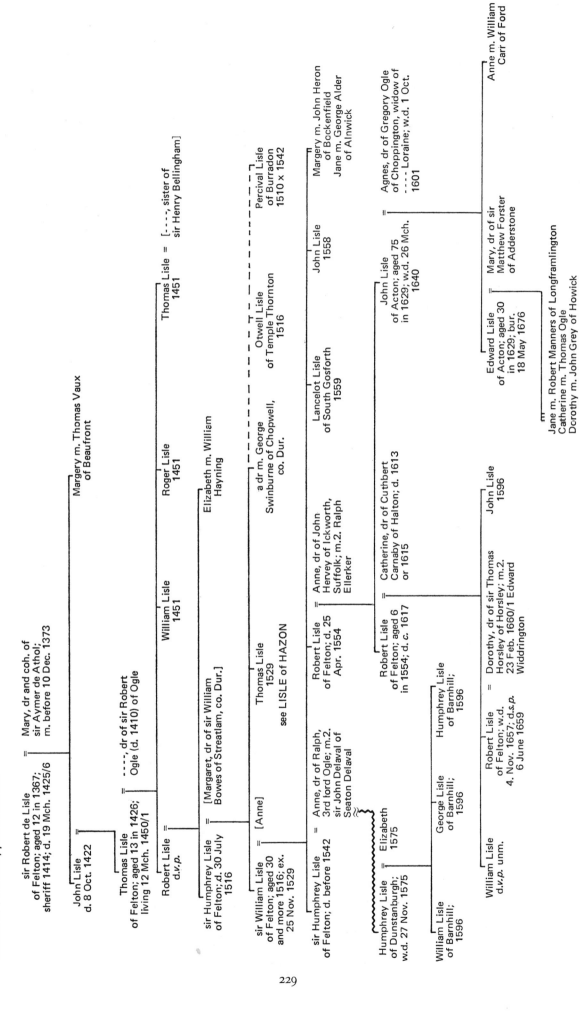

LISLE of HAZON, par. SHILBOTTLE

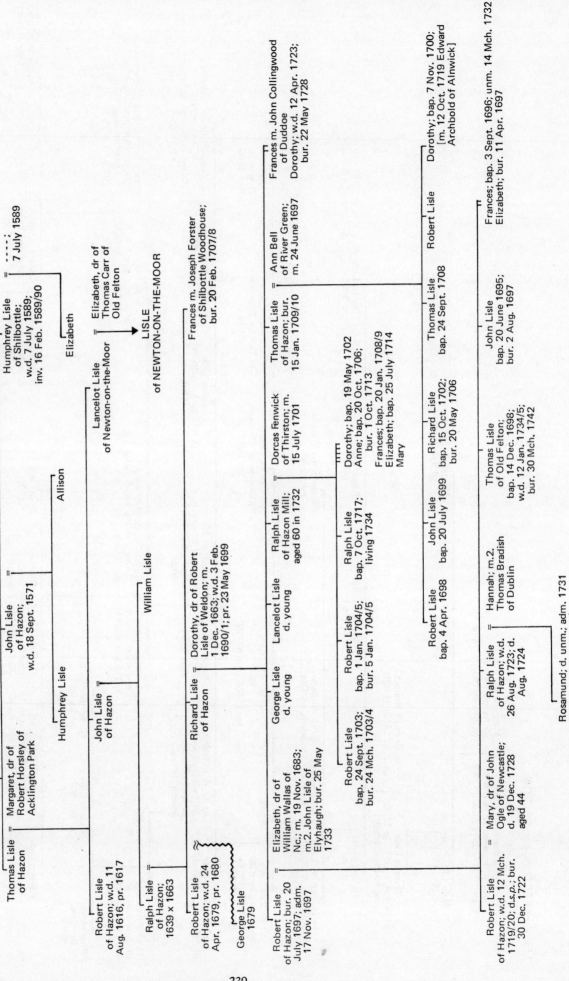

August 1616. He gives his lands in Thirston to William Lisle, younger son of his brother John Lisle, and the rest of his property to his great nephew Robert Lisle son of Ralph Lisle and grandson of John Lisle. To Margaret Lisle daughter of Lancelot Lisle of Newton-on-the-Moor, he leaves a horse 'and if Lancelot Lisleye, her father, and John Lisleye do think her to deserve more, then they in their discretion to mend the same'. He directs that his brother Lancelot Lisle is 'to endeavour to purchase Marmaduke Thirkeld's lands in Haison for the use of Robert son of Ralph Lisleye'. Administration of Robert Lisle of Hazon's personal estate was granted 15 November 1617 to his brothers John and Lancelot Lisle and to Robert Lisle son of the deceased's nephew Ralph Lisle. The personal estate was valued at £13. 18s.

John Lisle's son, Ralph Lisle, was a freeholder in Hazon in 1639. He was amerced in the sum of 3s. 4d. for not appearing at Alnwick manor court in 1661 to do suit and service for his lands in Hazon. Frances daughter of Ralph Lisle married as his second wife Joseph Forster of Shilbottle Woodhouse (b.ofm. 6 August 1670) and she by her w.d. 11 January 1702 leaves all her goods to her step-daughter, she paying to Ralph Lisle of Hazon, gent., £3, to Thomas Lisle of Newton-on-the-Moor £3 and to Frances wife of Ralph Storey of Abberwick £2 (NCH. II, p.101). Her step-son Ralph Forster of Elford appoints 'my kinsman Richard Lisle of Hazon' to be one of the trustees of his w.d. 19 March 1678/9 (Ib., p.102).

Ralph Lisle's son and successor Robert Lisle enlarged his property in Hazon by purchase of other lands there, 28 June 1669, from sir Henry St Quintin. By his w.d. 24 April 1679 Robert leaves his lands to his brother Richard's son Robert Lisle. To two other nephews, George and Lancelot he leaves legacies 'to bring them up with learning and trades'; Lancelot was apprenticed 25 February 1687 to Thomas Emerson of Newcastle, mercer, but both he and his brother George died in their minority. Robert Lisle's brother Richard Lisle had married Dorothy sister of Robert Lisle of Weldon. Dorothy was a widow when she made her w.d. 3 February 1690/1; her son Ralph Lisle is left to the tuition of her eldest son Robert Lisle; her son Thomas Lisle is left to the tuition of her sister Frances Lisle of Weldon; her daughters Frances and Dorothy Lisle are left to the tuition of her sister-in-law Mrs Frances Forster of Hartlaw. She also mentions in her will her son Lancelot Lisle. The will was proved 23 May 1699 by her daughter Frances wife of John Collingwood of Duddoe, the bondsmen being Thomas Lisle of Hazon, gent., and John Lisle of Elyhaugh, gent. (Dur. Prob. Off. by C.R.H.). Robert Lisle was buried in the chancel of Shilbottle church 20 July 1697 and administration of his personal estate was granted 17 November 1697 to Elizabeth Lisle, his widow. She was daughter of William Wallas of Newcastle, merchant, and on 19 November 1683 she married for her second husband John Lisle of Elyhaugh. Robert and Elizabeth Lisle's eldest son was Robert Lisle of Hazon who died in 1722 s.p. Their second son Ralph Lisle died two years later, leaving an only child, a posthumous daughter Rosamond, who died before 30 May 1734. The third son Thomas Lisle died unmarried at Old Felton in 1742.

Thomas Lisle by his w.d. 12 January 1734 leaves his 'real estate, if any, to Ralph Lisle, eldest son of my uncle, Ralph Lisle of Hazon', and then in trust for Frances and Elizabeth daughters of his said uncle Ralph (Neasham, Wills p.381).

Thomas Lisle had been concerned in the Jacobite Rising of 1715 and it was reported of him, 14 January 1718, that he had absconded or otherwise concealed himself. Thomas was right in believing that he would have no real estate to leave, for his brother Robert had died greatly in debt and his other brother Ralph had sold Hazon, 10 February 1723/4, to John Bacon of Staward. On 19 March 1725/6 a notice appeared in the *Newcastle Courant* to the effect 'That a commission issuing out of the High Court of Chancery will be executed between John Bacon, esq., complainant, and Thomas Lisle, and others, defendants, at the White Hart, Flesh Market, Newcastle, 24, 25, 26 March, inst., when and where the creditors of Robert Lisle of Hazon, gent., deceased, are desired to come and prove their several demands' (*PSAN*3. V. p.135). Robert Lisle's debts were the subject of a Chancery Suit of 1733; at one time, Robert had been indisposed for about 14 days and during that time had lodged in the house of Richard Strother of Alnwick, apothecary; 'several ointments, oils and other medicines used and prepared by the said Richard Strother in the cure of the said Robert Lisle' to the value of £3 were still unpaid for in 1733. In his last illness Robert had been attended by doctor Ogle of Kirkley who frequently visited him.

After the death of Thomas Lisle in 1742 it seems uncertain if there were any male heirs of his family. His uncle Ralph Lisle of Hazon Mill was aged 60 in 1732 and although Ralph had an eldest surviving son Ralph living in 1734, no descendants are known. For a cadet branch of the Lisles of Hazon *see* LISLE of NEWTON-ON-THE-MOOR.

LISLE OF NEWTON-ON-THE-MOOR, PAR. SHILBOTTLE

AT the Herald's Visitation of 1615, Lancelot Lisle of Newton-on-the-Moor registered his pedigree. He was a younger son of Thomas Lisle of Hazon by his wife Margaret daughter of Robert Horsley of Acklington Park. By his wife Elizabeth daughter of Thomas Carr of Old Felton, Lancelot Lisle then had three sons Ralf, George and John and a daughter Margaret. Ralf Lisle, the son and heir, married Ann daughter of David Crowe of Berwick, by whom he had a son Robert, aged 3 years in 1615, and a daughter Margaret. Annis daughter of David Craw was baptised at Berwick-on-Tweed 30 January 1588/9, but there is no record there of her marriage to Ralph Lisle.

A George Lisle, perhaps Lancelot Lisle's second son, was a freeholder at Newton-on-the-Moor in 1539 and was still living in 1643. Administration of the personal estate of a Lancelot Lisle of Newton-on-the-Moor was granted in 1650 to Joseph Heselrigge.

The Lisle lands at Newton became the property of George Lisle of Newton-on-the-Moor, who by his w.d. 15 December 1677 leaves them to his wife for life and then to his 'well-beloved nephew and sister's son Lancelot Strother'. George Lisle's wife was Susanna Adston of Alnwick whom he married at Felton 13 January 1656/7. The descendants of the nephew Lancelot Strother continued to own their lands in Newton until 1811.

231

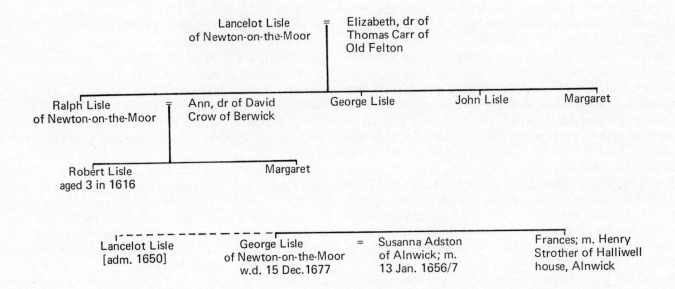

Lancelot Lisle of Newton-on-the-Moor = Elizabeth, dr of Thomas Carr of Old Felton

Ralph Lisle of Newton-on-the-Moor = Ann, dr of David Crow of Berwick | George Lisle | John Lisle | Margaret

Robert Lisle aged 3 in 1616 | Margaret

Lancelot Lisle [adm. 1650] | George Lisle of Newton-on-the-Moor w.d. 15 Dec. 1677 = Susanna Adston of Alnwick; m. 13 Jan. 1656/7 | Frances; m. Henry Strother of Halliwell house, Alnwick

LISLE OF ELYHAUGH, PAR. FELTON

ON 10 July 1573 Robert Lisle of Felton granted a 21 years lease of Elyhaugh to Lancelot Lisley of Hazon, brother of Robert Lyle of Hazon. It had originally been intended that Robert Lyle should be the lessee but he 'then stood in some danger about the suspicion of killing one —— Heron.' Elyhaugh was included in the estates settled by Robert Lisle of Felton on 17 January 1595/6 one of the remainder men being his third son John Lisle. In 1663 a John Lisle was rated for Elyhaugh and it has been suggested that he was the third and youngest son of Robert Lisle of Felton mentioned in the settlement of 1596. This identification is uncertain and the ancestry of the Lisles of Elyhaugh must therefore remain in doubt.

John Lisle (d.1672) had an only son and heir William Lisle who was buried at Felton 3 September 1683. Mrs Jane Lisle of Elyhaugh, buried at Felton 20 February 1710/1, was perhaps William's widow. William's only surviving son and heir, John Lisle, married Elizabeth daughter of William Wallas of Newcastle, widow of Robert Lisle of Hazon, by whom he had an only daughter Elizabeth who survived her father by two years and died unmarried in 1723. Elizabeth's heir at law was her father's youngest sister Elizabeth wife of Thomas Lisle of Weldon. John Lisle (d.1721) had by his w.d. 18 April 1720 settled his lands at Elyhaugh, Felton and Old Felton on his daughter Elizabeth for life and because he was 'extremely desirous that the estates should continue in the family of Lisle, who have for many generations enjoyed the same, I injoin and earnestly entreat my said daughter to marry and take to husband Robert, the eldest son of my late friend, Robert Lisle of Weldon, esq., or any other son of the said Robert Lisle.' Failing issue of his daughter Elizabeth, John Lisle leaves his estates to his sister Elizabeth who was already married to Thomas Lisle of Weldon. Further remainders are appointed to the testator's natural son John Lisle, late of Weldon, esq., deceased, and his heirs male; to William, second son of the said Robert Lisle, deceased; remainder to George Lisle, youngest son of Robert Lisle, deceased;

remainder to Robert Lisle, son of Thomas Lisle, late of Newton-on-the-Moor, gent., deceased; and to John Lisle, son of William Lisle, late of Long Framlington, gent., deceased. The testator leaves '£10 per annum to Dorothy Lisle of Hazon, the mother of my three natural children'.

Thomas Lisle of Weldon died in 1748 having survived his wife Elizabeth who had died in 1738. Elyhaugh and the other lands then passed to John Lisle of Morpeth, the illegitimate son of John Lisle (d.1721). By his w.d. 7 December 1756 John Lisle then of Morpeth gives his dwelling house at Morpeth to his wife Elizabeth for life, and after her death to his son Robert Lisle. John Lisle died in 1759 and must have been predeceased by his wife Elizabeth, for his widow Margaret proved his will in 1760 and was living at Morpeth 4 March 1762. John Lisle's only surviving son Robert was apprenticed 4 March 1762 to Thomas Airey of Newcastle, hostman, and died s.p. When he made his w.d. 12 May 1792 he was living at West Denton; he leaves his lands in trust for his wife for life and then to be equally divided between his nephews and nieces, the children of his sister Mary wife of William Coulson of Newcastle.

In spite of the elaborate entail of 1720 Elyhaugh had passed from the Lisle family in less than 80 years. Old Felton had been sold by Robert Lisle of Newcastle in his lifetime to Robert Lisle of Weldon.

LISLE OF WELDON, CHAP. BRINKBURN

FOR over three centuries a cadet branch of the Lisles of Felton owned Weldon Hall which had been part of the possessions of the prior and convent of Brinkburn. At the dissolution of the monasteries the messuage called Weldon hall and the land belonging to it, in the occupation of Thomas Lisle and of the yearly value of 26s. 8d. was granted by the Crown 9 March 1551/2 to sir John Horsley of Horsley. Thomas Lisle, the occupier of 1552, cannot be identified in the pedigree of the Lisles of Felton. On 21 December 1609 Tristram Lisle, gent., of Weldon hall, purchased from the

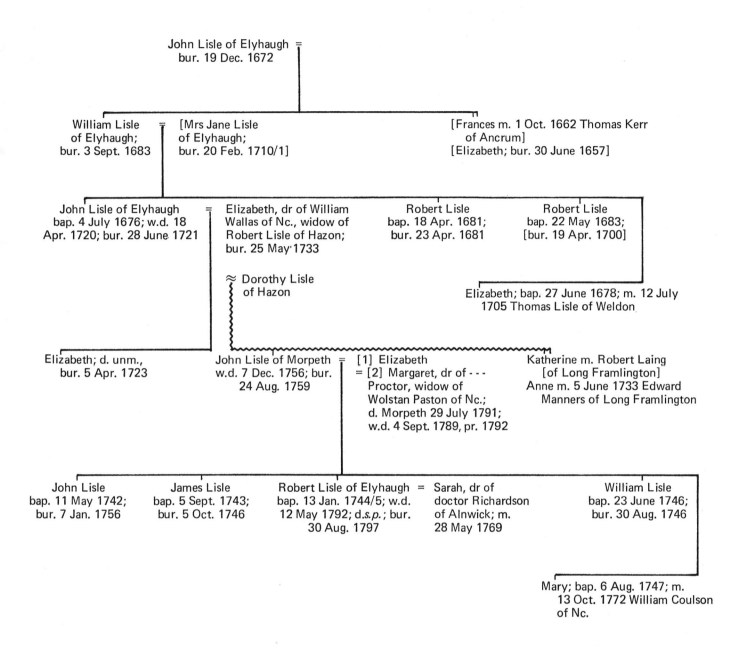

John Lisle of Elyhaugh =
bur. 19 Dec. 1672

William Lisle ╤ [Mrs Jane Lisle
of Elyhaugh; of Elyhaugh;
bur. 3 Sept. 1683 bur. 20 Feb. 1710/1]

[Frances m. 1 Oct. 1662 Thomas Kerr
of Ancrum]
[Elizabeth; bur. 30 June 1657]

John Lisle of Elyhaugh = Elizabeth, dr of William
bap. 4 July 1676; w.d. 18 Wallas of Nc., widow of
Apr. 1720; bur. 28 June 1721 Robert Lisle of Hazon;
bur. 25 May 1733

Robert Lisle
bap. 18 Apr. 1681;
bur. 23 Apr. 1681

Robert Lisle
bap. 22 May 1683;
[bur. 19 Apr. 1700]

≈ Dorothy Lisle
of Hazon

Elizabeth; bap. 27 June 1678; m. 12 July
1705 Thomas Lisle of Weldon

Elizabeth; d. unm.,
bur. 5 Apr. 1723

John Lisle of Morpeth =
w.d. 7 Dec. 1756; bur.
24 Aug. 1759

[1] Elizabeth
= [2] Margaret, dr of - - -
Proctor, widow of
Wolstan Paston of Nc.;
d. Morpeth 29 July 1791;
w.d. 4 Sept. 1789, pr. 1792

Katherine m. Robert Laing
[of Long Framlington]
Anne m. 5 June 1733 Edward
Manners of Long Framlington

John Lisle
bap. 11 May 1742;
bur. 7 Jan. 1756

James Lisle
bap. 5 Sept. 1743;
bur. 5 Oct. 1746

Robert Lisle of Elyhaugh =
bap. 13 Jan. 1744/5; w.d.
12 May 1792; d.*s.p.*; bur.
30 Aug. 1797

Sarah, dr of
doctor Richardson
of Alnwick; m.
28 May 1769

William Lisle
bap. 23 June 1746;
bur. 30 Aug. 1746

Mary; bap. 6 Aug. 1747; m.
13 Oct. 1772 William Coulson
of Nc.

Crown grantees some of the tithes which had belonged to Brinkburn priory; on 15 February 1615/6 he purchased other tithes and lands in Todstead, Okehaugh and Wester Brenkheugh. Tristram Liselye of Weldon, gent., made his w.d. 5 October 1619, by which he directs that he is to be buried 'in the parish church of Brinkburn where the rest of my ancestors are buried'; he leaves to his eldest daughter Isable 'all such goods going about the house as are called her own except two oxen in the draught'; she is to have 'four kine and calves, one red stott, one white whye and a red branded whye and all the clothes and bedding except the best bed and the furniture which I give to my son Robert Lisely'. Besides these Isable is to have all the pewter vessels now remaining in the house and one cauldron. His son Robert Liselye is to have the rest of his goods and is appointed sole executor. Tristram died before the end of the year for the inventory of his goods was exhibited on 21 December 1619. The goods

were only worth £10. 8s. 2d.; one of the appraisers, Wm Lisle, was unable to write and made his mark (*Dur. Prob. Off.* by C.R.H.).

The son Robert Lisle perhaps married a daughter of Ralph Carr of Lesbury for the latter in his w.d. 11 April 1644 leaves 'my chests etc., at Weldon to my daughters' (*NCH.* II, p.433).

Robert Lisle was still alive in 1646. A kinsman of his, Ralph Lisle of Low Framlington, yeoman, made his w.d. 31 March 1646 by which he leaves 'to my cousin Robert Lisleis son of Weldon, one colt'; he appoints his 'friends and kinsmen, Robert Lisley of Weldon and Ralph Dodd of the Heugh, executors'; he is to be buried 'in the parish church of Brinkburn where my father was buried'; his friend Dorathie Lisley of Elyhaugh is to have one quie; he leaves his mother 'all the two parts of goods which my father left me in his last will'. Robert Lisle of Weldon had been succeeded by his son Robert Lisle by 1657 when Robert Lisle of Felton by his will gives to his 'loving cousin Robert Lisle of Weldon' his lands adjoining Weldon called the New Intack, together with the farms of Catheugh, Turnerstead and Todstead. The relationship between the two families must indeed have been close to have warranted such a substantial legacy.

Robert Lisle of Weldon's will is dated 6 March 1668/9 by which he directs that his body is 'to be buried among the bones of my ancestors in Brinkburn'. His eldest son Robert Lisle is to have his real estate, and the house in Newcastle which he had bought from his aunt Eleanor Bell, widow, is to go to the two daughters Dorothy and Frances by his first wife; his younger children Thomas, William, Ann and Dorothy are to have £40 each. The supervisors of the will are sir Thomas Horsley of Horsley, the testator's two brothers-in-law William Carr of Eshot, esquire, and Mr John Carr of Lesbury, and his cousin Mr Robert Lisle of Hazon. Written in the margin of the will, presumably by one of the brothers-in-law, is the statement 'my brother Lisle of Weldon departed this world one Wednesday at night about 9 of the clock at night, it being the 10th day of this month of March in the year of God, 1668' (i.e. 1668/9). We notice that the Lisles of Hazon as well as the Lisles of Felton were reckoned as 'cousins' by the Lisles of Weldon in the 17th century.

The heir, Robert Lisle, had some dispute about his ownership of the tithes of Weldon hall and other places in the chapelry of Brinkburn. In an undated petition to the lord chancellor Hampden he declared that he was 'son and heir of R. Lisle, late of Weldon, aforesaid, gent., deceased, who was son and heir of R. Lisle of Weldon, aforesaid, gent., deceased, your orator's grandfather, who was son and heir of Tristram Lisle, late of Weldon, aforesaid, gent., also deceased, your orator's great grandfather'. By his wife Margaret daughter of William Brown of Bolton (m.1704) he had three sons Robert, William and George and two daughters Margaret (wife of Edward Mather of Framlington) and Anne wife of Robert Embleton of Shilbottle. The eldest son, Robert Lisle, a Morpeth solicitor, died in 1779. The second son, William Lisle, was a surgeon. On 10 August 1726 when he was 'now on an intended voyage from Bristol to Guinea' he made his will by which he leaves everything he possesses to his brother Robert. At the same time he wrote to his brother—'I should have been very glad to have settled in the country had not my unfortunate misconduct reduced my circumstances to such a state as to require such desperate adventures, and I also sincerely assure you without any adulation I should scarcely care to return to England if I did not think of seeing you alive and my voyage turned out to both our satisfactions. I set out tomorrow for Bristol to go Surgeon in the ship *Queen Elizabeth*, Chas Tweedy, master, to Guinea and Barbadoes. I have £4 per mens. wages, and 1 shilling for every slave, which is 600, viz. £30. . . . Your most affectionate brother, Will. Lesle'. The third son, George Lisle of Carville died s.p. in 1776.

The heir-at-law of these three brothers was Robert Lisle of Acton who is described in an indenture of 31 December 1784 as 'devisee of the will of Robert Lisle, late of Morpeth, esq., deceased, who died a bachelor and without issue, and second cousin and heir-at-law of George Lisle, late of Carville, esq., deceased, i.e. eldest son and heir-at-law of John Lisle, late of Newcastle, joiner and cabinet maker, deceased, who was eldest son and heir-at-law of William Lisle, late of Low Framlington, gent., deceased, who was third brother of Robert Lisle, late of Weldon, esq., deceased, who was father of the said Robert Lisle of Morpeth, and of the said George Lisle, deceased, and which said Robert Lisle, late of Morpeth, survived his brother, the said George, who died a bachelor without issue'.

Robert Lisle of Acton, who succeeded to Weldon in 1779, died in 1800. His only son Robert was born at Newcastle 24 December 1793 and educated at Eton and Magdalen College, Oxford. Whilst still under age he married at St George's, Hanover Square, 29 July 1812, Anne daughter of Anthony Salvin, a general in the army. A special Act of Parliament was passed 52 George III to enable him to make a valid settlement on his intended marriage, notwithstanding his minority. He assumed the territorial 'de' in front of his surname Lisle.

Robert de Lisle died s.p. at Edinburgh 7 May 1860, the last male heir of his family. His sister Isabella and her husband Hugh Moises, assumed the name of Lisle on succeeding to the Weldon estate, but they died s.p. The next heir was William Beresford Orde, son of John Bertram Orde by Eliza half sister of Robert de Lisle. He assumed the name and arms of Lisle in 1882 and at his death on 12 January 1903 was succeeded by his grandson William Beresford Orde Lisle.

LISLE OF CHIPCHASE, PAR. CHOLLERTON

BEFORE 1226 Richard de Umframvill gave the vill of Ray, par. Kirkwhelpington, to Peter de Insula and Margery his wife (*NDD*. p.110, No. 77; *NCH*. IV, p.333). Peter also had a grant from Richard de Umframvill of lands called Rowchester in Birtley and a fishery in the Tyne at Ovingham (*Greenwich Hospital deeds*, bundle 117; *NCH*. XII, pp.89, 145). In these two grants Peter de Insula is called nephew by Richard de Umframvill, and it has been assumed that it was his wife Margery who was in fact Richard's niece, but this cannot be taken as certain. His relationship to the Lisles of Woodburn is, however, certain for in Finchale Priory Chartulary is the entry *Otwelus de Insula et Petrus frater eius* (*Finchale Priory*, p.82). In 1231 Peter de Insula and Margaret his wife were charged 20s., for an amercement by four justices (*Pipe Roll*). As sir Peter de Insula he witnesses 21 January 1241 a covenant made by his brother sir Otower (*NDD*. p. 124, No. 11). In 1242 Peter de Insula held of Gilbert de Umframville, Chipchase and Whittle by a third part of a knight's fee of the old feoffment (*Book of Fees*, II, pp. 1114-5). The fact that these two places were held of the old feoffment means that they had been subinfeudated, perhaps to the Insulas, before the death of Henry I.

In 1243 the prior and convent of Hexham granted to Peter de Insula and Robert his son and heir, licence to have a perpetual chantry in the chapel of Chipchase (*NCH*. IV, p.330 and n.). Sir Peter must have been a good age when on 18 July 1261 he is said to have had a licence from Alexander III, king of Scots, to strengthen his mill dam; at this time the kings of Scotland held the lordship of Tyndale, the North Tyne, in which the dam lay being the boundary between this lordship and the manor of Chipchase. The date of this licence is uncertain as it is merely dated 1 July in the 11th year of king Alexander; Dodsworth made a marginal

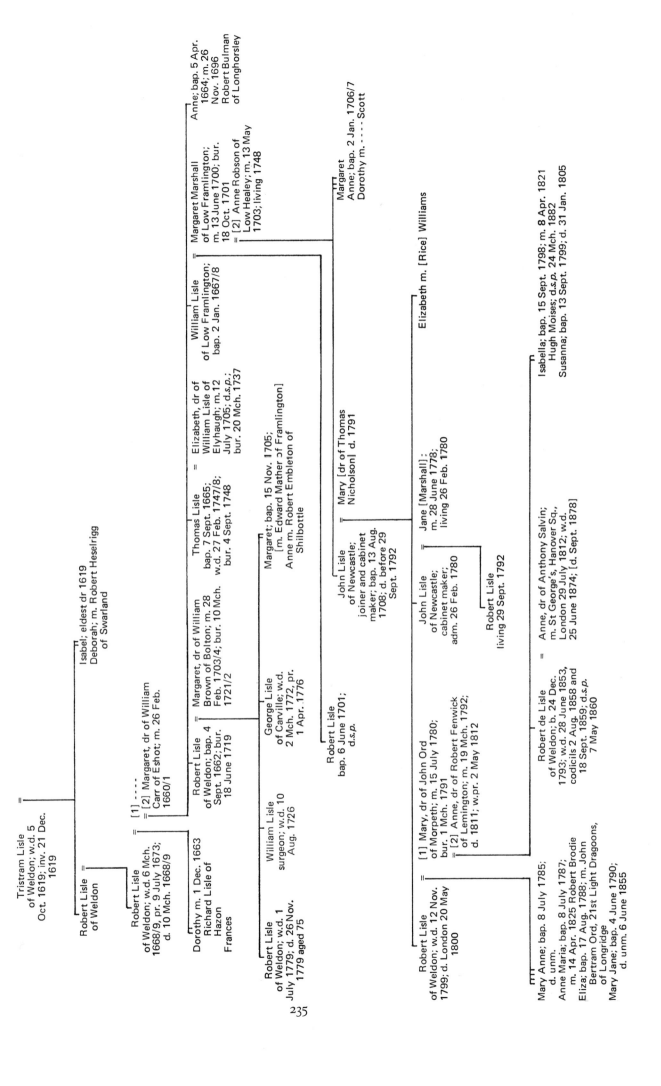

235

note to his extract *Fuit rex a 33 Hen. 3 ad 13 Ed. I* meaning that he identified Alexander as the third king of that name. 11 Alexander II 1224-5 seems too early. Sir Peter certainly survived his son and heir, Robert de Insula, for sometime after 1252 he claimed the wardship of Robert's daughter Margery. The son Robert was alive in 1262 when he held 1½ knight's fees an eighth part of a fee being subtracted, and held six vills of Hugh de Bolbec, baron of Styford, but was dead in 1269 (*NCH.* VI, p.225n.).

Robert de Insula was twice married. His first wife was Joan daughter and heiress of Simon de Welteden of Welton; when she died between 1241 and 1252 her only daughter Margery de Insula was her heiress; Margery married before 1257 Walter le Scot de Middleton and their descendants took the name of Welteden. Robert de Insula's second wife Margery, whose parentage is unknown, was living a widow in 1269 when her son, also called Robert, is described as son and heir of Margery, who was wife of Robert de Insula (*Assize Roll* 1269; *SS.* 88, p.180).

In 1279 Robert de Insula paid half a mark for licence to make a concord (*Ib.*, p.391). In 1284 he charged his guardian Robert de Insula of Woodburn with having wasted his lands at Chipchase (*de Banco Roll*, 12-13 E.I., m.54; *NCH.* IV, p.331 and n.). It is probable that Robert had recently attained his majority when this claim was made; during his minority he appears to have lived at Welton (*NDD.* p.125). As a knight he witnesses a deed dated 29 September 1290 (*NCH.* X, p.420n.). For the Subsidy of 1296 he paid on goods valued at £9. 9s. 8d. (*NCH.* IV, p.332). A grant of free warren in his lands was given to him in 1306/7 (*HN.* iii. II, p.394). A sir Robert de Lisle of Chipchase witnesses a Denton deed

of 24 May 1324 (*NDD.* p.250, No. 129; noted, with mistaken date, *HN.* ii. II, p.225n.).

It was probably sir Robert de Insula's son and successor, the third Robert at Chipchase, who paid the Subsidy for Chipchase in 1336 as Robert del Isle (*NCH.* IV, p.332). He witnesses as a knight a Colwell deed of December 1339 (*NDD.* p.248, No. 118) and a Kirkheaton deed of 13 June 1343 (*Ib.*, p.57, No. 42). For the Subsidy of 1346 there appears an inexplicable entry that Robert heir of John de Insula was assessed for Chipchase and Whitchester; Whitchester is certainly an error for Whittle, but John de Insula is otherwise unknown and his name may also be an error. On 22 February 1347 Robert de Insula of Chipchase granted to Nicholas his son for life, a messuage and land in Chipchase, quit of multure (*NDD.* p.112, No. 86; *NCH.* IV, p.332, note 3). It is possible that the son Nicholas died shortly after this, for on 24 March 1348 his father Robert quitclaimed to Roger del Spense his right in land in Chipchase which Roger had of the gift of Nicholas, grantor's son (*Ib.*, note 4; *NDD.* p.112, No. 87), and in the same year sir Robert made his grand-daughter Cecily daughter of John de Insula, his heir.

On 9 September 1348 sir Robert conveyed to sir William Heroun, lord of Ford, the custody and marriage of Cecily daughter of John de Lisle of Chipchase; sir Robert had entailed the manor of Chipchase on Cecily and she was to marry William or John or Walter, the sons of sir William Heroun, if God permitted them to live until Cecily and one of them should be of age to consort with her (*NDD.* p.113, No. 91; *NCH.* IV, p.332, note 6). The transaction was completed by a deed dated at Chipchase on the Sunday

LISLE of CHIPCHASE, par. CHOLLERTON

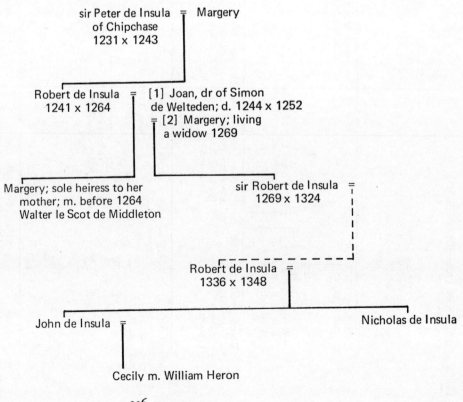

next after the feast of Dionysius (11 October) 1348 when Robert de Insula of Chipchase, *chevaler*, remitted to sir William Heroun, lord of Ford, all the rights he had in the manor of Chipchase with Rouchester (*NDD.* p.113, No. 92; *NCH.* IV, p.333, n.1). Cecily married Walter Heron and their descendants remained in possession of Chipchase until 1718.

LISLE OF BARMESTON, CO. DURHAM

On 11 February 1509/10 Gerard Fenwick took a 21 years' lease of lands in Burradon, par. Alwinton, from Percival Lisle and Elizabeth his wife who was one of the daughters and coheirs of John Burradon. Fenwick undertook that he would not assign the lease to, amongst others, Roger Fenwick, son of the said Elizabeth (*HN.* ii. II, p.115). In 1541 the tower at Burradon was 'of the inheritance of George Fenwycke and Percyvall Lysle in the right of his wife' (*AA2.* XIV, p.43). In 1542 Anna widow of sir Humphrey Lisle of Felton claimed dower against Robert Lisle esq., Anna widow of William Lisle, Percival Lisle gent., Anthony Fenwick gent., and Humphrey Lisle, gent. (*de Banco Roll, AA3.* VI, p.87). Of these, Robert Lisle was sir Humphrey Lisle's brother and heir, Anna widow of William Lisle was sir Humphrey's mother, and Humphrey Lisle was presumably sir Humphrey's illegitimate son of that name. It can be taken as reasonably certain that Percival Lisle was also a near relative, and as a matter of fact it has always been assumed that he was an uncle of this sir Humphrey Lisle, and a younger son of an earlier sir Humphrey (d.1516). There is no proof of this but the assumption seems reasonable.

When Robert Lisle made a settlement of his estates on 17 January 1595/6, the estates were settled after his three sons and his brother on Percival Lisle's three grandsons. Philpot's copy of the Visitation of Durham, 1615, No. ii, *fol.* 154 quoted in a family pedigree of Lisle, belonging to Mr Beresford Lisle, 1903, (*NCH.* VII, p.259n.) definitely states that Percival Lisle of Hart, co. Durham, was second son of sir Humphrey Lisle (d.1516). From this same source we learn that Percival Lisle's son was Robert Lisle of Biddick, co. Durham. This was the Robert Lisle who conveyed a moiety of his lands in Thornton to Anthony Fenwick, which moiety was reconveyed 9 May 1579 by Stephen Fenwick son of Anthony, to James Lisle, son of the said Robert, and the heirs male of his body, who finally sold Thornton, 8th September 1589. Anthony Fenwick was no doubt the Anthony Fenwick mentioned in the dower claim of 1542.

Robert Lisle was dead by 17 October 1582, when Bernard Gilpin, rector of Houghton, in his will of that date states that he 'bought of Mr James Lisle, and his mother, one other fine (in Houghton-le-Spring), lying unto the churchyard upon the east side, and at the end of the school and garthing, for this I paid to Mr Lisle and his mother £15, of this I remain finer myself, trusting that it should or now have been fined unto the school and governors thereof' (*SS.* 38, p.91). Robert Lisle's three sons James, John and Robert were remainder men in the settlement of Felton on 17 January 1595/6. Of the youngest son, Robert, nothing further is known. John Lisle was a Durham attorney and bailiff of Darlington 1606-1622; he married Barbara daughter of

Thomas Turner of Darlington, widow of William Barnes of Bedborne, co. Dur., and of Ralph Evers of Edgknole; John died *s.p.* and his widow proved his will on 8 May 1623 and was buried in Darlington church 19 July 1630.

Robert Lisle's eldest son and heir, James Lisle of Barmeston died in Durham gaol and was buried at St Mary-le-Bow, Durham, 30 March 1616. James' son Talbot Lisle was living at Barmeston, of which he was the lessee, in 1623; in 1636 he was presented for unlawfully baptising his children. These children were four sons, Talbot, Ralph, James and Robert, and a daughter Mary, their mother being Anne daughter of sir William Blakiston of Blakiston, widow of Topp Heath of Little Eden. A half-sister of the Lisle children was Ann Heath of Barmeston, co. Durham who died in 1633. In her w.d. 22 January 1632/3 she remembers her Lisle relations—'I give to my four brothers, Talbot, Ralph, James and Robert Liell, each of them five pounds a piece. I give to my sister, Mary Liell, twenty pounds. I give to my father-in-law, Mr Talbot Liell, ten pounds. To Mr Gilford Liell, a twenty shilling piece to be bestowed in a ring'. . . . 'I give to the poor of the parish of Washington, ten shillings, to be disposed of by my father, Mr Talbot Liell. To my mother, Mrs Ann Liell, ten pounds and all the monies due for the interest of my portion that shall be overplus more than the legacies amounts unto' (*SS.* 142, p.246).

The second Talbot Lisle married Catherine daughter of William Carr of Eshot, par. Felton, by his wife Anne daughter of John Lisle of Acton. Talbot Lisle's children are mentioned in the w.d. 3 August 1681 of their grandmother Anne Carr, the children being John, Charles, Mary (m. Cuthbert Close of Chipchase), Barbara (m. . . . . Dawson), Anne (m. Alexander Falconer, vicar of Felton), Magdalen, and Catherine (m. John Wightman of Edinburgh). The eldest son, John Lisle, is mentioned in the will of his uncle John Carr of Hetton, who desires him to be put to school at Berwick and at the age of 18 years to be bound to a counsellor.

John Lisle was probably the last male heir of his family for his only son Robert died in infancy in 1679.

LISLE—BIBLIOGRAPHY

of East Woodburn par. Corsenside. *HN.* ii. I, pp.171-174 (with pedigree).

of Chipchase, par. Chollerton. *NCH.* IV, pp.330-333 (with pedigree).

of Newton Hall, par. Bywell St Peter. *NCH.* IV, pp.122-125.

of Felton, par. Felton. *NCH.* VII, pp.244-262 (with pedigree); J. C. Hodgson *MSS pedigrees* I, 69, 472; III, 110, 228; A.398.

of Barmeston, co. Durham. *NCH.* VII, p.259 (pedigree).

of Elyhaugh, par. Felton. *NCH.* VII, pp.379-382 (with pedigree), J. C. Hodgson *MSS Pedigrees* I. 396, 399.

of Weldon, chap. Brinkburn. *NCH.* VII, pp. 498-504 (with pedigree); J. C. Hodgson *MSS pedigrees* I. 396-8.

of Acton, par. Felton. *NCH.* VII, pp.371-373; J. C. Hodgson *MSS pedigrees* I. 452-4, A.124.

of Hazon, par. Shilbottle. *NCH.* V, pp.463-472 (with pedigree); J. C. Hodgson *MSS pedigrees* I. 105.

of Newton-on-the-Moor. *NCH.* V, p.449 (with pedigree);

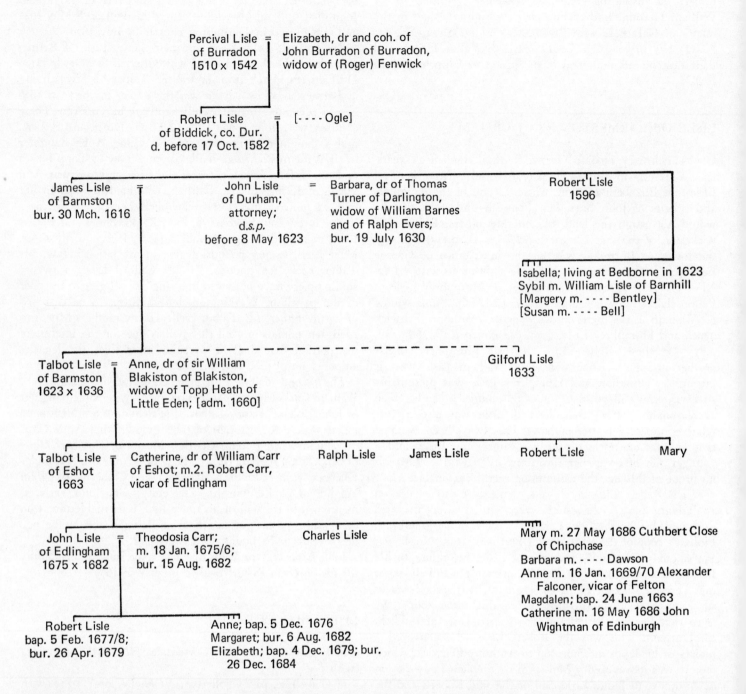

Percival Lisle = Elizabeth, dr and coh. of
of Burradon .... John Burradon of Burradon,
1510 x 1542 .... widow of (Roger) Fenwick

Robert Lisle = [- - - - Ogle]
of Biddick, co. Dur.
d. before 17 Oct. 1582

James Lisle = ... John Lisle = Barbara, dr of Thomas .... Robert Lisle
of Barmston .... of Durham; ... Turner of Darlington, ... 1596
bur. 30 Mch. 1616 .. attorney; .... widow of William Barnes
.... d.s.p. .... and of Ralph Evers;
.... before 8 May 1623 . bur. 19 July 1630

Isabella; living at Bedborne in 1623
Sybil m. William Lisle of Barnhill
[Margery m. - - - - Bentley]
[Susan m. - - - - Bell]

Talbot Lisle = Anne, dr of sir William .... Gilford Lisle
of Barmston ... Blakiston of Blakiston, ... 1633
1623 x 1636 ... widow of Topp Heath of
.... Little Eden; [adm. 1660]

Talbot Lisle = Catherine, dr of William Carr .. Ralph Lisle ... James Lisle ... Robert Lisle ... Mary
of Eshot ..... of Eshot; m.2. Robert Carr,
1663 .... vicar of Edlingham

John Lisle = Theodosia Carr; .... Charles Lisle
of Edlingham . m. 18 Jan. 1675/6;
1675 x 1682 .. bur. 15 Aug. 1682

Mary m. 27 May 1686 Cuthbert Close
   of Chipchase
Barbara m. - - - - Dawson
Anne m. 16 Jan. 1669/70 Alexander
   Falconer, vicar of Felton
Magdalen; bap. 24 June 1663
Catherine m. 16 May 1686 John
   Wightman of Edinburgh

Robert Lisle .... Anne; bap. 5 Dec. 1676
bap. 5 Feb. 1677/8; .. Margaret; bur. 6 Aug. 1682
bur. 26 Apr. 1679 .... Elizabeth; bap. 4 Dec. 1679; bur.
.... 26 Dec. 1684

pedigree registered by Lancelot Lisle in 1615 (Foster. p.80).

GENERAL. John Hodgson's *MSS notebook* T, pp.9-18; New-castle upon Tyne Record Series vol.VII—*Northumberland and Durham deeds*, pp.118-134. J. C. Hodgson's pedigrees—(Felton) I, 69, 472; (Hazon) I, 105; (Acton) I, 452-4, 478; (Weldon) I, 396-8; (Elyhaugh) I, 396, 399; (Felton) III, 110, 228; (Acton) A.124; (Gosforth) A.398.

LISLE—FREEHOLDERS

P.B.1628. William Lisley of Shothaugh, gent.; Robte Lisle of Felton, esq.; Edward Lisle of Acton, gent.; Lancelot Lisle of Hayson, gent.

P.B.1639. Robert Lisle of Felton, esq.; Edward Lisle of Acton, gent; Raph Lisle of Hason, gent; George Lisle of Newton on ye Moore, gent.

P.B.1698. none.

P.B.1710. John Lisle of Elishaw (*sic* for Elyhaugh); Robert Lisle of Weldon, arm., par. Framlington.

P.B.1715. Ra. Lisle of Hazon; John Lisle of Elyhaugh.

P.B.1721. John Lisle of Eihaugh (*sic*), esq; Robert Lisle of Hason, esq.

P.B.1748. Thomas Lisle, Elihaugh; Robert Lisle, gent., Morpeth, for Weldon; John Lisle, Morpeth.

P.B.1774. Robert Lisle esq., Newcastle, for Old Felton; George Lisle, esq., Carville, for Connefield; Robert Lisle, esq., Morpeth, for Weldon.

P.B.1826. Robert de Lisle, Kirsewell Ho. Lanark, for Acton; Aaron Lisle, Belford; William Lisle, Ancroft, for Wooler; John Lisle, Twizel Mill, for Wooler.

KNIGHTS OF 1166

BARONY OF BOLAM—KNIGHTS OF 1166

IN his *carta* of 1166 Gilbert de Boolun reported that he held his lands as three knights' fees of which he made service for one knight from his demesne; William son of Bernier made service for a second knight, and Robert de Bellesso for the third knight (*Lib. Nig.* p.329).

The barony of Bolam included Bebside, Cowpen, East Hartford and West Hartford in the chapelry of Horton; East Brunton in the parish of Gosforth; Elswick and Westgate in the parish of St John's, Newcastle; Fenham in the parish of St Andrew's, Newcastle; Bolam (with Bolam Vicarage and Gallowhill), Belsay, Bradford, Trewick and Shortflatt in the parish of Bolam; Aydon (with Aydon Castle), Thornbrough and Little Whittington in the parish of Corbridge; Deanham in the parish of Hartburn; and Tunstal in co. Durham. Henry II had granted to the lord of Bolam, probably 1157 x 1162, three vills belonging to his manor of Corbridge in exchange for Coniscliffe and certain other vills (in co. Durham). The three vills thus added to the barony of Bolam must have been Aydon, Thornbrough and Little Whittington.

William son of Bernier's fee has not been identified, and by the middle of the 13th century the only holding by knights' service in the barony of Bolam, was the manor of Thornbrough.

The knight's fee held by Robert de Bellesso in 1166 comprised the two vills of Thornbrough and Belsay. In 1171 Robert de Belesho paid 20s. for a plea (*Pipe Roll*). He was succeeded by his son William le Scot who had a confirmation of his two vills from his overlord Gilbert son of Gilbert. It is stated in the confirmation that Gilbert's grandfather James had given the vills to Robert, father of William le Scot for his homage and service making service of one knight's fee in the county and one third of a fee outside of the county (*NCH.* X, p.308n.). William le Scot's son and heir Walter Scot made agreement with John de Mydelton whereby Walter's two daughters and coheiresses were to marry the two sons of John de Mydelton. In 1242 the Middletons held the manor of Belsay in socage and the manor of Thornbrough as one knight's fee.

BARONY OF STYFORD—KNIGHTS OF 1166

IN 1166 Walter de Bolebec reported that in his barony there were 4½ fees of old feoffment, of which Gilebert de Bolum held 2½ fees, Hugh de Croudene 1 fee and William son of Boius 1 fee; of the new feoffment Ot(wel) de Insula had 1½ fees, Reginald son of Wimund ½ a fee, John Morel ⅓ of a fee, Gospatric ⅓ of a fee and Wibert de Slaveleia 1 fee.

The vills in this barony were more scattered than in any other Northumberland barony and included the following:—

Par. Bywell St Andrew. —Bearl, Broomhaugh, Riding, Styford and half of Bywell.

Chap. Blanchland. —Newbegin and Blanchland (called High Quarter).

Chap. Shotley. —Shotley Low Quarter.

Chap. Slaley. —Slaley Town and Slaley Out Quarter.

Par. Stamfordham. —Fenwick, Hawkwell and East Matfen.

Par. Heddon-on-the-Wall. —Eachwick, Heddon-on-the-Wall, East Heddon, West Heddon, Houghton (with Close House) and Whitchester.

Par. St John's, Newcastle. —Benwell.

Par. St Nicholas', Newcastle. —West Brunton.

Par. Kirkharle. —Hawick and Kirkharle.

Par. Hartburn. —Cambo, Farnlaw, Greenlighton, Hartington, Hartington Hall, Harwood, East Shaftoe, West Shaftoe, Wallington Demesne, Angerton (High and Low), Corridge, Hartburn, Hartburn Grange, Highlaws, North Middleton, South Middleton, Rothley, Thornton (East and West), Todridge and Whitridge.

Par. Kirkwhelpington. —Fawns.

Par. Bolam. —Harnham.

Gilbert de Bolum held the barony of Bolam, and his 2½ fees in the barony of Styford comprised the vills of Cambo, South Middleton (with Corridge and Highlaws), Shafto (East and West), Hartington (with Hartington Hall), Rothley, Hartburn, Hartburn Grange (formerly called Newton Grange), Harwood, Greenlighton, Harnham and Hawick. An account of Gilbert's family has already been given amongst the barons.

Hugh de Craudene's holding was Houghton, Whitchester, Wallington, Fawns and Farnlaw. The surname of Craudene was derived from Croydon near Royston in Cambridgeshire. A later Hugh de Crauden, who died before 1236, left a daughter and heiress Sibil wife of Robert de Beverley. Philip son and heir of Sibil succeeded to her property and surname, but dying 1278 x 1285 without legitimate issue, his heirs were his sister Isabel de Crauden and his nephew Richard Turpin (*NCH.* XIII, pp.101-102, 112).

The knight's fee held by William son of Boius in 1166 was perhaps half of Bywell, but William founded no known family and by 1242 this part of Bywell was held in moieties.

In 1166 Otwel de Insula was a considerable landowner in Northumberland but he held no lands *in capite*. In the barony of Styford he held Bearl, East Heddon, Fenwick, Hawkwell, East Matfen, Angerton, Thornton, West Brunton and two carucates in Kirkharle, perhaps two thirds of the vill. An account of the Insulas and their descendants, the Lisles, has already been given under the barony of Whalton.

Reginald son of Wimund, also called Reginald de Kenebell, held the manor of Heddon-on-the-Wall, but exchanged it with his lord, Walter de Bolebec, for half the manor of Benwell. The name Kenebell is derived from a place in the Bolebec fee in Buckinghamshire now called Kimble. Before the end of the 14th century the family had parted with their manor of Benwell, and was probably extinct.

The manor of North Middleton was at one time called Middleton Morel after John Morel who held it as one third of a knight's fee in 1166. His surname may have been a patronymic and occurs in Domesday Book. The family seems to have died out in the early 13th century.

West Heddon, held by Gospatric as one third of a knight's fee in 1166, provided the surname of Hidewyn for its later owners who were probably descended from Gospatric. His name is sufficient evidence that he was native born, but his successors bore such Norman-French Christian names as Robert and William. The family survived until the early 15th century. A family called Hidewyn holding lands in East Heddon was probably unrelated to the owners of West Heddon.

The knight's fee held by Wibert de Slaveleia in 1166 was the manor of Slaley. That the name is Wibert rather than Gilbert, sometimes borne by his descendants, is proved by an entry in the *Pipe Roll* for 1170 where Wibt de Slavle is charged 5m. that he enter not into the pleas made in time of war. In the early part of the 13th century the family of Slaveley was of some local importance. On 15 July 1308 the treasurer and the barons of the exchequer were ordered not to intermeddle further with the lands in Slaley and Steel which had been taken into the late king's hands on account of the madness of John de Slaveley. In consideration that his death had been certified to them and that the lands were not held of the king in chief, the officers were ordered to revoke any sequestration of the lands which they might have made (*Close Roll*). The unfortunate John was perhaps the last male heir of his family.

BARONY OF MITFORD—KNIGHTS OF 1166

In 1166 Roger Bertram reported to the king that in his barony six and a half knights had been enfeoffed in the time of Henry I by his grandfather and father, but that he himself had not created any more. Radulf de St Peter held two knights' fees, William de Fraglinton one fee, William de Diffleston one fee, Wihelard de Trophil one fee, John son of Simeon one fee, and Pagan de Hallesdure half a fee.

The lands comprising the barony of Mitford were:—

Par. Ponteland. —Ponteland (with Little Eland and Great Eland), Mason, High Callerton, Little Callerton, Darras Hall (originally called Calverdon Darreyns), Kirkley, Prestwick, Horton Grange, Dinnington, Brenkley, Milbourne, Berwick Hill, Higham Dykes and Milbourne Grange (formerly North Milbourne).

Par. Mitford. —Mitford, Newton Underwood, Nunriding, Molesden, Benridge, Espley, Throphill, Pigdon and Edington.

Par. Felton. —Felton, Old Felton (formerly Little Felton), Acton, Thirston, Overgrass, Swarland, Eshot, Bockenfield, Greens and Glantlees.

Chap. Hebron. —Causey Park.

Chap. Brinkburn. —Brinkburn.

Chap. Framlington. —Framlington.

Par. Meldon. —Meldon.

The two knights' fees held by Radulf de St Peter were the vills of Berwick Hill, Pigdon and Edington. The direct male line of the St Peters became extinct before the end of the 13th century. For an account of the St Peter family *see NCH.* XII, pp.511-513.

William de Fraglinton (*recte* Framlington), who held the vill of Framlington, now called Longframlington, was a great benefactor of Brinkburn priory and Newminster abbey. William Bertram II of Mitford confirmed to the canons of Brinkburn all the donations made to them by Radulph de Hechelaw and William de Framlyngton his son (*SS.* 90, p.3). One of the gifts to Brinkburn was two lands called 'Akehalgh' and 'Lynehalgh' which he gave for his own soul, the souls of his father and mother, the souls of his wife Cecilia and his son Michael, those of William Bertram and Roger Bertram his son, of William Bertram son of the said Roger, of all his own heirs, and all his parents and all the faithful dead (*Ib.,* p.99). William de Framlington's only son, Michael, evidently died in his father's lifetime. William died shortly before 1196 leaving five daughters, coheiresses, amongst whom his lands were divided.

The single knight's fee held by William de Diffleston (*recte* Dyveliston) was the manor of North Milbourne, which covered the modern townships of Higham Dykes and Milbourne Grange. William de Dyveliston held the small barony of Dilston.

Wihelard de Trophil took his surname from the manor of Throphill in the parish of Mitford, which he held as one knight's fee in 1166. He was apparently son of Wydhelard, sub-tenant of Hickleton, Yorks., under the Bailliols. This earlier Wydhelard had three sons, Ranulf, Wydhelard and Roger, of whom Ranulf had lands in Stamfordham which he gave to Brinkburn priory, Wydhelard held Throphill and Roger was probably father of Hugh son of Roger who held the Delaval barony of Callerton in right of his wife, and of Ralph son of Roger who held Rugley in the barony of Alnwick. No descendants of Wihelard de Trophill have been identified.

John son of Simeon held the manor of Meldon, perhaps with other lands. The name of John's father seems more correctly to have been Seman. John son of Seman witnesses a grant of land by William Bertram to the prior and convent of Brinkburn (*SS.* 90, p.41), and with Symon son of the said John witnesses two grants by William de Framlington to the same priory (*Ib.*, pp.12, 63). Symon son of John was succeeded by sir John son of Symon who witnesses many grants to Brinkburn between 1242 and 1257; he was a knight before 1246 (*Ib.*, pp.10, 11, 34, 37, 46, 77, 79). John son of Seman had acquired half the manor of Whittingham with its dependant vills of Thrunton and Barton, and in 1258 his grandson gave these lands to Brinkburn. It would seem that he had no male descendants (*NCH.* XIV, pp.508-510).

The half knight's fee held by Pagan de Hallesdure in 1166 may have been part of the vill of Little Felton. His descendants certainly held lands there in the 13th century though not by knights' service. In 1242 William de Schauceby and William son of Payn held 40 acres in Little Felton. Roger Bertram gave the vill of Little Felton to Brinkburn, except the service of two free men in the said vill, namely the services of William son of Roger son of Pagan and William de Stanceby, which he and heirs were to retain intact (*SS.* 90, p.26). W. Pagani de Hallesdur witnesses a grant to Brinkburn made by William de Framlington (d.*circa* 1195), and later grants are witnessed by William son of Pagan and by William son of Roger son of Pagan (*Ib.*, pp.33, 50, 63).

BARONY OF CHEVINGTON—KNIGHTS OF 1166

IN 1166 Ernulf de Morewic reported to the king that from his one knight's fee in Northumberland, a certain David held half of old feoffment. David is otherwise unknown. In 1242 a certain William de Bamburg held a quarter of Chevington (*i.e.* West Chevington) as one quarter of a knight's fee, but there is no reason to suggest that he was David's descendant.

The barony of Chevington comprised the single vill of West Chevington, chap. Chevington, although its lords took their surname from Morwick, which they held of the barony of Alnwick. The small township of Bullock's Hall was at one time part of West Chevington.

BARONY OF ELLINGHAM—KNIGHTS OF 1166

FOR this barony both Hugh de Ellington and Radulf de Gaugi made returns in 1166. The former reported that he held half the barony which had been William de Grainvills. Of this half, reckoned at one and a half knights' fees, Emma widow of William de Grainvill held half a knight's fee as her dower. Hugh had given to Ralph Baard and Robert de Bulmer in marriage with his two daughters half a knight's fee between them retaining in his own hands the remaining half fee.

At the same time Radulf de Gaugi reported that in the time of Henry I his antecessors had held his fee by the service of three knights. A certain knight called Galon held of old feoffment a quarter of a knight's fee. The whole barony had been divided between two sisters, one being his mother, and in her right he made service from his demesne for one and a half fees less an eighth part. Nothing had been alienated by himself of the new feoffment, but Hugh de Ellington who had married the other sister had enfeoffed Radulf Baard of a sixth part of a fee, and Gilbert de Heton of a twelfth part of a fee.

It will be seen that the two returns do not tally. Hugh de Ellington's wife had died before 1166 so that he only held her half of the barony as tenant by the courtesy. His two daughters, who had married Ralph Baard and Robert de Bulmer, were not daughters of the Grainvill heiress, so that their holdings could only be for the lifetime of their father-in-law. Gilbert de Heton's holding was presumably part of Heaton, par. All Saints', Newcastle; there is no evidence that he left descendants.

The holding, a quarter fee, held by Galon in 1166 was perhaps in Hartley, par. Earsdon. At a much later period there was a landowning family in Northumberland called Galon, but there is no reason to suppose that they were descended from this Galon.

The barony of Ellingham included the modern townships of Doxford and Ellingham in the parish of Ellingham; Newstead (originally called Osberwick), par. Bamburgh; Heaton, par. All Saints', Newcastle; Jesmond, par. St Andrew's, Newcastle; Cramlington, chap. Cramlington; and Hartley, par. Earsdon.

BARONY OF WOOLER—KNIGHTS OF 1166

THE barony of Wooler extended over the following townships:—

Par. Bamburgh. —Outchester, Warenford and Ratchwood.

Par. Belford. —Belford, Detchant, Easington, Easington Grange, Elwick and Middleton.

Par. Doddington. —Humbleton.

Par. Lowick. —Barmoor, Bowsdon, Holburn and Lowick.

Par. Wooler. —Fenton and Wooler.

Par. Brankston. —Brankston.

Par. Ford. —Broomridge, Crookham, Etal, Ford, Hetherslaw (and Flodden), and Kimmerstone.

Par. Kirknewton. —Akeld, Coupland, Grey's Forest, Selby's Forest, Yeavering and Hethpool.

In 1166 Stephen de Bulemer reported that the fees in his barony of the old feoffment were those of Liulf son of Alwold 1 fee, Helias son of Alvred 1 fee, Robert de Maneriis and Hugh de Dichende 1 fee, John son of Odard and Simon son of Ernulf 1 fee, and Robert Murdac 1 fee; and of the new feoffment, Thomas son of Roger ½ fee, Thomas son of Stephen de Bulemer 1 fee of which Radulf son of William holds ½ a fee and Robert Poher ¼ of a fee.

Liulf son of Alwold who held a single knight's fee in 1166 is otherwise unknown, but was evidently of native extraction. Helias son of Alvred can perhaps be identified with Helias de Achelda whose name occurs in the *Pipe Rolls* for 1170 and 1171. In 1242 William de Akild held a knight's fee in the barony of Wooler, the fee consisting of the vills of Akeld, Coupland and Yeavering. It seems likely that the family of Akeld ended in four coheiresses before the end of the 13th century.

Robert de Maneriis who with Hugh de Dichende held one fee in 1166 was presumably antecessor in title to Robert de Manerio who held the manor of Etal in 1254 as half a knight's fee (*see* MANNERS OF ETAL).

Hugh de Dichende acquired his surname from Detchant, par. Belford. In 1242 Henry de Dichend held Detchant for a quarter and a sixteenth of a fee. Sir John de Dichend, living in 1349, was apparently the last member of the family to own the manor (*NCH.* I, p.402), but much later there was a local family called Dotchin that may have taken its name from Detchant.

The knight's fee held by John son of Odard and Simon son of Ernulf in 1166 was the manor of Fenton. Simon son of Ernulf is otherwise unknown but John son of Odard was the baron of Embleton and ancestor of the family of Viscount.

Robert Murdac can be identified with Robert son of Bodin who held the manor of Outchester *circa* 1160 x 1168 (*Rot. Cart.* 35 E.I. No. 25 in *NCH.* I, p.200n.). Robert son of

Bodin gave half a carucate of his demesne in Outchester to Alnwick abbey, and the grant was confirmed by Alfred son of Robert son of Bodin. Bodin's descendants apparently acquired the surname of Ulcestre from their estate. The last of the family was Robert de Ulcestre, living in 1315, whose five daughters were his coheiresses.

In 1242 Odenel de Ford held Ford, Crookham, Kimmerston and a quarter of Hethpool as one knight's fee of old feoffment. This holding can hardly be other than the fee held by Liulf son of Alwold in 1166, but there is no evidence that Odenel was descended from Liulf. The family of Ford was extinct in the male line before the end of the 13th century.

The half fee of new feoffment held in 1166 by Thomas son of Roger has not been identified. Thomas son of Stephen de Bulemer held the manor of Barmoor which remained in the possession of his descendants, the Muschamps of Barmoor, until the middle of the 17th century.

MANNERS

A FAMILY taking its name from Mesnieres, Seine-Inf. arr. and cant. Neufchatel were feudal tenants of the counts of Eu both in Normandy before 1066 and in England after the Conquest. Before 1066 Robert de Maineriis witnesses a charter of Robert, count of Eu, for the abbey of Le Treport. William, count of Eu, was lord of the honour of Hastings at the time of the Domesday Survey, and died about 1095. His son, Henry, count of Eu, in 1166 gave the manor of Hooe, Sussex, to the priory of S. Martin-du-Bosc, the charter being witnessed by Tirel de Maneriis. In 1107 Henry, count of Eu, confirmed to the abbey of Le Treport a gift of Ramelin de Mesnils of land in Sept Meules *concessu Walterii Tirelli de Maisnerii domini sui*. Count Henry died in 1140, and was succeeded by his son John (d.1170). Count John, in the year of his death, confirmed his father's gift to the priory of S. Martin-du-Bosc, by a charter witnessed by Roger de Maneriis (*Harl. Soc.*, 103, p.63; Sanders, *English Baronies*, p.119).

About 1180 Reginald de Meiniers and Maud his wife gave to the abbey of Robertsbridge lands in the rape of Hastings, held of the count of Eu, which Maud's father Ingelran de Fressenvile gave her as a *maritagium*, and in exchange Reginald gave to Maud a rent of £12 *angevin* from his mill of Meiniers. In the 13th century Mesnieres occurs as Maneriis and in the 14th century as Mainieres (*Harl. Soc.*, 103, p.63). That the Manners family of Etal was descended from that of Sussex is rendered almost certain by the fact that a charter of Reginald de Maneriis, *temp.* Henry II, relating to lands in Sussex, remains amongst the duke of Rutland's muniments at Belvoir castle.

In 1166 Stephen de Bulemer, in his *carta* for the barony of Wooler, reported that Robert de Maneriis and Hugh de Dichende held one knight's fee in the barony. There can be little doubt that Robert de Maneriis belonged to the family deriving its surname from Mesnieres that had come to England in the time of William I with the count of Eu. The family holding in the barony of Wooler in Northumberland was of new feoffment and it is therefore possible that the first member of the family to come north had come with Stephen de Bulemer.

Raine, a very capable genealogist, states of the Manners family 'In addition to the unconnected and contradictory descents of this noble family contained in the Peerages, there are two MS. pedigrees of Manners, the one by Glover, *MS. Harl. 807, fol.* 30b, and the other by Vincent, in Coll. Arm; but these again vary much from each other, and in other respects seem of such questionable authority that I have been recommended by a herald, "to believe just so much of their early matches and descents as can be proved by better evidence". I deem it necessary, however, to lay before my readers the upper or doubtful part of Vincent's pedigree in that by Glover, preparatory to a more authentic genealogy' (Raine, *North Durham*, p.208).

The first six generations of Vincent's pedigree are:—

1. Sir Robert Manners, knt, lord of Etal, m. Philippa dr of sir Bartholomew Montboucher.
2. Sir Robert Manners, m. Hawise dr of baron Muschamp.
3. Sir Eustace Manners, m. Elizabeth dr of sir Henry or sir Hugh Prefene.
4. Sir Henry Manners.
5. Sir Robert Manners, m. Agnes dr of sir Davy Coupland.
6. Sir Robert Manners, dead in 36 E.III (1362), m. Alicia dr of sir Alan Heton, Alicia said to have died *circa* 29 E.III (1355).

These six generations must cover about 180 years and it is quite safe to say that the entire section of the pedigree is completely imaginary and has no relation whatever to the known facts. This is an example, unfortunately all too common, where the exercise of imagination has replaced a lack of knowledge.

In Vincent's pedigree, sir Robert Manners (No. 6 above) is given two sons. The elder is sir John Manners, aged one year (when he succeeded his father); his wife correctly is called Alicia but Alicia's son by her first husband, William de Whitchester, is oddly given as a son of sir John. Glover, perhaps correctly, states that sir John Manners died *s.p.*

Sir Robert's younger son, according to Vincent, was William Manners of Etal married to Jennet, daughter of 'Davy Baxter of Northumberland'. The maker of this pedigree may have had some information which has not survived, for in 1388 a Robert Manners appended to a charter his armorial seal of Manners and Baxter quarterly.

The later generations in Vincent's pedigree are:—

8. Sir Robert Manners, living 1402; m. Jane dr of sir Henry Strother.
9. Sir John Manners; m. Anne dr of sir John (Glover calls him sir Piers) Myddleton.

(9a. Glover introduces another sir Robert between these generations).

10. Sir Robert Manners, m. Jane dr of sir Robert Ogle, knt, and Maud his wife dr of sir John Grey.

We shall see later that this part of the pedigree is not seriously inaccurate.

Camden thought that the Manners family came originally from Manor-house, near Lanchester, co. Durham, and the idea that the surname was derived from some manor or other is hardly yet dead.

In order to explain why the Manners' coat of arms differs in tinctures only from that of the Muschamps, lords of Wooler, Raine (p.212) states that an heiress of the Muschamps carried Etal to the family of Maners. This explanation cannot be accepted. It was quite usual for a family to adopt the arms of its feudal superiors with only a small change, usually of tincture.

THE one knight's fee held by Robert de Maneriis and Hugh de Dichande in 1166 probably included the manor of Etal long held by the family of Manners and perhaps other lands, for in the 13th century Etal was held as half a knight's fee.

In the *Pipe Roll* for 1179 the sheriff records that Henry de Manerio rendered account of 80 marks for seisin of the lands of his wife's father *p.saisina tre patris uxoris sue*. Henry made annual payments towards his debt until 1186; he then owed 40s., one half of which was pardoned by breve of the king. With this assistance the debt was finally paid off in 1187. Between 1199 and 1216, perhaps *circa* 1200 Henry de Manerio and other knights who were sent to Carham to see if the infirmity whereof earl David (of Huntingdon, d.1210) *essoins* himself *de malo lecti*, is sickness or not, came to York and reported that they neither found the earl at Carham nor any one who knew about it (*CDS*. I, p.115). Henry de Manerio and Isabel his wife were considerable benefactors to Kirkham priory. Their gift to the priory of 4 bovates in Kilham was confirmed by Robert de Ros, and another gift was confirmed by Isabel de Kilham. In 1234 Thomas de Kilham also confirmed a gift to Kirkham made by Henry and Isabel de Manerio.

Throughout the greater part of the 13th and 14th centuries there was a succession of Robert de Manners holding the manor of Etal, and it is not easy to identify them separately. The second generation after Henry de Manerio was a Robert de Maneriis I 1232 x 1269. In 1232 he had a boundary dispute with William Muschamp of Barmoor. In 1242 Robert de Maneriis held Etal as half a knight's fee of new feoffment, in the barony of Muschamp, and was a juror for earl Walter Cumin *circa* 1244 (*CDS*. I, p.552). In 1250 he held half a knight's fee in the barony of Wooler of Robert Muschamp, deceased. As Robert de Manerio he was one of the jurors, 4 May 1251, to make an extent of the lands of Isabella widow of Adam de Wygeton (*Ib*., p.334), and on 20 March 1254/5 he was as a knight a juror for the *i.p.m.* of Isabella de Forde (*Ib*., p.374). About this time he was an important man on the border, and on 10 August 1255 the earls of Gloucester and Albemarle were accredited to Robert de Mesneres and others to Alexander, king of Scots, against those who would do him damage (*Ib*., p.381). He was appointed 20 September 1255 to the council of the Scots king, and was given letters of protection the next day (*Ib*., pp.387, 388). In 1256 and again in 1269 he was a juror at the assizes, his surname appearing in many different forms, Man', Maner', Maners, Manerio and Maneriis (*SS*. 88, pp.2, 52, 66, 137, 186, 192). Robert de Mesneres was still on the council of the Scots king, 6 November 1258, when Henry III made a declaration that he would afford them his counsel and aid when required (*CDS*. I, p.418).

On 16 October 1248 David de Meynners, knight, and others of the queen of Scots' retinue, were granted safe conduct to go to France (*Ib*., p.323). It is probable that sir David was a near relative, perhaps a younger brother, of the lord of Etal. The surname Menzies, pronounced Mengies, of a well known Scots family was at one time written as Meynners and kindred forms, and it is likely that they were cadets of the Manners of Etal, perhaps even descended from this sir David. In 1242 the heirs of Eustace de Maneriis held of the barony of Alnwick, Lyham, except two bovates, as one third of a knight's fee. Sir Robert de Menyres, sheriff of Berwick, witnesses in 1255 a grant to Coldingham priory by Gregory son of the marshal (*Raine*, app. p.46).

Sir Robert de Manners I evidently died before 1274, in which year Robert son of Robert Manners, was called upon to keep an agreement made by his father with Philip Haliburton about the mill of Etal. On 22 September 1278, Robert de Maners, holding 20 librates of land, not *in capite*, was distrained to take up knighthood; his sureties that he would do so were John son of Tyoch of Etal, William Scot of the same, Gilbert de Crookum and Adam Futurus (*HN*. I, p.295). He was a knight before 1281. In 1296 the goods of *domini Roberti de Manerio* at Etal were worth £27. 10s. 6d., and he was thus one of the richest men in the county (*Subsidy Roll*).

By 1328 we can be certain that the era of Robert de Manners III has been reached. In that year a Robert de Manners called on John Florison of Etal and Adam Waselesegh of Branxton to account for the moneys they had received as bailiffs of Etal. Sir Roger Heron, lord of Ford, on 21 September 1330, granted his manor of Hedgeley to Robert de Maners and his heirs (*NDD*. p.98, No. 23); this may have been a settlement as Hedgeley remained in the hands of the Heron family.

An exemplification of a fine made in 1336 was entered on the *Patent Roll*. By this Robert de Manners conveyed the manor of Etal to Hugh Sotevill, chaplain, in trust for Robert the grantor, with successive remainders to Robert son of Robert de Maners, Robert son of Adam de Maners, William son of Robert de Maners, with final remainder to the right heirs of the settlor. It is certain that Robert, the first remainder man, and William, the third remainder man, were sons of the settlor, and it is reasonable to suggest that between these two sons there was another son Adam who had died, leaving a son Robert, named after his grandfather.

The eldest son, Robert IV, was already a grown man, for in 1331 Robert de Manors, constable of Norham, and his father, petitioned the king, that for their services in the Scottish war, they should have the forfeited vill of Learmouth in the barony of Wark. Robert de Maners occurs as constable of Norham several times between 1333 and 1342, and on 18 May 1343 was appointed a justice of the peace for Norhamshire.

Sir Robert de Manners III in his lifetime acquired considerable estates. On 4 February 1335/6 William, prior of the church and convent of Durham, gave to sir Robert de Manoirs, for his good and laudable services to the church of Durham, the reversion of one and a half husbandlands in Berrington and three messuages and 46 acres in Buckton, after the death of Thomas de Gosewyk who holds the same for the term of his life (*Belvoir Deeds*). On 31 January 1334/5 king Edward III gave him, no doubt as a reward for his services in the Scottish war, two parts of the vill of Paxton in Berwickshire, lately belonging to Adam de Paxton and Alexander de Chesehelm, rebels. He also obtained lands in Goswick and Kyloe. It would seem that Robert son of Adam de Maners died before 1342, when bishop Bury gave a licence to Robert de Maners, *chevaler*, to settle two parts of the manors of Berrington and Kyloe (excepting 18 messuages and three carucates of land) on himself for life; remainder to Robert his son for life, and the heirs of his body; remainder to William the second son, and his heirs; remainder to the right heirs of Robert the elder; the reserved messuages and carucates were to be settled by Robert the son of sir Robert on himself and Margaret his wife and the survivor of them, with the same remainders.

In the proctor's roll for Norham for the 10th year of bishop Bury (1344/5) there is the record of the receipt of a palfrey for the mortuary of lady Ada de Maners. She must have been the first wife of sir Robert de Manners III. The death of his wife and the death of his eldest son Robert in 1345 or 1346 decided sir Robert to make a revised settlement of his lands in Berrington, Goswick and Kyloe. In 1346 he had a licence to settle the manor of Berrington, 12 messuages, 20 bovates and 50 acres of land there and in Goswick (subject to the life estate of Margaret widow of Robert Maners the younger) on himself for life; remainder to William Maners of Etal and the heirs of his body; remainder to Gilbert Heron and the heirs of his body; remainder to Henry de Cardoil and the heirs of his body; remainder to the right heirs of sir Robert Maners. Heron and Cardoil may have been the next heirs in the female line.

At this time William Maners, the only surviving son of sir Robert Maners was living at Etal. In 1348 a licence was given by John the prior and the convent of Durham to sir Robert de Maners to enfeoff William de Maners of Etal and Alianor his wife, in lands in Paxton, co. Berwick, held of them by military service. The same prior, on 2 October 1352, conveyed to sir Robert Maners and Elyne his wife, the third part of the demesne lands of Paxton, a third part of the fisheries in the Tweed called Streme Orrett and Brad, and lands in Auldencrawe, with remainder to Robert son of William de Maners, remainder to the right heirs of the said Robert, rendering to the prior of Coldingham the ancient rent. This is the first mention of sir Robert's second wife Elyne, and of his grandson Robert son of William de Maners. The latter was perhaps the Robert de Maners appointed constable of Norham castle and sheriff and escheator of Norhamshire 1 August 1345. Robert may have already received some of the outlying portions of the estate for in 1345 Robert de Maners, *chevaler*, made fine with the king for 10 marks for permission to assign to a certain chaplain to hold by mortmain 5 messuages and 170 acres in Hetherslaw and Brankston (*Exch. Roll* 19E.III, ro.34). Raine, and he has been followed by many later historians, has derived the later Manners of Etal from this Robert, but when sir Robert de Manners III died in 1355 the heir to his lands in Berrington, Kyloe, Buckton and Goswick, a messuage in Holy Island and the eighth part of fisheries in the Tweed called Blakewell and Twedemuthstell, was his son John, stated in the *i.p.m.* of 10 March 1355 to be 1½ years old. Margaret widow of Robert, and Eleanor widow of William, sons of Robert de Maners, held lands in Berrington for the term of their lives, no doubt in respect of their dowers.

Quite late in life, sir Robert de Maners III had taken a second wife, by name Ellen (Eleanor or Elyne) but we have no record of her parentage. Early in 1354 they had a son John, who became his father's heir. In a proof of age of the heir taken in 1375 he is stated to have been twenty-one on 28 September last (*AA1*, IV, p.328). An inquest taken on 19 April 1355 states that John was one year and three weeks old (*PRO. Chancery i.p.m.* Edw.III, file 130). Another inquest makes him one and a half years old on 10 March 1355 (*Durham i.p.m. 10 Hatfield, Dep. Keeper's Rep.* vol.xlv, app.i, p.235). The proof of age of 1375 was taken at Felton. William de Rodom deposed that the said John was 21 years old on Friday the Vigil of St Michael last; he was born at Etal and baptised in the church of Ford, when Roger Heroun was rector; he recollected the day because he saw the said John baptised by John de Clyfford, *chivaler*, who was his godfather. Thomas de Witton deposed that he had been at the burial of Robert Maners, father of the said John, at Ford, and heard people compute the age of the said John, and that he was a year and three weeks old on the day his father died.

In 1358 Ellen widow of Robert Maners, fined £20 to have the marriage of her son John; she married secondly John de la More of More, Lancs., and died 3 August 1362. The king then committed to Edward Letham custody of a carucate of land in Etal which Alma (*sic*) who was wife of Robert de Man's deceased, and one carucate of land in the same vill and 4s., rent in Tosson, and also the third part of the manor of Etal to hold until the heir was of age, rendering to the king £10 a year and providing for the sustenance of the heir (*Exch. Roll* 36 E.III, ro. 9, in *HN.* iii, II, p.329). Johanna widow of Edward Letham, married Robert Clavering.

We have already seen that John Maners, the heir, came of age in 1375. In 1379 William Heron, *chivaler*, was plaintiff in a suit against John son and heir of Robert de Maners, about the marriage of the said John which Heron claimed should appertain to him by the demise of John de la Mora, sometime husband of Elene de la Mora to whom Edward III demised the same. Heron's claim was that Robert de Maners had held of him by military service (*de Banco Roll*). Although their main property of Etal was not held of the Herons, the Manners may have held other lands as their feudal tenants. In 1381 John Maners sued Robert de Clavering and Johanna his wife about waste lands in Etal (*de Banco Roll*).

John Manners had married Alice daughter of sir William Delaval (d.1349), sister and heiress of sir Henry Delaval of Seaton Delaval. When her brother sir Henry died in 1388 she was about 40 years of age and then wife of John de Whitchester. In 1390 John Maners, *chivaler*, and Alicia his wife, by William de Soulby, their attorney, claimed half the manor of Newsham from John de la Vale and Margaret his wife, and a fourth part of the manor of Benwell from William de la Vale (*de Banco Roll*). Alice was quite a few years older than her second husband, and it is unlikely that they had any children, for if there had been any they would eventually have been heirs to some of the Delaval estates.

The inquisitions taken after Alice's death on 26 December 1402 describe her as a widow. If this description is correct, her husband John Manners was already dead. He was alive earlier in 1402 when John Wilkynson of Tynemouth had a suit against John Manners, esquire, and Alicia his wife, concerning the goods and chattels of the said John (*de Banco Roll*).

References to a Robert Maners, apparently the next owner of Etal, occur from 1387 onwards. In February 1387 the king's escheator reported that certain persons had entered Chillingham castle by guile and had shut up sir Alan de Heton in a tower there; four months later Henry, earl of Northumberland, and John Nevill of Raby were appointed to go with the escheator to free sir Alan and arrest ten persons, including Robert Maners, who were holding the castle by force (*Cal. Pat. Rolls*). On 12 May 1388 Robert Manners appended to a charter his seal of Manners and Baxter quarterly (*Laing Charters*, No. 80).

The place of Robert Manners in the pedigree has never been satisfactorily explained. Raine thought that he was the son and heir of William Manners of Etal mentioned in 1352. This cannot be right for when sir Robert Manners died in 1354 his heir was his infant son John, so that there could not then have been surviving male descendants of sir Robert's two elder sons, Robert and William. As John Maners came of age in 1374 and did not marry Alice de Whitchestre until about 1389 it might be thought possible that she was not his first wife. He was apparently unmarried in 1379 when his marriage was claimed by William Heron.

If John Maners had been married when he was eighteen years old, he could have had a son born in 1372. At the taking of Chillingham castle in May 1387 such son would only have been fifteen and thus hardly old enough to have engaged in an enterprise of this nature as one of the principals. It is much more likely that Robert of 1387 was a younger brother of John Manners. John was one year and three weeks old when his father died and could have had a younger brother, perhaps posthumous, born in 1354 who in 1387 would have been 33 years old. Vincent may have had some information, not now available to us, when he stated that John Maners was succeeded by his brother Robert.

On 28 July 1407 Robert de Maners was appointed a justice of assize in Norhamshire and Islandshire; a justice for gaol delivery at Norham 24 May 1421; a justice of the peace for Norhamshire and Islandshire 6 September 1421. In 1402 Robert de Maners the father (*le pier*), gave his son John de Maners, esquire, and Agnes his wife, daughter of John de Midylton in frank marriage, the manor of Humbleton, lands and burgages in Wooler, the fortlet of Lanton, lands in Coupland and Coupland mill (*Belvoir Deeds*). These must be the lands acquired by marriage with the Baxter heiress.

The description of Robert de Maners in 1402 as *le pier* might suggest that he had a son also called Robert. If this was so Robert the son may have been the eldest son, and the person of this name who owned the castle of Etal and the tower of Hethpool in 1415 (*Border Holds*, pp.14, 17). He was perhaps the Robert de Maners appointed a justice of gaol delivery at Norham 24 May 1421 and a justice of the peace for Norhamshire and Islandshire 6 September 1421.

The younger son of Robert de Maners *le pier* was John Maners, sheriff of Northumberland in 1413, who had married in 1402 Agnes daughter of sir John Midylton of Belsay.

This John Maners of Etal was concerned in the violent death of his neighbour William Heron of Ford on 20 January 1427/8. Isabella Heron, William's widow, complained that her husband had been 'maliciously slain by the said John Maners and his adherents'. Maners' reply to the charge was that neither he, John his son, nor William Andrewson his servant were guilty. He claimed that Heron with his servant 'and others with them came the day of the deed from Norham to Etal, in the town of the said John, with force and arms, and in his men and servants great assault made in shooting of arrows, striking with swords, and proposed to have slain them'. He asserted that neither he nor his son John were near hand Heron 'by a spear length or more' when the latter

was killed. Eventually the prior of Durham and the prior of Tynemouth were called in to arbitrate, who declared that John Maners, John Maners his son and heir, sir John of Medilton and all his sons of age being in England, all the sons-in-law of John Maners, Thomas Ilderton, Wm Strother, Will. Carnaby, Henr. Fenwyk and John Fenwyk of kin to Maners were to 'lawfully submit them with words and deeds of humbleness and submission'; and Maners was to cause 500 masses to be sung within the year for the relieving of the soul of William Heron (Raine, *North Durham*, pp.210-211).

Wm Strother and Henry Fenwyk were second cousins for their grandmothers were sisters. John Fenwyk was Henry Fenwick's uncle; and William Carnaby's wife is said to have been a daughter of Henry Fenwick. It is not known how any of these were 'of kin' to the Maners.

John Maners married (secondly) before 1404 Margery widow of Edward Ilderton; Thomas Ilderton of 1428 was no doubt a relative of John Maners' wife.

Sir John Maners died 6 September 1438 when Robert Maners, his son and heir, was aged 30. John Maners who had been son and heir in 1428 must have died in his father's lifetime. It is evident however that sir John Maners had a younger son, also called John, as in 1440 William Craustur sued Thomas Ramys, son of John Ramys, late of Shortflat, executor of the will of the said John Ramys, and John Maners the elder, gentleman, son of sir John Maners of Etall, knt., and Margaret his wife, coexecutrix of the said will, for 40s. (*de Banco Roll*, 717 mem. 346d. quoted *NCH*. X, p.349). This John Maners the elder, gentleman, may have been ancestor of the Manners of Cheswick.

Sir Robert Maners was justice of the peace in Norhamshire 1438, sheriff of Northumberland 1454 and MP for Northumberland in 1459. The writ for his *i.p.m.* was issued in 1461. According to Stow he was buried in the church of the Augustinian Friars in London. He married Johanna daughter of sir Robert Ogle (d.1436) of Ogle. The brief for her *i.p.m.* is dated 24 March 1488.

Their children seem to have been Robert (son and heir), John, Gilbert, Thomas and Jane. According to Dalton's Visitation of 1558 Jane married William Swynnoe of Cornhill, and from the same source we learn that Gylberte Manners, 2nd brother to sir Robert Manners of Etal, had a base and sole daughter Ewffema who married Raufe Bradford of Bradford. Gilbert may have been the man of this name who was bailiff of Embleton 1478 x 1485 (*NCH*. II, p.36). John son of sir Robert Manners, is said to have been *serviens* of Richard Nevill, earl of Warwick and Salisbury; he died in June 1492 and was buried in the Collegiate Church of St Mary at Warwick; an engraving of his monument is in Dugdale's *Warwickshire*, 348. For Thomas son of sir Robert Manners *see* MANNERS OF BERRINGTON.

Sir Robert Manners, eldest son of sir Robert Manners (d.1461), was sheriff of Northumberland 1463, 1464 and 1485. His marriage brought him into the ranks of the lesser nobility, for his wife was Eleanor daughter of Thomas lord Roos, and eldest sister and coheiress of Edmund, lord Roos. Her mother was Philippa daughter of John, lord Tiptoft, earl of Worcester. According to the *i.p.m.* of sir Robert Manners taken on 8 October 1495 he had died about the feast of St Bartholomew last past. George Manners, of full age, was his son and next heir.

MANNERS of ETAL, par. FORD

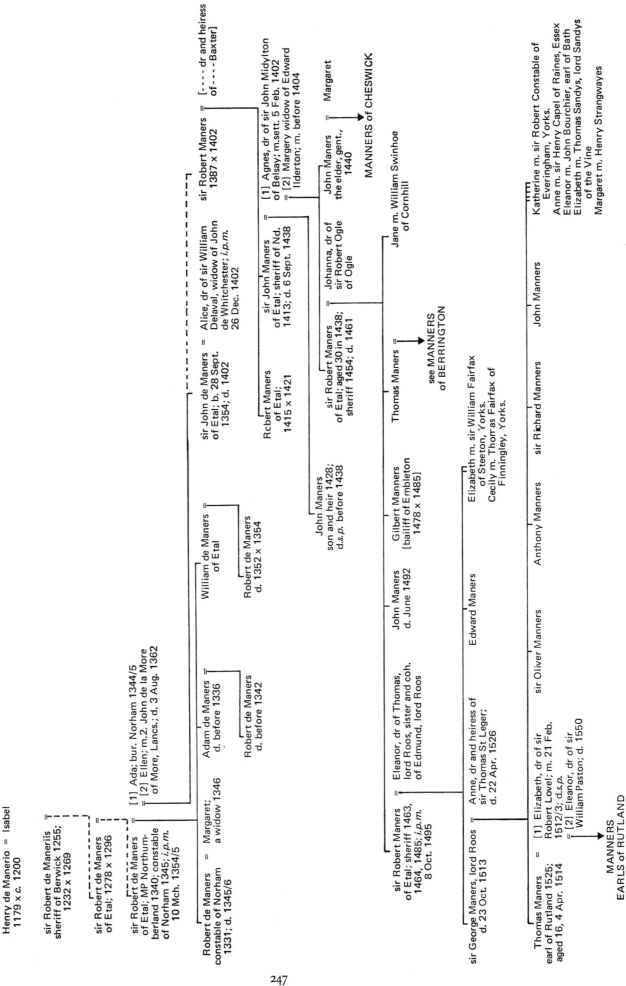

By 1501 George Manners was a knight and licence was granted to him to enter without inquest upon lands lately held by his father and he had pardon for all intrusions on the same. On the death of his maternal aunt Isabel Lovel, probably in 1512, sir George became 11th lord Roos. He died 23 October 1513 and was buried in St George's Chapel at Windsor. An *i.p.m.* taken at Holy Island 4 April 1514 found that Thomas Manners, aged 16, was his son and heir. Thomas' mother was Anne only daughter and heiress of sir Thomas St Leger, by Anne daughter of Richard, duke of York, and sister to Edward IV.

Lady Anne Ros died in 1526 and an *i.p.m.* was taken at Scremerston on 15 December 1528. A rough draft of an inquest signed by Wyllem Heron has survived 'We xij men find that my lady Ann Royse died vj day of May and the xviij year of king Herre the viijth and she was in possession at the said day in Berrington xxiiij *li.* In Buckton xls. and in Island and Norhamshire xxxs. and Thomas, lord Rousse, her son and heir, being of the age of xxiiij years or more; and for the holding of these lands we know not whether that holds be socage or knightservice, by the evidence we can get'.

In 1525 (18 June) Thomas Manners, lord Roos, was created earl of Rutland. Previous to this the Manners' coat of arms had been Sable, two bars azure, a chief gules, but by letters patent 18 June 1525 the earl of Rutland, on account of his royal descent, was granted in place of the original chief, a chief quarterly azure and gules, on the first and fourth two fleur de lys or, on the second and third a lion passant guardant of the first.

At this time the family was no longer resident at Etal and in 1547 they exchanged it with the Crown for lands elsewhere. The later descent of the family will be found in the peerages.

MANNERS OF CHESWICK, CHAP. ANCROFT

ABOUT 1208 x 1210 the vill of Cheswick was held in thirds. Patric de Chesewic and John de Hagardestun (decd) each held one of the thirds in socage at annual rents of 33s. 4d. The remaining third was a freehold held by William son of Adam de Chesewic at a rent of 33s. 4d.

An *i.p.m.* on 6 May 1403 found that Patric de Cheswick died seised of a capital messuage and demesne and other lands in Cheswick held as one twentieth of a knight's fee. His heirs were his two daughters Matilda, aged 20, and Elizabeth, aged 3. Matilda was already married to Robert de Strangways whose homage was taken for his wife's lands on 28 May 1403. Elizabeth married Robert de Maners, no doubt a cadet of the Maners of Etal. Elizabeth Maners died 19 October 1459, (*i.p.m.* 18 December 1459), when the heir to her one-sixth of Cheswick was her son John, then aged 22. This John Maners is described as John son of Robert son of John Maners when he gave lands in Cheswick to his brother Robert.

Raine (*North Durham*, p.230) suggests that Robert de Maners who married the Cheswick heiress was probably son of the sir John Maners of Etal 'who died before 1438'. This is perhaps correct for in 1440 John Manners the elder, gentleman, son of sir John Maners of Etal, knt., and Margaret his wife, who was co-executrix of the will of John Ramys, late

of Shortflatt, esquire, were sued for 40s. (*de Banco Roll*, 717 mem., 346d., quoted in *NCH*. X, p.349). Margaret was presumably a Raymes of Shortflatt.

John Maners of Cheswick died in 1470 or 1471 (*i.p.m.* 17 October 1471) when his son and heir Robert was four years old. The latter died young and *s.p.* leaving his two sisters, Margaret and Elizabeth as his coheiresses. The former married Henry Swinhoe (*i.p.m.* 18 November 1544), and the latter her kinsman Thomas Maners, and after his death, Ralph Haggerston. An inquisition taken at Holy Island 8 June 1538 after the death of Elizabeth widow of Thomas Manners and of Ralph Haggerston, and one of the daughters and heiresses of John Manners, late lord of Cheswick, found that Thomas Manners aged 30 is her son by Thomas Manners her former husband, and next heir. Besides her eldest son Thomas, she had two younger sons William and Henry. William Manners was one of the gentlemen of Bamburghshire in 1560. He was living at Orde in Norhamshire 7 August 1570 when he made his will. After directing that he is to be buried in the church of Tweedmouth he leaves his cott house and the sixth part of South Yerrowe to his son Thomas and for default of him to his son Nicholas. Nicholas, evidently the eldest son, is to have all his lands with successive remainders to the testator's son Thomas, his brother Henry and his cousin George. William Manners had a house in Berwick for his lifetime from his brother Thomas, late of Cheswick, and had since bought it from his 'cousin' Thomas son and heir of his said brother Thomas; William had since then sold the house to his brother Henry. He gives his son Richard a legacy of 40s., to his sister of Orde, to William Manners and to Henrie Manners of Holderness each 10s. He mentions in his will that he owes John Manners of London four barrels of salmon. The fact that his son Richard is only to have a small legacy and is omitted from the entail of the estates might suggest that he was illegitimate (*SS*. 38, p.218n.).

William Manners may have survived the making of his will for some years, for it was not until 29 May 1584 that an *i.p.m.* was held at Tweedmouth to determine who was heir to his lands. This was his son Nicholas aged 30. Martyn Garnett of Berwick, alderman, in his w.d. 17 February 1581/2 refers to 'my farmhold in Orde both water and land which I have of Nicholas Manners'. In the inventory of the debts owing to Luke Ogle of Eglingham attached to his w.d. 5 July 1596 is the item 'Nychollas Manners for a fine for one farm in Burton' (*SS*. 112, p.161).

Nicholas Manners of the Newtown (par. Bamburgh) had 114 sheep stolen by Scots raiders on 19 September 1589. Although described as of the Newtown, he was living at Burton when he made his w.d. 29 July 1598. He was then 'sick in body but perfect in memory'. The whole of his lands, his goods moveable and unmoveable, his houses, corn and cattle are to go to his wife Jane during her lifetime 'and unto the child that she is with presently, if it shall please God that the child shall come into the world heritably' (*Dur. Prob. Off.* by C.R.H.). The expected child was a daughter Isabella, born posthumously.

In 1631 John Ord esq., held lands in Orde, late Burrell's and Nicholas Manners', at a rent of £4. 8s.; George Manners paid 44s. 4d. for lands in Orde (*Raine*, app. p.156).

In 1542 the tower at Branxton and part of the town belonged to John Selby, gent., the remainder being of the inheritance of the earl of Rutland and Thomas Manors, gent. At Cheswick there was a little tower of the inheritance of one Thomas Mannors and others but it was in decay for a lack of reparations.

An *i.p.m.* taken at Norham 20 May 1546 after the death of Thomas Maners of Cheswick found that his heir was his son Thomas aged 21. Thomas' will dated 3 July 1545 is recited in the *i.p.m.* 'First I bequeath my soul to God Almighty which did redeem me with his precious blood, to the holy and blessed Virgin Marie his mother and to all the celestial company in heaven and my body to be buried in the quire of the Church of Holy Island before the glass windows where my father and mother with all other my predecessors doth lie, with soul mass and dirge the day of my burial, for my soul and all Christian souls and my coat armour to be set upon my grave for remembrance which they shall cause to be made with blue and yellow colours of canvas'. It is unfortunate that at this point the will is partly illegible for Maners proceeds to describe the armorial bearings to be placed on his shield, *viz.* 'a Rede bare a bow in the—sant thre—thre swerells thre salmonds and a —owe'. The testator continues 'if God call upon my wife to his mercy' she was to 'be buried as near my grave as may be'. The version of the will as printed in *SS*. 2. is wrong. The correct reading is not 'Jone my wife' but 'if God caull apone my wyief to his m'cye'. His son Thomas is to be heir to all his lands and failing him and the issue of his body lawfully begotten, to his other sons Alexander, Oliver, Henry and George in entail in succession 'then to return to such issue as it shall please God that my bedfellow and I shall have, and failing of all my issue lawfully begotten then to remain to my brother William Man(er)s,' and 'then to remain to the next true descent of lineage'. His wife is to have a third part of his lands and goods. The supervisors of the will are to be his brother William Maners and his brother-in-law George Carr. Thomas Maners died on 6 July 1545. It is not known whether George Carr was a brother of Thomas Maners' wife or had married a sister of his; Raine states that it was the former.

The blue and yellow colours of the canvas for the shield no doubt were to represent the tinctures of the Manners coat of arms—Or two bars azure and a chief gules. The shield to be displayed at the funeral was perhaps a quarterly one. The three salmon undoubtedly represent the arms of Orde of Ord—Sable three salmon paleways argent. Raine suggested that the three squirrels must represent Creswell—Gules three roundels argent each charged with a squirrel gules, sitting and cracking a nut. There was however a family of Langton that held one sixth of Orde in the 15th and 16th centuries, and a David Langeton used a seal on which was a squirrel sitting erect (*AA3*. VI, p.119). In 1443 bishop Langley granted his licence to Thomas Langton of Orde in Norhamshire to settle a sixth part of Orde and other lands. By 1451 Langton had died leaving Alice and Johanna his daughters under age (*Raine*, p.249). In 1532 Orde was held by George Orde, Thomas Manners, John Langton and John Burrell (*Ib.*, p.251n.). In 1560 William Maners, Widow Maners and Roland Burrell each held one-sixth of Orde and John Orde held one half (*Ib.*, p.23). Presumably a Langton married an Orde heiress, and at a later date a Manners married a Langton heiress, so that Thomas Maners in 1545 could quarter the arms of both families. In 1580 Orde was a village of John Orde's

and Thomas Manners', Nicholas Maners' and Rowland Burrell's with 10 tenants all unfurnished with arms (*CBP*. I, p.18).

The third Thomas Manners, who had been 21 years old in 1546 only survived his father a matter of five years. An *i.p.m.* taken at Norham on 16 April 1551 found that his heir was his son Thomas aged 2. Henry Ogle and Maryane his wife were seised for the life of Maryane of lands in Orde and Unthank in satisfaction of her dower as widow of Thomas Maners father of the said Thomas. Mention is made of Thomas' uncles William and Henry. Maryane was evidently widow of Thomas Manners (d.1545).

In one of his MS volumes of wills and inventories (VI, p.7) Raine gives extracts of the will dated 6 Nov. 1551 4 E.VI of Thomas Maners of Cheswick. The will does not now appear to be in the Durham Probate Office, but this particular volume of Raine's has on the front cover a pencil note 'Also contains wills from Prerogative Court Canterbury and from Hunter MSS 32'. The will may therefore be from one of these other sources. 4 E.VI is 1550 not 1551.

Raine's precis of the will is as follows—'my wife and my child exors—my uncle Will. Maners & Hen. ——supervisors —To my brother Henry Maners xxs. worth of land in Branxton for life rem. to my child—I give him the water of South Yarrowe—to my ii brether ——'.

Thomas Manners IV of Cheswick is stated by Raine to have married Margaret daughter of Henry Orde of Orde but this is incorrect. When Thomas Gray of Kyloe registered his pedigree in 1615 he recorded that his mother was Fortune daughter of Thomas Manners of Cheswick and that his father's sister Anne had married Thomas Manners—a case of sister and brother marrying brother and sister. Manners' wife was therefore Anne daughter of Raphe Grey of Kyloe. This is confirmed in Thomas Manners' will for in it he mentions 'my brother Henrye Graye'.

The will of Thomas Manners is dated 12 January 1592/3. By it he leaves to his eldest son George all his lands, waters and hereditiments in Orde, Cheswick, Branxton, Paston, Tweedmouth, Unthank, Holy Island and elsewhere in any other place 'to him and the heirs of his body lawfully begotten and failing thereof to my son Henry and his heirs'. Henry who was evidently under age, is to have £40 'to be paid unto him within six years next coming, and I commit him to my brother George Carleton, if he please to accept and take him'. George Carleton was son of Guy Carleton, captain of Norham. Guy had married '(blank) daughter and heiress of Rodham, widow of (blank) Manners' (*Harleian Soc.* 53. pp.147-148); she was Phelyx daughter of John Roddam (*NCH*. XIV, p.284). George Carleton became bishop of Chichester.

Manners' four daughters Agnes, Isabell, Margarett and Elizabeth are each to have £40. He had covenanted with his good friend Mr George Morton, alderman, that his son George should marry one of Morton's daughters. In consideration of this Morton is to pay £100 as dowry to redeem from mortgage for the use of the said George Manners and his wife the eighth share of the fishing water of South Yarrow. The testator gives his uncle George Manners 5 marks yearly during his life (*SS*. 38, p.218).

It is not known for certain that George Manners married a daughter of George Morton. The latter in his w.d. 21 April 1613 leaves £200 each to his daughters Jane, Ellinor and Mary but does not mention if they are married. Ellinor died unmarried before 24 July 1637, and Jane married Peter Jones of Holy Island. Mary may have married George Manners.

Thomas Manners IV was buried at Holy Island 19 January 1592/3. Although his son and heir George died 6 May 1633 his *i.p.m.* was not held until 6 December 1639. In the printed calendar his name is given as Thomas in error. Henry, aged 40, was his son and next heir. Henry Manners sold some of his property to Thomas Fenwick of Tweedmouth, for the latter in his w.d. 3 October 1626 mentions 'the land and waters purchased of Mr Henry Manners'.

After the death of Henry Manners, his widow Dorothy and Jane Manners, spinster, their daughter, sold two farms called Tenland and Twelveland farms to Henry Shell, gent., in return for an annuity, 13 June C.II (1688) (*Raine*, p.232n.). There must have been an earlier sale to Henry Shell of Berwick for he by his w.d. 12 March 1672 gives to his son Henry and his heirs for ever 'my land of Cheswick he paying Mrs Mannors and her daughters that which I owe them for the said land and £15 to my wife which I paid Jane Manners in part'. On 9 August 1693 John Davy, gent., and Jane his wife, late Jane Manners, executrix of Elizabeth Parlett, alias Manners, her late sister, deceased, and Eleanor Ford conveyed their interest in the two Cheswick farms to Edward Haggerston. It would seem that Jane Davy, Eleanor Ford and Elizabeth Parlett were the three daughters and co-heiresses of Henry Manners.

MANNERS OF BERRINGTON, CHAP. KYLOE

We have already noticed that bishop Beaumont in 1327 gave the manor of Berrington to sir Robert de Maners III for his lifetime. On 4 February 1335 William, prior of the church and convent of Durham, for the good and laudable services that Robert de Manoirs, *miles*, had given to our church of Durham, gave and conceded to the said Robert the reversion of all lands and tenements with appurtenances that Thomas de Gosewyk holds for his lifetime in the vills of Berrington and Buckton by our gift, *viz.*, in Berrington one and a half husbandlands which were Thomas son of Margarets, and in Buckton three messuages and 46 acres of land, to hold the said lands, tenements and messuages after the death of the said Thomas to the said Robert and his heirs in perpetuity of the chief lord of the fee by ancient services (*Belvoir Deeds*). At a later date, probably in the late 15th century these lands seem to have been used as a portion for a younger son. Before 1342 sir Robert had apparently acquired the whole manor for he settled two parts of it on his sons Robert and William successively.

About the beginning of the 16th century a cadet branch of the Manners held lands in Berrington direct of the bishop of Durham. In the first year of bishop Bainbridge (1507) there was a writ of *diem clausit extremum* concerning Isabella widow of Thomas Maners of Berrington esq. This is a writ to the escheator to summon a jury to inquire as to what lands a tenant was seised of at the time of his death. In the Durham Records of Chancery Enrolments this document is erroneously described in the margin as a writ *de dote assignada* (*i.e.* a writ to assign dower). Raine has accepted the incorrect marginal note. It is evident that it was the widow Isabella who had

died in 1507, not her husband. This is proved by the fact that in the same year (1507) there was issued to Thomas Maners, son and heir of Isabella widow of Thomas Maners, late of Berrington, licence of entry into the lands of his late mother in Islandshire and Norhamshire without prosecution of livery.

In 13 bishop Ruthal (1522) there was a precept issued for an *i.p.m.* in respect of Thomas Maners and in the following year (1 bishop Wolsey) Thomas Maners, son and heir of Thomas Maners, esq., was given a licence to enter without proof of age on lands lately held by his father.

It seems almost certain that the second Thomas Maners of Berrington married Elizabeth sister and coheiress of Robert Maners of Cheswick, and founded the second line of Manners of Cheswick. In 1509 Elizabeth widow of Thomas Maners, late of Cheswick, esquire, was to have an assignment of dower out of the lands of her late husband. The Berrington lands passed in some way to the Manners of Etal for in 1560 it was reported that Berrington had been held by Henry, earl of Rutland, but 'is now in demesnes to the Queen's Majesty —and no other man hath any part on inheritance or rent in the same'.

Raine in his pedigree of Manners of Etal suggested that the first Thomas Maners of Berrington was a younger son of sir John Maners (d.1438) of Etal, but the dates are hardly suitable for this identification. In 1458 Robert Maners, junior, esquire, and Thomas Maners, esquire, charged Richard Baynbryge of Brancepeth, co. Durham, with detaining six horses, five mules etc. at Overgrass (*de Banco Roll*). Robert and Thomas were probably both sons of sir Robert Manners (sheriff 1454), and Thomas was perhaps the first Thomas Manners of Berrington, who died about 1507.

MANNERS OF FRAMLINGTON, PAR. FELTON

About the middle of the 16th century a branch of the Manners family acquired property at Longframlington, and there seems little doubt that they were cadets of the Manners of Cheswick. The exact connection however is unknown. John Manners (d.1470) and Thomas Manners (d.1545) both of Cheswick owned property in Holy Island. Certain lands in Holy Island are described, 19 July 1583, as lying *inter terras Umfridi Mayners* (Raine, *North Durham*, p.183n.). In a rental of Norhamshire and Islandshire drawn up in 1631 John Swinhoe paid a rent of 2d. for Manners' land of Longframlington. In the inventory of the goods dated 25 August 1649 of Roger Manners of Newmoor House, par. Longframlington, gent., it is recorded that the tenant at Holy Island owed 13s. 4d. for one half year's rent due at Whitsuntide (*NCH.* VII, p.443). In the 16th century the families of Manners and Burrell had been neighbours at Orde, and John Burrell of Longframlington by his w.d. 13 May 1551 appoints Wm Maners, gent., a supervisor. No one of the name of Manners had attended the muster of 1538 from Framlington.

William Maners of Framlington made his will 2 March 1572/3 (proved 1574). He gives his soul 'to Almighty God and to all the holy company of heaven' and his body 'to be buried within my parish church of Our Lady at Framlington within the quere with my duty accustomed by the law'. All his lands are to go to his son Umfray Maners, and his daughter Jane Maners is to have 7s. of land belonging to the

MANNERS of CHESWICK, chap. ANCROFT, and of BERRINGTON, chap. KYLOE

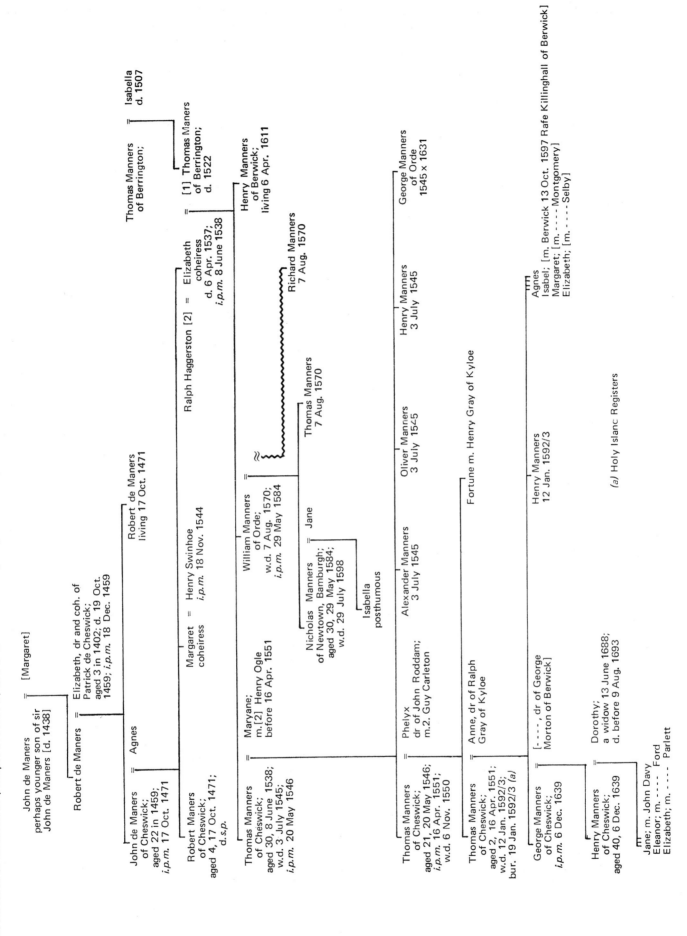

John de Maners
perhaps younger son of sir
John de Maners [d. 1438]   =   [Margaret]

Robert de Maners   =   Elizabeth, dr and coh. of
                          Patrick de Cheswick;
                          aged 3 in 1402; d. 19 Oct.
                          1459; *i.p.m.* 18 Dec. 1459

Robert de Maners
living 17 Oct. 1471

Thomas Maners
of Berrington;   Isabella
                                  d. 1507

[1] Thomas Maners
of Berrington;
d. 1522

John de Maners
of Cheswick;
aged 22 in 1459;
i.p.m. 17 Oct. 1471   =   Agnes

Robert Maners
of Cheswick;
aged 4, 17 Oct. 1471;
d.s.p.

Margaret   =   Henry Swinhoe
coheiress   *i.p.m.* 18 Nov. 1544

Ralph Haggerston [2]   =   Elizabeth
                             coheiress
                             d. 6 Apr. 1537;
                             i.p.m. 8 June 1538

Henry Manners
of Berwick;
living 6 Apr. 1611

Thomas Manners
of Cheswick;
aged 30, 8 June 1538;
w.d. 3 July 1545;
i.p.m. 20 May 1546   =   Maryane;
                             m.[2] Henry Ogle
                             before 16 Apr. 1551

William Manners
of Orde;
w.d. 7 Aug. 1570;
i.p.m. 29 May 1584

Richard Manners
7 Aug. 1570

Thomas Manners
7 Aug. 1570

Nicholas Manners
of Newtown, Bamburgh;
aged 30, 29 May 1584;
w.d. 29 July 1598

Jane

Isabella
posthumous

Thomas Manners
of Cheswick;
aged 21, 20 May 1546;
i.p.m. 16 Apr. 1551;
w.d. 6 Nov. 1550   =   Phelyx
                         dr of John Roddam;
                         m.2. Guy Carleton

Alexander Manners
3 July 1545

Oliver Manners
3 July 1545

Henry Manners
3 July 1545

George Manners
of Orde
1545 × 1631

Thomas Manners
of Cheswick;
aged 2, 16 Apr. 1551;
w.d. 12 Jan. 1592/3;
bur. 19 Jan. 1592/3 (a)   =   Anne, dr of Ralph
                                Gray of Kyloe

Fortune m. Henry Gray of Kyloe

George Manners
of Cheswick;
i.p.m. 6 Dec. 1639   =   [- - -, dr of George
                              Morton of Berwick]

Henry Manners
12 Jan. 1592/3

Agnes
Isabel; [m. Berwick 13 Oct. 1597 Rafe Killinghall of Berwick]
Margaret; [m. - - - - Montgomery]
Elizabeth; [m. - - - - Selby]

Henry Manners
of Cheswick;
aged 40, 6 Dec. 1639   =   Dorothy;
                             a widow 13 June 1688;
                             d. before 9 Aug. 1693

Jane; m. John Davy
Eleanor; m. - - - - Ford
Elizabeth; m. - - - - Parlett

(a) Holy Island Registers

demesnes for her life natural. Henry Muschampe's three children are to have three stirks of a year old to be kept to the children's behalf. His wife Elizabeth and his son Umfray are to be executors, 'they to dispone the rest of my goods to the honour of God and for the weal of my soul'.

Humphrey Manners was party to a deed with Thomas Arnold of Brinkburn 1590/1. The next member of the family to own property in Framlington was Lancelot Manners who is first mentioned 13 December 1609 as a witness to the will of Lancelot Creswell of Framlington.

The Christian names of William, Humphrey and Lancelot of the three earliest known members of the family of Manners of Framlington might suggest a close connection with the family of Lisle of Felton; two of the sons of sir William Lisle (d.1529) of Felton were called Humphrey and Lancelot. An inventory of the chattels of Mr Launcelott Maners of Long Framlington was made on 17 June 1611. Sequestration of his goods was granted to Anne his widow on 30 June 1612 and a further grant on 15 October 1612. Not until 11 March 1612/3 was administration of the will issued, and as the executor named was John Maners, son of the deceased and a minor, administration was issued to Agnes Maners, mother of John and to his uncle William Carr, and they were to be guardians of the young son during his minority. The two administrators were also to have tuition of the younger children, Roger, Barbara, Delbora and Dorothy (*Dur. Prob. Off.* by C.R.H.—the will is no longer extant). Lancelot Manners' wife was Agnes daughter of John Carr of Woodhall. In the pedigree registered by Agnes' brother William Carr in 1615, she is wrongly called Ann. Another brother, Roger Carr of Newmoor House, in his w.d. 1 April 1620 mentions Mrs Mayners of Framlington and Barbary Mayners of the same. Mrs Annas Manners is mentioned as a creditor of William Carr of Hetton in his w.d. 15 November 1624.

On 26 October 1633 Roger Manners of Framlington entered into a bond of marriage with Jane Heselrigg. She was a daughter of Robert Heselrig (d.1638) of Swarland. Henry Heselrigge of Swarland in his w.d. 20 March 1637/8 mentions his sister Mrs Jane Manners. It seems evident that John Manners, Lancelot's eldest son, died *s.p.* An inventory of the goods of Rodger Maners, gent., late of Newmoor House in the chapelry of Long Framlington was exhibited on 25 August 1649. His main assets were his farming stock but he had instruments of wood, worth £6, two pairs of new wheels with some other small wood lately cut, £2. 10s.; the bedding, linning with all such moveables were valued at £16 and his raiment at £5. The expenses at the funeral were £16. 7s. 7d. It is in this inventory that the rent due from the tenant at Holy Island is mentioned. This small property was still owned by the family in 1787.

On 23 August 1649 Robert Manners natural and legitimate son of Roger Manners of Long Framlington, par. Felton, deceased, personally appeared in the place of the consistory in Durham and saying that he was 15 years old chose Wm Hesilrigg, esq., his uncle as his guardian (*Dur. Prob. Off.* by C.R.H.). On 8 September 1649 commission was issued to take oath of Anne Manners, late wife of Roger Manners, gent., and four days later she received grant of administration; no children are mentioned, but besides the eldest son Robert, there was a younger son Roger.

The younger son Roger was living at Newmoor House 1674-1682 and at Smallburn 1689-1700. He married at Bolam 10 September 1667, Elizabeth (blank) and she was buried 23 February 1680/1 at Felton. It is unknown where Roger Manners was living between his marriage at Bolam in September 1667 and the death of his daughter Jane at Newmoor House in May 1673, but it is evident that he had children born during this period. Unfortunately the Longhorsley registers have a hiatus 1670-1694 due to 'an illiterate parish clerk' who had been entrusted with the job of transcribing the first register, which was in poor repair, but failed to do so in a satisfactory way; he omitted the entries he could not decipher and then burnt the original. No Manners entries survived. (Inf. from Mr Gordon Matthews). There are no records of baptisms of any of his children at Bolam or Felton in this interval; John Manners living at Newmoor House in 1719 and at Windy Banke in 1720 must have been a son of Roger and born 1667 x 1673.

Roger married secondly, at Felton 11 March 1681/2, Catherine Strangeways; she was daughter of Edward Strangways of Cheswick who in his w.d. 11 March 1682/3 gives £20 to his grandchild Thomas Manners. A son of Roger Manners was Edward Manners at one time of Swarland Fence who died at Smalldean in 1737. Another son Roger, bap. 8 June 1693, was perhaps Roger Manners 'a schoolboy at Mr Widdrington's' bur. Alnwick 11 May 1706.

Robert Manners, who had been aged 15 in 1649, married at Felton, 12 June 1660, Jane daughter and coheiress of Edward Lisle of Acton, and with her acquired lands in North Acton and Old Felton. Mr Robert Maners was one of the four and twenty of Felton church 1659-1661 and 1683. In 1681 a collection was made in Framlington chapelry for the ransom of the captive Christians in Algiers. Mr Robt Manners gave 6d, his two men servants 1½d, his two maids 1d, and Mr Roger Manners 2d. (*Felton Registers*). By his w.d. 26 March 1716 Robert leaves all his lands to his son Edward. His godson William Manners son of his nephew John Manners is to have a legacy.

Edward Manners of Long Framlington made his will 29 May 1727 and he was buried at Framlington 19 July 1727. His son John is to have his lands of North Acton and Newmoor House, paying his debt of £1800 to Henry Rawlings, £300 to Alexander Collingwood and £100 to his sister Mary Richardson (wife of John Richardson of Rothbury). His wife Jane Manners is to have his lands in Long Framlington, and after her death to be divided between their sons Edward and John. His lands at Smallburn are to go to his son Edward for life with remainder to John.

John Manners died at Newmoor House, intestate, and administration of his personal estate was granted to his widow Anne, 9 August 1739. He left four daughters his coheiresses, Jane (d. unmarried 19 December 1807), Elizabeth (d. unmarried 1801), Ann (wife of Robert Alnwick of Elyhaugh) and Margaret, who married her cousin John Manners of Long Framlington. A decree in the Court of Chancery ordered his estate to be sold, and an Act of Parliament, 19 Geo.II, was obtained to give valid conveyance. Only part of the estate was sold, the remainder being divided amongst the coheiresses.

John Manners who married his cousin Jane was son of Edward Manners (d.1741) and was an ensign in the 24th regiment of foot when he made his w.d. 14 October 1764 be-

MANNERS of FRAMLINGTON, par. FELTON

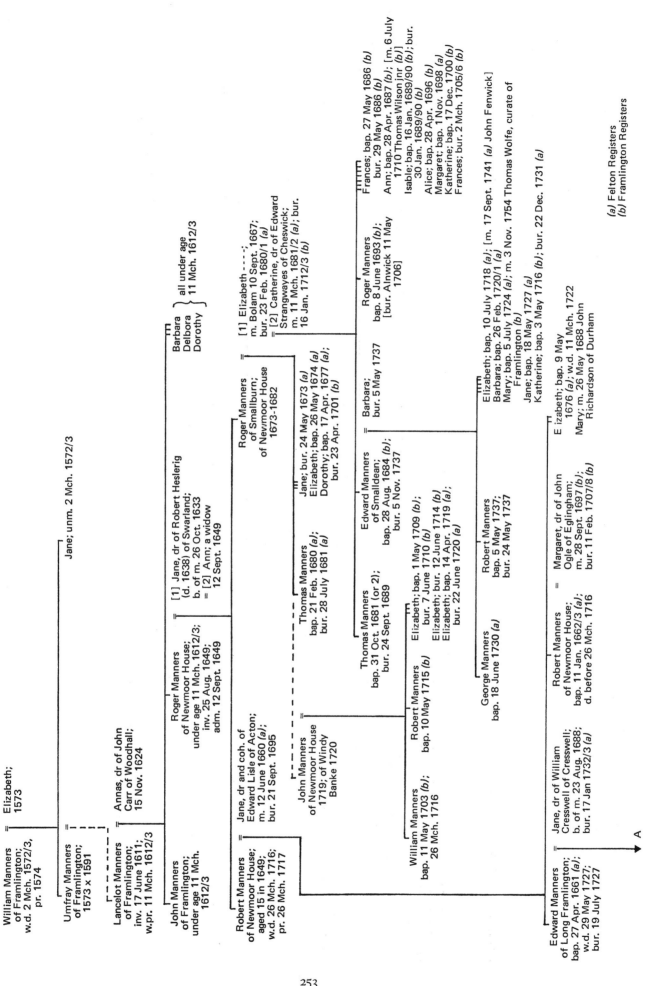

Frances; bap. 27 May 1686 *(b)*
bur. 29 May 1686 *(b)*
Ann; bap. 28 Apr. 1687 *(b)*; [m. 6 July 1710 Thomas Wilson jnr *(b)*]
Isable; bap. 16 Jan. 1689/90 *(b)*; bur. 30 Jan. 1689/90 *(b)*
Alice; bap. 28 Apr. 1696 *(b)*
Margaret; bap. 1 Nov. 1698 *(a)*
Katherine; bap. 17 Dec. 1700 *(b)*
Frances; bur. 2 Mch. 1705/6 *(b)*

Barbara ⎫
Delbora ⎬ all under age 11 Mch. 1612/3
Dorothy ⎭

[1] Elizabeth ----; m. Bolam 10 Sept. 1667; bur. 23 Feb. 1680/1 *(a)*
= [2] Catherine, dr of Edward Strangwayes of Cheswick; m. 11 Mch. 1681/2 *(a)*; bur. 16 Jan. 1712/3 *(b)*

Roger Manners
of Smallburn; of Newmoor House
1673-1682

Jane; unm. 2 Mch. 1572/3

Roger Manners
bap. 8 June 1693 *(b)*
[bur. Alnwick 11 May 1706]

Elizabeth; bap. 10 July 1718 *(a)*; [m. 17 Sept. 1741 *(a)* John Fenwick]
Barbara; bap. 26 Feb. 1720/1 *(a)*
Mary; bap. 5 July 1724 *(a)*; m. 3 Nov. 1754 Thomas Wolfe, curate of Framlington *(b)*
Jane; bap. 18 May 1727 *(a)*
Katherine; bap. 3 May 1716 *(b)*; bur. 22 Dec. 1731 *(a)*

Barbara; bur. 5 May 1737

[1] Jane, dr of Robert Heslerig (d. 1638) of Swarland; b. of m. 26 Oct. 1633
= [2] Ann; a widow 12 Sept. 1649

Jane; bur. 24 May 1673 *(a)*
Elizabeth; bap. 26 May 1674 *(a)*
Dorothy; bap. 17 Apr. 1677 *(a)*; bur. 23 Apr. 1701 *(b)*

Roger Manners
of Newmoor House;
under age 11 Mch. 1612/3;
inv. 25 Aug. 1649;
adm. 12 Sept. 1649

Edward Manners
of Smalldean;
bap. 28 Aug. 1684 *(b)*;
bur. 5 Nov. 1737

Thomas Manners
bap. 21 Feb. 1680 *(a)*;
bur. 28 July 1681 *(a)*

Thomas Manners
bap. 31 Oct. 1681 (or 2);
bur. 24 Sept. 1689

Elizabeth; bap. 1 May 1709 *(b)*;
bur. 7 June 1710 *(b)*
Elizabeth; bur. 12 June 1714 *(b)*
Elizabeth; bap. 14 Apr. 1719 *(a)*;
bur. 22 June 1720 *(a)*

Annas, dr of John
Carr of Woodhall;
15 Nov. 1624

Robert Manners
bap. 5 May 1737;
bur. 24 May 1737

John Manners
of Framlington;
under age 11 Mch.
1612/3

Jane, dr and coh. of
Edward Lisle of Acton;
m. 12 June 1660 *(a)*;
bur. 21 Sept. 1695

John Manners
of Newmoor House
1719; of Windy
Banke 1720

Robert Manners
bap. 10 May 1715 *(b)*

George Manners
bap. 18 June 1730 *(a)*

Robert Manners
of Newmoor House;
aged 15 in 1649;
w.d. 26 Mch. 1716;
pr. 26 Mch. 1717

William Manners
bap. 11 May 1703 *(b)*;
26 Mch. 1716

Robert Manners
of Newmoor House;
bap. 11 Jan. 1662/3 *(a)*;
d. before 26 Mch. 1716

Margaret, dr of John
Ogle of Eglingham;
m. 28 Sept. 1697 *(b)*;
bur. 11 Feb. 1707/8 *(b)*

Elizabeth; bap. 9 May
1676 *(a)*; w.d. 11 Mch. 1722
Mary; m. 26 May 1688 John
Richardson of Durham

Jane, dr of William
Cresswell of Cresswell;
b. of m. 23 Aug. 1688;
bur. 17 Jan 1732/3 *(a)*

Edward Manners
of Long Framlington;
bap. 27 Apr. 1661 *(a)*;
w.d. 29 May 1727;
bur. 19 July 1727

A ➤

William Manners
of Framlington;
w.d. 2 Mch. 1572/3,
pr. 1574

= Elizabeth;
1573

Umfray Manners
of Framlington;
1573 × 1591

Lancelot Manners
of Framlington;
inv. 17 June 1611;
w.pr. 11 Mch. 1612/3

(a) Felton Registers
(b) Framlington Registers

MANNERS of FRAMLINGTON, cont.

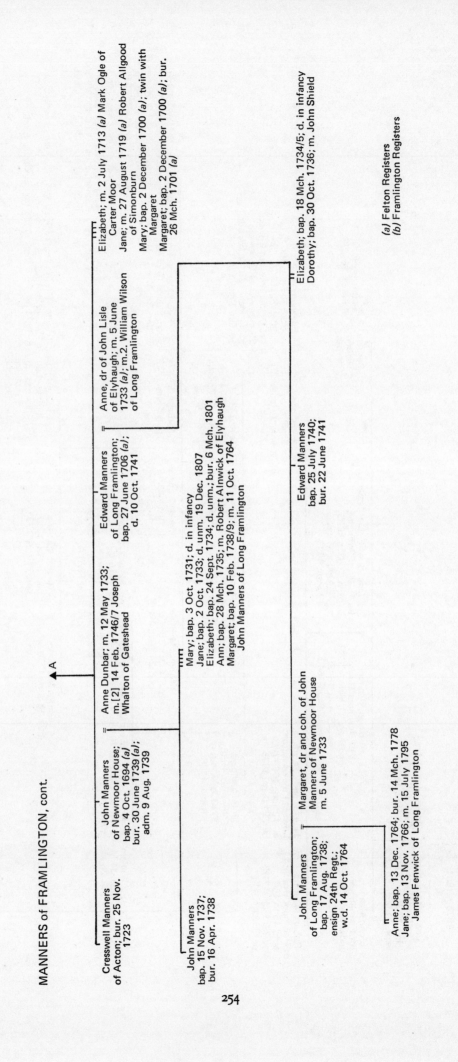

Cresswell Manners
of Acton; bur. 25 Nov.
1723

John Manners
of Newmoor House;
bap. 4 Oct. 1694 (a)
bur. 30 June 1739 (a);
adm. 9 Aug. 1739

=

Anne Dunbar; m. 12 May 1733;
m.[2] 14 Feb. 1746/7 Joseph
Whalton of Gateshead

Edward Manners
of Long Framlington;
bap. 27 June 1706 (a);
d. 10 Oct. 1741

=

Anne, dr of John Lisle
of Elyhaugh; m. 5 June
1733 (a); m.2. William Wilson
of Long Framlington

Elizabeth; m. 2 July 1713 (a) Mark Ogle of
Carter Moor
Jane; m. 27 August 1719 (a) Robert Allgood
of Simonburn
Mary; bap. 2 December 1700 (a); twin with
Margaret
Margaret; bap. 2 December 1700 (a); bur.
26 Mch. 1701 (a)

John Manners
bap. 15 Nov. 1737;
bur. 16 Apr. 1738

Mary; bap. 3 Oct. 1731; d. in infancy
Jane; bap. 2 Oct. 1733; d, unm. 19 Dec. 1807
Elizabeth; bap. 24 Sept. 1734; d. unm.; bur. 6 Mch. 1801
Ann; bap. 28 Mch. 1735; m. Robert Alnwick of Elyhaugh
Margaret; bap. 10 Feb. 1738/9; m. 11 Oct. 1764
John Manners of Long Framlington

Edward Manners
bap. 25 July 1740;
bur. 22 June 1741

John Manners
of Long Framlington;
bap. 17 Aug. 1738;
ensign 24th Regt.;
w.d. 14 Oct. 1764

=

Margaret, dr and coh. of John
Manners of Newmoor House
m. 5 June 1733

Anne; bap. 13 Dec. 1764; bur. 14 Mch. 1778
Jane; bap. 13 Nov. 1766; m. 15 July 1795
James Fenwick of Long Framlington

Elizabeth; bap. 18 Mch. 1734/5; d. in infancy
Dorothy; bap. 30 Oct. 1736; m. John Shield

A

(a) Felton Registers
(b) Framlington Registers

254

fore proceeding to join his regiment at Gibraltar. He died at Gibraltar leaving two infant daughters, Anne (died aged 14) and Jane who married 15 July 1795 James Fenwick of Long-framlington.

OTHER MANNERS

IN 1451 Robert Manners of Etal claimed from Gerard Manners 340 acres of land, 40 acres of meadow, 400 acres of pasture, 10 acres of wood, 300 acres of moor, 20 acres of marsh, 10 acres of older (?alder) grove and the moiety of the mill in Shotton by gift of the crown (*de Banco Roll*, No. 763, m.280, do. quoted in *NCH*. XI, p.185n.).

Younger sons for whom there was no available land or who felt the deep attraction of the town and its opportunities appear in Berwick in the second half of the 16th century and in Newcastle a little later. Henry Manners younger son of Thomas Manners of Cheswick, was a burgess of Berwick in 1570 and was living there 6 April 1611. He may have left descendants for early in the 17th century John, George, Thomas and Henry Manners were living in Berwick, where they had children baptised between 1589 and 1625.

At Durham Consistory Court on 16 February 1626 Henry Maners of Newcastle, aged 17 and upwards mentions his mother Ellinor Harrup and her sister Ann Brown. Mary Rennyson called Ellinor, Andrew Harrup's whore, saying that she parted the said Andrew and his wife and that Ellinor never had any children but bastards. Alice Dacres of Newcastle, widow, aged 50 and upwards deposed that she was somewhat of kindred to Ellinor, but with what degree she knoweth not (C.R.H.).

Henry Manners may have been Henry Manners, tanner, who became a freeman of Newcastle in 1631 and the man of this name who married at St Nicholas', Newcastle, 5 May 1633 Kathren Harup. The description of Henry Manners as a tanner may be a mistake, for on 26 April 1652 James son of Henry Manners, butcher, was admitted to his freedom by patrimony. James Manners paid the chimney tax on one hearth in Fickett Tower Ward, Newcastle, in 1665. Later Manners freemen of Newcastle were all masons. Henry Maners, mason, achieved his freedom in 1679 and was still taking apprentices in 1707 and 1709. Two sons, both masons, were made free by patrimony, Edward on 12 October 1702 and James on 17 January 1714/5. Moses Manners who became freeman on 13 July 1733 was probably a son of one of these two brothers for his sons Edward and Moses were both made freemen by patrimony, Edward on 15 January 1759 and Moses on 14 January 1765. Edward had two sons, Edward (free 17 January 1780) and James (free 14 January 1782). No doubt an examination of the various parish registers of Newcastle could fill in many details of the pedigree of these Newcastle masons.

A family of Manners owned lands in Newtown, par. Edlingham, and Milbourne, par. Ponteland, in the 16th century. In 1531 there was a dispute between John Maners and Roger Swynborn, esq., of Edlingham concerning the impounding of cattle in the field of Roughlees called 'Dolycroke'; judgement was given 8 October 1531 by the President and Council of the North against Maners (*Swinburne Deeds*, 3/14). Amongst the Border watches appointed in 1552 were those from Newtown to Learchild and from Learchild to Bolton; for the former there were appointed the town of Edlingham and the Newtown, the setters and searchers of the two watches being Robert Manners and Robert Killingworthe (*Leges Marchiarum*, p.285). George Carr of Lesbury in his w.d. 10 March 1559/60 mentions that 'Concerning the children of Robert Manners of Newtown, the tuition of whom was committed to me by their mother; the eldest of them I give to my cousin Robert Carr of Kimmerston, and the other two to the order of William Harrison, clerk, and John Carr of Boulmer, and I give to each of the said children 20s.' (*NCH*. II, p.431).

It would seem that Robert Manners, the setter and searcher of 1552, had died before 10 March 1559/60 leaving three young children under age, the tuition of whom had been given by their mother to George Carr of Lesbury. In the pedigree of Carr of Lesbury (*NCH*. II, p.429) it is suggested that George Carr had a sister Isabel who married firstly Robert Manners and secondly (blank) Ogle. There is some mix-up here; *Thomas* Manners of Cheswick by his w.d. 3 July 1545 appoints George Carr, his brother-in-law, to be a supervisor; after Thomas Manners' death, his widow Maryane married Henry Ogle.

There is a possibility that Robert Manners of Newtown was related to William Manners of Framlington, for the latter by his w.d. 2 March 1572/3 leaves a legacy to Henry Muschampe's three children, and George Carr of Lesbury leaves 20s., to his 'cousin' Henry Muschance. George Carr may have had a sister who married Robert Manners of Newtown but she is not specifically mentioned as such in his will. Of course if both Robert Manners and his wife were dead, he was doing the best he could for their three children. A close relationship between the Manners of Longframlington and those of Cheswick has already been postulated. The Manners of Newtown also seem to have had a similar origin.

On 18 January 1565/6 Edward Manors of the Newtown exchanged a house in Newtown with Thomas Swynborne of Edlingham for a messuage in Milbourne and on 4 January 1568/9 he exchanged with him the tower of Newtown for a messuage in Milbourne. The two parties had already, on 15 January 1565/6, made a confirmation of various exchanges in Newtown and Milbourne (*Swinburne Deeds* 3/36 to 3/44). In 1568 Thomas Manners held of the Crown certain lands and tenements in Milbourne, and also the vill called Newtown (*Liber Feodarii*). Edward and Thomas were perhaps two of the children of Robert Manners (d.1552 x 1560) of Newtown.

On 20 October 1582 Edward Manners pledged a tenement in Milbourne to Thomas Bates. He apparently failed to redeem his property, for Bates died in 1587 seised of five messuages and lands in Milbourne, late of the inheritance of Anthony Birde and Edward Maners (*i.p.m.* 35 Eliz. vol.236, No. 93). It was probably the same Edward Manners, living at Jesmond, and aged 70, who deposed 2 October 1611 about the bounds of Edlingham.

Another descendant of the knightly family of Manners must have been Robert Manners of South Hebborne, administration of whose goods was granted 19 January 1638/9 to his widow Anne Manners (*Dur. Prob. Off.* by C.R.H.). Robert was servant to alderman Richard Hodgson of Hebburn, co. Durham. Both he and his wife were recusants; Anne (Agnes) was convicted of recusancy 1606/7, presented by the church-wardens of Jarrow 1609, convicted 1615-1616; Robert and his wife were convicted 1624, 1625, 1630 (*SS.* 175, p.176). In one instance Robert is described as 'laborer'. Elizabeth Manners, also of the parish of Jarrow was convicted of recusancy in 1624 (E.377/32); her name is not coupled with those of Robert and his wife, so she may not have been related to them.

MANNERS—FREEHOLDERS

1698. Robert Manners of Newmoor House.

1710. Robert Manners of Newmoor House; Edwd Mannours of Acton.

1715. Edw. Manners of Smallburn for Longhorsley; Edw. Manners of Acton; Cresswell Manners of Acton.

1721. Edward Manners of Acton, gent.

MANNERS—BIBLIOGRAPHY

William Dugdale, Norroy King of Arms—*The Baronage of England.* 1676. Dugdale has little to say about the early members of the family, noting that 'Though none of this family arrived to the dignity of Peerage, until the Reign of King Henry the Eighth, yet were they persons of great note in Northumberland for many Ages before'. An ancient pedigree in *Monasticon*, vol.v. p.281 records a younger son Edward and two daughters Elizabeth and Cecily of sir Robert Manners (d.1495); also Oliver, Antony, Richard, John, Elizabeth, Catherine, Eleanor, Cicely and Margaret, younger children of George Manners, lord Roos (d.1514).

Rev. James Raine, MA.—*The History and Antiquities of North Durham.* 1852. Manners of Cheswick with pedigree, p.230. A careless mistake is made in the pedigree where the children of Henry Swinhoe and his wife Margaret Manners are called Manners instead of Swinhoe.

NCH. XI. pp.442-452. Manners of Etal, with pedigree. There are some errors in the pedigree. George Manners, lord Roos, is stated to have married secondly Elizabeth, daughter and co-heir of John Manners, lord of Cheswick; actually Elizabeth married Thomas Manners of Berrington.

NCH. VII. pp.443-447. Manners of Newmoor-house and Framlington, with pedigree.

J. Crawford Hodgson, *MSS pedigrees*, viii, 196; Newcastle, A.281; B.220.

MANNERS—NOTE

1. Robert Manners of Newmoor House, par. Felton, attaches to his w.d. 26 March 1716 a seal bearing the arms of the senior lines of Manners of Belvoir with the special augmentation granted to Thomas Manners, earl of Rutland, on account of his royal descent. It is certain that the Manners of Newmoor House could not have any right to these armorials, for the Manners of Newmoor House were cadets of the Manners of Cheswick descended from a great uncle of Thomas, earl of Rutland, the first to bear the special augmentation.

KNIGHTS OF 1166

BARONY OF GOSFORTH—KNIGHTS OF 1166

THERE were no knights holding fees in this barony in 1166. In that year William son of Siward reported to the king that he held a certain vill called Goseford and half of another vill called Mileton by the fee and service of one knight which his antecessors had made to the king's antecessors; nothing had been feoffed but all was in his own demesne.

The only part of this barony that lay in Northumberland was the vill of North Gosforth, par. St Nicholas', Newcastle. The vill of Mileton (Middleton) was at Middleton in Teesdale, co. Durham.

BARONY OF HADSTON—KNIGHTS OF 1166

RADULF DE WIRECESTRE held a single knight's fee in 1166 of which Jordan Hairun made a quarter part of a knight's service of new feoffment and Pagan de Wirecestre held a quarter also of new feoffment. The monks of Tynemouth had a seventh part of a fee and William son of Adam a third part of a fee. The vills comprising this barony were Hadston (chap. Chevington), Little Benton (par. Longbenton), West Chirton (par. Tynemouth), and West Swinburne and Colwell (par. Chollerton).

Jordan Hairun married Radulf de Wirecestre's daughter and heiress and succeeded him in the barony of Hadston. Pagan de Wirecestre seems to have been Radulf's younger brother or other near relation, and his descendants adopted the surname of Swinburne from their manor of West Swinburne. The families of HAIRUN (later Heron) and SWINBURNE have already been dealt with.

William son of Adam probably held in 1166 the vill of Little Benton, and his descendants adopted the surname of Benton. The family only survived for a few generations.

BARONY OF EMBLETON—KNIGHTS OF 1166

JOHN son of Odard reported in 1166 that of the three knights' fees held by him in chief he had enfeoffed of the new feoffment one and a half fees, namely William son of Adam half a fee, Albert half a fee and Ernulf and Aelard half a fee. The barony included Burton and Warenton (par. Bamburgh), and Craster, Dunstan, Embleton and Stamford (par. Embleton).

In 1166 William son of Adam held the vill of Warenton (perhaps excepting one carucate). Albert's half fee was the vill of Craster. His descendants held Craster in an unbroken male line until the death of Shafto Craster in 1837. Shafto Craster was succeeded by his nephew Thomas Wood, whose descendants assumed the surname of Craster and still own Craster. The half fee held by Ernulf and Aelard in 1166 was held in 1242 by William de Rok and Reyner de Dunstan, the former holding a quarter of Embleton and the latter a quarter of Dunstan and two bovates there.

William de Rok no doubt took his surname from Rock (par. Embleton) in the barony of Alnwick. The family died out before the end of the 13th century. The family of Dunstan survived a little longer, but is last heard of at Dunstan in 1336.

Simon de Warentham, probably descended from William son of Adam of 1166, was living in 1296 and seems to have been the last of his surname to hold Warenton.

CRASTER

The original holding of the Crasters was a small one, for the township of Craster is only 695 acres. In spite of this we have here an example of the remarkable tenacity with which a family could retain its ancestral estate for more than 800 years. There is evidence that throughout most of this period the family farmed the bulk of their lands themselves and this seems to have kept them away from politics. In the 14th century two successive owners became knights, one of them unwillingly, but not until 1681 did a member of the family become sheriff of the county, a distinction which has been held six times since then.

In the 15th century the attachment of the family to the House of York brought an addition to their estates in the form of the forfeited lands of sir John Beaumont. Although the normal extravagances of the 17th century rendered it necessary to part with all their outlying properties, Craster itself was retained although not without difficulty.

During the Civil War the Crasters were royalist but somehow avoided sequestration under the Commonwealth. The owners of Craster seem to have ignored the Jacobite Risings of 1715 and 1745; a young cousin William Craster was out in the '15 but escaped retribution.

The marriage in 1727 of John Craster and Catherine Villiers introduced the family to London and Continental society but by then the estate rents and the prestige of Catherine's family avoided the accumulation of further debts. About the same time John succeeded to half the considerable estates of his distant cousin dame Dorothy Windsor.

CRASTER OF CRASTER, PAR. EMBLETON

The Christian name Albert borne by the first known member of the family is an unusual one in the 12th century in Northumberland. It is Old German Adalbert, compound of *athal*, 'noble' and *berhta*, 'bright', equivalent to Old English Aethelbeorht. Withycombe (*The Oxford Dictionary of English Christian Names*, p.9) has suggested that the use of the name in England in the 12th and 13th centuries is more likely to be an importation of the continental form of the name. Sir Edmund Craster has also stated that the name is not specifically Anglo-Saxon, 'and there is therefore no necessity for supposing that the first owner of Craster was a native Northumbrian' (*AA*4. xxx, p.120). Ernulf and Aelard who together held half a knight's fee in the barony of Embleton in 1166 also bore names more likely to be German than Anglo-Saxon or French. The former is perhaps the same as Arnold from Old German Arenvald, compound of *arin*, 'eagle' and *vald* 'power' (Withycombe, *op. cit.*, p.30). Aelard is more certainly from the Old German Adalhard, compound of *athal*, 'noble' and *hardu*, 'hard' (*Ib.*, p.8).

In the decade 1165-1175 William de Argentom, who held a knight's fee in Yorkshire from William de Perci, gave to Albert de Craucestre in marriage with Christiana sister of the grantor, 25 acres of land at Redcar to hold in fee (Farrer, *Early Yorkshire Charters*, II, p.106, No. 768). Amongst the witnesses to this charter are Hugh *nepos* of Albert and William de Craucestria. Christiana was daughter of Roger son of Peter de Upleatham by his wife Agnes daughter and coheiress of William de Argentom. Another of Roger's daughters was Agnes Argentyn, lady of Upleatham, who gave all her lands in Upleatham, Merske and Ugthorpe to her kinsman John Herband; she included the homage and service of Albert de Craucestre for six tofts and crofts and 30 bovates of land in Upleatham and Redcar (*Percy Chartulary*, DCXXVII).

It is likely that Christiana de Argentom was Albert's second wife, and that William de Craucestria who witnesses her marriage settlement was Albert's son by a previous wife. Albert and Christiana had a son Ivo de Redeker (Redcar, Yorks) living in 1231. Yvo gave to Gisburne Priory with the consent of his brother William, land in Redcar which he had by his mother's gift. He also gave land in Redcar to Fountains Abbey. Albert and Christiana gave to the Augustinian canons of Guisborough a plot of land at Redcar on which they were to build a chapel (*SS.* 89, pp.231, 233). It seems that Albert de Crawcestre in later life entered religion and was the Albert who occurs as a canon of Guisborough in 1175.

For four generations after Albert, the Craster pedigree is proved by a law-suit of 1292. In that year Richard de Crawcestre claimed as his serf a certain William son of Robert. According to Richard's statement William son of Robert was descended from Egardus who had been a serf of Albert de Crawcestre's. The possession of Egardus and his heirs had descended from Albert de Crawcestre 'to William as son and heir, and from William to one William as son and heir, and from William to one John as son and heir', and from John to his son and heir, Richard, the claimant (*Assize Roll*, 21 E.I.).

The first William de Craucestre was party to a suit in the *curia regis* in 1214 (*Cur. Reg. Rolls*, VII, p.276), but it was probably William II who at the *curia regis* at Trinity 1224 with Thomas de Warnetham was to attach John le Viscount who had failed to put in an appearance in a plea brought against him by the abbot of Alnwick (*Northumberland Pleas*). In 1242 William de Craucestre held Craster as half a knight's fee in the barony of Embleton (*Testa de Nevill*). By 1245 he had been succeeded by his son John whose services to the lord of Embleton are mentioned in the *i.p.m.* of John Viscount taken that year. At Michaelmas Term 1253 John de Crawecestre and others were charged by William de Valence with attacking his men coming to the fair at Alnwick and beating and imprisoning them (*Nd Pleas*). John was alive twenty years later so that this might have been a youthful escapade.

In 1278 Richard de Crawcestre, as a landowner whose income from his land was over £20 a year, was distrained to take up knighthood. It was this Richard who in 1292 unsuccessfully claimed William son of Robert as his serf. As a knight he witnesses, 11 January 1282/3, an inspeximus of Adam Ribaud of Howick to sir John de Vesci of Alnwick (*Percy Chartulary* DCCVI). *Dominus* Richard de Craucestre was charged for the subsidy of 1296. Sir Richard probably died in 1314 for the bailiff of Embleton in his accounts to Michaelmas that year entered his name as supplying labour to the demesne lands at Embleton, but the name of Edmund de Craucestre appears on the debit side.

For the next two hundred years each successive Craster of Craster was called Edmund, a name no doubt derived from Edmund, earl of Lancaster (d.1298), owner of the barony of Embleton. It is difficult to identify separately these four Edmunds.

Edmund I was serving in 1319 as a man-at-arms under sir John Cromwell, Warden of the Marches, and he was still a man-at-arms in 1323. He was a knight by 1328. He married Maud widow of William de Clavering of Callaly and in 1335 was appointed guardian of his step-son Robert de Clavering (born 3 Feb. 1325/6). His wife died 28 November 1351. It was perhaps Edmund II who in 1368 deposed at the proof of age of John son and heir of John Musgrave of Heaton; he knew that John had been born on 14 February 1345/6 and had been present at his baptism in All Saints church, Newcastle (*AA*1. IV, p.326). An Edmund Craster was living in 1377.

For the next twenty four years we have no information about the owners of Craster. An Edmund Craster witnesses deeds of 25 May 1401, 11 November 1405, 10 January 1406 and 10 April 1407 (*NDD*. pp.155, 156). It might be presumed that this Edmund was a grandson of Edmund I who had been under age when his grandfather died. In 1415 a tower at Craster, no doubt the one still standing, was owned by Edmund Craster (*AA*2. XIV, p.19). Edmund de Crawcestre *armiger* witnesses a deed of 24 August 1424 (*NCH*. II, p.244n.). It has been stated that William Harding and Edmund Craster held half a knight's fee in Beadnell in 1427 (Surtees, *Durham*, II, p.250); this is difficult to understand for at no other time was Beadnell held by military service. The demesne lands attached to Embleton church were let for seven years from 1443 to Edmund Craster, esq., 'of Durham'.

On 26 November 1465 Edward IV gave to Edmund Craucestre and Richard Craucestre in grateful recognition of their services to him, the estates of John Beaumont forfeited by him after the battle of Towton; these lands comprised the manor of North Charlton and 4 messuages, 100 acres of land and 60 acres of wood in West Ditchburn (*Rot. Pat.*5 E.IV). Edmund Craucestre was apparently the third person of this name and Richard was presumably his brother. Richard had been appointed bailiff of Bamburgh castle 15 July 1461. It is evident that both brothers had performed signal service for the Yorkists, perhaps in the taking of Dunstanburgh castle in 1461. Edmund died before 1477 and his widow Margery married Ralph Carr of Newlands, par.

Bamburgh. Carr brought an action to recover his wife's dower in lands at Craster, Warenton, Beadnell, Bamburgh, Spindlestone, Budle and Ditchburn (*de Banco Roll*).

Edmund Craster IV was appointed constable of Dunstanburgh castle on 8 July 1489 at a fee of 20 marks a year, and was still constable in 1506. On 31 July 1509 he made a settlement of his lands at Craster, Spindlestone, Adderstone, Falloden and Howick on his eldest son Edmund in tail male with successive remainders to his other sons Jasper, Anthony, William and Thomas, and failing them on his daughter Edith. On 12 September following he gave to his son Jasper all his lands and tenements, rents services with appurtenances in the vill, territory and fields of Newton-by-the-Sea (Foster, *The Heralds' Visitation of Northumberland*, p.36).

An inquisition taken on 5 June 1511 after the death of Edmund Craster found that he had held Craster in fee, and certain lands on lease from the duchy of Lancaster in Embleton and Dunstan and half of Warenton. Edmund Craster was his son and heir and aged 5. There is evidently a mistake in the age of the heir, for Edmund's grandson was born in 1515; perhaps 5 should be read as 50.

Jasper Craster, second son of Edmund Craster (d.1511), was murdered by Richard Storey in 1521. In 1523 Robert Carr, bailiff of Alnwick, rendered account of 20s. the value of a horse which he had seized in 1521 from the goods of the fugitive felon, Richard Storey, who had fled on account of the death of Jasper Craster, the earl of Northumberland's servant. Edmund Craster's youngest son, Thomas, became guardian to his great-nephew Edmund VII with an allowance of £10 a year for the boy's maintenance. At one time he farmed the tithes of Ellington, but lived in Alnwick where he carried on the trade of a tanner. By his w.d. 19 May 1557 he leaves his house in Alnwick to his wife Margaret with reversion to their son William. The residue of all his goods is to go to 'my wife and my childer to be distributed among them equally' (*SS*. 112, p.13). Later Crasters living in Alnwick were perhaps descended from Thomas' 'childer'.

According to the 1615 visitation pedigree Edmund Craster VI married (blank) daughter of (blank) Widdrington of Widdrington. Elsewhere she is called Marion Widdrington. When Edmund Craster died on 9 November 1520 his heir was his son George, aged 5. George married Eleanor, daughter of sir Thomas Forster of Adderstone; after George's death she married Robert Widdrington of Wearmouth.

George Crawster of Craster was 'hale in my remembrance and in my body' when he made his w.d. 10 April 1544. He gives £4 to a priest to sing a year for him and all Christian souls. Each of his servants is to have 6s. All his lands and goods moveable and immoveable are to go to his wife Eleanor and his son Edmund. Eleanor is to have the ordering of his son's lands as long as she remains a widow. If she should marry, then John Forster, Thomas Forster and Thomas Crawster are jointly to have the ordering of him with his lands and goods. Eleanor was pregnant. If she should have a man child he is to have the farmhold in Embleton that Henry had; if the expected child should be a girl she is to have £60 of the rent of all the testator's lands. The child was in fact a girl who was named Margaret and eventually married Michael Hebburne of Hebburn. It was no doubt as a result of this marriage that in 1588 Eleanor's brother was called in to arbitrate in a long standing blood feud between the Hebburnes and Storeys. In the inventory dated 10 August 1619 of the goods of Margaret Heborne there is mention of a 'legacy or portion given and left due by the last will of George Craister to Margrete Craister his daughter then unborn at his death the sum of 60s. or thereabouts' (*SS.* 142, p.130); (60s., is perhaps a mistake for £60).

Edmund Craster VII was constable of Warkworth in 1569. He was present at the Wardens' meeting on 27 July 1585 when lord Francis Russell was killed by the Scots. This was a time of almost continuous raiding across the Border. The 'laird of Crawster' was raided about Christmas 1587 (*CBP.* I, p.360) and he suffered again on 29 October 1588 (*Ib.,* p.361). Although he had sold most of the small outlying properties in Northumberland he had bought a property at Barton in Richmondshire, Yorks. By his w.d. 7 November 1594 he leaves his 'lordship of Craster' and his other lands in Northumberland to his son John. His lands at Barton are left to his wife for life with remainder to his younger sons Edmund and Thomas, who are also to have £60 each for their portions. Two married daughters are to have £10 each. and five unmarried daughters each 100 marks. He leaves 10s. to his schoolmaster Sir Thomas, and to his sons John Craister and Henrie Collingwood each one old ryall. Edmund Craster's daughters were:—

1. Jane wife of Bertram Anderson of Newcastle; she died before 10 Oct. 1606.

2. Margaret wife of Henry Collingwood of Etal.

3. Grace wife of William Armorer. (He was probably William Armorer of Cornhill; w.d. 20 Dec. 1607). In the pedigree of Armorer of Belford (*NCH.* I, p.390) his wife is called Grace Ogle, almost certainly in error. No doubt this has been suggested because William Armorer in his will mentions his 'brother' Edward Ogle. This Edward Ogle was second husband of William Armorer's wife's sister Isabella.

4. Eleanor (Ellen, Helen); unmarried 1597, 1606.

5. Isabell wife of Luke Ogle (d.1604) of Eglingham. (m.2. Edward Ogle).

6. Barbara; m. St Nicholas', Newcastle, 8 May 1599, Cuthbert Bewick, merchant.

7. Catherine; she d. before 23 September 1597.

The two younger sons of Edmund Craster VII were apprenticed to Newcastle merchants, Edmund on 1 August 1592 to Henry Fenkell, boothman, and Thomas on 1 August 1594 to Peter Thompson, mercer. Edmund Craster's widow seems to have made a home for herself in the half ruined castle of Dunstanburgh, presumably in the constable's lodgings. Here she made her will on 23 September 1597. She leaves to each of her sons-in-law an angel. Her son John Craister is to have her bedding and pots and pans; and her daughter Grace Armorer all her linen. To her sons Edmond and Thomas she leaves £20 apiece, to her daughters Barbara Craister and Ellen Craister each £33. 13s. 4d., and to her daughters Ellen Craister, Jane Anderson, Margaret Collingwood and Isabell Ogle each £20. Alice Craister's mother was still alive and Alice leaves her a ryall (*SS.* 112, p.165).

Alice Craster's mother Jane widow of Christopher Mytford of Newcastle, alderman, made her will on 16 October 1606 (pr.4 May 1608). She was a very wealthy old lady with goods worth £1839. 7s. 3d., and she leaves substantial legacies to her Craster grandchildren. John, Edmond and Thomas Craister are to have £20 each and she leaves similar legacies to her grand daughters Margaret Collingwood, Isabel Ogle, Barbara Bewick and Grace Armorer. Her grand daughter Jane Anderson had died, so her children are to have £16. Eleanor Craster who was still unmarried is to have £20 (*SS.* 38, p.31n.).

John Craster, Edmund VII's eldest son, had been at Queen's College, Cambridge. In 1615 he registered his pedigree at Richard St George, Norroy King of Arms' visitation of Northumberland. By his wife Margaret daughter of William Carr of Ford, he had then living four sons Edmond, John, William and George, and two daughters Margaret and Jane; Edmond, the eldest son, was then 15 years old. He was one of the Commissioners of the Middle Marches who signed a letter to the Privy Council 24 April 1618 (*S.P.*14/97/37). During John Craster's lifetime much of the family estates was sold and what remained was heavily mortgaged. It is not known when John Craster died. He was alive in 1638 when he gave evidence in a chancery suit on behalf of his wife's nephew William Carr. Before 1642 Craster was in the possession of Edmund Craster, John's eldest son, who in that year paid the hearth tax there.

Edmund Craster married Edith daughter of sir Matthew Forster of Adderstone, but died *s.p.* and was succeeded by his eldest surviving brother William. His brother John had been a colonel in the army of Gustavus Adolphus and there is a tradition in the family that he was killed in the battle of Lutzen in 1632. The youngest brother George had a five years' lease at £8 a year of Edlingham South Demesne in 1652 (*SS.* 111, p.350). He married Pollie, illegitimate daughter of Robert Fenwick and widow of William Fenwick of Lesbury. Thomas Fenwick of Foxton Hall by his w.d. 7 July 1654 leaves his eldest son to be brought up by 'my father-in-law Mr Geo. Craster'. George Craster was living at Little Houghton in 1664.

At the time of the Civil War, William Craster was a royalist, and lord Widdrington appointed him a major in the regiment he raised for the king. There is some evidence that he was at one time in command of the garrison of Morpeth Castle. By his w.d. 19 June 1650 William Craster leaves all his lands in Craster and Dunstan to his wife Anne until his son Edmond should become 21 and then Edmond is to pay his mother £700 or otherwise she should continue to have the lands for seven years longer for the payment of the testator's debts and the advancement of his younger children. His wife Anne is to be sole executrix and his brother Mr George Craster and Henry Strother trustees to see the will discharged. The inventory of William Craster's goods is dated 4 December 1650 (*Dur. Prob. Off.* by C.R.H.). His wife Ann was sister of Arthur Kellam of Firth house in Cawledge park, Alnwick, who by his w.d. 13 October 1648 devises to his nephew Edmund Craister, son of William Craister, esq., 'one black snipt fille'. Besides his eldest son Edmund, colonel Craster seems to have had three other sons, William, John and Daniel. Margaret wife of Nathaniel Salkeld of Hulne Park House, Phillis wife of Thomas Marley of Kyo, co. Durham, and Elizabeth wife of Ralph Grieve of Hulne Park were probably his daughters.

William son of William Crayster of Crayster, Nd, esq., decd, was apprenticed 1 June 1655 to Henry Slynger of Newcastle, boothman; he was perhaps William Craster of Stamford, buried at Embleton 7 October 1721.

John son of William Craster died in 1651 and was buried at Berwick. The descendants of Daniel Craster, William's other son, eventually succeeded to the Craster estate, and will be dealt with later.

Edmund Craster the heir is mentioned in the list of non-conformists of Alnwick in 1662 but was evidently a dissenter and not a papist; he and his wife are among those persons indicted for recusancy at Quarter Sessions, October 1683, but here again many dissenters are included. Edmund's wife was Barbara daughter of Martin Fenwick (d.1680) of Butterley. Besides their eldest son and heir John, they had two younger sons Edmund and Thomas and a daughter Anne. Edmund married at Embleton 7 April 1702 Margaret Steward of Stamford.

At York Assizes on 8 March 1679/80 Eleanor Gilchrist deposed that upon Thursday last, betwixt three and four o'clock after noon, she being in Esquire Craster's garden and there she heard a noise. Thereupon she went to the top of the garden wall to see what made the noise. There she saw Mr Edward Forster lying, and she also saw one Mr Thomas Craster walking from him; and she saw two swords drawn lying besides Mr Edward Forster. Then she called unto Mr Craster saying, 'What have you done to Mr Forster?' but she heard no answer.

Henry Strother in his w.d. 24 April 1689 leaves 'To my coz., Mrs Anne Craister, one guinea as a token, to be paid when her father Edmund Craister of Craister, esq., doth pay and satisfy a bond for £28. 18s. 1d., penalty for the payment of £14. 9s. and one halfpenny principal'. Later Anne married William Grey of Stamford. Barbara wife of Nicholas Whitehead of Lesbury Field House (b. of m. 21 May 1689) and Mary wife of John Atkinson of Gateshead (b. of m. 13 September 1701) may have been Anne's sisters.

Administration of the goods of Edmund Craster was granted 4 September 1694 to his son Edmund. His eldest son John matriculated at Merton College, Oxford, 10 December 1680. In November 1689 John entered into a bond of marriage with Mary daughter of John Ayton of Fawside, co. Durham. He had evidently followed the religious tenets of his father and was married by a nonconformist minister. More than four years later his wife insisted upon a more regular church service and this was performed at St. Nicholas', Newcastle, on 13 February 1693/4. The entry in the parish register reads, 'John Craister, gentleman, and Mrs Mary Ayton having been married some time ago by a Nonconformist Minister, this was done to satisfy the scruples of the gentlewoman'.

John Craster lived permanently at Fawside, his wife's home, and there he made his will on 2 July 1722. He had been a sick man for some time, and on 21 October 1720 (or 1721) he wrote to his eldest son 'Mr John Craster at John's Coffee House in Foulwood's Rents, near Grey's Inn, London' to inform him of his ill health. 'Son, the time of dissolution seems to approach. I am so ill that I have not strength nor time to order my affairs as I would. I have told your sister what I desire, which she will inform you of. You partly know what I desire. Your sisters two thousand pounds apiece and for your brothers your aunt's estate and Boulden land. They are to pay you five hundred pounds apiece at (the) expiration of eight years, which your sister will tell you which way you are to dispose of it. As this is your father's

command I charge you perform it, as you tender his pies (sic) who is your affectionate father John Craster'.

When the time came to make his will, John had changed his ideas. He is to be buried in Craster's porch in Embleton church. Craster Tower is to go to his eldest son John, 'now of Gray's Inn, esquire' together with the lease of Shoreswood Hall and the corn tithes there, paying £80 per annum to the second son William, of Oriel College, Oxford, and £80 per annum to the youngest son Bartholomew, of Lincoln college, Oxford. His daughter Isabel wife of John Mylott of Whithill is to have the land at East Bowdon, and his second daughter Elizabeth Craster is to have the land at Newfield called Minikins Newfield. John Craster was buried at Embleton 22 July 1722. The two younger sons William and Bartholomew (also called Bertram) died unmarried, and another son Edmund had died in his father's lifetime.

After John Craster's death, his widow Mary lived at Shoreswood, par. Norham, and there she made her will on 1 December 1730. She leaves her daughter Elizabeth £200, her daughter Anne £250, and Mary daughter of her son John £50.

John Craster the younger matriculated at Merton college, Oxford, 4 July 1712 at the age of 15, and entered Gray's Inn on 3 July 1716. He married in 1727 Catherine daughter of Henry Villiers. Catherine's grandfather sir Edward Villiers had been appointed governor of Tynemouth castle in 1661, and her father succeeded to the appointment and died 11 August 1707. The Villiers family had a close connection with the royal court, both that of Charles II and that of William of Orange. Sir Edward Villiers was nephew by the half-blood to George Villiers, first duke of Buckingham, and was uncle to Barbara Villiers, later duchess of Cleveland, one of the mistresses of Charles II. A sister of Henry Villiers was Elizabeth, mistress of William of Orange; when Elizabeth was sent away from the Court at queen Mary's dying request, she married lord George Hamilton, one of Marlborough's generals, later created earl of Orkney. Another of Henry's sisters was Ann who married William of Orange's closest friend, William Bentinck, afterwards earl of Portland.

The lighthouse in Tynemouth castle was a valuable asset to the Villiers family, being maintained by a toll of fourpence per ship owned by his majesty's subjects and twelvepence by strangers and foreigners. On the death of Catherine Craster's brother Henry Villiers on 29 May 1753, the lighthouse became the property of his widow Mary. She, by her w.d. 22 October 1766, leaves it to trustees for the benefit of her godson William Fowke, subject to the payment of an annuity of £40 to Catherine Craster, widow, for life.

It is not surprising with such connections that John and Catherine Craster spent most of their married life in London where they maintained a town house in Carey Street and later at number 40 Lincoln's Inn Fields. They also had a country house at Taplow in Buckinghamshire. John continued his legal work and was made a Bencher of his Inn in 1742. Through the help of his wife's relations, John Craster was elected Member of Parliament in 1757 for lord Weymouth's pocket borough at Weobley in Herefordshire, and retained his seat until 1761. A kinsman of his wife, Thomas Villiers, afterwards earl of Clarendon, wrote to John Craster from the Admiralty on 3 April 1757 about the election expenses. 'My dear sir. I have talked with ld Granville on your expense at the election. He agrees with me that it shall be limited and not exceed on your part 800 pds, but nothing must be spared towards securing success, and I shall write to Mr Cox to assist you with what money you may want, I am dear sir, most affectionately yours Thos Villiers.'

On 26 December 1756 died Dorothy, widow of the hon. Dixie Windsor. She was the last surviving sister and coheiress of Bertram Stote (d.1707) of Newcastle. Dorothy Windsor owned extensive estates at Kirkheaton, Longbenton, Willington and Jesmond, in all about 3,200 acres. After some litigation, John Craster and sir Robert Bewick of Close House were found to be heirs to the estates as descendants of dame Dorothy Windsor's great-great-grandfather, Cuthbert Bewick of Newcastle.

John Craster died at Taplow 31 December 1763. Of three sons and two daughters only his son George survived, the other children having died in infancy. Mrs Catherine Craster's will was found 'in a closet in her apartments in Windsor Castle'; she died there 1 October 1772. She appoints her nephew (actually her husband's nephew) John Wood of Beadnell to be executor, and administration was granted to him on 8 September 1810.

John Craster had literary tastes and 'amassed a respectable gentleman's library which remains, reasonably intact, at Craster'. He also pursued genealogical researches of his own family and has left behind him a fairly accurate account of his ancestry based on public records, wills and his estate deeds. There has also survived an account of a three-day ride through Lincolnshire. At the end of the third day he wrote:—

'How happy is the tough skin which wears like a buff skin
    Without crack or flaw;
For there's no abiding the torment of riding
    When buttocks are raw.'

John Craster's son was the first of the family to be given the Christian name of George, derived from his two godfathers. At his baptism at St Andrew's, Holborn, his godparents were George, earl of Orkney, George, lord Lansdown, and lady Clanronald. George was educated at Eton and on 24 May 1754 was entered at Gray's Inn. In 1756 his father bought him a commission in the Royal Troop of Horse Guards for which he paid £2000.

On 3 February 1757 he married at St Clement Danes, London, Olive, daughter of John Sharpe, Solicitor of the Treasury and MP for Callington. She was said to have a fortune of £30,000. On the occasion of the marriage John Craster gave his son an annuity of £400 during his own lifetime, and the reversion, after his death, of his Northumberland and Durham estates. This was the time of the 'grand tour' when all young men of family toured the continent. The young couple set out for Paris in 1760 and then visited at their leisure the principal cities of western Europe—Bordeaux, Marseilles, Aix, Genoa, Naples, Rome, Venice, Milan and Turin—only returning to England in the summer of 1763. The next two years were employed in renovating the family home of Craster Tower and adding thereto a new Georgian wing.

In March 1769 Olive fell ill, and a visit to the hot wells at Bristol proving of no avail, they moved to Paris for the winter months. There Mrs Craster died, her body being brought home to England for burial in the Craster vault in Embleton church. The funeral expenses of £288. 18s. 1d. included 'a hearse and pair to move the body from the Custom House at Long Acre and thence to Embleton'. It may have been about this time that George Craster drew up a draft petition, apparently for a title, for submission to George III. He stated that 'your petitioner's family from whom he received his existence and his fortune have been usefully employed in the service of their king and country ever since the time of king Henry the first, and your petitioner hoping to imitate their industry and virtues earnestly wishes to add to their glory and to obtain the testimony of your majesty's approbation of their good conduct by the honour bestowed on their name'. There is no evidence that the petition ever reached more than draft form.

For the rest of his short life, George Craster lived principally in Paris with short autumn visits to Craster. On 22 July 1771 he made his will in London and then returned to Craster to die there on 9 May 1772. As he had no children, the estates passed under the terms of his father's settlement to Daniel Craster of Embleton, son of his great-great-uncle Daniel Craster (d.1702) of Alnwick Abbey.

Daniel Craster of Alnwick Abbey was buried at Alnwick 21 August 1702, and administration of his goods was granted on 3 November 1702 to his widow. She was Elizabeth daughter of Mark Fenwick of Denton. It was their eldest son Daniel who succeeded to the Craster estates in 1772 when he was 91 years old.

A younger son, William Craster, was out in the Jacobite Rising of 1715. 'He was at this time a half pay officer was taken prisoner and ordered to be executed' (Sir David Smith's MSS). According to Patten, the historian of the Rising, 'William Craster of Craster, Northumberland, came with Mr Forster, and two others, into the Rebellion; these being all that gentleman brought into the same fate with himself' (Patten, *History of the Rebellion in 1715*, 3rd edition, p.118). How William Craster escaped execution is not known. He was living at Rock Moor house when he made his w.d. 14 April 1725. His wife Susannah is to have all his estate and all the profits and benefits of his lease of the farm now occupied by William at Rock moor house and of the lease now contracted for and at present occupied under sir John Swinburne. He leaves legacies of 20s. each to his brothers Daniel, John and Edmund, the last two to have theirs 'if living'. His three sisters Elizabeth Morley, Magdalene and Anne Craster are also to have 20s. each. The widow Susanna, who had been appointed sole executrix, proved the will 18 October 1725 (*Dur. Prob. Off.* by C.R.H.). (For Edmund see CRASTER OF NEWCASTLE UPON TYNE.)

Daniel Craster, who succeeded to Craster in 1772, died 13 October 1777 aged 96 and was succeeded by his second but eldest surviving son Daniel III. The latter was sheriff of Northumberland in 1779 and died in 1784. By his wife Ann daughter of John Coulter of Newcastle, merchant, he had five sons, John, Daniel IV, Shafto, William and Edmund, and four daughters, Mary, Barbara, Elizabeth and Ann. John, Daniel and William died in infancy. Shafto Craster who succeeded to Craster in 1784 died 7 May 1837 leaving an only daughter Frances Isabella who died unmarried 23 June 1860 aged 75. The youngest brother Edmund had died in 1824; his wife Phillis daughter of Thomas Buston of Buston, par. Warkworth, died 20 December 1813 'in the 23 year of her

CRASTER of CRASTER, par. EMBLETON

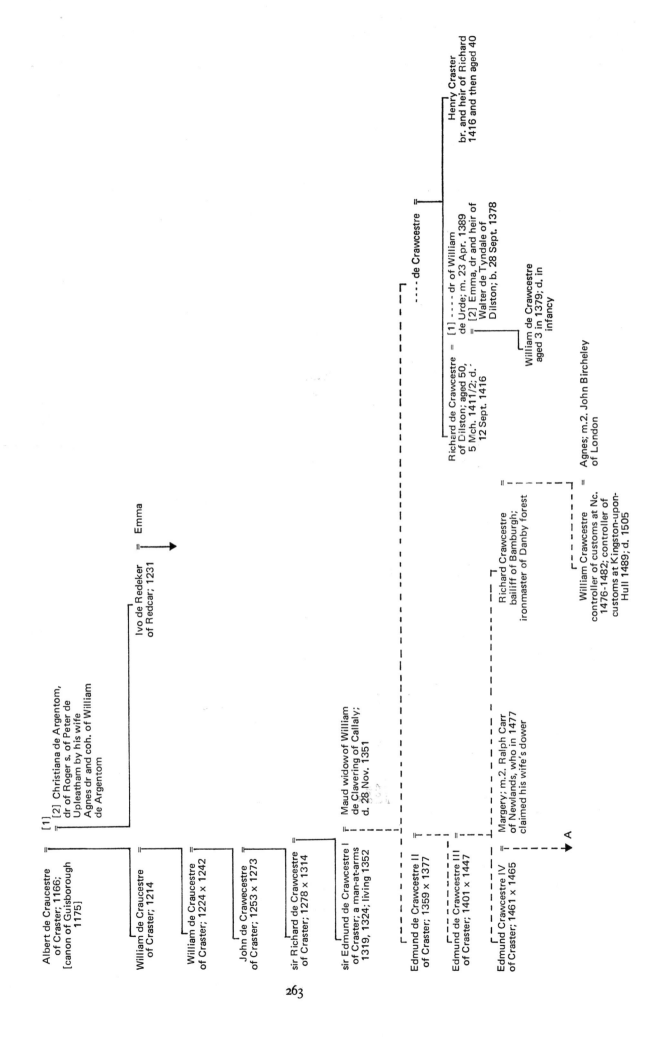

Albert de Craucestre
of Craster; 1166;
[canon of Guisborough
1175]

[1]
[2] Christiana de Argentom,
dr of Roger s. of Peter de
Upleatham by his wife
Agnes dr and coh. of William
de Argentom

Ivo de Redeker
of Redcar; 1231   = Emma

William de Craucestre
of Craster; 1214

William de Craucestre
of Craster; 1224 x 1242

John de Crawecestre
of Craster; 1253 x 1273

sir Richard de Crawcestre
of Craster; 1278 x 1314

Maud widow of William
de Clavering of Callaly;
d. 28 Nov. 1351

sir Edmund de Crawcestre I
of Craster; a man-at-arms
1319, 1324; living 1352

- - - - de Crawcestre

Edmund de Crawcestre II
of Craster; 1359 x 1377

Edmund de Crawcestre III
of Craster; 1401 x 1447

Richard de Crawcestre   =   [1] - - - dr of William
of Dilston; aged 50,   de Urde; m. 23 Apr. 1389
5 Mch. 1411/2; d.   = [2] Emma, dr and heir of
12 Sept. 1416   Walter de Tyndale of
                                Dilston; b. 28 Sept. 1378

William de Crawcestre
aged 3 in 1379; d. in
infancy

Henry Craster
br. and heir of Richard
1416 and then aged 40

Richard Crawcestre
bailiff of Bamburgh;
ironmaster of Danby forest

Edmund Crawcestre IV   =   Margery; m.2. Ralph Carr
of Craster; 1461 x 1465   of Newlands, who in 1477
                           claimed his wife's dower

William Crawcestre   =   Agnes; m.2. John Bircheley
controller of customs at Nc.   of London
1476-1482; controller of
customs at Kingston-upon-
Hull 1489; d. 1505

A

263

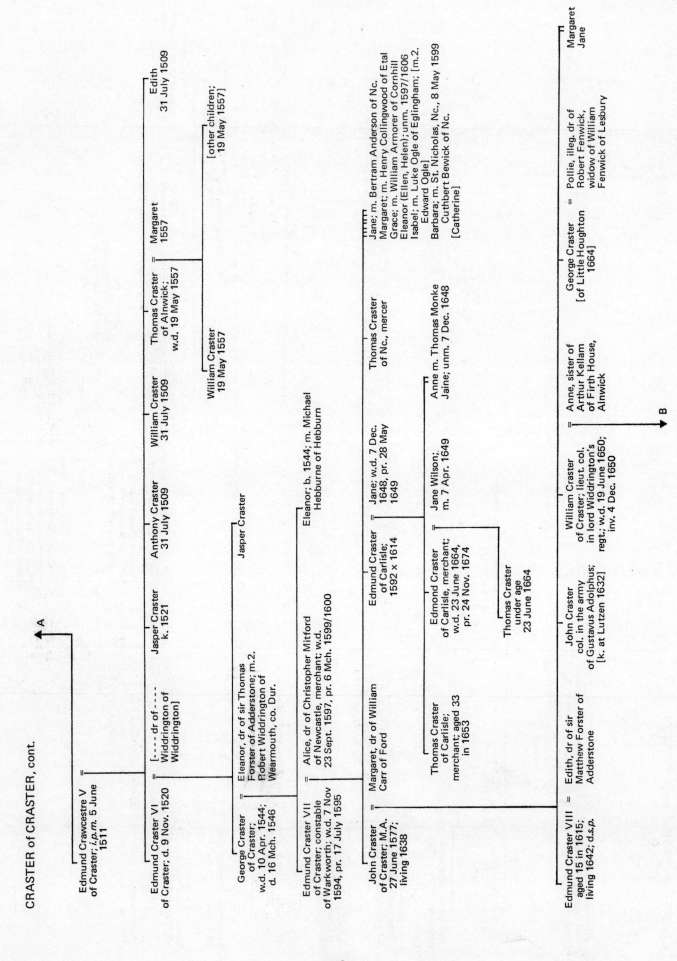

A

Edmund Crawcestre V of Craster; i.p.m. 5 June 1511

Edmund Craster VI of Craster; d. 9 Nov. 1520 = [---- dr of ---- Widdrington of Widdrington]

Jasper Craster k. 1521

Anthony Craster 31 July 1509

William Craster 31 July 1509

Thomas Craster of Alnwick; w.d. 19 May 1557 = Margaret 1557

Edith 31 July 1509

William Craster 19 May 1557

[other children; 19 May 1557]

George Craster of Craster; w.d. 10 Apr. 1544; d. 16 Mch. 1546 = Eleanor, dr of sir Thomas Forster of Adderstone; m.2. Robert Widdrington of Wearmouth, co. Dur.

Jasper Craster

Edmund Craster VII of Craster; constable of Warkworth; w.d. 7 Nov 1594, pr. 17 July 1595 = Alice, dr of Christopher Mitford of Newcastle, merchant; w.d. 23 Sept. 1597, pr. 6 Mch. 1599/1600

Eleanor; b. 1544; m. Michael Hebburne of Hebburn

John Craster of Craster; M.A. 27 June 1577; living 1638 = Margaret, dr of William Carr of Ford

Edmund Craster of Carlisle; 1592 x 1614 = Jane; w.d. 7 Dec. 1648, pr. 28 May 1649

Thomas Craster of Nc., mercer

Jane; m. Bertram Anderson of Nc.
Margaret; m. Henry Collingwood of Etal
Grace; m. William Armorer of Cornhill
Eleanor (Ellen); unm. 1597/1606
Isabel; m. Luke Ogle of Eglingham; [m.2. Edward Ogle]
Barbara; m. St. Nicholas, Nc., 8 May 1599 Cuthbert Bewick of Nc.
[Catherine]

Thomas Craster of Carlisle; merchant; aged 33 in 1653

Edmond Craster of Carlisle, merchant; w.d. 23 June 1664, pr. 24 Nov. 1674 = Jane Wilson; m. 7 Apr. 1649

Anne m. Thomas Monke
Jaine; unm. 7 Dec. 1648

Thomas Craster under age 23 June 1664

John Craster col. in the army of Gustavus Adolphus; [k. at Lutzen 1632]

William Craster of Craster; lieut. col. in lord Widdrington's regt.; w.d. 19 June 1650; inv. 4 Dec. 1650 = Anne, sister of Arthur Kellam of Firth House, Alnwick

George Craster [of Little Houghton 1664] = Pollie, illeg. dr of Robert Fenwick, widow of William Fenwick of Lesbury

Margaret
Jane

Edmund Craster VIII aged 15 in 1615; living 1642; d.s.p. = Edith, dr of sir Matthew Forster of Adderstone

B

CRASTER of CRASTER, cont.

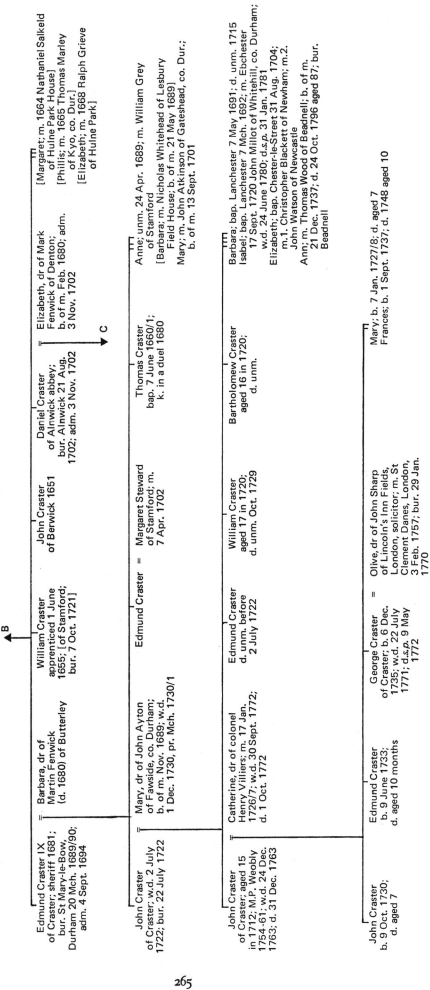

B →

C →

Edmund Craster IX of Craster; sheriff 1681; bur. St Mary-le-Bow, Durham 20 Mch. 1689/90; adm. 4 Sept. 1694
= Barbara, dr of Martin Fenwick (d. 1680) of Butterley

William Craster apprenticed 1 June 1655; [of Stamford; bur. 7 Oct. 1721]

John Craster of Berwick 1651

Daniel Craster of Alnwick abbey; bur. Alnwick 21 Aug. 1702; adm. 3 Nov. 1702
= Elizabeth, dr of Mark Fenwick of Denton; b. of m. Feb. 1680; adm. 3 Nov. 1702

[Margaret; m. 1664 Nathaniel Salkeld of Hulne Park House]
[Phillis; m. 1665 Thomas Marley of Kyo, co. Dur.]
[Elizabeth; m. 1668 Ralph Grieve of Hulne Park]

John Craster of Craster; w.d. 2 July 1722; bur. 22 July 1722
= Mary, dr of John Ayton of Fawside, co. Durham; b. of m. Nov. 1689; w.d. 1 Dec. 1730, pr. Mch. 1730/1

Edmund Craster = Margaret Steward of Stamford; m. 7 Apr. 1702

Thomas Craster bap. 7 June 1660/1; k. in a duel 1680

Anne; unm. 24 Apr. 1689; m. William Grey of Stamford
[Barbara; m. Nicholas Whitehead of Lesbury Field House; b. of m. 21 May 1689]
Mary; m. John Atkinson of Gateshead, co. Dur.; b. of m. 13 Sept. 1701

John Craster of Craster; aged 15 in 1712; M.P. Weobly 1754-61; w.d. 24 Dec. 1763; d. 31 Dec. 1763
= Catherine, dr of colonel Henry Villiers; m. 17 Jan. 1726/7; w.d. 30 Sept. 1772; d. 1 Oct. 1772

Edmund Craster d. unm. before 2 July 1722

William Craster aged 17 in 1720; d. unm. Oct. 1729

Bartholomew Craster aged 16 in 1720; d. unm.

Barbara; bap. Lanchester 7 May 1691; d. unm. 1715
Isabel; bap. Lanchester 7 Mch. 1692; m. Ebchester 17 Sept. 1720 John Millot of Whitehill, co. Durham; w.d. 24 June 1780; d.s.p. 31 Jan. 1781
Elizabeth; bap. Chester-le-Street 31 Aug. 1704; m.1. Christopher Blackett of Newham; m.2. John Watson of Newcastle
Ann; m. Thomas Wood of Beadnell; b. of m. 21 Dec. 1737; d. 24 Oct. 1796 aged 87; bur. Beadnell

Edmund Craster b. 9 June 1733; d. aged 10 months

George Craster of Craster; b. 6 Dec. 1735; w.d. 22 July 1771; d.s.p. 9 May 1772
= Olive, dr of John Sharp of Lincoln's Inn Fields, London, solicitor; m. St Clement Danes, London, 3 Feb. 1757; bur. 29 Jan. 1770

John Craster b. 9 Oct. 1730; d. aged 7

Mary; b. 7 Jan. 1727/8; d. aged 7
Frances; b. 1 Sept. 1737; d. 1748 aged 10

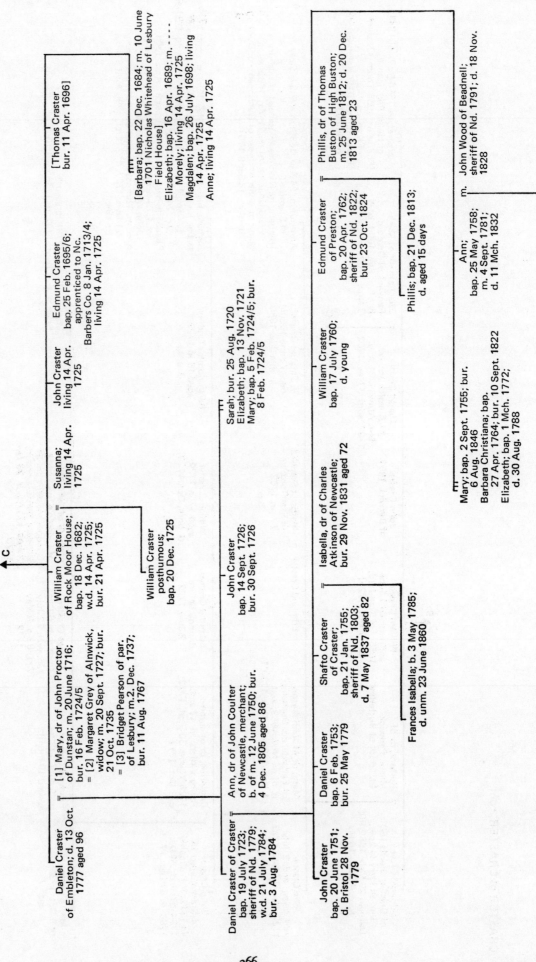

C →

Daniel Craster of Embleton; d. 13 Oct. 1777 aged 96

William Craster of Rock Moor House; bap. 18 Dec. 1682; w.d. 14 Apr. 1725; bur. 21 Apr. 1725

[1] Mary, dr of John Proctor of Dunstan; m. 20 June 1716; bur. 16 Feb. 1724/5
= [2] Margaret Grey of Alnwick, widow; m. 20 Sept. 1727; bur. 21 Oct. 1735
= [3] Bridget Pearson of par. of Lesbury; m.2. Dec. 1737; bur. 11 Aug. 1767

[Thomas Craster bur. 11 Apr. 1696]

Edmund Craster bap. 25 Feb. 1695/6; apprenticed to Nc. Barbers Co. 8 Jan. 1713/4; living 14 Apr. 1725

John Craster living 14 Apr. 1725

Susanna; living 14 Apr. 1725

[Barbara; bap. 22 Dec. 1684; m. 10 June 1701 Nicholas Whitehead of Lesbury Field House]
Elizabeth; bap. 16 Apr. 1689; m. - - - - Morely; living 14 Apr. 1725
Magdalen; bap. 26 July 1698; living 14 Apr. 1725
Anne; living 14 Apr. 1725

William Craster posthumous; bap. 20 Dec. 1725

Daniel Craster of Craster bap. 19 July 1723; sheriff of Nd. 1779; w.d. 21 July 1784; bur. 3 Aug. 1784

Ann, dr of John Coulter of Newcastle, merchant; b. of m. 12 June 1750; bur. 4 Dec. 1805 aged 86

Sarah; bur. 25 Aug. 1720
Elizabeth; bap. 13 Nov. 1721
Mary; bap. 5 Feb. 1724/5; bur. 8 Feb. 1724/5

John Craster bap. 14 Sept. 1726; bur. 30 Sept. 1726

John Craster bap. 20 June 1751; d. Bristol 28 Nov. 1779

Daniel Craster bap. 6 Feb. 1753; bur. 25 May 1779

Shafto Craster of Craster; bap. 21 Jan. 1755; sheriff of Nd. 1803; d. 7 May 1837 aged 82

Isabella, dr of Charles Atkinson of Newcastle; bur. 29 Nov. 1831 aged 72

William Craster bap. 17 July 1760; d. young

Edmund Craster of Preston; bap. 20 Apr. 1762; sheriff of Nd. 1822; bur. 23 Oct. 1824

Phillis, dr of Thomas Buston of High Buston; m. 25 June 1812; d. 20 Dec. 1813 aged 23

Phillis; bap. 21 Dec. 1813; d. aged 15 days

Ann; bap. 25 May 1758; m. 4 Sept. 1781; d. 11 Mch. 1832

m. John Wood of Beadnell; sheriff of Nd. 1791; d. 18 Nov. 1828

Mary; bap. 2 Sept. 1755; bur. 6 Aug. 1846
Barbara Christiana; bap. 27 Apr. 1764; bur. 10 Sept. 1822
Elizabeth; bap. 1 Mch. 1772; d. 30 Aug. 1788

Frances Isabella; b. 3 May 1785; d. unm. 23 June 1860

CRASTER [WOOD] of CRASTER →

CRASTER [WOOD] of CRASTER, cont.

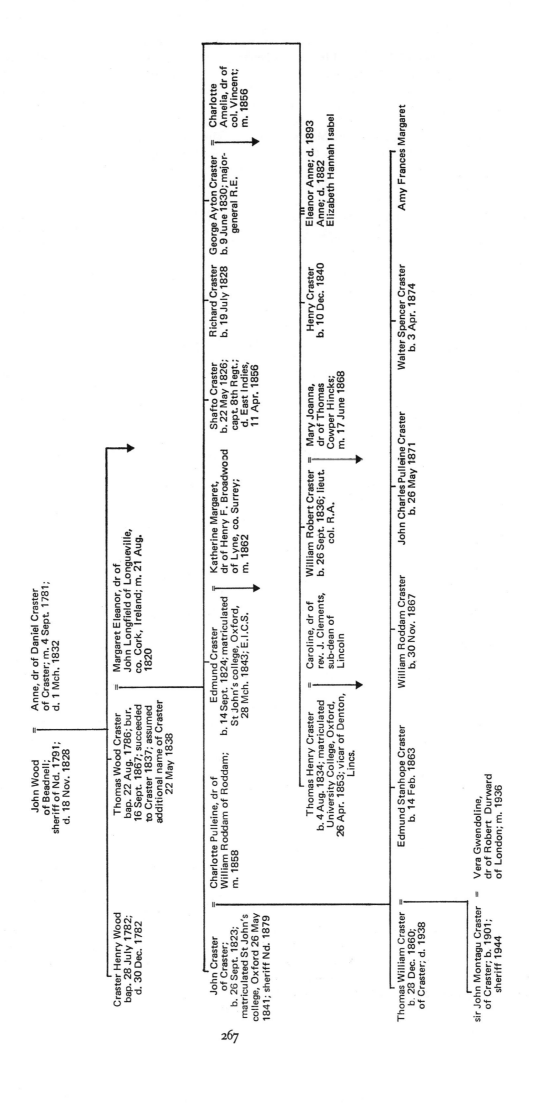

267

age, leaving a daughter who at her baptism received the name of her dear mother, and soon after followed her into a better world, aged only 15 days' (M.I. Ellingham).

On the death of Shafto Craster in 1837 the heir to Craster was his nephew Thomas Wood, eldest surviving son of John Wood of Beadnell by his wife Ann Craster. Thomas Wood had a grant of arms 2 May 1838, and on 22 May had licence to use the surname of Craster in addition to that of Wood. Thomas Wood's great grandson sir John Montagu Craster is now the owner of Craster. He is probably the 22nd generation from Albert de Crawcestre of 1166 and Craster has been owned by his direct ancestors for at least 800 years.

CRASTER OF NEWCASTLE UPON TYNE

EDMUND CRASTER, bap. 25 February 1695/6, 3rd son of Daniel Craster of Craster (d.1702) by his wife Elizabeth Fenwick, was apprenticed 8 January 1713/4 to the Barber Surgeons Company of Newcastle. It would appear that Edmund had not kept contact with his family, for when his brother William made his w.d. 14 April 1725 he left Edmund 20s., 'if living'.

A family of Craster living at Penicuik, Midlothian, in the 19th century had a tradition that they represented the Crasters of Craster in the male line and it has been suggested that they were descended from Edmund the barber surgeon. Mr Robert Greaves Craster living at Spencer Lodge, Bromley, Kent, in 1894 had in his possession a 'Breeches' Bible, printed at London in 1576. The book had been given in 1577 by Robert Johnson, bachelor of divinity, parson of North Luffenham in Rutland, to the aldermen of Stamford, Morice Johnson, Robert Johnson's father, having been some time one of them. At a later date the bible was used as a family bible by an Edward Christer, and at the end, on the middle of the cover is the note 'Edward Christer his Bible. This Bible was given by my grandmother the 21 of September 1746'. The name of Edward Craster's grandmother seems to have been Margaret Whorledge and there is a note on the fly-leaf 'Edward Whorledge his book 1752'.

The family record in the Bible commences with the children born between 1745 and 1760, of an Edward Craster. The second son, John, born 24 December 1747 was baptised at St John's, Newcastle, 17 January 1747/8 and married at St Nicholas', Newcastle, 27 June 1769, Hannah Fenwick. Their eldest son John married at Hexham 15 September 1799 Jane Robson, and these two became the parents of Thomas Craster, master of the Eye Infirmary at Newcastle in 1851, where he died on 9 December 1882.

Thomas' eldest son John moved to Wellington, Penicuik, Midlothian, and died there on 2 July 1890. Thomas' second son was a doctor in Middlesbrough, and died 15 October 1888.

OTHER CRASTERS

A DESCENDANT of Thomas Craster (w.d. 19 May 1557) the Alnwick tanner or of one of his brothers may have been Batholmew Craster of Stobswood, par. Morpeth, who seems to have been a farmer. Batholmew made his will on 26 July 1579 in which he directs that he is to be buried within the parish church of Ulgham, paying my accustomed duties'. He leaves to his youngest brother Lewes Crastor 'one lin loome and one pott'. His daughter Jane, apparently his only child, is to have a cow and calf, and John Craster, William Craster and Christofer Craster are to have the offspring and proof of the cow until Jane comes of lawful age. Jane is also to have a presser, an 'almire' and a 'cawell'. The rest of his goods moveable and unmoveable are to go to Margret Craster, his wife, and Jane Craster, his daughter. One of the witnesses to the will which was proved on 7 April 1580 is Wylliam Craster (SS. 112, p.82).

Edmonde son of Edmonde Craster of Craster, who had been apprenticed on 1 August 1592 to Henry Fenkell of Newcastle, boothman, seems to have moved to Carlisle where an Edmound Craister was admitted to the Merchant's Gild of Carlisle in 1614. He married at St Mary's, Carlisle, 7 April 1649, Jane Wilson, and it was evidently his widow, Jaine Craister of the city of Carlisle, widow, who made her w.d. 7 December 1648. She leaves to Ales Porter the elder her gold ring, 'which now I wear upon my finger'. Her god daughter Mary Jackson is to have a silver spoon, and her godmothers Jackson and Mary Wilkinson each a 5s. piece of gold. To her grandchild Edmond Norman she leaves £20 when of age, and to her grandchild Dolly Monke one 'how back whie' (i.e. a hollow backed young heifer). Her son Thomas Craister is to have all her heirable lands, and she appoints as her executors her daughters Anne wife of Thomas Monke, and Jaine Craister, and her son Edmond Craister. The will was proved 28 May 1649. Thomas Craister the son of Edmond Craister was admitted a brother of the Carlisle Merchant's Gild on 30 March 1638, and Edmond Craister the son of Edmond Craister on 6 July 1655. Thomas was aged 33 when at Michaelmas 1653 he deposed about the taking of Carlisle for the King in April 1648 (Westmorland Note Book, p.83, quoting from Exch. Dep. Cumb. No. 17). Edmond Craister the son describes himself as of the city of Carlisle, merchant, in his w.d. 23 June 1664. He is to be buried in St Cuthbert's church 'where my ancestors have been buried'. All the bedsteads, tables, frames, chairs, buffets, leads, grates, fatts (i.e. vats), brewing vessels, cubbards, chists, brass mortar and pestell are to remain as heirlooms 'to the house I now dwell in'. His wife is to have this dwelling house for her natural life, except for the two foreshopps and one parlour which his son Thomas is to have 'so soon as he shall accomplish the age of twenty one years'. The will was proved by the widow and son on 23 November 1674 (Record Office, Carlisle).

Jaine Craister's son Thomas Craister was probably Thomas Craister of the city of Carlisle, merchant, who on 26 April 1653 purchased from Ralph Dowson of Loftus, Yorks., the socage manor of Carlisle (Howard of Naworth MSS at Durham). Thomas was an important Parliamentarian and served on the Committee appointed by the Roundheads for the propagation of the Gospel in Northumberland, Cumberland, Westmorland and Durham (Nightingale's Ejected in Cumberland and Westmorland). At one time Thomas was a magistrate for Cumberland and mayor of Carlisle.

A John Craster 'of Cumberland' matriculated from Queen's College, Cambridge, in Michaelmas 1589.

CRASTER of NEWCASTLE UPON TYNE

Edward Craster

John Craster
b. 24 Dec. 1747;
bap. St John's, Nc.,
17 Jan. 1747/8

= Hannah Fenwick;
m. St Nicholas, Nc.;
27 June 1769

William Craster = [Arabella Gow;
b. 25 Nov. 1750   m. 12 Feb. 1774]

Margaret; b. 7 Mch. 1753; [bur. St John's,
Nc., 26 Feb. 1766]
Ann; b. 18 Nov. 1760

Edward Craster
b. 12 Sept. 1745

Edward Craster
b. 23 Apr. 1776;
d. 10 Mch. 1777

Edward Craster
b. 21 Apr. 1778

William Craster
b. 26 Dec. 177 [9]

Fenwick Craster
b. 12 May 1781

Jane; b. 4 Aug. 1770
Sarah; b. 24 Apr. 1772; bap. St John's,
Nc., 14 June 1772

John Craster
b. 23 Apr. 1774

= Jane Robson;
m. Hexham
15 Sept. 1799

John Craster
b. 11 Dec. 1807

Hannah; b. 12 June 1800
Sarah; b. 6 Feb. 1806
Francis; b. 3 Dec. 1810

Thomas Craster
b. 22 Jan. 1803;
master of Nc. Eye
Infirmary 1851; d.
9 Dec. 1882

= Elizabeth Shipley;
m. Oct. 1822

Jane Greaves;
m. St James's chapel,
Blackett St., Nc.,
5 June 1849

Thomas W. Craster
of Middlesborough;
b. 23 Mch. 1829; M.D.;
d. 15 Oct. 1888

= Adelaide Vaughan;
m. Escombe, co. Dur.,
30 Nov. 1857

Jane; b. Feb. 1823

Thomas Vaughan Craster
b. 17 Apr. 1859; d. 19 Oct. 1881

Edward Ernest Craster
of Carwood house, Grange Road,
Middlesborough, L.R.C.P.; born
6 Dec. 1861

3 other sons

two drs.

John Craster
b. 24 Mch. 1824;
bap. St Mary's,
Gateshead; d. Wellington,
Penicuik, Midlothian,
2 July 1890

= Marie, dr of Dr Daniel
McKechnie of Witton Park,
Kent, 1894; b. Barrack Sq.,
Nc., 10 Oct. 1854

John Craster
of Wellington, Penicuik,
Midlothian, 1894; b.
Barrack Square, Nc.,
19 Oct. 1856

Mary; d. young
Elizabeth; b. 5 Sept. 1852; m. Penicuik, Apr. 1880,
Alfred Blechynden
Hannah Jane; b. Rose Street, Inverness,
25 Nov. 1859
Mary; b. Wellington, Penicuik, Midlothian,
6 June 1863
Jane Greaves; b. Penicuik, 28 Nov. 1868

Robert Greaves Craster
of Spencer Lodge, Bromley,
Kent, 1894; b. Barrack Sq.,
Nc., 10 Oct. 1854

Albert Kenneth Greaves Craster
b. 19 July 1890; bap. 15 Aug. 1890

Marie Evelyn

John Geoffrey Craster
b. Woodburn, Penicuik, 27 May
1888; bap. 28 June 1888

CRASTER—BIBLIOGRAPHY

Northumberland County History II, p.166-182 with pedigree. This account of the Craster family was compiled by Cadwallader John Bates.

The Early History of the Craster Family. By sir Edmund Craster. In *AA*4. XXX, pp.118-148.

The Craster Family—Three Generations. By sir Edmund Craster. In *AA*4. XXXI, pp.23-47.

The Contents of a Northumbrian Mansion 1772. By sir Edmund Craster. In *AA*4. XXXIII, pp.17-26.

CRASTER—NOTES

1. It has been thought advisable to reserve for a note the amusing statement by the gossip Spearman written in a copy of Hutchinson's *History of Northumberland* in the Broome Park library. He states 'I have seen an account that the Craucesters were standard bearers to Canute our Danish King, and thence had the Badge of the Raven'. The Craster arms are in fact—Quarterly or and gules, a crow in the first quarter, the crow being undoubtedly a punning allusion to the 'craw' of Crawcestre. The Craster shield is first blasoned in Jenyn's Roll at the time of Edward III.

2. There are no Craster wills or administrations between 1638 and 1700 in the Principal Probate Registry at Somerset House.

3. In 1598 Thomas Cryston was a freeholder in Embleton. When the common fields and the moor were divided in 1730 Ralph Christon had 1 11/12 farms and Robert Christon 1/6th of a farm. It seems likely that these Christons were cadets of the Crasters of Craster. Robert Craister who was a freeholder in Embleton in 1710 is evidently the Robert Christon, a freeholder there in 1715—the names Craister and Christon must have been interchangeable. This is to some extent confirmed by the statement in the w.d. 21 April 1722 of Robert Christon that he leaves to his son Ralph 'all my freehold lands in Embleton called Craister lands'. The Christons belonged to the Society of Friends. Their farm called Christon Bank was sold 1 May 1759 by John Criston of Newcastle, cordwainer, the last male of the family. There is a pedigree of the family in *NCH*. II, p.47.

CRASTER—FREEHOLDERS

1628. John Craister, of Craister, esq.

1639. John Craster, of Craster, esq.

1698. John Craister of Craister, esq.

1710. Robert Craister of Embleton; Tho. Craister of Alnwick; Tho. Craister of Alnwick (*sic*); Wm Craister of Craister, par. Embleton; John Craister of Alnwick; David Craister of Alnwick.

1715. Wm Craister of Craister; Tho. Craiston of Alnwick; John Craister of Alnwick; Robert Christon of Embleton.

1721. Robt. Craisten of Embleton, quaker.

1748. Ralph Christon, Embleton; Robert Christon, Embleton.

1774. Dan. Craster esq., Craster.

1826. Shafto Craster esq., Craster.

KNIGHTS OF 1166

BARONY OF DILSTON—KNIGHTS OF 1166

WILLIAM son of Aluric de Dovelston in 1166 held a third part of one knight's fee, of which nothing had been sub-enfeoffed.

The barony consisted of the single township of Dilston, par. Corbridge.

BARONY OF CALLERTON—KNIGHTS OF 1166

GILBERT DE LANVALE's barony was held in 1166 by the service of two knights, and he reported that a certain knight (*miles*) held a quarter part of one fee. Neither the 'certain knight' nor the location of his holding is known. In 1242 the sheriff reported that the tenants of old feoffment (*i.e.* created before 1135) in the barony were Richard de Neusum who held 3½ carucates of land, presumably in Newsham, by 1/6th of a fee, and Robert son of Ranulph who held a carucate in Callerton by 1/16th of a fee. Neither of these holdings seems to fit with the quarter fee of 1166. However in 1208 Gilbert Delaval made an agreement with Adam de Neusum about the six carucates contained in the manor of Newsham. The result of this division was to give Adam three and a half carucates for which he agreed to render the service of a sixth part of a knight's fee. It is possible that the holding of the Neusum family had previously been a quarter fee.

The townships included in the barony of Callerton were:—

Par. Newburn. —Black Callerton, North Dissington and South Dissington.

Par. Earsdon. —Seaton Delaval and Newsham (with South Blyth).

BARONY OF WARKWORTH—KNIGHTS OF 1166

ROGER son of Richard's *carta* in 1166 was the briefest made by any of the Northumberland barons. He states 'I Roger son of Richard hold *in capite* of the king, Warkworth by the service of one knight'. Evidently nothing had been sub-enfeoffed.

The barony extended over the modern townships of Warkworth, Acklington, Acklington Park and Gloster Hill.

BARONY OF BOTHAL—KNIGHTS OF 1166

RICHARD BERTRAM reported in 1166 that he held his fee by three knights of old feoffment; the whole barony was in his own hands and no knights held under him. The modern townships included in the barony were Ashington, Bothal Demesne, Longhurst, Oldmoor, Pegswood and Sheepwash

in the parish of Bothal; and Earsdon, Fenrother, Hebron and Tritlington, chap. Hebron.

The return of 1166 may not have been strictly accurate in stating that there were no sub-enfeoffments, for in the return made in 1242 it was said that Peter de Crikelston (*sic*) and Eve his wife then held Tritlington and Earsdon by one knight's fee of *old* feoffment.

BARONY OF MORPETH—KNIGHTS OF 1166

ROGER DE MERLAI reported in 1166 that of the old feoffment William de Clifton held one knight's fee, Reiner held two fees of new feoffment, Roger de Merlai a quarter part of a fee and Robert son of Peter a third part of one fee. The balance to make up the four knights' fees by which Roger held the barony lay in his demesne lands.

The following townships were in the barony:—

Par. Morpeth. —Morpeth, Buller's Green, Hepscott, Morpeth Castle (with Catchburn, Stobhill and Parkhouses), Newminster Abbey, Shilvington, Tranwell (and High Church) and Twizell.

Par. Stannington. —Bellasis, Blagdon, Clifton (with Coldwell), Duddoe (East and West), Saltwick, Stannington (East and West Side), Shotton and Plessey.

Par. Longbenton. —Long Benton, Killingworth, Walker and Weetslet.

Par. Newburn. —Woolsington.

Chap. Ulgham. —Stobswood, Ulgham and Ulgham Grange.

The knight's fee held by William de Clifton in 1166 comprised the two vills of Clifton and Coldwell, held throughout the 13th century by the family of Conyers, no doubt the same family that held Sockburn, co. Durham, throughout the Middle Ages and later. William de Clifton was probably a Conyers. The name of Henry de Coisners appears in the *Pipe Roll* for 1178, and in 1188 he and William de Coisners witness a deed of Roger de Merlay. The anniversaries of Henry Conyers and Eda his wife were observed at Newminster Abbey. William de Coyners gave lands to Newminster for the health of his own soul and those of his wife Eva and his son Henry (*SS. 66*, p.19); this was apparently the William de Clifton (or Conyers) of 1166. William son of Henry de Coyners gave an inspeximus to Newminster of the charter of the land of Scharplawe in Clifton which had been given to the abbey by his grandfather William Coyners (*Ib.*, p.21). This proves three generations of the family— William I 1166; Henry (son) 1178 x 1188; and William II (son). The name of the second William occurs in the *Pipe Rolls* 1210-1219; he was surety for Godfrey Mauduit in 1201 (*Nd Pleas*), a pledge for Alice de Stutevill in 1206 (*Ib.*) and a knight for the grand assize in 1208 (*Ib.*). He gave lands in Clifton to Newminster in exchange for the grange of Coldwell. A later William Conyers held Clifton and Coldwell in 1242 as one knight's fee of old feoffment. In 1281/2 Elizabeth Conyers held the manor of Clifton by the service of one knight. An undated deed in the *Newminster Chartulary* records a confirmation by Richard de Coyners of the gifts to Newminster made by his ancestors (*SS*. 66, p.22). No later connections between the Conyers family and Clifton have been found.

The rev. John Hodgson thought that there could be no doubt that Shotton, Blagdon and North Weetslade formed part of the lands held by Reiner in 1166 as two knights' fees of old feoffment. There is no evidence for this. In 1242 these three vills were held by John de Plessys as *one* fee of old feoffment. The name of Adam de Plaeizeiz appears in the *Pipe Roll* for 1170. The last of the family, Richard de Plessetis, died in 1349 and his estates passed by a previous settlement to the Widdringtons.

The one-third of a fee held in 1166 by Robert son of Peter may have been the one-third of a fee (South Weetslade) held by Galfrid de Wydesdale in 1242. The family of Weetslade continued to hold lands in South Weetslade until 1360 when the king's escheator seised for the Crown the lands there which had belonged to John de Wetslad in 1317 on the grounds that John had taken part in the rebellion of Gilbert de Middleton (*NCH*. XIII, p.432).

BARONY OF ALNWICK—KNIGHTS OF 1166

IN 1166 William de Vesci by his *carta* reported that he held twenty knights' fees of the king of old feoffment which his father had held on the year and day that king Henry (Henry I) was alive and dead. The twenty fees included the barony of Malton in Yorkshire as well as that of Alnwick in Northumberland. To cover the knights' service which was due to the Crown his ancestors had enfeoffed before 2 December 1135, twenty fees. Thirteen of these fees can be identified as being in the barony of Alnwick. They are:—

Herevicus Coleman—1 fee: Bilton, par. Lesbury.

William Tisun—2 fees: Shilbottle (with Woodhouse and Whittle), Hazon (with Hartlaw) and Newton-on-the-Moor, par. Shilbottle; Guizance, chap. Brainshaugh, and Rennington, par. Embleton.

Ernald de Morewic—1 fee: Morwick, par. Warkworth, and East Chevington, chap. Chevington.

Adam Ribalt—1 fee: Howick, par. Howick.

Richard de Roc—1 fee: Rock, par. Embleton.

John son of Odard—2 fees: Newton-by-the-Sea, par. Embleton, and Earle, par. Doddington.

Walter Bataile—1 fee: Preston, par. Ellingham, and Brunton, par. Embleton.

Radulf son of Man—1 fee: Adderstone, par. Bamburgh, and North Charlton, par. Ellingham.

Simon son of Ernold de Lucre—1 fee: Lucker (with Hoppen), par. Bamburgh, and South Charlton, par. Ellingham.

Odenell de Dunframvill—2 fees: Ingram (with Reaveley and Clinch and Hartside) and Fawdon, par. Ingram; Alwinton, Biddlestone, Burradon, Clennell, Farnham, 'Chirmundisden', Netherton (North Side and South Side)

and Sharperton, par. Alwinton.

Since the enfeoffment of the original twenty knights' fees, William de Vesci and his ancestors had enfeoffed certain others lands out of their demesne. The enfeoffments by Yvo and by Eustace son of John seem all to have been in Yorkshire, but William himself had created the following holdings by knights' service in the barony of Alnwick:

William de Tubervill—1 fee: Horton, par. Chatton.

Galfrid de Vall(oignes)—½ fee: Newham, par. Bamburgh.

Radulf son of Roger—½ fee: Rugley (part of Alnwick), par. Alnwick.

Besides the above holdings by military service, the barony of Alnwick included many vills either held in demesne or let to socage tenants. These were:—

Par. Bamburgh —Swinhoe and Tuggal.

Par. Alnwick —Alnwick (with Abbey lands, Alnwick South Side, Canongate and Huln Parks) and Denwick.

Par. Embleton —Broxfield and Falloden.

Par. Lesbury —Alnmouth, Lesbury and Wooden.

Par. Longhoughton —Boomer (with Seaton House), Littlehoughton and Longhoughton.

Par. Alnham —Alnham, Prendwick, Skrenwood and Unthank.

Par. Chatton —Chatton, Coldmartin, Fowberry, Heslerigg, Hetton, Hetton House, Lyham and Weetwood.

Par. Chillingham —Chillingham, Hebburn and Newtown.

Par. Doddington —Doddington, Ewart and Nesbit.

Par. Warkworth —Amble and Hauxley.

Before 1242 many more holdings by knights' service had been created from the demesne lands.

Between 1139 and 1142 Henry son of the king of Scots, granted and restored to Eustace son of John and his heirs after him in fee and inheritance, all the lands in Northumberland which he held in chief of Henry, king of England, and after him of king Stephen. He granted in addition, in augmentation of Eustace's other fee, but for no additional service the lands of Bertune and Pottunam, Pachestune and Stivecheam (*PRO*. C.47/9/5 (*Chancery Miscellanea*) in *Regesta Regum Scottorum*, p.138). A copy of this charter appears in the 14th century *Percy Chartulary* (*SS*. vol.117), but here the place-names have been deliberately altered to support the Percy claim to the Vesci inheritance, the names there being given as Breneton, Proportunam, Pachestenam and Scrimeston. The editor of *Percy Chartulary* guessed the modern equivalents of three of these places as Branton, par. Eglingham, Paston, par. Kirknewton, and Scremerston 'on the coast south of Berwick'. The lands conveyed by earl Henry to Eustace son of John are in fact four manors of the Honour of Huntingdon, Earls Barton, Northants, Potton, Beds, and Paxton and Stukeley, Hunts.

Spindleston and Budle, par. Bamburgh, are often referred to as members of the barony of Alnwick. They had formed part of the demesnes of Bamburgh, but Henry I gave to Eustace son of John 'the land Archaristam, which I have in my demesne in Bamburgh, to wit, the land of Spilestona and the mill of Warnet, which render to me yearly sixty shillings, and the land of Bolla with appurtenances, which was wont to render to me forty shillings'.

Some of the military tenants in the barony of Alnwick were themselves holders of other local baronies. Ernald de

Morewic held the small barony of Chevington, John son of Odard was baron of Embleton, and Odenell de Dunframvill held the barony of Prudhoe and the lordship of Redesdale. Radulf son of Man (Main) was a king's forester and as such held the serjeanty holding of Ditchburn. Accounts of the families of these persons have already been given. The Valoignes of Newham have appeared amongst 'Other Baronial Families'.

The Herevicus Coleman who in 1166 held Bilton, par. Lesbury, as one knight's fee left descendants who adopted the territorial surname of Bilton. In 1242 Hervic de Bilton was owner of Bilton. In 1352 Eleanor widow of Richard de Bilton had become the owner. William son of Henry de Bilton, in 1358, conveyed to sir Robert de Umfreville the reversion of the township of Bilton which John de Belyngham held during the life of Eleanor widow of Richard de Bilton (*NCH*. II, p.452).

The same 14th century monk of Alnwick Abbey who compiled the fictitious pedigree of the Vescis did the same disservice for the Tisuns who had been great benefactors of the abbey. The pedigree is such a typical production of the times that it deserves to be quoted in full.

'William, duke of Normandy, called the Bastard, associating with himself the lords Ivo de Vescy and Eustace son of John, with knights assembled together from all places, with the people of Normandy and other countries, passed over the sea with a strong band into England, and having joined battle with Harold and his army, obtained it, and so was adorned with the Crown of the Kingdom. In this battle William Tisoune fell, whose brother, that is to say, Richard Tisoune was the founder of the chapel of the monks of Gysyns about the years (*sic*) of our Lord 1000, whose father was called Gisbright Tisonne, the founder, namely, of the abbeys of Malton, Walton and Bridlington. This Gisbright gave to Richard, his son, the village of Shilbottell, together with the church of Gisyng etc. This Richard begat William Tisoune, and William begat German Tisoune, and German begat the Lady Bone of Hilton, who was the wife of William de Hilton. This changed the surname Tisoune to Hilton, and William de Hilton begat Alexander, and Alexander begat sir Robert de Hilton. And the aforesaid king gave Ivo de Vescy his knight, for his service, to wife, the only daughter of the said William Tisoune, killed in the said battle, with the baronies of Alnwick and Malton, which before that time belonged to Gisbright Tisoune, the father of William and Richard Tisoune' (*AA1*. III, p.135).

The inaccuracies are obvious. We are expected to believe that Gisbright Tisoune, a man with a typical Norman-French name, founded abbeys in Yorkshire more than 66 years before the Conquest. One of his sons, Richard, is said to have founded the chapel of Guyzance in AD 1000 and another son, William, to have fallen at Hastings 66 years later, apparently fighting for king Harold. Even if the date 1000 is a mistake for 1100 the discrepancies are evident.

The surname Tisoune is probably a nickname derived from the French *taisson*, a badger. It occurs in Normandy before the Conquest. Rodulf Taisson and his brother Ernis are witnesses to a charter of Robert, duke of Normandy, and *circa* 1048 Radulf Taison, presumably the same person, witnesses a grant of William, duke of Normandy, to the abbot of Marmoutier (Ewen, *A History of Surnames*, pp.78-79).

Another fantastic story about the Tisons is that 'Descended from the lords of Le Cinglais in Calvados, Gisbright or Gilbert Tison occupied the distinguished office of standard-bearer in the host which followed the Conqueror and he shared in the lands wrested from their Saxon owners (*NCH*. V, p.416).

A charter in the *Selby Chartulary* describes Gilbert Tison as *domini regis Anglie summus vexillator* but the charter is palpably fictitious (*Early Yorkshire Charters*, XII, p.49). At the time of the Domesday Survey, Gilbert Tison, although not one of the great landowners of the time, held 27 manors in Yorkshire, 6 in Nottinghamshire and one in Lincolnshire. If in fact Gisbright was descended from the lords of le Cinglais in Calvados, he may have been a companion in arms of the first Vesci to come to England, for the surname of Vesci is probably derived from Vassy, also in the department of Calvados.

In his *carta* of 1166 William de Vesci specifies first of all the knights of old feoffment that had held from his father in 1135. Then he schedules the feoffments that had been made by Yvo de Vesci, Eustace son of John and by himself. As William Tisun's fees are included in the first schedule there is the presumption that the Tisun feoffment had not only been before 1135 but before the time of Yvo de Vesci. Unfortunately it is not known who owned the barony before Yvo. Eustace son of John confirmed to Alnwick abbey the grant made to it by Richard Tysone of the church of St Wilfrid at Guyzance. One of the witnesses to the confirmation is Adam the sheriff who held that office *c.* 1141-1147. Richard Tysone must therefore have held his fees earlier than this.

The name of Ricard Tisun appears in the *Durham Liber Vitae* (SS. 13, p.52). A gift made shortly before 1100, by Gilbert Tison, the Yorkshire baron, to Selby abbey is witnessed by *Adam filio meo et Willelmo et Everardo cappellano et Ricardo Tisun*, and others. It has been supposed that Richard Tisun was a younger son of Gilbert and founder of the Tisun family that held Shilbottle. As no relationship is specified for Richard in the charter, Farrer deduced that he was not a legitimate son of Gilbert, though doubtless of the same family (*Early Yorkshire Charters*, XII, p.15). It seems likely that William Tison who held Shilbottle in 1166 was Richard's son. Another son may have been Guy Tison, coroner for Northumberland 1165-1177. Before 1184 the names of German Tisun and Richard Tisun appear as witnesses together with William. They were probably both sons of William; German certainly was. *William Tisone et Germano filio suo* witness the grant of Morwick and East Chevington by William de Vesci to Ernulph de Morwick. The grant has been dated 'before the year 1135' on the strength of a confirmation of it by Henry, king of England (*NCH*. V, p.345). As William de Vesci held the barony of Alnwick 1157-1184 the royal confirmation must have been made by Henry II.

German Tisun's only daughter and heiress Bone (or Benita) married William de Hilton of Hilton, co. Durham, a baron of the bishopric, and the manor of Shilbottle passed to the Hilton family. A late reminder of the Tisun's benefaction to Alnwick abbey appears in the *Northumberland Pleas* for Michaelmas 1261 when Robert de Hilton had a plea against the abbot of Alnwick, that he hold to him the covenant made between Patrick, sometime abbot of Alnwick, the said abbot's predecessor, and William Tysun, great grandfather of the said Robert, whose heir he is, concerning the advowson of the priory of the nuns of Guyzance.

Adam Ribalt who held Howick as one knight's fee in 1166 left descendants who retained possession of Howick until late in the 13th century. Adam Rybaud *tertius* held Howick in 1242 (*Percy Chartulary* MCII), but before 1279 had given it to his son William, who in that year is called 'lord of Howick' (*SS.* 88, p.315). On 12 January 1282/3 William Rybaud gave to John de Vesci the homage of Robert Mautalent for lands in Howick. His father Adam witnesses the grant, and on the same day confirmed his son's grant. Mautalent's lands in Howick seem to have been half the manor. The other half belonged to German Rybaud whose daughter and heiress, Margery, carried it by marriage to the family of Harang. At the assizes in 1279 John Harang claimed from Robert Harang 4 messuages, 60 acres of land, one acre of meadow and one twelfth part of the mill in Howick of which German Rybaud, grandfather of the said John had been seised (*Ib.*, p.284).

The Rybauds also owned a quarter of the manor of Embleton and certain lands in Broxfield. In 1279 Adam Rybaud and Isabella his wife conveyed the quarter of Embleton to Robert Swethop of Embleton in exchange for 40s. a year and one quarter of corn to Adam and Isabella for their lives. On 7 March 1332/3 Henry de Percy of Alnwick gave to the abbot and convent of Alnwick licence to acquire from sir Alexander Hilton all that land which Adam son of Hugh Rybaude had held in Broxfield (Tate, *History of Alnwick*, II, app. xviii).

Richard de Roc, the holder of Rock in 1166 was the founder of a family that held the manor of Rock throughout most of the 13th century. The owner in 1242 was William de Rok, and his successor was probably Thomas de Rok who was distrained for knighthood in 1278. For the Subsidy of 1296 Michael de Rock was one of the twelve jurors for the barony of Embleton. Two years later a Thomas de Rock held a quarter of Embleton for a quarter of a knight's fee. After this the family seems to have died out. In the middle of the 14th century the manor of Rock was the property of Robert de Tuggal.

The family of Batail besides holding the manors of Preston and Brunton had lands in many other parts of the county. Some details regarding the pedigree of the family were given in a law suit *curia regis* at Michaelmas '1207'. Richard de Umframvill complained that Eustace de Vesci 'deforces him of the wardship of the heir of Henry Bataill, who ought to be in his wardship by reason of the feoffment which Robert *cum barba*, Richard's great-grandfather, made to Gilbert Bataill, the heir's ancestor. Because the said Robert, when Gilbert came with him to the conquest of England, enfeoffed him of Fawdon and of the moiety of Netherton to hold of him and his heirs by service of a knight; so that Gilbert held that land all his life and after him Walter Bataill his son, and after him Henry Bataill, father of the said heir' (*Nd Pleas*). Fawdon and Netherton were two of the vills in the barony of Alnwick sub-enfeoffed by the Vescis to the Umframvills. The Batails seem to have died out in the 14th century.

A pedigree of the Batails 'to some extent conjectural' is given in *NCH.* XV, p.441. The name has been perpetuated in the farm of Battleshield Haugh, par. Linbridge. The derivation of the surname from the battle of Hastings is quite impossible.

Simon son of Ernald de Lucre who in 1166 held Lucker and South Charlton as one knight's fee left descendants who retained possession of Lucker for nearly 200 years. Three generations bore the Christian name of Simon. 'Symon de Lucre the third' gave two tofts and three bovates of his demesnes in Lucker to the church and canons of St Oswald de Nostel. He was also a benefactor to the canons of Alnwick abbey giving them also three bovates in Lucker. It was this Simon de Lucre who in 1242 held Lucker with Hoppen its member, South Charlton and Falloden as one knight's fee of the barony of Alnwick. In 1258 sir Simon III augmented his gift to Alnwick abbey with pasturage rights for eight cows, given for the health of his soul, that of his wife Juliane and those of all his ancestors. His wife was a daughter of Thomas de Warentham. Sir Simon was succeeded by his brother Robert, referred to as lord of Lucker in 1296 and 1325.

In 1336 John de Loccre was living at Lucker. On 25 July 1339 John de Loker, aged 30, deposed at the proof of age of Thomas de Bradford, baron of Bradford; he stated that Thomas had been baptised on 14 July 1316 and remembered the date because it was then that his own father, Robert de Loker, had been erecting a new hall in his manor of Lucker (*AA3.* III, p.304). He died on 20 April 1352 seised of the manor of Lucker and lands in South Charlton and Warenford, his heir being his son John then of full age. The second John was succeeded by his brother David, and he by his son also called David. The son David died under age on 21 August 1379, when his heir was his uncle Henry aged 40 years and more. Henry was concerned in the killing of John de Coupland, a warden of the marches, in 1362. He was declared an outlaw at Newcastle in January 1365 and fled to Scotland. His lands escheated to the lord of Alnwick.

In his *carta* of 1166 William de Vesci reported that he had enfeoffed William de Tubervill of a knight's fee in his barony. The grant of the fee must have been after 1157 when William de Vesci had succeeded to the barony. The fee was the manor of Horton, par. Chatton, known in the 13th and 14th centuries as Horton Turbervill. The Turbervills retained possession of Horton until the middle of the 14th century. The first three or four generations of the family were all called William. It was perhaps the second William who on the Feast of St Michael (29 September) 1210 witnesses a convention made between Eustace de Vesci and William son of Roger; the convention was signed at Gillingham in Dorset, where William de Turberville was no doubt in attendance on his lord (*Percy Chartulary*, p.348). At Easter term 1278 Aline widow of William de Turbervill had a plea against Alice de Middleton for dower in the mill of Horton. In 1289 John de Cambo held Horton for half a knight's fee and 6s. 8d. rent. He may have held Horton in right of his wife whilst the heir was under age. In 1317 Robert Turberville died seised of two parts of the manor of Horton except 129 acres of arable and 7 acres of meadow. After this there follows in the inquisition the statement that he held by knight's service from Edmund Turberville and that Robert's heir is John Turberville aged 8 years. Edmund must have sublet the manor to a relative and there must have been a widow of a previous owner holding her dower thirds. The relationship between Edmund, Robert and John cannot even be guessed at. John Turberville was still owner of Horton in 1352, although for the feudal aid of 1346 David Grey and Joan his wife were assessed for half a knight's fee in Horton Turberville, and John Turberville was similarly assessed at Horton. Although the feudal aid was imposed in 1346 it was several years before it was collected and we can presume that Joan wife of David Grey and Joan Turberville were one and the same person, the heiress of the Turbervilles. The ownership of Horton certainly passed at this time to the Greys, and Turberville as a surname disappears from Northumberland.

Radulf son of Roger who held Rugley in Alnwick in 1166 belonged to a family that never adopted a surname. Although the family was not of baronial status, members of it intermarried with local baronial families. Radulf son of Roger had three brothers Hugh, Richard and William. Hugh seems to have married twice. In 1166 he held the barony of Callerton, perhaps as husband of a Delaval widow. His sons Roger and John are called nephews of Bernard de Baliol, lord of Bywell, so their mother must have been Bernard's sister. A certain Wielard held under the Baliols the manor of Hickleton, Yorks. Wielard had three sons, Ranulf, lord of Stamfordham, Wielard, lord of Throphill and a certain Roger. It is probable that this Roger was father of Radulf son of Roger, lord of Rugley and his three brothers.

Radulf died before 1196. About 1209/10 in the *curia regis* the assize came to recognise if Radulf son of Roger, uncle of John son of Hugh, was seised in his demesne as of fee of the town of Rugley on the day of his death. Eustace de Vescy, of whom the land was held, stated by his attorney that Radulf had two brothers Richard and William who each held Rugley in turn, and that William received an exchange from Eustace which he still holds. The decision of the court was apparently in favour of Eustace de Vescy. It is not known what

land William received in exchange for Rugley. In 1242 Reyner Teutonicus held Rugley as one quarter of a knight's fee.

BARONIES OF BYWELL, PRUDHOE, BRADFORD, WARK, LANGLEY AND GRAYSTOKE— KNIGHTS OF 1166

THE holders of these six baronies failed to make the requisite returns in 1166 or if they did make them they have not survived. Some of these baronies undoubtedly had tenants by knight's service in 1166 and earlier for the sheriff's returns of 1242 lists tenants of old feoffments by military service. It will be more convenient to deal with the families of these tenants with the 1242 returns.

LORDSHIPS OF TYNDALE AND REDESDALE— KNIGHTS OF 1166

IN the middle of the 13th century both these lordships had military tenants. No return was made for Tyndale in 1242. Gilbert de Humframvill had six tenants holding by knight's service in Redesdale but it is not recorded whether they held by old or new feoffment. The families of these tenants will be reserved for detailed account under the 1242 returns.

SERJEANTIES, THEGNAGES, DRENGAGES, CROWN LANDS AND CHURCH LANDS— KNIGHTS OF 1166

AT least one of the serjeanties had military tenants of old feoffment in 1242, but naturally there would not have been any in the holdings of thegns and drengs. There is no evidence of knight's service in the Crown or Church lands.

INDEX

For simplification the territorial *de* and the descriptive *le* are all omitted, and in order to avoid making the index unnecessarily long, only the *first* Christian name of each person is used; the title sir is also omitted. Place names in Northumberland are defined by the original parish in which they were situated: (from Wards, Divisions, Parishes and Townships of Northumberland according to the Ancient and Modern Divisions: By William Dickson of Alnwick, 1833).

Bayfeld, Juliana, 223-225; Michael, 223-225
Beadnell, par. Bamburgh, 198, 259
Beadnell, Catherine, 130; George, 92, 166, 167; John, 51; Margaret, 165-167; Rowland, 130
Beal, Islandshire, 76
Beamish, co. Dur., 189
Beanley, par. Eglingham, 186; serjeanty, 8, 10
Bearl, par. Bywell St Andrew's, 222-224, 226, 239
Beaufront, par. St John Lee, 108
Beaumont, Cassandra, 210; Francis, 210; John, 258, 259
Bebside, chap. Horton, 162, 165, 166, 168, 169, 239
Becham, Lincs., 222
Bedford, duke of, 10
Bedlington, Bedlingtonshire, 166, 168, 169; mill, 53, 139; steward of, 166
Bek, Anthony, bishop of Durham, 1
Bekard, John, 31
Belesme, Robert, 9
Belford, par. Belford, 209, 241
Belgrave, Francis, 91
Belise, Margaret, 214
Bell, Ann, 83, 230; Eleanor, 212, 234; Elizabeth, 66, 68, 83, 128; James, 166, 167; Jane, 166, 167; John, 66, 68, 91, 137; Margaret, 84; Richard, 218; Robert, 69, 199, 201, 212; Samuel, 121; Sarah, 199, 201; Susan, 238; Thomas, 128
Bellasis, par. Stannington, 271
Bellingham, chap. Bellingham, 48; church, 134; Doddheaps in, 134; Redeswood Scroggs in, 134
Bellingham, family, 91; Henry, 229; John, 273; Margaret, 147, 154; Margery, 154; Nicholas, 154; Robert, 145
Bells Kirk, wardens meeting at, 54
Belsay, par. Bolam, 143, 239; manor, 49
Belsay (Bellesso), Maria, 143; Robert, 239; Thomas, 143
Belvoir, castle, 243
Bendish, Ann, 210; Robert, 210
Benington, Herts., 33; barony, 1, 33
Bennet, of Nc., 91; Agnes, 200; Elizabeth, 120; Isabel(la), 120, 122; Katherine, 120; Richard, 196, 200; William, 120, 122
Benridge, par. Mitford, 168, 175, 177, 240
Bentinck, William, 261
Bentley, Margery, 238
Benwell, par. St John's, Nc., 44, 239; manor, 76, 240
Bermingham, Alice, 13; Ralph, 13
Bernaby, Margaret, 187; William, 185, 187
Berrington, 244, 245, 248; manor, 250
Bertie, Bridget, 102, 105; Elizabeth, 102, 105; Peregrine, 102, 105
Bertram, of Bothal, 89, 154; Elena, 145, 154; Edward, 31; Isabel, 76; John, 49, 76, 145-147, 154; Richard, 141; Robert, 145, 154; Roger, 95, 240; William, 71, 240
Bervie, Scot., 33
Berwick-on-the-Hill, par. Ponteland, 174, 240
Berwick-on-Tweed, 10, 53, 98, 124, 150, 159, 218, 248, 255; chamberlain of, 25, 78; chancellor of, 25; constable of, 52, 99; garrison, 129; governor of, 12, 99, 102, 126, 203; keeper of castle, 44; marshal, 99, 129, 149; mayor, 52; provost marshal, 99, 114, 115; recorder, 199, 203; treasurer, 52, 53; vicar, 203, 204
Betagh Keppocke, Ireland, 217
Bevans, Mary, 204
Beverley, Yorks., 12, 14, 19, 76; prebendary of, 14, 16
Beverley, Philip, 239; Robert, 239; Sibil, 239
Bewclay, par. St John Lee, 48
Bewick(e), Barbara, 260, 264; Christopher, 124, 125; Cuthbert, 260, 262, 264; Elizabeth, 124; Isabel, 124, 125; Joseph, 86; Robert, 106, 262; Thomas, 92, 106
Bexstede, Petronella, 24; Richard, 24
Bickerton (Bykertoun), Alice, 6; Hugh, 4, 6; Thomas, 4

Biddlestone, par. Alwinton, 272
Bigge, Charles, 205, 206; Katherina, 206
Bilton, par. Lesbury, 272, 273
Bilton, surname, 273; Eleanor, 273; Henry, 273; Hervic, 273; Richard, 273; William, 273
Bilton, Lincs., 185
Bingfield, par. St John Lee, 96, 111, 125
Birde, Anthony, 255
Birkbeck, Gervase, 192; Thomas, 192
Birkeley, Agnes, 263; John, 263
Birkhead(s), chap. Netherwitton, 117, 118, 128
Birtley, chap. Birtley, 58, 63, 64, 86, 124; manor, 50, 52; Shields, 86
Bishop, Susan, 179
Bishop's Waltham, rector, 181
Bishop Wearmouth, co. Dur., alms house, 193; curate, 192
Blackaburn in North Tyndale, 56
Blackadder, Scot., 150
Blackberd, Thomas, 111
Blackburn, Lancs., 192
Blackburne, Frances, 210
Black Callerton, par. Newburn, 97, 100, 271
Black Death, 25
Blackett, Christopher, 265; Elizabeth, 265; Henry, 177; William, 83
Blackhall, par. Hexham, 64
Blackhall in Kirkheaton, 62
Blackhall in Ray, 56
Black Heddon, par. Stamfordham, 123, 132, 222
Blagdon, par. Stannington, 96, 97, 99, 123, 271, 272
Blaikden, Robert, 123, 124, 127
Blakelock, Mary, 214; Ralph, 214
Blakewell, fishery in the Tweed, 245
Blakiston, Ann, 237, 238; William, 237, 238
Blaklamb, Joan, 133; William, 133
Blanchland, chap. Blanchland, 239; abbey, 223
Bland Close, Yorks., 192
Blankney, Lincs., 101; lord of, 9
Blechynden, Alfred, 269; Elizabeth, 269
Blenkinsop, George, 92; John, 146; Thomas, 92
Block, Allen, 214 Parthenia, 214
Blount, Elizabeth, 5, 7; John, 5, 7
Bloxam, Mary, 202; William, 202
Blund, Robert, 31
Blyth, St Mary of, 222
Bockenfield, par. Felton, 31, 43, 72, 86, 240; manor, 1, 44, 71, 74; moor, 74, 118, 126
Bogles Gaire, in Chirdon, 56, 57
Bolam, par. Bolam, 26, 239; barons, 1; barony, 23, 90, 195, 239; church, 23; manor, 23, 25, 26; vicar, 23
Bolam (Bolum), Gilbert, 239
Bolam Vicarage, par. Bolam, 239
Bold, Frances, 208; Richard, 208
Bolebec, fee in Bucks., 240
Bolebec, Hugh, 222, 223, 236; Walter, 222, 223, 239, 240
Boleyn, Ann, 12
Bolingbroke, Lincs., 4
Bolton, par. Edlingham, 132, 195, 196, 255
Bon-Jedburgh, co. Rox.; town, 10; laird, 173
Bonus Hill, in Whalton, 205
Boolun, Gilbert, 239
Booth (Bothe), John, 209; Margaret, 208, 209; Robert, 209; Roger, 78, 208, 209; Thomas, 209
Borough, Thomas, 5, 7, 148
Bosworth Field, battle, 12, 22
Boteler, Elizabeth, 79; lord, 78, 79
Botetourt, Johanna, 143; Ralph, 143
Bothal, par. Bothal, 271; advowson, 152; baron of 145, 154; barony, 90, 146, 271; castle, 146, 152; church, 125, 128, 141, 149, 151, 152, 159, 195; Earsdon Hill in, 159; manor, 152, 195; mill, 150; rector, 177, 195
Bothwell, earl of, 109
Boulmer, par. Longhoughton, 272
Bourchier, Eleanor, 247; John, 247
Bourne, Dorothy, 135; John, 135; Joseph, 135; Widdrington, 145

Boutflower, Dorothy, 176, 179; Joan, 179; Nathaniel, 176, 177, 179; Thomas, 179
Bouverie, Arabella, 181; Edward, 181
Bowden, J., 218
Bowes, Agnes, 60; George, 55; Henry, 54, 55, 60; Margaret, 229; Robert, 50, 51, 124, 151; William, 229
Bowey, Margaret, 136; Thomas, 136
Bowman, Isabel, 219; Mark, 219
Bowsdon, par. Lowick, 203, 241
Boyd, John, 40; Nora, 40; Thomas, 145
Boyes, Elizabeth, 215; William, 215
Boyne, battle, 106
Boynton, Christopher, 97, 98, 104; Elizabeth, 75, 97, 98, 104; Matthew, 75
Boythorpe, Alice, 11; Hugh, 8, 11
Brabant, dukedom, 9; duke of, 9, 22
Bracebridge, Harriet, 180; Walter, 180
Brad, fishery in the Tweed, 245
Brader, Daniel, 166
Bradford, par. Bolam, 25, 173, 186, 190, 239
Bradford, of Bradford, 91; Euphemia, 246; Jasper, 185, 187; Margaret, 185, 187; Ralph, 246; Thomas, 91, 159, 274
Bradish, Hannah, 230; Thomas, 230
Bradley Hall, co. Dur., 49
Brailes, Warw., manor, 5
Braithwaite, Mariana, 176; Mary, 176, 179; Richard, 176, 179
Bramham Moor, Yorks., battle, 10
Brampton, John, 145
Brandling, of Nc., 91; Anne, 115, 116; Charles, 115, 116, 121; Eleanor, 201; John, 120; Ralph, 201; Robert, 91, 98, 120, 169, 171, 227; Thomas, 116
Branton, par. Eglingham, 78; minister of, 121, 122
Branxton, par. Branxton, 241, 245, 249; tower, 248
Branxton, Margery, 74; William, 74
Bray, Ireland, 217
Bray, Alice, 216; Thomas, 216
Brechin, bishop of, 180
Brecknock, Elizabeth, 76, 77; Thomas, 76, 77
Brenan, Gerald, 8
Brende, John, 53
Brenkley, par. Ponteland, 174, 240
Bridlington, Yorks., abbey, 273
de Briedenbach, baron, 181
Brinkburn, chap. Brinkburn, 234, 240; canon of, 226; church of, 233; prior of, 95, 148; prior and convent, 95, 224, 226, 232; priory, 240, 241
Briwere, Joan, 13; William, 13
Brody, Anne, 235; Robert, 235
Broomepark, par. Edlingham, 132
Broomhaugh, par. Bywell St Andrew, 239
Broomhope, chap. Birtley, 56, 112, 133, 224, 226
Broomhouse, 199
Broomley, par. Bywell St Peter, 97
Broomridge, par. Ford, 241
Brotherwick, par. Warkworth, 217
Broughton, John, 203-205; Mary, 203, 204
Brown(e), Anne, 211, 255; Bridget, 210; Dorothy, 169, 192, 194; Edward, 121-123; Frances, 121, 122; Hannah, 201; Jane, 69, 70; John, 68, 169, 192, 194; Leonard, 211; Margaret, 137, 138, 234, 235; Martha, 215; Richard, 210; Sarah, 123; Thomas, 137, 138, 192; William, 215, 234, 235; general, 205; rear admiral, 201
Broxfield, par. Embleton, 272, 274
Bruce (Brus), Adam, 10, 13; David, 144, 145; Henrietta, 211; Isabel(la), 10, 13
Bruges, church of the Capuchin monks, 109
Brun, Randulf, 94
Brunton, par. Embleton, 272, 274
Brunton, par. Gosforth, 222, 223, 239
Brussels, prioress of British convent, 17
Bryan, barony, 10
Bryan, Ann, 210; William, 210

Dissington, par. Newbourn, 49, 97, 145

Ditchburn, par. Eglingham, 100, 101; serjeanty of, 272

Dixon (Dickson), Anne, 218; Isabel, 149; John, 52; Thomas, 121, 218

Dobson, Jane, 137, 138; John, 92, 137, 138; Thomas, 86

Dodd, Barrodall, 40; Cuthbert, 54; Edward, 87; Eleanor, 40

Doddington, par. Doddington, 272; curate of, 199, 201

Dodhill in Chirdon, 56

Dodsworth, Anthony, 131; Eleanor, 131; Roger, 141

Dolfinston, Scot., 51, 62

Domesday Survey, 1, 4, 8, 22, 23, 33, 243

Donkin, Joshua, 198

Dotchin, family, 241

Douglas, John, 145; Joshua, 175; Isabel, 84; earl, 145

Doughty, Alice, 211; Anthony, 210; Jane; 210; Robert, 211

Downe, viscount, 74

Downham, par. Carham, 195-197

Down(e)s, John, 80; J. M., 216; Mary, 216

Doxford, par. Ellingham, 241

Draper, Henry, 92

Drogo, s. of Ponz, 2

Drogheda, Ireland, 217

Druridge, chap. Widdrington, 93-100

Druridge, Alan, 94

Dublin, Ireland, 14; county, 213; lord mayor, 18

Dudgale, William, 18, 22

Duddo(e), par. Stannington, 45, 78, 118, 271

Dugdale, William, 18, 22

Dukesfield in Slaley, 124, 131

Dunbar, Anne, 254

Dunbar and March, earl of, 10

Dundonald, earl of, 88

Dunley in Chipchase, 56

Dunstan, par. Embleton, 257, 259

Dunstan, family, 257; Reyner, 257

Dunstanburgh, castle, 259, 260; constable of, 14, 259

Durham, archdeacon, 37; bishop of, 41, 43, 51, 72, 76, 100, 135, 147, 168, 186, 244, 245, 250; castle, 116; church of St Margaret's, 65; monks of St Cuthbert, 41; prebendary, 180; prior of, 41, 44, 114, 223, 224, 244, 246, 250; prior and convent, 2, 41, 245; vice admiral of Palatinate, 26

Durtrees in Elsdon, 85

Dymoke, Anne, 7; Edward, 7

Dyveleston, Aluric, 271; Lucy, 41-43; Simon, 41, 143; Thomas, 41-43, 142; William, 240, 271

Eachwick, par. Heddon-on-the-Wall, 239

Eachwick, William, 95

Earl, Elizabeth, 164; John, 164

Earle, par. Doddington, 272

Earls Barton, Northants, 272

Earsdon, par. Earsdon, 31, 151, 156

Earsdon, chap. Hebron, 193, 271; Forest, 151, 156, 159; Hills, 160, 161

Earsdon, Humphrey, 218; William, 218

Easington, par. Belford, 209, 241

Easington Grange, par. Belford, 241

East Bowdon, co. Dur., 261

East Brunton, par. Gosforth, 23

East Chevington, chap. Chevington, 96, 97, 99, 272, 273

East Hartford, chap. Horton, 239

East Hartington, par. Hartburn, 148

Easter Kilbride, Scot., 33, 34

East Heddon, par. Heddon-on-the-Wall, 239, 240

East Lilburn, par. Eglingham, 189

East Marches, 51; lieutenant of, 45; muster of, 196; survey of, 50; warden of, 129, 147, 171

East Matfen, par. Stamfordham, 222-224, 226, 239

East Newton, par. Bywell St Peter, 222, 224, 226

East Shaftoe, par. Hartburn, 239

East Sleekburn, Bedlingtonshire, 168, 169

East (Little) Swinburne, par. Chollerton, 96, 99, 111

East Thirston, par. Felton, 86

East Woodburn, par. Corsenside, 223

Eddie, Blanch, 202; George, 202

Eden, Isabel, 114; 115; Katherine, 207, 209; Robert, 114, 115, 207, 208

Edgehill, Arthur, 216; Mildred, 216

Edinburgh, 50

Edington, par. Mitford, 240

Edlingham, par. Edlingham, 143, 260; manor, 190; vicar, 238

Edmonston, Scot., laird of, 50

Edward I of England, 9, 10, 23, 98

Edward III of England, 10, 96, 145, 244

Edward IV of England, 147, 248

Edward VI of England, 93

Edwards, Edward, 208; Elizabeth, 208; Grace, 214; Thomas, 214

Egardus, a serf, 258

Eglingham par. Eglingham, 196-199; manor, 193; mill, 196, 197; rectory, 185, 186; tithes, 186, 189, 190

Egremont, Cumb., 205

Egremont, baron, 14, 16

Eland, Robert, 145

Eldred, John, 63

Elgin and Aylesbury, earl of, 211

Elizabeth dr of William, 1, 4, 6

Elizabeth I of England, 12, 52, 90, 93

Elkington, Charles, 216; Lucie, 216

Ellerker, Ann, 228, 229; Frances, 21; James, 21; Margery, 16, 98, 104; Ralph, 50, 124, 152, 185, 228, 229; William, 16, 98, 104, 226, 228

Ellingham, par. Ellingham, 147, 241; barons of, 2; barony of, 1, 36, 89, 90, 241; church of St Maurice, 41; manor, 2

Ellington, par. Woodhorn, 94, 95, 97, 98, 100, 168, 169, 259

Ellington, Edmund, 95; Hugh, 1, 36, 37, 241; Jo(h)anna, 1, 36, 37

Elliott, family, 54; Robert, 87

Ellis, Mary, 214

Ellison, of Nc., 91; Cuthbert, 91; John, 86; Robert, 92

Elmeden, Elizabeth, 36, 38; William, 36, 38

Elsdon, par. Elsdon, 4

Elsdon, Ann, 206; Edmund, 206

Elswick, par. St John's, Nc., 239

Elwick, par. Belford, 241

Elyhaugh, par. Felton, 227, 232

Emblehope in North Tyndale, 111

Embleton, par. Embleton, 129, 257, 259, 274; bailiff of, 14, 16, 246, 247, 259; baron of, 241; barony of, 90, 257, 258, 272, 274

Embleton, Anne, 234, 235; Robert, 234, 235

Embree, Joseph, 58

Emerson, Thomas, 231

Emothill, manor, 78

Emsworth, Hants, 69

England, chancellor, 72; constable, 10, 15; lord high chamberlain, 12; marshal, 10; vice admiral, 93

England, Anne, 20; Roger, 20

Epplerwoodhope in Wark, 54

Eppleton, Co. Dur., 78

Ernald s. of Adelin, 222

Ernisius, 223

Ernulf, 257

Errington, of Beaufront, 57; Anthony, 50, 57, 92, 205, 207, 209; Catherine, 126; Dorothy, 100, 105, 110-112, 209; Edward, 126; Frances, 57, 60; George, 57; Gilbert, 118, 119, 126; Henry, 100; Isabel(la), 57, 72, 73, 118, 119; John, 92, 100, 105, 110, 112, 129, 175; Katherine, 62, 63; Lucy, 120, 122; Luke, 116; Margaret, 109, 110, 205, 207; Mark, 92, 109, 171; Nicholas, 52, 57, 60, 92, 109, 110, 118; Ralph, 57, 62, 63, 111, 125; Richard, 126; Roger, 120; Thomas, 111, 124; Ursula, 62; William, 157; Mr of Beaufront, 117

Eshells in Hexhamshire, 196

Eshot, par. Felton, 31, 240; manor, 1, 31, 78

Eshot, Edmund, 31

Eslington, par. Whittingham, 78

Eslington, Elizabeth, 78, 79; John, 95; Robert, 78, 79

E(a)son, Anne, 18, 20

Espec, Adeline, 1; Walter, 1

Espley, par. Mitford, 240

Espleywood, 43

Essex, earl of, 17, 33, 100, 161; countess of, 34; House, 18

Essingdon, Ralph, 95

Eston Gosebekes, Suffolk, 23; rector, 24

Etal, par. Ford, 241, 243-245, 248; castle, 44, 246; mill, 244

Ettrick, Anne, 193, 194

Eu, counts of, 243

Eure, family, 90; of Kirkley, 91; of Witton, co. Dur., 171; Agnes, 225; Constance, 16; Francis, 174; Hugh, 143; Johanna, 148, 154; John, 225; Matilda, 148; Ralph, 48, 148, 171, 224; William, 16, 97, 98, 117, 148, 154, 174, 226; lady, 174; lord, 52, 53, 55, 91, 100, 117, 120, 152, 173, 174, 182

Eustace s. of John, 33, 41, 272, 273

Everest, Dora, 40; Richard, 40

Evers, Barbara, 237, 238; Ralph, 237, 238

Evett, James, 216; Katherine, 216

Evington, Frances, 210; Nicholas, 210

Ewart, par. Doddington, 272

Ewbancke, Mary, 113; Toby, 113

Eyncurt (Aincourt), Agnes, 9, 13; John, 9, 13

Eyre, Mary, 102, 105; Rowland, 102, 105, 106; Thomas, 102

Fairfax, Alathea, 102, 105; Cecily, 247; Charles, 102, 105; Elizabeth, 247; Ferdinando, 131; Frances, 131; Guy, 148; Thomas, 247; William, 247; of Cameron, lord, 131, 132; viscount, 102, 105

Falaise, treaty of, 33

Falconer, Alexander, 237, 238; Anne, 237, 238

Faldingworth, Lincs, 5

Fallesley, Elizabeth, 78, 79; John, 78, 79

Falloden, par. Embleton, 130, 259, 272

Fallowfield, John, 144; Richard, 144

Faneside, widow, 218

Fanning, Ann, 102, 105; John, 102, 105

Farendon, Elizabeth, 4, 6; Nicholas, 4, 6

Farinley in Bickerton, par. Rothbury, 4

Farnham see Thirnham

Farnlaw, par. Hartburn, 239

Farrdon, Alice, 63, 65

Fauconberg, Isabel, 223, 225

Faudon, Peter, 95, 224

Faule, Geoffrey, 145

Fawdon, par. Ingram, 5, 272, 274; manor, 31

Fawdon, par. St Nicholas', Nc., 93, 133

Fawns, par. Kirkwhelpington, 239

Fearnley, Benjamin, 76, 77; Elizabeth, 76, 77

Fell, Alice, 36

Felling in Broomhope, 56, 111

Felton, par. Felton, 159, 232, 240; church, 228; manor, 106, 147, 148, 224, 226-228; Moor, 86; rectory, 228; St Michael's Church, 31, 85; vicar, 224, 238

Felton, Anthony, 74, 75, 228; Jane, 74, 75; John, 10

Fenham, par. St Andrew's, Nc., 239

Fenkell, Henry, 260

Fenrother, chap. Hebron, 71, 72, 98, 151, 159, 271

Fenton, par. Wooler, 241

Fenton, Anne, 212

Fenwick, par. Stamfordham, 123, 222, 223, 239

Fenwick, of Fenwick, 89, 91; of Langshaws, 161; of Middleton, 91; Alan, 71; Alice, 180; Ann, 163, 235; Anthony, 237; Arthur, 135; Barbara, 121, 122, 186, 188, 261, 265; Blanch, 205, 206; Catherine, 111; Claudius, 92; Constance, 98, 104, 111; Cuthbert, 176, 179, 206; Dorcas, 230;

Ogle, *cont.*

264; Lydia, 211, 213, 214; Lyonel, 186, 189, 190, 191; Mabel, 166, 167, 186-188, 191; Magdalen, 178, 188, 191, 211, 219; Margaret, 25, 28, 114, 115, 144, 147, 149, 151, 153-155, 159-170, 172-175, 178, 182, 184, 185, 187, 188, 190, 191, 196, 198, 200, 201, 205-210, 214, 217, 218, 220, 226, 253; Margery, 147, 151-155, 159, 163, 167, 169, 172, 178, 180, 185-187, 190, 191, 208; Maria, 217; Marian, 197; Mark, 63, 65, 93, 171-175, 178, 182, 183, 195, 196, 200, 209, 212, 220, 254; Martha, 177, 179, 193, 194, 215; Martin, 156, 159, 166, 168-170, 192, 217; Mary, 120, 122, 159, 161-167, 170, 173-176, 178-182, 184, 188, 190, 191, 193, 194, 196-206, 210-212, 214-216, 218, 219, 230; Maryann, 161, 249, 251, 255; Matilda, 147, 154, 182, 187, 191; Matthew, 93, 159, 160, 162, 163, 165, 166, 168-170, 185, 186, 188, 190, 191, 195, 200; May, 215; Maud, 214; Melchoir, 212; Melora, 204; Merriell, 152, 187, 196, 200; Metcalf, 219; Michael, 162, 173, 174, 178, 182; Mildred, 216; Millicent, 211; Nancy, 212; Nathaniel, 177, 179-181, 220; Newton, 177, 179, 180, 220; Nicholas, 197-201, 203, 204, 210; Nina, 216; Norman, 215; Octavius, 214; Oliver, 92, 165, 173, 185, 186, 188-191, 196, 200; Oswald, 157, 218; Oswin, 149-152, 155-158, 173, 185, 207, 218; Owen, 147, 151, 154; Parthenia, 214; Patrick, 168; Pelham, 216; Percy, 202, 215, 216; Peter, 93, 195, 200, 220; Philip, 188; Phillis, 163, 165-167, 188, 191, 218; Phoebe, 212; Ponsonby, 216; Rachel, 191, 211; Ralph, 116, 148, 151, 152, 154, 155, 157, 158, 160, 162, 166, 167, 173, 176, 177, 179, 185-188, 190, 191, 198, 199, 201, 209, 217, 219, 220, 227, 229; Reginald, 196; Richard, 143, 144, 153, 161, 180, 189-191, 198, 201, 202, 208-211, 213, 214, 216, 219, 220; Robert, 5, 25, 28, 46, 49, 98, 104, 114, 115, 123, 127, 141-161, 163, 165-167, 169, 171-174, 182, 186-189, 193-202, 204, 205, 208-211, 213, 214, 217, 219, 220, 229, 243, 246, 247; Roger, 116, 142, 153, 158, 169, 172, 208, 220; Rowland (Roland), 205, 206; St John, 216; Sally, 216; Samuel, 160-163, 203-205, 215, 217; Sarah, 164, 166, 167, 179, 180, 194, 199, 201, 205-209, 214-216, 219; Savile, 180; Sberletta, 208; Sence, 181, 211; Sibil, 49, 59, 155, 171, 173, 178, 184; Sophia, 180, 181, 211; Stephen, 209, 217; Susan(nah), 171, 179-181, 208, 211; Temple, 211; Theophilus, 203, 204; Thomas, 92, 142, 143, 146-156, 158, 159, 161-163, 165-172, 174-176, 178-182, 184-187, 189-194, 196-198, 200, 201, 203-220, 228, 229; Thomasine, 186, 187, 197, 200, 212; Timothy, 220; Trajectina, 211; Tristram, 196, 197, 200; Ursula, 203, 204; Utricia, 211; Valentine, 210; Walter, 215; Wentworth, 192-194; Wilfred, 215; William, 120, 122, 143, 147-151, 153-156, 159-164, 166, 167, 169-172, 175-177, 179, 181-185, 187-189, 191, 193, 196, 199, 201, 203-210, 212, 214-218, 200; —, 238; admiral, 176, 177, 213; baron, 147; captain, 217; Dr, 231; earl, 19, 102, 141, 153, 161; land, 49, 123, 148, 150, 152, 226; lord, 14, 18, 49, 59, 97, 98, 104, 114, 115, 123, 127, 141, 148-160, 162, 163, 168, 171, 173, 178, 182, 185-187, 189, 193, 195, 205, 207, 209, 213, 217, 221, 227, 229; Mistress, 185; Parson, 51, 151, 171, 195; sergeant maj, gen, 213; viscount, 207, 209, 217

Ogleborough in Fowberry, 161, 195

Okehaugh, 233, 240

Old Beanley, par. Eglingham, 186, 190

Old Bewick

Old Felton, par. Felton, 218, 228, 232, 240, 252

Oldmoor. par. Bothal, 149, 152, 185, 193, 271

Oliver, Christian, 80, 82; John, 80, 82

Orby, Joan, 15; John, 15

Orde, Norhamshire, 248, 249

Ord(e), Ann, 161, 164; Catherine, 117, 188, 191; Clara, 109, 110; Eliza, 234, 235; Elizabeth, 117; George, 117, 126, 188, 191, 249; Henry, 2, 249; John, 234, 235, 248, 249; Margaret, 249;

Orde, *cont.*

Mary, 161, 164, 235; Robert, 112; Thomas, 117; William, 109, 110, 161, 164, 234, 263; coat of arms, 249

Orkney, earl of, 261, 262

Osberwick, now Newstead, par. Bamburgh, 241

Ostilly, Durand, 33, 35; Gunnora, 33, 35

Otterburn, battle of, 10

Outchester, par. Bamburgh, 241, 242

Outchester (Ulcestre), Robert, 242

Overgrass, par. Felton, 240, 250

Overton, 222

Ovingham, par. Ovingham, 139; chantry of St Mary, 223; vicar, 83

Ovingham, Thomas, 223

Owen, Anne, 216; Hugh, 17; Lucy, 17; Thomas, 216

Oxford, earl of, 23, 24, 222

Oxley, Amor, 129

Oxnam, co. Rox., 9

Oxton, Lincs., manor of, 5

Pagan, s. of John, 33; William, 241

Palmer, Alice, 160, 163; Beatrice, 214; Gervase, 160; Joseph, 214; Matthew, 160

Panierheugh, Scot., battle of, 151, 157

Panmure, Scot., 33

Panton, Catherine, 61; —, 58, 61

Pape, Anne, 211

Paris, Matthew, 43

Park, Agnes, 31, 32; Gilbert, 128; Richard, 31, 32.

Park End in Simonburn, 62

Parker, Mary, 206

Parkhouses, par. Morpeth, 271

Parkinson, George, 113; Henry, 113, 115; Margery, 113, 115

Parlett, Elizabeth, 250, 251

Parr, —, 51

Parsons, Martha, 58

Parttrers, Roger, 196

Paston, par. Kirknewton, 249

Paston, Eleanor, 247; Elizabeth, 53, 59; Francis, 176, 179; Margaret, 233; Percival, 53, 59; Sarah, 176, 179; William, 247; Wolstan, 177, 233

Patten, Robert, 102

Pavenham, Bury, Beds., 14

Pawtoune, Edward, 64; Margery, 64, 65

Paxton, Berwickshire, 244, 245

Paxton, Adam, 244

Paxton, Hunts., 272

Payne, Mary, 216; Thomas 216

Paynel, William, 11

Peachell, Ann, 77; John, 77

Peacock(e), Ann(e), 38; Margaret, 38

Pearson (Pereson), Barbara, 207, 209; Bridget, 266; Janet, 111; Jenkyn, 111; Roger, 198; Thomas, 207, 209

Peeris, William, 8

Pegswood, par. Bothal, 151, 271

Pellew, George, 214; Henrietta, 214

Pembroke, countess of, 14; earl of, 16

Peninsular War, 199

Pennington, Joan, 148; Johanna, 154; John, 148, 154

Penson, Jane, 214

Pepper, Catherine, 131; Cuthbert, 131

Perci-en-Auge, Normandy, 8

Percy (Perci), barons of Alnwick, 10; family, 8 90; of Alnwick, 91; of Beverley, 12, 16, 18, 21; of Bolton Percy, 22; of Dunslay, 8, 11, 22; of Pavenham, 22; of Scotton, 22; Adelidis, 9; Adeliza, 11; Agnes, 9, 11, 13; Alan, 8, 9, 11-17, 19; Alexander, 9, 13, 18; Algernon, 12, 17, 20; Alice (Alicia), 8, 11, 13, 20; Anastasia, 13; Ann(e), 12, 14, 16-18, 20; Anthony, 18; Avice, 11; Catherine (Katherine), 12, 14, 16, 17; Charles, 14, 17, 19-21; Constance, 16, 98; Dorothy, 17; Edward, 19, 21; Eleanor (Alianora), 12-18, 20, 21, 148, 149, 154; Elizabeth, 14-22; Ellen, 21; Emma, 8, 11, 20; Ernald, 22;

Percy, *cont.*

Frances 21; Francis, 18, 20-22; Gaufrid, 9, 11; Geoffrey, 8, 9, 13; George, 12, 14, 16, 17, 98, 148, 154; Gosfrid, 9, 11; Grace, 16; Guischard, 17, 18; Henrietta, 19; Henry, 1, 9-22, 91, 98, 104, 128, 145, 148, 274; Hugh, 9; Idonea, 15; Ingelram, 12-14, 17, 18; Isabel(la), 10, 13-15, 17, 18; James, 14, 18, 20; Jane, 14, 16, 17, 20; Jasper, 21; Joan (Johanna), 13, 15-17; Jocelyn, 12-14, 16-21; John, 9, 14, 16, 18, 20, 21; Laurence, 20; Lionel, 12; Lucy, 17; Lydia, 14, 20; Mainfred, 8; Margaret, 10, 14-17, 20-22, 123; Margery, 16, 98, 104; Maria, 17; Martha, 19-21; Mary, 15-17, 20, 21; Maud, 9, 11, 15-17; Peter, 22; Philippa, 14, 15; Picot, 22; Ralph, 10, 12-16, 148; Richard, 8-11, 13-18, 20, 22; Robert, 9, 11, 15, 18, 20-22; Roger, 10, 15, 18, 20; Sarah, 20; Serlo, 8, 11; Simon, 22; Thomas, 10, 12, 14-22, 50, 55, 108, 149, 195, 217; Tryce, 20; Walter, 8, 9, 11, 13; William, 8-20, 22, 27, 150, 210, 258; baron, 12, 13, 17, 19, 22; of Cockermouth, baron, 14

Percy de Poynings, baron, 11, 16

Perfect, A., 214; Edith, 214

Perkins, Elizabeth, 20; Dr, 20

Perrot, Dorothy, 17; Thomas, 17

Peterborough, bishop of, 177, 179, 181

Petworth, Sussex, 12, 19; honour of, 8, 9; lord of, 13

Petyt, Mr, 69

Philip s. of Hamund, 41

Philippa, queen of England, 144, 145

Philipott, Joan, 145; John, 145

Philips, Ann, 105, 106; Charity, 207, 209; George, 105; Helen, 216; Joseph, 216; Louisa, 216; Thomas, 207, 209; W.H., 216

Piborne, Mary, 20; Richard, 20

Pickering, John, 148

Picts Wall, 56

Pigdon, par. Mitford, 43, 49, 53, 54, 56, 240; manor of, 44, 48

Pilgrimage of Grace, 12, 14, 50, 195

Pilkington, Elizabeth, 212

Pilsbury, Jonathan, 199, 201; Sarah, 199, 201

Pinchbeck, Lincs., 209

Piperden, battle of, 147

Plankey, 110

Plantagenet, Henry, 15; Mary, 10, 15

Plantagenet-Harrison, gen., 137, 139

Plessey, par. Stannington, 97, 99, 112, 114, 116, 271; manor, 96

Plessis, Adam, 272; John, 272; Richard, 272

Plumbe, Francis, 211; Jane, 211

Plumpton Park in Inglewood, 23

Plumpton, Robert, 148

Plymouth, earl of, 131

Poher, Robert, 241

Pontefract, Yorks., castle, 226

Ponteland, par. Ponteland, 240; church, 145

Pontoise, abbess of, 102, 105

Popple nr Haddington, Scot., 213

Port, Emma, 8, 11; Hugh, 8

Portgate, par. St John Lee, 48, 110, 126

Portland, duke of, 156; earl of, 261

Potton, Beds., 272

Pott(s), Agnes, 124, 125; Edward, 126; Eleanor, 126-128; Elizabeth, 128; George, 118, 126, 127; Mark, 124, 125; Mary, 126-128; Michael, 126; Robert, 128; Thomas, 128; William, 126-128

Poulter, Edmund, 181; Elizabeth, 181

Powys, lord, 17, 147

Poynings, baron, 10, 16; barony, 10; manor, 19

Poynings, Eleanor, 10; Richard, 10

Poyntz, family, 2

Pratt, Mary, 212; Michael, 118; Robert, 212

Prefene, Elizabeth, 243; Henry, 243; Hugh, 243

Prendwick, par. Alnham, 272

Presfen, Mary, 2; Michael, 2; William, 2

Preston, par. Ellingham, 33, 272, 274

Preston, Margaret, 208; Thomas, 108, 208

Preston, battle, 102; viscount, 102, 105

Prestwick, par. Ponteland, 168, 240

Scarisbrick, Elizabeth, 208
Schauceby, William, 240, 241
Scotherskelf, John, 69
Scotland, Edward Baliol, king of, 10; chamberlain of, 33, 34
Scot(t), Alexander, 63; Anne, 180, 206; Dorothy, 235; Henry, 180; Isabel, 180; J., 206; John, 63; Margery, 63; Matthew, 22; Richard, 76; Walter, 45, 239; William, 239, 244
Scouland, Ellen, 133; Richard, 133
Scourfield, Ralph, 199, 201; Sarah, 199, 201
Scrampston, Yorks., 222
Scremerston, Islandshire, 99
Screnwood, par. Alnham, 272; manor of, 106
Scrope of Bolton, lord, 16
Scrope, Geoffrey, 133
Scryvane, William, 49, 146
Scurfield, Andrew, 69; Frances, 69, 70
Scurr, Jonathon, 64, 65; Mary Ann, 64, 65
Seagram, J. H., 216; Sally, 216
Seamer, Elizabeth, 20
Seaton Delaval, par. Earsdon, 97, 271; chapel of, 162
Sedman, Alice, 212; John, 212
Selby, Yoks., abbey, 273
Selby, Alexander, 92, 117-119, 135; Annabel, 143; Charles, 135, 205; Christopher, 159; Eleanor, 159; Elizabeth, 57, 60, 101, 105, 251; Helen, 118, 135; Jane, 118; Joan, 117-119, 135; John, 25, 196, 248; Katherine, 25; Mary, 135; Oliver, 218; Robert, 117, 135; Roger, 57, 60; Thomas, 135; Walter, 25, 143; William, 72, 101, 105, 135
Selby's Forest, par. Kirknewton, 241
Semar, Yorks., 8
Sept Meules, Normandy, 243
Sergeant, Elizabeth, 210 —, 210
Sewingshields, par. Simonburn, 43, 55, 58, 146; castle, 50, 54, 56; manor, 54, 56
Seymour, Algernon, 19; Charles, 19; Elizabeth, 19; Henry, 17; Jane, 17
Shafto, of Bavington, 91; Ann, 130, 186, 191; Catherine, 131; Charles, 126; Cuthbert, 59, 63, 65; Dorothy, 123, 127; Edward, 53, 59, 64, 116, 186, 191; Elizabeth, 64, 65; Esther, 65; George, 219; Grace, 124; Isabel, 26, 29, 64; James, 124; John, 58, 91; Mally, 59, 63, 65; Margaret, 65, 67; Margery, 53, 59; Mark, 85; Mary, 80, 81; Percival, 52, 53; Phillis, 64, 65; Reynold, 123, 124, 127; Robert, 131, 168; Thomas, 80; Ursula, 126; William, 58, 64, 65, 92, 96, 111, 124, 166, 226
Sharpe, John, 262, 265; Olive, 262, 265
Sharperton, par. Alwinton, 272
Sharples, Eleanor, 215
Sharpley in Simonburn, 56, 57, 78
Shaw, Bernard, 162, 164; Margaret, 162, 164
Shawbush in Bellingham, 86
Sheepwash, par. Bothal, 271; advowson of, 153
Shell, Henry, 250
Sheridan, Hester, 180; Richard, 180
Sherwell, Thomas, 92; William, 91
Shevell, David, 160, 161, 163; Ralph, 137
Shield, Dorothy, 254; John, 254
Shieldhall, par. Slaley, 63, 64, 87
Shilbottle, par. Shilbottle, 272, 273
Shilmore, par. Alwinton, 109
Shilvington, par. Morpeth, 98, 143-146, 148, 150-152, 157, 186, 205, 271
Shipley, par. Eglingham, 196
Shipley, Elizabeth, 269
Shireburne, Mary, 102, 105; Nicholas, 85, 102, 105
Shitlington, 55; manor of, 54, 56-58
Shoreston, par. Bamburgh, 124
Shoreswood, Norhamshire, 261
Short, Alice, 145; Robert, 145
Shortflatt, par. Bolam, 25, 26, 175, 239; manor of, 23, 26; tower, of, 25
Shortmoor in Chipchase, 57, 58
Shothaugh, par. Felton, 227
Shotley High Quarter, chap. Blanchland, 239

Shotley Low Quarter, chap. Shotley, 239
Shotton, par. Stannington, 96, 97, 99, 114, 116, 120, 271, 272
Shrewsbury, 10, battle of, 10; countess of, 152, 219; earl of, 14, 153, 155, 171
Sidney, Dorothy, 17; Robert, 17
Silksworth, co. Dur., 41
Simon s. of Ernulf, 241; s. of John, 240; s. of Ponz, 2; s. of William, 143
Simonburn, par. Simonburn, 52, 55, 87; bailiff of, 87; castle, 56, 57, 62; church, 57; manor of, 43, 52, 54, 56; parson, 87; Rector, 128
Simpson, George, 180; Maria, 180; Robert, 191
Skelton, Yorks., 38; baron of, 10, 13
Skipwith, Margaret, 5; William, 5
Skynner, Audrey, 210; Vincent, 210
Slackhouses, 168, 186
Slaley, par. Slaley, 64, 85, 87, 240
Slaley (Slaveleia), John, 240; Wibert, 239, 240
Slaterfield in Simonburn, 52, 56, 87
Sligo Co., Ireland, 213
Slingsby, Francis, 17; Mary, 17
Slynger, Henry, 260
Smalesmouth, par. Greystead, 80, 83
Smallburn in Longhorsley, 252
Smart, Peter, 171, 172; Susan, 172
Smathwaite, Mary, 115, 116; Samuel, 115, 116
Smelt, Elizabeth, 166, 167; Thomas, 166, 167
Smith, Albert, 215; Alethea, 211; Ann, 88; Barbara, 86; Catherine (Katherine), 61, 65, 208; David, 228; Dorothy, 121, 122; Elizabeth, 215; John, 116; Francis, 65; Isabel, 81, 157, 158; Mary, 212; Ralph, 116; Robert, 88; Roger, 211; Thomas, 121, 122; William, 81, 86
Smithson, Elizabeth, 19; Hugh, 9, 19
Snabdough in Chirdon, 54, 56-58
Snape in Hexhamshire, 83
Sneyd, Catherine, 180; Edward, 180
Snitter, par. Rothbury, 107
Snookbank in Framlington, 219
Snowden, Dorothy, 192, 194
Solley, Catherine, 179; Joseph, 179
Somerset, Anne, 12, 17; Arthur, 180; Edith, 180; Henry, 12, 17; duchess of, 219; duke of, 18, 19, 205, 219
Soppitt, par. Elsdon, 109
Soppitt, Thomas, 218
Sorsbie, Robert, 83
Sotevill, Hugh, 244
Soulby, William, 245
Soulis (Sules), Ranulf, 41
Soulsby, John, 206; Mary, 206
Southampton, earl of, 19
Southcott, Catherine, 102, 105; Edward, 102, 105
South Charlton, par. Ellingham, 228, 272, 274
South Dissington, par. Newburn, 149, 171, 173, 186, 189, 190, 271
South Gosforth, par. Gosforth, 120, 222-224, 226, 227
South Middleton, par. Hartburn, 23, 25, 26, 239
South Middleton, par. Ilderton, 195
Southwark, White Lion, 161
South Weetslade, par. Longbenton, 272
Sowerby, Jane, 179
Sparke, Jane, 83, 84; Ralph, 83, 84
Spence (Spense), John, 196; Roger, 236
Spencer, Catherine, 12, 16; Robert, 12, 16; lord, 153
Spindlestone, par. Bamburgh, 259, 272
Spink, Jane, 75; William, 75
Spire, Thomas, 147
Spofforth, Yorks., 8
Spurnam, Jane, 205, 206
Stablertowne, Ireland, 217
Stafford, Alice, 6; Edward, 16; Eleanor, 16; Humphrey, 6
Stagg, Mary, 206; Thomas, 206
Staindrop, co. Dur., 113
Stamford, par. Embleton, 257
Stamfordham, par. Stamfordham, 132, 240; school, 131
Standard, battle of the, 9

Standen, Thomas, 78
Standish, Edward, 106; Elizabeth, 208
Stanhope, co. Dur., parson of, 195; rector of, 193
Stanhope, lord, 17
Stanley, Charles, 101, 106; Edward, 17; Jane, 101, 105; Lucy, 17
Stannington, par. Stannington, 190, 217, 271; church, 190
Stannington, John, 96
Stanton, par. Longhorsley, manor, 71
Stapelton, Brian, 90
Starbotton in Craven, Yorks., manor, 10
Star Chamber at Westminster, 173
de Starck, baron, 179
Starhead, —, 45
Staunton, 145
Staunton, Notts, parson of, 160
Steel in Buteland, 58, 111, 112, 133
Stelling, par. Bywell St Peter, 55, 56
Stephen of England, 272
Stevens, William, 171
Steward, Margaret, 261, 265
Stewart (Stuart), Alexander, 45; Christiana, 109, 110; John, 109, 110; James, 12
Stewkley, Hugh, 207; Sarah, 207
Steyward, Roger, 143; Thomas, 144, 145
Stickley, par. Horton, 142
Stidley Hill, par. Corsenside, 111, 112
Still, Margaret, 48
Stirrup, Notts., 76
Stixwould Prior, 13
Stobhill, par. Morpeth, 271
Stobswood, chap. Ulgham, 271
Stockar, Henry, 192
Stockwell, Frances, 164; governor, 162, 164
Stoke Charity, Hants., 209
Stoke, juxta Newark, battle of, 148
Stokershaugh, par. Alwinton, 117
Stokes, Ralph, 95
Stokoe, Anthony, 111; Henry, 64, 65, 111; Margery, 80, 81; Mary, 80; Richard, 80, 81
Stonecroft, chap. Newbrough, 48, 94, 96, 98, 110, 111
Stonehall, 99
Storey, family, 260; Anne, 207, 209; Frances, 231; John, 197, 207, 209; Ralph, 231; Richard, 259
Stote, Richard, 92
Strachan (Stragan), Alexander, 144
Stranguish, Anne, 130; Agnes (Annes), 130; Catherine, 252, 258; Edward, 252, 253; Henry, 247; Margaret, 247; Matilda, 248; Robert, 248
Strathbogie (Strabolgy), David, 14, 15; Elizabeth, 15; Philippa, 15
Streatfield, Catherine, 180; Charles, 180; Elizabeth, 180
Streme Orrett, fishery in the Tweed, 245
Stringer, Francis, 202; Mary, 202
Strother, family, 195; Eleanor, 117, 119; Elizabeth, 57, 60, 161, 163; Frances, 232; Henry, 232, 243, 260, 261; Jane, 243; John, 53, 57, 60, 92; Lancelot, 117, 119, 231; Mabel, 120; Matilda, 120, 122; Maud, 104, 120; Richard, 231; Robert, 161; Thomas, 85, 120, 122; William, 57, 145, 161, 163, 220, 246
Stubton, Lincs., 76
Stukeley, Hunts., 272
Sturton Grange, par. Warkworth, 120
Stuteville, Alice, 271; Robert, 35; Sibilla, 35
Styford, par. Bywell St Andrew, 239; barony of, 56, 90, 93, 222, 223
Suffolk, earl of, 14, 51, 108
Sunderland, earl of, 156
Surrey, earl of, 149
Surtees, Thomas, 96
Sussex, earl of, 52
Sutton, lord, 16; Francis, 112, 113; Mary, 112, 113
Sutton in the Forest, Yorks., 33
Swalwell, co. Dur., 59, 166
Swan, Jane, 162, 165; Utricia, 211; William, 211
Swanne, Bertram, 53; Dorothy, 53, 59

Widdrington, *cont.*
139; Timothy, 121, 122; Ursula, 100, 101, 104-106, 110-113, 131, 137, 139; William, 94, 97, 99-102, 104-107, 111-113, 115, 117-119, 121-123, 125-129, 131-136, 139, 140, 160, 171; lady, 99-102, 109, 113, 135; lady Widdrington of Blankney, 94; lord, 80, 101, 102, 107, 109-111, 125, 126, 131, 140, 160, 203, 260; lord Widdrington of Blankney, 94, 101, 105, 106; Mr, 152, 171, 252
Wigan, battle of, 101
Wight, Alice, 220; Nicholas, 220
Wightman, Catherine, 237, 238; John, 237, 238
Wigton (Wygeton), Adam, 244; Isabella, 244
Wilkinson, Barbara, 212; Gabriel, 212; John, 217, 245; Matthew, 66
William I of England, 2, 8, 9, 141, 142, 243, 273
William II of England, 4, 223
William of Orange, 261
William the Lion, king of Scots., 33, 34, 93
William s. of Adam, 89, 257; s. of Bernier, 239; s. of Boius, 239; s. of Payne, 240; s. of Robert, a serf, 258, 259; s. of Roger, 241, 274, 275; s. of Siward, 257; s. of Stur, 222, s. of Waltheof, 1, 4, 6; s. of William, 1, 4, 6
William the Atheling, 9
Williams, Elizabeth, 235; Rice, 235
Williamson, Ann, 212; Gertrude, 40; Matthew, 212
Willington, par. Wallsend, 262
Willoughby, Christopher, 7; Elizabeth, 7; —, 118
Wilmot, Ann, 77; Barbarina, 181; Edward, 77; Valentine, 181
Wilsing, Elinor, 215

Wilson, Ann, 253, 254; Cuthbert, 80; Jane, 264; John, 195; Mary, 64, 65, 125, 127, 180; Ralph, 125, 127; Thomas, 253; William, 254; —, 185
Wilthew, Mary, 64, 65
Wilton, family, 37; Anfrida, 37; Ralph, 37
Winchester, bishop, 5; dean, 179; earl, 34; prebendary of, 79, 181
Winckles, Jane, 175, 178; Mary, 175, 178; Thomas, 175, 178
Windebank, secretary, 108
Winship, Lionel, 40; Margaret, 40
Windsor, castle, 262
Windsor, Dixie, 262; Dorothy, 258, 262
Winter House, Hexhamshire, 196
Wintoun, earl of, 102
Wintrick in Bockenfield, 74
Windwood, secretary, 108
Wirecestre, Pagan, 257; Radulf, 1, 41, 42, 257
Witton, David, 23, 28; Joan, 25, 26, 28; Thomas, 245
Wolfe, Mary, 253; Thomas, 253
Wolsey, bishop, 218; cardinal, 12
Wolsingham, co. Dur., curate of, 192
Woolsington, par. Newburn, 271
Wood, Ann, 262, 265, 266; Guy, 214; John, 262, 266; Mary, 214; Thomas, 257, 263, 265
Woodburn, par. Corsenside, 222, 224, 226, 227
Woodburne, William, 192
Wooden, par. Lesbury, 272; manor, 96
Woodhorn, par. Woodhorn, 95, 100, 111; bailiff of, 98; demesne, 116; manor, 97, 99; vicar, 107
Woodhouse in Shilbottle, 272
Woodman, Alan, 143
Woodroffe, Elizabeth, 17; Francis, 139; Margaret,

Woodroffe, *cont.*
139; Richard, 17
Woodyear, Joseph, 206
Woolascott, Ann, 132; Martin, 132
Wooler, par. Wooler, 241, 246; baron, 36; barony, 1, 44, 90, 241, 243, 244; haugh, 149
Wooley, par. Slaley, 87
Worcester, 14; earl of, 12, 15, 17, 246
Worteley, Maud, 23, 28; Nicholas, 23, 28
Worthington, Christopher, 209
Worthy Park, Hants., 177
Wotton, John, 17; Lucy, 17
Wrangham, Jane, 162; William, 218
Wrenne, Jane, 74, 75; William, 74, 75
Wright, David, 218; Hilda, 88; Jane, 218; Martha, 19, 21; Robert, 19, 21
Wriothlesley, Elizabeth, 19; **Thomas**, **19**
Wudeham, Alice, 24; William, 23, 24
Wydhelard s. of Wydhelard, 240, 275
Wymbyshe, Elizabeth, 5, 7; Thomas, 5, 7
Wyndham, Dorothy, 211; John, 211; earls of Egremont, 9
Wythill, Alice, 95; Gilbert, 95

Yarrow, Cuthbert, 80
Yates, Elizabeth, 212; John, 212
Yeavering, par. Kirknewton, 241
York, 10, 12, 244; abbey of St Mary, 4, 222; abbot of St Mary's, 11, archbishop of, 49, 52, 65, 123, 224; buildings co., 102; duke of 10, 139, 248; gaol, 129; hospital of St Peter, 41; recorder, 131
Young, Ann, 121, 122; Christopher, 92; Edward, 121, 122; Julia, 206; Lambton, 206